U. C. Knoepflmacher

INTO *C*HILDLAND

Victorians, Fairy Tales, and Femininity

THE UNIVERSITY OF CHICAGO PRESS ♦ CHICAGO AND LONDON

U. C. Knoepflmacher is Professor of English and Paton Foundation Professor of Ancient and Modern Literature at Princeton University. He is author, most recently, of *Wuthering Heights: A Study* and coeditor of *Forbidden Journeys: Fairy Tales and Fantasies by Victorian Women Writers,* the latter also published by the University of Chicago Press.

The University of Chicago Press, Chicago 60637
The University of Chicago Press, Ltd., London
© 1998 by The University of Chicago
All rights reserved. Published 1998
Printed in the United States of America
07 06 05 04 03 02 01 00 99 98   5 4 3 2 1

ISBN (cloth): 0-226-44815-0

Library of Congress Cataloging-in-Publication Data

Knoepflmacher, U. C.
     Ventures into childland : Victorians, fairy tales, and femininity / U. C. Knoepflmacher.
          p.   cm.
     Includes bibliographical references and index.
     ISBN 0-226-44815-0 (cloth : acid-free paper)
     1. Children's literature, English—History and criticism.   2. Girls—Great Britain—Books and reading—History—19th century.   3. English literature—19th century—History and criticism.   4. Fantastic literature, English—History and criticism.   5. Children's literature, English—Illustrations.   6. Children's literature—Psychological aspects.   7. Great Britain—History—Victoria, 1837–1901.   8. Femininity (Psychology) in literature.   9.Fairy tales—History and criticism.   10. Authorship—Sex differences.   11. Sex role in literature.   I. Title.
PR990.K58   1998
820.9'9282'09034—dc21   97-32030
                                                                        CIP

∞ The paper used in this publication meets the minimum requirements of the American National Standard for Information Sciences—Permanence of Paper for Printed Library Materials, ANSI Z39.48-1992.

Contents

Illustrations

Buttonholing the Reader:
A Preface of Sorts

"By thy long grey beard and glittering eye,
Now wherefore stopp'st thou me?"
 —SAMUEL TAYLOR COLERIDGE

"Eins, Zwei, Drei, Vier, Fünf, Sechs, Sieben,
Wo ist denn die Acht geblieben?
Ausgewandert in die Ferne,
In Europa nicht mehr gerne."
 —WALTER BENJAMIN *(adapted)*

May I detain you? Perhaps you've already thumbed through this book, pausing at an illustration here and there, maybe even checking out the index for some clues as to its contents. What is my narrative about? For whom is it intended? Let me try to be of some help. I shall not be too equivocal; but like that other buttonholer, Coleridge's Ancient Mariner, I may turn out to be a bit circuitous. You must forgive me. Since this is a fairly hefty book, I somehow feel that my enterprise deserves a longish preamble.

This book takes a very close look at the stories, poems, and illustrations that seven British children's authors created within a span of twenty years, from the early 1850s to the early 1870s. And it looks just as closely at the interrelations among their texts, all of which are fantasies or fairy tales. These post-Romantic constructs are fascinating in their own right, and I treat them as seriously as the Romantic poems and Victorian novels I often haul in as parallels and foils. But I also consider them as an integral part of a nineteenth-century debate about the nature of childhood that eventually pitted women authors against male predecessors who had already challenged each other on ideological and artistic grounds. Far from being outdated, their disputes are poignant at a time when our inherited notion of childhood as a precious preserve seems seriously threatened.

There are considerable differences among John Ruskin and the three male successors I examine here—William Makepeace Thackeray, George MacDonald, and Lewis Carroll. Yet all four writers created constructions of childhood that were shaped by their common longing for a lost feminine complement. That longing, prompted by personal circumstances as well as by the special conditions under which nineteenth-century boys were raised, was embodied in the fantasies and fairy tales these men created and was reflected in their choice of young girls as their prime auditors and readers.

In 1865, the publication of *Alice in Wonderland* completed the erosion of a didactic and empirical tradition of children's literature that had been dominated by female authors for over a century. The enormous success of Carroll's fantasy thus presented a creative challenge for the three women writers I consider in the second half of this book—Jean Ingelow, Christina Rossetti, and Juliana Horatia Ewing. By creating fantasies that were covertly anti-fantastic in their emphasis, these women reasserted their belief in a child's orderly progression towards maturity within a temporal world marked by boundaries and limits. Moreover, by contesting male idealizations of a feminized innocence, they also tried to wrest child-texts away from the fantasists who had come to dominate the market. Their own imaginative constructs thus involve an indirect reappropriation of a literature that had once been their own.

The ten chapters I devote to intertextual readings thus chart a progression that falls into two distinct movements, each of which takes up five chapters. The first movement (chapters 2 through 6) starts with my discussion of Ruskin's *The King of the Golden River* as a text that banishes the female, the erotic, and the parental, and culminates with my consideration of *Through the Looking-Glass* as a text in which Carroll at least partially accepts that he can no longer hold out against the possibility of Alice's passage into adulthood. The second movement (chapters 7 through 11) retreats chronologically by beginning with MacDonald's *At the Back of the North Wind,* a work published a few years before *Looking-Glass.* In that novel, which features an androgynous boy much like Ruskin's protagonist, MacDonald reverses the earlier emphasis of his own "The Light Princess" (discussed in chapter 4); he now resists maturation, and yet at the same time also offers a corrective to Ruskin's and Carroll's ambivalence about adult female power.

MacDonald thus opens up, as much as Carroll had, the literary field; what is more, he facilitates the intervention of new women writers. Jean Ingelow deliberately uses *At the Back of the North Wind,* rather than the first *Alice* book, as her prime foil for her *Mopsa the Fairy.* Instead of a numinous female figure leading a fragile androgyne into a realm of the imagination, a matriarchal fairy queen must banish the sturdy English boy Jack and push him back into a social reality whose clear demarcations are understood and accepted by his biological mother. That realistic world, grounded in time, is also emphasized in the works of Rossetti and Ewing, taken up in my last three chapters. It is Ewing, however, rather than the anti-Carrollian Rossetti, who ultimately manages to realign the fairy tale with earlier literary and cultural forms. Her grasp of a folkloric tradition based on female transmission and her relation to the practices of her own literary mother allow her to revitalize the didactic texts of the earlier Enlightenment women who wrote for children.

In working out the complicated interrelationships among the major texts through which these seven authors signaled their differences, I may well have produced the most comprehensive history (literary and cultural) yet written about the so-called golden age of children's literature. That history, to be sure, is hardly all-inclusive, given the omission of important works such as Charles Kingsley's *Water Babies* (1863), and given, too, my decision not to consider the prolific Mary Louisa Molesworth's entry, in 1875, into the field of children's literature. Moreover, for reasons which my chosen texts greatly help to illuminate, I even find myself seriously questioning the label of "children's literature" that we bestow on a branch of writing that simultaneously appeals to children and adults—a dual audience which the mid-Victorians, who capitalized on that pleasurable appeal, liked to call "the young of all ages."

The notion that "adult" and "juvenile" texts should be kept apart did not become prevalent until the end of the nineteenth century. Convenient for publishers as well as for highbrow aesthetes who, like Henry James, wanted to detach a smaller elite audience from an "unreflective" readership at large, the distinction nonetheless proved to be more honored in the breach than in the observance. Many of the twentieth century's finest children's authors—Edith Nesbit and Rudyard Kipling at the beginning of the century, or, later, E. B. White, Russell Hoban, and Maurice Sendak—continued to appeal to a dual authorship. And writers whose sophistication would have met James's strictest standards—Virginia Woolf, Gertrude Stein, or Randall Jarrell—valued the opportunity to address younger readers. Nor is the separation of adult- and child-texts really observed by any adult reader who rereads a childhood favorite with a renewed appreciation that may even enhance the book's earlier appeal. Such a reader may also find unexpected intensities of delight in texts created for a new generation of boys and girls.

Yet the segregation has nonetheless been detrimental to the serious study of children's books in our schools and colleges. Trained to teach *Hamlet* rather than *Charlotte's Web,* only a handful of innovative schoolteachers have recognized that their students might learn more from the ironies that mark weepy Wilbur's linguistic redemption in a credulous world ruled by advertising than from the soliloquies of a moody and suicidal prince in a remote Danish castle. At the university level, the segregation is even more absolutely enforced. Although English departments have gleefully discovered that "kiddie lit" will fill classrooms, they have also made sure that children's classics not contaminate the high seriousness of canonized masterpieces such as *Paradise Lost* or *Middlemarch.*

Even books that quite overtly tap childhood energies, such as *Jane Eyre* or *Gulliver's Travels* (reprinted as a children's book from the eighteenth century onward), thus are exclusively treated as adult fare by college professors. In American studies, as far as I know, no one has yet considered Henry James's *What Maisie Knew* to be perfectly teachable in conjunction with *A Little Princess,* the novel written by James's brash neighbor Frances Hodgson Burnett. And courses in women's studies seldom dwell on a field that drew such a large number of women writers from the eighteenth century to the present: the children's books of major authors such as Mary Wollstonecraft, Maria Edgeworth, Burnett, Nesbit, or even Louisa May Alcott, and the contributions of influential editors like Mary Mapes Dodge, whose *St. Nicholas Magazine* shaped the outlooks of two generations of Americans, are somehow relegated to a lesser status by virtue of their "unreflective" audience. If *The Awakening* has become standard fare in such courses, the many stories and novellas Kate Chopin published in magazines for children are not. In like manner Christina Rossetti's book of nursery rhymes, *Sing-Song,* is seldom alluded to in current revalidations of her poetry even though, as I try to show in my ninth chapter, that volume allowed her to realize an "adult" agenda that she had previously been unable to disseminate.

"There was a ship," begins the Ancient Mariner in order to hold his auditor. At this point in my own narrative there are two truisms you should pause to consider. Let me present them in the form of a syllogism:

1. All "children's books" are written by adults.
2. All "adults" are former children.
3. Therefore, it follows that all children's books involve, in varied combinations and to varied degrees, an adult reactivation of childhood selves all of us harbor.

Now the notion of such "selves" creates considerable discomfort for several kinds of poststructuralist literary critics, who distance the text from the author by insisting on the impersonality of all writing. But since I never look at biography as being in any way independent of culture and history, and since my biographical forays always allow the instability and incompleteness of any author's ostensible design, I hope that you will not be too put off by my occasional probings into adult and child selves.

Authors who write (and illustrate) books for children inevitably depict a traffic between childhood and maturity. Lewis Carroll, in a photograph I analyze in chapter 5, tried to flatten himself into a child-shape. Yet such flattenings, clearly related to the compressions imposed on the *Wonderland* Alice or on the miniaturized males through which Ruskin hoped to reduce his aversion towards an aggressive adult masculinity, cannot remove a self-consciousness marked by hindsight and experience. Only one of my seven authors, Juliana Horatia Ewing, wrote strictly for children. Ruskin was far better known as a critic of art and society; Thackeray and Mac-Donald as novelists and essayists; Ingelow and Rossetti as poets whose verses were aimed at an adult readership; even the madcap Lewis Carroll had to share his identity with the staid Reverend Charles Dodgson, a mathematician, photographer, and Oxford don.

The traffic between adult and child was, in effect, an intrinsic part of all the authorial identities the Victorians concocted in their public efforts to make sense of their world. Dickens, to take just one prime example, wrote very few texts expressly designed for children, and yet, like Blake and Wordsworth in the generations before him, he persistently resorted to the creative energies of the child in his major literary constructions. Does the adult fantasist always cling to defenses first developed as an imaginative child? George Eliot, in a passage I discuss in chapter 1, seemed to think so. Whether a parent (like Thackeray and MacDonald) or childless (like Ruskin, Carroll, Ingelow, Rossetti, and Ewing), the writer who addresses children is inevitably involved in a reconstruction of his or her own early selves. Maurice Sendak, whose stake in the nineteenth century is so considerable, claims that his own work, both as a graphic artist and as a writer, stems from his persistent efforts to maintain contact with "the psychic reality of my own childhood." The remark might easily have been made by any one of my Victorian Seven. It even applies to the personal anecdote about *Dumbo* with which I open chapter 1.

Given the self-reflexive nature of our constructions of childhood, it should not surprise you to find that I will often draw on biographical matters in the chapters that follow. Carroll's Alice may be an eroticized Other concocted by a child-lover, as James R. Kincaid has cogently argued. But she is also the little girl Carroll would have liked to have been had his culture not demanded that he grow into a man. Unlike Kincaid, I believe in authorial selves, and hence have no compunction in weaving some biographical strands into the textual narratives I offer. The childlands my authors construct and the child selves they choose to feature have much to do, directly or indirectly, with their early relations to their parents or siblings, their own parenting (in the case of Thackeray and MacDonald), and their avuncular interest in a special child.

This seems to be the proper point to make a personal confession. You have probably guessed by now that my adoption of an archaic mode in addressing you as a "you" was quite calculated. Like Lewis Carroll's Gnat, I was trying to evade adult formulations by presenting myself as a child-like and trustful believer in I-you bonds. Even the decision to press the Ancient Mariner into service was decidedly non-adult: "He readeth best / Who knoweth best / That creatures big are creatures small" seems to be my own version of the moral that Coleridge himself dismissed as being far too simple. Yet I also know that my all-too-serious handling of texts written for the young will expose me to the contrary accusation that I have somehow robbed them of their "wonder" or "enchantment."

"We murder to dissect," said Wordsworth, who regarded the poet as a "man speaking to men" and yet never relinquished the child within, or, for that matter, the powerful feminine components of his imagination. A student once told me, "You are a white-haired child." I took her observation as a compliment, although she may not have meant it as such. Childishness and childlikeness are hardly identical, as George MacDonald usefully observed quite long ago. Indeed, it is the conflation of the two which not only MacDonald but also Thackeray and the women writers I discuss in my last chapters strenuously resisted. As one who has supervised the growth of four children, both as a single parent and as a *paterfamilias,* I've had a special stake in what might be called the dialectics of growth. I have wanted my children never to let go of all their early strengths, and yet I have also desperately wanted them to mature. As a refugee from Nazi Europe, I felt a personal urgency in helping replenish a stock that Hitler sought to terminate. My children, more than I, deserve to take their place in—and to contribute to—a productive society of grown-up women and men. And this leads me to a much more somber note.

Long before the arrival of a fourth child, when I was still raising my first three, an acquaintance chided me for having ignored the ecological goals of "zero" population growth. I did not respond. It seemed improper to claim a special privilege. How could I tell him what that "zero"—the German word is *Null* as in "an*nul*ment"—evoked for me? I shall continue to be haunted by a frequently reproduced photograph of a little Jewish boy in the Warsaw ghetto. The boy is being herded, with arms over his head, by a helmeted Nazi soldier armed with a submachine gun. I am obsessed by that child: he seems to have been exactly my own age in 1941 or 1942; he is dressed in a coat and cap quite similar to those I wore around that time; and he even looks remarkably as I did. This boy is my special double, my alter ego, my dream-child. His parents could not flee Europe, as mine managed to do. His family surely perished at Auschwitz or in some other death camp. What would this child and one million others like him have become had they been granted adolescence, maturity, the gift of life?

It is here where I part company with the idolaters of childhood, past and present. The Victorian child-lovers who fantasized about keeping their Alices and Peter Pans ever young did not have to face the horrors of a systematic policy of extermination that insured that all "undesirable" children would never reach maturity. The sentimentality of the nineteenth century seems cruelly subverted by our own century's atrocities. I am dedicating this book to the dream-children our post-Victorian century created in a nightmare we cannot afford to forget. Junita Vismnyatsky, Anne Frank, Hanusz Weinberg, and the nameless boy of the photograph, submitting to his adult captor with arms over his head, were branded as aliens and denied the temporary shelter we call childhood or adolescence. There were no escapist childlands for them to find. Instead, the adult horror they were forced to experience aged them instantly, in a burning flash. And yet, "the bush was not consumed." Their memory must not be extinguished.

U. C. K.

Acknowledgments

Given this book's long gestation, I have benefited from so many supporters and helpers that my acknowledgments must seem incomplete. Relatives, friends, and mentors who would have rejoiced in the end-product are no more: Edith Fleischman, Mel Tumin, Dudley Johnson, Coral Lansbury, and George H. Ford are greatly missed. I owe much to Allen Fitchen's and Barbara J. Hanrahan's early enthusiasm for this project and to Alan Thomas's exemplary patience and encouragement; the unusual care shown by the two readers who reported on the manuscript proved to be a wonderful boon. To my indebtedness for the generous support of fellowships from the Rockefeller Foundation at its outset and from the National Endowment for the Humanities near its termination, I must add my grateful memories of my stay at the National Humanities Center in North Carolina; the book's last chapters will always be associated with a host of friendly faces I shall never forget.

I must devote a special paragraph to a special friend, James R. Kincaid, lest my dialogue with his provocative *Child-Loving* be misread as churlish ingratitude. Jim's meticulous and incisive page-by-page comments on early drafts of chapters 3, 4, and 5 proved invaluable. His openness to ideas that often were contrary to his own greatly helped me in clarifying their murky exposition. I know no other scholar as selfless and giving as this fellow-Victorianist.

Linda Shires, partner in things Victorian and domestic, also deserves a paragraph of her own. I am not just indebted to her for her infallibly sound judgments, her greater adeptness in word-processing and theorizing, her patience with my impatience, but also for her fine job in mothering the young subject whose *Dumbo*-watchings I discuss in my first chapter.

Others, I fear, will have to be bunched together. I am obliged to the Beinecke Library at Yale University and the Berg Collection at the New York Public Library for allowing me to reproduce excerpts from manuscript letters cited in chapters 4 and 9, to the Pierpont Morgan Library for the reproduction of a Thackeray sketch in chapter 3, to the Harry Ransom Humanities Research Center at the University of Teaxas for the reproduction of a George MacDonald photograph in chapter 5, and to the editors of *Children's Literature* and *Nineteenth-Century Literature* for their permission to reprint, albeit in altered form, those portions of chapters 2 and 10 that appeared in their journals. My thanks, also, to Princeton University's Committee on Research in the Humanities and Social Sciences for assistance in the preparation of the final copy.

I have benefited, too, from my collaborations with Mitzi Myers and Nina Auerbach, my co-editors on two projects involving texts and authors considered here. And I am grateful to Margaret Higonnet, J. Hillis Miller, and Elaine Showalter for their faith in this project. My obligations to others are often acknowledged in my notes, but many valuable suggestions, comments, and bits of information given to me by colleagues, students, members of my NEH summer seminars for college and school teachers, audiences at sundry locations in the United States, Canada, and England, and curators in those three countries, have become so intermingled with ideas of my own that it is difficult, at this point, to retrace these stimuli to their original begetters.

Let me end by thanking my four children, Julie, Paul, Daniel, and Alexander Knoepflmacher, for letting me grow by parenting them.

Abbreviations

AC George MacDonald. *Adela Cathcart*. New York: George Routledge, n.d.

AD Juliana Horatia Ewing. "Amelia and the Dwarfs." In *Forbidden Journeys: Fairy Tales and Fantasies by Victorian Women Writers*. Edited by Nina Auerbach and U. C. Knoepflmacher. Chicago: University of Chicago Press, 1992.

AW Lewis Carroll. *Alice in Wonderland*. In *Alice in Wonderland: Authoritative Texts*. Edited by Donald J. Gray. New York: Norton and Company, 1992.

B Juliana Horatia Ewing. "The Brownies." In *The Brownies and Other Tales*. London: George Bell, 1875.

BB Juliana Horatia Ewing. "Benjy in Beastland." *Aunt Judy's Magazine* 8, nos. 49 and 50 (May and June 1870).

BNW George MacDonald. *At the Back of the North Wind*. New York: Macmillan, 1964.

CW The Complete Works of John Ruskin. Edited by E. T. Cook and Alexander Wedderburn. 39 vols. London: George Allen, 1903–12.

FB Juliana Horatia Ewing. "Friedrich's Ballad." In *Mrs. Overtheway's Remembrances and Other Tales by J. H. Ewing*. London: Dent, n.d.

IM Juliana Horatia Ewing. "In Memoriam, Margaret Gatty." *Aunt Judy's Magazine* 12 (November 1873): ; Reprinted in *A Peculiar Gift: Nineteenth Century Writings on Books for Children*. Edited by Lance Salway. Hammondsworth, Indiana: Kestrel Books, 1976.

KGR John Ruskin. *The King of the Golden River, or, The Black Brothers: A Legend of Stiria*. New York: Dover Publications, 1974.

LG Lewis Carroll. *Through the Looking Glass, and What Alice Found There*. In *Alice in Wonderland: Authoritative Texts*. Edited by Donald J. Gray. New York: Norton and Company, 1992.

LP George MacDonald. "The Light Princess." In *Works of Fancy and Imagination*. Vol. 8. London: Strahan, 1871.

MF Jean Ingelow. *Mopsa the Fairy*. In *Forbidden Journeys: Fairy Tales and Fantasies by Victorian Women Writers*. Edited by Nina Auerbach and U. C. Knoepflmacher. Chicago: University of Chicago Press, 1992.

NA Lewis Carroll. *The Nursery "Alice."* Introduction by Martin Gardner. New York: Dover Publications, 1966.

RR   William Makepeace Thackeray. *The Rose and the Ring, or, The History of Prince Giglio and Prince Bulbo: A Fireside Pantomime for Great and Small Children.* Harmondsworth, Indiana: Puffin Books, 1988.

RR Fac.   William Makepeace Thackeray. *The Rose and the Ring, Reproduced in Facsimile from the Author's Original Manuscript in the Pierpont Morgan Library.* New York: Pierpont Morgan, 1947.

SL   Christina Rossetti. *Speaking Likenesses.* In *Forbidden Journeys: Fairy Tales and Fantasies by Victorian Women Writers.* Edited by Nina Auerbach and U. C. Knoepflmacher. Chicago: University of Chicago Press, 1992.

S-S   Christina Rossetti. *Sing-Song: A Nursery Rhyme Book.* New York: Dover Publications, 1968.

STC   Jean Ingelow. *Stories Told To a Child.* London: Wells Gardner, Darton and Co., 1896.

TS   Juliana Horatia Ewing. "Timothy's Shoes." *Aunt Judy's Magazine* 9, nos. 55 and 56 (November and December 1870): 3–12; 81–87.

UG   Lewis Carroll. *Alice's Adventures Under Ground.* Facsimile edition with an introduction by Martin Gardner. New York: Dover Publications, 1965.

WFI   George MacDonald. *Works of Fancy and Imagination.* London: Strahan, 1871.

WMB   "Wee Meg Barnileg and the Fairies." Reprinted in *The Way of the Storyteller* by Ruth Sawyer. London: Penguin Books, 1986.

O N E

Entering Childland: The Double Perspectives of Generation and Sex

And he beheld the moon, and, hushed at once,
Suspends his sobs
. . . .
Well! / It is a father's tale.
——SAMUEL TAYLOR COLERIDGE,
"The Nightingale"

Motherless baby and babyless mother,
Bring them together to love one another.
——CHRISTINA ROSSETTI,
Sing-Song: A Nursery Rhyme Book

I

Let me begin this book with a personal anecdote. Some years ago I decided to show a videotape of *Dumbo* to my youngest child, not yet quite two years old. Seeing the 1941 film through the eyes of a toddler who was beginning to master the structures of language proved to be instructive. I had forgotten that Dumbo never speaks throughout the film, that—unlike the hyperbolic circus master or the huffy lady elephants whose circumlocutions are as hurtful as their sneers—the newly arrived baby is quite literally "dumb." Although, by the film's last frame, Dumbo has fully mastered the art of flying, the narrative allows him to remain a linguistic innocent. His silence, however, only enhances his appeal. For the multiple *feelings* of this mute infant—contentment, shame, loss, timidity, loneliness, yearning, humiliation, surprise at unexpected skills, playful exultation, and the bliss that follows a restored symbiosis between mother and child—are perfectly captured by the expressiveness of the animator's art and the composer's musical score.

As I watched my child watching Dumbo, I was startled to see his face mirror every phase in this complex succession. Riveted by all scenes involving the baby elephant, he faithfully reflected their emotional content. Although, like Dumbo, he lacked the language to describe his feelings, my son "understood" the emotive rhythms established early in the film: he was gratified by the delivery of different babies to the circus animals, became mildly disturbed by Mrs. Jumbo's unfulfilled expectations, and yet, as a result, also became deeply involved in the new mother's joyful welcoming of her tardy infant. The sharply changed attitude of the elephant ladies towards this blue-eyed innocent seemed to puzzle him. But, once again, any potential anxiety was quickly dissipated by the comforting tenderness with which Dumbo's mother reassures the baby she rocks to sleep after gently swaddling him in his oversized ears.

Yet the film's main story proved far more difficult for my son to manage than those first scenes. I had not foreseen the powerful effect of loss that could be induced by a fiction that, as I knew from the advantage of my own experience, would pleasurably convert all losses into gains. My child's unmediated capacity for empathy and identification now almost became a handicap. Unaware of fairy-tale formulas, unable to rely on defenses readily available to an older child or to adults, he fell subject to the melodramatic mood swings of a film that held him spellbound through its visual and musical powers. I reproached myself for not having anticipated his vulnerability. It was too late to stop the film. The mesmerized little viewer demanded the story in full: a fantasy of mastery and compensation now had to be seen in its entirety. There were to be no breaks or interruptions. Only the sight of Dumbo's soft landing in his mother's lap in the film's final scene helped to restore my son to our living room. He beamed as the little elephant, now sporting aviator's goggles, slid down Mrs. Jumbo's extended trunk in order to be nuzzled and once more enveloped by maternal warmth.

Yet was this happy ending worth the trembling underlip and brimming eyes which had marked my child's earlier responses to the scenes of Dumbo's separation and loneliness? Recalling my own childhood responses, I had unhesitatingly chosen *Dumbo* over other Disney films such as *Bambi* or *Snow White*. I trusted my early recollections: the traumatic death of Bambi's mother and the deformation of a beautiful mother into a hideous witch still vitiate my attraction to those films. *Dumbo,* however, was remembered as an untarnished jewel. I was convinced that the film would be received with unalloyed pleasure by the boy I uncritically equated with my former self. My rationalizations seemed foolproof. In a mental rerun of the film, I had satisfied myself that those huffy lady elephants displayed none of the viciousness shown by the female villains of later Disney films I had uneasily watched with my older children. Nasty and snobbish pachyderms they were, to be sure, but hardly as disturbing as Cruella Deville, the sadistic skinner of Dalmatian puppies.

Why, given such caution, had I been utterly unable to foresee my little boy's overidentification with Dumbo's pathos? The answer was simple: I had myself first seen *Dumbo* as a ten-year-old, already armed with protective devices unavailable to my son. For me, as a child already familiar with circus masks and carnival disguises, the sad expression on a little elephant-clown's face could not have had the impact it obviously had for a two-year-old. What is more, I could avail myself of the multiple visual and tonal distractions the film provides for older viewers: the surrealistic parade of pink elephants during the dream sequence that marks Dumbo's intoxication, for example, or the funny patter of Dumbo's allies and fellow outcasts, Timothy Mouse and the friendly black crows.

But for a child still too young to detach himself from Dumbo's melo-drama, the stylized and metamorphic ballet of elephants who startle the viewer by assuming unexpected shapes offers no comic relief. Quite to the contrary, to judge from my boy's expression, the dream sequence appar-ently struck him as a pointless diversion from his overriding interest in the fate of babies separated from their mothers. And even though my son seemed to welcome Timothy Mouse and the five crows as creatures capable of sympathizing with Dumbo's plight almost as intensely as he did, he could hardly be expected to be amused by Timothy's Brooklynese twang or by the crows' raucous adoption of African-American rhythms of speech and song. The evocation of wartime magazine covers and the allu-sion to FDR's "fireside chats" were historical touches probably lost on me when I had first seen Dumbo, but for my two-year-old they obviously held no interest whatsoever. It was Dumbo's well-being that quite clearly preoccupied my son as he looked for images that might restore that well-being. Even the last-minute loss of the "magic feather," which the credu-lous Dumbo credits for his flying skills, unsettled him. And it continued to unsettle him—though admittedly less and less so—on subsequent re-showings of the film.

For "Dumbo" now *had* to be reshown. It had become fetishized. The attempts to substitute other films or shorter cartoons were emphatically resisted. Although the sequence of events became increasingly familiar to my son, although he also became more adept at explaining what pleased and what displeased him about the story, he still demanded its incessant repetition. His concurrent acquisition of language—and, with that acqui-sition, his expanding grasp of the consequences of separation and individ-uation—fueled his interest. He sensed what I had also sensed: the psycho-logical relevance to a developing child of the story of a little elephant who grows up and yet manages to return to a pre-linguistic oneness with his mother. More and more consciously than at the film's first showings, he came to regard Dumbo as an agent for continuing conflicts of his own.

By addressing these universal childhood conflicts, then, *Dumbo* ap-pealed, albeit on different levels, to a two-year-old as much as to the father who had so unwisely chosen to show him the film at too early an age. Why had I selected this particular film? I began to see that I had not activated its restorative fantasy solely for the gratification of the child sitting next to me. I had coerced him into becoming my partner, much like John Ruskin, William Makepeace Thackeray, and Lewis Carroll did when they enticed an older special child—Effie Gray, Anny Thackeray, and Alice Liddell—with fantasy-constructs that might embody a shared childhood preoccupation with loss and recovery. Was the being I have repeatedly been calling, in such proprietary fashion, "*my* boy," "*my* son," and "*my* child" therefore not merely an agent for a journey of my own? If "my" Alex was as much a surrogate for yearning and hindsight as Lewis Carroll's dream-child, Alice, did not his vulnerability also act as a decoy for my very own?

In George Eliot's *Middlemarch,* that novel for "grown-up people," as Virginia Woolf liked to call it,[1] the narrator repeatedly exposes the vulnerable child-selves that lurk beneath the veneer of a magnified adult experience. Borrowing her metaphor from the Greek stage, this narrator suggests that "behind the big mask and the speaking-trumpet, there must always be our poor little eyes peeping as usual and our timorous lips more or less under anxious control."[2] But such a defensive armature also is necessary, as George Eliot implies elsewhere in the same novel, if we are not to be overwhelmed by an excessive flow of feeling. In viewing *Dumbo* with my son, I clung to controls unavailable to a two-year-old. Unlike him, I could fall back on the frames and filters provided by memory, irony, and analogical habits of mind; I also possessed an awareness of the fictionality of fiction, of the distortions of subjectivity, of the weight of inscribed cultural codes.

As a professional student of narratives, I even could detect affinities between the Disney film and tales relying on similar character types or plot configurations. Was not the little creature called "Dumbo" merely another version of that "Dummling" figure so prominent in folk tales and invented *Kunstmärchen?* Was not levitation a power bestowed on those over-towered by adults in many a liberating fantasy? The aggressive pleasure my son and I felt when the flying elephant-child strafes his former adult torturers with a barrage of peanuts was equally keen for us both. But for me, at work on a scholarly book about Victorian fantasies for children, it carried associations he certainly would not be making for years to come.

Classic fairy tales often end when a youngest and simplest child bests older rivals who have been conniving, cruel, and manipulative. In fact, in

1. Virginia Woolf, "George Eliot," in *Collected Essays* (New York: Harcourt, 1967), 1:201.

2. George Eliot, *Middlemarch* (1871–72; reprint, Boston: Houghton Mifflin, 1956), chap. 29, 207.

the next chapter of this book, I shall make much of John Ruskin's decision to borrow precisely such a plot device from the Brothers Grimm for the 1841 fairy tale he fashioned for a "very young lady" while himself a young man still tied to parental apron strings. In *The King of the Golden River,* a tale of innocence rewarded, Ruskin assigns to the abused boy-Cinderella he calls "little Gluck" essentially the same passive role of a victim of commercial greed that little Dumbo comes to play, exactly a hundred years later, in the Disney film. If Dumbo is at the mercy of the whip-cracking circus master, Gluck is even more cruelly exploited by his rapacious older brothers, whom Ruskin also identifies with a sadistic masculinity. Helped by tiny yet potent allies, each of these innocents is ultimately rewarded with a return to maternal origins.

The restorative fantasy which Ruskin activates in *The King of the Golden River* (which Disney found of sufficient interest to merit a spin-off called *Uncle Scrooge and the Golden River*)[3] can, moreover, like *Dumbo,* be fully shared by children and grownups. Adults aware of Ruskin's importance as an influential critic of Victorian culture may read into the text several levels of meaning unavailable to the child reader. However apt, such sophisticated layerings—whether socio-political or religious or even ecological—nonetheless remain mere elaborations for a core fantasy. Ruskin's narratives always gratify a primal yearning for the restoration of a lost "purity." Paradoxically, then, an adult reader is drawn into a fantasy that remains essentially anti-adult in its regressive hostility to growth and sexual division.

Ruskin furnishes me with an ideal starting point for the sequence I shall be tracing. Later Victorian writers who wrote for children drew—directly or indirectly—on *The King of the Golden River,* which Ruskin did not publish until 1851, by which time his notoriety as the author of *Modern Painters* and *Stones of Venice* lent respectability to his venture into juvenile fiction. The six successors of Ruskin I will consider—three men and three women—shared his Romantic nostalgia for a "pure" and undifferentiated childhood Eden; but they also challenged his resistance to maturation as well as his resulting idealization of a passive—and dubiously asexual— prepubescence. Skeptical of the deformation of traditional fairy tales by Charles Perrault and the Grimms, these six successors devised original

---

3. Created by Disney artist Carl Barks, the story appeared in comic book form on January 19, 1958, as the fourth in a series of "Uncle Scrooge Adventures"; it was reprinted in April 1988. I am grateful to Professor James Addison for this information.

constructs that were more subversive of fairy-tale conventions than Ruskin's purported transcription of a "legend of Stiria."

Still, despite their innovativeness, the children's books I consider after *The King of the Golden River* are best read with Ruskin's precedent in mind. Thackeray, for instance, deliberately evokes that precedent in *The Rose and the Ring,* as does George MacDonald in "The Light Princess," a work which Ruskin found both attractive and offensive. For the women writers, too, Ruskin's insistent identification of childhood with femininity and his consequent belief that women artists were better suited to bring forth "the radiance and innocence of reinstated infant divinity" among the "the flowers of English meadows" presented considerable difficulties (*CW,* 33:340). His patronage (as the artist Kate Greenaway knew all too well) could be as obstructive as his derision. In their efforts to reclaim what they considered to be a female tradition of fantasies and fairy tales, Jean Ingelow and Juliana Horatia Ewing (whose work he supported) and Christina Rossetti (whose *Speaking Likenesses* he derogated for being so unlike her "pretty nursery rhymes" in *Sing-Song*)[4] had to contend with his appropriations of the feminine. All six of these writers, however, remained indebted to Ruskin. The double perspective of child and adult he had implanted in his 1841 text would be perfected in their more complicated fantasies for young readers of both sexes. By turning to such child readers, these writers tried, as had Ruskin, to confront their own self-division between adult and child selves.

II

The dual perspective that operates in *The King of the Golden River* and in later Victorian narratives for children, however, was already being refined half a century earlier in literary texts primarily intended not for children, but for adult readers. Major English Romantic poets such as William Blake, Samuel Taylor Coleridge, and William Wordsworth wrote poems that relied on the interpenetration of those contrary yet complementary states of perception that Blake had labeled Innocence and Experience. In these revisionary poems, children are no longer seen as miniature grown-ups. Instead, in a major reversal of a catechistic literature of instruction

4. Ruskin to F. S. Ellis, 21 January 1875, *CW,* 37:155.

that had flourished in the eighteenth century, the child now could act as a corrective for adult presuppositions about the constitution of reality, value, and meaning.

Both versions of Blake's "Nurse's Song," for example, rely on a contrast between the blended "voices of children" and the single voice of an adult speaker. The Nurse who speaks in *Songs of Experience* is disturbed by the gap between an adult self-consciousness that stems from hindsight and the child's total obliviousness to impending change. Turning "green and pale" at the "fresh" recollection of her own "youth," she jealously derides the children for spending hours and days "wasted in play" (lines 4, 3, 11).[5] But this speaker's counterpart in *Songs of Innocence* (a volume that, unlike *Songs of Experience,* Blake had intended for a dual audience of adults and children) lets herself be overruled by her wards. She engages in a dialogue with the children, whose plea for a prolongation of play she not only re- produces but winds up indulging: "Well, well, go & play till the light fades away" (line 15). The poem ends by stressing the unrestraint of childhood: "The little ones leaped & shouted & laugh'd / And all the hills ecchoed" (lines 15–16).

Child readers or auditors might well regard such an ending as a tacit endorsement of their strong wish to circumvent the limits imposed by adult authority. An older reader, however, senses that, for all her permis- siveness, the Nurse of *Innocence* cannot surrender herself to a wishful be- lief in a never-ending day. Despite her deference to the children's desire for an elongation of present pleasures, she also displays, in more muted form, the temporal awareness that governs the jaundiced Nurse of *Experi- ence.* Although she refuses to treat the children as if they were incipient adults, she can only "echo" a desire emanating from innocents oblivious to time. Neither speaker's point of view can therefore be fully endorsed by the poet. The human progress through "contraries" has to avoid both a sentimental reversion to falsified memories of pure Innocence and a cyni- cal imposition of dictates based on the excessive constraints of Experience.

Blake, then, considers regression to be as limited and limiting as repres- sion. Even when, in poems such as "The Lamb" or "Infant Joy," he directly adopts the voice of an innocent child or infant, he always introduces a com- pensatory awareness that qualifies the attractive naiveté of such a speaker.

---

5. This and all subsequent quotations from Blake, Wordsworth, and Coleridge are taken from David Perkins, ed., *English Romantic Writers* (New York: Harcourt, 1967). Line references will be given in the text.

The injection of an implied adult perspective acts as counterweight to an utterance that appeals precisely by its confident immaturity, its seeming ability to strip away doubts and hesitations that come with an awareness of a more complex cluster of knowledge. What appears, on the surface, to be a self-assured monologue by an innocent blissfully free of the disenchantments of Experience thus turns out to be, after all, a dialectical construct that stresses the unresolved opposition between the perceptions of the child and the adult.[6]

Blake's capacity to keep such contraries in suspension is strongly in evidence in most of the Victorian books for the "young of all ages" I shall be considering in subsequent chapters of this book. It is no coincidence that writers such as George MacDonald, Lewis Carroll, and Christina Rossetti were intimately familiar with Blake's poetry. Yet the balance achieved by these and other writers of fantasies for children and adults is often far more precarious than in Blake. The same abrupt tonal shifts one encounters in a poem such as Tennyson's "Two Voices" mark the alternations between irony and nostalgia that one finds in the *Alice* books or in Jean Ingelow's *Mopsa the Fairy*. As in Margaret Gatty's "See-Saw," a story I have extensively discussed elsewhere as a paradigm for this uneasy balancing act,[7] such to-and-fro oscillations suggest how much more difficult it had become for the Victorians to maintain an equipoise between the two voices of Experience and Innocence.

Even though innocents like Ruskin's "little Gluck," Carroll's "little Alice," George MacDonald's "little Diamond," and Jean Ingelow's "young Jack" are valued for their imperviousness to adult formulations, such child-protagonists are presented by omniscient narrators whose superior sophistication is as manifest as that of the magical figures who act as authorial surrogates. Although these adult narrators and adult (or quasi-adult) agents are hardly prone to denigrate the young in the bitterly reductive

---

6. As Alan Richardson has persuasively shown, Blake reintroduces a dialogic process that had become lost in late eighteenth-century catechistic texts that purported to follow the format of a dialogue yet were, in fact, highly monologic ("The Politics of Childhood: Wordsworth, Blake, and Catechistic Method," *ELH* 56 (Winter 1989): 861ff. For an excellent collection of essays devoted to the Romantic perception of childhood, see James Holt McGavran, Jr., ed., *Romanticism and Children's Literature in Nineteenth-Century England* (Athens: University of Georgia Press, 1991).

7. See U. C. Knoepflmacher, "The Balancing of Child and Adult: An Approach to Victorian Fantasies for Children," *Nineteenth-Century Fiction* 37 (March 1983): 497–530.

manner of Blake's Nurse of *Experience,* their treatment of children often verges on the condescending and dismissive. Thus, both the narrator of *The Rose and the Ring* as well as the Fairy Blackstick openly mock the naiveté of the tale's hero and heroine; similarly, in *Alice in Wonderland,* the narrator who delights in repeatedly exposing Alice's ignorance of geography or mathematics is a distinct cousin of the rude Hatter who calls her "stupid."

Still, male ironists as sophisticated as Thackeray and Carroll (or as distrustful of the very medium of the fairy tale as George MacDonald) remain far more sentimentally attached to childhood and children than female ironists such as Juliana Horatia Ewing and Christina Rossetti. For, unlike women authors who could look back at generations of maternal storytellers and identify themselves with an adult female authority,[8] Victorian male writers turned to the child in order to find compensations for a middle-class culture's division of the sexes into separate spheres. Whereas girls were kept at home and taught by mothers or governesses or older sisters, their brothers were sent away to school at an early age. The imaginative deprivation such boys felt is captured in a plaintive letter written from school by the eleven-year-old Alfred Gatty to his older sister Julie (the future "Mrs. Ewing"): "Do you mind writing me a story when you are well, for I can very seldom get a story book here."[9] The nursery from which this boy has been exiled is equated with a sustaining female imagination he wishes to recover.

It is no coincidence, therefore, that the "special children" for whom Ruskin, Thackeray, MacDonald, and Carroll wrote their fantasies should all have been young girls. Each man's particular relationship to his prime auditor/reader differs in nature as well as in its intensity. In Thackeray's and MacDonald's case, an identification with an oldest and favorite daughter—Isabella or "Anny" Thackeray and Lilia or "Lily" MacDonald—did not preclude a simultaneous involvement with younger readers, fit though few. *The Rose and the Ring* was also created for Minny Thackeray and her American friend Edith Story; the original child-audience for "The Light Princess" included Lily's younger sister Mary and her brother

---

8. For the best discussion of that female authority, see Mitzi Myers, "Impeccable Governesses, Rational Dames, and Moral Mothers: Mary Wollstonecraft and the Female Tradition in Georgian Children's Literature," *Children's Literature* 14 (1986): 31–59.

9. Quoted in Christabel Maxwell, *Mrs. Gatty and Mrs. Ewing* (London: Constable, 1949), 112.

Greville. Nor is the father-child relation that may have spawned these fictions for children ultimately as important as each fantasy's reactivation of the author's own relation to a mother who enters the story as a powerful figure seen in both her good and bad aspects.

In the case of Carroll and Ruskin, however, Alice Liddell and Effie Gray were the objects of a more exclusive identification. Each girl received a manuscript copy of a tale specially crafted for her. It is true that Lewis Carroll's obsession with the dream-child who continued to haunt him "phantomwise" was much more powerful and enduring than Ruskin's emotional involvement in the young girl he eventually married and then all too readily agreed to divorce. Ruskin's own flickering interest in Alice Liddell, whom he briefly wooed as an avuncular suitor later in his life, pales even more when compared with Carroll's lifelong infatuation. For Carroll clung to the "evening of July" of his 1861 story-telling outing for almost three more decades. In 1871, he made Alice the heroine of *Through the Looking-Glass,* even though her real-life original was by then almost twenty years old. And, as if to compensate for his and her aging, Carroll went back in time by printing, in 1886, a facsimile of *Alice's Adventures Underground,* the manuscript he had given Alice Liddell in 1864, and by creating, in 1889, still another *Alice* book, *The Nursery "Alice."* If, in the Wonderland stories, he had tried to reduce the size of a growing seven-year-old who, at one point, fears that she may altogether shrink away, he now produced a shrunken text he wished to be "thumbed, to be cooed over, to be dogs'-eared, to be rumpled, to be kissed," and perhaps even "to be read by Children aged from Nought to Five."[10]

Unlike such public displays of the "dear Alice" from whom Carroll is still parting at the end of this 1889 text, Ruskin deliberately obscured the identity of the "very young lady" for whom he had privately written his fairy tale in 1841. Although during the composition of *The King of the Golden River* Ruskin referred to the story as "Phemy's fairy tale" (Euphemia Gray was then known as "Phemy" rather than "Effie"), he failed to identify this prime reader both in the published 1851 version and in the section of *Praeterita,* his 1885 autobiography, in which he discusses that youthful production. What is more, the tale itself conceals his affiliation. Unlike Carroll's Alice-dominated stories, Ruskin's plot offers no female characters whatsoever, relying instead on miniaturized male agents to re-

---

10. Lewis Carroll, "Preface (Addressed to Any Mother)," in *The Nursery "Alice"* (New York: Dover, 1966), xxi–xxii.

ward "little Gluck" and punish his brothers. Still, notwithstanding such concealments, Ruskin originally regarded the thirteen-year-old Euphemia Gray as an alter ego. In writing a fairy tale for himself and a girl who had lost her siblings, he dramatized a return to a purified Eden he renders as a feminine and maternal space. As an indulged only child of parents he would later accuse of having demasculinized him, Ruskin thus engaged in an act of projection not unlike that which Carroll undertook when he "projected his own femininity"[11] on a girl comfortably nestled, as he had once been, between older and younger sisters. Held back from puberty, Ruskin's boy-androgyne and Carroll's dream-child allow their creators to resist the gender division that comes with sexual maturation.

The Victorian male authors who sought to recover a lost "femininity" preferred to follow, understandably, the examples set by Coleridge and Wordsworth rather than by Blake. The two coauthors of *Lyrical Ballads* had, after all, launched their careers by stressing the incompleteness experienced by the adult man. To counter that incompleteness, each had invoked childhood and femininity as restoratives. Wordsworth's chief contribution to their 1798 collaboration, his celebrated "Lines Composed a Few Miles Above Tintern Abbey," acquires an added significance if read with the hindsight Ruskin's and Carroll's child-pastorals provide. Like Ruskin's Gluck, Wordsworth's speaker returns from civilization to a secluded and unsullied mountain enclave he associates with his childhood. Although, unlike little Gluck, this speaker is a full-grown man, he has retained the "purer mind" of his "boyish days" in Nature while living in "towns and cities" (lines 29, 73, 26). Gluck's own unhappy exile in a "populous," "large city" stems from the male violation and sterilization of a female Eden (*KGR*, 32, 14). The rapacity of his older brothers has separated him from a nurturant Treasure Valley, described as having once been perennially moist, sheltered by peaks "always covered with snow," and beautified by the Golden River's "constant cataracts" (*KGR*, 13, 14). Similarly cut off from the "deep rivers" and "sounding cataract" that fertilized his early imagination, Wordsworth's speaker once more can "hear / These waters" upon revisiting the Wye valley (lines 69, 76, 2–3). But only adult memory now can preserve this aureate "dwelling-place" (line 141). Gluck, however, as his German name indicates, is more fortunate. He can assume sole possession of the paradise he regains when, through a miracle

11. Michael Hancher, "Alice's Audiences," in McGavran, *Romanticism and Children's Literature*, 200.

that is both natural and supernatural, "The Treasure Valley became a garden again" (*KGR,* 67).

Such a fairy-tale ending is impossible in a poem as firmly grounded in a temporal reality as "Tintern Abbey." To reconcile himself to the matured manhood he associates with loss, Wordsworth's speaker invokes a sororal self on whose "wild eyes" he can at least project his "former pleasures" (lines 119, 118). His act of projection very much resembles that which shaped Lewis Carroll's *Alice* books. To "behold" in a younger female Other "what I was once" (line 120), each writer must create an imaginary dream-child. Only a year and a half younger than her brother William, Dorothy Wordsworth was no unreflective child of Nature as he blessed her "wild ecstasies" on a special day in July of 1798. Almost twenty-seven, she was hardly as young as the "Child of the pure unclouded brow / And dreaming eyes of wonder" who, on another memorable July day, so impressed Carroll that he continued to celebrate her as a girl in the introductory verses of *Through the Looking Glass.*

The actual features of an adult Dorothy Wordsworth and a growing Alice Liddell were less consequential to Wordsworth and Carroll than the distorted self-reflection these alter egos offered. Each male writer extracts from youthful female "eyes" some "gleams" of his own "past existence" (lines 148–49). The image of an arrested girl allows each elegist to idealize his own lost childhood oneness. The mesmeric eyes of a beautiful ten-year-old stare at the reader in the oval photograph that Carroll so carefully placed at the end of the manuscript copy of *Alice's Adventures Under Ground,* a narrative about a seven-year-old that he presented to the "Dear Child" after she had passed the age of twelve. The oval, flanked by hand-drawn decorations that resemble the curved frame of a mirror, pierces the last line of the story, sundering the words "happy summer" from "days." Separated more than ever from "the little Alice of long-ago" (*UG,* 90) by her imminent puberty, Carroll wants to leave Alice Liddell with a record of his vain effort to arrest her growth through photograph and story.

As love-gifts, Wordsworth's and Carroll's elaborate constructs are as sincere as they are selfish. Like Wordsworth, who convinces himself that a matured Dorothy will surely find "healing thoughts / Of tender joy" by remembering "me, / And these my exhortations" (lines 144–47), Carroll draws comfort from securing a perennial listener for a text he now can set out to refine. Gradually, in revising their original fantasies of loss and compensation, each writer dispenses with the actual female figure who was so important to him as a catalyst. Their signification as characters can now be transferred to types less dependent on such real-life originals. Just as Wordsworth transforms the Dorothy of "Tintern Abbey" into the unaging ghost-child Lucy Gray, hazily seen at dawn by a speaker no longer as firmly bound to the contours of a temporal reality, so does Carroll turn a dream-child, freed from her dependence on an aging Mrs. Alice Liddell Hargreaves, into the fairy-child Sylvie of the *Sylvie and Bruno* books, written at the end of his career.

And a similar transference takes place when each of the women cast in the role of addressee and reader is replaced by a wider audience. For, however genuinely prized as self-extensions of each writer, these "dear, dear" friends not only give way to unknown readers of both sexes but also are used as lure for an imaginative partnership with another wounded male ego. As Wordsworth reminded Coleridge in *The Prelude,* the two men had shared the therapeutic treasure of his sister Gift of God as a stimulus for their collaborations. For his part, by sharing a copy of the *Underground* manuscript with George MacDonald only a few months after he had bestowed his precious and exclusive love-gift on Alice Liddell, Carroll helped to launch new careers as authors of children's fiction for both himself and a fellow fantasist.

III

Wordsworth's and Carroll's identification with a sororal self, however, stems from an antecedent act of displacement. The word "mother" appears in neither "Tintern Abbey" nor in the original *Alice's Adventures Under Ground.*[12] Although the spaces into which Wordsworth and Carroll thrust Dorothy and Alice are as maternal as Ruskin's Treasure Valley, the reliance on a female surrogate marks each writer's alienation, as a male, from the primal shelter that magically reopens for Gluck at the end of *The King of the Golden River.* Indeed, not only Wordsworth's speaker and Carroll's narrator, but Dorothy and Alice as well, are denied the symbiosis that Ruskin's self-effacing narrator grants the hero of his fairy tale. Wordsworth insists on the inevitability of his sister's eventual fall: the day will

---

12. Although the Queen of Hearts, followed by ten "Royal children," all "ornamented with hearts," is as fecund a matriarch as Queen Victoria herself (*UG*, 70).

come when the maternal Nature of which she is still a part must give way to compensatory linguistic constructs, "by thought supplied," that only his fraternal imagination can provide. Exerting an even stronger imaginative control over Alice, Carroll forces his own frustrations on the falling girl. Although he eventually allows her to squeeze herself into the "small passage, not much larger than a rat-hole" that leads into "the loveliest garden you ever saw" (*AW,* 6), he also makes that garden a most inhospitable Eden, unfit for a child stamped by adult presuppositions she cannot shed in her regressive descent into a netherworld.

To a Romantic poet eager to assert unity in the face of division, the brother-sister relation can offer a blending that recapitulates the primal union between mother and child. Not only were William and Dorothy formed in the same womb, but they also were imprinted by the same parent before being pressed into different gender roles. In a passage that captures the plight of later imaginative nineteenth-century orphans such as the Brontë children, Wordsworth notes in *The Prelude* that the early loss of their "honoured Mother, she who was the heart / And hinge of all our learnings and our loves" could only be compensated by the interplay of siblings.[13] The maternal presence that Wordsworth so forcefully dramatized in subsequent poems is not directly invoked in "Tintern Abbey." It is immanent, however, in a Nature described, much like the matriarch of *The Prelude,* as the "anchor of my purest thoughts, the nurse, / The guide, the guardian of my heart" (lines 109–10).

Carroll's own regressive yearning for a maternal nesting place is clearly related to his lifelong interest in the poetry of Wordsworth (and also of Tennyson, himself a purveyor of what Wordsworth calls the "eagerness of infantine desire").[14] "Solitude," the earnest and self-indulgent 1856 poem that was Charles Lutwidge Dodgson's first publication under the pseudonym of "Lewis Carroll," seems much closer to the nostalgic frame-poems of the *Alice* books than to the ironic narratives themselves. Written shortly before he first met his little Alice, these sentimental verses significantly expose the vulnerability and self-pity that always lie on the other side of the comic control and witty deflections of Carroll's art. Significantly, "Solitude" not only employs a stitch-work of phrases culled from Wordsworth's poetry but also erects a Wordsworthian landscape as a wishful yet impossible refuge from adult life:

13. William Wordsworth, *The Prelude* (1850 version), book 5, lines 257–58.
14. Ibid., book 2, line 26.

Here from the world I win release,
Nor scorn of men, nor footstep rude,
Break in to mar the holy peace
Of this great solitude.

Here may the silent tears I weep
Lull the vexed spirit into rest,
As infants sob themselves to sleep
Upon a mother's breast.[15]

Anticipating the agent he would soon use in his Alice stories, Carroll ends the poem by wishing himself to be "once more a little child / For one bright summer day" (lines 39–40).

Yet, in the fiction of *Alice's Adventures Under Ground,* the little child who almost drowns in a pool formed by her own tears is hardly encouraged to yearn for a mother's breast. Quite to the contrary, even in her first venture into childland, Alice comes in collision with maternal figures whose behavior is every bit as "rude" as that of all the other creatures who make her visit so distinctly unpleasurable. The pigeon insists that Alice is a serpent who threatens the eggs hatching in her nest; the Queen who also happens to be "the Marchioness of Mock Turtles" (*UG,* 74) is so "crimson with fury" that she can barely be restrained by the meek husband who reminds her that Alice "is only a child" (*UG,* 72). By the time Carroll had expanded the manuscript of *Under Ground* into the *Wonderland* text, mother figures not only have proliferated but also have become even more threatening: the Marchioness/Queen has split into a Duchess who all but mutilates her baby and a Queen of Hearts whose lust for wholesale executions is now unbounded.

Carroll's intensified anti-matriarchal stance may have been fueled by his increased anger at Mrs. Lorina Liddell, Alice's mother, as I shall suggest when I contrast these two texts in my fifth chapter. But his resentment, I think, also stems from his retention—in adult life—of a much earlier sense of betrayal. Like other Victorian boys who found the necessary separation from a beloved mother difficult to weather, Carroll seems

---

15. Lewis Carroll, "Solitude," lines 13–20, in *The Collected Verse of Lewis Carroll* (London: Macmillan, 1930), 417. For a fuller discussion of this poem, see my "Revisiting Wordsworth: Lewis Carroll's 'The White Knight's Song,'" *Victorians Institute Journal* 14 (1986): 1–20.

to have blamed a parent who could not permit him to stay as closely bonded to her as his sisters were allowed to remain. Nineteenth-century middle-class culture charged mothers with the task of fostering the independence of boys who were expected to leave the domestic circle in order to prepare for a role in a world of paternal authority. As the appointed enforcer of the strict boundaries on which her culture insisted, the Victorian mother was compelled to discourage the eroticized bonds that had given her children an early sense of unbounded power. Cast out into a masculine sphere, stripped of his oneness with the feminine, the boy was led, simultaneously, to exaggerate the mother's omnipotence and to bemoan the sudden shattering of his own "aspiration for omnipotent control."[16]

Thus, in a reversal of actual gender roles, the power wielded by real-life patriarchs gets attributed to the mother in many a fictional construct of the Victorian era. The weakening of paternal authority is especially prominent in the fantasies that male authors wrote for children. In such fantasies, fathers could be written off as infantile, like Carroll's King of Hearts, or as weak and vulnerable, like the White and Red Kings in *Looking-Glass* or the blustering monarchs in Thackeray's *The Rose and the Ring*. Or they could be represented as obtuse and forgetful, like the King in MacDonald's "The Light Princess," or as severely incapacitated providers, like Diamond's father in *At the Back of the North Wind*.

By way of contrast, the matriarchs in these same fantasies are usually endowed with extraordinary powers. Magical figures such as Thackeray's Fairy Blackstick and MacDonald's North Wind are godlike in their omniscience and omnipotence. And although Alice exposes the shallow authority of both the *Wonderland* and *Looking-Glass* queens, she becomes their rival in a struggle for maternal dominance. The power of these matriarchs turns out to be illusory in the fantasylands they rule. Alice's true influence, however, should assert itself when, as "a grown woman" (*UG*, 90), she supposedly will imprint the dreams devised by Carroll on a new generation of child listeners. Like the older sister who confidently predicts Alice's future role, the girl will eventually become a mediator, a more natural and useful disseminator of fables than the marginalized bachelor who usurped a maternal imagination for his own nostalgic ends.

It is their remembrance of a mother's capacity to give and yet to with-

---

16. Jessica Benjamin, *The Bonds of Love: Psychoanalysis, Feminism, and the Problem of Domination* (New York: Pantheon, 1988), 152.

hold nurturance that led Victorian male authors to make her such a strong presence in their fantasies for child readers. Even the absence of a maternal character often attests to the writer's sense of her preeminence. Although eliding any reference to a human mother,[17] Ruskin could symbolically animate the desire to feed "upon a mother's breast" when he allowed Gluck to regain sole access to the nutriments offered by a newly oozing Treasure Valley. For their part, by trying to bring such infantile longing under some form of control, Carroll, Thackeray, and MacDonald preferred to justify a distancing process. To guard their child-protagonists against an excessive dependence on the mother, they represented her or her stand-ins as negligent or harmful to the child's development; or, alternatively, they created magical caretakers who merely seem indifferent to the fates of wards or godchildren. Moreover, even when repudiating a maternal dominance, they licensed their male narrators to appropriate for themselves a good measure of the mother's original authority and playful interactions with her child.

Still, given their ambivalent responses towards the world of nurturance from which so many Victorian males felt banished in early boyhood, it is not surprising to find that repudiation and endorsement are often hard to disentangle. Anger and longing, retaliation and idealization, satire and sentiment are inextricably intertwined, locked "arm-in-arm together."[18] Creatures such as Carroll's hideous Duchess, who refuses to nurture her small baby, or MacDonald's equally hideous Princess Makemnoit, who conjures a monster whose slow sucking brings death, ostensibly seem targets for the writer's (and male illustrator's) outrage. Drawn by John Tenniel as a monstrosity in her own right, the grotesque Duchess appears directly responsible for the transformation of an infant boy into a suckling pig; drawn by Maurice Sendak as a Gorgon who sprouts a phallic snake from her lap, Makemnoit directs this offspring to dry out Lake Lagobel as well as the milk of all nurturant mothers in the kingdom she wants to destroy. Yet the sadism of these phallic women is integral to the aggressiveness that the male writer himself displays in his parodic deformation of motherhood. Carroll and the smirking Cheshire Cat seem to relish the shock which the Duchess's behavior produces in Alice; they have an obvious stake in her utter subversion of Victorian maternal norms. Similarly,

17. Yet see p. 64 below.

18. John Sutherland, ed., *Vanity Fair: A Novel Without A Hero* (Oxford: Oxford University Press, 1983), chap. 17, 200.

the anger which the richly imaginative Makemnoit directs at the stupid and impotent parents of the Light Princess makes her the author's ally in a fable in which children must grow beyond the mindless infantilism of their elders.

The proximity and interchangeability of "bad" and beneficent incarnations of maternal power are often quite startling. In the original manuscript of *The Rose and the Ring*, where mothers of unattractive children much prefer the flattery of a hypocritical rival, the severe and judgmental Fairy Blackstick is reviled for her unvarnished truth-telling. And even in the published version of Thackeray's comic fairy tale, Blackstick continues to be branded as an "odious Fairy" by those she has offended by her resolution to withdraw her former favors; she is ostensibly cruel to godchildren to whom she now seems to bequeath nothing more than "a *little misfortune*" (*RR,* 19; Thackeray's italics). MacDonald's North Wind, too, is at first erroneously regarded as a destroyer whose cruelty is as strong as that of the vindictive Makemnoit in his earlier story. Only gradually does it become apparent that MacDonald wants us to accept North Wind as a kinder version of the Mother Goddess: the deaths she brings about are presumably placed in the service of a recuperative order.

The process of revision at work in these texts is related to the male writer's redefinition of a maternal space. As I shall show, Thackeray challenges Ruskin's construction of that space as passively "feminine" by making women, rather than sadistic men, the prime contenders in his fairy tale, and by reintroducing the sexuality Ruskin had tried to expunge. For their part, MacDonald and Carroll not only fructify each other but also engage in a process of authorial self-revision. Unlike Ruskin and Thackeray, each of whom wrote but a single children's book, Carroll and Mac-Donald cannot be adequately represented without a look at their development as fantasists. A full overview of their evolving obsession with the feminine, however, would certainly demand a discussion of their problematic final books: Carroll's *Sylvie and Bruno* (1889) and *Sylvie and Bruno, Concluded* (1893) and MacDonald's much-revised adult fantasy *Lilith* (1895). Since I restrict myself to works that span from Ruskin's 1851 to Rossetti's 1874 texts, these later productions fall outside my time frame.

But by sandwiching the sequence formed by Carroll's first three *Alice* books (discussed in chapters 5 and 6) between chapters devoted to Mac-Donald's "The Light Princess" and *At the Back of the North Wind* (chapters 4 and 7), I am able to do some justice to major modifications in each writer's stance. MacDonald's tonal shift in "The Light Princess," where a

Thackerayan ironist abruptly turns into a Ruskinian lyricist, gives way, in *North Wind,* to the sustained uncontrol of a narrative that mythifies a little boy's deadly infatuation with the mighty mother whose appearances he increasingly covets. Carroll himself would eventually flirt with mystical encounters in the *Sylvie and Bruno* books. But, as fairy Sylvie's adoration of Lady Muriel suggests, he had by then softened his angry attitude towards grown-up women. That anger is already less pronounced in the text of *Through the Looking-Glass.* Still, even though Carroll now accepts an older girl's strong identification with Dinah's mothering of her kittens, he also tries to subvert Alice's steady progress towards queenship. As Humpty Dumpty ominously reminds Alice, "with proper assistance," she might have left off growing altogether (*LG,* 162).

IV

In their imaginative ventures into remothered childlands, Ruskin, Thackeray, MacDonald, and Carroll not only appropriated "femininity" for their own ends but also came into collision with the women writers and educators who had for more than a century been charged with the moral upbringing of British children of both sexes. Until quite recently, that collision was seen by historians of children's literature as part of a wider contest between Romantic fantasists (all men) and didactic rationalists (most of whom were women). In this traditional view, still held by Geoffrey Summerfield and Humphrey Carpenter in the 1980s, Romantic and post-Romantic fantasists who advanced "the epistemology of Innocence, so to speak," are to be infinitely preferred to the dry-as-dust realists who insisted on the child's "development of adult, critical thought."[19]

Summerfield and Carpenter also follow previous historians of children's literature when they endorse Charles Lamb's derision of writers such as Anna Barbauld and Sarah Trimmer as malignant censors of the child's unreason.[20] In a much-quoted letter to Coleridge in which he

19. Geoffrey Summerfield, *Fantasy and Reason: Children's Literature in the Eighteenth Century* (Athens: University of Georgia Press, 1985), 53.

20. Humphrey Carpenter, *Secret Gardens: The Golden Age of Children's Literature* (Boston: Houghton Mifflin, 1965), 3. Summerfield, however, shrewdly notes that Lamb tailors his "contempt for blue-stockings" to suit Coleridge's own prejudices (*Fantasy and Reason,* 248).

excoriates "the cursed Barbauld crew" for having "banished all the classics of the nursery," Lamb insists that a "vapid" utilitarian knowledge threatens to drive away "that beautiful Interest in wild tales which made the child a *man* while all the time *he* suspected himself to be no bigger than a child."[21] Lamb's choice of gender for that hypothetical child is significant. He and his sister Mary had been selecting books for Hartley Coleridge, who was being introduced to fairy tales by his father. Appealing to Coleridge, Lamb thus rhetorically asks: "Think what you would have been now, if instead of being fed with Tales and old wives' fables in childhood, you had been crammed with geography and natural history?"[22]

Yet Hartley Coleridge, the romantic child in whom his father, the Lambs, and the Wordsworths had placed such inordinate hopes, would not grow up to be an empowered male genius. Fixated on childhood, always dressed in boy's clothes, preferring the company of small girls and smaller boys to that of adults, Hartley achieved, in Judith Plotz's words, "neither fortune nor profession, nor reputation, nor wife, nor child, nor self-respect"; as poet, he became an imitative "eulogist of childhood, surpassing even Wordsworth," whom he echoed in countless poems about children and "minimal forms of life such as small animals, birds, fragile flowers, wasps, fleas, microscopic sea creatures."[23] Hartley's notion of adulthood as a "state of steady decline" is epitomized in "Adolf and Annette," the unpublished fairy-tale fragment he wrote sometime between 1835 and 1849—close in time to the young Ruskin's 1841 composition of *The King of the Golden River,* a story that it resembles.[24] Unlike Ruskin's Gluck, however, Hartley's "forlorn" twins cannot return to the "divine air" of the mountain Eden where they were raised by a mysterious White Lady.[25] Deprived of "all energy and initiative," these romantic child-protagonists mirror, as Plotz notes, the creative impotence of a fantasist unable to match his sister Sara, whose bold *Phantasmion* (1837) features dreams that at least constitute "a kind of action."[26]

21. Lamb to Coleridge, 23 October 1802, *The Letters of Charles Lamb,* ed. E. V. Lucas (London: Dent, 1935), 1:326; italics added.

22. Ibid.

23. Judith Plotz, "Childhood Lost, Childhood Regained: Hartley Coleridge's Fable of Defeat," *Children's Literature* 14 (1986): 139, 138.

24. Ibid., 139; Plotz reprints "Adolf and Annette" after her essay, 151–61.

25. Hartley Coleridge, "Adolf and Annette," 161.

26. Plotz, "Childhood Lost," 146.

Hartley, of course, was the toddler whose joyous oneness with a feminized Nature his father had celebrated in 1798 in both "The Nightingale: A Conversation Poem" and "Frost at Midnight," the poems Coleridge shared with Wordsworth before the latter's composition of "Tintern Abbey." The conclusion of "Frost at Midnight" offers what is arguably the most powerfully condensed construction of a space designed to blur the binaries of both age and gender. And, not coincidentally, Coleridge's great poem also presents the most pronounced male appropriation of a maternal imagination. Left alone with the peacefully slumbering infant "cradled by my side," the speaker evades all other "inmates of my cottage," including the mother whose role he assumes as he watches, with "tender gladness," the "gentle breathings" of his "so beautiful" babe (lines 44, 4, 49, 45, 48). The speaker's closeness to the cradled boy only sharpens his sense of paralyzed adulthood. He feels mired in a present irreparably removed from a vital, androgynous childhood in which he and a sister, now dead, were playmates "clothed alike" (line 43). Through an extraordinary manipulation of layerings of time and space, the alienated speaker tries to become whole again by projecting a future for his sleeping son. No longer a passive watcher, he activates a shaping imagination as fecund as the "brooding" maternal force Milton apostrophized in *Paradise Lost*. Father and son are now jointly infused with a new vitality. Reborn within a matrix that is immune to seasonal change, Hartley is freed to wander under the protection of a "quiet Moon" (an action that also culminates the garrulous "father's tale" of "The Nightingale"). And, having animated a new Adam, the god-like poet has also managed to remother himself.

Lamb's letter to Coleridge, then, involves more than an attack on the presumed unimaginativeness of certain women pedagogues. For, in denouncing "the cursed Barbauld crew," Lamb knowingly takes sides in an emerging conflict between male and female writers vying for possession over the unformed child. That contest, as recent criticism has shown, also informs major Romantic texts such as Mary Shelley's *Frankenstein* (1818). Born a year after Hartley Coleridge, the daughter of Mary Wollstonecraft and William Godwin (both of whom wrote and published books for children) had a firsthand knowledge of male mothering after losing her mother in infancy.[27] It is therefore hardly coincidental that she chose to

27. See William Veeder, *Mary Shelley and 'Frankenstein'* (University of Chicago Press, 1986); U. C. Knoepflmacher, "Thoughts on the Aggression of Daughters," in George Levine and U. C. Knoepflmacher, *The Endurance of 'Frankenstein'* (Berkeley: University

give a distinctly Coleridgean cast to Frankenstein's Adamic creature. For Shelley has the creature remember how, newly formed, with arms outstretched, he stood naked in a moon-bathed landscape. The posture, which mimics that which Coleridge adopted for little Hartley in both "The Nightingale" and "Frost at Midnight," deliberately links Shelley's "hideous progeny" to that earlier object of Romantic experimentation. The fictional giant who wants to live a child-life with little William and the miniaturist who would celebrate microscopic forms of life are, after all, distinct cousins. Both are child-men compelled to see themselves as deformities, monsters unfit for adult life in a heterosexual order.

Writing to Coleridge as a personal friend and as one of Hartley's mentors, Charles Lamb poses as a partisan of those male anti-didacticists who wished to reclaim a "wild" childhood domain, free from all female authority. But his partisanship also remains equivocal. The original books for children that he and his sister Mary produced for Godwin after the success of their *Tales from Shakespear* in 1807—the stories collected in *Mrs. Leicester's School* and the verses gathered in *Poetry for Children* (both 1809)— place them squarely in the rival camp of the female moralists. Lamb may have been correct to assume that Hartley deserved something better than the props he would have found in the works of Barbauld and Trimmer; but given his own practice as a didactic writer for children, he also appears to have sensed that "wild tales" alone were not sufficient to make "the child a man."

But for a historian like Humphrey Carpenter to equate the children's books of Anna Barbauld with those of Maria Edgeworth, and "one or two [unnamed] others" who "tried their best" yet with "limp" results, is as dubious a sleight-of-hand as Summerfield's similarly dismissive coupling of the religious Barbauld and the rationalist Mary Wollstonecraft, whose *Original Stories* for children (which Blake engraved in 1791) he characterizes as being "permeated by a grim, humourless, tyrannical spirit."[28] As Mitzi Myers has suggested in a review of Summerfield's book, a double standard seems to operate whenever male commentators refuse to distinguish the work of an Edgeworth or Wollstonecraft from the more pedestrian efforts of Barbauld. Instead of exploring the cultural causes that led women who wrote for children in the late eighteenth and early nineteenth

---

of California Press, 1979), 88–119; Anne K. Mellor, *Mary Shelley: Her Life, Her Fiction, Her Monsters* (London: Routledge, 1988).

28. Carpenter, *Secret Gardens,* 2; Summerfield, *Fantasy and Reason,* 299.

century to endorse realism, reason, and the "grown-up values associated with mature reflection," critics prefer to denounce all such efforts for their resistance to fantasy.[29] Myers's own rehabilitation of the child-texts of Wollstonecraft and Edgeworth is a welcome antidote. Her careful anatomy of the conventions that operate in these works should halt further bouts of dismissive contempt for writers who, at their finest, were able to offer their juvenile readers an equivalent of the sophisticated domestic moralism that Jane Austen propagated in her novels for adults.

But what about those post-Romantic women authors whose writings for children could hardly remain unaffected by the success of male fantasists such as MacDonald and Carroll? At the beginning of the nineteenth century, Edgeworth could resist the magic of the "wild tales" that Lamb extols in his letter to Coleridge. But by the mid-century, a new generation of writers saw themselves not only as the descendants of the literary foremothers who had shaped what Summerfield calls the "Edgeworthian, empiricist view of what can be said to constitute 'reality,'"[30] but also as the rightful heirs of the unlettered female storytellers, peasant women or nursemaids, whose materials Perrault and the Grimms had co-opted. Whether these lower-class spinners of tales—presented as informants, witnesses, narrators, or even inventors of the magical events they relay— were not themselves a literary invention matters less than the new authority such a personage seemed to confer on women writers. As Nina Auerbach and I have shown, the fairy tale was reclaimed as a literature of their own by mid-Victorian women writers eager to tap its rich mythical resources.[31]

Still, even in their imaginative fairy-tale adaptations for children or for adults, these women authors continued to respect the "Edgeworthian" tradition. Fairy tales, to be sure, could offer unaging princes and princesses as well as gardens and castles so well conserved that they hardly needed repair. By way of contrast, as Anne Thackeray Ritchie humorously remarked at the outset of her *Fairy Tales for Grown Folks* (written around

29. Mitzi Myers, "Wise Child, Wise Peasant, Wise Guy: Geoffrey Summerfield's Case Against the Eighteenth Century," *Children's Literature Association Quarterly* 12 (1987): 108–9.

30. Summerfield, *Fantasy and Reason,* 305.

31. Nina Auerbach and U. C. Knoepflmacher, eds., *Forbidden Journeys: Fairy Tales and Fantasies by Victorian Women Writers* (Chicago: University of Chicago Press, 1992), 11–20, 135–38.

the time that Carroll finished *Wonderland*), the "realistic stories for children" had become badly frayed: "Little Henry and his Bearer, Poor Harry and Lucy, have very nearly given up their little artless ghosts and prattle, and ceased making their own beds for the instruction of less excellently brought up little boys and girls."[32] Still, despite her ironic allusion to Mary Martha Sherwood's 1814 Evangelical best-seller and to Edgeworth's own 1801 text, Ritchie is by no means suggesting that the earlier literature of instruction had become extinct. Sherwood's work was simply updated, as Patricia Demers has shown, by the less sermonizing, but still heavily didactic, Evangelical children's books of Hesba Stratton, whose popular *Little Meg's Children* (1868) handled social issues treated in a far more fantastic vein by George MacDonald.[33] And the poetry of earlier domestic moralists continued to be reissued. Anne and Jane Taylor's *Original Poems for Infant Minds* (1804–5), for instance, included perennial favorites such as Ann's "My Mother" and Jane's "Twinkle, Twinkle, Little Star," verses whose appeal remained undiminished by Carroll's *Wonderland* parodies and which met no competition until the appearance of Christina Rossetti's *Sing-Song* in 1872. Even Ritchie herself not only edited and wrote about Edgeworth's work, but also aligned herself with the Edgeworthian tradition by converting old fairy tales into domestic narratives about ordinary lives—minutely detailed, closely observed psychological studies worthy of an Elizabeth Gaskell or George Eliot.

Given the receptivity of audiences who welcomed the retold folk tales and invented *Kunstmärchen* that had begun to flood the market ever since the 1823 translation of the Grimms, and, given, too, their own powerful attraction to romance, why did imaginative Victorian women writers approach fantasy so much more guardedly than their male counterparts? Just as Gaskell and George Eliot respected the norms of causality much more than Dickens, so did Jean Ingelow, Christina Rossetti, and Juliana

32. Anne Thackeray Ritchie, "The Sleeping Beauty in the Wood," in Auerbach and Knoepflmacher, *Forbidden Journeys,* 21–22. Mary Martha Sherwood's *Little Henry and His Bearer* (1814) is the story of an Anglo-Indian boy who converts his Hindoo bearer to Christianity before dying. As didactic but less sentimental was Maria Edgeworth's *Harry and Lucy* (1801).

33. See Patricia Demers, "The Letter and the Spirit of Evangelical Writing of and for Children," in McGavran, *Romanticism and Children's Literature,* 129–49. Juliana Horatia Ewing's *The Story of a Short Life* (1885), which Judith Plotz discusses in the same volume ("A Victorian Comfort Book," 168–89), can also be seen as a more sophisticated Victorian updating of Sherwood's cruder *Little Henry.*

Horatia Ewing create children's stories that handle with much greater circumspection the fantastical elements freely deployed by Ruskin, Mac-Donald, and Carroll. Some of this guardedness undoubtedly stemmed from their affiliation with religious publishing houses and journals that could guarantee women writers a wider juvenile audience. But Carroll's and MacDonald's religious credentials were just as impeccable, and they even contributed to some of the same magazines for which Ingelow and Ewing wrote. We therefore need to turn to other cultural explanations to help us understand the caution of post-Romantic women writers in their ventures into the fantastic.

V

In fashioning their narratives for and about children, Victorian women relied on a rather different experience of childhood than that which had influenced the fantasies created by their male counterparts. Whereas the male fantasists discussed above were eager to blur and dissolve sexual differences, their female competitors were more likely to insist on the reality of gender binaries. Unlike sons whom a nineteenth-century middle-class culture pushed out of the maternal sphere at an early age, daughters remained attached to the mother for a much longer period. Some girls, like their brothers, were sent off to educational establishments away from home, while others received their instruction from domestic tutors, governesses, or older members of their family. But even when the middle-class matriarch did not directly undertake her own daughter's instruction—as many well-educated women, such as Jean Ingelow's mother, for example, felt compelled to do—the Victorian mother usually maintained a more extended dominance than her twentieth-century equivalent. In 1886, when work outside the home was becoming acceptable for many young women, the anonymous author of an essay entitled "Between School and Marriage" still urged the female offspring of the gentry and the middle class to stay at home and "pay her way by filling in the little spaces in home life as only a dear daughter can, by lifting the weight of care from her mother."[34]

The average Victorian matron who zealously guarded her unmarried

---

34. "Between School and Marriage," *Girl's Own Paper,* 4 September 1886, 769. I am grateful to Professor Sally Mitchell for this quotation.

daughters until they might pass into the control of a husband thus exerted powers that resulted in a double identification. As Nancy Chodorow and Jessica Benjamin have noted in discussing mother-daughter relations in our own times, an internal bond with the same-sex parent makes sexual maturation less problematic for girls than for boys; yet a prolongation of the original childhood dependence into the years of adolescence—and, in mid-Victorian times, often far beyond—can hamper a daughter's need to assert her independence. For nineteenth-century women who never underwent the separation so keenly felt by growing Victorian males, there was no similar allure in a wishful merger with the mother or with fantasized substitutes. The fusions and projections so prominent in the fantasy-constructions of male desire thus were more likely to be resisted or even opposed by women who had already faced the more complicated task of simultaneously affiliating and disaffiliating themselves from a maternal influence that insisted on their submission.[35]

Even in a fantastic masterpiece such as *Wuthering Heights,* Emily Brontë distances herself from the intense desire for gender transcendence she dramatizes through Heathcliff and Catherine. Like their Romantic precursors, these bifurcated halves of a single "I" want to recover a sexually undifferentiated childhood oneness. Yet if *Wuthering Heights* seems close to "Tintern Abbey" in its longing for a fusion of male and female selves, it also ironizes that very desire through the figure of that would-be Wordsworthian, young Lockwood. Snugly sequestered in Catherine's oak bed, this Carrollian bachelor first identifies himself with—and then cruelly repudiates—a female dream-child. Drawn to Catherine's old diary, "scrawled in an unformed, childish hand,"[36] Lockwood carries her own defiance of adult male authority into the first of his two dreams. Yet when she materializes in his second dream, Lockwood becomes terrified by her touch. He resists her pleas to enter the bed that was once her own with the same cruel desperation shown, in the Grimm fairy tale, by the princess who tries to smash the slimy frog who has crept into her chamber.

Having at first regarded the girl as a desexualized playfellow, an ally for his own circumvention of an adult masculinity, Lockwood now views

35. Nancy Chodorow, *The Reproduction of Mothering: Psychoanalysis and the Sociology of Gender* (Berkeley and Los Angeles: University of California Press, 1979), 96–97; Benjamin, *Bonds of Love,* 77–79, 151–56.

36. Emily Brontë, *Wuthering Heights,* ed. William M. Sale, Jr. and Richard J. Dunn, 3d ed. (New York: W. W. Norton, 1990), 16.

her as an erotic invader of the female space he has usurped. Her reclamation of that space threatens his own sexual identity. The woman who returns to his bed in a child's shape challenges Lockwood's feminization of childhood. Although this specter chooses to appear as a small girl, Lockwood finds himself confronting the ghost of an adult woman torn between the allurements offered by rival male lovers. Moreover, by trying to cut off the penetrating limb whose touch he finds so repellent, he is driven to reverse her (and his own) sexual identity. Terrified by the unforeseen outcome of his earlier affiliation with a defiant little girl, Lockwood flees the Heights in order to be calmed by a maternal older woman, Nelly Dean.

Emily Brontë's reliance on this female realist to take over a narrative that the imbalanced Lockwood can no longer control bears an interesting relation to the many nineteenth-century child-texts governed by the authority figure whom Mitzi Myers calls a "mentoria."[37] If Nelly assumes the function discharged by the educated aunts, governesses, teachers, godmothers, grandmothers, and mothers in the narratives of the Edgeworthian school, her class origins also make her the equivalent of less learned dispensers of folk wisdom, the legendary spinners of "old wives tales" so dear to the eighteenth- and nineteenth-century imagination. For his part, Lockwood is relegated to the dependency of those youngsters represented as eager, though passive, listeners of the fabulous tales by a Mother Bunch or Mother Goose. Resting in bed, ministered and fed by Nelly, he needs a nurse's tale more than a wholesome meal to stabilize his disordered imagination. But his sexual immaturity also will prompt Lockwood to escape Nelly's efforts to interest him in the second Cathy, a widowed virgin. As a childish adult, a boy-man who fears female sexuality, Lockwood concludes that there is no place for him in the generative realm over which Nelly presides.

Brontë, of course, does not unreservedly endorse the woman who brags about her "reasonable" outlook. Nelly's lack of sympathy with adolescent longings she dismisses as irrational makes her resemble the repressive Nurse in Blake's *Songs of Experience*. Indeed, her narratorial authority is strongly challenged by the more imaginative Catherine, who predicts that the temporal order Nelly always invokes will eventually transform her into a "withered hag."[38] Still, despite Brontë's own qualms about Nelly and her undeniable sympathy with Heathcliff, it is significant that the

---

37. Myers, "Impeccable Governesses," 31–59.
38. Brontë, *Wuthering Heights,* 95.

novelist should qualify her assent to a Romantic wishfulness she rightly genders as masculine.

In his clever treatise on "child-loving," James Kincaid has fun with the notion of Heathcliff and Catherine as bedroom partners in childhood: their union, he asserts, is simply that of "genderless angels" on which "we" project "our erotic figurings."[39] As Kincaid knows from our many friendly exchanges, I have difficulties with his all-inclusive "we," particularly when women readers and women authors are excluded from his attempts to make pedophilia a prime link between "Victorian culture and ours." After allowing "us" to project our "figurings," not really on young Heathcliff, that rather grimy lad, but on the more adorable "boy David" Copperfield, Kincaid is ready to spring a big claim: "Gender," he concludes, "or any other set figure of sexual opposition is of very little importance to child-loving."[40] The remark might have been made by the witty Lockwood just before he was so severely unsettled by his second dream. For Brontë, after all, is no more a purveyor of pedophilic interest than are Edgeworth, Ingelow, Rossetti, and Ewing, or, for that matter, Thackeray and MacDonald. Despite my absolute delight in Kincaid's playful textual readings, my own ventures into Victorian child-texts lead me to conclusions contrary to his own. (As my discussion of *Through the Looking Glass* in chapter 6 makes clear, we even disagree about the one author both of us consider at length.) For, unlike Kincaid, I firmly believe, and expect to show throughout this study, that gender does indeed very much figure in the Victorian constructions—and deconstructions—of childhood and even of child-loving.

Unlike motherless orphans such as Emily Brontë and Mary Shelley, compelled to avail themselves at least partly of the constructions of desire devised by male imaginations, the three women writers I consider in this book remained closely linked to their mothers. As unmarried women, Jean Ingelow and Christina Rossetti did their most significant writing while residing with strong-willed and highly religious matriarchs from whom they were seldom separated. Ingelow was fifty-six when her namesake, Jean Kilgour Ingelow, died at the age of seventy-seven, and so was Rossetti when her own mother, Frances Polidori Rossetti, died at the age

---

39. James Kincaid, *Child-Loving: The Erotic Child and Victorian Culture* (London: Routledge, 1992),13.

40. Ibid.

of eighty-five. Although Juliana Horatia Gatty left her parents after finding "a double of myself" in Colonel Alexander Ewing, whom she married at the age of twenty-six,[41] her writing career continued to be intertwined with that of her enterprising mother, an author of considerable standing both as a naturalist and a writer for juveniles. As editor of *Aunt Judy's Magazine* until her death in 1873 at the age of sixty-seven, Margaret Scott Gatty helped to disseminate the work of the daughter whose superior literary talents she had recognized and fostered.

Ewing's terse but moving tribute to this literary mother, "In Memoriam, Margaret Gatty," more fully discussed in my last chapter, avoids the more intimate note Christina Rossetti always adopts in her own acts of homage to "my first Love, my Mother, on whose knee / I learnt love-lore that is not troublesome; / Whose service is my special dignity."[42] For, unlike Rossetti or Ingelow, Ewing can view her mother as a public figure. Despite her access to personal details unknown to other eulogists, she prefers to assess a woman of letters whose sensibility and cultural interests overlap with her own. Margaret Gatty is treated as a much-respected forerunner, not as the object of a worshipful daughter's first love.

By assessing her mother with the empirical objectivity that Margaret Gatty displayed in her own writings, Ewing can indirectly attest to that forerunner's influence. As an intellectual model, this mentoria thus could be kept apart from the more fallible woman whose occasional lapses in mothering did not escape her sharp-eyed daughter. As I argue in my last chapter, Ewing's brilliant "Amelia and the Dwarfs" owes much of its success to precisely such a separation. In this astute comic fable about the transmission of female authority, the asocial Amelia acquires the identity of a grown-up woman despite the obstacle posed by her mother's dubious example as an enforcer of domestic order.

The transmission of authority made possible by a mother or by maternal surrogates also preoccupies Ingelow and Rossetti in their own fables for the young. In Ingelow's *Mopsa the Fairy* there is no single maternal domain such as Ruskin's Treasure Valley or MacDonald's land at the back

41. Quoted in Maxwell, *Mrs. Gatty and Mrs. Ewing,* 163.

42. Christina Rossetti, "Sonnets Are Full of Love," lines 5–7; this dedicatory sonnet introduced the 1881 edition of *A Pageant and Other Poems; The Complete Poems of Christina Rossetti, A Variorum Edition,* ed. R. W. Crump (Baton Rouge: Louisiana State University Press, 1986), 2:59.

of North Wind. Instead, the blurred boundaries of the maternal fairylands Jack visits only contribute to his and the reader's disorientation. The boy's relief at finding himself safely back in a Victorian domestic present is a little like the relief Lockwood feels when his return to the domestic Grange provides him with the antidote to the seamless nightmares and shifting snowdrifts that threatened to erase all identity markers. Like Lockwood, Jack now yields gratefully to a storyteller who stabilizes his imagination. His mother's familiar voice —the last of many female voices heard in Ingelow's narrative—soothes Jack as much as Nelly had calmed Lockwood.

But the mother whose final song is about separation and loss seems more imaginative than Nelly Dean. For, like the poet-narrator who tells the story of Jack and Mopsa, she seems to understand the plight of a boy whose development lags behind that of his beloved Mopsa, the girl who grew up before he did, just as Catherine preceded Heathhcliff in her mental and sexual maturation. Ingelow empathizes with Jack, but she strongly identifies with Queen Mopsa's Catherine-like nostalgia. Whereas Carroll undercuts the authority of queens who irritate him as much as they do Alice, Ingelow prefers to stress the painful constraints placed on their authority. In *Mopsa,* neither fairy queens nor a human refugee who has fled to fairyland to escape the inequities of class and gender are ever given the absolute power that Thackeray grants to Fairy Blackstick or MacDonald to Princess Makemnoit. Still, despite their inhibited power and their deference to an ordinary Victorian boy, these adult women possess the linguistic authority he lacks.

That authority is wielded with angry forcefulness by the didactic Aunt whom Rossetti casts as the narrator of the three linked stories of *Speaking Likenesses.* Rossetti's subversiveness, already apparent in her poetry for adults and in the deceptively "innocent" lyrics of *Sing-Song,* is much more pronounced than Ingelow's or Ewing's. The reader of *Mopsa* gradually discovers that a fantasy named after the fairy-princess who outgrows Jack is no more a boy's book than *Alice in Wonderland* was a fiction for girls. Rossetti, however, never pretends that the tales told by an autocratic narrator to her little nieces belong anywhere else than in a girl's book. More hostile than Ingelow or Ewing towards the possessiveness of male sentimentalists who tried to endear themselves to special girl-friends, Rossetti has her unsentimental narrator take absolute charge. By steadily undermining a hunger for the fabulous, she refuses to mend—as Ingelow and

Ewing preferred to do—the fantasies for children devised by her male contemporaries.

Unlike Rossetti, both Ingelow and Ewing willingly adopt fantastic forms in order to repossess an imaginative tradition they regard as their own. By working within the modes of Carroll and MacDonald, Ingelow both signifies and masks her conflicts with the male texts she tries to counter. By rescuing and recasting an old Irish folk tale that had been transmitted by generations of female storytellers, Ewing can indirectly offer a corrective to Ruskin's fabrication of a pseudo-folk tale that elides all female authority. Rossetti, however, repossesses fairy-tale motifs to thwart the expectations of little girls whose imaginings, she feels, have been excessively conditioned by Carroll. The boys in *Speaking Likenesses* are as sadistic and possessive as the goblin men who try to lure Lizzie in Rossetti's "Goblin Market."

Speaking Likenesses carries a dedication "To My Dearest Mother in Grateful Remembrance of the Stories with which She Used to Entertain Her Children." Had the author of this excessively deferential dedication conveniently forgotten that she had once despised, as vehemently as Lewis Carroll or her own brothers did, the moral fables her mother insisted on reading to the four Rossetti children?[43] Nor could a narrative that includes figures as bizarre as the Medusa-headed goddess of discourse who plagues little Flora really be anchored in a "remembrance" of Mary Martha Sherwood's *Fairchild Family* or Thomas Day's *Sandford and Merton,* as Rossetti's dedication seems to hint. It was her own anger at what she perceived as a male usurpation of a maternal discourse that led Rossetti to place her powers of fantasy in the service of an anti-fantastical ideology.

Despite their discrepant strategies, however, Rossetti, Ingelow, and Ewing are at one in their desire to reclaim the female authority appropriated in Romantic poems about childhood and in those post-Romantic fictions in which an Effie Gray and Alice Liddell could act as catalysts for male self-projections. It is lamentable that the textual reappropriations these women authors undertook should have been so steadily ignored by the critics and literary historians who write about children's books. The innovativeness of the child-texts I consider in my last four chapters has been greatly underestimated. Texts designed to challenge what was, and still

---

43. See Georgina Battiscombe, *Christina Rossetti: A Divided Life* (New York: Holt, Rinehart, and Winston, 1981), 21.

remains, by far the most popular children's book of the 1860s have been dismissed, paradoxically, for presumably offering little more than lame "imitations" of *Alice in Wonderland*.[44]

That misconception, ironically enough, has above all hurt the reputation of the most subversive of these counter-texts, *Speaking Likenesses*. Missing the sarcasm of Rossetti's self-deprecating remark that her book was fashioned in the "likeness" of Carroll's, critics felt justified in seeing it as little more than an imperfect copy. Unlike Ingelow's or Ewing's writings for children, the text remained unreprinted for over a century until reissued in 1991—with *Mopsa*, "Amelia," and other works—by Nina Auerbach and myself. As we suggest in our introduction to *Speaking Likenesses*, Rossetti uses the last of her three stories as a parable that calls attention to her defiance of the male predecessors whose minds had feasted on a feminized childhood. Maggie, the most ideal of her three little protagonists, stoutly resists the insatiable Mouth-Boy who threatens to ingest the provisions entrusted to her by her grandmother. By fending off a creature whose horrible mouth is even wider than those of Carroll's Duchess and Humpty Dumpty combined, this Little Red Riding Hood repudiates a Wolf who stands for the devouring imaginations of the Grimms and their male successors.

Ingelow and Ewing are less overt in their reclamations. By turning Jack's fantastic adventures into a bildungsroman about Mopsa's growth, Ingelow tries to preserve a realm of the female imagination free from incursions by a loving but immature male. Mopsa is not just segregated, however, from the boy who returns to his Victorian "mamma"; she is also cast as a foil of the *Wonderland* Alice who trudged off, even more gladly, to a home where she might forget her increasingly unpleasant adventures. Unlike Alice, Mopsa remains in a wonderland she cannot flee. Accepting the crown that Carroll will wrest away from the *Looking-Glass* Alice, this wiser but sadder figure proves that the rulers of female fantasylands need not be deformed into grotesque caricatures of adult women.

Ewing's Amelia is another anti-Alice. This curious and determined child also aborts her sojourn among sadistic underground creatures in order to

44. Joining *Speaking Likenesses* and *Mopsa the Fairy* in a short paragraph on "imitations" so "far from *Alice* in character and intention that they tell us little," Humphry Carpenter fails to see that it is precisely through their distancings from Carroll that texts "which blend Carrollian fantasy with moral earnestness" tell something very worth understanding (*Secret Gardens*, 57).

return to Victorian domesticity. But, unlike the girl who tries to impress the Wonderland creatures with the inanities of her elders, Amelia is not a conformist. Instead, the underworld into which she is thrust mirrors her own anarchist leanings. Hence, unlike Alice and more like Mopsa, Ewing's heroine finds that her venture into fantasyland allows her to remake herself into a responsible adult. Whereas Alice offends the arrested denizens of the world into which Carroll has pressed her, Amelia uses her sexual charms to outwit besotted dwarfs as eager to detain her as Carroll had been to detain his dream-child. Amelia's relation to the dwarfs is Ewing's version of Maggie's relation to the Mouth-Boy, for it acts as an emblem for a woman writer who emulates in order to repudiate. By adapting an authentic old wives' tale and by highlighting Amelia's resourcefulness, Ewing restores an activist matriarchalism suppressed by Perrault, the Grimms, and the Victorian inventors of pseudo-*märchen*.[45] And, willing to educate sadistic boys as much as aggressive girls, Ewing tames a Mouth-Boy in "Benjy in Beastland," the pendant she devised for "Amelia and the Dwarfs." As a reconciler who managed to recombine the traditions of fantasy and domestic realism, Ewing effected a synthesis that would prove helpful to later writers for children. It is no coincidence that, in the next generation, both Edith Nesbit and Rudyard Kipling should have regarded her as a prime source of inspiration.

When, in the closure of Nesbit's Psammead fantasies or at the end of Kipling's Mowgli stories, a mother materializes to revalidate her children, we are reminded of a feature of common interest to the Victorian women and men who wrote for the young. Ewing's Amelia and Ingelow's Jack embrace their mothers after their sojourn in fantasylands; Rossetti's Maggie resists grotesques before she returns to the welcoming arms of her grandmother. Although, as I have been insisting, the recovery of the maternal meant something substantially different for women authors of children's books than it did for their male counterparts, it is also true that this quest remained a common denominator for writers—and readers—of both sexes. Although the fantasies I shall examine in the next ten chapters

45. Ewing counters the passivity which the Grimms had enforced on the once-active folk-heroines they also silenced. See Maria Tatar, "Paradigms for Powerlessness," in *The Hard Facts of the Grimms' Fairy Tales* (Princeton: Princeton University Press, 1987), 71–80; and Ruth Bottigheimer, "Silenced Women in the Grimms' Tales," in *Fairy Tales and Society: Illusion, Allusion, and Paradigm,* ed. Ruth Bottigheimer (Philadelphia: University of Pennsylvania Press, 1986), 115–31.

are conditioned by differences in gender, they go back to the imaginings of a shared early childhood. The scene in which a little elephant is nuzzled by Mrs. Jumbo has, I am prepared to believe, the same emotional appeal for all watchers of *Dumbo*—for girls and their mothers as much as for little boys and their imprudent fathers.

T W O

Resisting Growth: Ruskin's
The King of the Golden River

*It was in this mood that he conceived those oft-
reiterated regrets for a half-ideal childhood, when
the relics of Paradise still clung about the soul—a
childhood, as it seemed, full of the fruits of old age,
lost for all, in a degree, in the passing away of the
youth of the world, lost for each one, over again, in
the passing away of actual youth.*
        —WALTER PATER, *"Wordsworth"*

*It may indeed be questioned whether we have any
memories at all* from *our childhood: memories* relating
to *our childhood may be all that we possess.*
        —SIGMUND FREUD, *"Screen Memories"*

I

"How things bind and blend themselves together!" mused a seventy-year-old John Ruskin in the last paragraph of *Praeterita,* the lyrical autobiography he concluded in 1889. In this remembrance of things past, Ruskin's most resolute attempt to come to terms with his origins, realism blends with an intense wishfulness. A lifetime's desire to retrieve the emblems of cultural wholeness and purity now takes the shape of a personal quest as an old man rummages through the residual layerings of his backward-looking, richly evocative mind. Landscapes interpenetrate, merged by memory. Young faces dissolve into old ones. Juxtaposition, always Ruskin's forte, yields likeness in unlikeness. Although the final vision is, appropriately enough, one of approaching darkness, a golden radiance confers eternity on a moment in time: "Through the sunset that faded into thunderous night as I entered Siena three days before, the white edges of the mountainous clouds still lighted from the west, and the openly golden sky calm behind the Gate of Siena's heart, with its golden words, *Cor magis tibi Sena pandit,* and the fireflies everywhere in sky and cloud rising and falling, mixed with the lightning, and more intense than the stars" (*CW,* 35:561–62).

Ruskin is alone as he imaginatively crosses the gate to this golden Eden. But, in the previous paragraph, where he reconstructs still another refuge from darkness, his garden at Denmark Hill, he becomes rejuvenated by the company, not of one, but of two Eves: "I draw back to my own home, twenty years ago, permitted to thank Heaven once more for the peace, and hope, and loveliness of it, and the Elysian walks with Joanie, and Paradisiacal with Rosie, under the peach-blossom branches by the little glittering stream which I had paved for them" (*CW,* 35:560). Here, too, nature and artifice fuse. Yet the awed observer of a skyscape is presented as the lord of his own garden. He can pave the glittering stream. And he can screen the entering inmates. For it is significant that Ruskin's two companions should be remembered as children only, still "girlish" figures (*CW,* 35:542). His cousin "Joanie" Agnew is not yet Mrs. Arthur Severn, the matronly caretaker of Ruskin's aged mother and, later, of himself. Ruskin bars that older incarnation from the garden so precious to his memory; he will place her children but not the adult woman into that privileged space.[1] "Rosie" La Touche, the second companion, remains similarly arrested in time. She is closer to the graceful ten-year-old he first met in 1859 than to the young woman whose painful references to a briefly shared "Eden-land" now sting the "sorrowful" old man and remind him of having ever since "lost sight of that peach-blossom avenue" (*CW,* 35:561). He can reopen that avenue only by retreating into a precarious realm of imagined innocence.

Almost half a century before he composed *Praeterita,* Ruskin had fashioned another golden blending of art and nature as a preserve for the desexualized "innocence" of childhood. If *Praeterita* enlists the nostalgia of memory, *The King of the Golden River, or, The Black Brothers,* though similarly retrogressive, activates those "forward-looking thoughts" and "stirrings of inquietude" which the growing child evokes, according to Wordsworth, in the maturing adult.[2] The little book ostensibly intended for the thirteen-year-old Euphemia Gray was written in 1841 before Ruskin's delayed graduation from Oxford and before his propulsion into eminence with the publication of the first two volumes of *Modern Painters* (1843, 1846). Yet despite his later disparagement of the work, it anticipates many of the central ideas Ruskin was to develop in his more serious, theoretical writings.

Still, as Jane Merrill Filstrup has rightly suggested, *The King of the Golden River* also is shaped by the incipient fears that beset Ruskin during his "early manhood."[3] And these fears not only stemmed from doubts about his "aesthetic appreciation of nature," as Filstrup shows, but also involved far more elementary insecurities about assuming the identity of

---

1. When Ruskin celebrates Joan Agnew, he deliberately infantilizes her movements. Her "beautiful dancing," he notes, was childlike and "right," devoid of the coquetry that has "disgraced all feminine motion for the last quarter of a century" (*CW,* 35:560). To characterize such "rightness," he reproduces his description of a child-dancer from the 1867 *Time and Tide:* "She caricatured *no older person,* [but] looked and behaved *innocently,*—and she danced her joyful dance with perfect grace, spirit, sweetness, and *self-forgetfulness*" (ibid., 559; also *CW,* 17:337–38; italics added).

2. William Wordsworth, "Michael," lines 148–49.

3. Merrill Filstrup, "Thirst for Enchanted Views in Ruskin's *The King of the Golden River,*" *Children's Literature* 8 (1980): 77–78. Filstrup's emphasis on the "aesthetic morality" of Ruskin's fairy tale is shared by George P. Landow in "And the World Became Strange: Realms of Literary Fancy," *Georgia Review* 33 (Spring 1979): 12–15.

an adult male. "Phemy's fairy tale," as the young author called it at the time, acted as an important emotional outlet for the over-nurtured only child of Margaret and John James Ruskin. By casting himself as the deprived and parentless child Gluck, the boy-Cinderella, Ruskin could indulge emotions that did not fully erupt into his consciousness until 1863, when cloaked self-pity turned into open anger and recrimination. Only then, after the failure of his marriage, the hopelessness of his love for Rose LaTouche, and his consequent displacement of that love onto the little girls at the school of Winnington Hall, did Ruskin squarely blame his parents for having made him unfit "for the duties of middle life." He accused his father for the "two terrific mistakes which mamma & you involuntarily fell into" in the supervising of his growth. Instead of having been taught how to be steeled against adversity, "severely disciplined and exercised in the sternest way," forced "to lie on stone beds and eat black soup," he had—he complained—been raised as an overindulged middle-class child: "You fed me *effeminately* and luxuriously," he insisted (italics added). A parental insistence on the religious denial of "all the earnest fire of passion and life" had presumably rendered him passive and volitionless: "for I thought it my duty to be thwarted—it was the religion that led me all wrong here . . . . Now, my power of *duty* has been exhausted in vain."[4]

Ruskin's long-delayed 1863 outburst at the "dearest Father" to whom he had so dutifully submitted all of his writings, including "Phemy's fairy tale," and whom he would again idealize in *Praeterita,* was written, significantly enough, from the precincts of Winnington Hall, the girls' school in which he had assumed the avuncular role of mentor and guardian of his "little birds." It was in the same year that Lewis Carroll launched "Alice's Adventures Under Ground," his own avuncular confrontation with a female dream-child. But the young Ruskin who had authored *The King of the Golden River* in 1841, more than two decades earlier, was not yet the child-lover of the 1860s. He had accepted the lively Phemy Gray's challenge to write a fairy tale because he was eager to ward off personal anxieties about change and death. They were both in need of therapeutic relief. She had just lost three younger sisters to scarlet fever; he, then twenty-

4. John Ruskin to John James Ruskin, 17 December 1863, *The Winnington Letters: John Ruskin's Correspondence with Margaret Alexis Bell and the Children at Winnington Hall,* ed. Van Akin Burd (Cambridge: Harvard University Press, 1969), 458–59.

two, was convalescing at Leamington after a bout of what his ever-solici-
tous parents feared might turn into fatal tuberculosis.[5]

Although *The King of the Golden River* was composed at Euphemia
Gray's express request, its prime readers were Ruskin's parents, who made
sure to retain a manuscript copy for themselves before forwarding Phemy
her own. The elder Ruskins appreciated the tale as a reassuring token of
their son's uncorrupted—and incorruptible—"innocence." *The King of
the Golden River* ends on a note of submission. Only when Gluck, the passive young protagonist, accepts the authority of the paternalistic little King
can a lost Eden be restored: "And thus the Treasure Valley became a garden again, and the inheritance, which had been lost by cruelty, was regained by love" (*KGR,* 67). Margaret Ruskin wrote to John, "I like your
Fairy Tale amazingly." And, to signify that she had fully grasped the implications of that ending about an inheritance regained by love, she added:
"The latter part I think quite equal to the beginning—did I mention this
before?"[6] Her husband proudly concurred: "I almost wish Fairy Tale was
printed . . . —very moral and descriptive."[7] But it was not to get printed
in 1841, despite the elder Ruskin's attempts to bring it to the attention of
a friendly publisher.[8]

On the surface, then, Ruskin's story about an effeminate boy eventually
rewarded for his charitable behavior was addressed to a double audience
of child and adult by a writer whose delayed adolescence caused him to
continue to hover between the opposed states of innocence and experience.
Despite his eagerness to obtain the approval of this dual readership, how-

5. He was also recovering from an infection of a different sort—his unreciprocated
infatuation with Adele Domecq, the daughter of his father's business partner, who attracted him far more than the younger Euphemia Gray.

6. Margaret Ruskin to John Ruskin, 7 October 1841, *The Ruskin Family Letters,* ed.
Van Akin Burd (Ithaca: Cornell University Press, 1973), 2:695.

7. John James Ruskin to John Ruskin, 9 October 1841, *Ruskin Family Letters,* 700. In
the previous paragraph, Ruskin's father instructs his twenty-two-year-old "boy": "*Eat
slowly masticate well* especially minced Collops."

8. John James Ruskin apparently had his wife write out still another copy of his son's
fairy tale for the benefit of W. H. Harrison, the editor of an annual. In a letter informing
John that "Harrison comes today to read Fairy Tale," the elder Ruskin also saw fit to
copy out a long poem in which Harrison's own "lame boy" displays a submissiveness
that well exceeds that of the fictional Gluck: "I am a fragile, feeble boy; / And many
[lads?] I see / Who while the hours with sport and toy / Too manful all for me" (*Ruskin
Family Letters,* 696–98).

ever, Ruskin was not wholly able to prevent quite contrary emotions from piercing through this acquiescent offering of a fable that was itself about acquiescence. The angry rebelliousness that would openly erupt in his later career already lurks in *The King of the Golden River,* as half-submerged as those threatening black rocks over which waters swirl "wildly into the night" (*KGR,* 54, 59).

II

Ruskin's realization that *The King of the Golden River* was shaped by something more than pure filial "duty" may well account for his later attempts to distance himself from that youthful production. Literature written for children, he increasingly came to believe, should not trouble "the sweet peace of youth with premature glimpses of uncomprehended passion," but rather uphold the "unquestioning innocence" of its prime audience.[9] Unlike the women didacticists of the Edgeworthian school of realism, Ruskin regarded fairy tales as ideal child fare and insisted that they ought not be moralized "to suit particular tastes, or inculcate favourite doctrines." Any "retouching" of such old stories, he felt, would disturb meanings that had evolved "naturally"; by simply confirming the innate morality—"unsullied and unhesitating"—of the very young, fairy tales could prepare children "submissively, and with no bitterness of astonishment, to behold, in later years, the mystery—divinely appointed to remain such to all human thought—of the fates that happen alike to evil and to good."[10] Neither the pronounced ideological outlook nor the satiric energies that powered Ruskin's writings for adults thus were to be admitted in texts for "unsullied" child readers.

But Ruskin's motives for distancing himself from his 1841 fairy tale were not confined to his notions about pure and impure child-texts. There were compelling personal reasons for him to play down his authorship of the story that had so greatly pleased his initial readers. When *The King of the Golden River* finally did appear in December of 1850, nine years after its composition, lavishly illustrated by Richard Doyle, its author was no longer a youth writing for a private audience, fit though few. At work on *The Stones of Venice,* he had become a literary celebrity with the publica-

---

9. John Ruskin, "Fairy Stories" (1868; *CW,* 19:234, 235).
10. Ibid., 236, 235.

tion of the first two volumes of *Modern Painters* and *The Seven Lamps of Architecture* (1849), issued by Smith, Elder, and Company, who now also published his fairy tale. There was, moreover, an additional change in circumstances. Little Phemy Gray had turned into sensual Effie Ruskin. For Ruskin's 1841 child reader had become the alluring young bride he married, with the reluctant approval of his parents, on April 10, 1848, the day of one of the largest Chartist political protests.

The story of Ruskin's ill-fated marriage to Effie, of its annulment on grounds of his failure to consummate it, of her remarriage to John Everett Millais, has been often and well told.[11] There is no need to rehearse it once more. But one question remains. By the time *The King of the Golden River* appeared in print, Ruskin's disaffection for his young wife had become more than manifest. The flirtatious woman he still tried to treat as a desexualized "Sweet Sister" now seemed to belong to the same "adult reality" he had resisted in his fairy tale, where his exaltation of "unquestioning innocence" could still bind him to a thirteen-year-old. Why, then, did he agree to publish a book that had been ostensibly written for her at such a markedly different phase of his emotional life?

The 1850 version of *The King of the Golden River* carried a prefatory "Advertisement" by its "Publishers" rather than an introduction by its unnamed "Author." This author, who is characterized as having composed the story "solely" to amuse a "very young lady," similarly unidentified, supposedly never entertained "any idea of publication." He is described as having at best given a "passive assent" to the "suggestion" made by an anonymous "friend" that the manuscript, which remained in that friend's private "possession," be at last made public. Given the author's distancing from his handiwork, the task of promoting the book and of conveying its meaning seems to have been left to the discretion of his publishers and to the artistry of the story's chosen illustrator. The "Advertisement" thus ends by stressing the prominent part played by this one named figure: "The illustrations, by Mr. Richard Doyle, will, it is hoped, be found to embody the Author's ideas with characteristic spirit" (*KGR,* 7).

11. See, especially, Mary Lutyens, *The Ruskins and the Grays* (London: John Murray, 1972), and Jeffrey L. Spear, "Ruskin on His Marriage: the Acland Letter," *Times Literary Supplement,* 10 February 1978, as well as the same author's *The Dreams of an English Eden: Ruskin and His Tradition in Social Criticism* (New York: Columbia University Press, 1984), 54–64. A popularized account of the marriage can also be found in Phyllis Rose, *Parallel Lives* (New York: Random House, 1983), 45–94.

In its suppressions, the "Advertisement" succeeds in depersonalizing all that is personal. It prevents the reader from speculating why such a volitionless author should have at last agreed to publish his story, nine years after its composition, at the suggestion of his anonymous "friend," a figure who has been identified as none other than Ruskin's father.[12] There is no hint that the "very young lady" at whose express "request" he originally wrote the story had later become the author's own wife, a touch that certainly would have endeared the project to sentimental Victorian readers. The two figures—a male adult and a female child—seem purposely unrelated, kept apart from each other, as well as from an "Author" somehow unwilling to be identified in his intimate relations as son and husband.

When, decades later in *Praeterita,* Ruskin was forced to take a stance towards *The King of the Golden River,* he continued to play down all emotional associations. Only after a seeming digression on the "comforts and restoratives" he found in Dickens's writings as a young man does Ruskin at last assess his own first effort as a fabulist. His botanical expeditions are made to appear far more significant than any creative efforts: "Under these peaceful conditions I began to look carefully at cornflowers, thistles, and hollyhocks; and find, by entry on Sep. 15th, that I was writing a bit of *The King of the Golden River*" (*CW,* 35:303). The author who must resort to a diary entry to bring himself to recall this little "bit" of original writing soon depreciates his creativity:

> The King of the Golden River was written to amuse a little girl; and being a fairly good imitation of Grimm and Dickens, mixed with a little true Alpine feeling of my own, has been rightly pleasing to nice children, and good for them. But it is totally valueless, for all that. I can no more write a story than compose a picture (*CW,* 35:303–4).

Ruskin's derogation of his book is excessive, as is his characterization of its derivativeness. That *The King of the Golden River* is highly imitative of the form of a German *Märchen* is certainly true. But Ruskin's adaptation of the Grimm stories he had found, as a child, in Edgar Taylor's *German Popular Tales* (1823, 1826) also involves significant departures. His changes,

---

12. See James S. Dearden, "*The King of the Golden River:* A Bio-Bibliographical Study," in *Studies in Ruskin: Essays in Honor of Van Akin Burd,* ed. Robert E. Rhodes and Del Ivan Janik (Athens: Ohio University Press, 1982), 32–59.

as we shall soon see, have much to do with the aggressive underpinnings of the tale his parents valued as a token of filial submission.

By giving his "passive assent" to his father's renewed plea that he publish *The King of the Golden River,* Ruskin seems to have hoped to erase fissures that had become more marked after a Venetian vacation he had taken in 1850 with Effie. Two years after his marriage, the man who eventually would devalue a work "pleasing to nice children" still found himself preferring the role of a "nice" child to that of a sexual adult. It seems significant that, in order to recapture the bond that had existed between himself and his father, Ruskin should have considered including in *Praeterita* a birthday letter that John James Ruskin had sent to Venice in 1850. In it, the elder Ruskin movingly described the intense happiness his only son "had given him in thirty-one years." Yet this treasured letter also had a slight flaw as a relic. For, in it, John James Ruskin made much of "Effie's beautifully written and graphically given account" of a Venetian ball the couple had recently attended.[13]

That vivid account, in which Effie describes dancing so energetically with the officers of the Austrian occupation army that "my toes have been sore ever since," is sexually charged. Effie proudly singles out the attentions she received from a Russian prince who, she notes, was the lover of the famous ballerina Taglioni. After thanking Ruskin "for the Honour of dancing with me," this aristocrat, "a fine young man and gentlemanly in his manners," manages to detain Effie for almost three more hours after "John left the ball" to retire to their rooms. The Prince offers Effie a "very fine supper" at one o'clock in the morning, begs her to become "engaged to him" for two more polkas, only to let this Cinderella flee the ball on the condition that he might see her again. When he reappears in a later letter, he strikes the young woman as someone capable of "making love" most "cleverly."[14]

In considering his father's letter for inclusion in *Praeterita,* Ruskin was prompted into making an identifying note: "The 'Effie' of this letter is the Phemy for whom *The King of the Golden River* was written when she was twelve years old."[15] Yet the need to connect publicly the "nice" girl who had urged him to write a fairy tale with the woman who divorced him for

13. Mary Lutyens, ed., *Young Mrs. Ruskin in Venice: Her Picture of Society and Life with John Ruskin, 1849–1852* (New York: Vanguard Press, 1965), 131n.

14. Ibid., 130–31, 137.

15. Ibid., 131n.

failing to consummate their marriage apparently proved too disturbing for the autobiographer. Ruskin's decision to omit any references to Effie in *Praeterita,* a work that, after all, was supposedly designed to stress only pleasurable remembrances of things past, thus led him to leave out his father's pleasing letter.

In 1850, Ruskin still could not bring himself to blame on his parental upbringing his demasculinization and unfitness "for the duties of middle life." The Edenic purity he so ardently coveted required one last gesture of reaffirmation. From 1850 onward, however, Ruskin chose to adopt the guise of a maturer self, the sophisticated critic of architecture and culture, in his search for a pristine Treasure Valley. Instead of resettling little Gluck in a paradisiacal garden, he could now guide adult readers to recognize the shards of an organic past still embedded in the present as the visible emblems of an earlier era of untainted, childlike belief. And instead of magically reducing Gluck's overgrown brothers into two huge and frozen black boulders, he could animate the stones of medieval Venice by stripping them free from the accumulated detritus of subsequent layers of civilization. Magic could now be carried into history. The imaginative man who professed to be wholly unable to tap his creativity ("I can no more write a story than compose a picture") could at least signify his socialization through the extraordinary process of *re*creativity by which he might distill a cultural "innocence" from the anxious manifestations of modernity. Not until *Praeterita,* near the very end of his writing career, would he again devise a narrative construct to recover, as Wordsworth had in *The Prelude,* the special, but threatened, childhood self of an elect.

Ruskin's eagerness to protect such a childhood self, with a fierceness that bordered on falsification, provides a key to his long and rich career. Read in that context, *The King of the Golden River* was a crucial undertaking. In 1841, the young Ruskin had naively thought that he could "bind and blend" himself with an unspoiled young girl; as yet barely conscious of the strong misgivings his story betrayed, he had proudly offered this fictional blending to his delighted parents. By 1850, though considerably chastened, Ruskin still tried to tell himself that not only the manuscript of his fairy tale, but also his better childhood self, had somehow "remained" intact "in the possession" of friends far more precious than any wife. It was a pious myth. But by believing in it Ruskin only succeeded in delaying the encroaching recognition that his adult development had been severely stunted. When he subsequently brought himself to acknowledge that fact, he turned his wrath outwards. By excoriating modernity's adulterations,

he could remain steadfast in clinging to his earlier idealization of innocence. Childhood still needed to be insulated from a destructiveness that
Ruskin persisted in identifying with an adult modality: "Children should
laugh but not mock," he asserted in "Fairy Stories" in 1868, and "when
they laugh it should not be at weaknesses and faults of others" (*CW,*
19:234).

Earnestness is rewarded in *The King of the Golden River.* Although the
magical agents who punish and reward are capable of a sardonic humor,
Ruskin's story lacks the ironic playfulness of most of his male and female
successors. Unlike the Thackeray of *The Rose and the Ring,* the Carroll of
the Alice books, and unlike the two witty women writers, Ingelow and
Ewing, whose children's tales he considered to be far superior to the productions of Thackeray and Carroll, Ruskin never regards the child reader
as a fellow humorist who is capable of enjoying an anarchic wit. Nor is
his view of traditional fairy tales as irreverent as that of George MacDonald. As eager to maintain the "purity" of his boy-hero as that of the fairy
tale medium, Ruskin feels compelled to deny the actual subversiveness of
his tale for "nice children." Instead of acknowledging the anger that lurks
in his tale or of transmuting that anger into the controlled aggression of
parody and satire, as Thackeray or Carroll would soon do, he preferred
to turn his negativity on the book itself by depreciating its value.

But is the tale truly as "valueless" a creative endeavor as Ruskin maintained? Is it only designed to confirm nice children in their niceness? The
story can certainly be read in that fashion. My students give *The King of
the Golden River* their rather unenthusiastic respect. They value it for its
craftsmanship: its symmetry and control, its mastery of language, its lyrical
descriptions of landscape, its color and design. A handful (usually those
who also cherish C. S. Lewis) even praise the work for its quasi-Christian
"message" about the rewards of charity. But the majority find the tale to
be too pietistic. They particularly dislike Gluck as an excessively bland
and bloodless figure whose acquiescence they unfavorably contrast to the
behavior of later Victorian child protagonists, from Carroll's Alice and
Ewing's Amelia to Kipling's Mowgli and Burnett's Mary Lennox, all figures capable of indignation and spunk, as well as considerable ingenuity
and self-reliance. Their response seems justified. And yet they fail to recognize that the story's ostensible tameness is in conflict with the extraordinarily powerful violence which Ruskin activates and then barely subdues
in order to reward his child-hero.

III

At first glance, the oppositions that Ruskin establishes in the introductory paragraphs of *The King of the Golden River* seem amply familiar. Innocence is juxtaposed to experience. The fecund Eden "commonly called the Treasure Valley" is immediately set apart from the "broad plains" and "populous cities" that lie on the other side of the mountains sheltering this agrarian enclave. And, just as predictably, of the "three brothers, called Schwartz, Hans, and Gluck," who own the "whole of this little valley," the youngest is "completely opposed" to his "seniors," both in "appearance and character" (*KGR,* 14, 16). As in the Grimm *Märchen* which Ruskin so well remembered from his boyhood reading of *German Popular Tales*— stories such as "The Golden Goose," "The Queen Bee," and "The Golden Bird"—a youngest brother epitomizes the trust and openness of the Innocent.[16]

The elder brothers, Schwartz and Hans, are powerful adult males whose distrust is as pronounced as their desire for domination. Their masculinity is shown to be repulsive. They are described as "very ugly men, with over-hanging eyebrows and small dull eyes, which were always half shut, so that you couldn't see into *them,* and always fancied they saw very far into *you*" (*KGR,* 15). The narrator's description assumes the vantage point of a powerless child who vainly tries to fathom the thoughts of domineering adults who tower over him. That such an identification is taking place is soon confirmed by the ensuing description of "little Gluck" himself. As a pre-pubescent child, "not above twelve years old" (like Phemy Gray at the time), "fair, blue-eyed" (like John Ruskin), he is still unmarked by suspicion, still unworldly, and, above all, wholly unmasculine.

16. The lifelong impact on Ruskin of Edgar Taylor's translation of the Grimm fairy tales is evident from his frequent use of individual stories as frames for letters and publications in which he assumes that his readers share his own intimate familiarity with these texts. Yet the impact of *German Popular Tales* on Ruskin was visual as well as literary. In *Praeterita,* he recalls how he copied, "when I was between ten and eleven," George Cruikshank's illustrations to Grimm, "with great, and to most people now incredible, exactness" (*CW,* 35:74–75). When Ruskin decided to reissue (albeit in larger print suited for young readers) the original 1823 and 1826 volumes of Taylor, he also retained the original designs, which he hailed in his preface as belonging to "the best period of Cruikshank's genius" (*CW,* 19:239). He regarded that preface, later reprinted as "Fairy Stories," the essay I have quoted above, as one of his best pieces of prose.

The contrast between this androgynous youngster and his adult siblings is reinforced by Richard Doyle's carefully differentiated drawings of the three brothers. Ruskin's choice of this young illustrator for the work he had written at the age of twenty-two was apt. Doyle himself was twenty-one when he succeeded George Cruikshank (Ruskin's childhood favorite) as the prime English illustrator of the Grimms. *The Fairy Ring* (1845) had appeared five years before the publication of *The King of the Golden River*. At the time, in a review that stressed the "child-like simplicity and wonder" of such fairy tales, Thackeray had praised "Dicky" Doyle as an ideal illustrator by taking note of the precocious artist's own capacity for wonder.[17]

Depicted by Doyle as highly developed athletic figures whose short-cropped hair accentuates their muscularity, the ugly older brothers are exposed in Ruskin's text as rapacious sadists who kill "everything that did not pay for its eating": blackbirds, hedgehogs, crickets, even the harmless cicadas, "which used to sing all summer in the lime trees" (*KGR,* 15). With the exception of the sketch in which a shackled Schwartz is brought before the magistrate, every drawing of the two men portrays them as holding on to weapons. There are staffs, flagons, sticks (with which they beat Gluck [fig. 1]), rolling pins (with which they try to assault their first visitor, "the little gentleman"), and swords and daggers (with which they fight each other [fig. 2]).

Gluck, in contrast, respects the ways of a feminine Nature. Unlike Hans and Schwartz, he is "kind in temper to every living thing" (*KGR,* 16). While they hoard both corn and gold, and will later adulterate metals in "the large city," the boy-Cinderella is forced to "clean shoes, floors, and

---

17. "A very young man, we believe scarcely twenty, he has produced in the course of a few years, in the pages of *Punch* and elsewhere, a series of designs so remarkable for grace, variety, fancy, and wild picturesqueness—drawings of such beauty and in such profusion, as we believe are quite unexampled hitherto" (Gordon N. Ray, ed., *William Makepeace Thackeray: Contributions to the "Morning Chronicle"* [Urbana: University of Illinois Press, 1966], 98). Doyle's only fault, according to Thackeray, was a trait which Ruskin would have regarded as a virtue—an excessive "gentleness of disposition" that leads the artist to shy away from grotesque drawings of hags and witches. When Doyle adopted a more satirical style in some of his later work, Ruskin became predictably cooler. Doyle's 1864 *Birds' Eye Views of Society,* a work reminiscent of Thackeray's own *Book of Snobs,* struck Ruskin as "full of power, but entirely wrong in feeling" (*CW,* 36:463). Rodney Engen's *Richard Doyle* (Stroud, Gloucester: Catalpa Press, 1983) offers the fullest discussion of Doyle's remarkable career.

sometimes the plates, occasionally getting what was left on them, by way of encouragement, and a wholesome quantity of dry blows, by way of education" (*KGR,* 33, 16). Drawn by Doyle as a decidedly girlish figure, with a soft swelling breast and long flowing hair, Gluck curiously anticipates John Tenniel's far more famous rendering of the young Alice. In one illustration, depicting Gluck after he has been transported to the city by his brothers, the boy assumes the pose of a sequestered Rapunzel, looking nostalgically from an ivy-encased window in the direction of the lost Treasure Valley (fig. 3).

In three other drawings, in each of which he stands against the cavity of the goldsmith's furnace (so like the larger concave of the fireplace against which he is depicted in the first chapter), Gluck disregards a large sword that leans, unused, next to him (figs. 4, 5, and 6). Whereas that weapon will soon be wielded by one of his brothers, a puzzled Gluck winds up gazing, in the last of these three drawings, into the hollow furnace out of which he has previously extracted the baby-sized King of the Golden River. The midget he helped to deliver had arrived in a kind of breach-birth: "instead of a liquid stream, there came out, first, a pair of pretty yellow legs" (*KGR,* 39). But he has now mysteriously "disappeared" again into the red-hot hole from which he originated (*KGR,* 3).

As the first and foremost of the oppositions on which Ruskin relies for his plot, the contrast between Gluck and his two brothers would seem to be clear-cut. For Ruskin quite overtly prepares readers conditioned by the traditional form of the *Märchen* to expect that the youngest and weakest of three brothers will eventually obtain some prize denied to his more powerful elders. That this rewarded innocent should be called "Gluck" rather than "Dummling" (or Simpleton), as in the story of "The Golden Goose," also seems in keeping with established conventions. In the fifth volume of *Modern Painters* Ruskin rightly recalled that the "latest descent" of a "youngest child" was habitually regarded as "a sign of fortunateness" in the Scandinavian and Germanic sagas on which so many Grimm folktales are based (*CW,* 7:396). The German word for such luck is, of course, "Glück." The noun by which the little boy is "called" thus also helps to separate him, and his calling, from the unfortunate fates of Schwartz, the oldest brother whose adjectival name acts as a surname for both "Black Brothers," and of Hans, the middle brother, who pushes himself ahead of Schwartz by becoming the first of the three questers. (That this defier of traditional rank should be the only one to bear a Christian name, and that this name should should correspond to that of "John"—Ruskin's own first

1 Richard Doyle, Gluck Beaten

2 Richard Doyle, The Brothers Fighting

3 Richard Doyle, Gluck as Rapunzel

name and also that of his father—may have something to do with the
aggressive masculine identity the fable tries to repress.)[18]

Yet, as even the specificity of this symbolic naming suggests, Ruskin
markedly departs from the German models he later professed to have followed as submissively as Gluck follows the authority of his elders. In the
Grimm stories, the fortunate youngster who vies with his brothers not
only bests them but invariably acquires the power explicitly associated
with an even stronger father figure. In "The Golden Goose," for example,
Dummling, "despised and ill-treated by the whole family," dutifully asks
his father's permission to replace the brothers who had ventured into the
enchanted forest. Yet the woodcutter cruelly reminds the boy of his inferiority to the elder children both parents favor: "Your brothers have
lamed themselves; you had better stay at home, for you know nothing of
the business." When Dummling stubbornly insists on being given the
same chance available to "brighter" brothers who nonetheless have
maimed themselves with the father's sharp ax, the woodcutter gruffly dismisses him: "Go your way; you will be wiser when you have suffered your

18. Like the fictional Hans, John James Ruskin was a second child. The existence of
a Grimm protagonist, "Hans im Glück," whose name combines those of both characters,
complicates even further the resonance these associations might have held for the
young author.

4 Richard Doyle, Gluck at the Furnace (I)

folly."[19] He regards the boy as valueless. Whereas the older sons had been given cake and wine by their parents, Dummling is merely granted some stale bread and sour beer. But by sharing his coarse provisions with one who seems as powerless as he has been, a "little old man" much like Gluck's two tiny supernatural visitors, the dwarf-king and South-West Wind, Esquire, Dummling soon excels his crippled brothers. Moreover, by winning a princess and becoming *her* father's heir, he obtains far greater powers than those which his own surly father might have bestowed on him.

If, as Bruno Bettelheim contends, tales such as "The Golden Goose"

19. *Grimms' Fairy Tales Translated by Edgar Taylor and Illustrated by George Cruikshank,* reproduced in facsimile from the first English edition, 1823, 1826, 2 vols. (London: Scolar Press, 1979), 1:180. In the German version, Dummling's folly is more pointedly contrasted to the behavior of the older brothers, ironically called "klug" and "verständig" (i.e., clever). For the German text of the tales I rely on *Grimms Märchen: Vollständige Ausgabe,* 2 vols. (Zurich: Manasse Verlag, n.d.).

5 Richard Doyle, Gluck at the Furnace (II)

6 Richard Doyle, Gluck at the Furnace (III)

encourage a growing child to overcome feelings of insignificance by fostering the belief that "small real achievements are important," these tales also
tend to equate such achievements, much more than either Ruskin or Bettelheim wants to allow, with a gained male potency that has decided sexual
overtones.[20] When Dummling cuts down an old tree to find the golden
goose "in a hollow under the roots" his axe-wielding produces results that
neither his father nor his father's male heirs could have obtained. His
prowess does not stem from the acquisition of adult skills but relies instead
on the primal energy that makes him the sharer of the forest dwarf's own
powers. He can thus reverse the rules of male primogeniture that operate
in a social organization. The goose emerges from a hollow that leads to a
princess's bed.

The same pattern of reversal also operates in "The Queen Bee" and in
"The Golden Bird," two other Grimm stories. In the first, the youngest
and weakest of three princes (he even assumes the shape of a "little insignificant dwarf" in the Taylor translation that Ruskin read as a child) wins
the "youngest" but "best" of three princesses. Although he generously
grants the other two princesses to the brothers he rescues, it is he who will
rule as "king after her father's death."[21] A princess also goes (as well as a
golden steed and a golden bird) to the kindly youngest son of the king's
gardener in "The Golden Bird." In the German original, the protagonist
is himself a "Königssohn" or prince, and it is his royal father who executes
his treacherous older brothers and allows him to succeed to the throne.[22]

If *The King of the Golden River* follows the formula established by these
fantasies of magically achieved male power, it nonetheless greatly qualifies
that power. It is true that the meek and feminized Gluck will, by the
story's end, inherit the earth his violent brothers have turned into sterile
"red sand and grey mud" through their unnatural greed and cruelty

---

20. Bruno Bettelheim, *The Uses of Enchantment: The Meaning and Importance of Fairy
Tales* (New York: Knopf, 1976), 73, 186.

21. *Grimms' Fairy Tales,* 1:86, 90.

22. The implausibility of a gardener's son becoming the heir of a king stems from
Taylor's excessive condensation of "Der Goldene Vogel." As elsewhere in his translations, Taylor also softens the fate of the older brothers. By converting "ergriffen und
hingerichtet" into "seized and *punished*" (ibid., 1:27), he robs the story of its final parallelism: in the German version, the "godless" brothers executed by their father are replaced
by the kindly fox who turns into the princess's long-lost brother. He and the prince and
their sister/wife thus form a new trinity: "Und nun fehlte nichts mehr zu ihrem *Glück,*
solange sie lebten" (*Grimms Märchen,* 1:405; italics added).

(*KGR*, 30). Yet Ruskin pointedly departs from his German models by omitting two of their prime features. He carefully removes any reference to the father figure who, in the German *Märchen,* is always needed to confirm the fantasy of mastery: Gluck is a brother but never a son. Although he eventually recovers, through love, "the inheritance" which "had been lost by cruelty," that land, though called a "patrimony" (*KGR*, 33), is given distinctly female characteristics. What is more, Ruskin denies Gluck the princess habitually bestowed on the younger son as a token of his sexual maturation. Indeed, in its avoidance of any female figure whatsoever, Ruskin's fairy tale not only differs from the three stories just mentioned (or from "The Water of Life" and "The King of the Golden Mountain," which contain parallels I will discuss later) but also from most other Grimm *Märchen.* Given the fact that Ruskin wrote *The King of the Golden River* for his father, mother, and little Phemy, the omission of either parents or of a female mate in the story's plot must be regarded with considerable suspicion.

Why did a tale written by this dutiful son elide the elementary identification of child with parent, so central, as Bettelheim and others have shown, to the basic format of the fairy tale? And why did this offering "to a very young lady" so pointedly avoid the obligatory use of both genders? The answer to these questions is quite simple. Ruskin tried to rid his story of the "impurities" of aggression and sexuality he found in his originals. And yet his attempts at purification through displacement merely call attention to his vicarious attraction to the same violent and erotic elements so much more overtly handled in the folk tales he hoped to refine.

Indeed, displacements occur throughout the plot of *The King of the Golden River.* Previous questers in the Grimm *Märchen* always obtain totemic objects of power—golden animals or artifacts with magical properties—that bring about material enrichment. But the "Golden River" of the book's title yields no tangible hoard. A waterfall that merely looks "*like* a shower of gold" and does not even fall into the Treasure Valley itself remains a fluid metaphor. As Ruskin makes clear at the outset, the valley does not need this stream for its irrigation; the enclave's original fertility is derived directly from heaven: moist clouds linger on the virginal, always "snowy hills." When Gluck undertakes his quest, near the end of the story, he falsely assumes, as his brothers had done, that he will be rewarded with a literal store of gold, the traditional source of power. What he will gain, instead, is something Ruskin considers to be far more precious. Free from the rigidity identified with the materialism and lust for power of his brothers, Gluck now benefits from a natural diversion of waters: "Behold, a river, *like* the Golden River, was springing from a new cleft of the rocks above it, and was flowing in innumerable streams among the dry heaps of sand" (*KGR,* 67; italics added). Like the dwarf's release from the liquid streams of gold that poured out of a hollow furnace, this new emanation involves a rebirth.

The feminized boy who has not sought male power is thus rewarded by the waters that issue from this "new cleft." He can return to a renovated Eden better far than that which his brothers, but not he, had lost. He has remained as pure as ever. No princess is needed to mark his final maturation as a male, for he can bypass the very process of maturation. He has not altered. Like the "fresh grass" and "moistening soil" around him, he has merely become refertilized. Like the little King whose "pretty yellow legs" Gluck had pulled from the furnace, he can be reborn as a child. It is his two older brothers who must remain forever frozen as "two black stones," the hardened emblems of their callous male rigidity.

IV

Despite its harmonious ending, *The King of the Golden River, or, The Black Brothers* owes its imaginative energy less to Gluck's beatification than to the punishments meted out to his brothers by the boy's two supernatural allies. Ruskin's reliance on two magical agents to take the place of the single figure who operates in stories like "The Golden Goose" and "The Golden Bird" befits his use of parallelism throughout the meticulously crafted five-part structure of his story. The success of Gluck's quest in the last chapter obviously builds on the failure of the preceding expeditions undertaken by Hans and Schwartz in chapters 4 and 5. Yet these two chapters also form a paired pendant that contains its own pleasing variations within repetition. And if, as noted, the opening chapter sets up the opposition between the older brothers and their young sibling, it also introduces Gluck's first visitor, South-West Wind, Esquire, and prepares the reader for the appearance of the King of the Golden River in chapter 2.

Both magical figures are sufficiently alike to be occasionally confused with each other by unwary readers. (Until the very last line of the first chapter, when the name of South-West Wind, Esquire is finally made known, it might be thought that he is the King of the book's title.) Since each visitor is presented as small in size, he also becomes associated with the boy repeatedly called "little" Gluck. When the first one appears, he strikes Gluck as "the most extraordinary looking *little* gentleman he had ever seen"; when the second one assembles his legs, arms, and "the well-known head" of Gluck's golden mug into a unified body, he rises "in the shape of a *little* golden dwarf" (*KGR,* 19, 39, italics added). Yet despite their minuteness and drollness, each figure also assumes an authoritative stance that makes Gluck behave just as "submissively" towards them as he behaves towards Schwartz and Hans (*KGR,* 41). The first visitor speaks "petulantly," "gruffly," and "drily" to the boy, even though he initially addresses the older brothers "very modestly" (*KGR,* 20, 22, 23, 26.) The second visitor soon proves to be equally "pertinacious" and "intractable" in speech as in demeanor (*KGR,* 40). Each figure thus combines Gluck's physical slightness with the superior strength of his brothers. Indeed, by prevailing over the older brothers, both of these allies can enact a hostility which Gluck is not allowed to display. Whereas the dwarf who leads Dummling to the Golden Goose or the fox who secures treasures for the youngest brother in "The Golden Bird" may indirectly cause the maiming or punishment of the older siblings, Ruskin's two little magical figures delight in their overt role as sadistic avengers.

Despite their similar roles, however, South-West Wind Esquire and the King of the Golden River differ considerably in their appearance and in the extent of their power. Gluck's first visitor is as grotesque as the older brothers he will so relentlessly humiliate. Measuring "about four feet six in height," he may seem even smaller than the petite Gluck; yet his actual size is greatly enlarged by a series of protuberances. He wears "a conical pointed cap" of "nearly" his own "altitude," further extended by a "black feather some three feet long"; the "enormous black, glossy-looking cloak" ("much too long" even in calm weather) is spread out horizontally by the gusts "to about four times his own length" (*KGR,* 19). What is more, "the little gentleman" sports "a very large nose, slightly brass-coloured," which Ruskin originally went on to describe as "expanding towards its termination into a development not unlike the lower extremity of a key bugle" (*CW,* 1:316; 316n; *KGR,* 18). When Richard Doyle accordingly drew that protuberant nose as a long, metallic, trumpet-like snout, a suddenly prudish Ruskin deleted the description, forcing Doyle to redraw the phallic proboscis, now shortened and naturalized, in three illustrations. Yet Ruskin retained sufficient allusions to South-West Wind's "dripping" appendages to prepare the reader for the stranger's mode of vanquishing Schwartz and Hans.

7 Richard Doyle, South West Wind, Esquire *(first version)*

Unlike his grotesque predecessor, Gluck's second supernatural visitor seems "exquisitely delicate." Only his facial features are "rather coarse, slightly inclining to coppery in complexion, and indicative, in expression," of his own pugnacious temperament (*KGR,* 40). For he retains the "very fierce little face" on the original mug that an uncle (rather than a father) had given "to little Gluck, and which he was very fond of" (*KGR,* 34). Having never drunk "anything out of it but milk and water," Gluck is appalled when ordered to melt down his "old friend." Unlike Schwartz, who has been made uncomfortable by the mug's "intense gaze," the mild boy seems oblivious to the "malicious" aspect of its lifelike eyes. Noting

8 Richard Doyle, South West Wind, Esquire *(second version)*

that the "flowing hair" (so like his own golden locks) has disappeared in the melting-pot, Gluck regards the eyes, "which looked more malicious than ever," as those of a fellow-victim: "'And no wonder,' thought Gluck, 'after being treated in that way'" (*KGR,* 35). Incapable of voicing any resentment over his own mistreatment, the boy finds himself shocked by the pugnacity the King displays as soon as he regains the fluidity already associated with the bellicose South West Wind. The disabled King may have been, as Gluck still is, paralyzed: "The shape you saw me in," he explains, "was owing to the malice of a stronger king" (*KGR,* 42). But, unlike Gluck, he will not hesitate to use his regained might to force on

9 Richard Doyle, South West Wind and the Black Brothers *(first version)*

10 Richard Doyle, South West Wind and the Black Brothers *(second version)*

the boy's "wicked brothers" the same arrested condition from which he has been released.

Ruskin carefully contrasts the sizes of Gluck's two small visitors. If South-West Wind is four and a half feet tall, the golden dwarf is exactly one third in size, "about a foot and a half high." Yet the tinier creature makes better use of his regained magical powers. South-West Wind's energies are purely destructive. He overpowers Gluck's brothers and ravages the Treasure Valley. Although he spares Gluck, he is unconcerned with the boy's ultimate fate. The King of the Golden River, on the other hand, by turning Hans and Schwartz into huge black boulders and then rewarding Gluck, mixes violence with beneficence by liberating his own unwitting liberator. What is more, by allowing Hans and Schwartz one further chance before each man's self-destruction, he grants them free will, in the manner of Milton's God. This Lilliputian deity thus seems, superficially at least, more benevolent than South-West Wind who resentfully wrecks an Eden.

Still, each of these acerbic and quarrelsome figures paradoxically displays the same aggressiveness that Ruskin's narrator professes to condemn in the litigious Schwartz and Hans. Just as Doyle's drawing shows a nervous, finger-biting Gluck stand by passively as the first of his surrogates is about to fight his virile brothers, so does the narrator try to screen his feminized hero from a male contentiousness attributed alike to the boy's tormentors and allies. Yet the dissociation seems somewhat spurious: the non-violent Gluck, after all, is not just the victim but also the beneficiary of intense violence. Others merely act out the vengeful anger he will not show.

Ruskin's investment in the sadistic manifestations of his story thus seems undeniable. Although that investment is not as openly acknowledged as in the narratives of Thackeray, Carroll, or Christina Rossetti, it cannot be concealed in a plot that dwells as much on the brutality of the Black Brothers as on their disablement. South-West Wind overwhelms them, not once, but twice. He first vanquishes them in combat and then, in a sequence given unmistakable sexual overtones, violates the domestic enclosure into which Gluck had so reluctantly admitted him. The first encounter ends swiftly. When Schwartz seizes the rolling pin to beat Gluck for letting the dripping stranger sit by the hearth, "the old gentleman" uses the huge conical cap he had previously stuck "up the chimney" to parry the blow and send the weapon "spinning like a straw" into a corner. When Hans tries to grab the intruder, he is sent flying after the rolling pin, and soon a "very angry" Schwartz follows him there, hitting "his head against the wall as he tumbled into the corner" (*KGR,* 21, 25, 27). On his second visit, South-West Wind produces far greater damage. For he now not only batters the house in which he has been so inhospitably treated but also reduces the Edenic Treasure Valley into "one mass of ruin, and desolation" (*KGR,* 30).

The mighty gale that makes the barred door "burst open with a violence" that shakes the entire structure also rips off the roof of the bedroom of the older brothers and drenches their beds:

The two brothers sat up on their bolster, and stared into the darkness. The room was full of water and by a misty moonbeam, which found its way through a hole in the shutter, they could see in the midst of it, an enormous foam globe, spinning round, and bobbing up and down like a cork, on which, as on a most luxurious cushion, reclined the little old gentleman, cap and all. There was plenty of room for it now, for the roof was off.

"Sorry to incommode you," said their visitor, ironically. "I'm afraid your beds are dampish; perhaps you had better go to your brother's room; I've left the ceiling on there." (*KGR,* 29–30)

The symbolism speaks for itself. Two adults are commanded to take refuge in a child's room. The bed of the virginal Gluck is not "dampish"; no conical cap has deflowered the enclosure into which his older brothers, "wet through, and in an agony of terror," flee for their safety. The situation reverses that in which a small child, on awaking either in discomfort or in terror over some overpowering "bad" dream, seeks shelter in the dry and warm bed of reassuring parents presumably better equipped, as grown-ups, to defuse anxiety or shame. It is Schwartz and Hans, however, who have suffered from something not unlike what Wordsworth (who yoked the imagination to "the sexual appetite, and all the passions connected with it") called a "spontaneous overflow of powerful feelings."[23] As their sarcastic visitor reminds them, the brothers have met their match.

But Gluck himself, though physically spared, is not immune to the aftereffects of this imaginative overflow. The waters emitted by South-West Wind's spillage have "gutted" the rest of the house in which Gluck has so unquestioningly labored as a docile domestic. Outside, they have "swept away trees, crops, and cattle" (*KGR,* 30, 31). The Treasure Valley has turned sterile: "What had once been the richest soil in the kingdom, be-

---

23. William Wordsworth, preface to the second edition of *Lyrical Ballads* (1800).

came a shifting heap of red sand" (*KGR,* 33). All three brothers must now be exiled from an Eden that has turned into a "desert." Although the youngest and most feminine retains a "paradise within," he suffers even more acutely than his self-reliant siblings from the deprivations caused by a violent and violating masculinity. Only his charity—and the agency of a more benign protector—can restore the garden that will be entrusted to his care.

Yet even the kindlier King of the Golden River displays none of the charitable feelings that he ostensibly rewards in Gluck. It is no coincidence that Gluck's crowning act of goodness to the dying dog who will turn into the King himself should be presented as his only timid act of defiance. On deciding to give the dog the last drops of the water he has saved for his quest, Gluck denounces the instigator of that quest: "Confound the King and his gold too." Although, ironically enough, he has unwittingly nurtured the very figure he purports to condemn, it seems noteworthy that Gluck has at last displayed some of the anger from which he has, until then, so carefully been screened. When the King of the Golden River promptly materializes, the boy is afraid. After reassuring Gluck not to feel guilty for having cursed him, the dwarf goes on to give vent to his own far more unencumbered irascibility: "Why didn't you come before," he demands, "instead of sending me those rascally brothers of yours, for me to have the trouble of turning into stones? Very hard stones they make too." When Gluck protests, horrified, "Oh dear me! . . . have you really been so cruel?," the dwarf-king becomes "stern." Cruelty, he insists, was a proper retaliation against those who abused the innocent (*KGR,* 64, 65).

V

In an epilogue to *The King of the Golden River* that he decided never to print, Ruskin shifts from the earnest biblical cadences of the book's last sentences to a more satirical, Thackerayan tone.[24] In this discarded closure,

24. Addressed to a "Gentle Reader," this epilogue resumes the tone adopted in a prefatory address to a "Fair and Gentle Reader" (who is clearly the young Phemy Gray), which Ruskin also kept out of the printed text. He also rephrased some expressions presumably designed to amuse a twelve-year-old. Thus, for instance, a morning described as being so lovely that it "might have made any one happy" originally was described as having possibly "put spirits into a wet blanket" (*KGR,* 47; *CW,* 1:335n). Fearful that a self-conscious levity might jar with the earnest "purity" of his fable, Ruskin shied

the narrator sides with the child reader by mocking the "acumen" of several "old people," fictitious adult commentators, who vainly tried to make sense of "the more mysterious circumstances above related" (*CW,* 1:346n). Old ladies, learned parish clerks, even "the mater"[25] who added her "many and edifying comments" to the narrative, seem so befuddled that Ruskin asks his child reader "to form your own conclusions." Yet there are moral issues Ruskin does not want to leave unsettled. The narrator thus insists that Hans and Schwartz were not unduly punished. He stresses that it was their refusal to heed three appeals of "increasing strength" that led to their doom; by way of contrast, Gluck's response to three appeals *"diminishing in their claims"* has led to his reward (*CW,* 1:348n; Ruskin's italics).

Diminution is, in *The King of the Golden River* as much in *Alice in Wonderland,* both an imaginative feature as well as a mode of defense against growth. Ruskin's fantasy of "little" Gluck and the "little" allies who defeat the boy's overgrown tormentors was more than a love-gift for a special child. For, as I have been suggesting, Ruskin enlisted the form of the fairy tales he had loved as a boy in order to reconfront the disabling childhood conflicts he had never fully resolved in the process of growing up. As an only child, he saw himself as the weakest member of a tightly knit trinity formed by himself and his adoring parents. The security he derived from their unqualified support was both an asset as well as a liability. The strength of their backing convinced him of his own election as a treasured dweller in an Edenic space. At the same time, however, he could not avoid resenting the Gluck-like debility and overdependence that was the result of their loving domination.

Ruskin openly faced that ambivalence in *Praeterita,* where he compares at one point the formation of his character to that of the "youngest" of four boy cousins: "Charles, like the last-born in a fairy tale," he notes, was given rather cruel lessons in self-sufficiency by an older brother (*CW,* 35:88–89). Ruskin contrasts this rough schooling to his own upbringing. His mother, he recalls, congratulated herself for her overprotectiveness: "In her own son's education, she had sacrificed her pride in his heroism to her anxiety for his safety; and never allowed me to go to the edge of a pond, or be in the same field with a pony" (*CW,* 35:89). Describing how

---

away from the tonal mixtures of "The Light Princess," as his reaction to MacDonald's tale (discussed on pp. 138–39, below) suggests.

25. In the manuscript, Ruskin changed "mater" to "relative," which, as Cook and Wedderburn rightly note, "does not read quite right" (*CW,* 1:348n).

he was wrested away from the wild Welsh landscape that seeded in him the "Alpine feeling" later implanted in *The King of the Golden River,* Ruskin stops his narrative in order to indulge in the wishfulness of an "if only" fantasy:

And if only then my father and mother had seen the real strengths and weaknesses of their little John;—if they had given me but a shaggy scrap of a Welsh pony, and left me in charge of a good Welsh guide, and of his wife, if I needed any coddling, they would have made a man out of me there and then, and afterwards the comfort of their own hearts, and probably the first geologist of my time in Europe.

If only! But they could no more have done it than throw me like my cousin Charles into Croydon Canal, trusting me to find my way out by the laws of nature.

Instead, they took me back to London, and my father spared time from his business hours, once or twice a week, to take me to a four-square, sky-lighted, sawdust-floored prison of a riding-school. (*CW,* 35:96)

This section of *Praeterita* furnishes a better gloss to *The King of the Golden River* than does Ruskin's brief, dismissive account of the book later in the same volume, or, for that matter, than do both the published preface and the suppressed epilogue to his tale.

Ruskin used the fairy tale mode to explore a childhood utterly different from that which he had experienced as the much-coddled child of Margaret and John James Ruskin. His early reading of *German Popular Tales* had peopled his fantasy life with a rich and variegated series of alternate identities. In 1841, the sophisticated young Oxonian thus could briefly shed his learning by seeing himself as a kindly Dummling rewarded by "fortunateness." And he could also translate himself into filial figures who, even when maligned, abandoned, or deceived, remained steadfast in their allegiances. The protagonist of "The Water of Life," another youngest son of three, risks his life to bring the sick king, his father, a potion "that he might drink and be healed."[26] The hero of "The King of the Golden Mountain," an only son, does not resent being traded to a dwarf by the impoverished merchant father who wants to replenish his sagging fortunes. As victims of injustice, both of these figures resemble Gluck. If Gluck harbors no grudge toward the older brothers who have assumed parental control over his life, the youths in Grimm do not resent the fathers whose weakness they pity—the sick king who mistakes his youngest

---

26. *Grimms' Fairy Tales,* 1:86, 90.

son's deep love for parricidal enmity and the imprudent merchant who cannot protect the only son he turns "adrift." Yet these spurned sons use their dispossession to exhibit the self-reliance that Gluck so sorely lacks.

Gluck hesitates before he covertly feeds South West Wind in defiance of his brothers; he animates the little king by sheer accident, having agreed to melt down his mug. The protagonist of "The Water of Life," on the other hand, actively embraces the role of nurturer. Resolved to cure his ill father, he also feeds the starving inhabitants of three entire nations with a magical loaf of bread he has found, together with a magical sword, at the same spot where he obtained the elixir of life. His kindness knows no limits. Whereas Gluck readily accepts the petrifaction of his brothers, the prince in the Grimm story so fervently pleads with a dwarf who has immobilized his treacherous siblings that he gains their release. Promptly betrayed by them and banished by the father they have deceived, he nonetheless triumphs when emissaries from the lands he saved and a princess who exposes his brothers persuade his Lear-like father of this youngest child's nobility.

The hero of "The King of the Golden Mountain" also overcomes betrayal. After besting a dwarf he served, the deserted son uses a magical ring to impress his father with tokens of his maturity—a queen whose wealth he has acquired and a little son of his own. But like the hero of "The Water of Life," this protagonist is stripped of his accomplishments at the parental home to which he has returned. Shamed by his wife's desertion, bereft of his ring, he must start out anew. He outwits three gigantic brothers and steals their invisible cloak, seven-mile boots, and a magical sword which allows him to decapitate enemies with great abandon. Confronting his unfaithful wife and the suitors who have gathered at her palace, this invisible Ulysses slays all his rivals and recovers his throne. The Cruikshank drawing, possibly one of those illustrations that Ruskin diligently copied as a boy, depicts with gory realism the slaughter that culminates this fantasy of male omnipotence.

The folk-tale originals of these two Grimm stories probably were directed at adult consumers who welcomed them as fantasies of upward mobility. For a middle-class child, however, there was an added appeal. Both tales assuage the guilt such a child might feel when it wishes to free itself from parental domination by rising above its parents in strength and status. By insisting that it is pure "love" that earns Gluck sole possession of the Valley, *The King of the Golden River,* too, can soften a power-fantasy that requires the desirable death of a child's nearest kin. Yet in promoting that fantasy Ruskin's tale remains far more tentative than his German models, or, for that matter, than Juliana Ewing's tough-minded adaptations of folk tales I consider in the last chapter of this book. For Ruskin's uneasy handling of the conflict between strength and weakness betrays his difficulties in resolving the gender-division the growing child must negotiate in the formation of a sexual identity of its own.

The trinity formed by a boy and his two parents is replaced, at first, by the trinity formed by Gluck and the two brothers who exhibit to such an exaggerated degree the mercantile mindset that Ruskin came to resent in his father.[27] In placing Gluck into a second trinity formed through his association with his two revengeful "little" allies, Ruskin again elides the female power that Thackeray, Carroll, and George MacDonald more openly confronted in their own fantasies for children. Whether positive or negative, that power needs to be faced by growing boys and girls—and hence by writers who want to address a juvenile audience.

Ruskin's handling of femininity, however, not only differs from that of his Victorian successors but also from his German originals. The hero of "The Water of Life" is saved by the princess whose intervention vindicates him in the eyes of his father; the hero of "The King of the Golden Mountain" must overcome the sexual betrayal of his child's mother in order to reassert his threatened masculinity. By stressing Gluck's own femininity, Ruskin tries to insert a feminine element into each of the male triangles on which his plot relies. But this device is ineffectual. Shown first by Gluck's adoption of a domestic role usually assigned to a younger sister in many folk tales and then signified by his act of midwifery in bringing about the "birth" of the tiny King, the boy's assumed femininity fails to compensate for the absence of any actual female figures. Unlike MacDonald, who would deliberately convert South-West Wind, Esquire into the sensuous, all-powerful maternal figure of North Wind, Ruskin insists on masculinizing those "laws of nature" he wanted his parents to harness in order to make "a man out of me." Even the miraculous opening of the moist "cleft" that restores the Treasure Valley's fecundity is brought about by the

---

27. In a letter in which he reproached the wine merchant for an excessive concern with status, the son protested that he had been encouraged as a child to prefer high-placed "brutes" to the company of humbler folk "whose life is as pure as an archangel's" (John Ruskin to John James Ruskin, 12 August 1862, *Winnington Letters,* 370).

dwarf-king, who thus assumes a role that would have been much better discharged by a strong female agent such as Thackeray's Fairy Blackstick. The "exquisitely delicate," yet feisty, dwarf whom Gluck frees from an arrest like his own could easily have been given a female gender.

Ruskin's anger at—and later idealization of—his father suggests that he found male identification safer and easier than a confrontation with the strong "mater" whose name he had so mockingly introduced, but then changed to a more innocuous "relative," in his suppressed epilogue. In *Praeterita,* he astutely noted a trait which had set the two male Ruskins apart from the third member of their family trinity. The Wordsworthian delight of father and son in the "bolder scenery" of Wales through which they roamed made the boy guiltily conscious of a pagan bond he could not have established with his strict and self-denying Calvinist mother:

The joy of a walk with my father in the Sunday afternoon toward Hafod [was] dashed only with some alarmed sense of the sin of being so happy among the hills, instead of writing out a sermon at home;—my father's presence and countenance not wholly comforting me, for we both of us had alike a subdued consciousness of being profane and rebellious characters, compared to my mother. (*CW,* 35:95)

The masculine model John James Ruskin tried to provide for his only son vied with the strong grip on both men held by Margaret Ruskin, domestic sermonizer and instiller of guilt. Although he may not have plunged the boy on a bareback pony, the elder Ruskin did take him to an urban riding school to develop his confidence. But as *The King of the Golden River* shows, Ruskin continued to identify masculinity with an aggressiveness he both courted and feared as being "too profane and rebellious" in character. If his rebellion against his father came too late in his development, his disengagement from his mother never took place at all. It is significant that Gluck should win his release through the agency of a fellow-victim, dominated by someone more "powerful" than he. And the final identity Gluck obtains through this tiny patriarch is that of a matriarchal provider. No potent overspill but a mere "three drops of holy dew" convert Gluck into the harvester of the feminine Treasure Valley over which he presides, still unmarried, still pure and childlike. That Margaret Ruskin should have stressed her pleasure over the tale's outcome hardly seems surprising.

In a seminal 1933 essay, "The Early Development of Conscience in the Child," Melanie Klein relied on her "numerous analyses of children of all ages" to propose that the "evil monsters out of myths and fairy-stories" that take such a hold on the child's imagination did not just stem, as even Freud had supposed, from primal fears of "being devoured, or cut up, or torn to pieces" or "from repressed impulses of aggression." Instead, she argued, such creations were also attributable to the growing child's conscious censorship of its asocial and destructive feelings. She remarked: "I have no doubt from my own analytic observations that the real object behind those imaginary, terrifying figures are the child's own parents, and that those dreadful shapes in some way or other reflect the features of its father and mother, however distorted and fantastic the resemblance may be."[28] Her observation applies in interesting ways to *The King of the Golden River,* a fantasy in which Ruskin reaffirmed his own apparent irresolution, much earlier in his development, of a stage of character-formation that Klein, in another essay, calls the boy's "femininity-phase." Such irresolution may lead to a gradually channeled expression of "excessive aggression" that results from the anxious subjection to "the tyranny of a super-ego which devours, dismembers, and castrates and is formed from the image of father and mother alike."[29]

By excessively feminizing "little Gluck" and by making him the passive recipient of the Treasure Valley, Ruskin injected the very imbalances he tried to subdue in his parable about a boy's acquisition of an adult identity. Even more than the Grimm prototypes on which he is based, Gluck resembles the heroine of "The Golden Water" in *The Arabian Nights,* which Ruskin singled out, in his last published work, as "quite a favourite story with me" and one "that has had an immense power over my own life" (*CW,* 35:639). But even in that lengthy tale, which Sir Richard Burton reprinted, heavily annotated, under the title of "The Two Sisters Who Envied Their Cadette," Princess Perizadah is given, like Carroll's Alice or Ewing's Amelia, a far more active role than that accorded to Gluck. As the prime restorer of her family's broken unity, she acts as a foil to her tyrannical father as well as to her jealous maternal aunts. The princess rescues her older two brothers and then brings about her mother's reinstatement in the graces of the Shah who has allowed his wife to be unjustly defamed. If Ruskin cherished, as he says he did, this fable of a family's

---

28. Melanie Klein, *Love, Guilt, Reparation and Other Works* (New York: Dell, 1977), 249.

29. Melanie Klein, "Early Stages of the Oedipus Complex," in ibid., 189, 190.

reunification, he nonetheless endowed Gluck with none of Perizadah's wit, preferring instead simply to associate the boy with the redemptive Golden Water that the princess manages to recover.

Despite Ruskin's derogation, his tale for "nice" children became an influential Victorian text. Both its content and its form carried a cultural significance that went beyond the personal elements I have been stressing. By screening his child-protagonist from an adult reality portrayed as "cruel," Ruskin hoped to proclaim that future members of the Victorian middle-class could somehow stay unsullied by the acquisitive, mercantile world of their fathers. Yet that bourgeois order had, of course, carefully nurtured the author of the lavish publications financed by John James Ruskin. That paradox could hardly escape the notice of professional writers such as Thackeray, MacDonald, Ingelow, or Ewing; for them, children's books offered a means to make the money on which the wealthy Ruskin could so freely draw.

The insulation that Ruskin's fairy tale promotes was also ideologically suspect to some of his successors in the field of children's literature. They recognized what he also came to see, namely, that a tale that so lyrically upholds nature over artifice nonetheless remains unnatural at its core. For all its emphasis on fluidity, Ruskin's fairy tale sadly bypasses the natural flow that changes the growing child into an adult. Like the King who was frozen into a golden mug, Gluck remains arrested in his aureate purity; shuttled back and forth, he is thrust into the City of Experience yet deposited back into his native paradise. It was no wonder that Thackeray, always a parodist, would soon employ Ruskin's earnest tale as a prime foil for his comic *The Rose and the Ring*.

As we shall see in the next chapter, Thackeray playfully accentuates the adult authorial self-consciousness that Ruskin saw as defiling the purity of child-texts. In an essay entitled "Gold Growing," Ruskin wishes that calligraphers might be "appointed to write down for us words really worth setting down—Nursery Songs, Grimms' Popular Stories, and the like"; the result, he claims, would be "not, perhaps, a cheap literature, but at least an innocent one."[30] Yet Ruskin's own venture into a mode he regarded as innocent is hardly unself-conscious. The triplets he injects into his story of a cinder-fellow go far beyond those found in Perrault (three sisters, three mothers) or the Grimms (Aschenputtel's three visits to the ball). From the

---

30. *Fors Clavigera*, Letter 16 (*CW*, 27:284).

triune setting (valley / mountains / torrents) Ruskin establishes at the start to the last three words ("THE BLACK BROTHERS"), the profusion of trinities seems overwhelming.[31] Again, his exquisite descriptions of the Alpine landscapes traversed by the questers have a visual precision and rhetorical complexity that befit the author of *Modern Painters,* but that surely seem out of place in a construct professedly shaped by a primitive and child-like simplicity.

Ruskin's belief in the organic purity of a fairy-tale form that could pre-serve the child's "unquestioning innocence" is a mark of his Romanticism. Wordsworth had held that children and rustics were far closer to "the essential passions of the heart" than the civilized adult; Coleridge had con-tended that an early reading of fairy tales might habituate the mind to a "love of the great and the *whole.*"[32] Like these predecessors, Ruskin re-sented the intrusion of an adult point of view in "the best stories recently written for the young" (*CW,* 19:233). His remark, made in the 1868 essay on "Fairy Stories," suggests that he was quite possibly thinking of the works by Thackeray, Carroll, and MacDonald which appeared in the de-cade that ran from 1854 to 1865. The narrators used by all three of these writers certainly follow a practice that Ruskin excoriates—the habit of "the author's addressing himself to children bred in school-rooms and drawing-rooms, instead of fields and woods—children whose favourite amusements are premature imitations of the vanities of elder people" (*CW,* 19:233).

Ruskin's eagerness to block out such an adult point of view leads him to comment on the ways in which writers for children may impose alien values or introduce a diction foreign to the child. Yet his defensiveness also leads him, both in his later criticism as well as in his own 1850 publica-tion of "Phemy's fairy tale" into the opposite extreme. For Ruskin's sepa-

31. In addition to the character triads and the three-to-one ratio in the sizes of Gluck's two visitors, each of the three questers takes three hours to meet three figures, the last of whom changes his appearance in "three seconds" before he squeezes three drops of dew into the river. South-West Wind, Esquire, who knocks three times, wears a three-foot feather on the cap he uses to tumble a trio formed by Hans, Schwarz, and a rolling pin. For his part, the dwarf-king takes turns "of three feet long" after thrice addressing Gluck as "My boy." Hans is punished after lightning "thrice" shakes the sky; Schwartz is punished after thrice saying, "Water, indeed!" Even Gluck's lamentations come in threes: "Oh dear, dear, dear me"; "My mug, my mug, my mug."

32. William Wordsworth, preface to the second edition of *Lyrical Ballads;* S. T. Cole-ridge to Thomas Poole, 16 October 1797.

ration of innocence from experience denies the important interplay between phases that, in true Romantic fashion, he prefers to regard as incompatible. It therefore took a more reality-oriented observer of the growing child to seek out the common interests of child and adult selves that Ruskin so assiduously prefers to keep apart.

For a realist such as Thackeray (like Ruskin, a strong matriarch's only child), "the vanities of elder peoples" are not all that alien to the young whom Ruskin wants to screen from the contamination of adult experience. In *The Rose and the Ring,* originally written for his two daughters, Thackeray boldly extends the satirical mode of *Vanity Fair* into Ruskin's world of innocence. Treating his child readers as incipient ironists, he allows his skeptical imagination to repose in a realm of magic. But Thackeray's own tale about power lost and regained also admits what Ruskin's wants to deny—namely, that children can be just as power-hungry as adults. Aggression and sexuality, handled so circumspectly by Ruskin, are therefore given prominence by Thackeray in his anarchic fairy tale. His playful partnership with young readers allows him to inject a dynamic that the earnest, richly symbolical yet ultimately arrested mode of *The King of the Golden River* had failed to activate.

THREE

Growing Up Ironic: Thackeray's *The Rose and the Ring*

Three illnesses of my own and two of my girls, and four numbers of Newcomes and a Christmas book written in 3 months—I think I have had enough to do. . . . To be father and mother too is too much for any one: let alone such a lazy fellow as me—But the discipline is good à quelque chose let us trust. . . .

. . . If it had not been for a nonsensical Xmas book I have been writing I don't know what I should have done in these last dreary weeks.
—WILLIAM MAKEPEACE THACKERAY,
8 and 17 March, 1854

I

On March 1, 1854, William Makepeace Thackeray, residing in Italy with his two teenage daughters, anxiously recorded in his diary: "Yesterday Anny fell ill for the first time since we have been together. A good deal of fever & restlessness today. Minny a dear little nurse." Soon, the thirteen-year-old Minny (Harriet Marian) also became confined to bed "with Scarletina caught from Anny," her elder by three years; and, to make matters worse, Thackeray found himself unable to minister to either daughter after a sudden "attack of spasms" had left him painfully crippled.[1] Yet before his and Minny's confinement, he had found a way to soothe his afflicted daughter and to allay his own fears: "Wrote these days in the Fairy Tale, and amused Anny with it. It is wonderful how easy this folly trickles from the pen."[2] Buoyed by Anny's quick recovery, Thackeray was able to send off a cheerful report to "My dearest Mammy," the grandmother with whom the girls had lived in Paris from 1840 to 1846 after the separation enforced by their own mother's mental illness and confinement. Minny, her father breezily assured Anne Carmichael-Smyth, would soon be quite as comfortable "as her sister who lies in my bed in the next room grinning like a Cheshire Cat with a face as round as a ditto cheese."[3]

Thackeray's turn to a "nonsensical" fairy tale during a crisis that required him to provide the highest form of child care was to have an extended therapeutic value. Despite occasional bouts of self-pity, he had welcomed the opportunity to "be father and mother too" of the girls he had reclaimed eight years earlier; their life together had reinstated a gratifying feminine presence in the home of a man who was wifeless and yet unable to remarry. Thackeray had lovingly discharged the role of caretaker that he had inherited from the children's mother and his own. The Italian tour

1. "Diary for 1854," 1, 6, and 7 March 1854, *The Letters and Private Papers of William Makepeace Thackeray,* ed. Gordon N. Ray (London: Oxford University Press, 1946), 3:672.

2. Ibid., 2 March 1854, 673.

3. Thackeray to Anne Carmichael-Smyth, 7–8 March 1854, *Letters and Private Papers,* 3:352.

with his daughters had been preceded by a separation necessitated by his frantic American travels in 1853. Their illnesses took all by surprise. The severe threat to Anny's and Minny's health and the renewal of his "old malady" suddenly raised for Thackeray the specter of more permanent separations and revived earlier memories of abandonment and loss. To blend childhood and manhood, and to reinstate the maternal femininity from which both boy and adult man felt so profoundly cut off, Thackeray composed, as Ruskin had done in 1841, a compensatory fantasy of reclamation.

The forty-three-year-old Thackeray, who had lost his Anglo-Indian father at the age of four, hardly resembled the sheltered young author who had privately presented his parents with the manuscript of *The King of the Golden River*. Nor, despite her similar exercise of an ironclad matriarchal authority, did Thackeray's mother much resemble the overprotective Margaret Ruskin: after sending her only child away from India when he was just five years old, the young and attractive Anne Carmichael-Smyth, who promptly remarried, did not see William again for another four years. The absence of a maternal guardian, so prominent a motif in *The Rose and the Ring,* thus was as familiar to Thackeray as to his daughters. Anny was almost four when her grandmother replaced the mother she vividly remembered; Minny was six when Thackeray reclaimed her from Mrs. Carmichael-Smyth, the only mother she had known. The experience of maternal absenteeism—desertion would be too strong a word, given Anne Carmichael-Smyth's genuine solicitude and Isabella Thackeray's incapacitation—thus created a bond between Thackeray and his two daughters. That bond undoubtedly encouraged his reliance on both Anny and Minny as his agents in a fantasy about a pair of adolescent orphans whose destitution actually helps them grow up, while two other young people, though provided with parents, remain woefully arrested as infantile caricatures.

Although deprivation also figured prominently in *The King of the Golden River,* Thackeray makes it essential to a developing self-reliance that Ruskin's Gluck notably lacked. As passive recipient of the King's legacy, Gluck resembled his young creator, who was totally dependent on his father's financial wealth and social influence. Thackeray's two protagonists, however, are fortified by the parental neglect they experience. The dose of "a little misfortune" each receives from Fairy Blackstick at their christening is as important a gift as the kingdoms they eventually regain with the help of a matriarch whose magical powers greatly exceed those of Ruskin's diminutive king. That dose of misfortune is a dilution of Thackeray's remembrance of his own years of motherless (and wifeless) flounderings. Financially insecure, chronically ill, sexually unfulfilled, the deracinated gentleman turned hack writer and cartoonist had been exposed to a full share of those hardships that Ruskin so fervently wished he might have endured in order to attain a more masculine "middle life."

Still, the circumstances that led Thackeray and Ruskin to write fairy tales for young women bear greater resemblance than might be surmised from the radically different textures of their lives and their art. In each case, illness acted as a catalyst for the composition of a fairy tale. And, in each case, too, the writer's attempts to repair a male identity in need of feminine restoration required the mediation of a young female reader. As we saw in the last chapter, Ruskin's attempt to recover a feminine space through the agency of young Effie Gray was brought about by their shared experiences of disease: his brief bout of tuberculosis and her own, more frightening encounter with scarlet fever—the same disease from which Anny and Minny Thackeray recovered so speedily but which had killed Effie's three sisters. Ruskin associated the restoration of health with maternal nurturance in *The King of the Golden River:* Gluck assumes the female role his brothers had spurned when he ministers to the three enfeebled creatures he meets on his quest. His nurturance is rewarded by the regeneration of the feminine Treasure Valley.

For Thackeray, the unexpected illness of his daughters also led to a fantasy of maternal recovery. His emotional stake in his offspring was obviously far more intense than Ruskin's rather lukewarm attraction to the girl for whom he ostensibly had written "Phemy's tale." Nor was that investment as desexualized as Ruskin's. In Anny and Minny, Thackeray confided to his mother, he had "perhaps" acquired partners better suited in temperament "than the wife whose want has made me so uncomfortable these many years past."[4] Indeed, the masculine worldling, whose own "womanliness" was so often stressed by friends and detractors alike,[5] went

---

4. Thackeray to Carmichael-Smyth, 2 February 1855, *Letters and Private Papers,* 3:415.

5. Thackeray's "tenderness" was deemed to be "almost womanly" by Sir Theodore Martin and prompted his friends to love him "almost as one loves a woman," according to Trollope; his "loving-kindness" was also associated by Herman Merivale with "all the nervous susceptibilities ... of a woman" (Philip Collins, ed., *Thackeray: Interviews and*

further by suggesting, only half in jest, that his girls were actually more satisfying to him as mates than any adult female companion might have been: "I have 2 little wives not jealous of each other; and am at last most comfortable in my *harem*."[6]

This sense of conjugal intimacy—evident in Thackeray's unself-conscious reference to his round-faced, older daughter contentedly convalescing "in my bed in the next room"—is borne out by the letters he wrote to "my dearest women" whenever away from them. Later in 1854, he shared with his daughter "dearest Nan" the most recent details of his search for a third female resident, a suitable governess: "And to night— where do you think I'm going? To meet a Miss MacWhirter at tea. A clergymans daughter independent, clever."[7] Thackeray enjoys teasing Anny about the possible enlargement of his little harem. His interest in this available candidate is certainly innocent. Yet he also toys with the prurience that might cause others to misconstrue a harmless association into something more sexually charged—as certain reviewers of *Jane Eyre* had done when they fabricated stories about Thackeray's presumed liaison with another clever and independent clergyman's daughter, much to Charlotte Brontë's embarrassment and to his own mischievous delight.

To nullify the potentially erotic subtext he has injected into his letter to Anny, Thackeray unexpectedly alters his self-representation as an adult caretaker of the family's fortunes. He asks his daughter to see him as a boy whose appetite is better satisfied by a passion for rich desserts than by any involvement with clever women he might meet over tea: "Henry Davison and I dined at home together and had roly poly pudding so good that I says I wish I had my girls here says I—so he says I should like to see them very much but *after the roly poly* pudding so we ate it all up."[8] The

---

Recollections [London: Macmillan, 1983], 2:206, 332, 350). It was that hypersensitivity that led Walter Bagehot to dismiss Thackeray as a thinker in a sexist remark that also stereotypes women writers such as Charlotte Brontë and George Eliot, both of whom greatly admired Thackeray: "His mind was, to a considerable extent, like a woman's mind. It could comprehend abstractions when they were unrolled and explained . . . , but it never naturally created them. . . . He acutely felt every passing fact—every trivial interlude" (Walter Bagehot, "Sterne and Thackeray," *National Review* 18 [April 1864]: 546).

6. Thackeray to Carmichael-Smyth, 2 February 1855, *Letters and Private Papers,* 3:415.

7. Thackeray to Anny Thackeray, 28 August 1854, *Letters and Private Papers,* 3: 386, 385.

8. Ibid., 385.

account of such boyish feasting also allows Thackeray to remind his daughters that he has been dutifully recasting the fairy tale they shared with him—a tale that begins with gluttonous characters who indulge themselves at the breakfast table and that relies throughout on funny allusions to foods attractive and offensive to young stomachs.

In readying *The Rose and the Ring* for publication, Thackeray informs Anny, he has lately been redrawing the pictures he fashioned, while still in Italy, for her and Minny and the smaller children who attended their pantomime: "I have done a mort of wood-blocks though for Giglio and Bulbo." Thackeray ends his letter by proposing that the original threesome consider putting on a repeat performance of the private theatricals he is transforming into a public book. He offers them a trans-generational Christmas "benefit" to be staged as soon as he can join "my daughters and parents" with the printed text in hand.[9] The proposed revival of the original pantomime thus might, Thackeray seems to suggest, also reactivate the comic purgation he has tried to extend in his nearly completed book to a joint audience of old and young, "great and small children" alike. All painful wants, yearnings, memories of loss may be wishfully erased if the three generations of family survivors—his mother, stepfather, daughters, and Thackeray himself—allow laughter to remove the traces of division or strife.

II

The Rose and the Ring, or, the History of Prince Giglio and Prince Bulbo was issued as a Christmas book by Smith, Elder, & Co. in December of 1854, exactly four years after the same publishers had printed Ruskin's *King of the Golden River*. Thackeray's comic fairy tale, however, not only uses Ruskin's work as an occasional foil but also significantly departs from his own previous Christmas books, all five of which had been, as Gordon N. Ray puts it, "*hors d'oeuvres* in his realistic manner, not markedly different except in their slightness, from his novels of modern life" (*RR Fac.,* xii). Indeed, the fourth of these Christmas books, *Rebecca and Rowena: A Romance Upon a Romance* (1849), which he offered as a playful sequel to Sir Walter Scott's *Ivanhoe,* is an antecedent that Thackeray may well have

9. Ibid.

wanted to reconsider as much as Ruskin's adoption of the outward contours of a Grimm fairy tale.

The Rose and the Ring can actually be read as Thackeray's attempt to
strike a balance between the contrary perspectives of *Rebecca and Rowena*
and *The King of the Golden River,* two books also linked by virtue of their
having been illustrated by the very same artist, Richard Doyle.[10] That
Thackeray was skeptical about the arrested innocence promoted in *The
King of the Golden River* seems evident from some of his comic emenda-
tions of Ruskin's plot that we shall later consider. But by 1854 Thackeray
also appears to have become less disposed to uphold the disenchantments
of adult experience as a criterion that justified his earlier, dismissive treatment of a romance such as *Ivanhoe.* Buttressed by his respect for the imagination of children and adolescents, Thackeray had become more willing
to accommodate the claims of fantasy.

In *Rebecca and Rowena,* Thackeray does not yet display the tolerance
for fairy-tale wishfulness that he would adopt in *The Rose and the Ring.*
Although he admits the appeal that "extremely juvenile legends" like
Scott's once held for him, Thackeray regards such materials with the same
ironic hindsight that had marked his handling of the boy Dobbin's infatuation with *The Arabian Nights* in *Vanity Fair* (1847–48). By fashioning a
"middle-aged" sequel to *Ivanhoe,* he can demote his original to the rank
of a juvenile book. For Scott's romance, according to the narrator of
Rebecca and Rowena, ends with a falsification. From an adult perspective,
Ivanhoe's living ever happily after with "that icy, faultless, prim, niminy-
piminy Rowena"[11] is an impossibility that Thackeray satirically sets out
to redress.

Still, as always, Thackeray is more duplicitous than his narrator allows,
for his parody surreptitiously serves the very wishfulness he professes to
expunge. By rearranging Scott's plot and eventually allowing Ivanhoe to

10. A bout of illness in 1849 had prevented Thackeray from cutting wood blocks
based on his own drawings; he therefore delegated the art work to "my friend Mr. RICH-
ARD DOYLE" (William Makepeace Thackeray, *Rebecca and Rowena: A Romance upon Romance* [London: Chapman and Hall, 1850], 5). For Thackeray's and Ruskin's opposing
views on the early Doyle's "gentleness of disposition" and the later Doyle's satirical craft,
see pp. 48 and 48n, above. As Gordon N. Ray notes in *Thackeray: The Age of Wisdom:
1847–1863* (London: Oxford University Press, 1958), 470n, Doyle's emerging "disillu-
sionment with the great world" chimed with the tone of *The Newcomes,* which he also
illustrated for Thackeray.

11. Thackeray, *Rebecca and Rowena,* 3, 5.

marry Rebecca, he can also fashion, however much tongue in cheek, "a romance upon romance." It is Rebecca and not Rowena, the narrator professes, who has been the true feminine ideal, "so admirable, so tender, so heroic, so beautiful," he had unremittingly worshipped ever since he devoured the novel in his boyhood.[12] By now placing her in a burlesque that mocks all male aspirations of heroism, Thackeray tries to keep alive something resembling his original devotion.

Given his ironic deflation of chivalric prowess, however, Thackeray cannot wholly prevent Rebecca's ideality from becoming tarnished by the grotesques who surround her. Although her image is less sullied than that of the girl in white to which Dobbin so dubiously clings in *Vanity Fair,* she also lacks the vitality of Amelia's antitype, the resilient Rebecca Sharp. In *Vanity Fair,* Dobbin's infatuation and Amelia's own cult of her worthless dead husband were rendered as adolescent fantasies that each should have shed. In *Rebecca and Rowena,* however, Thackeray himself attempts to preserve a bland and bloodless literary stereotype of ideal femininity.

There were personal reasons for Thackeray's hungering after the very romance he dismissed as "extremely juvenile." His immersion in a genre he professes to subvert in the name of adult "reality" helped him relieve a painful emotional deprivation: Thackeray and Jane Octavia Brookfield, who was unhappily married to a close friend of his, though admitting their need for each other, also decided that "the iron frame of propriety established by respectable Victorian society" barred them from becoming lovers.[13] The same society that soon applauded Effie Ruskin's decision to replace her mate with John Everett Millais would have condemned any liaison between a clergyman's wife and a grass widower whose public image and reputation always seemed tenuous to those aware of his years of Parisian bohemianism. When Charlotte Brontë chose to dedicate the second edition of *Jane Eyre* (1847) to Thackeray, she was unaware of the private history of the novelist she admired. The man she cast as a fiery Hebrew prophet actually resembled the fictional Rochester in more ways than one. Like Rochester, whose flighty *amours* in wicked Paris Brontë contrasts to his new sincerity of feeling, the middle-aged Thackeray had fallen in love with a Jane he could not marry because chained to a wife as hopelessly insane as the Madwoman in the Attic. Brontë's romance, like Scott's, thus only seemed to mock the reality of Thackeray's position.

12. Ibid., 4.
13. Ray, *Thackeray: Age of Wisdom,* 70.

It is hardly coincidental that *Rebecca and Rowena* should have been composed immediately after Jane Brookfield attended Thackeray's sick bed. Fever-wracked and debilitated, he was as vulnerable as Scott's Ivanhoe was when nursed back to health by the beautiful Rebecca of York or as the comatose Rochester whom Jane saves from a burning bed. If Brontë could kill Bertha Mason to unite her Jane and Rochester, Thackeray would eliminate Rowena to license Ivanhoe's search for his true elective affinity, an idealized equivalent of Jane Brookfield. By casting himself as El Desdichado, Wilfrid the Disinherited, another Will could be freed to indulge his thwarted desire. In the safe realm of a romance disguised as an anti-romantic burlesque, Thackeray could obtain his own coveted Jane, now transformed into Rebecca the Unattainable, the Forbidden.

It was, as the narrator of *Rebecca and Rowena* avows, "a simple plan for setting matters right."[14] Life itself, however, offered no such simple solutions, only further displacements. In the letters Thackeray wrote to correspondents that even included her husband and his own mother, Jane Brookfield, though still childless at the time, is persistently metamorphosed into an idealized maternal figure. His love for her, Thackeray incongruously proclaims at one point, is as "pure" as his love for his youngest daughter.[15] In these and other such protestations, Thackeray not only denies the erotics that enter even the purest forms of father-daughter love but also refuses to consider the eroticized relation between a son and his mother (especially a mother as young and seductive as his own had been). There is a good amount of self-delusion when he asks Jane Brookfield whether the innocent voices of little boy choristers, which charm him so much "that they set all my sensibilities aquiver," have the same effect on her, only to answer his own question for her: "I am sure they do."[16]

Eventually, however, Thackeray seems to have understood that it was best to nurture his desire in private. Invoking still another major Brontë romance, *Wuthering Heights,* Thackeray announced: "It's happier that we should love each other in the grave, as it were, than that we should meet by sham-chance, and that there should be secrets or deceits." In the same letter, written in October of 1853 just before his trip to Rome with Anny and Minny, he tells two confidantes that his daughters are aware of his

---

14. Thackeray, *Rebecca and Rowena,* 5.
15. See Ray, *Thackeray: The Age of Wisdom,* 66.
16. Thackeray to Jane Brookfield, 14 October 1848, *Letters and Private Papers,* 2:447.

infatuation: "My girls I suppose see all about it; but they love her all the same." With such understanding supporters close by, Thackeray can now claim that he feels closer to "Dear J." when away "than when sitting by her." Such displacements allow him to convert her into a mere abstraction: "I admire human nature in thinking of her."[17]

The best strategy, however, involved a radical reversal of Thackeray's previous relation to the feminine. Instead of periodically rekindling his adolescent worship of a female ideal constructed out of a yearning for fusion with an unattainable mother, he began to assume an interest in adolescents of the opposite sex. By assuming the persona of a fatherly or avuncular older male, Thackeray discovered that his attraction to younger women might be safely maintained without any sense of transgressing the bounds of propriety. Thus, around the same time that Thackeray distanced himself from Jane Brookfield, he found unexpectedly joyous compensations in the company of young women. The nostalgia, self-pity, sentimentality, as well as the repressed sexual desire inevitably stirred up by his infatuation with grown-up, maternal women could be minimized by what Thackeray now described to a medical friend as a much smaller "dose" of the old love-malady.[18]

While still in the United States, away from Anny and Minny, Thackeray found in the sixteen-year-old Lucy Baxter and her cousin Libbie Strong worthy substitutes for Jane as well as for his own daughters. But the allurements of the older Sally Baxter (who, at nineteen, was close in age to the young mother ever-engraved in Thackeray's childhood memories of India) had to be resisted. He therefore needs to assure himself—in a letter to the mother to whom he had always reported his self-justifications—that even though he has been "in love for 3 days with a pretty wild girl of 19 (and was never more delighted to discover that I could have this malady again,)" his flirtation has ended.[19] Yet his letter of farewell to Sally is as "sentimental and fond" as the two drafts he claims to have burned.[20] By way of contrast, when Thackeray writes illustrated

17. Thackeray to Mrs. Elliot and Kate Perry, October 1853, *Letters and Private Papers,* 4:437.

18. Thackeray to Dr. John Brown, 25 March 1853, *Letters and Private Papers,* 3:245.

19. Thackeray to Charmichael-Smyth, 20 December 1852, *Letters and Private Papers,* 3:149.

20. Thackeray to Sally Baxter, 22 December 1852, *Letters and Private Papers,* 3:151.

letters to Lucy Baxter and Libby Strong, he engages in a flirtatious animation that very much anticipates Lewis Carroll's inventiveness in his own
playful correspondence with his many little girlfriends.

Yet in addressing his "little absurd birds (I wish I could hear you pronounce them 2 woerds absuerd buerds in your New York tone!)," Thackeray is also more overtly sexual than Carroll ever allows himself to be
(and, certainly, than Ruskin is in his exchanges with his own little birds at
Winnington). He invents naughty liaisons for the girls whom he marries
off to lower-class suitors of other races. He even extends his tasteless remarks about racial miscegenation to the daughters he has by then rejoined:
"we have our prejudices in Europe," he tells Libby and Lucy, "when my
youngest girl [Minny is only thirteen at the time!] was married to the black
footman I was for a long time inconsolable but the little tawny graces of
my infantile grandson have reconciled me to his mother's choice and the
bandy legs and woolly head of his father." The jocular tone Thackeray
adopts to describe his daughter's presumed impregnation by a black footman barely conceals a fascination with taboos that certainly go beyond
interracial marriage.[21]

The licenses that Thackeray takes in these letters to young women are
put to far better advantage in *The Rose and the Ring.* A fairy tale whose plot
depends on male lust—as well as the lust that an older woman, Barbara
Gruffanuff, feels for the young Prince Giglio—remains inoffensive, as attractive to adolescents as well as to much younger readers. While still in
Italy, Thackeray had tested the tale on the younger children of English-
speaking exiles, notably the little American Edith Story (convalescing
from the same epidemic that had killed her brother and infected the
Thackerays). In England, if one is to trust the memory of Blanche Warre
Cornish, the daughter of one of Thackeray's Anglo-Indian cousins, she
was offered a "foretaste" of *The Rose and the Ring* by being shown drawings of the female characters. In a sketch Thackeray specially drew for
her, little Blanche was given a somewhat different foretaste: although the
figures represented were those of little girls, the representation somehow
allowed her to anticipate the mature perspective of a "grown woman."[22]

It is precisely Thackeray's blending of the perspectives of childhood,
adolescence, and maturity that makes *The Rose and the Ring* so much more

21. Thackeray to Libby Strong and Lucy Baxter, 17–18 October to 3 November 1853,
Letters and Private Papers, 3:311.

22. Collins, *Thackeray: Interviews and Recollections,* 2:194.

elastic than either *Rebecca or Rowena* or *The King of the Golden River*. The tale that he concocted for his teenage daughters and for little Edith never lingers in a childhood Eden. Growth is all. Using adolescence as his primary vantage point, the story's narrator can simultaneously look backwards and forwards, at the simplicities of childhood and the complications of maturity. Thackeray's "Fireside Pantomime for Great and Small Children" thus always navigates between opposing perspectives. Edith Story herself later recalled the "great benevolent giant" who read his fairy tale in her sick-room as a sort of mediator between that sequestered space and the "all-absorbing interests" of the busy city-world to which he belonged.[23] Her remark contradicts the sentimental myth that arose after Thackeray's death, a myth that exaggerated the regressiveness of *The Rose and the Ring* by converting Edith into the exclusive recipient of a story as much designed for "Great" children as for the "Small."

After Thackeray's death on December 24, 1863, the poet Frederick Locker Lampson penned a tribute in which he deliberately adopted the point of view of Edith Story. In "The Rose and the Ring (Christmas, 1854, and Christmas, 1863)," Locker has Edith, now a young woman soon to become the Countess Peruzzi, reread the fable that "the kind Wizard" had presented to her as the "last and best of his Toys."[24] For his part, the same Richard Doyle who had illustrated *Rebecca and Rowena* and *The King of the Golden River* furnished a woodcut for the poem as his own tribute to his former associate. Instead of the sharp antitheses of Doyle's drawings of Gluck and his brothers, we are offered a composition that insists on harmonizing contraries. The vertical posture of the huge male storyteller who hovers over the little girl is not at odds with her horizontal placement on the couch that acts as a sickbed. Instead, his inclined back runs in a near-parallel to the axis formed by her propped-up torso and sagging skirt (fig. 11).

The two figures are further united by the open window that frames them. In *The King of the Golden River,* Doyle had portrayed a feminized Gluck looking out longingly at the distant mountains (fig. 3). In this portrait, however, the emphasis is on inwardness. The myopic reader who strains to read his own text and the listener who contentedly closes her eyes can avert their gaze from the window centered on the basilica of St.

23. Ibid., 255.

24. Frederick Locker Lampson, *London Lyrics* (London: Macmillan, 1904), 147; the lines quoted are 17 and 18.

11 Richard Doyle, Thackeray and Edith Story

Peter's in Rome, the city of visible history. The reclining miniature of a Sleeping Beauty does not yet have to venture into the outside from which her visitor has come. But his own stiff, unsettled posture suggests that he cannot linger for long. Though droll, like the long-nosed South-West Wind in Ruskin's fable, and as capable of sarcasm, this adult male with a broken nose is highly vulnerable.

The juxtaposition of the spellbound girl and the erection that looms high above the cityscape at her back may also be Doyle's way of hinting that a tension exists between Thackeray's disparate activities as a regressive storyteller for children and a determined man of letters moving in a world of adult sexuality. (Locker's poem similarly offers a contrast between the friend of "innocent maidens and boys" and the mighty "scorner" of the vanities of men and women.) If so, however, the opposition says more about Victorian culture's separation of innocence and experience than about Thackeray's actual practice. *The Rose and the Ring* and *Vanity Fair* are not antithetical extremes. For Thackeray consistently regarded children and grown-ups as travelers on different stretches of the selfsame road. He deliberately addresses "children" when asking his readers to shut the puppet-box in the last sentence of *Vanity Fair*. And he offers a portrait of Anny and Minny, then eleven and eight, doing just that in the final illustration to *Vanity Fair*.

Vanity Fair, like *The Newcomes*, portions of which Thackeray wrote while working on *The Rose and the Ring*, is told by a world-weary narrator whose skeptical outlook prevents him from embracing the child-play to which adults would like to revert. To indulge in such play, Thackeray suggests at the end of *The Newcomes* (1853–55), grown-ups must activate a wishfulness that requires a suspension of disbelief. He therefore directs his "Friendly reader" to the outskirts of a "happy, harmless Fable-land," in which "you and the author" might meet "some future day." But that distant realm, where heroes and heroines can live ever happily after and "annoying folk are gotten out of the way," is not in the purview of adult ironists compelled to dwell on the discrepancies between the ideal and the real.[25]

As *The Rose and the Ring* demonstrates, however, irony need not be ruled out if adults agree to enter Fable-land together with the child. Convinced that all mockery was detrimental to the childlike earnestness he wanted to preserve, Ruskin excised the ironic epilogue to *The King of the Golden River*. And, what is more, much later in his career and long after Thackeray's death, he peevishly contended that, "of all writers whatsoever of any people or language, I should most strictly forbid Thackeray" to young readers of both sexes (*CW,* 34:588). Yet the narrator of *The Rose and the Ring* respects the child reader and, especially, the adolescent reader as incipient fellow-ironists. He therefore refuses to filter the contradictions that Ruskin had regarded as impurities in need of refinement. Instead, he tries to effect a bond between juveniles and grown-ups by jointly inviting them to participate in a gratifying game that will both question and yet also indulge the improbabilities of make-believe.

III

In *Rebecca and Rowena,* male rivalry had been paramount; despite its tribute to Rebecca, the story had appropriated for its own mock-heroic purposes the jousts and combats and sexual jealousies of *Ivanhoe*. Thackeray

---

25. William Makepeace Thackeray, *The Newcomes: Memoirs of a Most Respectable Family,* Kensington Limited Edition (Boston: Estes & Lauriat, 1891), 3:416–17.

himself had thus become Sir Walter Scott's rival. In *The Rose and the Ring*, however, where the contest between two powerful female figures makes male heroics seem even more inconsequential, Thackeray credits a female collaborator for inspiring his plot. Asked to toss off some caricatures by his "friend Miss Bunch, governess of a large family that lived in the *Piano Nobile* of the house inhabited by myself and my young charges" (*RR*, "Prelude," 5),[26] he soon found himself pressed into the responsibilities of sustaining an entire narrative. This "lady of great fancy and droll imagination" (*RR*, "Prelude," 7), named after the traditional Dame Bunch, thus acts as a muse for the carefree graphic artist whose casual drawings assumed a larger life of their own. Whether based on reality or fictitious, this ally resembles another governess of great fancy and droll imagination. But the Showman of *Vanity Fair* had to repudiate the adulterous, child-hating Miss Sharp. Here, however, a father eager to entertain his motherless offspring and a mother-surrogate who knows how to amuse her own charges become partners. Through their wedded imaginations, they can, though as chaste as any fairy-tale innocents, become fruitful and multiply.

The narrator of Thackeray's "Prelude" hopes that a tiny band at a Twelfth-Night "child's party" in distant Rome will sprout into a much larger audience back in the home-country: "If these children are pleased, thought I, why should not others be amused also?" (*RR*, "Prelude," 8). These multiplied "others" replace the original children as well as the collaborating adults. For Thackeray—or rather the pseudonymous "M. A. Titmarsh"[27]—invites a host of English (and American) parents and governesses to share the printed text along with their young: "And you elder folks—a little joking, and dancing, and fooling will do even you no harm" (*RR*, "Prelude," 6). Diminution was the means by which an earnest young Ruskin tried to regain the purity of childhood lost. But the "nonsensical Xmas book" a "dear giant" told to little Edith Story relies on a comic bloating to endorse the process of growth. The narrative begins with an indoor scene that parodies petty bourgeois domesticity by seating a king, queen, and princess at "their royal breakfast-table" (*RR*, chap. 1, 7). It ends

---

26. The Puffin Books edition of *The Rose and the Ring* will be cited in the text by both chapter and page number. Miss Bunch is also mentioned in the verse that ends chapter 2 of the manuscript version (*RR Fac.*, 7).

27. On Thackeray's use of this *nom de plume* for his Christmas books, see Ray, *Thackeray: Age of Wisdom*, 98–100. If "M. A. Titmarsh" is a crabby bachelor who makes a "book speak like a man" (98), his name also carries decidedly maternal associations.

with an outdoor procession as all "principal officers of state" (*RR*, chap. 19, 140) accompany a new king and queen to the wedding that will unite them and the lands they have regained.

This emphasis on progress, on the growth of characters who move from a domestic realm to a public domain, is extended to the account of the book's own transformation from private to public pantomime. Thackeray's "Prelude" positively exults in its first-person account of his fairy tale's evolution. His eagerness to buttonhole his readers markedly differs from the elision that led the nameless "Author" of *The King of the Golden River* to rely on an "Advertisement" in which his publishers obliquely allude to his fairy tale's origins. Ruskin's need, in 1851, to conceal the personal underpinnings of his fantasy was, as noted in the previous chapter, very much related to his initial effort, in 1841, to keep Gluck free from all contamination with violence and adult sexuality. By having Gluck return to a re-virginized Treasure Valley, Ruskin not only hopes to regain innocence but also to restore his insulation. We are not allowed to see the crowds that reportedly flock to the boy's opened granaries. The recovered shelter merely replaces the cradle that Hans and Schwartz had polluted.

By way of contrast, the matured Giglio and Rosalba adapt themselves to the contours of the acquisitive, strife-ridden, urban world that Ruskin's boy-hero was encouraged to flee. Not only do their responsibilities exceed Gluck's, but they also gain a self-knowledge he never required. Although their final happiness, like Gluck's, depends on the aid of a superior and wiser magical figure, they eventually manage to lead their own lives without the insurance provided by fairy roses and fairy rings, marital aids required by their immature antitypes, Prince Bulbo and Princess Angelica.

The wedding ceremony that Thackeray uses at the end of his story is a feature common to the happy endings of both fairy tales and "adult" social comedies. Yet his reinstatement of a closure that Ruskin had pointedly avoided also suggests that Thackeray understood the error of deforming into "innocent" *Kindermärchen* a genre that did not segregate the interests of the young from those of the old in its original folk-tale format.[28] Thack-

---

28. This recognition, as we shall see in chapter 11, also informs Juliana Ewing's fairy tales for children and is a salient point of difference between her and Ruskin's work in the genre. Anne Thackeray's impish *Fairy Tales for Adult Folks* (1867) restores fairy tales for adult consumption. The ageless fairies she calls "centenarians" appeal equally to children and their elders through their "fund of spirits and perennial youth" ("The Sleeping Beauty in the Wood," in Nina Auerbach and U. C. Knoepflmacher, eds., *For-*

eray mocks the exaggerated passions that grip the many suitors over-whelmed by Rosalba's magically enhanced beauty. Notwithstanding such mockery (intensified perhaps by a need to make light of his own sexual frustrations), it seems clear that he believed that the representation of sex-ual desire had a definite place in tales intended for growing children. The adolescent infatuations Thackeray depicts as silly are therefore regarded with an amused toleration. Like George MacDonald in "The Light Prin-cess" (discussed in the next chapter), Thackeray regards youthful erotics as a necessary phase in the formation of an adult identity.

Even though Thackeray's prime auditors were his teenage daughters, the adult identity taking shape in *The Rose and the Ring* is that of a young male. Despite his efforts to chart the progress of Rosalba's growth as care-fully as Giglio's, it is clear that the education of the immature prince lies at the center of the book. The story that carries the subtitle "The History of Prince Giglio and Prince Bulbo" is a fairy-tale version of the male *Bil-dungsroman* Thackeray tackled in *Pendennis* (1848–1850) and again at-tempted in *Philip* (1861–1862), his last complete novel. Giglio's passage from adolescence into maturity is not completed until the last pages. He starts out as a teenage naif who has already been outstripped by his quicker cousin Angelica and will soon lag behind the self-aware and self-educated Rosalba. Despite his own gradual education and eventual pretensions to leadership, the young prince remains an object of contestation for two older female figures, an omnipotent Fairy Blackstick and a conniving Countess Gruffanuff, until the book's last pages. Although his psychologi-cal roundness makes him more attractive than the grotesque Bulbo, he seems as dependent on the superior wit of the four female characters as the writer who professed to rely on Miss Bunch's aid and encouragement. Femininity, in *The Rose and the Ring,* possesses attributes that are innately adult, authoritative, fully developed. The feminine is therefore coveted as an aid in the formation of a more rounded masculine self.

In the drawing Thackeray devised for his book's title page, the reclin-ing posture adopted by a teenage boy makes him as central as the recum-bent figure of Edith Story was in the Doyle drawing discussed above. The central position the boy occupies in front of a hearth that blazes with shad-owy shapes allows him to crowd out the other six figures in the composi-tion. The relaxed youngster is framed by two groupings, in each of which

bidden Journeys: Fairy Tales and Fantasies by Victorian Women Writers [Chicago: Univer-sity of Chicago Press, 1992], 22).

12 W. M. Thackeray, Frontispiece to *The Rose and the Ring*

there is a woman and two children. The woman seated behind him and against whose chair the boy is propped holds up what seems to be a male child; placed next to her and to the boy is a rapt teenage girl, about his own age. The seated woman who faces the boy is an older storyteller, a Miss Bunch who has adopted the by now familiar Mother Goose stance depicted by previous illustrators; she is flanked by two smaller children, another paired boy and girl (fig. 12).

Although all the listeners depicted in the drawing seem equally attentive, the female teller's prime auditor appears to be the mesmerized young man with whom she maintains exclusive eye contact. Her imaginative powers have clearly animated the shapes dancing in the fireplace, yet these fluttering "strangers" also seem to emanate from the cooperating fancy of the adolescent who lies beneath them. The shapes are themselves masculine, though mock-heroic, for they correspond to the two princes of the subtitle. The horseman represents Prince Giglio at the dubious moment of his highest accomplishment when, mounted on a "fairy horse" given to him by Fairy Blackstick, he is allowed to topple the "royal ruffian and usurper, who has such a bad cause, and who was so cruel to women" (*RR,* chap. 17, 128–29). The bulbous-headed figure in the foreground is unmistakably Prince Bulbo, possibly holding on to the magical Rose that had been Blackstick's present to his mother.

The double plot of *The Rose and the Ring* sets its two male protagonists in apposition to each other. Though competing at one point for the chambermaid Betsinda (not yet revealed as Princess Rosalba), Giglio and Bulbo are more profitably seen as doubles, higher and lower versions of the same adolescent strivings. Both have been the recipients of the talismans which Fairy Blackstick had originally awarded to their mothers. Yet the fairy ring and fairy rose awarded to her god-daughters "to render them charming in the eyes of their husbands" soon made them so absurdly vain that they began to patronize their donor. Alienated by the childish vanity of these mothers, Blackstick declines all "further magical performances" and scarcely uses "her wand at all except as a cane to walk about with" (*RR,* chap. 3, 20). Aware that her gifts only perpetuate, rather than correct, the immaturity and propensity for self-delusion of her recipients, the Fairy withholds her favors from both Rosalba and Angelica. As a result, each girl-princess becomes far more self-reliant than the boy-princes whose dependence on their dubious maternal legacy greatly impedes their growth.

Yet Giglio is less stifled by his parentage than Bulbo. Orphaned as a youngster, neglected by the scheming uncle who stripped him of his throne and fortune, the prince actually benefits from his lack of filial bonds. Unlike Bulbo, he does not have to conform to the expectations of a domineering father. And he can eventually recover his patrimony, as well as Rosalba's, because he has never been as dependent as Bulbo on the magical crutch passed on from mother to son. The handsome Giglio finds it easy to part with his dead mother's fairy ring, "when, as quite a child, he gave it to Angelica," the ungainly cousin who is King Valoroso's daughter (*RR,* chap. 7, 45). The ill-favored Bulbo, however, cannot wean himself from his own mother's deathbed injunction "never to part" with her fairy rose (*RR,* chap. 11, 79). To seem "irresistibly beautiful," she had herself relied on the rose to conceal the "ridiculous" and "hideous" features she passed on to her son (*RR,* chap. 3, 18).

Giglio's transference of his mother's ring to Angelica leads everyone, including Giglio himself, excessively to "love and admire" that resourceful but unaccomplished and unattractive princess. The displacement significantly repeats a shift that occurred in Giglio's childhood when his own father "transferred all his love" from wife to offspring as soon as the boy began to wear her magical ring (*RR,* chap. 7, 45). By having the ring quickly change hands again, as it passes from Angelica to Barbara Gruffanuff and from "Gruffy" to a Rosalba still masked as Betsinda, Thackeray can question the depth of Giglio's attachment to a succession of love-objects, much as Shakespeare had undercut the steadfastness of his romantic lovers through the magic confusions of *A Midsummer Night's Dream*. The deflecting propensities Thackeray displayed whenever wracked by his old love-"malady" probably sharpened his acute awareness of the dynamics of transference: the sickness of Anny and Minny may well have reactivated a history of unfulfilled attachments that had traveled from mother to wife to Jane Brookfield, and, most recently, to young Sally Baxter.

Thackeray contrasts Rosalba's exclusive (and silent) devotion to Giglio with his own loud professions of rapture to three successive love-objects. Whereas his ring-induced love for her is initially as artificial as his infatuation with Angelica and Gruffanuff, her love for him has evolved naturally. In a situation that replicates Thackeray's earlier fantasies of sickbed romances, Rosalba finds herself drawn to Giglio while nursing him back to health. But the previous fantasies are also revised. The maturity of Rosalba's love not only exposes Giglio's fickleness, but also contrasts with the adolescent behavior of the earlier male patients: Ivanhoe's / Thackeray's protestations of undying love for Rebecca / Jane were belied by the prompt turn to more suitable substitutes (Rowena / Sally Baxter). Rosalba avoids the romantic displacements of her male counterparts. Her devotion is essentially maternal. She replicates the bond that exists between parents and children, a bond recently reconfirmed for the father-and-mother-too who was nursing, and being nursed by, his two daughters.

Thackeray suggests that Giglio's illness stems from emotional deprivation. The young man is convinced that the female affection he requires as a primary prop has been withdrawn from him. With his mother dead, Fairy Blackstick seemingly removed, Gruffanuff still hostile to him, Betsinda still perceived as a mere background figure, and the Queen Mother, "his royal but weak-minded aunt" (*RR,* chap. 6, 37), more interested in jewels and whist parties than in his well-being, Giglio has become excessively dependent on his cousin Angelica's approval. When Angelica spurns him, this "good-natured" but "thoughtless youth" falls apart (*RR,* chap. 6, 32). Never "much inclined to politics or any learning," excelling only in horsemanship, fencing, and dancing, he cannot parry the accusations of those who remark "how he was so ignorant that he could not spell the commonest words . . . ; how he drank a great deal too much wine at dinner . . . ; how he owed ever so much money at the pastrycook's and the haberdasher's . . . ; how he was fond of playing cards with the pages." When Angelica, too, begins to "scorn him for being so stupid" (*RR,* chap. 6, 32, 36), and, what is worse, to show a decided preference for the silly Bulbo, Giglio becomes unmanned.

Confined to his sickbed, "bled and physicked" by the court physician, forgotten by all courtiers but the brainless captain of the guard, Count Hedzoff, Giglio finds himself attended by one as neglected as himself, the loyal Betsinda (Rosalba). When she discovers that the love-starved patient is profiting neither from the doctor's "horrible medicines" nor from "the gruel" she is commanded to bring him, this fellow-Cinderella takes the task of nourishment into her own hands. Aware of Giglio's infatuation with his cousin, Betsinda tells him that the roast chicken and jellies she has herself prepared were made by Angelica "with her own hands, on purpose for" him (*RR,* chap. 7, 43). The fiction works: Giglio gobbles up the jellies and picks the chicken to its last bone, only to become disenchanted with the ringless Angelica and enamored of the ring's new possessor, Gruffanuff, who then gives it to Betsinda.

Only when Queen Rosalba (no longer Betsinda) assures herself that King Giglio (no longer dethroned) does not require her to wear his mother's ring can the couple bestow it upon a permanently immature "poor youth" (*RR,* chap. 17, 130). Bulbo welcomes the magical ring Giglio and Rosalba were about to throw away. Having accidentally lost his fairy rose to Angelica, he has become repulsive to her while she has become greatly enhanced in his eyes. Whereas Angelica's derision of Giglio led him to shed his torpor and made him eager to become worthy of Rosalba, her similar scorn of the ungainly Bulbo only confirms him in his sloth and self-abasement. Giglio therefore awards the fairy ring to his hapless double: "no sooner had Bulbo put it on, but lo and behold, he appeared a personable, agreeable young Prince enough—with a fine complexion, fair hair, rather stout, and with bandy legs; but these were encased in such a beautiful pair of yellow morocco boots that nobody remarked them" (*RR,* chap. 17, 126–27). Unlike the illusionless Giglio and Rosalba, Bulbo and Angelica require artifice to find the fairy tale happiness they would otherwise not obtain.

Like *Vanity Fair,* with its double plot and counterpointed heroines, *The Rose and the Ring* plays with Victorian gender stereotypes. Males may be active on the battlefield, whether at Waterloo and Crimea or in mock-heroic encounters in fable-lands called Paflagonia and Crim Tartary. But when set against true activists of the opposite sex, they are almost as paralyzed as Ruskin's Gluck. Thackeray's view of himself as a "lazy fellow" is as much inscribed in this children's book as in his adult novels. Like Jos Sedley, Bulbo is an exaggerated physical caricature of a "rather stout," appetite-driven, and effeminate Thackeray. Yet the portrait of Giglio as a clumsy young man crippled by his sentimental yearning for an idealized female complement relies, like the presentation of William Dobbin, on a more psychologically negative self-image. A fatherless only child, whose early indolence and Bohemianism has led him to forfeit his patrimony, Giglio replicates Thackeray's own wants even more directly than Dobbin; and his later prowess as a university prize student and his future as Rosalba's happily reformed husband rather sardonically invert the fate of the Cambridge dropout who became a "widower" tied to a living wife.

Yet Giglio's prime relation is not to Rosalba. The plot of *The Rose and the Ring* depends on the presence of a maternal authority figure who seems removed and uninvolved, yet who turns out to be as much the shaper of a young man's destiny as the actual Mrs. Carmichael-Smyth had been in Thackeray's emotional life. The Fairy Blackstick lets her godson flounder on his own before she decisively intervenes at the eleventh hour to prevent him from relapsing into the insecurities of adolescence. Paradoxically enough, although her intervention secures Giglio's independence, it only reaffirms his slavish dependence on her powers. It is this paradox that fascinates Thackeray. The formative process he recreates through young Giglio's story furnished the middle-aged novelist with an amused, if bittersweet, insight into his own past.

IV

The character who underwent the greatest change in Thackeray's transformation of his illustrated manuscript into a printed text was Fairy Blackstick. This figure, at first called "Alethea" (Truth)[29] as well as Blackstick, originally had to vie with her rival Fairy Hopstick or "Lusingha" (Deceitful Flattery) in her role as the *deus ex machina* who, like Ruskin's King of the Golden River, ensures the happiness of a disenfranchised youth. Hopstick, whom Thackeray removed from the final version, proves to be popular with women to whose parties she (and seldom Blackstick)

29. Samuel Butler assigned the same name to Ernest Pontifex's aunt and surrogate mother in *The Way of All Flesh*.

gets invited. Always encouraging her hosts to think of themselves as worthier and more beautiful than they actually are, she also flatters "ladies' children" by vowing that "nothing was ever so charming and good and lovely" (*RR Fac.*, 10). Blackstick, by contrast, is a blunt truth-teller (as Thackeray's mother was known to be).[30] She tells a "fond mamma" that "I cannot think that yours is a very pretty and clever child and I think you give Anny too many sweet meats, and it is time Tommy was in bed" (*RR Fac.*, 10).

Gordon N. Ray suggests that Thackeray dispensed with Fairy Hopstick because the satire of the adult vanities to which she caters might have seemed "beyond the range of at least the juvenile part of his audience" (*RR Fac.*, ix). The suggestion, however, loses force if one considers how overtly such vanities, even those of a sexual nature, continue to be satirized in the remainder of the published book. It seems more likely that Thackeray decided that a foil to Blackstick only diluted that figure's needed preeminence. Originally, he appears to have wanted to show that the godmother hailed as "good" bestows favors that turn out to be noxious, while the traditionally aloof fairy declared to be "bad" actually helps to promote a child's independence.

Thackeray describes Blackstick's godmotherly practices in a long passage he later excluded:

Alethea had the drollest way of treating her god children and many people grumbled at her practice, as we do sometimes at the prescriptions of the Physician when he is called in. For instance she would drive up in her chariot (no fairy in all the world had such a plain one) to a cottage where the family were starving, and instead of giving them money and clothes cakes hams sausages and so forth, she would bid the children look in the boot, whence they would take out a quantity of dirty clothes, and a piece of soap, and a hammer and an axe, and bid the good wife wash the clothes, and the husband break the stones for a road to Blackstick castle; and when the linen was washed and the stones broken her steward would come and pay for the work done: fetching more clothes, and showing more stones in another road which the cottagers might wash and break. (*RR Fac.*, 11)

This utilitarian philosophy of self-help is not, however, limited to the lower classes, for Blackstick uses the same practical schooling for an effete godchild named "Odicolonio."

30. See Gordon N. Ray, *Thackeray: The Uses of Adversity: 1811–1846* (London: Oxford University Press, 1958), 109–110; Winifred Gerin, *Anne Thackeray Ritchie: A Biography* (Oxford: Oxford University Press, 1983), 279, 281.

The figure with "sober dress and keen severe eyes" whom her detractors call "That horrid *Methodist* of a Fairy!" originally resembled the female didacticists of the anti-fantastical school of Edgeworth or Wollstonecraft.[31] Although her philosophy of self-help remains unchanged, Blackstick becomes a far more magical and mysterious personage in revision. Her restraint is now attributed to her awareness of the futility of the awesome metamorphic powers she can unleash. She has become a female Prospero, an artist disillusioned by human nature. Thackeray now chooses to endow this figure with a history of her own:

> When she was young, and had been first taught the art of conjuring, by the necromancer her father, she was always practising her skill, whizzing about from one kingdom to another upon her black stick, and conferring her fairy favors upon this prince or that. She had scores of royal godchildren; turned numberless wicked people into beasts, birds, millstones, clocks, pumps, bootjacks, umbrellas or other absurd shapes; and, in a word, was one of the most active and officious of the whole college of fairies.
>
> But after two or three thousand years of this sport, I suppose Blackstick grew tired of it. Or perhaps she thought, "What good am I doing by sending this princess to sleep for a hundred years? by fixing a black pudding on to that booby's nose? by causing diamonds and pearls to drop from one little girl's mouth, and vipers and toads from another's? I begin to think I do as much harm as good by my performances. I might as well shut my incantations up, and allow things to take their natural course." (*RR,* chap. 3, 17)

What is noteworthy about this revision is not just the livelier prose, but also the narrator's underlying identification with Blackstick's "I." Her creativity and simultaneous distrust of wishfulness are Thackeray's very own. Whereas the earlier version of "Alethea" only seemed to accentuate the aloofness of the outspoken and humorless Evangelical mother to whose "hard" dictates Thackeray habitually deferred,[32] the later version makes this maternal superego seem more accessible. The *mater abscondita* who seems so remote in the first version becomes internalized. By concluding that the best she can wish for Giglio and Rosalba is a "little misfortune," Blackstick can pass on to her wards what Thackeray learned from the adored mother who had sent him away at such a young age and what he, in turn, was now able to pass on to his daughters—a self-reliance without which he might have remained as arrested as Bulbo. If Blackstick de-

---

31. See pp. 22–23, above.
32. Thackeray to Carmichael-Smyth, May 1840, *Letters and Private Papers,* 1:443.

rives her powers from the necromancer-father who taught her his art, Anny and Minny might acquire a hard-earned independence from an artist-father distrustful of artifice. The boundaries between generations—and genders—could thus be traversed. Sons can become mothers by passing on to their daughters the "natural" wisdom of a grandmother whose own "unfinished novel for children" was destined never to appear in print.[33]

Like Ruskin before him, then, Thackeray regards femininity as essential for the recovery of a male psyche. But whereas Ruskin's fear of masculinity leads him to remove the powerful males who had oppressed his boy-Cinderella, Thackeray simply empowers those female elements he values in himself. If M. A. Titmarsh defers to Miss Bunch and the narrator lets Fairy Blackstick carry out his plot, the story's male characters engage in empty declamations while their female counterparts determine the course of events. Not only Fairy Blackstick is skilled in art. As a small waif, Rosalba shrewdly gets herself adopted as "Betsinda" by staging an impromptu dance on her single slipper. After lisping, "I can dance, and I can sing, and I can do all sorts of ting," the little Cinderella makes herself a flower-wreath and dances "so drolly and prettily, that everybody was delighted" (*RR,* chap. 5, 27–28).

Although she is not the daughter of a French dancing girl like the Becky Sharp of *Vanity Fair,* this tiny *danseuse* has also mastered the arts of enchantment. Like Becky, who learned drawing from her father, Rosalba is a skilled graphic artist who embellishes the sketches Angelica then passes as her own; like Becky, she is also a quick learner, mastering the lessons Angelica finds boring; and like Becky again, she is adept in the art of concealment, allowing Giglio to believe that she is but a menial chambermaid. Although she refuses to flaunt the sexual allurements that inflame all males enchanted by her ring, Rosalba relies on her physical charms more than on her legitimate claims to the throne in trying to rally a loyalist army.

Far craftier and more Becky-like, however, is the upstart "Countess" Gruffanuff whose insincerities and quickness of invention serve her so well. It is she who shows the stupid Hedzoff how to circumvent the order to execute Giglio and she who finds a means to become queen of Paflagonia. Taking advantage of Giglio's wine-aided intoxication with the illusory beauty the ring has bestowed on her, Barbara Griselda Gruff-

---

33. Ray, *Thackeray: Uses of Adversity,* 109.

anuff seizes her chance. When Giglio pays her "most outrageous compliments" and vows to marry her, despite the disparities in age and standing, she resorts to the same device that the low-born Becky so deftly exploited when she relied on hoarded notes from admirers to secure her future:

> To marry the heir to the throne! Here was a chance! The artful hussy actually got a sheet of paper and wrote upon it, "This is to give notice that I, Giglio, only son of Savio, hereby promise to marry the charming and virtuous Barbara Griselda Countess Gruffanuff, and widow of the late Jenkins Gruffanuff, Esq."
>
> "What is it you are writing? you charming Gruffy!" says Giglio, who was lolling on the sofa by the writing-table.
>
> "Only an order for you to sign, dear Prince, for giving coal and blankets to the poor, this cold weather. Look! the King and Queen are both asleep, and your Royal Highness's orders will do."
>
> So Giglio, who was very good-natured, as Gruffy well knew, signed the order immediately; and, when she had it in her pocket, you may fancy the airs she gave herself. (*RR,* chap. 8, 54–55)

Just as, in the denouement of *Vanity Fair,* Thackeray had joined forces with Becky Sharp by having her produce an incriminating letter that painfully revives what both readers and Amelia had long forgotten, so does he, near the end of *The Rose and the Ring,* have Barbara Gruffanuff, demurely dressed in white, resuscitate the note that threatens the expected union of Giglio and the "high-principled" Rosalba. By pretending to undermine the happy closure of a fairy tale through the intrusion of an alien, "adult" reality, Thackeray twits his audience of young and old. His chief target in the story, however, remains an impossibly smug Giglio, whose eagerness to take credit for his rise to eminence makes him disregard the debt he owes to Fairy Blackstick. The prince who so excessively depends on female approbation now badly overestimates his male self-sufficiency.

Regarding Rosalba as a well-deserved guerdon, Giglio not only has forgotten the promissory note that Gruffanuff produces but also has conveniently repressed his indebtedness to the Fairy who oversaw his transformation from near illiteracy to stardom at Bosforo University, shielded his bride from coming to any harm, and protected him with a "suit of armor, which was not only embroidered all over with jewels, and blind to your eyes to look at, but was also water-proof, gun-proof, and sword-proof" (*RR,* chap. 17, 127–28). Blackstick has, moreover, equipped Giglio with a remarkable instrument, a fairy sword "which elongated itself at will." It is with this weapon that Giglio manages to overpower the "justly irritated" King Padella, Bulbo's mighty father, who is amazed to find that his own "most enormous weapon" has become utterly "impotent" (*RR,* chap. 17, 129).

Small wonder, then, that Giglio's benefactress assumes that she has earned the right to advise her godson in the business of kingship. But, "fancying it was his own valor and merits which had put him on his throne, and conquered Padella," Giglio behaves like a petulant son chafing at what he considers to be excessive maternal interference (*RR,* chap. 18, 133). When Rosalba adoringly confirms his self-image as a "pattern of perfection," he disregards her advice to keep his "testy observations" out of Blackstick's hearing: "'Why is Fairy Blackstick always advising me, and telling me how to manage my government, and warning me to keep my word? Does she suppose that I am not a man of sense, and a man of honor?' asks Giglio testily. 'Methinks she rather presumes upon her position'" (*RR,* chap. 18, 133).

Soon, however, this "man of sense" relapses into whining boyhood. He falters when confronted with the incriminating document produced by Barbara Gruffanuff:

> "Is it your handwriting, Giglio?" cries the Fairy Blackstick, with an awful severity of countenance.
>
> "Y-y-y-es," poor Giglio gasps out. "I had quite forgotten the confounded paper: she can't mean to hold me by it. You old wretch, what will you take to let me off?" (*RR,* chap. 18, 136)

When Gruffanuff's sexual lust proves to be as strong as her hunger for money, Giglio meekly turns to his godmother for help. But Blackstick seems as unrelenting:

> Giglio was half mad with rage by this time. "I will not marry her," says he. "Oh, Fairy, Fairy, give me counsel!" And as he spoke, he looked wildly round at the severe face of the Fairy Blackstick.
>
> "'Why is Fairy Blackstick always advising me, and warning me to keep my word? Does she suppose that I am not a man of honor?'" said the Fairy, quoting Giglio's own words. He quailed under the brightness of her eyes: he felt that there was no escape from that awful Inquisition. (*RR,* chap. 18, 137)

The seeming alliance between Blackstick and Gruffanuff causes Giglio's inflated self-esteem to collapse. Considering himself to be forever deserted by his godmother and irreparably separated from his swooning bride, he falls back melodramatically on a manly code of "honor": he will marry the hideous Gruffanuff, he vows, but will die as soon as the ceremony has taken place.

Having humiliated Giglio, Blackstick can unleash the powers she has held in abeyance and rescue the imprudent young man from his "horrible bride." She is, after all, far more adept at the game in which Barbara Gruffanuff seemed to excel. For the Fairy, too, can rely on a past action to alter the plot. Just as Giglio's memory had to be jostled into remembering, by chapter 18, the letter that "dear Gruffy" made him sign in chapter 8, so must any reader with a short attention span now be reminded, by chapter 19, of the sadistic punishment that Blackstick had inflicted on an insolent male as far back as chapter 4. Her act of dominance—which condemned Barbara Gruffanuff's surly husband, the porter Jenkins Gruffanuff, into a painful, shrunken existence as a brass door-knocker—will now be turned against the female rival who has presumed to take control of Giglio. Their combat proves fiercer than the prince's flourishes with his silly fairy sword.

When a frowning Blackstick places herself at the threshold of the palace in which the marriage contract is about to be signed, Giglio misreads her protective posture as still another affront to his deflated self: he is sure that she wants "to insult his misery" (*RR,* chap. 19, 146). But the Fairy is ready to release her anger on his behalf:

"Are you determined to make this poor young man unhappy?" says Blackstick.

"To marry him, yes! What business is it of yours? Pray, madam, don't say 'you' to a Queen," cries Gruffanuff.

"You won't take the money he offered you?"

"No."

"You won't let him off his bargain, though you know you cheated when you made him sign the paper?"

"Impudence! Policemen, remove this woman!" cries Gruffanuff. And the policemen were rushing forward, but with a wave of her wand the Fairy struck them all like so many statues in their places.

"You won't take anything in exchange for your bond, Mrs Gruffanuff," cries the Fairy, with awful severity. "I speak for the last time."

"No!" shrieks Gruffanuff, stamping with her foot. "I'll have my husband, my husband, my husband!"

"YOU SHALL HAVE YOUR HUSBAND!" the Fairy Blackstick cried; and advancing a step, laid her hand upon the nose of the KNOCKER.

As she touched it, the brass nose seemed to elongate, the open mouth opened still wider, and uttered a roar which made everybody start. The eyes rolled wildly; the arms and legs uncurled themselves, writhed about, and seemed to lengthen with each twist; the knocker expanded into a figure in yellow livery, six feet high; the screws by which it was fixed to the door unloosed themselves, and JENKINS GRUFFANUFF once more trod the threshold off which he had been lifted more than twenty years ago! (*RR,* chap. 19, 149)

The law invoked by Barbara Gruffanuff to force Giglio into marriage now turns against her: legally married to a man everyone assumed to have disappeared long ago, she cannot hold Giglio to his contract. By releasing Jenkins and restoring his large size, Blackstick permits Giglio to grow into manhood.

This dramatic outcome of Thackeray's fairy tale can be read on a variety of levels—personal, cultural, and literary. There is a double self-mockery in his account of Barbara Gruffanuff's thwarted desire, for Thackeray not only identified himself with Giglio's (and Jenkins's) paralysis but also with Gruffy's sexual frustrations. He, too, is someone whose chains to an absent yet living mate prevented him from looking for fresh partners. On a broader level, *The History of Prince Giglio and Prince Bulbo* satirizes the male empowerment the story purports to dramatize. The Prince whose name means "lily" (and can also be read as a contraction of "Guglielmo" and hence the equivalent of "Willie" Thackeray) is not the heroic vanquisher of warrior-kings in a boy's fantasy. Instead, this good-natured but giggly naif is easily outwitted by an opportunistic older woman who covets him as a sexual gigolo as much as Lady Bellaston coveted Tom Jones. He thus is simultaneously the hero of a racy comedy of manners as well as a fairy tale "Dummling" like Ruskin's Gluck.

In his own way, then, Giglio exhibits the same passivity Ruskin valued in Gluck and Thackeray mocked in Bulbo. Like Bulbo and Jenkins Gruffanuff and all the other posturing males in the story Thackeray wrote for his daughters, Giglio lacks the resilience and inventiveness that are so unequivocally identified with the feminine. By making this femininity aggressive in the characters of Blackstick and Gruffanuff, Thackeray exploits the same reversal of gender stereotypes that would become a staple of the comic operas of Gilbert and Sullivan two decades later. His deformation of stereotypical notions of masculinity anticipates a play like *Iolanthe,* where female fairies are similarly enlisted to expose male pretensions of sexual and political power.

Yet, as I have been suggesting, *The Rose and the Ring* above all embodies a psychological understanding of the process of growing up that stemmed from Thackeray's sharpened awareness of his own development. The broken-nosed satirist who mocks himself when he flattens the nose of the over-amorous King Valoroso, who assigns Jenkyns Gruffanuff his own height, or who endows Giglio and Bulbo with his adolescent waverings is not merely deflating his own masculinity. Instead, he celebrates a feminine identification that has become strengthened and complicated by his relation to his daughters. In both her early and final incarnations, the "severe" Fairy Blackstick, as I have hinted, is endowed with features that Thackeray drew from his perceptions of his own mother and then blended with the creativity and restraint of desire that he found in himself.[34]

Thackeray's reliance on the Fairy as artificer and ideologue suggests that he had come to recognize the source of his affectual and creative energies in that early "relationship of trust" mothers create as a "playground" for their children's "gradual control of the actual."[35] The Fairy Blackstick who makes a "dumb," fetally positioned, tiny door-knocker grow into a six-foot man possesses the powers of animation of one who is both a parent and a novelist. As supervisor of his daughters' growth, Thackeray seems to have rediscovered the crucial function of play in his own identity formation. His fable thus dramatizes what D. W. Winnicott so well articulates: "The thing about playing is always the precariousness of the interplay of personal psychic reality and the experience of control of actual objects. This is the precariousness of magic itself, magic that arises in intimacy, in a relationship that is found to be reliable. To be reliable the relationship is necessarily motivated by the mother's love, or her love-hate, or her object-relating."[36] By alternately withholding and employing magic in a game that involves children and grown-ups, Blackstick / Thackeray can take his/her characters through the difficult steps of a process of mediation re-enacted whenever conflicting orders of reality unsettle the child we all carry within.

Not only Blackstick, however, but Barbara Gruffanuff, too, is needed

---

34. Even Thackeray's drawings of Blackstick establish correspondences Anny and Minny might be expected to notice: the handsome face and figure that make the Fairy so much more dignified than Gruffy and the Queen resemble those of Anne Carmichael-Smyth, who, though sixty-two in 1854, had retained her regal beauty; moreover, the long wand Blackstick uses as a cane would have reminded Thackeray's daughters of the crutch-like black walking stick their lame grandmother began to use in her late forties.

35. D. W. Winnicott, *Playing and Reality* (London: Tavistock, 1980), 48, 47.

36. Ibid., 47.

to help Giglio—and us—balance wishfulness and experience. A more powerful antagonist than the falsifying Hopstick, Gruffanuff acts as a foil to the childishness Blackstick also combats. Her realism is as unblinking as that of Becky Sharp, and Thackeray's respect for it is evident in his handling of her downfall. To have Barbara Gruffanuff carried away or transformed by the touch of Blackstick's magic wand would have falsified that realism. It is significant, therefore, that this figure should be undone by the same marital situation that Thackeray had come to regard, in his life, as the hard, adamantine fact against which all his wishful evasions and displacements foundered. Indeed, it is not Gruffy's realism but rather her indulgence of Thackeray's own desire to find a new love-object that Blackstick so cruelly shatters by reminding the "widow of the late Jenkins Gruffanuff, Esq." that she is not widowed at all.

Blackstick predominates over the childless Gruffy by repossessing Giglio. In 1846, after he had wrested his daughters away from his "dearest Mammy," Thackeray told Mrs. Carmichael-Smyth that even though he empathized with her "pangs" on losing her grandchildren to him, "it is best that they should be away from you." Possibly referring to his own early separation from her, he allowed that her pain had "brought back all sorts of early times, and induced an irresistible burst of tears on my part," which the onlooking Anny, however, whose "eyes were quite dry," failed to understand. But this separation, Thackeray insisted, was absolutely necessary: "There can't be two first principles in a house. We would be secretly jealous of each other." Although eager to console "my dearest old Mother in her bereavement," Thackeray also remained firm in asserting that her displacement had been imperative: "the children are in their natural place: with their nearest friend working their natural influence."[37] Whether Thackeray still recalled this forceful letter when, eight years later, he first made the fairies Alethea and Lusingha, and then Blackstick and Gruffanuff, fight over the control of a Prince "Lily" and a Princess "White Rose" is doubtful. But the intervening years had only confirmed his intuitive sense of the importance of supervision by "their nearest friend" of children residing in a "natural place."

Ruskin had transported Gluck back to a feminized "natural" space after hardening the Black Brothers into two giant stones. But although Thackeray frees Rosalba's female domain from male usurpation, he tells a story

---

37. Thackeray to Carmichael-Smyth, 4 December 1846, *Letters and Private Papers,* 2:255–56.

that not only relies on different means than Ruskin's but also seems expressly designed to subvert *The King of the Golden River.* Parody was as irresistible to Thackeray as to George MacDonald and Lewis Carroll. Just as MacDonald would convert Ruskin's droll South-West Wind, Esquire, into the mighty and beautiful maternal figure of North Wind, so does Thackeray convert the little King of the Golden River into a Fairy Blackstick. In Ruskin's fairy tale, the King has been frozen into the golden mug by one he acknowledges to be mightier than himself; in Thackeray's revision, it is the mighty Blackstick who both freezes and unfreezes the "figure in yellow" that is so much taller than the "gruffly" speaking dwarf whose "pretty little yellow legs" materialize in Gluck's furnace. Thackeray's creation of female figures who take over the aggressive roles that Ruskin reserves for males suggests his dissatisfaction with the polarized gender stereotypes his predecessor had tried to preserve.

Although, like Ruskin, Thackeray introduces male sadists whom he is eager to overthrow, the brutal behavior of Count Hogginarmo and King Padella is treated with a deliciously comic exaggeration that makes them seem incapable of producing the real pain that Hans and Schwartz inflict on Gluck. Hogginarmo vainly woos Rosalba by promising to deposit at their "bridal table the head of King Padella, the eyes and nose of his son Prince Bulbo, the right hand and ears of the usurping Sovereign of Paflagonia" (*RR,* chap. 13, 88). Padella, for his part, so relishes the prospect of executing Rosalba that he indulges in a catalogue of the most outlandish tortures which his retaliating opponents might inflict on his hostage son. Even the ironically named Valoroso, Padella's timid fellow-usurper, regards the beheading of his nephew Giglio with the same equanimity he had shown on decapitating the eggs arrayed on his breakfast table.

By comically blurring the traditional oppositions between adults and children, as well as between the sexes, Thackeray distances his fairy tale from Ruskin's. Ruskin ended his story by returning to the enveloping topography of the Treasure Valley. Thackeray reserves his last sentence for the Fairy who sails away on her cane and never again returns to Paflagonia or Crim Tartary. The difference is telling. Whereas the solitary Gluck can preside over his Valley because his masculine brothers have been forever removed, Giglio and Rosalba can jointly rule over their united kingdoms because the godmother who removes herself has at long last certified them as grown-ups.

V

The tone and texture of *The Rose and the Ring* playfully defract the fairy-tale mythos that Ruskin had tried to capture in its pristine purity. Rather than follow the mode of a Grimm *märchen*, Thackeray remains as eclectic as possible, gleefully exploiting the frictions that result from a wide and arcane set of references. Although he retains the lineaments of a fairy tale, these vie with allusions to a Victorian present as well as to "adult" classics such as *Hamlet* and *Tom Jones*. We start out in Paflagonia "ten or twenty thousand years ago." But the kingdom first mentioned in Sir Philip Sidney's *Arcadia* (another fable about a conflict between children and parents) is no refined mythical abode such as Ruskin's Treasure Valley. It adjoins Crim Tartary, a region whose name permits Thackeray to introduce a host of comical references to eating, cooking, and vegetables—like spinach, cauliflower, and broccoli—notoriously detested by children. And to add to the incongruity, the hostilities between the two kingdoms carry distinctly contemporary resonances (the Crimean War being still under way in 1854).

Thackeray's anachronisms serve a multiple purpose. They contribute to a contravention of probability that both sharpens and diffuses the sense of what is and is not real. By releasing both child and adult readers from consistency and logic, the protean text produces something akin to that "magic" pleasure which Roland Barthes locates in linguistic variation produced by a "galaxy of signifiers." Thackeray's game is less "grammatical" than those played by MacDonald in "The Light Princess" or by Carroll in the Alice books, where meanings are destabilized through puns and verbal subversions. But by heaping together competing frames of reference, Thackeray "acrobatically" presents "the plural diversity of possibilities" that free his readership from being constrained by any single typology.[38]

Although we are ostensibly taken to an *Ur*-world, "ten or twenty thousand years ago," Thackeray makes his characters smoke cigars, consume breakfast sausages, read newspapers such as the *Bosforo Chronicle,* quote Shakespeare, refer to Victorian circuses and zoos, and derive their elementary knowledge from that educational catch-all, *Mangnall's Questions.* Contradictions abound. The narrator twice informs us that Princess Angelica is, like Giglio and Rosalba (or Thackeray and Ruskin), "an only child"

---

38. Roland Barthes, *S/Z: An Essay,* transl. Richard Miller (New York: Hill and Wang, 1974), 4, 5, 58.

(*RR,* chap. 1, 7; chap. 2, 11). Yet a few pages later we are casually told that the knocker that once had been Jenkins Gruffanuff was muffled "when the princess Angelica's little sister was born". When Gruffanuff disappears, those who recall his beer guzzling, his marital quarreling, and his "debt to the tradesmen," assume that he has emigrated, as many a Victorian derelict might have done, "to Australia or America" (*RR,* chap. 4, 25). But when Giglio later rhapsodizes about his love for Betsinda, he introduces a geographical fine point unobserved before: "What woman in all Europe, Asia, Africa, and America—nay, in Australia, only it is not yet discovered—can be presumed to be thy equal?" (*RR,* chap. 9, 61). Victorian child readers still conditioned to find dry history and geography lessons pressed into books ostensibly designed for their amusement would have reveled at such calculated freedoms.

Thackeray's drawings similarly undermine expectations of consistency and decorum. The costumes worn by the characters may be mid-Victorian (as in the opening illustration of the breakfast scene) or medieval (as in the depiction of "The Terrific Combat Between King Giglio and King Padella"), or, more likely, an amalgam. Thackeray's first two drawings of Prince Bulbo subvert, in their grotesqueness, the idealized Renaissance portrait that the court painter Sir Tomaso Lorenzo, K.P. (Knight of the Pumpkin) had earlier unveiled to impress Angelica. But if Thackeray mocks an actual Sir Thomas Lawrence whose stylized work he deflates as much as the pseudo-Shakesperean rantings of a novelist like G. P. R. James, the two cartoons are themselves inconsistent: entering the story as a ruffled seventeenth-century cavalier, Bulbo reemerges in the coat and tails worn in modern drawing rooms. Elsewhere, garbs are mixed within the same illustration: Napoleonic hussars with bayoneted rifles stand next to plumed warriors accoutered in the heaviest coats of armor; in the scene depicting Bulbo's stay of execution, a helmeted guard with halberd is seen on the Gothic battlements contentedly puffing his pipe. Since the fairy ring and the fairy rose can consistently alter the characters' real appearance, apparel may also take shapes that can arbitrarily be affixed to cardboard dolls. Veracity is exposed as theatricality. Placed in compositions that follow Victorian genre paintings that purportedly represent historical events, the figures reveal their Commedia dell'Arte origins as types still around in Christmas pantomimes.

Such subversive touches convey more than the comic chaos of a *Punch* humorist. They kindle a pleasurable alertness that makes the reader—and especially the juvenile reader who enjoys detecting sham and trickery—

an eager accomplice of a winking author. Thackeray respects the intelligence of his child readers. He encourages them to see beyond a cast of characters whose limited comprehension often makes them downright infantile. Thus, the narrator's carefully seeded clues allow us to detect that Betsinda is none other than the lost Rosalba long before the characters do. When the castaway Betsinda tells the old woodman into whose hut she has stumbled that she "had been left, when quite a little child," with the cloak and shoe she now again is forced to wear, her host is "so astonished, it was quite curious to see how astonished he was" (*RR,* chap. 12, 82). Producing a coin bearing the likeness of the deposed king of Crim Tartary, he vows it to be "exactly like the young woman," even though Thackeray's drawing of the five-shilling piece depicts a hook-nosed creature who bears no resemblance whatsoever to Rosalba. The woodman then produces a "shoe and the piece of velvet he had kept so long" and places them against the little shoe that Betsinda carries around her neck and the torn cloak that barely covers her shoulders. Only after such strained analogical efforts does the "dear old woodman" finally fall down on his knees, rub his "venerable nose three times on the ground," and acknowledge as "my princess" the shabby stranger who is invited to put her "foot on his head" (*RR,* chap. 12, 83). Having long ago pieced together the puzzle this slow-witted man has so laboriously reconstructed, Thackeray's child readers can exult in their superior knowledge and savor the revelation's mock fanfare.

But Thackeray allows them further gratifications by injecting a wider set of analogies than those which the happy woodman will ever manage. For the scene in which a man kneels before a young woman dressed in rags contains icons familiar to any discerning child: the restoration of a second slipper has converted a Cinderella into a princess. At the same time, however, these icons are rent as severely as Rosalba's baby cloak. For the kneeling figure is not a young prince who confers his status on a cinder-scullion, but a decrepit woodman whom his "rightful Queen" immediately recognizes as one of her father's disgraced retainers: "For in her lowly retreat, and under the name of Betsinda, HER MAJESTY ROSALBA, Queen of Crim Tartary, had read of the customs of all foreign courts and nations" (*RR,* chap. 12, 83–84).

The shrewdness and artfulness that we have learned to prize in the author and in ourselves are thus displayed by Rosalba herself. By reading the books that Angelica and Giglio neglected, we now discover, she has been long aware of her ancestry and her empire's history. As fellow-readers whose knowledge of similar plots led us to suspect her identity and to associate a one-shoed waif with the heroine of the fairy tale that Thackeray regarded as "the sweetest of all stories,"[39] we are ready to embrace this smart princess as one of our own. Moreover, we remain aware of what is still missing. The kneeling old woodman to whom Rosalba graciously restores the former title of Lord Spinachi must still be replaced by a kneeling prince who has yet to be elevated from his own Cinderella status. And, to merit such an elevation, that prince must acquire the superior knowledge Rosalba and the reader already possess. Giglio's course of studies lies still before him. As Thackeray knew from observing his daughters, girls mature well before boys.

Thackeray repeatedly encourages his readers to participate in a game of inference and detection. It may not take an extraordinary amount of perspicacity to predict that the fierce lions who gobble up Hogginarmo will nuzzle up like gentle kittens to a Rosalba who, while still a lisping naif, had volunteered, "Little lion was my brudder; great big lioness my mudder; neber heard of any udder" (*RR,* chap. 5, 28). Yet the narrator feigns unbounded surprise: "But O strange event! O extraordinary coincidence, which I am sure none of you could *by any possibility* have divined! When the lions came to Rosalba, instead of devouring her with their great teeth, it was with kisses they gobbled her up! They licked her pretty feet, nuzzled their noses in her lap, they moo'd, they seemed to say, 'Dear, dear sister, don't you recollect your brothers in the forest?'" (*RR,* chap. 15, 112; Thackeray's italics). The mock profession of surprise confirms us as fellow-players and fellow-ironists. We are as close to the implied author as Rosalba is to the fraternizing lions. Precisely because we know that Thackeray knows that his readers have fully "divined" the lure he has cast to test their alertness we trust him as our comrade in a shared world of incongruities.

The bonding of reader and author is also advanced by Thackeray's eclectic use of literary allusion. And that bond again distances us from a Giglio so unself-conscious that he lacks even the most rudimentary tools to read himself as a character in a narrative. Denied the familiarity with Shakespeare available to any middle-class Victorian child raised on Charles and Mary Lamb, the guileless freshman known as "Mr. Giles" must imbibe a prodigious university education before he can spot the literary archetype best suited to his situation. Whereas Thackeray's one year

---

39. Quoted in Ray, *Thackeray: Uses of Adversity,* 206.

at Cambridge was marked by the alienation that led him to parody the prize poem by a fellow student called Alfred Tennyson, young Giles turns into an unwitting parody of the Dutiful Boy of didactic tracts when he amasses the following awards in his first year at college:

The Spelling Prize	The French Prize
The Writing Prize	The Arithmetic Prize
The History Prize	The Latin Prize
The Catechism Prize	The Good Conduct Prize

Having presumably learned the best that has been thought and said, Giglio knows his Shakespeare at last: he recognizes how, "all young and careless of my rights," he enacted the role of "hapless Hamlet, Prince of Denmark" by permitting an uncle to deprive him of his throne (RR, chap. 14, 105). The identification—which fits Thackeray better than Giglio[40]— is belated. As always, Giglio is a step behind. What has taken him fourteen chapters to locate was easily spotted in the first chapter, where his guilty uncle, imitating Claudius, cited "England's dramatist" in a blank verse soliloquy. Giglio's own decision hereafter to speak in blank verse and to mark his exits with rhymed couplets make his conversion to Shakespeare as ridiculous as his frequent pauses "to suck an orange" while haranguing his troops in the manner of Henry V (RR, chap. 14, 108). His tardy discovery of a literary matrix seems even more absurd in the original manuscript, which had featured a fine drawing in which the prince, clad in inky black, stands aloof from a rotund Gertrude-like Queen, an Ophelia-like Angelica, and a Claudius-like Valoroso (fig. 13).

If Thackeray teased Victorian child readers with Giglio's Shakespearian antecedents, he invites adult readers to recognize that this "good-natured" but "thoughtless youth" is also a version of Henry Fielding's Tom Jones. Unable to learn either classics or mathematics from a tutor called "Squaretoso," entangled with a married woman, this version of

40. Unlike Hamlet or Thackeray, Giglio does not have to reckon with the remarriage of an attractive young mother to a masculine figure taking his father's place (and his own). Whatever love Giglio may have felt for his biological mother, long dead and "ordinary looking," was transferred to his "stout" aunt, whose still "pleasing" features suggest that she "must have been lovely in her youth" (RR, chap. 2, 12). This distancing from the central situation in Hamlet, the play that Ernest Jones would use to illustrate Freud's ideas about the Oedipus complex, has the effect of also distancing Giglio from a Thackeray who often was made uneasy by the self-reflections he habitually saw in texts by other writers.

1 3 W. M. Thackeray, Giglio as Prince Hamlet
(The Pierpont Morgan Library, New York; MA 926)

Squire Allworthy's imprudent nephew will require the combined efforts of a wiser Sophia-figure and a god-like novelist called Blackstick to set him on the road to happiness. Whereas Gruffanuff covets this young man as a sexual toy, Rosalba has loved ever since she first saw him—as Sophia did Tom—in a garden, "when she was quite a little child" (*RR,* chap. 9, 65). The eighteenth-century novelist, from whose sexual frankness Charlotte Brontë, George Henry Lewes, and Thackeray himself professed to shy away,[41] can, paradoxically, be enlisted with impunity in a book for children whom Victorian culture perceived as incorruptibly innocent.

The frictions and impurities injected throughout *The Rose and the Ring* have, just as paradoxically, a unifying effect. By calling attention to the arbitrariness of our tendency to separate adult fictions from those that ap-

41. For two approaches to Thackeray's relation to Fielding, see Ralph Wilson Rader, "Thackeray's Injustice to Fielding," *JEGP* 56, no. 2 (April 1957): 203–212, and E. D. H. Johnson, "*Vanity Fair* and *Amelia,*" *Modern Philology* 59, no. 2 (November 1961): 100–113.

peal to the child, Thackeray creates a common ground. Both "great and small children" should divest themselves of the falsifying illusions of omnipotence promoted by an adherence to any single system of meaning. Irony alone can check such delusions and define the limits of true power. Whereas Ruskin nourished a secret fantasy of abolishing all adult power, Thackeray prefers to use his own power in an effort to expose its shortcomings. The hunger for unlimited might that grips children as much as grown-ups is corrected by a Fairy Blackstick who, like that other all-powerful artificer, Prospero, relinquishes her powers. For, like Thackeray himself, she distrusts her capacity to alter human nature through the uses of enchantment.

In a review written shortly after the publication of *The Rose and the Ring,* Margaret Oliphant welcomed the story for its avowed difference from *Vanity Fair,* "that clever, unbelieving, disagreeable book."[42] The fairy tale, she contended, was free from "Mr. Thackeray's wicked and witty comments upon the world." She liked the story's "obeisance to True Love," yet hailed it for its failure to push a "moral," as some "other Christmas carols of our acquaintance," written "in the vein of teaching," had been prone to do.[43] Oliphant's remarks seem suspect. Despite its antididactic vein, the narrative of *The Rose and the Ring* is didactic in promoting, not just "True Love," but also the liberating pleasures of self-awareness. Yet the self-awareness Thackeray associates with growth is also a liability. Despite Oliphant's assertion, the weary "Vanitas, Vanitatum," which marks the end of the "disagreeable" *Vanity Fair,* always lurks as a subtext in this agreeable fairy tale.

For Thackeray extends his skepticism to the very beliefs he promotes. Giglio's mastery of textbooks may be a more honorable outlet for his energies than his physical assault on sexual rivals. But the callow young man who can only succeed as Blackstick's pawn is never called upon to prove that his maturation is definitive. With Blackstick removed, an unassisted Rosalba may find it difficult to extricate her husband from new lapses. Fielding's Tom Jones was a potential Captain Booth, the husband of a suffering Amelia; Giglio remains a potential George Osborne. Adult readers thus cannot avoid inferences which child readers may gloss over. The

---

42. Margaret Oliphant, "Mr. Thackeray and His Novels," in *Thackeray: The Critical Heritage,* ed. Geoffrey Tillotson and Donald Hawes (London: Routledge, 1968), 204; first published in *Blackwood's Magazine* 58 (January 1855): 86–89.

43. Oliphant, "Mr. Thackeray," 203.

alliance between innocence and experience totters whenever Thackeray admits the instability of the process of growth that his story endorses.

"True Love" is not immune to the sentimental falsifications of fairy props. Thackeray reverts to the Victorian stereotype of an unquestioning angelic helpmeet when he deprives Rosalba of the common sense she had shown as the independent Betsinda. The young woman who shrewdly assessed Giglio's weaknesses now regards him a paragon of virtue. After recovering from the swoon induced by Giglio's expected marriage to Gruffanuff, Rosalba utters a renunciation speech so unnaturally "noble" that Thackeray cannot refrain from treating it with tongue in cheek:

"I cannot marry him, but I shall love him always; . . . I will go and be present at his marriage with the Countess, and sign the book. . . . I will see, when I get home, whether I cannot make the new Queen some handsome presents. The Crim Tartary crown diamonds are uncommonly fine, and I shall never have any use for them. I will live and die unmarried like Queen Elizabeth, and, of course I shall leave my crown to Giglio when I quit this world." (*RR,* chap. 19, 139)

Such devotion seems anomalous in a world in which the bourgeois Valoroso, who extols marital bliss, abruptly vows to slaughter his harmless wife. Even the loyalty of Captain Hedzoff appears questionable, as he mindlessly repeats the selfsame refrain, "a soldier, sir, knows but his duty," to competing masters. Indeed, the figures least blinded by illusion are the story's villains: Hogginarmo and Padella never mask their crass ambition. And Gruffy's frank lust for Giglio makes her seem far more honest than "True Love's" votaries.

Thackeray's revalidation of the fairy tale as an amalgam combining irony and wishfulness appealed to later women writers, notably to the older daughter he first amused with *The Rose and the Ring.* Anne Thackeray Ritchie wittily transported figures such as Sleeping Beauty, Cinderella, and Blue Beard into a Victorian present. And she eventually adopted the persona of "Blackstick herself," a truth-teller of the "school of Miss Edgeworth and Mrs. Barbauld," to link the essays in her *Blackstick Papers* (1908).[44] Her occasional references to her father in essays on Felicia Hemans, George Sand, and Elizabeth Gaskell suggest her desire to stress his compatibility with a realistic female tradition that spanned from Edgeworth and Austen to her own "niece," Virginia Woolf, and also included, as we shall see, Juliana Horatia Ewing.

44. Anne Thackeray Ritchie, *Blackstick Papers* (London: Smith, Elder, 1909), 47, 2.

Women who wrote for children welcomed Thackeray's comic accommodations of the real. Not only Ewing, but also Frances Hodgson Burnett and Edith Nesbit (the last, like Thackeray, an inveterate parodist) found themselves far less resistant, ideologically and formally, to *The Rose and the Ring* than to the fairy tales of Ruskin, MacDonald, and Carroll. It is true that MacDonald and Carroll also shared Thackeray's distrust of a culture that sundered the child from the grown-up and the masculine from the feminine. And both men learned much from his ironic and parodic subversions of literary precedents. But they rejected his guarded view of magical "fable-lands" in their own ventures into childlands designed to reshape the relation between genders and generations.

FOUR

Mixing Levity and the Grave: MacDonald's "The Light Princess"

I

In "De Juventute," an essay in a series called "Roundabout Papers" that he ran after assuming the editorship of the *Cornhill Magazine,* Thackeray reflects on the lasting impressions made by texts read in childhood. Acknowledging that he might like to write "a story which boys would relish for the next few dozen of centuries," he reminds himself that boys have always enjoyed texts written for girls. Does a new generation, he wonders, have "anything so good and kindly as dear Miss Edgeworth's *Frank?*" That work may have belonged "to a fellow's sisters," but it remained irresistible. Even the grown-up man must admit that he would be as affected as ever: "I think there were one or two passages that would try my eyes now, were I to meet with the little book." Thackeray's nostalgia has a serious cultural edge. Where are the writers for new generations of imaginative children? Thackeray wants future authors to supply the romance he had found in the books of his own childhood: "I meet people who don't care for Sir Walter Scott, or the *Arabian Nights;* I am sorry for them, unless they in their time have found *their* romancer—their charming Scheherazade."[1]

Thackeray, who died in 1863, did not live long enough to find out that a writer whose adult romance he had recently accepted for the *Cornhill* would soon become a major author of fiction for children. George MacDonald had been recommended to him by Richard Monckton Milnes as "the author of *Phantastes* and *Within and Without,*" a man of "very fine fancy, high education, and good taste," bound to come up with some good "poetical prose."[2] It is doubtful whether Thackeray bothered to look up the two works mentioned by Milnes. Like MacDonald's Scottish ghost story "The Portent," which Thackeray printed in the May, June, and July issues of the 1860 *Cornhill,* they belong to a literary tradition at odds with

1. William Makepeace Thackeray, "De Juventute," *The Cornhill Magazine* 2 (October 1860): 509.

2. Richard Monckton Milnes to Thackeray, 27 December 1859, *The Letters and Private Papers of William Makepeace Thackeray,* ed. Gordon N. Ray (London: Oxford University Press, 1946), 4:170.

his own. *Within and Without* (1855), the Shelleian verse drama that gained its impoverished and tubercular author the respect of literati like Milnes, and *Phantastes: A Faerie Romance for Men and Women* (1858), the disjointed prose narrative which followed Novalis's prescriptions for the shaping of *einem echten Mährchen* [*sic*] (*WFI*, 5:2), insist on a hazy dreamworld's superiority to everyday reality. Although both works feature male seekers as much in need of a female complement as Thackeray's own heroes, their quest for a mystical "Fairy land" is wholly alien to his mode.

As writers for adults, MacDonald and Thackeray had little in common, even though a group portrait of nine male Victorian authors positions the bearded young Scotsman right behind the author of *Vanity Fair*.[3] As writers for children, however, they shared important affinities. The comical first half of "The Light Princess," written in 1862 but not published until 1864, resembles *The Rose and the Ring* in its playful irreverence towards the traditional form of the fairy tale. Although that irreverence, in MacDonald's case, may owe more to the Romantic irony of German writers such as E. T. A. Hoffmann, it results in generic and tonal mixtures that recall Thackeray's own. MacDonald also tested Thackeray's notion that a children's book should equally appeal to readers of "large and small growth" when he read "The Light Princess" to his own children as well as to Bedford College undergraduates who had expected to hear him lecture on *The Faerie Queene*.

"The Light Princess" offers a fantasy of parental restitution, since, like Thackeray, MacDonald uses the fairy-tale mode to seek compensation for early losses. Still, his own yearning for a complementary femininity stems from a sense of maternal deprivation that is more intensely traumatic than Thackeray's had been. Thackeray relied on Fairy Blackstick to prepare her adolescent godchildren for the realities of adult life. MacDonald, however, prefers to locate the feminine in an anterior state of being that also brings out his fascination with death and transcendence.

This fascination, first played out in *Within and Without, Phantastes,* and

---

3. The "photograph" (more likely a composite paste-up) entitled "Group of Contemporary Writers" can be found facing page 353 in Greville MacDonald's *George MacDonald and His Wife* (London: George Allen & Unwin, 1924). Robert Lee Wolff, who also reproduces the illustration (facing page 6 of *The Golden Key: A Study of the Fiction of George MacDonald* [New Haven: Yale University Press, 1961]), claims that it "surely" antedates 1859, which seems rather doubtful. The other three writers standing behind their sitting elders are J. A. Froude, Wilkie Collins, and Anthony Trollope.

"The Portent," eventually found its way into "The Light Princess" and *At the Back of the North Wind,* the longer children's romance I discuss in chapter 7. In *Within and Without,* Julian, a nobleman who wants to become reunited with Lilia, the wife he had doubted, dies at the end of the fourth act (or part four, as MacDonald prefers to call the divisions of his verse drama), yet reappears in the next act, set in "a world not realized." There, Julian is taken by his and Lilia's child, the little girl Lily, into a fog, where they come upon Lilia and all three "are clasped in an infinite embrace." The drama ends with directions that call attention to its unstageable climax: "[*The moon and stars and the blue night close around them; and the Poet awakes from his dream*]" (*WFI,* 2:261, 271, 272).

In *Phantastes,* MacDonald combines the roles of Julian and Poet, quester and dreamer, through the figure of Anodos. Like Julian, Anodos dies in the next-to-last installment of his wanderings; like the Poet, he wakes up "once again conscious of a more limited, even a bodily and earthly life" (*WFI,* 6:209). Anodos asks whether he can "translate" his visionary adventure "into common life." Is he expected to "live it all over again, and learn it all over again," in a "world of men, whose experience yet runs parallel to that of Fairy land?" (*WFI,* 6:213–14). The question is of obvious importance to MacDonald's artistic self-definition. The dominant "forms" of Victorian fiction are better suited to the depiction of a "world of men" than to the Romantic dream-scapes Anodos traverses in his search for an elusive female essence.[4]

The insufficiency of patriarchal constructions of reality are impressed on Anodos at the start of his travels. Having recently attained manhood and become invested with "legal rights," the youth takes possession of keys that might unlock his patrimonial inheritance: "Perhaps I was to learn how my father, whose personal history was unknown to me, had woven his web of story; how he had found the world, and how the world had left him. Perhaps I was to find only the records of lands and money, how gotten and how secured; coming down from strange men" (*WFI,* 5:5). But when he unlocks his father's desk, Anodos comes upon, not the records he expected to find, but an unsuspected female presence. Hovering over withered rose leaves and a faded packet of papers is a "tiny woman-form" who immediately rebukes Anodos for doubting her existence.

---

4. The discontinuities of Anodos's narrative owe much to Shelley's *Alastor* (cited in an epigraph for the opening chapter) and to the "*Erzählung ohne Zusammenhang*" advocated by Novalis, Ludwig Tieck, and E. T. A. Hoffmann.

When this tiny lady promises to grant him a wish, Anodos becomes even more skeptical, for he associates power with both size and masculinity:

"How can such a very little creature as you, grant or refuse anything?"

"Is that all the philosophy you have gained in twenty-one years?" said she. "Form is much, but size is nothing. It is a mere matter of relation. I suppose your six-foot lordship does not feel altogether insignificant, though to others you do look small beside your old Uncle Ralph, who rises above you a great half-foot at least. But size is of so little consequence to me, that I may as well accommodate myself to your foolish prejudices."

So saying, she leaped from the desk upon the floor; where she stood a tall, gracious lady, with pale face and large blue eyes. Her dark hair flowed behind, wavy but uncurled, down to her waist, and against it her form stood clear in its robe of white.

"Now," said she, "you will believe me." (*WFI*, 5:9–10)

By altering her form, however, this female figure also alters Anodos's perception of her. His earlier condescension, so like an adult's patronizing stance towards a tiny child, now turns into eroticized longing. When, overcome by her "irresistible" beauty, he steps forward to embrace her, she checks his ardor by apprising him of their relation. Her disclosure completes the reversal of Anodos's expectations. Instead of the male identity he had hoped to strengthen, he has uncovered a suppressed female lineage. For the figure before him is a foremother who treats him as an uncomprehending child:

"Foolish boy, if you could touch me, I should hurt you. Besides, I was two hundred and thirty-seven years old last Midsummer-eve; and a man must not fall in love with his grandmother, you know."

"But you are not my grandmother," said I.

"How do you know that?" she retorted. "I dare say you know something of your greatgrandfathers a good deal further back than that; but you know very little about your greatgrandmothers on either side. Now, to the point. Your little sister was reading a fairy-tale to you last night."

"She was."

"When she had finished, she said, as she closed the book, 'Is there a fairy-country, brother?' You replied with a sigh, 'I suppose there is, if one could find the way into it.'"

"I did; but I meant something quite different from what you seem to think."

"Never mind what I seem to think. You shall find the way into Fairy land tomorrow. Now look into my eyes." (*WFI*, 5:10–11)

I have reproduced this exchange so fully because of its relevance to MacDonald's later writings for children, notably *At the Back of the North Wind*, as well as to Jean Ingelow's *Mopsa the Fairy*, a work that culminates with a similar generational shift by making a patronizing male become subservient to the female fairy who outgrows him. Although the passage introduces a "Faerie Romance" designed for "Men and Women," MacDonald already stresses the importance of what he would soon call the "childlike." Like Diamond, Mossy, and Curdie, the trusting boy-questers of the later tales, Anodos can venture into Fairy land only by submitting to the powers of a maternal mentoria. Even the little sister who read Anodos a fairy tale proves to be a better guide than the father—or great grandfathers—whose "web of story" Anodos had expected to disentangle. Like the girl Lily, who reunited Julian with his wife in *Within and Without,* she acts as a mediatrix who can connect Anodos to unknown matriarchs. Just as Thackeray welcomed the agency of his daughters in his own quest for the feminine, so can Anodos's sister feel more readily than he the ancestral "fairy blood" that courses through both their veins.

II

MacDonald's readiness to consider the fairy tale as a form of female transmission anticipates Juliana Horatia Ewing's recovery of matriarchal folk tales, discussed in the last chapter of this study. But unlike Ewing, and more like Ruskin before him and Lewis Carroll after him, MacDonald is governed by his desire to recover a femininity he associates with a primal symbiosis. When asked to look into the eyes of his mysterious fairy "grandmother," Anodos finds himself overcome by "an unknown longing" for a suppressed and half-forgotten relationship: "I remembered somehow that my mother died when I was a baby." He recounts how, as he looked "deeper and deeper" into the fairy's mesmeric eyes, "they spread around me like seas, and I sank in their waters." When a "sea, still as death" turns out to be "a low fog burnished by the moon," a "low, sweet voice" informs Anodos that he has arrived in "Fairy land" (*WFI*, 5:11–12). That a dead mother should be recalled as soon as the young man looks into the stranger's eyes, that the "longing" he feels should find spatial correlatives his flowing imagination liquefies, that his wish for an oceanic fusion should recapitulate his little sister's wish for a fairyland, are associations that seem to originate in George MacDonald's obsessive reenactment of desires he located in his own early childhood. Although his mother, the well-educated and beautiful Helen MacKay, died of tuberculosis when he was eight rather than a mere "baby," he nonetheless placed an enormous importance on the separation that had occurred when, as an infant, he was weaned from her breast and turned over to a wet-nurse.

In his 1924 *George MacDonald and His Wife,* Greville MacDonald describes how he replayed the role of Anodos when he lifted a letter, then nearly "a century old," out of "my father's cabinet with its secret nest of drawers" in order to recover the voice of Helen MacKay MacDonald and to document "her son's adoration of her memory." To Greville, the letter's content suggests that the "infant George" already displayed "some real heroism in the facing of adversity." But its importance rather lies in what it tells us about MacDonald's later constructions of reality, when he secreted the letter away in his desk, "along with a golden brown lock of that mother's hair and her wedding gift to her husband, a little silver-set seal with his name *George* engraved on its red stone." In her letter, Helen MacDonald responds to the mother-in-law who had sternly insisted that she wean "our little Boy." Protesting that she was not even allowed "three months" to fulfill her desire to nurse her child, the young mother nonetheless acquiesces to advice that may have been well intentioned. (After two further pregnancies, the weakened mother was no longer able to resist the tuberculosis that claimed so many MacDonalds and periodically threatened her long-lived son.)[5]

George MacDonald seems to have cherished his mother's letter as proof of her special relation to him. Professing herself to have been "very unwilling" to deny the child who, she notes, "has not got anything from me since," Helen MacDonald appears acutely aware of his need for the absent breast. She regards their desire for each other, as well as their stoicism, as a bond. Absence becomes a form of communion, blending mother and child: "But I cannot help my heart being very much grieved for him yet, for he has not forgot it: poor little fellow he is behaving wonderfully as yet. He cryed desperate a while the first night, but he has cryed little since and I hope the worst is over now."[6] Rather than a testimonial of infant "heroism," as Greville MacDonald would have it, the letter documents a separation that MacDonald's fictions enact in order to annul. Robert Lee Wolff thus seems correct in regarding the episode as a major "clue,"

5. MacDonald, *George MacDonald and His Wife,* 33, 31.
6. Ibid., 32.

though he is perhaps too trusting about Greville's narrative of the "secret drawer."[7]

By the time MacDonald contributed "The Portent" to Thackeray's 1860 *Cornhill Magazine,* he had finished a new volume of verses, written while he was recovering from tuberculosis in Algiers. The main poem, a blank verse narrative entitled "A Hidden Life," dwells on the visionary martyrdom of still another seeker of "essential womanhood," a tubercular young farmer who composes his epitaph while dying "in his father's room" and who, having worshipped the unattainable in life, is "content to know the vision / Had lifted me above myself who saw." (The name "Anodos"—from the Greek words for *up* and *road*—suggests the same upward motion.) In a reversal, the dying young man leaves his final thoughts in a "letter in his desk / With seal and superscription." When read, near his grave, by the lady he loved, their delayed communion is again supervised by a child, a "little boy" now, who, significantly enough, has watched "a cow near by / Gather her milk" from the clover fields (*WFI,* 1:337, 335, 342, 344).

"The Portent," too, at least in its *Cornhill* version (for MacDonald later altered the story), dwells on the severance of a mysteriously connected man and woman. Subject to identical dreams, Duncan Campbell, the protagonist, and Lady Alice, discover that they "were born the same hour, and our mothers died the same day."[8] Wrenched away from Lady Alice by her guardians, then maimed at Waterloo, Campbell thinks he sees Alice's face behind a barred window of a Brussels building that turns out to be "an asylum for the insane" (a touch that Thackeray probably appreciated even less than the dedication of *Jane Eyre*). Yet when his elusive lover is not to be found among the inmates, nor in the "haunted room" in which he and she first experienced identical visions, Campbell becomes a Heathcliff vainly pursuing a female specter. He finds some comfort in his mental act of interiorization, the "single intensity of will, that she should come to me", but he desists when he considers the "torture" his calls might inflict

---

7. Wolff, *Golden Key,* 13. There were good reasons for Greville to imitate *Phantastes.* As the full title of his biography indicates, he, too, stresses the filial relation to a special mother, the gifted Louisa Powell MacDonald, whose "maternal sense in loverhood" and beauty "in old age" he puts forward with some of the "adoration" he attributes to his father (MacDonald, *George MacDonald and His Wife,* 125, 126).

8. George MacDonald, "The Portent: III.—The Omen Fulfilled," *Cornhill Magazine* 2 (July 1860): 82.

on this alter-ego.[9] Has Lady Alice merely been an embodiment of desire, the adult equivalent of her namesake, Lewis Carroll's dream-child? By earlier teaching Alice how to translate her intuitions into language, Campbell traduced her into letters. The story's final paragraph hints that, like the "tiny woman-form" who rose above the faded letters in the secret compartment of a desk, Alice remains an emblem for male longing:[10]

They say that Time and Space exist not, save in our thoughts. If so, then which has been, is, and the past can never cease. She is mine, and I shall find her—what matters it where, or when, or how? Till then, my soul is but a moon-lighted chamber of ghosts; and I sit within, the dreariest of them all. When she enters, it will be a home of love; and I wait—I wait.[11]

Thackeray's editorial arrangements for "The Portent" suggest that he had grasped the import of MacDonald's novella. He positioned it between poems by women authors by printing Emily Brontë's posthumous "The Outcast Mother" before its first installment and Elizabeth Barrett Browning's "A Musical Instrument" right after its ending.[12] He also seemed to regard MacDonald's tale important enough to merit one of the two full-page illustrations inserted into the May issue. Entitled "Legend of the Portent," the drawing (facing page 617) depicts the huge figure of a woman who turns away from minuscule males fighting at the edge of a precipice in a distant and darker background (fig. 14). The legendary figure, a foremother familiar to Campbell and Alice from narratives relayed by their Gaelic-speaking nurses, thus assumes an even greater prominence than in the story itself.

Thackeray may have wanted to pair this illustration with "Bedford to the Rescue," the other tipped-in, full-page drawing (facing page 583),

9. Ibid., 83.

10. As such, she resembles the goddess Eos in Tennyson's "Tithonus," the poem that first appeared in the February 1860 issue of the *Cornhill*. The links between "The Portent" and Tennyson's *Maud* (1855) are also inescapable.

11. MacDonald, "The Portent," 83.

12. The May 1860 issue also featured Anne Thackeray's first published essay, "Little Scholars." In her account of London schools she had visited, she singles out a Jewish institution for teaching its students how to become "independent and self-respecting in their dealings with the grown-up people who came to look at them." The concluding thanks to a "fatherly Providence" for such lessons in self-reliance must have been appreciated by the father-editor who had tried to instill in Anne the independence of mind both she and he valued (*Cornhill Magazine* 1 (May 1860): 556).

which accompanied the monthly installment of his own realistic *Lovel the Widower*. There, the male combatants are now foregrounded, while a young woman and an inactive male stand behind them (fig. 15). Although the expression of the two female figures is quite similar, the composition of each drawing makes them seem antithetical. Bessy, the drab figure in "Bedford to the Rescue," is subsidiary to the men engaged in a comic free-for-all. The representation of the noble maiden in "The Legend of the Portent," on the other hand, befits her idealized and legendary status. Her flowing hair and huge size anticipate Arthur Hughes's even more stylized representations of North Wind in *At the Back of the North Wind*.

Having learned that the work of graphic artists might help market his "poetical prose," MacDonald soon enlisted Arthur Hughes to illustrate his first story for children. On July 9, 1862, Lewis Carroll recorded in his diary that he had run into Mr. MacDonald "on his way to a publisher with the MS. of his fairy tale 'The Light Princess' in which he showed me some exquisite drawings by Hughes."[13] Although Carroll apparently was already familiar with the text, his interest in the illustrations suggests that they were new to him.[14] But even Arthur Hughes's truly "exquisite" drawings failed to attract the unnamed publisher (perhaps Smith and Elder, who had printed *The King of the Golden River, The Rose and the Ring,* and the *Cornhill Magazine*). When "The Light Princess" finally did appear in 1864, it was as one of a dozen interpolations in MacDonald's adult novel *Adela Cathcart*.

Indeed, not until another male "Scheherazade" had created a huge market with the success of *Alice in Wonderland* (1865) did George MacDonald finally become the "romancer" for children for whom Thackeray had called in "De Juventute." Since the MacDonald family had played such an important role in the evolution of Carroll's book,[15] it seemed fitting that the popularity of *Alice* should now facilitate MacDonald's new

13. *The Diaries of Lewis Carroll,* ed. Roger Lancelyn Green (Westport, Connecticut: Greenwood Press, 1971), 1:184.

14. According to Roger Lancelyn Green, two volumes of Carroll's diaries covering a four-year period from 18 April 1858 to 8 May 1862, still available to his nephew Stuart Dodgson Collingwood for the 1898 biography, were lost (ibid., 1:143). It was during this time that Carroll's interactions with the MacDonald family appear to have been at their most intense.

15. For more on that role, see pp. 151–56, below.

14 "Legend of the Portent" *(Cornhill Magazine)*

career. In 1867, MacDonald lifted "The Light Princess" and two other interpolated fairy tales, "The Giant's Heart" and "The Shadows," out of *Adela Cathcart,* added two more, and restored Hughes's fine woodcuts in his first full book for children, *Dealings with the Fairies.* In a brief preface, signed "YOUR PAPA," he addressed his own children, the older of whom

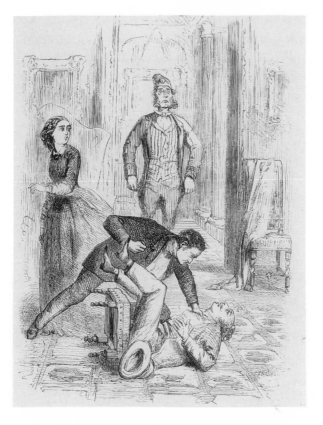

15 "Bedford to the Rescue" *(Cornhill Magazine)*

had already been part of Lewis Carroll's trial audience for "Alice's Adventure Under Ground":

You know I do not tell you stories as some papas do. Therefore, I give you a book of stories. You have read them all before, except the last. But you have not seen Mr. Hughes's drawings before.

If plenty of children like this volume, you shall have another soon.[16]

After the success of *Dealings with the Fairies,* MacDonald was soon publishing *At the Back of the North Wind,* even more lavishly illustrated by Hughes's wood-cuts, in serial installments from 1868 to 1869 in a newly

16. George MacDonald, *Dealings with the Fairies* (London: Alexander Strahan & Company: 1868), iii. The "last" story to which MacDonald refers was "The Golden Key." The four others were "The Light Princess," "The Giant's Heart," "The Shadows," and "Cross Purposes."

founded magazine for juvenile readers, *Good Words for the Young*. By 1869 he had become that periodical's editor and was busily recruiting contributors, just as Thackeray had done for the *Cornhill* a decade before. The journal's cover, with its Wordsworthian epigraph, "The Child is Father of the Man," soon boasted the names of Hans Christian Andersen, Charles Kingsley, Jean Ingelow, William Gilbert (before his partnership with Arthur Sullivan), and, of course, MacDonald himself. In "The Child and the Man," an elaboration on the poem from which he had drawn the magazine's motto, MacDonald forcefully laid down his editorial aims:

This Magazine, then, devotes itself to the literature of natural piety between child and man and man and child. It is a periodical for the young—and even the very young will be cared for by us—but in such sort for the young that full-chorded harmony we aim at will not be struck out unless the mature can also take their places at our Round Table of GOOD THINGS. We shall speak not merely to the Child in the presence of the Man, but to the Child who is father of the Man, believing that there is one music which will thrill both together; one "rainbow in the sky," at which their hearts will "leap up" together.[17]

Although MacDonald eventually relinquished his editorship of the magazine, he continued to contribute shorter and longer pieces (such as the serialized novels *Ranald Bannerman's Boyhood* and *Guttapercha Willie,* not among his most notable efforts). The appearance in book form of *At the Back of the North Wind* (in 1871, the year of Carroll's *Through the Looking Glass*), *The Princess and the Goblin* (1872), and *The Wise Woman* (1875, later renamed *The Lost Princess*), consolidated his stature as a major children's author.

That the Victorian public had taken notice of the shift in MacDonald's career seems borne out by an 1872 cartoon for *Once a Week*. The caricature by Frederick Waddy shows a gigantic but benevolent-looking writer in the act of proffering *Good Words For the Young* to a pair of children (fig. 16). MacDonald's latest adult novel, *The Vicar's Daughter* (1872), lies neglected on the floor. It is difficult to ascertain whether, in rendering MacDonald's still divided output, the cartoonist means to be critical or complimentary or merely to make a neutral comment on existing tastes. In other

---

17. George MacDonald, "The Child and the Man," *Good Things for the Young of All Ages* (January 1873): 2. The magazine had undergone one of several name changes, with "*Things*" replacing "*Words*" perhaps because it now featured, in addition to poetry and prose, more puzzles, riddles, and visual materials than before.

16 Frederick Waddy, "MacDonald as Giant 'Goody-Goody'"

words, is the Scotsman in his tartan suit being depicted as a canny exploiter of a burgeoning new literary market or as a kindly moralist who prefers to dole out his "goody-goody" goods to children rather than to entertain adult readers with novels of sensation?

Regardless of its intended emphasis, the cartoon associates MacDonald's career with the success of Lewis Carroll. As Glenn E. Sadler has noted, the association is quite overtly made.[18] It is not just that the giant looms above the children much in the way that Alice towered over the childish

18. George MacDonald, *The Gifts of the Christ Child: Fairy Tales and Stories for the Childlike,* ed. Glenn Edward Sadler (Grand Rapids, Michigan: Eerdmans, 1973), 1:8.

Wonderland creatures; the very girl to whom this giant proffers his magazine decidedly resembles Tenniel's Alice. Still, as the cartoonist may well have remembered, there had also been an abundance of larger-than-life female forms in MacDonald's own fictions: the "tall, gracious lady" who directs Anodos back to Fairy land; the "mighty woman, with a face / As calm as life," who waits for the dying protagonist in "A Hidden Life"; the huge maiden in the illustration for "The Portent"; the sky-bound North Wind who is so enormous that Diamond can nestle in her hair; the ogress who warns Tricksee-Wee in "The Giant's Heart" that her husband is "fond of little children, particularly little girls."[19] Had Frederick Waddy endowed his gigantic editor-author with a kilt rather than a pair of tartan trousers, the cartoon might have more explicitly captured MacDonald's fondness for soaring female projections. That fondness is just as evident in "The Light Princess." And yet, as we shall soon see, MacDonald's first fairy tale for children also acts as an antidote for his earlier fantasies. By grounding a magically levitating female child, MacDonald managed to check his own desire for disengagement from a mundane reality.

The claims of reality were undoubtedly accentuated for MacDonald by his increasing contact with growing children. By the time he addressed his offspring in the preamble to *Dealings with the Fairies,* the eleventh and last of George and Louisa MacDonald's children had arrived. Of the seven children born before MacDonald wrote "The Light Princess," five had been girls. Among these, his favorite by far remained his firstborn, Lilia (or Lily) Scott MacDonald (1852–1891). Greville MacDonald refers to his sister's "genius," an estimate confirmed by Lewis Carroll.[20] To MacDonald himself, however, this "little mother" to the younger children seemed to betoken a femininity regained, a precious compensation for what he had lost.[21] Her value to him thus resembled, perhaps even exceeded, the

19. "The Giant's Heart," ibid., 2:55. C. Robertson had portrayed the ogress as a Brobdingnagian when the story appeared in *The Illustrated London News* (reproduced on p. 54).

20. MacDonald, *George MacDonald and His Wife,* 327. Carroll likened Lilia's acting talents to those of Ellen Terry; after attending theatricals put on by the family, he noted that "Lily appeared in all the pieces, and was the only one who could act" (26 July 1879, *Diaries of Lewis Carroll,* 2:382). For a discussion of Carroll's photograph of MacDonald and his daughter, and of his letter of condolence after Lilia's death, see pages 159–60 and 154–58, below.

21. See George MacDonald's remarks about Lily in his 1862 letters to his wife (MacDonald, *George MacDonald and His Wife,* 326, 327).

investment that Thackeray had placed in his own firstborn daughter. He called her his "White Lily" and bestowed her alternate names on both the mother and the daughter of Julian in *Within and Without*.[22] In a letter MacDonald wrote to Lilia on the occasion of her twenty-ninth birthday, the last one she would experience, he deplores the "cactus-hedge" that had often prevented him from expressing the full depth of his attachment: "I can only tell you I love you with full heart fervently, and love you far more because you are God's child than because you are mine.—I don't thank you for coming to us, for you could not help it, but the whole universe is 'tented' with love, and you hold one of the corners of the great love-canopy for your mother and me."[23]

Lilia's death, eleven years before that of his wife and fourteen years before his own, shattered MacDonald. He had already completed his last major work, *Lilith* (where Lilith's daughter Lona, rather than Lilith herself, becomes another fictional conflation of Helen MacDonald and Lilia). He kept rewriting the book until its publication in 1895. He would write little thereafter. Presumably to comfort the widower who by then had stopped speaking to all surviving members of his family, another daughter, Winifred Troup, decided to publish an anthology she entitled *Babies' Classics Chosen by Lilia Scott MacDonald*. It appeared in 1904, MacDonald's last year alive. Explaining that the collection of poems, newly illustrated by a superannuated Arthur Hughes, had been started long ago by "my sister whose name is on the title-page," Winifred modestly downplayed her own editorial efforts.[24] And, by including four of George MacDonald's own poems among the selection, she managed to couple a father and his favor-

22. At the close of Tennyson's *The Princess* (1847), "little Lilia, rising quietly," reinstates gender-divisions briefly blurred by androgynous and "gynandrous" men and women. Lilia's birth may have facilitated MacDonald's grudging acceptance of genderbinaries. One would have expected him to name his best beloved after his dead mother.

23. MacDonald, *George MacDonald and His Wife*, 517. Lilia was in America, where she was helping a widowed brother nurse his young; she died later that year (Greville's account of his father's grief after Lilia's burial is painful to read). When MacDonald characterizes Lilia as an elect, he uses terms he had applied to "God's baby," Diamond, in *At the Back of the North Wind*.

24. Winifred Troup, *Babies' Classics Chosen by Lilia Scott MacDonald* (London: Longmans, Green and Company, 1904), vii. Represented by "A Baby Sermon," "Up and Down," "Baby," and "Lesson for a Child," MacDonald was the only living poet among selections that ran from the Renaissance to mid-Victorians such as Tennyson and Browning.

ite child as collaborators. Her gesture seems a fitting closure for the career of a writer who had all along counted on the collaboration of female ghosts.

III

George MacDonald's attachment to living children acted as a much-needed counterweight to his desire for union with a maternal essence beyond "Time and Space." The ballast is apparent in "The Light Princess," written when Lilia was ten years old. Although MacDonald's first children's fairy tale retains a good many of the aspects found in his fantasies for adults, it also significantly reverses the numinous quests of Julian, Anodos, or Campbell. The prince who becomes infatuated with the Light Princess may still display the obsessiveness that characterized these earlier seekers; but by grounding his beloved in the actuality she has tried to evade, he insists on the primacy of everyday life. What is more, the princess herself acts as a foil for the evanescent females of the earlier fictions. Comically treated, this giddy child is encouraged to grow up rather than to soar away or dissolve into a different dimension. Whereas a this-worldly union proved impossible in MacDonald's adult fantasies, "The Light Princess" follows the format of traditional fairy tales (or of *Kunstmärchen* such as *The Rose and the Ring*) by closing with the marriage of a matured royal couple.

It seems rather significant that the very first character we encounter in "The Light Princess" should act as a parodic counterpart to the males who, in MacDonald's adult romances, yearned for a female self-extension. The king who addresses his queen in the dialogue that opens the mini-chapter called "What! No Children?" proves to be even more ridiculous than Thackeray's King Valoroso. Valoroso became inflamed by the beauty of his daughter's chambermaid, in a burlesque in which Thackeray mocked such lustful excesses. At the opposite extreme is MacDonald's nameless king, so sexually naive that he does not know how to go about begetting the offspring he thinks he desires. He thus reproaches his wife for not having instantly presented him with what all other "queens of my acquaintance" seemed to be able to produce: "'Why don't you have any daughters, at least?' said he. 'I don't say *sons*; that might be too much to expect.'" The smiling queen hints that she may not be able to oblige her consort "immediately" with what he wants. Like a mother who must dampen a little boy's demand that a baby sister be instantly presented to him, she advises "patience." The chapter ends with the king's receiving "more than he deserved," when, "at last, the queen gave him a daughter— as lovely a little princess as ever cried" (LP, chap. 1, 3–5).

MacDonald's wonderfully comic characterization of this "little king with a great throne" links the mindless monarch to his newborn daughter and helps explain her predicament (LP, chap. 3, 12). For the king's failure to remember the existence of a powerful sister soon brings about his child's emotional retardation and a loss of physicality. Under the spell of the king's sister, "as lovely a princess as ever cried" promptly loses the sensibility to cry, and is made to be lighter than air. The child develops into an unfeeling, narcissistic, increasingly shallow young woman, whose shrill and grating baby-laughter persists almost until the very end of the tale. This levitating princess will have to undergo changes far more radical than those which allowed Giglio and Rosalba to outgrow the childish behavior of the adults in *The Rose and the Ring*.

If the Light Princess resembles her light-haired father both physically and temperamentally, the dark-haired queen proves to be as deficient a parent as soon as she turns her "light-aired" child over to a nurse and prefers to best her husband in devising puns built around the word "light" (LP, chap. 5, 19–21). Although "much cleverer than the King," she remains just as one-dimensional. Neither can break free from their nursery-rhyme origins: while he counts out his money in the counting-house, she spends her time eating bread and honey in her parlor (LP, chap. 3, 11; chap. 5, 18). The puerility of these parents thus remains their prime function. Whereas the princess eventually acquires the gravity that will allow her to escape a perpetual childhood, the king and queen drop out of the story without ever witnessing her cathartic transformation. Permissible in babies but deplorable in adults, childishness must be superseded by the "divine childlikeness" that MacDonald prizes as the true bond between young and old.[25]

If the childishness the king passes on to his infant daughter represents Innocence at its worst, his spurned sister stands for an equally undesirable deformation of the state of Experience. A witch who can easily "beat all

---

25. George MacDonald, "The Child in the Midst," in *Unspoken Sermons* (London: Strahan & Company, 1868), 3.

the wicked fairies in wickedness, and all the clever ones in cleverness" (LP, chap. 2, 7), Princess Makemnoit is Fairy Blackstick and Gruffanuff rolled into one. By far the most compelling figure in the tale, this dispossessed outsider, banished by her father and totally forgotten by her witless brother, is a negative version of the magical foremothers idealized in fictions like *Phantastes*. When she invites herself to her niece's christening to cast the spell that, she fervently hopes, "will make the whole family miserable" (LP, chap. 2, 7), she enacts the role played by Fairy Blackstick, similarly eager to bestow a "little misery" on the infants Giglio and Rosalba at their christenings. MacDonald imparts his own subversive handling of literary convention to Makemnoit when he assures us that she knowingly scorns "all the modes we read of in history, in which offended fairies and witches have taken their revenges" (LP, chap. 2, 7). If Blackstick was cast as a dignified maternal surrogate who seemed cruel only to turn kind, this "disagreeable" hag, whose disproportionately huge forehead suggests both her superior intelligence as well as a Satanic pride, is a confirmed hater, incapable of "loving anybody but herself" (LP, chap. 2, 7).

MacDonald invests Makemnoit with emotional energies every bit as strong as those that had gone into the maternal "essences" of his adult fantasies. Both types offer compensations for loss. The desire to find a substitute for Helen MacDonald's nurture has become a desire for revenge as unmitigated as that which motivates the slighted Makemnoit herself. Earlier, male seekers wanted to fuse with an etherealized femininity; now, a displaced female insists on assuming masculine characteristics. To reclaim her ascendancy, Makemnoit acts out a travesty of the maternal. Her second and more calculated act of revenge converts her into a phallic mother as grotesque as the demoniacal figure to whom MacDonald devoted *Lilith,* his last and most eerie novel.

In chapter 11, MacDonald produces his own version of classic monster-mothers such as Spenser's Error or Milton's Sin. Descending into a cave on "the underside of the bottom of the lake" that has become the only refuge for her niece's emerging femininity (LP, chap. 11, 75), Makemnoit gives birth to a gigantic drill. Cackling so ferociously that her black cat's hairs "stand erect with terror," she raises the "huge gray snake" out of seaweed powder and then coaxes the creature—whom she kisses, presses against her body, and calls "my beauty"—to attach its mouth to the cavern's roof, where it clings "like a huge leech, sucking at the stone" (LP, chap. 11, 72). As her excited cat looks upward, its stiff tail "like a piece of cable," Makemnoit asks the sucking snake to drain dry the rocky roof and starts to "mutter"[26] runic incantations. Only after the entire Lake Lagobel has trickled through the orifice it has pierced does the serpent shrivel up to be "again like a dry piece of seaweed" (LP, chap. 11, 75–76).

The mixture of nurturance with phallic aggression is as unpleasant here as in Spenser's depiction of Error and her brood or Milton's portrait of Sin and Death. Hostile to a female water-world, this pseudo-mother is far more masculine than the brother-king whose ignorance about the production of babies had bordered on the idiotic. In Maurice Sendak's powerful illustration of the scene, the huge snake directly rises from the lap of the woman with the Satanic brow. Makemnoit's aggressiveness gives impetus to the entire plot of "The Light Princess." A "maker," as her name indicates, as well as a "Mac," her father's true son, she serves her male creator's design as much as Fairy Blackstick had served Thackeray's. Blackstick, too, could enlarge and shrivel masculine appendages; as a combination of William Makepeace Thackeray and his living mother, she was a puppeteer capable of granting or denying men their masculinity. But whereas Thackeray needed to appease the cane-wielding power he had originally cast as the unpleasant Hopstick, George MacDonald's own sense of betrayal does not permit him to make "Make-'em-know-it" a restorer of harmony and peace. She remains a version of the "bad" mother.

Makemnoit's extraordinary power as a villainess thus stems from anger that "The Light Princess" sets out to exorcise and to replace with a more gender-balanced alternative. It is hardly coincidental that Makemnoit's final death, so casually introduced, should have no direct bearing on the tale's outcome, and that, moreover, it should have been caused by an accident produced by her own overreaching. She has been far too potent to be dismissed, like the princess's parents, or to be allowed to make her exit, like Fairy Blackstick, by riding out of the story on a broom or a cane. Makemnoit is the story's only major character who is given a name. We never discover what Christian name the unnamed king and queen might have bestowed on their daughter. Since it is Makemnoit's spell which makes the child at the baptismal font both "Light of spirit" as well as "Light of body," the witch actually endows the Light Princess with her titular first name. When, by chapter 9, another nameless figure enters the story, "the son of a king, who . . . set out to look for the daughter of a

26. Given his total command of the German language, MacDonald's use of the German noun for "mother" as an English verb may well have been intended as one more bit of wordplay in this pun-filled story.

queen," this archetypal seeker, immediately treated with the same levity that marked the narrator's handling of the royal couple and their light daughter, hardly seems capable of becoming Makemnoit's foil.

The narrator quickly mocks the young prince for the same dematerialized yearning that had made the princess's father look so absurd. No flesh-and-blood princess fits this versifying idealist's blueprint. The female love-object he seeks remains a hazy abstraction. And rumors about the Light Princess have disqualified her in his mind. He has heard "some reports about our princess," we are told, "but as everybody said she was bewitched, he never dreamed she could bewitch him" (LP, chap. 9, 49). Bringing in his hero at the story's midpoint, MacDonald teases his readers with a figure who appears to be flat and generic. By calling him a "fine, handsome, brave, generous, well-bred, and well-behaved youth, as all princes are," the narrator only accentuates the young man's seeming predictability:

One day he lost sight of his retinue in a great forest. These forests are very useful in delivering princes from their courtiers, like a sieve that keeps back the bran. Then the princes get away to follow their fortunes. In this they have the advantage of the princesses, who are forced to marry before they have had a bit of fun. I wish our princesses got lost in a forest sometimes. (LP, chap. 9, 49–50)

MacDonald's irreverent attitude towards fairy-tale conventions should alert any readers who might assume that this prince will never break the mold of princely stereotypes. For such readers, the transformation that takes place in the concluding chapters must come as a total surprise. Mac-Donald wants to sift new meanings out of conventions he dismisses as mere "bran." His story abruptly shifts from light to grave when a callow story-book prince turns into a Christ-like martyr. The prince's unexpected readiness to sacrifice himself nullifies Makemnoit's magic and redeems the Light Princess from a life of shallowness.

Still, in a passage rife with ironies, MacDonald initially stresses the prince's conventionality. The young man, we learn, has chosen to "make no inquiries" about the Light Princess because he is convinced that creatures under a magic spell make rather undesirable brides:

For what indeed could a prince do with a princess that had lost her gravity? Who could tell what she might not lose next? She might lose her visibility, or her tangibility; or, in short, the power of making impressions upon the radical sensorium; so that he should never be able to tell whether she was dead or alive. (LP, chap. 9, 49)

The narrator whose voice filters the thoughts of this naif introduces several levels of irony. There is, first of all, a direct mockery of someone so unprepared for a fleshly princess. Since the abstract female ideal the prince seeks already lacks visibility and tangibility, he ought to welcome a bride as immaterial as Lady Alice became at the end of "The Portent." His confusion about what she might lose therefore differs from the narrator's express wish that princesses be allowed the freedom to get lost in a forest as much as princes. The passage thus also introduces a dramatic irony, for the prince's doubts will be removed as soon as he stumbles upon a swimmer who turns out to be "our" laughing princess. Upon hearing her ecstatic screams, his "sensorium" will become quite radically inflamed.

But there is also a third level of irony that arises from the prince's association of invisibility with death. Though he purports to reject a love-object who might be dead, he will actually offer his life when he sees hers on the wane, and, like Anodos in *Phantastes,* will undergo both death and resurrection. What is more, the princess will recover her gravity only when, in a reversal of the fear here attributed to the prince, it is *she* who cannot tell whether *he* is dead or alive. The prince must cease to show all signs of life in order to extricate both himself and the princess from their entanglement in a "light" comedy. His introduction as a comic figure thus jars with the ultra-earnestness of his final role.

Yet what first draws the prince to the princess in the chapter entitled "Put Me In Again" is an unmistakable erotic attraction. Aroused first by those shrill screams, then by the shape of "a lady," and finally by the touch of the body he hauls out of the waters "to lay her on the bank," the prince rapidly sheds all essentialist thoughts of female invisibility and intangibility. Even her anger at being removed from the only element that weighs her down makes the princess irresistibly attractive to her would-be rescuer:

But, her gravitation ceasing the moment she left the water, away she went up into the air, scolding and screaming.

"You naughty, *naughty,* NAUGHTY, NAUGHTY man!" she cried. No one had ever succeeded in putting her into a passion before.—When the prince saw her ascend, he thought he must have been bewitched, and have mistaken a great swan for a lady. (LP, chap. 9, 52)

Despite Arthur Hughes's lovely drawing of the princess's swan-like deportment in the water, it is Maurice Sendak's modern drawing of two skinny-dipping truants that somehow better captures the eroticized swimming that takes place as soon as the prince, "catching her up in his arms," springs back into the water (LP, chap. 9, 56). Their experience of a "fall" is, as this punning Adam and his Eve now discover, highly pleasurable:

"How do *you* like falling in?" said the princess.

"Beyond everything," answered he; "for I have fallen in with the only perfect creature I ever saw."

"No more of that; I am tired of it," said the princess. Perhaps she shared her father's aversion to punning.

"Don't you like falling in, then?" said the prince.

"It is the most delightful fun I ever had in my life," answered she. "I never fell before. I wish I could learn. To think I am the only person in my father's kingdom that can't fall!"

Here the poor princess looked almost sad.

"I shall be most happy to fall in with you any time you like," said the prince devotedly.

"Thank you. I don't know. Perhaps it would not be proper. But I don't care. At all events, as we have fallen in, let us have a swim together." (LP, chap. 9, 58)

John Ruskin, to whom MacDonald had shown the original manuscript of "The Light Princess" in 1863, felt convinced, after "trying to analyze the various qualities of mind" it displayed, that such overt eroticism made it unsuitable for children. As Ruskin explained in a letter to MacDonald, there were other reasons why the story "will not do for the public in its present form." First of all, he contended, MacDonald was not a humorist in the Thackerayan manner. His capacity to "see too deeply," a virtue in Ruskin's eyes, thus became a liability: "[Y]ou cannot laugh in any exuberant or infectious manner—and the parts which are intended to be laughable are weak." Secondly, having found its comedy excrescent and its "curious mixture of tempers" a weakness, Ruskin wanted the story to be refined into a more earnest narrative such as his own *King of the Golden River*.

But it was the explicit sexuality of "The Light Princess" that troubled Ruskin the most:

Then lastly, it is too amorous throughout—and to some temperaments would be quite mischievous. You are too pure-minded yourself to feel this—but I assure you the swimming scenes and love scenes would be to many children seriously harmful.—Not that they would have to be cut out—but to be done in a simpler and less telling way. We will chat over this. Pardon my positive way of stating these things—it is my inferiority to you in many noble things which enables *me* to feel them and prevents *you*.[27]

There were personal reasons for Ruskin's need to desexualize MacDonald's story. Curiously enough, his hopeless love for the sixteen-year-old Rose LaTouche had brought the two men together as much as the intellectual affinities she had shrewdly anticipated when she had acted as their intermediary.[28] After Ruskin began to tell his new friend about his passion for the young woman, he asked MacDonald's permission to meet her, against her parents' wishes, at his friend's home. After a scrupulous investigation of Ruskin's sexual history convinced MacDonald that this middle-aged lover's intentions were indeed quite "pure-minded," he agreed to chaperone encounters as stealthy as the meetings between the bathing prince and princess. Although MacDonald's sympathy for Ruskin's plight was genuine, it also offered a real-life analogue to his narratives of longing for female essences.[29]

MacDonald did little to tone down the sexuality of the scenes in "The Light Princess" that had disturbed Ruskin. Despite their growing friendship and mutual respect, the two men continued to disagree on ideological

27. Ruskin to MacDonald, 22 July 1863, unpublished manuscript letter, Beinecke Rare Book and Manuscript Library, Yale University.

28. Rose La Touche had been attending MacDonald's lectures on Shakespeare. She and her mother, Maria Price La Touche, who found MacDonald more "human" than Ruskin, wanted the men to meet. Rose hoped that MacDonald's religious certitude, though unorthodox, might help Ruskin overcome his unbelief: "if you want to know why I want you to see him,—I think he is good—has in him what you would—or would once, have thought good—is loving to other people, and is *sure* of things" (cited in Van Akin Burd, *John Ruskin and Rose La Touche: Her Unpublished Diaries of 1861 and 1867* [Oxford: Clarendon Press, 1979], 84, 85).

29. MacDonald asked Ruskin to tell him "the full story" of his annulled marriage to Effie Gray, an account that, according to Greville MacDonald, reflected "nothing but honour upon Ruskin—unless he lied to my father, or my father to me—one supposition as incredible as the other." Greville's similar idealization of Ruskin's love for Rose was no doubt filtered by his father's own construction of a "wonderful love-story." In that narrative, which bears a decided resemblance to MacDonald's favorite fictions, an "honourable and pure-hearted" Ruskin morbidly loves "the frail, strangely beautiful, sweetly smiling girl" who dies of "heartbreak" when their union cannot be consummated. (MacDonald, *George MacDonald and His Wife,* 331).

matters. On questions of theology, MacDonald remained the more conservative of the two, as Ruskin noted when he refused to act as godfather at the christening of Maurice MacDonald. Playing the role of a subversive Princess Makemnoit, Ruskin insisted that, as a confirmed "Pagan," he regarded "your font business merely as a very imperfect and unnecessary washing for that day." Were he to take on another god-child, he added, it would have "to be a girl—for I like girls, and they mostly like me—but I can't bear boys." Ruskin teasingly offered two alternatives: could one of the older MacDonald girls ("grown a little") perhaps be assigned to him as a substitute godchild and Maurice be reassigned to her own godfather? Or, might a sex-change possibly be imposed on the bald infant by fitting him with "crine Lycymnia" (one of Lycymnia's tresses)?[30]

On sexual matters, however, it was actually MacDonald who was the greater iconoclast. Although he implanted some stylistic changes upon inserting "The Light Princess" into *Adela Cathcart,* the 1864 novel for adults, he did not alter the text after offering it to child readers. Instead, he seems to have defended his position against censorship "on the question of passions," since, in an undated letter, Ruskin agrees: "I wholly feel with you that the harm of ignoring them has been fearful." Nonetheless, Ruskin remained adamant in his critique of "The Light Princess." As far as he was concerned, the passions had no place in a text intended for children: "But I think that they ought to be approached in a graver and grander manner—that fairy tales—and everything calculated for readers under 14 or 15, should be wholly free of every sexual thought—that afterwards passion should be given in serious and glorious truth—as the great law and sanctification of all bodily life."[31] After the publication of *Adela Cathcart,* he complained (correctly so, as we shall see in the next section) that MacDonald had actually assigned his objections to the heroine's prudish aunt.

When MacDonald stresses the unsuspected pleasure the Light Princess takes in her newly found swimming mate, he suggests that—though still childish and narcissistic—the young woman is capable of a sexual maturation that will lead to her eventual emotional growth. To squelch this de-

---

30. Ruskin to MacDonald, 13 April 1864, *The Winnington Letters: John Ruskin's Correspondence with Margaret Alexis Bell and the Children at Winnington Hall,* ed. Van Akin Burd (Cambridge: Harvard University Press, 1969), 486–87.

31. Ruskin to MacDonald, unpublished manuscript letter [1863?], Beinecke Rare Book and Manuscript Library, Yale University.

velopment, Makemnoit now sets out to destroy the element of water that MacDonald, like his Romantic precursors, regards as an emblem of femininity. Not content to drain Lake Lagobel with her snake, Makemnoit also curses the moon, the supervisor of tides, and prevents every spring in the country from continuing "to throb and bubble." Indeed, as all fluids dry at their source, humans themselves become depleted of vital juices. In a scenario of special meaning to George MacDonald, infants are deprived of maternal milk: "And not alone had the fountains of mother Earth ceased to flow; for all babies throughout the country were crying dreadfully—only without tears" (LP, chap. 11, 77). The desiccation Makemnoit visits on the land strongly resembles the rape of the Treasure Valley in *The King of the Golden River*. Here, too, what was once moist and fertile becomes a sterile landscape: "The lake went on sinking. Small slimy spots began to appear, which glittered steadily amidst the changeful shine of the water. These grew to broad patches of mud, which widened and spread, with rocks here and there and floundering fishes and crawling eels swarming" (LP, chap. 12, 80–81).

In Ruskin's fable, the passivity that separated the girlish Gluck from his power-hungry brothers was rewarded when the valley drained by male sadism became freshly irrigated. In "The Light Princess," however, a passive purity cannot restore fecundity. The prince mocked earlier for his numinous idealism becomes an active votary of love when he discovers the princess to be "wasting away with the lake, sinking as it sank, withering as it dried". Hence, when informed that the "body of a living man" must be sacrificed to "stanch the flow" of the seeping water, the prince offers himself as the "one hero" ready to "give himself of his own will" (LP, chap. 12, 78, 82). He will "cork," "put a stopper—plug—what you call it, in your leaky lake, grand monarch," he explains to the uncomprehending king, in one of the story's last bits of levity (LP, chap. 13, 86). Rather than redeem the silly king's "nation," the prince only wants to save the despairing young woman who finds her soul "drying up within her, first to mud, then to madness and death". Determined to overcome her death wish, he knows that success demands his own self-sacrifice, a renunciation of all hope for a sexual consummation: "Love is death, and so is brave. / Love can fill the deepest grave. / Love loves on beneath the wave" (LP, chap. 12, 80, 81).

IV

The resolve to preserve the life of a dying female links "The Light Princess" to the frame-narrative that MacDonald had devised in his 1864 *Adela Cathcart*. There, the fairy tale is told by the book's narrator, a jolly Pickwickian bachelor called John Smith, who offers it as his first contribution to a story-telling group formed to cure the heroine, his twenty-one-year-old niece Adela, from literally "dying of ennui" (*AC*, 343). Like the other tales (which range from parables to vampire stories and include John Smith's other "child's story," "The Giant's Heart"), "The Light Princess" is meant as a cathartic for Adela (whose last name seems an anagram of that very word). With a clinical eye at his niece, Smith hints that his tale might be "fitter for grown than for young children"; it is, he explains, "a Fairy-Tale Without Fairies" (*AC*, 53, 54).

The avuncular Mr. Smith finds himself persistently opposed by Mrs. Cathcart, Adela's aunt. She interrupts his account of the swimming scenes by branding them "very improper" and then casts a worried glance at her young son in attendance, "as if she were afraid of her boy's morals." Even "an indubitable snore from the youth" and Adela's own smiling defense ("We must not judge the people in fairy tales by precisely the same conventionalities we have") do not assuage Mrs. Cathcart's resistance (*AC*, 79). In the same letter in which Ruskin had vented his "awfully wicked humor" on the infant Maurice, he went on to protest: "You *did* make me into Mrs. Cathcart. She says the very thing I said about the fairy tale. It's the only time she's right in the book—you turned me into her first and then invented all the wrongs to choke up my poor little right with. I never knew anything so horrid."[32]

Despite his remonstrances, Ruskin must have recognized that the frame-story, like the fairy tale itself, is designed to combat a literal-mindedness that he opposed as strenuously as MacDonald. After observing the listless Adela perk up during a powerful Christmas sermon on the baby Lord Jesus, both Smith and a shrewd young physician, Harry Armstrong, arrive at an identical diagnosis: they decide that her "atrophy," though physical, actually stems from a profound spiritual malaise that can only be cured by an assault on the adult "conventionalities" her culture has imposed on her.

---

32. Ruskin to MacDonald, *Winnington Letters,* 487.

Rather resembling the morbid Rose La Touche,[33] Adela needs the alliance of Smith and Armstrong to convert her into the latter's bride. She suffers, as Armstrong notes, from her soul's "discontent" with the meagerness of "the theological nourishment" she has received (*AC*, 50). Armstrong welcomes Smith's story-telling plan as "a better mental table" for Adela's "strong" mind; Smith, in turn, is amazed at the young doctor's perspicacity: "You astonish me by the truth and rapidity of your judgments. But how did you, who like myself are a bachelor, come to know so much about the minds of women?" The doctor promptly answers: "I believe in part by reading Milton" (*AC*, 51).

Smith picks up the clue when he begins his literary reclamation of Adela by narrating "The Light Princess." He has already hinted that his niece will "see light again" as soon as she learns to restore meaning to a reality she has unduly darkened (*AC*, 26). Accordingly, when Mrs. Cathcart professes herself unable to understand the symbolic import of Smith's opening allusion to "Goody Gravity," he readily replaces it with a "more general, and indeed more applicable, motto," taken "from no worse authority than John Milton: 'Great bards besides / In sage and solemn times have sung / ... / Of forests and enchantments drear, / Where more is meant than meets the ear'" (*AC*, 54). Smith explicates his chosen touchstone: "Milton here refers to Spenser in particular, most likely. But what distinguishes the true bard in such work is, that *more is meant than meets the ear;* and, although I am no bard, I should scorn to write anything that spoke only to the *ear,* which signifies the surface understanding" (*AC*, 55). MacDonald's narrator here issues a warning to those who might underestimate his fable. A children's tale of seeming levity can become as grave as *Paradise Lost,* written by a bard who knew that Spenser's stories of errant princes, forests, and enchantments spoke to more than "surface understanding."

Smith thus tries to prepare the listeners of "The Light Princess" for the story's abrupt shift from Thackerayan comedy to Ruskinian high seriousness. Readers who encounter the story without its frame, however, may well find that shift as puzzling as Mrs. Cathcart did and hence object to the "curious mixture of tempers" that Ruskin had noted. The movement from comedy to pathos is certainly awkward. Resolved "to die like a

---

33. Using the hindsight of his own years of medical practice, Greville MacDonald insists that Rose died from "acute neurasthenia as, I think, the case would now be diagnosed" (MacDonald, *George MacDonald and His Wife,* 331).

prince," the youth who places himself in "the hole" of the lake to counter its defloration by Makemnoit sings a long love song while twisting his body into a most "uncomfortable position" (LP, chap. 14, 90, 92). But the bored princess responds neither to the young man's lyrics nor to his contorted efforts to kiss her fingertips. As insensitive to his plight as Adela Cathcart is to Harry Armstrong's love, she reluctantly feeds him "bits of biscuit and sips of wine" (LP, chap. 14, 97). When, with the water nearing his neck, he begs for a kiss, she grants one that is long and sweet but also very cold. The prince's discomfort resembles the reader's. What are we to make of the princess's continued treatment of him, not as a type of Christ, but as a silly sentimentalist who warbles an endless song before the rising waters finally cover his lips?

That MacDonald wanted such incongruities to shatter a too complacent attachment to "surface" story elements seems evident from one of the chief sources on which "The Light Princess" draws, E. T. A. Hoffmann's *Prinzessin Brambilla,* a novella that Thackeray may also have come across before introducing commedia dell'arte figures into *The Rose and the Ring.* Operating on several levels of reality, Hoffmann's intricate tale tries to revalidate a commedia that had preserved the fantastic. In it, MacDonald not only found the myth of a lake redeemed from a wizard's spell, as Wolff first noted, but also strong support for his own subversive intermingling of the *spasshaft* and *ernsthaft.*[34]

Hoffmann's protagonist, an actor called Giglio, resembles his Thackerayan namesake in that he is always manipulated by an ironic intelligence (who appears, depending on the level of reality at play, as a charlatan vendor, a Duke, a wizard, and a dramatist). This Giglio, however, also resembles MacDonald's young prince in his obsessive quest for a female ideal, the Princess Brambilla, who is both an illusory figure and an existing being. Dressed in commedia costumes (thus filling the outfits shown in Callot's accompanying etchings), Giglio at one point actually slays himself in a duel, only to become resurrected, as MacDonald's prince will be at the end of "The Light Princess." His ego or *Ich* is increasingly confused by the triple layering of realities the tale intersplices. Strutting about in *grenzenlose Gravität* (unbound gravity), Giglio is laughed at by others. Nonetheless, together with his bride Giacinta, he helps regenerate Lake Urdar and reanimates Urdarland's Queen Mystilis, who had replaced this Eden's

---

34. Wolff, *Golden Key,* 118–20; E. T. A. Hoffmann, *Prinzessin Brambilla: Ein Capriccio nach Jakob Callot,* ed. Wolfgang Nehring (Stuttgart: Reclam, 1971), chap. 7, 134.

former rulers, a too grave king and too light queen. Mystilis stands for a Fantasy liberated from epistemological division. According to Hoffmann, competing notions of reality are responsible for so badly splitting and befuddling Giglio's riven "I." A form of Fantasy that can simultaneously rely on humor and gravity thus can dissolve false dualisms. Hoffmann's bizarre "capriccio after Callot" exults in a metamorphic art that opposes all one-sided perceptions of what may or may not be "real."

In the lyrical ending to "The Light Princess," MacDonald follows both Hoffmann's and Ruskin's precedents when he depicts a symbolic irrigation as a return to a metaphoric order based on an overflow of feeling. Hoffmann had inundated the parched Urdarsee and Ruskin had flushed the arid Treasure Valley. MacDonald, however, directly links the rain he visits on the drought-stricken country to the princess's cathartic tears. Able to show emotion at last, she single-handedly pulls the prince out of the water; yet the young man seems to be past breathing even after her people carry him "to her own room, and lay him in her bed" (LP, chap. 14, 101). Deliberately excluding the king and queen ("fast asleep" during this climactic scene), MacDonald has her old nurse join the princess as they alone work over the young man's body. Their ministrations are handled with deliberate vagueness: the experienced older woman "knew what to do," we are told, and yet the task of bringing the prince back to life seems to devolve solely to the princess, who tries "on and on, one thing after another, and everything over and over again" (LP, chap. 14, 101–2). When the prince at last opens his eyes, the princess's own eyes stream with the tears she has so long suppressed.

In "The Light Princess," as in the ending of *The King of the Golden River,* this process of refertilization is now described in cadences that almost seem biblical. Yet unlike Ruskin, who insisted on preserving Gluck's virginal attributes, MacDonald links fecundity to the bedroom in which he has placed his young protagonists:

The princess burst into a passion of tears, and *fell* on the ground. There she lay for an hour, and her tears never ceased. All the pent-up crying of her life was spent now. And a rain came on, such as had never been seen in that country. The sun shone all the time, and the great drops which fell straight to the earth, shone likewise. The palace was in the heart of a rainbow.

It was a rain of rubies, and sapphires, and emeralds, and topazes. The torrents poured from the mountains like molten gold; and if it had not been for its subterraneous outlet the lake would have overflowed and inundated the country. It was full from shore to shore.

But the princess did not heed the lake. She lay on the floor and wept. And this rain within doors was far more wonderful than the rain out of doors. (LP, chap. 15, 102–3)

Despite its Christian typology, the passage does not exclude a dollop of Thackerayan comedy to leaven the seriousness of MacDonald's conclusion. The drama of the princess's recovery of her lost gravity is, after all, handled rather lightly. When she finds that she cannot rise from the floor, but keeps tumbling down, her old nurse "utters a yell of delight":

"My darling child! she's found her gravity!"
"Oh, that's it! is it? said the princess, rubbing her shoulder and knee alternately. "I consider it very unpleasant. I feel as if I should be crushed to pieces."
"Hurrah!" cried the prince from the bed. "If you've come round, princess, so have I. How's the lake?"
"Brimful," answered the nurse. (LP, chap. 15, 103–4)

The bed from which the prince shouts his approval at his bride's sudden "crushing" has become the center of gravity for a story which began with a king's innocence about the production of babies. Like the "brimful" lake, a marriage bed will soon brim over, as the last sentence of the story confirms:

So the prince and princess lived and were happy; and had crowns of gold, and clothes of cloth, and shoes of leather, and children of boys and girls, not one of whom was ever known, on the most critical occasion, to lose the smallest atom of his or her due proportion of gravity. (LP, chap. 15, 107)

This reassertion of the materiality of gold and cloth and leather and children of both sexes would not have been possible in MacDonald's adult fantasies. Even the priority given to boys over girls may suggest a deliberate attempt to check his earlier exaltations of the feminine. By writing for growing children, MacDonald had managed to ground that femininity, much as Tennyson, the impersonator of Marianas and Ladies of Shalott, had tried to do in *The Princess* (1847), where comedy and fairy tale also were enlisted to domesticate a princess who defied her culture's codes of behavior. As father to an ever-increasing host of "children of boys and girls," MacDonald had come to resemble, as his son Ronald noted, the "chief of a clan"; the "patriarchal idea" had all along been "in his blood."[35]

---

35. Ronald MacDonald, "George MacDonald," in *From A Northern Window*, ed. F. Watson (London: Nisbet, 1911), 84. .

Gravity and growth had displaced his regressive yearnings. But not completely. He would find new ways of recombining the polarities of "The Light Princess" in *At the Back of the North Wind*. Though responsive to the material city-world around him, little Diamond would also become the mystic fellow-traveler of a beautiful North Wind.

V

In a preface written for the 1904 edition of his father's fairy tales, Greville MacDonald tried to account for their continued popularity. Why would stories such as "The Light Princess," which he reprinted, "appeal to the young" if they actually reflect the concerns of much "older persons"? Stripped of ornate phrases about the child's "aeolian chords of being," Greville's answer still remains remarkably astute. Children, he argues, want to confront "the unknown" without having it explicitly codified or explained. As a result, MacDonald's handling of complexities he neither simplifies nor overtly allegorizes seems ideally suited to their intuitive understanding:

> In *The Light Princess,* for instance, though the child know nothing of the laws of gravity and have no notion of the essential sisterhood of joy and gravity, he yet gets some of the fitness of law and the futility of life without weight, of mirth without the possibility of tears.[36]

His erudition and superior intelligence notwithstanding, MacDonald respects the child's receptivity to a sense of wonder and open play. Indeed, according to his son, he even values the transgressive tendencies that didactic texts so often tend to correct:

> The popular literature for children makes small appeal to the germinal power: it tickles the fancy and fosters the intellectual laziness which ever prefers the easy semblance of work to the doing of deeds, which mistakes things for the energy that makes them, the letter for the law, the symbol for the idea symbolized, the material for the spirit. In brief, it is the unconsciously realized truth of my father's fairy stories that makes them appeal to the child for acceptation and love.[37]

36. Greville MacDonald, preface to *The Fairy Tales of George MacDonald* (London: Arthur C. Fifield, 1904), 1:v.
37. Ibid., vi.

Conscious of dogmatizing about "my father's intentions," Greville refers us to George MacDonald's own remarks about the operations of an imagination that is open to the unconscious. Indeed, the son's preface elaborates views his father had enunciated in a piece printed, towards the end of his career, to introduce the 1893 American edition of *The Light Princess and Other Fairy Tales,* and, earlier, within a collection of essays he called *A Dish of Orts.*[38] In the 1893 version of this essay, entitled "The Fantastic Imagination," MacDonald addresses himself to adults who might be puzzled by the fairy tales which follow, headed by "The Light Princess." Such tales, he contends, involve what he calls a process of "calling up" in both writer and reader. Dormant or forgotten materials are brought into consciousness through "new forms." Following both Coleridge and the German Romantics he knew so well, MacDonald claims that "when such forms are new embodiments of old truths, we call them the product of the Imagination; when they are mere invention, however lovely, I should call them the work of the Fancy."[39]

MacDonald then proceeds to anticipate, and to answer in catechistic fashion, three objections an adult reader might raise. When his putative reader is made to say, "You write as if a fairy tale were a thing of importance: must it have a meaning?" MacDonald quickly replies that all meaning remains relative: "one man will read one meaning in it, another will read another." Aware that his emphasis on the subjectivism of literary responses only may discomfit his implied reader, MacDonald has that reader raise a second question (still asked by students eager to get *the* "correct message"): "If so, how am I to assure myself that I am not reading my own meaning into it, but yours out of it?" Again, MacDonald's reply takes the form of a challenge: "Why should you be so assured? It may be better that you should read your meaning into it. That may be a higher operation of your intellect than the mere reading of mine out of it: your meaning may be superior to mine."[40]

By now, MacDonald's hypothetical reader has become unsettled. If these fairy tales are to be disseminated among children, how can their adult guardians act as expositors of such lax and slippery "meanings"?

38. *Orts* had appeared in 1882, and *A Dish of Orts,* an enlarged edition, in 1893. "Orts" are table leftovers, so that modified pieces like the 1886 article "The Imagination" are to be regarded as undigested materials warmed up and served over again.

39. MacDonald, "The Fantastic Imagination," in *Gifts of the Christ Child,* 1:24.

40. Ibid., 25.

Might not grownups merely pass on their own confusion to the child? And so this straw man asks the question for which MacDonald has cleverly reserved his third and most elaborate answer:

"Suppose my child ask me what the fairy tale means, what am I to say?"

"If you do not know what it means, what is easier than to say so? If you do see a meaning in it, there it is for you to give him. A genuine work of art must mean many things; the truer its art, the more things it will mean. If my drawing, on the other hand, is so far from being a work of art that it needs THIS IS A HORSE written under it, what can it matter that neither you nor your child should know what it means? It is there not so much to convey a meaning as to wake a meaning."[41]

Warming up to his subject, MacDonald now taunts his hypothetical reader by suggesting that the child may be capable of a response that is superior, in its receptivity, to that of such a cautious and literal-minded guardian:

"But indeed your children are not likely to trouble you about the meaning. They find what they are capable of finding, and more would be too much. For my part, I do not write for children, but for the childlike, whether of five, or fifty, or seventy-five."[42]

In an earlier version of this same essay, MacDonald introduced an anecdote to illustrate his contention that a "childlike" receptivity could intuitively allow an imaginative adult to "glimpse" the truth of laws even before these could be ascertained as laws. Adducing the example of "a mathematical friend, a lecturer at one of the universities," he noted that this nameless don "had lately guessed that a certain algebraic process could be shortened exceedingly if the method which his imagination suggested should prove to be a true one." The experiment was put to a test, the method found to be true, and the work accepted by the Royal Society. As R. B. Shaberman points out, the work in question was the 1866 *Condensation of Determinants,* published under the name Dodgson, by a writer who had become better known a year earlier as Lewis Carroll.[43] The *Alice* books by this "mathematical friend" will be taken up in the next two chapters. And our consideration of Carroll's work will begin, appropriately enough, with a review of the relation between these two associates of the "childlike" imagination.

41. Ibid.
42. Ibid.
43. R. B. Shaberman, "Lewis Carroll and George MacDonald," *Jabberwocky: The Journal of the Lewis Carroll Society* 5 (Summer 1976): 79.

F I V E

Expanding Alice: From Underground to Wonderland

I should be very glad if you could help me in fixing a name for my fairy-tale. . . . The heroine spends an hour underground, and meets various birds, beasts, etc. (no fairies), endowed with speech. The whole things is a dream, but that I don't want revealed till the end. I first thought of "Alice's Adventures Under Ground," but that was pronounced too like a lesson-book, in which instruction about mines would be administered in the form of a grill.
——CHARLES LUTWIDGE DODGSON

"I do wonder what can have happened to me! When I used to read fairy tales, I fancied that kind of thing never happened, and now here I am in the middle of one! There ought to be a book written about me, that there ought. And when I grow up, I'll write one——but I'm grown up now," she added in a sorrowful tone: "at least there's no room to grow up any more here."
——LEWIS CARROLL

I

In July 1879, Mark Twain met Lewis Carroll and George MacDonald at a London theatrical produced by Louisa MacDonald and her family, back from Italy where they had settled since 1877. Carroll noted in his diary that he felt "pleased and interested" in meeting "Mr. Clemens." Twain's response, however, was lukewarm: "We met a great many other interesting people, among them Lewis Carroll, author of the immortal *Alice*— but he was only interesting to look at, for he was the stillest and shyest full-grown man I have ever met except 'Uncle Remus.' Doctor MacDonald and several other lively talkers went briskly on for a couple of hours, but Carroll sat still all the while except that now and then he asked a question. His answers were brief. I do not remember any of them."[1]

In Twain's account, the sociable "Doctor MacDonald" (he had received an honorary LL.D. in 1868) is set in apposition to a "full-grown man" who behaves as timidly as a small child (or a shy White Rabbit) in the company of adults. This contrast between two writers who bonded precisely because of their shared ability to mediate between the child and the adult seems rather oversimplified. Although it is true that Carroll was more at ease in the company of children, he could be as gregarious as MacDonald whenever he sought out celebrities he wanted to cultivate. And his camera gave him access to adults as easily as to girls and boys. What is more, his friendship with the MacDonalds was unencumbered by the kind of reserve that marked his relation to Alice Liddell's wary parents, Canon Henry George Liddell and Lorina Liddell. Carroll cherished the opportunity of frequenting a household in which he could almost be as open with Louisa and George MacDonald as with Mary and Greville, his favorites among their brood. That he availed himself of MacDonald's offer to have the entire family respond to the *Ur*-copy of "Alice's Adventures Under Ground," which he then recopied and illustrated before presenting it to Alice Liddell in November of 1864, indicates the extent of his trust.

Despite its dubiousness, Twain's distinction between the two men

1. *The Diaries of Lewis Carroll,* ed. Roger Lancelyn Green (Westport, Conn.: Greenwood Press, 1971), 2:382.

nonetheless has a distinct bearing on my own movement from Mac-
Donald's "The Light Princess" to Carroll's first Wonderland ventures. For
if Twain appreciated both the man and the writer in MacDonald (from
whom he obtained an autographed copy of *At the Back of the North Wind*
to bring to his own children), he regarded the "author of the immortal
Alice" as someone whose wit was to be found in a text rather than in a
Victorian drawing room. This cleavage—like that which separates the
uninteresting C. L. Dodgson from the seductive Lewis Carroll—has a
bearing on any critical effort to gain access to a mind more familiar to
us as a pseudonymous presence in the *Alice* books. George MacDonald's
preservation of his mother's letter about him furnished both his biogra-
pher-son and his future critics with a possible key to his mythologies. Yet
Carroll's reticence, evident even in his detailed yet guarded diary entries
and his most exuberant letters, tends to discourage the kind of burrowing
into personal life and childhood experience undertaken in my previous
chapters on Ruskin, Thackeray, and MacDonald.[2]

2. Some "burrowing," however, seems in order at this point. Unlike Ruskin and
Thackeray, who had no siblings, and unlike MacDonald, who was separated from his
brothers early in life, Charles Dodgson (1832–1898) grew up flanked by two older sisters,
Frances (1828–1903) and Elizabeth (1830–1916), on the one side, and two younger sisters, Caroline (1833–1904) and Mary (1835–1911), on the other. This position not only
seems relevant to his special identification with an Alice Liddell similarly flanked by
older and younger sisters, but was recreated in many of his group photographs, such as
the picture "Summer" I extensively discuss later in this chapter.

The sororal ambiance of his early childhood also makes Carroll's relation to "femininity" very different from that of the sisterless male writers I have so far discussed.
Whereas "femininity" is associated with mothers, lost or recreated, by Ruskin, Thackeray, and MacDonald, for Carroll it seems primarily associated with a girlhood from
which he was wrested when sent off to Richmond School, Rugby, and Oxford. His exile
from the feminine and his identity as "new boy" were first handled with comic indirection in early productions such the 1845 poem "Brother and Sister" or the half-
recriminatory drawing about "The only sister who *would* write to her brother" in the
1849 *Rectory Umbrella*. Reporting to his sister Elizabeth from Rugby upon reading the
first installment of "Dickens' new tale, 'Davy Copperfield,'" the boy refuses to identify
with David and his loss of a female world, claiming instead that the "poor plot" is happily offset by the sketch of Mrs. Gummidge, "a wretched melancholy person, who is
always crying, happen what will." This weeper, a precursor of the bi-specied Mock-
Turtle, Carroll singles out for having "amused me" (Charles Dodgson to Elizabeth
Dodgson, 24 May 1849, *The Letters of Lewis Carroll,* ed. Morton N. Cohen, with the
assistance of Roger Lancelyn Green [New York: Oxford University Press, 1978], 1:10).
Carroll's own creation of grotesque older women, his idealization of girls, and even the

Carroll himself calls attention to this protective self-suppression in *The Hunting of the Snark*, the "Agony in Eight Fits" he published in 1876, after the success of both the *Wonderland* and *Looking-Glass* texts. The amnesiac Baker who has forgotten his name is prevented from indulging in a narrative that might go back to his own childhood origins. His "antidiluvian" account ("My father and mother were honest, though poor—") is cut short when the Bellman commands him to "Skip all that!" The Baker submits, although "in tears,"[3] like that other Carrollian self-caricature, the Mock Turtle. He skips forty years, thus moving from infancy to his present, second childhood. The poem itself eventually comes to an abrupt halt when the Baker "softly and suddenly" vanishes in "the midst of the word he was trying to say." The last utterance of this Carrollian self-caricature thus takes the shape of an aborted stutter:

> "It's a Snark!" was the sound that first came to their ears,
>   And seemed almost too good to be true.
> Then followed a torrent of laughter and cheers:
>   Then the ominous words "It's a Boo—"
>
> Then, silence. Some fancied they heard in the air
>   A weary and wandering sigh
> That sounded like "—jum!" but the others declare
>   It was only a breeze that went by.[4]

There is much in this closure that links the two writers whom Twain arbitrarily chose to regard as opposites: a fascination with death, and, therefore, also with silence; a mixture of humor and morbidity; a distrust of narrative progression and of words themselves. For all their verbal wit, both Carroll and MacDonald tapped energies that originated from an anti-linguistic otherworld that each identified with the early phases of childhood. Greville MacDonald recalled his father's appreciation of Car-

---

"sororal" closures he devised for both the *Underground* and *Wonderland* texts, offended women writers such as Christina Rossetti, as we shall see in chapters 9 and 10. Yet these constructions clearly stemmed from primal affiliations and separations he continued to replay as a writer for children.

3. Lewis Carroll, *The Hunting of the Snark, An Agony in Eight Fits,* "Fit the Third: The Baker's Tale," stanzas 4 and 5, lines 13, 14, and 17, in *Alice in Wonderland: Authoritative Texts,* ed. Donald J. Gray (New York: Norton & Company, 1992), 225.

4. Ibid., "Fit the Eighth: The Vanishing," stanzas 6 and 7, 234.

roll's ability to mediate between the child to whom words are new and strange and an adult for whom language has lost all freshness:

How happily could my father laugh over this loving humorist's impromptu drawings, full of the absurdities, mock-maxims, and erratic logic so dear to the child-heart, young or old. While Dodgson, the shy, learned mathematician who hated inaccuracy, loved to question the very multiplication table's veracity, my father, who hated any touch of irreverence, could laugh till tears ran at his friend's ridicule of smug formalism and copy-book maxims.[5]

Whereas Carroll's levity touched the "child-hearts" of the MacDonalds, young and old, it was George MacDonald's sobriety that increasingly appealed to the writer who, in *Sylvie and Bruno* (1889), opted to stress "the graver cadences of Life."[6] Although Carroll tried to stay in contact with the MacDonalds after their move to Italy, the correspondence became as sporadic as their visits to London. His letter to Louisa MacDonald of 13 January 1892 movingly offers condolences on the loss of "dear Lily" before his expression of sorrow veers into self-pity:

You were so good as to say, in a letter I received on May 8, 1890 (which I have ever since had on record as one "to be answered") "come and see us." It would be a very pleasant thing to do: but I can see no prospect at all of my ever going outside England again. Life is wearing away fast (I shall be 60 in a few days), and more and more I grudge the hours that *must* be given to so many other things, when *I* would like to work, 24 hours a day, at the books I have on hand, nearly done, or half done, or only begun. Some, I suppose, I cannot hope to finish: but I *earnestly* long to complete the second (and concluding) volume of *Sylvie and Bruno.* Whether it is better, or worse, than the *Alice* books, I have no idea: but I take a far deeper interest in it, as having tried to put more real *thought* into it. Most of the *Sylvie and Bruno Concluded* is in type, though in the most chaotic order, and a good many of the pictures are drawn: and, if God grants me life, and enough brainpower, it is my *hope* to get the book out by Christmas next. I need not say that a copy will be sent out to *you,* directly it is ready.[7]

---

5. Greville MacDonald, *George MacDonald and His Wife* (London: George Allen & Unwin, 1924), 321–22. Still, as if afraid that such "irresponsible gaiety and fun" might diminish his father's reputed *gravitas,* Greville quickly insists that this Victorian sage never shed "the atmosphere of sadness so prevalent in his youth" (ibid., 343). If the Baker's voice dissipates into a breeze that completes his utterance, MacDonald spent his last years patiently—and silently—waiting for a reunion with North Wind.

6. Lewis Caroll, preface to *Sylvie and Bruno* (London and New York: Macmillan and Co., 1889), xiii.

7. Carroll to Louisa MacDonald, 13 January 1892, *Letters of Lewis Carroll,* 2:886.

That Carroll hoped that these lines might be noted by Louisa MacDonald's husband seems underscored by his self-characterization. He no longer wants to be seen as the "loving humorist" who has made MacDonald laugh at dinners, croquet games, and photographic sessions at Tudor Lodge. Instead, he seems to protest, he has become more of a metaphysician, a thinker brooding about questions of "far deeper interest" than the contents of the *Alice* books. He has moved from levity to gravity, and hence might be construed to resemble MacDonald himself.[8]

Small wonder, then, that in his letter to Louisa MacDonald Carroll should move from his account of *Sylvie and Bruno Concluded* to a consideration of his former associate. Carroll's appreciation of MacDonald's grief at being separated from his favorite daughter almost seems secondary to his sense of their own apartness:

How is your husband now? I am very glad he has found a climate that seems to suit his health so well, though it *does* put us very far apart. Please give my love to him, and Irene, and Winnie, and accept some it yourself also.[9]

Ostensibly a response to the news of Lilia MacDonald's death, Carroll's letter is all about death—his own waning life and curtailed ambitions, the *Sylvie and Bruno* books with their recurrent preoccupation with dying, his enforced separation from a MacDonald who refuses to give in to the consumption that has claimed three of his children. As Carroll belatedly seems to recognize, the idea of death had all along linked him and MacDonald. But another point of contact is just as strongly reaffirmed: the intense desire for an evanescent female self through whose loss and gain each writer defined his own imaginative identity.

The opening paragraph of Carroll's letter, in which he tries to process the emotional impact of Lilia's death, and a lengthy postscript, in which he boasts with rather unbecoming glee of having acquired two new "girl-friends" to gladden his old age, frame the sections I have so far quoted. Despite the remarkable discrepancy in tone, this opening and closure stem

---

8. In their allegorical mode and their obsession with evil, the two *Sylvie and Bruno* books do indeed seem closer to MacDonald's religious fantasies than to Carroll's earlier work. For connections, see R. B. Shaberman, "Lewis Carroll and George MacDonald," *Jabberwocky: The Journal of the Lewis Carroll Society* 5, no. 3 (Summer 1976): 78, 84–86; and John Docherty, *The Literary Products of the Lewis Carroll—George MacDonald Friendship* (Lewiston, NY: Edwin Mellen Press, 1995), 332–50.

9. Carroll to Louisa MacDonald.

from the same need to offset the preoccupation with loss that takes over the central portion of the letter. Both involve acts of translation that allow Carroll to replace Lilia, whom he had valued as "the only one who could act" in the theatricals he and Twain had witnessed,[10] with two new acquaintances, young actresses whose accomplishments on the stage he rather unfeelingly extols for the benefit of Louisa MacDonald.

Carroll begins his letter by transporting Lilia into a heavenly wonderland. By insisting that her demise should inspire joy rather than bereavement, he returns to a mode he had already adopted in the much-reprinted 1876 "Easter Greeting," in which he assured "every child who loves 'Alice'" that it would "see a brighter dawn" upon the moment of death:[11]

My dear Mrs. MacDonald,

It was only by chance that I learned, a few weeks ago, from Ronald, who called here, what a heavy sorrow has fallen on you all, in the death of dear Lily. And I have been meaning ever since (only every day brings its own pressure of occupation) to write a few words to tell you that your sorrow is very sincerely shared by me: yes, and your joy too (I am sure I may add); the holy joy that dwells on the present abiding peace that we cannot doubt is hers at the moment, and the sweet companionship of other holy ones, and *perhaps* (but how little we know for certain about the saints in Paradise!) of her dear Lord and ours.[12]

Lilia has been freed from "the pressure of occupation" that besets those whose temporal obligations make them tardy in their condolences and can cause them "to grudge the hours" spent on pursuits other than *Sylvie and Bruno Concluded.* The death of MacDonald's eldest child leads Carroll to think of his own mortality and of his separation from the fellow-writer who still has his daughters Irene and Winnie to prop him up as much as a devoted wife.

Yet Carroll's postscript unexpectedly proclaims that he, too, can still count on female companions to bring him this-worldly joy. The man who continued to market his youthful involvement with the three Liddell sisters has just found, thirty years later, still another set of substitute "girlfriends," having lately singled out two of four orphaned sisters, one of whom bears the same name as MacDonald's daughter Irene and both of whom are supposedly highly talented actresses, as Lilia MacDonald had

10. *Diaries of Lewis Carroll,* 2:382. See also 2:300 (1 July 1871).

11. Carroll, "An Easter Greeting to Every Child Who Loves 'Alice,'" in *AW,* 218.

12. Carroll to Louisa Macdonald.

been. This new relationship, Carroll insists, is impregnable, free of the misperceptions of presumed improprieties that affected his emotional investment in Alice and her sisters. Small girls have been replaced by young women, and he, so close to sixty, can no longer be misrepresented as a lusty young bachelor. He can therefore invite the young actresses to his quarters with total impunity. For his investment in them, Carroll rather disingenuously implies, is purely avuncular, as desexualized as the old Professor's relationship with the fairy-child Sylvie:

I have had Violet once, and Irene twice, as my guest in my lodgings at Eastbourne. For in my old age I have begun to set "Mrs Grundy" entirely at defiance, and to have girl-friends to brighten, one at a time, my lonely life by the sea: all ages from 10 to 24. Friends ask in astonishment, "did you ever hear of any *other* elderly clergyman having young-lady guests in this way?," and I am obliged to confess that I never *did;* but I really don't see why they shouldn't. It is, I think, one of the *great* advantages of being an old man, that one can do many pleasant things, which are, quite properly, forbidden to a younger man.[13]

The letter to Louisa MacDonald, with its final note of boastful exultation, dramatizes the same tug-of-war between thwarted and rekindled desire that also prompted Carroll's successive revisions of his *Alice* books. Unable to detain the passage of time, the child lover who projects himself on an actual girl is bound to be disappointed. Death, towards which a growing Alice moves so unwittingly, lies at the end of a process of change that steadily distances the original object of desire. Carroll can thus either indulge in nostalgia, as he does in the frame-poems of the *Alice* books, with their bittersweet memories of lost summer days, or he can express an ironic resentment, directed both at the girl who insists on becoming a woman and at himself for his inability to reclaim childhood as a permanent condition for himself and this female double. Only art can go beyond both nostalgia and mockery. By "eternizing" the child and converting her into an ever-youthful figure, Carroll's artistic reconstructions can offer him and her a perennial field of dreams open to other players similarly eager for renovation. But an actual Alice Liddell, like an actual Lilia MacDonald, is destined to fade and die. Since no immortal fairy-children such as Sylvie can be found at either Oxford or Eastbourne, an aging uncle-figure must periodically seek new surrogates he can then "have" as his guests.

13. Ibid., 887.

If Alice Liddell could be replaced by Alice Raikes and Alice Raikes be replaced, in turn, by Gertrude Chataway (two of his later child-companions), so can one actress eventually be replaced by another in Carroll's ongoing drama of self-rejuvenation. Lilia, the oldest of the MacDonald sisters, can thus give way to Irene, the youngest of the Barnes sisters. In an exquisite symmetry, Mr. Barnes, the clergyman whose death transformed four orphaned daughters into nieces to be wooed and cosseted, has provided an opening for the clergyman's son who, as a child, was flanked by two older and two younger sisters in the Dodgson household. Although he "shall be 60 in a few days," Carroll has found still another child-grouping into which he can, for a while at least, try to blend. Thirty years earlier, Canon and Mrs. Liddell were understandably disturbed by the lavish attentions paid to their stunningly beautiful daughters. Now, however, such interest can be conveniently presented as fully de-eroticized, even though eventually new candidates will have to be found for a re-kindling of pleasures "forbidden to a young man."

II

Despite Carroll's protestations to Louisa MacDonald, however, the "pleasant things" he could now pursue attest to the uniformity of his eagerness to play with younger associates of the opposite sex. The sixty-year-old patron of the Barnes sisters is driven by the same desire that led him earlier to entertain the Liddell girls or to crouch among the young MacDonalds at Tudor Lodge. Indeed, the letter's juxtaposition of two selves—a grave author-thinker who longs to be among his books, "24 hours a day," and a jolly host who banishes care by importing a steady flow of fellow-players—involves the same contrast Carroll had effected, three decades before, through an antithetical pair of photographs that featured the Mac-Donalds themselves. The pictures, which show George MacDonald with Lilia and position Carroll within a group formed by the younger children and Louisa MacDonald, were taken in 1863, the year in which Carroll copied out the *Ur*-text of "Alices Adventures Under Ground" for the family and in which MacDonald decided that he would place his own story of "The Light Princess" in the adult *Adela Cathcart*.

The group photograph of Carroll and the younger MacDonalds was taken a few months before its pendant. Since it is set on a lawn in late July of 1863, around the first anniversary of the rowing expedition to Godstow and the invention of the tale of *Alice,* I shall call it "Summer."[14] In it, Carroll lies flanked by two children on either side; Mrs. MacDonald, kneeling at the left and hence on a higher plane than the recumbent figures, provides, together with the small tree at her back, the photograph's sole vertical axis (fig. 17). Seen somewhat differently, the picture breaks down into two overlapping pyramids, each of which features one of the two adults (fig. 18). The first, formed by Louisa MacDonald, the tree, and the boy Greville, has the tree at its apex. The second and flatter pyramid, formed by the four children and Lewis Carroll, has Carroll at its apex, although his head is considerably lower than Mrs. MacDonald's and only barely higher than that of his special friend Mary, the oldest girl to his right (and the viewer's left).[15]

In the second photograph—which I shall call "Autumn," given its October date[16]—George MacDonald and Lilia, his "White Lily," form a vertical composition. Here, too, the female figure looms higher. But unlike her mother in the "Summer" photograph, who kneels apart from the others, Lilia seems cowed by the father who presses her tightly against his rib cage. Whereas her hand rests on his shoulder, his own left hand encircles her waist, his fingers fastened on her belt (fig. 19). Her slightly bent posture, her removed hat, and her eyes cast demurely down as she glances at his feet past the book he holds in his right hand, suggest an attitude of total submission.[17] She is unlike the free-floating Light Princess who

---

14. Cf. *Diaries of Lewis Carroll,* 1:201: *"July 31 (F).* Took a few more photographs: I have now done all the MacDonalds." Greville MacDonald's dating of the photograph as "1862" thus seems off by a year (MacDonald, *George MacDonald and His Wife,* 345). On 10 October 1863, Carroll went on another spree: "Took photographs of Lily, Mary, Greville, Winifred, Ronald, and Miss Powell [Louisa MacDonald's sister]" (*Diaries of Lewis Carroll,* 2:205).

15. Roger Lancelyn Green claims that the "three eldest girls" are in the photograph, in addition to Greville, Mrs. MacDonald, and "Dodgson himself" (*Diaries of Lewis Carroll,* 1:206). But Lilia is not part of the group.

16. Cf. *Diaries of Lewis Carroll,* 1:206: *"Oct: 14 (W).* Took a large picture of Mr. MacDonald and Lily."

17. Jan B. Gordon and Edward Guiliano astutely note that in photographs such as this one Carroll uses a book to act as a "structural center" or focal point for "the viewer's gaze" rather than for the gaze of his subjects. MacDonald thus sneaks "a look from the book" into the camera, while Lilia directs her eyes to "the right of the book" (Jan B.

soared beyond the grasp of her parents or the bored Alice who stared away from the book her sister was reading in the first illustration Carroll drew for his "Under Ground" manuscript. The volume that MacDonald holds—it may be the Bible or *Pilgrim's Progress,* a favourite, or even one of his own works—acts as an emblem of male authority.[18] Just as the foliage in the back leans against an austere brick wall, so does the child with a flower name lean on the austere man whose hypnotic eyes glare straight out of the picture. If she is an Eve restrained by a father-instructor, he is a visionary eager to surmount boundaries and frames.

If we return to "Summer," the first picture, with its horizontal line accentuated by the hedge-row at the back of the figures and its depth conferred by the recesses of multiple planes, our eyes tend to repose, not on Mrs. MacDonald, for all her eminence and the intensity of her own straight look into the camera, but on Carroll at the center of the flatter and more broadly based pyramid formed by the children. At the extreme right, a disembodied shoe appears, seemingly from nowhere. (It is often simply cropped off in other prints of this photograph, notably in Cohen's edition of Lewis Carroll's letters.) Without the foot, Carroll would seem to have no lower body whatsoever, to have simply sprouted out of the lawn, like a mushroom. Yet this mushroom-man does not want to loom over the adjacent children in the way that the mushroom on which the Caterpillar reposes looms over Alice in Carroll's and Tenniel's drawings. Unlike the adult male in "Autumn," this figure does not seek to dominate the young. Whereas the angular paterfamilias draws his "White Lily" into his autumnal field of gravity, Carroll tries to flatten himself as much as possible in order to remain as close as he can to the level of his vernal child-friends. Of these, only the tiniest (probably Winifred, MacDonald's sixth child, then aged five) still snuggles unreservedly against "Uncle Dodgson." Being older, Mary and Greville already sit apart, clumped together, stiffly wedged between Carroll and their mother. Irene (age eight—or maybe Caroline, age nine) balances Greville both spatially as

---

Gordon and Edward Guiliano, "From Victorian Text-Book to Ready-Made: Lewis Carroll and the Black Art," in *Soaring with the Dodo: Essays on Lewis Carroll's Life and Art,* ed. Edward Guiliano and James R. Kincaid [Charlottesville: The Lewis Carroll Society of America and University of Virginia Press, 1982], 20, 21).

18. The photograph thus also acts as a pendant to the maternal authority or inspiration emphasized in the picture of Christina Rossetti and her mother that Carroll also took in 1863. See pp. 166 and 339n, below.

17 C. L. Dodgson, Photograph of the MacDonald Family

18 Diagram of Figure 17

19 C. L. Dodgson, Photograph of George and Lily MacDonald
(Gernsheim Collection, Harry Ransome Humanities
Research Center, The University of Texas at Austin)

well as temporally, being closer in age to him than Mary. Nonetheless, she
threatens to remove herself from the child-pyramid by refusing to face the
camera and preferring to gaze in the direction of her mother.

Louisa MacDonald, however, is situated on a plane altogether different
from that formed by her four children and by the child-man in their
midst. Whereas Carroll's effort to adapt himself to the children seems
counteracted by a certain awkwardness in his pose, Mrs. MacDonald appears to fit more naturally into the triangular arrangement she shares with
Greville and the tree. (Indeed, the tree that grows behind her and her male
child seems to have sprouted from her half-extended hand.) As a seeder

and cultivator, she thus complements the husband who, in the "Autumn" photograph, can proudly pose with a still growing "White Lily." Her decoratively textured cape makes her stand out even further. It seems to invest her with the status and power which the man amidst her children, dressed in sober black, is trying to downplay. Yet it is he, of course, who has orchestrated the composition of the photograph, who has placed her at the periphery, and himself at the center, of the arrangement. The woman who kneels at the forefront thus can be seen in the subordinate position of an expositor who has drawn an invisible curtain to expose a *tableau* of five figures to an audience of viewers. Her attitude resembles that of the kneeling angel in religious portraits of the Annunciation; if so, the other adult, cradled among little children and trying to become like them, can assume an even more exalted role.

There is an unavoidable tension, then, between Louisa MacDonald as queen of her child-garden and the mushroom-man who has planted himself in that female space. The matriarch's power seems to be benign. She is closer to Fairy Blackstick than to Princess Makemnoit, Thackeray's and MacDonald's representations of the Good and the Bad Mother. Still, her resemblance to Carroll's Queen of Hearts, a power figure without power, seems suspicious. The authority of this other ruler associated with a garden (and a rose tree) was circumvented by truant subordinates who, by flattening themselves out, prevented her from being able to tell "whether they were gardeners, or soldiers, or courtiers, or three of her own children" (*AW,* chap. 8, 64; *UG,* chap. 4, 72). Yet the outsider who has tried to flatten himself among Louisa MacDonald's children is bound to be detected. Like Alice, he wants to fit in, but remains an alien. In Carroll's last drawing for the "Under Ground" text, the angry Queen who excludes Alice holds a flower in her fist. In the "Summer" photograph, the tree that rises out of a kindlier mother's hand spreads over her male offspring but excludes Lewis Carroll.

The "Summer" photograph thus also introduces another tension, similarly attenuated, between Carroll and Greville, the androgynous boy with female locks.[19] And this tension contributes to a further erosion of the

19. On noticing the long locks of the beautiful boy posing for the statue of "Boy and Dolphin" (still at Hyde Park), Carroll suggested that Greville consider trading his head for one of marble because it "would not have to be brushed and combed" (Stuart Dodgson Collingwood, *The Life and Letters of Lewis Carroll,* [London: T. Fisher Unwin, 1898], 83). To his immense delight, the child very seriously entertained the idea. Greville's

20 Revised Diagram of Figure 17

symmetries I have noted. For a third triangle, with Greville and the tree at its center and mother and sister on either side, robs the child-triangle with Carroll at its center of stability. Without the complement of the two children on the left, the child-frieze is broken (fig. 20). Greville, on the other hand, can still enjoy the female support of mother and sister. Himself feminine, though a boy, he is as enveloped by femininity as MacDonald's Diamond will be when nestling in North Wind's hair.[20] By way of contrast, the man against whom the smallest girl still snuggles seems incomplete. Without the prop of the two children to the left, the torso that has been severed from its foot may well topple over. The posture seems as unnatural as that into which the giantess Alice contorts herself when trying "the effect of lying down" on one elbow in the cramped quarters of the tiny White Rabbit (fig. 21). Unable to squeeze herself into the horizontal enclosure, she has to undergo a kind of amputation by sticking "one arm out of the window, and one foot up the chimney," all the while pondering how much better it would be if "one wasn't always growing larger and smaller" (*AW*, chap. 4, 28; *UG*, chap. 2, 34, 36).

Both the "Summer" and "Autumn" photographs acknowledge the process of growth that Carroll nonetheless finds so difficult to accept. The photographs are pendants, much as *Alice in Wonderland*, a summer book, would later be complemented by *Through the Looking Glass*, an autumn

---

"joyous memories" of the "adorable writer of *Alice*" are given full play in his *George MacDonald and His Wife*, 343.

20. See pp. 240–41, below.

21 Carroll vs. Tenniel: Alice at the White Rabbit's

book. And, as in the case of these two books, the earlier composition is the one that contains the greater amount of friction and strife. It is significant that Lily should be barred from the "Summer" photograph with its frieze of younger children. Like Lorina Liddell, Alice's older sister who was already thirteen at the time of the 1862 Godstow expedition, Lilia Mac-Donald is already removed from a childhood Eden. "Autumn" thus depicts a harmony that is easier to attain: a full-grown man holds his pubescent daughter against the left rib cage, the site from which Eve had sprung, wholly developed as a sexual adult. But if Carroll can honor a fellow-writer whose piercing eyes detect the essences that link the "childlike" of all ages, he cannot quite bring himself to pay the same tribute to a mother who supervises the growth of her living, sensitive plants. Kneeling before a tree, she is an Eve who brings life, as well as death, into the world. Although she may shelter Greville, cast as a mini-Adam, she seems at odds with the interloper who squats among her daughters, in an unwitting re-creation of the attitude assumed by the jealous archangel obsessed with the consequences of his fall. Unlike the sad figure who resents his lapse into manhood, the kneeling woman in the picture seems to accept the mutability that Carroll so badly wants to arrest or side-step. Louisa Mac-Donald thus is the figure his little girl-friends will inevitably become before wilting. As such, kind mother though she is, she also acts as a *memento mori*.

"Summer" thus depicts a contest that C. L. Dodgson must inevitably lose. There is no possibility here of a never-ending caucus race, with equal prizes for all. In competing with Carroll over the possession of her children, this mother knows that the process of growth is inevitably on her side. Although that growth will also dictate the inevitable loss of children who shall leave her (or even, like Lily, die before her), she can reign supreme at this brief moment in their development. In fact, the maternal supremacy Carroll acknowledges through this photograph will be tapped by those women writers who challenged him after the success of the *Alice* books and vied with him for possession of child-audiences and childhood itself. Carroll's portrait of Louisa MacDonald, like his portrait of Frances Rossetti and her daughter Christina, taken around the same time, thus seems proleptic as a harbinger of all those maternal surrogates who will guide the young in the poetry and fiction of Ingelow, Rossetti, and Ewing.

Try as he might, the flattened man at the center of the "Summer" composition cannot regain Childhood Lost. He is but a removed upper extremity, a detached intelligence, which, like the severed head of the Cheshire Cat, cannot fully reenter a child's mind or reduce itself into a child's body any more than Milton's envious angel could remain lodged in Eve's troublesome dream. It is that intelligence, after all, which has orchestrated this ironic composition. Whether Carroll had asked George MacDonald to snap the picture or whether he had actually used a timing device, as Morton Cohen contends,[21] it is his artist's control that remains dominant, for all his attempts to lose himself in a garland of unself-conscious children.

Still, if a timing device *was* used for the "Summer" photograph, the appropriateness seems all too evident. For the photograph wants to arrest the very growth it portrays as inevitable. It wants to stop time and stunt the upward movement that is so pronounced in the vertical pendant picture of a father and his adolescent daughter. In his "Under Ground" manuscript Carroll had also resorted to a photograph to freeze "the happy summer days" he experienced with "the little Alice of long-ago." The haunting oval portrait he pasted at the end of the manuscript depicts a face that can remain ever-young, even if the manuscript's recipient has altered in age and appearance (fig. 22). Yet the expansion of this text into *Alice's Adventures in Wonderland,* which the remainder of this chapter will take up, allowed Carroll to give vent to responses that belie the placidity of that earlier closure.

The introduction, in the *Wonderland* text, of new figures, such as the Duchess and her baby, the Cheshire Cat, the trio of Hatter / Hare / Dormouse, the alteration of pieces such as "The Mouse's Tale", the expansion of the trial scene, and the revision of the ending, bring out more forcefully than before the ambivalence with which Carroll regards Alice's willed return to a normal world of growth. In both versions of the story, Alice wakes up as the flat cards that come flying at her turn out to be "some dead leaves that had fluttered down from the trees upon [on to] her face" (*AW,* chap. 12, 98; *UG,* chap. 4, 88). Her older sister gently brushes away these emblems of a mutability that Alice, but not the reader, can still ignore. Although the narrator of *Wonderland* will still identify with this reality-oriented sister, his sharper ironies and more obsessive allusions to death suggest the increasing distance that separates him from the original recipient of his love-gift to a "Dear Child." Carroll knows that Alice must repudiate his desire to linger forever in a mid-summer dream world in

21. *Letters of Lewis Carroll,* 1:124.

find a pleasure in all their simple joys, remembering her own child-life, and the happy summer days.

22 Alice's Photograph in the Manuscript of *Alice's Adventures Under Ground*

which time can stand still. At the same time, however, by prolonging the attempt to detain his heroine "an hour underground," he also rebels against that inevitability.

III

When, on 26 November 1864, Lewis Carroll presented Alice Liddell with the handcrafted, painstakingly lettered and self-illustrated manuscript of "Alice's Adventures Under Ground," she was twelve-and-a-half years old. The photograph that he placed in a mirror-like oval at the end, however, was that of a girl of seven, and hence exactly the fictional Alice's age. Decorated with symmetrical festoons that resemble the signs for parentheses as well as the mathematical symbol for infinity, this mirror reflects a face that cannot age. Gazing back from the text in which he has placed her image, the ever-youthful Alice of the photograph remains as arrested as the figures on Keats's Grecian Urn. A private moment of desire has been forever frozen. Such a wishfulness, however, becomes less possible in the public *Wonderland* text of 1865, where the blonde Alice drawn by Tenniel has ceased to resemble either the mesmeric child of the oval photograph or the dark-haired and pensive Pre-Raphaelite dream-child whom Carroll tried to capture in his own 1864 drawings.[22] For the writer has become harsher, not just on Alice, but also on himself. If he is angry at his inability to contain Alice within the fantasy world into which he has thrust her, he also recoils from his sentimental yearning for a dreamland in which time might stand still.

No longer tied to the personal or private, Carroll has become less vulnerable. And his lesser vulnerability manifests itself through the altered characterization of the time-conscious agent who first draws the fictional Alice into a childland, the White Rabbit. In both the *Under Ground* and *Wonderland* texts this timid creature is startled when addressed by a nine-foot female. But whereas in Carroll's illustration for *Under Ground* the Rabbit very much looks like a tiny suitor who shyly proffers a bouquet of flowers to Alice, he only shows his retreating backside in Tenniel's corresponding illustration for *Wonderland* (see fig. 23). Though huge, the first Alice makes sure to lower herself to the eye-level of the Rabbit she has detained; the second Alice, however, looms far above the minute figure receding in the distance. The dropped "nosegay," which the first Alice found "so delicious that she kept smelling it" (*UG,* chap. 1, 13), has now turned into a fan which the second Alice merely uses to cool herself, "as the hall was very hot" (*AW,* chap. 2, 15). The change seems minor. But it introduces a subtle shift in emphasis that is corroborated by the altered pronoun used to describe the creature whom Alice addresses as "Sir" in both versions of the episode. Whereas the first Rabbit disappeared into the darkness "as hard as *it* could go," the second one runs away "as hard as *he* could go" from his gigantic and overheated interlocutor (*UG,* chap. 1, 13; *AW,* chap. 2, 15; italics added).[23] The Rabbit fears punishment by an adult figure called "Marchioness" in the *Under Ground* text and "Duchess" in the *Wonderland* version. This fear, however, becomes far more comprehensible in the later text, where we are allowed to witness the Duchess's

22. See Jeffrey Stern, "Lewis Carroll the Pre-Raphaelite: 'Fainting in Coils,'" in *Lewis Carroll Observed: A Collection of Unpublished Photographs, Drawings, Poetry, and New Essays,* ed. Edward Guiliano (New York: Clarkson N. Potter, 1976), 161–80. Stern's emphasis on Carroll's interest in Dante Gabriel Rossetti and on the "Hughesian" energies of his own illustrations (174) have a bearing on my discussion of the anti-Carrollian collaboration between Christina Rossetti and Arthur Hughes in chapters 9 and 10.

23. A similar change is made in the account of another Carrollian surrogate, the Mock Turtle, whose alienation becomes more pronounced in the *Wonderland* version.

dried her eyes to
see what was coming
It was the white
rabbit coming back
again, splendidly
dressed, with a
pair of white kid
gloves in one hand,
and a nosegay in
the other. Alice was ready to ask help of any
one. she felt so desperate, and as the rabbit

23 Carroll *(above)* vs. Tenniel *(opposite):* Alice with the White Rabbit

sadistic behavior towards her baby child. Although Alice is horrified by the actions of the Duchess and her cook, the behavior of these adult figures does not substantially differ from her own when, after attaining her largest size in the Rabbit's home, she turns both on him and on poor Bill the lizard.

The Rabbit whom Carroll had enlisted to draw a little girl into a genderless meeting place for adults and children is cast as a dubious agent in both versions of the story. When he trots back to recover his lost gloves and nosegay/fan, the Rabbit and Alice are, for a brief moment, almost identical in size, and both are shown to be obsessed with loss and aware of change. But the disparity between the *Under Ground* and *Wonderland* texts continues. As the Rabbit searches anxiously to recover the missing articles, Alice, who wants to help him, finds herself dispossessed of her own earlier markers which, in the first version alone, significantly include a "river-bank" fringed with "rushes and forget-me-nots," an obvious reminder of the river expedition Dodgson undertook with the Liddell children on an ever-receding summer day (*UG*, chap. 2, 32).

When Alice finds that she has grown so huge that she completely fills up the Rabbit's room, she ponders—in both versions of the text—how to reconcile herself to her discomfort. She reasons that if there is "no room to grow up any more *here*," she might not have to age, and adds, "That'll be a comfort, one way—never to be an old woman" (*UG*, chap. 2, 39; *AW*,

chap. 4, 29). Yet the two old women whom Carroll added in the *Wonderland* "Pig and Pepper" episode display an aggressiveness that seems to come with their greater size. When Alice shrinks to be nearly identical in size to the Rabbit, he orders her about in "a quick angry tone," mistaking her for his servant Mary Ann.[24] In a drawing for *Under Ground* that Ten-

---

24. Was Carroll, a stammerer in the presence of adults, reminded of Goldsmith's hero in *She Stoops to Conquer,* who loses his inhibitions and stutter when he mistakes his social equal for a serving maid? In his article, "Alice on the Stage," Carroll insisted that

niel chose not to replicate for Wonderland, Carroll shows the Rabbit extending a balled fist at a cowing and deferential Alice (*UG,* chap. 2, 33). Yet the tables are soon turned. Resembling the Duchess and the cook, an enlarged Alice becomes sadistic. When the cook flings objects at the Duchess and the Duchess tosses the baby at Alice, the girl worries about the safety of the child they might easily kill. But her own actions with the childlike Rabbit and Bill (the latter half-choked, like the baby), are just as unrestrained. The giant hand that drops the terrified Rabbit on the broken glass of the tiny greenhouse resembles, in Tenniel's drawing more than in Carroll's, a giant claw. The enlarged Alice has become as feral as Dinah, the female predator she invokes to intimidate the Mouse and the birds. In both versions of the text, power-relations have displaced play-relations. And, for Carroll, power always involves the gender distinctions on which society insists.

There is no reason to question the sincerity of Carroll's motives in offering Alice Liddell the love-gift of "Alice's Adventures Under Ground." Carroll wanted the adolescent never to forget the child-play through which a small girl and a grown-up man had erased, ever so fitfully and perhaps more in his mind than in hers, the categories of gender and age. But the resentment that Carroll felt over the parental and societal pressures that conspired against a continuance of this union burst out far more openly in *Wonderland.* Not only has a sentimental nosegay turned into a utilitarian fan, but a timid Rabbit has been replaced by the unsparing Mad Hatter:

> Alice sighed wearily. "I think you might do something better with the time," she said, "than wasting it in asking riddles that have no answers."
>
> "If you knew Time as well as I do," said the Hatter, "you wouldn't talk about wasting *it*. It's *him*."
>
> "I don't know what you mean," said Alice.
>
> "Of course you don't!" the Hatter said, tossing his head contemptuously. (*AW,* chap. 7, 56)

---

any actor playing the Rabbit should have a quavering voice and quivering knees (see *AW,* 282). And was the housemaid called "Mary Ann" because the name was of someone known to the Liddell children, or a generic name, or even a joke at the expense of Mary Anne Evans, whose moral claims and erudition as George Eliot were occasionally questioned by those who brought up her class origins? Dodgson / Carroll's extraordinary allusiveness, much like Evans / Eliot's own, encourages his readers to hunt for analogues that may well seem far-fetched.

Wasting time on answerless riddles and on circular caucus races where nobody wins, Carroll suggests, is preferable to progress into a world of sexual differentiation and domination. The seven preliminary stanzas that Carroll placed before the *Wonderland* narrative preserve some of the nostalgia still allowed throughout the *Under Ground* text. But even this celebration of a "golden afternoon" introduces discordancies that the new narrative will magnify. The number of bodily changes Alice experiences remains the same in both texts. But the expansion from four to twelve chapters and from 18,000 words to a novella that is twice as long also permits Carroll to increase Alice's discomforts. Harangued by the Duchess, insulted by Hatter and Hare, subjected to the exasperations and denigrations of a much longer trial, the later Alice becomes a far more frustrated figure than the heroine of *Under Ground.* The introductory verses insist on the "friendly" nature of her interactions with the Wonderland denizens. Yet this "land / Of wonders wild and new" has decidedly become far more unfriendly (*AW,* 3).

Infected by the hostility of her surroundings, the *Wonderland* Alice drops a politeness maintained much longer in the earlier version. Exasperated by their rudeness, she starts herself to speak "very angrily" to the Hatter and the Hare, before being rebuked for being uncivil (*AW,* chap. 7, 59). Alice's smoldering anger climaxes at the trial: her defiant "Who cares for *you?*" ruptures the civility she no longer needs to observe (*AW,* chap. 12, 97). In *Under Ground* that remark had almost seemed directed at an author fearful that Alice Pleasance Liddell may, by forgetting their summer days together, no longer care for *him.* In *Wonderland,* however, the remark seems a logical retaliation for the greater indignities to which the fictional Alice has been subjected. Her dream has been distinctly unpleasant. Whereas, at the end of the first version, Alice's older sister can still greet her by saying, "Wake up! Alice dear! ... what a nice long sleep you've had," the new phrasing pointedly omits the word "nice" from the speech (*UG,* chap. 4, 89; *AW,* chap. 12, 98).

Sufficiently detached by now from an actual girl on whom he could project his own desire for communion in a "nice," genderless childland, the Carroll of *Wonderland* has become less vulnerable than the author of *Under Ground.* Although he has retained agents that suggest his vulnerability—there are, in addition to the White Rabbit, those other victimized "its," the quivering Mouse and the sobbing Mock-Turtle—he has also added figures who are more suggestive of his anger. The lack of civility with which Alice is treated by the unremittingly hostile Hatter and Hare extends even to minor characters such as the "decidedly uncivil" Frog Footman, not found in the earlier version (*AW*, chap. 6, 46). By assuming the guise of several of the pseudo-adults Alice encounters, Carroll turns on his slippery alter ego, the girl who would be adult. Mixing love and anger, he compels her to undergo mutations she eventually transcends through sheer biological (rather than magical) growth. At the same time, however, he persistently surrounds her with his own protean self-transformations. Just as Milton's Satan adopts the shapes of sundry animals in order to insinuate himself into the company of the Edenic pair he both admires and resents, so does Carroll reappear in different guises to woo and yet to castigate the curious little Eve he can possess at least for the duration of a short dream.

Carroll's most memorable addition to the 1865 text, the Cheshire Cat, is neither a victim nor an aggressor. Both inviolable and genial, the Cat represents a comic mastery over feelings that would otherwise dissolve into Mock-Turtle tears or into Mad Hatter sarcasms. It is significant that the Cat should first appear, not perched on the outdoor tree where Alice later discovers it, but squatting indoors, next to the cook, the Duchess, and the baby. Yet it is also set apart from these grotesque parodies of domesticity. The Cat's grin—which Alice immediately notices and on which she "very politely" comments to the Duchess (*AW*, chap. 6, 48)—endows the creature with an ironic detachment similar to the narrator's own. Whereas the mouths of the hideous Duchess and the sour-faced cook, like the baby's, turn downward in Tenniel's illustration, the Cat's upward grin and upraised eyes convert it into an amused spectator.

Aloof from the deformation of maternity he witnesses in Duchess and baby, the Cat, unlike Alice, refuses to be drawn into domestic squabbles. By the time the Cat appears outdoors on the tree branch, the male baby whom Alice tried to protect from a non-nurturant mother has turned into a piglet. Moving her eyes from the trotting male porker to the Cat stationed above her, Alice recognizes that this "it" belongs to a very different order: "It looked good-natured, she thought: still it had *very* long claws and a great many teeth, so she felt that it ought to be treated with respect" (*AW*, chap.6, 51). The genderless dream-cat allows Alice to displace her respectful memory of an actual cat, Dinah, the aggressive hunter who will turn into a mother of kittens in the *Looking-Glass* text. For this new "it" seems to combine the aggressiveness that Carroll imputes to masculinized females, such as the Duchess, Queen of Hearts, and the Red Queen, with the solicitude he will attribute, in the later text, to feminized males such as the Gnat and the White Knight.

Whereas most of the other creatures Alice meets in Wonderland are either totally self-absorbed or downright hostile, the "good-natured" Cat seems willing to act as her guide to this childland's mad circularity. The anger that infects all others can be transcended by a metamorphic intelligence that equates madness with play. Whichever way Alice walks, the Cat informs her, madness lies. The teleology posited by adults does not operate in Wonderland:

> "Would you tell me, please, which way I ought to go from here?"
>
> "That depends a good deal on where you want to get to," said the Cat.
>
> "I don't much care where—" said Alice
>
> "Then it doesn't matter which way you go," said the Cat.
>
> "—so long as I get *somewhere*," Alice added as an explanation.
>
> "Oh, you're sure to do that," said the Cat, "if only you walk long enough."
>
> Alice felt that this could not be denied, so she tried another question. "What sort of people live about here?"
>
> "In *that* direction," the Cat said, waving its right paw round, "lives a Hatter: and in *that* direction," waving the other paw, "lives a March Hare. Visit either you like: they're both mad."
>
> "But I don't want to go among mad people," Alice remarked.
>
> "Oh, you ca'n't help that," said the Cat: "we're all mad here. I'm mad. You're mad."
>
> "How do you know I'm mad?" said Alice.
>
> "You must be," said the Cat, "or you wouldn't have come here."
>
> Alice didn't think that proved it at all: however, she went on: "And how do you know that you're mad?"
>
> "Well, then," the Cat went on, "you see a dog growls when it's angry, and wags its tail when it's pleased. Now *I* growl when I'm pleased, and wag my tail when I'm angry. Therefore I'm mad."
>
> "*I* call it purring, not growling," said Alice. (*AW*, chap. 6, 51)

If Alice were able to imitate a Cat who can convert anger into a pleasurable purr, she might have avoided the infectious madness of the Tea Party into which she is about to stumble. For, after some deliberation, she opts to go to the house of the March Hare, hoping to find him less offensive than a Hatter sure to be deranged.[25]

---

25. The word "mad" is not only associated with fury and derangement, but also, as James R. Kincaid remarks, with sexual excess: "in the mating season (March), hares . . .

The "Cheshire Puss" markedly differs from the mad trio at the Tea Party. Never as insulting as the Hatter and the Hare, the Cat also is more attentive than the dozing Dormouse who finds it difficult to sustain an interest in little girls. Unlike these creatures, the Cat is curious about Alice's immediate past. Told that its abrupt appearances and disappearances make her feel quite giddy, the Cheshire Cat obliges Alice by vanishing "quite slowly, beginning with the end of the tail" (*AW,* chap. 6, 53). Such self-castrating solicitude is akin to that of later Carrollian personations, such as the impotent Looking-Glass Gnat and the evanescent Baker in *The Hunting of the Snark.* And, in the *Wonderland* text, where the Cat even promises Alice that she will see him again at the Queen's croquet grounds, its kindness is in marked contrast to the sadism of a Hatter who relishes discomfiting her as much as scalding the Dormouse. Later, the Cat gratifies Alice even further by unabashedly sharing her own antipathy for the Wonderland royalty. Her decision to introduce it as "a friend of mine" at the croquet-party thus seems fully justified (*AW,* chap. 8, 67). Whereas before, all "friendly chat with bird or beast" had been aborted by Alice's invocation of Dinah's prowess, this fellow-feline remains her one steady Wonderland friend.

The Cheshire Cat signifies Lewis Carroll's ability to rise above the pull between nostalgia and resentment that had marked the *Under Ground* text. In casting this free spirit as a genderless embodiment of ludic wit, the doleful Charles Lutwidge Dodgson could counter the obsession with loss and death shown by other self-projections such as the White Rabbit, the fearful Mouse, and the tearful Mock-Turtle. Unlike these fragile personations, this "it" enjoys the mythical status of an immortal. Whereas animals such as the Dodo, the Caterpillar, or the Pigeon are imports from a Darwinian world of aggression, voracity, and sexual selection, the Cat is a product of pure imagination that can float, god-like, as an infinite "I am" aloof from all division and strife. Moving from its place by the Duchess's hearth to its perch on the tree from which it instructs Alice, the Cat eventually winds up—as shown in Tenniel's third illustration—as a mere head that hovers, ever aloof, above the domineering Queen, her deferential mate, and the timid White Rabbit.

---

are unusually wild" (*Alice's Adventures in Wonderland,* illustrated by Barry Moser [Berkeley: University of California Press, 1982], 79n). Even *marsh* hares are less inhibited, given their greater freedom of movement, as Kincaid also notes.

The Cat's playful aspect disturbs those Wonderland characters whose identity depends on a totally illusory sense of their status and power. On inspecting "the Cat's head with great curiosity," the King of Hearts concludes that he does not like "the look of it"; yet, in a feeble effort to assert his supremacy, he magnanimously proclaims that "it may kiss my hand, if it likes." The Cat not only rejects such shows of fealty, but also proceeds to undermine the dubious female power on which the King relies when he implores his wife to "have this cat removed" (*AW*, chap. 8, 67, 68). By invalidating the Queen's command, the Cat sets the stage for Alice's own defiance. The purple-faced monarch who wants to decapitate a talking head will be just as unsuccessful when she later orders the beheading of a girl who has by then reached her "full size" (*AW*, chap. 12, p. 97).[26] At the same time, however, the grinning creature also undermines Alice's own infatuation with power—an infatuation she retains in *Through the Looking-Glass,* where, once again, she will identify herself with the figure of Dinah.

Stung by the Cat's calculated insolence, the King pronounces its manner to be "impertinent" (*AW*, chap. 8, 68). But its unmannerly behavior is hardly devoid of pertinence, something which the King, who later confuses the words "unimportant" and "important" cannot be expected to notice (*AW*, chap. 12, 93). The Cat offers Alice the opportunity to recognize the limits of a gendered world of power. The Queen's erroneous attribution of male sex to the Cat makes her predictable command seem even more suspect: "'Off with *his* head!' she said *without even looking around*" (*AW*, chap. 8, 68; italics added). A closer look at the culprit might have made the "savage Queen" act less rashly. She can make the Hatter quake after she puts on her spectacles (*AW*, chap. 11, 88), and she can declare the Knave of Hearts to be guilty of a punishable transgression, as Mrs. Lorina Liddell presumably did in discouraging further exchanges between Dodgson and her children. But her inherently impossible command would be most difficult to execute on a transgressor who lacks a lower body. The only headless and brainless male around is the Queen's already emasculated husband.

26. Significantly enough, in the *Under Ground* text, the Queen never orders Alice's head to be cut off; the girl's defiance simply follows the milder "Hold your tongue!" (*UG*, chap. 4, 88). The greater irascibility of the *Wonderland* Queen is matched by the second Alice: the "little scream of fright" she uttered in the first version has now become a "little scream, half of fright *and half of anger*" (*AW*, chap. 12, 97; italics added).

The Queen's imperious edict thus proves every bit as futile as Mrs. Liddell's apparent resolve—with the support of her husband—to end Dodgson's imaginative play with her daughter. Like the Cat which, when first seen still whole in body, appears between the Duchess's baby and the cook's stove, an "aloof" Lewis Carroll could stay intact even after being physically "removed" from a matriarch's household. Although his eroticized interest in an actual girl had been deemed improper, he was no guiltier of a tangible offense than the Knave accused of stealing one of the Queen's "tarts." Mrs. Liddell is said to have destroyed the many letters and poems Dodgson wrote to his "little Alice." At the Knave's trial (a segment which, besides the Mad Tea-Party, is Carroll's longest addition to the original "Under Ground" text), a letter, which turns out to be a "set of verses," is deemed to be highly incriminating. Once again, the Queen is ready to pass a too hasty sentence:

> "That *proves* his guilt, of course," said the Queen, "so, off with—"
> "It doesn't prove anything of the sort!" said Alice. "Why you don't even know what they're about."
> "Read them," said the King.
> The White Rabbit put on his spectacles. "Where shall I begin, please your Majesty?" he asked.
> "Begin at the beginning," the King said, very gravely, "and go on till you come to the end: then stop." (*AW,* chap. 12, 94)

Yet when these verses are read, they epitomize Wonderland madness as much as the Cheshire Cat. The poem lacks a linear development: any one of its stanzas could be easily relocated. As circular and atemporal as the reality over which the Cat presides, this final bit of poetry competes with the nostalgic hindsight of the prefatory verses. There is really no way for anyone to begin at a true beginning. The poem thus resembles the fluidity of the Cat itself: having no head or tail, it might just as well be read backwards, "beginning with the end of the tail" (*AW,* chap. 6, 53). Like *The Hunting of the Snark* and the very different kind of nonsense verses that George MacDonald would insert in *At the Back of the North Wind,*[27] the poem offers no discernible message. If this is a letter, who is the speaker and who is the recipient? And what is their sex?

> My notion was that you had been
> (Before she had this fit)

---

27. See chapter 7, pp. 251–53, below.

An obstacle that came between
Him, and ourselves, and it.

Don't let him know she liked them best,
For this must ever be
A secret, kept from all the rest
Between yourself and me.

(*AW,* chap. 12, 95)

The poem mocks the literalism of executioners who require a palpable head. Like the Cheshire Cat, it can be freely truncated, and yet continue to grin defiantly at baffled readers prevented from affixing labels to the relations between an "I" and a "you."

As a protective Victorian mother, Mrs. Lorina Liddell adhered to the same socio-sexual reality embraced by the fictional Alice, for all her sympathy with the Cheshire Cat and indignation at the Queen. From his own vantage point, however, a Carroll still inexperienced in the ways of "Mrs. Grundy" obstinately refused to see any improprieties in his attachment to a child whose sexual development he could hardly arrest. As far as he was concerned, the "you" he had courted, appropriated, and made one with his "me" had already become an alien, a "she" subject to the same "fits" that made all grown women an "obstacle" for him. Just as male babies might turn into pigs, so could little Alices turn into Duchesses and Queens. But if Carroll smarted from the need to sunder the dream-child from his first and foremost "girl-friend," he had also learned how to transform this attachment—and loss—into ironic art. His move from the still private "Under Ground" to the public *Wonderland* allowed him to have the last grin.

By relying on his adult mind to reconstruct an analogue to the child's undifferentiated realm of the imaginary, Lewis Carroll could make it an inviolable trysting place. Like Keats, whose poetry he knew so well, he resorted to verbal play in order to preserve desire in "some untrodden region" of the psyche: by expanding the topography of Wonderland, he could consolidate an internal landscape where "branched thoughts, new grown with pleasant pain, / Instead of pines, shall murmur in the wind."[28] There, the playful head of the Cat could easily survive detachment from an actual physical body. Unbound to a world where, beyond sexual devel-

---

28. John Keats, "Ode to Psyche," lines 50–53.

opment, lies death, it could defy severance and mutilation. The "it"-ness of art resisted the threat of change and the frustration of desire by preserving, yet defusing, fear, anger, and self-pity.

The Cat dissolves, reappears, dissolves again, just as the *Wonderland* text becomes itself circular, ever renovating. The oval photograph of an ever-young Alice's head is no longer needed in a book that boasts the Cat's own round head. As an emblem of the unceasing pleasurableness of metamorphic play, the Cheshire Cat is unaffected by loss. It is thus unlike the melancholic "Uncle" Dodgson whose infatuation with children condemned him to a repetition of farewells. But the Cat also differs from the fictional Alice who, by choosing to return to the world above, ultimately blends with her real-life counterpart. Whereas the "Cheshire-Puss" remains a symbolic entity, itself the child of an atemporal dream, Alice rejects the "far-off land" to which her creator/suitor would forever like to consign her. Back in a temporal world where "dead leaves" flutter down from trees "upon her face" (*AW,* chap. 12, 98), she *will* lose her head. Like Eve, who hungered for the fruit whose mortal taste brought death into this world, Alice accepts a fate which Carroll's art cannot help her to withstand.

The Cheshire Cat is Carroll's prime means for asserting the supremacy of his desire for what James Kincaid has called the "child-who-ought-to-be."[29] That impossible and irrecoverable child is Alice's sole Wonderland friend and guide. Yet her humanity prevents her from becoming the Cat's perpetual playmate. The altered ending of the *Wonderland* text, like the altered "Mouse's Tale" that acts as Alice's first introduction to another's fantasy world, shows that Carroll could not simply laugh away the painful realities that growing children must come to accept. Alice's final scream, "half of fright and half of anger," may deprive her of a grinning partner who has gone beyond anger and fear. But the narrator of her story, as mortal as she, can no more remain forever grinning than the serious little girl who will, as her sister foresees, soon "be herself a grown woman," surrounded by a new crop of children (*UG,* chap. 4, 90; *AW,* chap. 12, 99).

---

29. See James R. Kincaid, *Child-Loving: The Erotic Child and Victorian Culture* (London: Routledge, 1992), 196.

IV

Unlike the fantastic Cheshire Cat, emblem of the self-sufficiency of care-free Play, the Mouse and Alice's older sister are cast as time-conscious and time-oppressed figures. The Mouse, a fellow-swimmer, shares its tale of victimization with a "ring" of other animals. These hunted species are not chimerical like the Gryphon or the Mock-Turtle or the Cat; even the rare Dodo owes its extinction to an unsentimental Nature red in tooth and claw. Alice's reality-oriented sister is similarly planted, at least in the revised *Wonderland* version, amidst a natural landscape near a "busy farm-yard" teeming with mortal animal life. Indeed, this concrete setting belatedly materializes to suggest that there has all along been a real-life foundation for the seemingly arbitrary components of Alice's hour-long dream: an actual "pool rippling to the waving of the reeds" is now shown to correspond to the dream-pool in which the "frightened Mouse splashed his way" through Alice's tears (*AW,* chap. 12, 99).[30]

Like Alice herself, the Mouse is keenly aware of the ways in which power determines place on a hierarchical ladder in which the stronger dominate the weak. Even before the Mouse begins to recite the drab details of William the Conqueror's consolidation of power, Alice has already associated the creature with history and the historically verifiable. Although still blessed with a child's ignorance of "how long ago anything had happened" (*UG,* chap. 1, 20; *AW,* chap. 3, 22), she gives the Mouse a lineage dating back to William. After her unsettling encounters and changes in size, and even though she is not quite sure whether a mouse might want to talk,[31] Alice wants to cling to something vaguely familiar.

Alice correctly identifies this new acquaintance as someone who knows the contours of her own world. Her mistake, however, is to share memories that hardly hold the same pleasant associations for the Mouse which they carry for her. The girl who wondered whether cats eat bats or bats eat cats as she fell down the rabbit-hole brings up her favorite emblem of power, Dinah, as well as the structures of killing and eating to which she has been conditioned in the world above. When, after realizing her blunder, Alice tries to soothe the Mouse by suggesting that a "nice" little rat-

---

30. Why "*his* way" rather than "its way"? Elsewhere, the Mouse is never given a male gender; perhaps the attribution is meant to reflect the older sister's perspective.

31. In the 1864 text, she feels that the Mouse might be more accessible than the White Rabbit; the contrast is removed in the 1865 version.

killing dog might possibly be another common acquaintance, she merely reveals her own semi-conscious capacities for aggression (*UG,* chap. 1, 20–21; *AW,* chap. 2, 19–20). As the pigeon later points out with considerable logic, Alice *must* be as rapacious as a snake if she is fond of eating eggs. Her affiliation with voracious predators persists throughout her adventures: whitings, she assumes, for example, come automatically breaded, with tails neatly tucked into their mouths.

Despite her identification with the strong who devour the weak, Alice confirms that, as she had suspected, she and the quivering Mouse belong to the same world of survival through power. And, perhaps precisely because of its own low position on the power-scale, the tiny Mouse has obtained "some authority" among their fellow survivors of the flood, all of whom, "wet, cross, and uncomfortable," almost resemble helpless newborns, still dripping amniotic fluid (*UG,* chap. 2, 25, 24; *AW,* chap. 3, 21). But the Mouse's story of the submission to William the Conqueror by the "English, who wanted leaders, and had been of late much accustomed to usurpation and conquest" hardly interests a girl more attracted to the predatory skills retained by domesticated dogs and cats (*UG,* chap. 2, 25; *AW,* chap. 3, 22). Unable to dry out its listeners with doleful chronicles of domination and submission, the obsessive Mouse, whose personal "history" will again stress victimization, yields to the kindly Dodo's suggestion, in the *Wonderland* version, that a Caucus Race might be more effective.[32]

In both versions, however, the Mouse acts as the group's prime storyteller. It fares better with the "long and sad tale" which Alice tries to follow yet cannot help but replace with her own visual "idea" of a diminishing "tail" (*UG,* chap. 2, 27; *AW,* chap. 3, 24). In both (very different) versions of this curtailed narrative, form deflects from content even if, on closer inspection, the two are quite related. When, in her phonetic confusion, Alice mistakes the Mouse's "not" for a "knot" in its kinky tail, the offended storyteller indignantly leaves the premises. She has been inattentive to the negative warnings it has tried to encode in its tail of a tale. Ensnared by the same wordplay used by such mythical figures as the Mock-Turtle and the Cheshire Cat, Alice has momentarily relaxed her

32. In the *Under Ground* version, the Dodo merely leads the group to a house where they can dry themselves (as Dodgson had done on an outing with the soaked Liddell children).

infatuation with power. Her forgetfulness is ironic, since both versions of the Mouse's tale are very much concerned with power and powerlessness.

In a passage from the *Under Ground* version which he preserved almost verbatim in the *Wonderland* text, Carroll has the Mouse's listeners vainly plead for the return of this offended storyteller:

"Please come back, and finish your story!" Alice called after it. And the others all joined in chorus. "Yes, please do!" But the Mouse only shook its [ears] head impatiently, and walked [quickly away, and was soon out of sight] a little quicker.

"What a pity it wouldn't stay!" sighed the Lory, as soon as it was quite out of sight. And an old Crab took the opportunity of saying to [its] her daughter "Ah, my dear! Let this be a lesson to you never to lose *your* temper!" "Hold your tongue, Ma!" said the young Crab, a little snappishly. "You're enough to try the patience of an oyster!"

"I wish I had our Dinah here, I know I do!" said Alice aloud, addressing nobody in particular. "*She'd* soon fetch it back." (*AW,* chap. 3, 26; *UG* variants given in brackets)

The call for a return of this self-banished teller of tales clashes with Alice's yearning for Dinah's fierce fetching powers. Yet offsetting both attitudes is the sudden interpolation of a young female Crab's defiance of her moralizing "Ma." The Lory's wistfulness is taken up, appropriately, by the older sister at the end of the book;[33] she will gently seek to make a vanished story "stay" by envisioning a child-surrounded, maternal Alice. The angry baby Crab, however, will not be soothed by a parental perspective. It snappishly counters the mother who wants to make the Mouse's departure a mere occasion for edifying remarks useful to growing daughters. The child's insolence is refreshing; whereas the Lory sighs for Mouse and Alice yearns for Dinah, this little creature insists on its self-sufficiency. Its impertinence, however, can no more be permitted in fictional figures such as the Lory and Alice than in the real-life daughters of Mrs. Lorina Liddell, even though this "Ma" had all too likely also used the recent departure of a mousy yet angry "Uncle" Dodgson as a means for giving her girls a "lesson" in proper conduct for future adults.

By clinging to her image of Dinah, Alice avoids both the Lory's nostalgia and the little Crab's rebelliousness. Just as she has failed to follow the

33. The Lory, after all, stands for that older sister, named Lorina after her mother, Lorina Hannah Reeve Liddell.

Mouse's tale, so will she later delegate the job of interpreting her own adventures to a sister better equipped to handle the traffic between past, present, and future. Alice is not a sentimentalist; her empathy is limited. She does not understand that the Magpie, the Canary, and even the kindly Dodo are hardly delighted to hear how Dinah would "eat a little bird as soon as look at it!" (*UG*, chap. 2, 30; *AW*, chap 3, 26). Even when, reduced in size, a Lilliputian Alice risks being "trampled" by a puppy as huge as a "cart-horse," she exploits the animal's playfulness with the cool aplomb of a professional bull-fighter (*UG*, chap. 2, 47; *AW*, chap. 4, 32). Though currently as tiny as a mouse, Alice is not about to regard herself, as the Mouse did, as one of the hunted.

The playfulness that made Alice look at the shape of the Mouse's "tail" suggests that she is still close enough to childhood to wean herself from the infatuation with empowerment she has derived from the world of her Victorian elders. For the downward spirals into which Carroll placed the two versions of the Mouse's story are, like the narrowing rabbit-hole, funnels designed to filter or lessen the strength of the forces operating in Alice's everyday world. In this sense, both ideograms resemble those ancient Hebrew amulets in which the reduction of phrases, word by word, and letter by letter, usually taken from a sacred text such as the Song of Songs (itself the celebration of a Female Other) was meant to produce a magic distillation that could restore the owner to a sense of the pristine and quintessential.[34] Still, even though the shape of each Mouse's tale is similar, their contents differ quite substantially (see fig. 24). The first tale, which the Dodo asks the Mouse to tell, dwells on the fortuitousness of an order in which dogs and cats might accidentally crush, by their sheer weight, those slighter than they are. The second tale, which Alice herself now requests from the Mouse, appears to hint that "cunning" can empower the weak as well as the powerful. There is a further difference, however, in that the two narratives curiously reverse the private emphasis of the "Under Ground" manuscript and the public accessibility of the printed and more widely disseminated *Wonderland* book. The story the Dodo extracts

---

34. On 11 May 1859, in a letter in which he recounted his visit with Tennyson, Dodgson mentioned that the Laureate had told him that "often on going to bed after being engaged on composition," he would dream long passages of poetry: "One was an enormously long one on fairies, where the lines from being very long at first, gradually got shorter and shorter, till it ended with 50 or 60 lines of two syllables each!" (Carroll to W. E. Wilcox, *Letters of Lewis Carroll*, 1:37).

seems more universal than its counterpart, since it involves the victimizing of a generic "We" by a nameless dog and cat. Although the plural pronoun clearly stands for mice living under a mat, it also seems to extend to the Mouse's childlike animal auditors, all subject to persecution by creatures more powerful than they. The story Alice expects to hear, however, is a more personal one. She wants the Mouse to explain to her—through some autobiographical reminiscences—the sources of its enmity towards mice-

<pre>
We lived beneath the mat
      Warm and snug and fat
            But one woe, & that
                  Was the cat!
                        To our joys
                        a clog, In
                      our eyes a
                   fog, On our
                 hearts a log
            Was the dog!
         When the
       cat's away,
      Then
     the mice
     will
      play,
        But, alas!
          one day, (So they say)
               Came the dog and
                     cat, Hunting
                          for a
                          rat,
                        Crushed
                      the mice
                    all flat,
                   Each
                  one
                 as
                 he
                 sat
                      Underneath the mat. Warm
                                              &
                                            snug
                                          &
                                        fat. Think of that!
</pre>

<pre>
                  "Fury said to
                    a mouse, That
                      he met in the
                       house, 'Let
                          us both go
                          to law: I
                           will prose-
                            cute you.—
                           Come, I'll
                         take no de-
                       nial: We
                     must have
                   the trial;
                  For really
                 this morn-
                ing I've
              nothing
             to do.'
            Said the
             mouse to
              the cur,
                Such a
                 trial, dear
                  sir, With
                   no jury
                    or judge,
                     w o u l d
                     be wast-
                    ing our
                   breath.
                  'I'll be
                 judge,
                I'll be
               jury,'
               said
              cun-
              ning
              old
              Fury:
              'I'll
               t r y
                the
                 whole
                  cause,
                  a n d
                 con-
                demn
               you to
              death.'
</pre>

24 Two versions of the Mouse's Tale

catchers such as Dinah or a "nice little dog." Her petition strongly suggests that Carroll has inserted a subtext which neither Alice nor the Mouse itself can fully fathom.

Trying to allay the Mouse's ruffled feelings, the second Alice says: "'You promised to tell me your history, you know, . . . and why it is you hate—C and D,' . . . half afraid that it would be offended again" (*AW*, chap. 3, 24). *C* and *D* here obviously stand for "Cat" and "Dog," the oppressors of the first Mouse's Tale. But the letters also stand for "Carroll" (Charles) and "Dodgson," the names of the authorial intelligence that goes beyond the limited perspectives of the Mouse and Alice. Exulting more freely in his ironic powers, the creator of the *Wonderland* text no longer is content simply to dwell on the fragility of White Rabbits, Mice, Mock-Turtles, and kindly Dodos, all self-parodies of the stammering Uncle Do-Do-Dodgson. The second Mouse's Tale is decidedly less sentimental. Unafraid of risking anger or "hate," freer from self-pity and self-mockery, Uncle Dog-son can now just as easily identify himself with the "cunning" cur named "Fury" as with a grinning Cheshire Cat.

Both versions of the Mouse's Tale stress "death," the word placed at the very tip of the second "tail." Yet death is problematic in each version, albeit for different reasons. Are the mice who, in the first version, wind up pressed as flat as playing cards, truly dead? If so, why do they remain as "warm and snug and fat" as before, even after their crushing? Could it be that they now survive in a safer alternate world? The flattening of a "we" in a cozy subterranean realm beneath an unstable surface seems more attractive than pathetic.

The second version of the Mouse's Tale more directly foreshadows the climactic trial scene which precipitates Alice's exit from the mad Hades of her dream. But whereas the death-sentences meted out in a Wonderland courtroom could easily be evaded, the fate of the mouse in the second tale seems preordained. For "cunning old Fury" remains in absolute control. Who is this doomster? Does he stand for the relentlessness of a process by which all life ends in death, that other word beginning with the letter *D*? Or is his the controlled fury of an aloof satirist who can loom over change just as the Cat can soar above the litigants below? If so, the sentences pronounced by this prosecutor, judge, and juror rolled into one may well free those he condemns and remove them from the world into which Alice chooses to return.

As both these versions of the Mouse's Tale help to remind us, and as Carroll's revision of his book's closing paragraphs tends to confirm, there are always two distinct threats of death present in his Alice books. The Cheshire Cat tells Alice that she will encounter madness no matter which Wonderland path she chooses to tread. The same remark might be made about the omnipresence of death: the worlds of temporal power and of eternal play that are always competing in Alice's mental wanderings equally threaten her individuality. Alice refuses to be flattened into a symbol. If she were to become absorbed by Wonderland's illogic and cast her lot among its chimerical inhabitants, she would forever be someone else's toy. Yet her decision to waken into a world where trees periodically shed their leaves and mortals, just as predictably, shed their lives is intensely painful, if not to her, then to her creator. For, as he knows, the extraordinary little girl who runs away from her dream has merely delayed the advent of her death as an ordinary human being.

Carroll's involvement with the actual Alice Liddell made it difficult for him to consign her fictional namesake to the condition of perpetual arrest he so fervently desired for herself and himself. Even in the *Wonderland* text, where he wrested himself away from the spell of the oval photograph he had pasted at the end of *Under Ground,* he was not prepared to give primacy to either one of Alice's two contrary realms. When other writers followed Carroll in depicting a clash between a dreamworld and a world of growth, they took a more decisive, though one-sided, stance. Death itself could now preserve dream-children such as MacDonald's Diamond, as we shall see in chapter 7 of this book. In *At the Back of the North Wind,* this androgyne is allowed to return to a hazy mythical domain from which he has simply been borrowed for his short sojourn among the living. Diamond, at least, must vigorously carry out a this-worldly social mission in a drab Victorian London; but, by the turn of the century, Peter Pan can remain untainted by the City of Experience, sheltered and immune on his island of never-growing boys.

For Carroll, however, such resolutions are no more acceptable than the concessions to a world of growth that his immediate female successors— Ingelow, Rossetti, and Ewing—would soon dramatize in their own brilliant books for children. Eager to blend the imaginary with the mundane, he therefore seizes on the figure of Alice's sister as a better mediator than the morbid Mouse. The closures he devised for both *Under Ground* and *Wonderland* invite the reader to occupy the same threshold position held by this older sister. We shift to her mental processes, because only the mind, capable of memory as well as of prediction, can graft the wishfulness of fantasy unto a temporal order. The last paragraph of each book, almost identical, deliberately aligns the young and the old: the immature Alice and her maturer sister; a past Alice and a future Alice; the child-protagonist and her adult creator; juvenile auditors and grown-up readers. These contraries are briefly balanced through the rhetorical expression of a wish—a tactic that Carroll was to deploy again in *Through the Looking-Glass*. Just as the older sister hopes that a future Alice would recognize meanings and continuities she cannot yet fathom, so does the *Looking-Glass* narrator expect that the impatient girl who wants no more delays in the progression to her crowning may some day come to appreciate the White Knight's love-gift of a self-indulgent Song.

The heavily revised paragraphs leading up to this final expression of wishfulness, however, once more call attention to differences in emphasis between *Underground* and *Wonderland*. Since the first, more intimate, text is still tied to shared memories, Carroll uses the sister's reverie to recall familiar landmarks. The same merry crew steering their boat into a "setting sun" evoked in the dedicatory verses of *Wonderland* is recalled by the *Under Ground* sister who "began dreaming after a fashion." Rather than being set apart from the prose-text in prefatory verses, the scene here acts as the sentimental climax to a tale of loss. Grounded on land and in the present, the sister can also see herself slowly floating down a "winding" river, on a path that recedes as much as the words that Carroll had placed in a narrowing Mouse's Tale. The sister joins Alice in listening for the words of "a tale that was being told" by an unidentified teller (*UG,* chap. 4, 89). She is thus, simultaneously, a former participant, as well as a stranded observer, like the knight Bedivere who watches a dream-king drift away in Tennyson's "The Passing of Arthur."

But, unlike Bedivere, the sister is still a dream-voyager herself: like one of the three queens who ferry Arthur's mortal / immortal remains to the wonder-isle of Avalon, she guards idealized yearnings. Fancy can dress nostalgia with poetic apparel. The "ancient city" in the background of the winding river, though a makeshift Camelot, is literally Oxford, with its medieval spires. And the "music of voices" that is heard, as the boat disappears "after many turnings of the stream," though recalling the joyous shouts that greeted the translated Arthur, are the shrieks of delight of three little girls who are no more (*UG,* chap. 4, 90).

Similarly elegiac, the second version avoids the sentimentality of the first. Keats, rather than Tennyson, now acts as a poetic correlative. Loss is as prominent as before, but it is treated, as in "To Autumn," as a bridge between art and life. The mythical dreamworld that Alice vacates is at one with the "dull reality" surrounding her pensive sister. In the first of the two paragraphs which Carroll added for the 1865 text, the sister rehearses the sounds of Wonderland. Beginning with the White Rabbit's nervous rustling in the grass and the Mouse's frantic splashings in the pool, the catalogue becomes increasingly high-pitched: "Once more the shrieking of the Gryphon, the squeaking of the Lizard's slate-pencil, and the choking of the suppressed guinea-pigs, filled the air, mixed up with the distant sob of the miserable Mock Turtle" (*AW*, chap. 12, 98). The final focus on this weeper, rather than on a Cheshire Cat, its laughing foil, is exquisitely positioned.

In the second of the added paragraphs, the sister who has heard unheard sounds locates their sources by opening her eyes to the mutable landscape around her. Each of these "queer noises" has had a discernible origin, identified in a new catalogue that also concludes with "the Mock Turtle's heavy sobs." Significantly enough, the sister does not follow the sequential order in which Alice met the "strange creatures" whose sounds have been rehearsed. Instead, the order she follows seems to adhere to the proximity of their real-life location. The grass, still "rustling in the wind," through which the White Rabbit had scurried, comes first, because closest to the sister; the "cattle" whose "lowing" seems to have inspired the Mock-Turtle's sobs, are "in the distance," at the farthest remove (*AW*, chap. 12, 99, 98).

Like the sights and sounds in Keats's "To Autumn," this landscape is at once mythical and mutable. The cattle, like the "full-grown lambs" that bleat so strongly in Keats's ode, may well be clamoring because of the impending removal of the young: taken to a slaughter-house, calves and heifers will be converted into mock-turtle soup. There is nothing decorative about this revised ending. Pathos and irony interpenetrate. Just as the "wailful choir" which concludes Keats's blending of death and renovation affirms the music of a dying day, so does Carroll's plaintive closure transform the "confused clamor" of animals real *and* imagined into a hymn at once psychic and seasonal. Alice is now ready for a quest that will be linear, rather than circular. Although the threat of death remains in the reversed reality behind the looking-glass, she and Carroll could join forces, and, as a collaborative we, could sever the head of the dreaded Jabberwock. Separation might still be mastered.

Placed at the entry and exit of the more unreal elements of Alice's dream, Mouse and sister belong to a sort of epistemological border patrol. They preserve distinctions between rival notions of reality, yet also facilitate a traffic between contraries. Carroll's revisions of both the Mouse's Tale as well as of the sister's reformulation of Alice's dream suggest his desire to connect the realms of Play and Power. Although tempted to do so, he was unwilling to break off all contact between a dreamworld where unsexed Cheshire Cats can reign supreme and a temporal order in which little girls are encouraged to adopt the socio-sexual powers exerted by Victorian matriarchs. His realism demanded the bridge he would dramatize through Alice's crossings in still another pendant, *Through the Looking-Glass.*

SIX

Shrinking Alice: From Wonderland to Looking-Glass Land

Therefore all seasons shall be sweet to thee,
. . . .
       whether the eave-drops fall
Heard only in the trances of the blast,
Or if the secret ministry of the frost
Shall hang them up in silent icicles,
Quietly shining to the quiet Moon.
         —SAMUEL TAYLOR COLERIDGE,
           "Frost at Midnight"

       meantime the frost-wind blows
Like Love's alarum pattering the sharp sleet
Against the window-panes; St. Agnes' moon hath set.
         —JOHN KEATS, *"The Eve of St. Agnes"*

I

Like the "Summer" and "Autumn" photographs analyzed in the previous chapter, *Alice's Adventures in Wonderland* (1865) and *Through the Looking-Glass* (1871) can be read as seasonal pendants. The prefatory verses of *Wonderland* match the vernal scenery with which the prose narrative opens: Alice and her sister sit on a grassy bank that may border the same river on which they had glided as members of a storyteller's merry crew. Similarly, the "frost" and "blinding snow" featured in the verses that head *Through the Looking-Glass* recur at the outset of a story that promises a genial shelter. "The storm-wind's moody madness," the rhymes proclaim, cannot affect "childhood's nest of gladness"; Carroll's "magic words" shall make "the raving blast" inaudible to child-ears. This assurance is promptly repeated by Alice herself, when she tells the black kitten that it has nothing to fear from the snowstorm raging outside their room. The girl who now assumes the role of a finger-wagging adult "angry" at the misdemeanors of the childish kitten quickly reassures this derelict that it will not be thrust outdoors. For Alice insists that wintry frosts can be beneficent: "Do you hear the snow against the window-panes, Kitty? How nice and soft it sounds! I wonder if the snow *loves* the trees and fields, that it kisses them so gently?" (*LG*, 103, 109).

Lewis Carroll here offers more modulations on the Romantic antecedents he knows so well. His opening address to an immortal dream-child and Alice's faith that a wintry "white quilt" (*LG*, 109) can preserve the greenness of summer follow Coleridge's paean to a wonder-boy immune to seasonal change. At the same time, however, there is a darker mirroring: the frost that patters against Alice's window-panes also recalls the more unsettling experiences of another young fantasist, Keats's Madeline. This older, more fully sexualized dreamer fears the "iced gusts" that "rave and beat" outside her chamber of maiden thought. Her seducer's claim that this is "an elfin storm from faery land, / Of haggard seeming, but a boon indeed,"[1] is not borne out by the closure of a poem that begins and ends with the chill of mortality.

1. John Keats, "The Eve of St. Agnes," stanzas 37 and 39, lines 327, 344–45.

Carroll's own closure to his prefatory poem promises that no such chills shall mar his new Alice's dreams. Nine years have passed since the July afternoon of the first telling of the *Wonderland* adventures. The Mock Turtle's heavy sobs have become attenuated, transformed into the barely audible sighs of a small, mournful gnat:

> And, though the shadow of a sigh
> May tremble through the story
> For "happy summer days" gone by,
> And vanished summer glory—
> It shall not touch with breath of bale,
> The pleasance of our fairy-tale.
>
> (*LG,* 103; lines 31–36)

Still, despite the assurance of this last stanza, the prefatory poem retains the time-consciousness of the *Wonderland* text. The child whose photograph was inserted between the words "happy summer" and "days" in the "Under Ground" manuscript has, by 1871, become a young woman who is almost twenty years old. Just as the six stanzas of the poem Carroll placed in between the conclusion and the beginning of the two prose narratives act as a sort of fulcrum, so do its middle two stanzas offer a demarcation between past and present. The third stanza obsessively recreates, once again, the ambiance of the story-telling expedition undertaken by Carroll and his girl-auditors in the summer of 1862. But the fourth stanza, although ostensibly dwelling on a small child, introduces adult connotations. The sad maiden summoned to bed may not just be a little girl, but also one who, like Sleeping Beauty or Keats's Madeline, finds her "nest" raided by a member of the opposite sex:[2]

> Come, hearken then, ere voice of dread,
> With bitter tidings laden,

---

2. As James R. Kincaid notes in his edition of *Through the Looking-Glass,* "melancholy maiden" originally read "wilful, weary maiden" ([Berkeley: University of California Press, 1983], xxiii). While critics from Empson to Kincaid have remarked on the triple meaning of a "bed" that can stand for a child's resting place, a marriage bed, and a death-place, the ironic echoes of "The Eve of St. Agnes," a poem that conflates sexual consummation with extinction, appear to have gone unnoticed. When Carroll claims that his words shall sustain "childhood's nest of gladness," he seems to be countering the false assurance Keats's Porphyro proffers to Madeline: "Though I have found, I will not rob thy nest" (stanza 38, line 340).

Shall summon to unwelcome bed
A melancholy maiden!
We are but older children, dear,
Who fret to find our bedtime near.
(*LG* 103; lines 19–24)

In its emotional control, *Through the Looking-Glass* is a text that continues the distancing process begun in *Wonderland*. Although twenty years
always separate Lewis Carroll from Alice Liddell, her own egress from
childhood made the gap between these two "older children" less painful
than before. Whereas both the *Under Ground* and *Wonderland* texts were
fueled by the recent memory of pains and resentments, Carroll's nostalgia
and anger diminished once a marriageable young woman forever replaced
the playmate who had inspired "a tale begun in other days." The female
Other addressed in the poems that frame *Through the Looking-Glass* is still
a version of that unforgettable child, the recipient of yet another "love-gift
of a fairy-tale." But Carroll can now segregate the actual Alice from a
fictional counterpart who has aged a mere six months in a span of seven
actual years. And, rather than indulge sentimental longings or an aggressive desire for domination, he can mock the manifestation of such emotional excesses in a new set of male personages. From the White King,
whose pencil Alice appropriates as soon as she crosses the looking-glass
border, to the White Knight and Old Wasp who try to detain her before
she undertakes her very last crossing, the male figures Alice now meets
are far more fragile and ineffectual than she. Although the Mad Hatter
and March Hare are allowed to return, they have become subdued replicas
of their old antic selves.

In *Through the Looking-Glass* Carroll seems closer, intellectually at least,
to a resolute seven-and-a-half-year-old pilgrim than he was to the seven-
year-old heroines of the previous two *Alice* books. For he and she have
now become associates in a new venture. The "we" who are but-older-
children can become better partners, as companionable spirits and fellow
problem-solvers, than the "we" who glided down a river. The rowboat
formerly plied by little arms with little skill has been replaced by chess
pieces whose rudimentary movements the new Alice at least has mastered.
She may have recently lost a game to an unnamed opponent: "when we
were playing just now," she ruefully reminds the black kitten, she might
have won, "if it hadn't been for that nasty Knight, that came wriggling
down my pieces" (*LG,* 110). Although Carroll suggests here, early in the

narrative, that he hardly intends to abdicate his control of the chess board on which his dream-child moves with such determination, this self-driven Alice is certainly less of a pawn than her much-tormented *Wonderland* and *Under Ground* counterparts.

There is even a certain looking-glass parity between Alice's handling of the Black Kitten and Carroll's handling of Alice. For Alice herself now possesses the deliberate skills of a fiction-maker. She invests the kitten with her own superiority when she converts the small creature into a Red Queen who has "grown" from "three inches high" to become "half a head taller than Alice herself" (*LG,* 123). Until the end of her dream, Alice will, as a self-appointed pawn, defer to the fictitious authority of this figure, the most powerful piece on the chess board. Only when her own queening still leaves her discontented does the waking Alice revoke the powers she has conferred. By shaking a shrunken Red Queen back into the shape of a small kitten, she now displays the same powers of enlargement and reduction that Carroll had exerted over Alice herself in Wonderland.

The implied author of *Looking-Glass* similarly agrees to a temporary divestment of his own control. Just as Alice ostensibly defers to a Red Queen whom she has endowed with her own power, Carroll purports to defer to Alice for the duration of the dream-game. His male personations—a dozing Red King, a feeble Gnat, the immature Tweedles, a Humpty Dumpty unable to do the simplest subtractions, and a hopelessly muddled White Knight—seem inferior to the determined little girl who has taken the infant Lily's place. Yet when Alice reclaims her powers by aborting her dream, Carroll drops his own mask of impotence. With the game over, a player who may have feigned his own sleep, as the spuriously dozing "Uncle" Dodgson was wont to do, reasserts the supremacy of his own design. Like Alice, he is fond of games which involve "Let's pretend."

When Alice's logical older sister, "being very exact," insists that a player can only pretend to be a single Other, Alice demurs: "Well, *you* can be one of them, then, and *I'll* be all the rest" (*LG,* 110). Lewis Carroll here seems to side with a younger child's infinite capacity for multiple impersonations. Yet, in Alice's dream-game, it is Carroll who adopts a variety of guises, while the girl can only "be one." Moreover, when at the end of the narrative, Carroll has Alice-the-dreamer concede that she may in fact have been dreamed by that non-player, the sleeping Red King, he suggests that this active girl may well be as much of a male self-projection as any of the story's passive and fragile men. If so, is not Alice's autonomy as spurious as that which she has chosen to give to the Red Queen? Christina Rossetti certainly thought so when she attributed to Carroll's imagination the same voracity shown by the Walrus and Carpenter. The hunger of the unsavory duo who continue to speak to oyster-others even after having consumed them with bread and butter was promptly transferred by Rossetti and her illustrator Arthur Hughes to the figure of the ever-hungry Mouth-Boy in *Speaking Likenesses*.[3]

Yet it is also possible to view Carroll's empowering of the *Looking-Glass* Alice in a less cannibalistic light. For, unlike the marooned male figures she bypasses, Alice engages in a "drive towards self-mastery" that is every bit as Carrollian as their solipsism.[4] Whereas the *Wonderland* Alice was subjected to the irrationality of childish figures she misread as adults, the *Looking-Glass* Alice embodies Carroll's much stronger endorsement of the mastery that comes through growth. She is therefore the forceful, forward-looking "one" who can counter "all the rest" in a self-division that pits her against Carroll's continued attraction to the arrested state of being he now represents through notoriously vulnerable surrogates rather than through an invulnerable Cheshire Cat. These childish and childlike figures are not only, as Donald Rackin would have it, Alice's "dead selves," the emblems of an infantilism she must discard, but also remain an integral component of Carroll's lingering fondness for the *Wonderland* circularities of madness and play that he, as much as she, had resolved to leave behind. The new Alice thus is crucial to a revisionary project in which "moody madness" can be resisted. Despite her subordination as dreamer to Carroll's own fictional dream-constructions, this Alice functions as an agent who persistently shows herself to be far more inventive and independent than her easily frustrated *Wonderland* predecessor. Placed in a mirror-world in which space and time are reversible, this intelligent child repeatedly finds herself called upon to decode rules and meanings she is eager to master.

The irrationality of the *Wonderland* denizens was matched by the abruptness with which unpredictable events were thrust upon a girl who had thoughtlessly stumbled down a rabbit-hole. But the *Looking-Glass* Alice, while still awake, is given a full chance to anticipate the potential consequence of her ventures into an alternate reality. This more reflective child, who seems highly interested in giving a structure to her experiences,

3. See chapter 10, pp. 369–71, below.

4. Donald Rackin, *Alice's Adventures in Wonderland and Through the Looking-Glass: Nonsense, Sense, and Meaning* (New York: Twayne Publishers, 1991), 78.

has already formed "ideas" about the topography of the place she explores in her waking imagination. From her observation of the books in the reflected drawing room, for instance, she has deduced what she will shrewdly put to use when she comes upon "Jabberwocky," namely that, in the world behind the mirror, "the words go the wrong way" (*LG,* 110).

Whereas the reckless *Wonderland* Alice, "burning with curiosity," never once considered the consequences of plopping down a rabbit-hole (*AW,* 8), her *Looking-Glass* counterpart gives curiosity an intellectual dimension. She is a mini-logician who can empirically build on received knowledge. The first Alice found that the lore her elders drilled into her proved useless in an underground where memorized poems came out ventriloquially altered. The chess-player of *Through the Looking-Glass,* however, relies on mental capacities she has already tested in her everyday world. Her understanding of "pretence"—the designation of arbitrary, yet consistent meanings that would allow her to convert herself into a hyaena and her "frightened old nurse" into a bone—makes her own ventures into fantasylands far less disconcerting. Although she cannot decode the words of "Jabberwocky" even after she has figured out that she must read the text from left to right, she remains sufficiently interested in "the meaning" of a poem that filled her "head with ideas" to consult Humpty Dumpty about it, five chapters and fifty pages later (*LG,* 164, 118).

Alice Raikes Wilson-Fox's often-quoted 1932 anecdote about the mirror-test to which she was subjected by Lewis Carroll may not validate her claim about having given him "his first idea for *Alice Through the Looking-Glass.*"[5] Nonetheless, it sheds light on an alliance not yet possible in the *Under Ground* and *Wonderland* texts by showing the contiguity between the thinking capacities of an adult mathematician and a precocious girl:

> One day, hearing my name, he called me to him, saying, "So you are another Alice. I'm very fond of Alices. Would you come and see something that is rather puzzling?" We followed him into his house, which opened, as ours did, upon a garden, into a room full of furniture with a tall mirror standing across one corner.
>
> "Now," he said, giving me an orange, "first tell me which hand you have got that in." "The right," I said. "Now," he said, "go and stand before that glass, and tell me which hand the little girl you see there has the orange in." After some perplexed

5. Alice Wilson-Fox, "So You Are Another Alice," reprinted in *Lewis Carroll: Interviews and Recollections,* ed. Morton N. Cohen (Iowa City: University of Iowa Press, 1989), 197.

contemplation, I said, "The left hand." "Exactly," he said. "And how do you explain that?" I couldn't explain it, but seeing that some solution was expected, I ventured, "If I was on the *other* side of the glass, wouldn't the orange still be in my right hand?" I can remember his laugh. "Well done, little Alice," he said. "The best answer I've had yet."[6]

Carroll's hope that Alice Raikes might come up with "some solution" to the puzzle he posed and his obvious delight in the resourceful way in which she had framed her answer show an investment in the child's reasoning capacities that is totally at odds with the Mad Hatter's utter lack of interest in the *Wonderland* Alice's ability to solve his riddle. Any attempt to find likenesses between ravens and writing desks must rely on ingenious wrenchings that remain funny because of the essential incongruity of the entities being yoked. Yet there *are* plausible ways to explain the asymmetry of reflected images, and, hence, to account for the unlikeness of fundamental likenesses. On a chess board, the facing figures are asymmetrical: what is left is right. And, by extension, as the *Looking-Glass* Alice soon discovers, progress can be made through regress, goals ahead can be reached by walking backwards, and, if one trusts the White Queen, even memory might move both ways: "It's a poor memory that only works backwards" (*LG,* 150). The elementary rules of reversal that a small chess player has mastered thus may eventually offer an emancipation from the tyrant Time who, according to the Mad (and maddening) Hatter, "wo'n't stand beating" (*AW,* 56). Therefore, Alice Raikes or the *Looking-Glass* Alice or any beginner capable of finding a logic in what seems illogical or antithetical already holds a key that an abstract thinker can use to unlock more sophisticated puzzles worthy of a Wittgenstein.

When Carroll delegates to the *Looking-Glass* Alice many of the commentaries and parenthetical asides that would have been made by the ironic narrator of *Wonderland,* he suggests that he and his forward-moving heroine have become far more alike than they were during her circular adventures underground. The condescension with which the *Wonderland* narrator had treated an error-prone "poor little thing" was manifest in his parenthetical glosses whenever she misused words such as "antipathies" or showed her ignorance of the actual meaning of "grand words" such as Latitude or Longitude, as well as in his mock-approval of her recollection that, "if you drink much from a bottle marked 'poison,' it is almost certain

6. Ibid., 196–97.

to disagree with you sooner or later" (*AW*, 12, 8, 11). In the *Looking-Glass* text, however, where Alice's inferences and thoughts are always treated with great respect, the narrator even apologizes for his brief intervention in chapter 1: "But this is taking us away from Alice's speech to the kitten" (*LG*, 110). His deference to her point of view is such that he professes himself unable to explain what sort of "wages" Humpty Dumpty might have paid to the words in his service: "Alice didn't venture to ask what he paid them with; and so you see I ca'n't tell you" (*LG*, 164). Although eventually Carroll pulls rank on Alice, he is perfectly content to let her be his stand-in for the duration of the *Looking-Glass* games. He can afford to nap while this able agent carries out his design.

II

The intimate connections between Carroll and the *Looking-Glass* Alice surface, curiously enough, in an episode devoid of any overtly Carrollian surrogates such as Humpty Dumpty or the White Knight. In chapter 3, Alice meets the Fawn within the wood "where things have no names" (*LG*, 135). The scene captures a brief moment of perfect symbiosis such as that which George MacDonald would have rendered through the total union between a child and its mother's body.[7] Alice's forward progress is halted when she suddenly loses her memory of signifiers. She has forgotten the name for "wood": enjoying the forest's shade, she tells herself that it was a comfort "to get into—into—the *what*"? As she places her "hand on the trunk of a tree," the object she touches becomes a mere "this," causing her to wonder what "it" might call "itself" (*LG*, 135). Immediately thereafter, her own name—and, with it, her gender—also vanishes. Indistinguishable from all others, she is ready to meet the genderless Fawn:

> She stood silent for a minute, thinking: then suddenly she began again.
> "Then it really *has* happened, after all! And now, who am I? I *will* remember, if I can! I'm determined to do it!" But being determined didn't help her much, and all she could say, after a great deal of puzzling was "L, I *know* it begins with L!"
> Just then a Fawn came wandering by: it looked at Alice with its large gentle eyes, but didn't seem at all frightened. "Here then! Here then!" Alice said, as she held out her hand and started to stroke it; but it only started back a little, and then stood looking at her again.

7. See the discussion in the next chapter, pp. 246–47, below.

"What do you call yourself?" the Fawn said at last. Such a soft sweet voice it had! "I wish I knew," thought poor Alice. She answered, rather sadly, "Nothing, just now."

"Think again," it said: "that won't do."

Alice thought but nothing came of it. "Please, would you tell me what *you* call yourself?" she said timidly. "I think that might help a little." (*LG*, 136)

Like Alice's encounter earlier in the same chapter with another "it," the minuscule Gnat, her relation to the Fawn allows Carroll to dramatize the arbitrariness of the names through which we signify individuation and difference. The Gnat had prepared Alice for the loss of identity that she would suffer in the wood where all things lack names, and, what is more, had shyly hinted that such a self-suppression might actually be desirable. (In fact, the Gnat's own self-erasure took place right after Alice dismissed its feeble pun about a nameless Miss who might go unmissed even when amiss in her obligations.) Yet whereas this puny punster can easily be construed as a Carrollian self-parody, there seems to be no such authorial delegate wandering in the wood in which Fawn and Alice briefly fuse before becoming separated again by the return of their self-consciousness.

Still, the momentary erasure of her name makes it possible for Alice's identity to touch that of the writer who would later cast himself as the amnesiac (and dissolving) Baker in "The Hunting of the Snark." Their contact in this scene is as brief as that between her hand and the tree trunk she touches but cannot name and even shorter than that between her arms and the creature whose neck she so "lovingly" clasps before it identifies itself as Fawn and calls her a "human child" (*LG*, 137). Aware of its insignificance, the puny Gnat knew that it would not be much missed by a determined young miss. And, indeed, although she is always concerned about injuries that larger beings might suffer (the fighting Tweedles, the dangerously perched Humpty Dumpty, even the trusting little oysters), Alice hardly seemed upset when the Gnat dissolved into nothingness after shedding "two large tears" (*LG*, 135). Whereas the Gnat's concern with separation seems as imbalanced as the Mock Turtle's morbidity in the previous book, Alice remains decidedly unsentimental.

Ostensibly, then, a dissolution of self might involve distancing rather than bonding. If the Carrollian Gnat's lapse into nothingness failed to affect Alice, the nothingness caused by her own momentary bout of amnesia might well further separate her from, rather than bring her closer to, the intelligence that calls itself "Lewis Carroll." Indeed, as soon as she fails to remember the words for "wood," "tree," and "Fawn," as well as for herself, Alice's role as Carroll's surrogate intelligence must necessarily weaken. No longer able to depend on her point of view, the reader now has to rely on Carroll's narrator for an identification of the objects—tree and fawn—touched by a child who finds herself, like a baby, suddenly incapable of separating Self from Other. Accordingly, the scene reenergizes a voice that, until this point in the narrative, had persistently deferred to Alice's alert self-musings. Like the *Wonderland* ironist who had mocked the earlier Alice's use of words that were totally inappropriate to her situation, the narrator activated in this scene now questions the vocabulary of an amnesiac. Carroll thus immediately undercuts Alice's resolute, "I'm determined to do it!," by wryly noting that "being determined didn't help her much" (*LG*, 136).

And yet, at the same time, this episode also confirms Alice's and Carroll's oneness. Straining to recall her name, Alice can come up only with one letter of the alphabet, *L*. In glossing her choice, recent editors of *Through the Looking-Glass* have not been quite as helpful as one might have expected from their diligence on so many other occasions: although Martin Gardner and James Kincaid are less laconic than Donald Gray, who simply tells us that "Liddell begins with *L*" (*LG*, 136n), they shed almost as little light on the matter. Gardner, to be sure, asks us to remember that "Lily," the name of the pawn whose place Alice has taken, also begins with *L*, while Kincaid directs his readers, with a glee that almost seems unbecoming, to Peter Heath's rather chilling deconstructive emphasis: "since the fictional Alice's name begins with an *A*, it is impossible that she should KNOW it to begin with anything else."[8]

Fortunately, however, there is a much wider range of possibilities, and since these happen to serve my own argument about Carroll's identification with the *Looking-Glass* Alice, I shall gladly el-ucidate. Carroll had already played with *L* anagrams in *Wonderland*, when he gave the names of Elsie and Lacie to Alice's older sister and herself in the story about three little girls told by the sleepy Dormouse (a Dodgson surrogate). By making "Elsie" out of "L. C.," he could signify kinship through the initials that Lorina Charlotte shared with himself as Lewis Carroll, the mirror image of "C. L." (Charles Lutwidge). And by pushing an *L* before the *A* in "Lacie," he could play with his favorite child's name by giving it the same

8. Martin Gardner, ed., *The Annotated Alice*, (New York: Clarkson N. Potter, 1960), 226n; Kincaid, ed., *Through the Looking-Glass*, 34, n. 11.

initial as "Lewis" (the pseudonymous *L*-name *he* had pushed before his *C*-name).[9] (The choice of "Lacie" also enabled him to approximate the name for the sororal alter ego Wordsworth had called "Lucy," and perhaps even allowed him to hint that Alice could quite possibly be closer to a torpid and "lazy" Dormouse than she might have supposed.)

In finding common letters for himself and female alter egos, Carroll was merely following a practice he had begun as a child: as Morton Cohen has recently pointed out, the boy built for his beloved older sister Elizabeth Lucy a miniature toolbox that he inscribed, "E. L. D. from C. L. D.," in order to stress their common middle initial.[10] Since Victorian older sisters often acted as surrogates for a mother distracted by the birth of subsequent children, the boy who clung to the maiden-name of his Lutwidge parent felt a special kinship with Elizabeth / Lucys or Lorina / Elsies as well as Lacies.[11] When, at the end of the *Wonderland* and *Under Ground* texts, he anticipates for an older Alice the role of children's storyteller he had

---

9. Donald Rackin rightly notes that the elimination of the paternal name and the inversion/conversion of "Charles Lutwidge" into "Lewis Carroll" created a "decided shift from an unambiguous masculinity to a surreptitious femininity," since Lutwidge was Dodgson's mother's maiden name and Carroll (or Carol) is often a feminine name. Rackin also finds it "very tempting" to speculate whether the very adoption of the "L. C." *nom de plume* might not have been stimulated by Dodgson's attraction to "Lacie" Liddell, although he acknowledges that the choice of pseudonym probably anteceded his first encounter with the four-year-old child (Rackin, *Alice's Adventures,* 158n).

10. Morton N. Cohen, *Lewis Carroll: A Biography* (New York: Alfred A. Knopf, 1995), 12.

11. Elsie, Lacie, and Tillie, the three little girls in the Dormouse's aborted tale, seem eager to recover a maternity lost when they draw "all manner of things—everything that begins with an M—"; when Alice wants to know, "Why with an M?," the March Hare silences her with, "Why not?" (*AW,* 60). A similar breakdown occurs in *Looking-Glass* when Alice asks Humpty Dumpty to explain the meaning of "*mome raths*": "Well, a '*rath*' is a sort of green pig: but '*mome*' I'm not certain about. I think it's short for "from home"—meaning that they'd lost their way, you know" (*LG,* 166). Why does Humpty Dumpty, so confident about his definitions, suddenly admit some uncertainty here? And why, after having expounded on "portmanteau" words such as "slithy" and "mimsy," is he so reluctant to link the loss of mom with the exile from home? As noted in my introductory chapter, Victorian boys suffered a loss of femininity by being sent to boarding schools while still too "green" and innocent. Did Carroll blame his mother for the indignities he suffered at Rugby, a place in which he saw abused boys turn into pigs? Humpty Dumpty's elision fits a book in which the anger at mothers such as the Duchess and the Queen of Hearts has been greatly diluted.

adopted for himself, Carroll tries to signify his kinship with the sustaining imagination of the mothers, governesses, maiden aunts, and older sisters dramatized in juvenile fictions as much as in actual nurseries of the Victorian middle-class.

The momentary loss of her full name allows the *Looking-Glass* Alice to experience the abolition of all barriers between self and not-self so coveted by Carroll's Romantic forebears and so evident in his own compulsive self-projections on prepubescent children. The little boy who ventures into "some far-distant wood" in Wordsworth's "Nutting" has been appareled in "cast-off weeds" that make him every bit as "quaint" a figure as the Tweedle twins whom Alice also swaddles in protective layerings after she resumes her role of quasi-adult caretaker (lines 8, 9). Yet as soon as this mini-knight stumbles upon "one dear nook / Unvisited" (lines 16–17), he forgets his mission. As a denuded Adamic child, he can merge with the "green stones" and "shady trees" around him, and even hear the sounds of eternal "fairy-water breaks" (lines 36, 35, 33). Upon waking from this state of suspension, the boy aggressively reasserts the masculine identity conferred to him by adults. With a violence that exceeds that of the tree-hitting Tweedles or the jousting Red and White Knights, he defaces the womb-like bower with "merciless ravage" (line 45). Nonetheless, for a moment as fleeting as Alice's own brief sojourn in the wood of unnaming, the boy had managed to recapture the state of oneness that exists before the onset of individuation and self-consciousness. His short-lived moment of bliss thus is akin to the short-lived harmony that Coleridge so differently represented, around the same time, in "Kubla Khan," with its celebration of the soon-shattered dome so perilously perched near the mazes of the sacred river Alph.

When Alice, similarly retreating into a magical wood and similarly treading back to the alpha of an earlier existence, forgets that her name begins with that first letter, she is following the laws of regress and reversal that operate elsewhere in Looking-Glass land. Since the name "Alice Pleasance Liddell," if held against a mirror, would read "Lleddil Ecnasaelp Ecila," and the initials "A. P. L." would turn into "L. P. A.," Alice is quite correct in assuming that the first letter of her name is an *L*. But this act of alphabetic reversal by a girl who has forgotten the names for "wood" and "tree" also betokens her identity with whatever she sees. Imprinted by her surroundings, she has herself become a stock. While still an undergraduate at Christ Church, Lewis Carroll had written a mock-epic, *The*

Ligniad, for a cherished college chum, George Girdlestone Woodhouse.[12] By using the Latin word for wood, *Lignum,* for his poem's title, he could simultaneously play with his friend's name and revive their shared fun with an ancient text that had featured a wooden horse almost as preposterous as a Rocking-horse-fly, which, as the Gnat so helpfully explains to Alice, "is made entirely of wood" (*LG,* 133). When Alice claims that "it begins with L," the child for whom wood and tree and her own name have blended as indistinguishable "its" has unwittingly acquired the Latin education of an Oxford don.

The "El" that Alice produces may also carry the religious resonance by which Coleridge tried to dignify his and Wordsworth's yearning for the dissolution of self. When he defined the primary imagination as "a repetition in the finite mind of the eternal act of creation in the infinite I AM,"[13] Coleridge was, of course, referring to the human or finite mind's replication of the divine or infinite spirit who in the Old Testament wants to go unnamed and hence to be known simply as "I am who I am." Whether singular as "Eloah" or plurally designated as "Elohim," this God is not only inscribed in the Hebrew name that Charles Lamb and Mary Ann Evans used for their own pseudonyms (from Elijah, Elia and Eliot), but also is embedded in all acts of relation between any mortal "I" and Himself, and, indeed, among all mortal egos. Once again, Alice, whether a Lacie or Lucy or Lily or Liddell (or the She who is "Elle"), seems quite correct in answering her own "who am I?" with the assertion that she knows "it begins with L!" For so does the identity of Lewis or Lutwidge, her invisible twin, or, for that matter, of the twins she next encounters, Dum and Dee, the Tweed-*el* boys.

Yet before she can face the two men who look "so exactly like a couple of great schoolboys" (*AW,* 139), Alice must separate herself from her fellow

---

12. See Anne Clark, *Lewis Carroll: A Biography* (New York: Schocken, 1979), 76; also, Richard Wallace, *The Agony of Lewis Carroll* (Melrose, Massachusetts: Gemini Press, 1990), 155. The friendship with Woodhouse, who died a year before Carroll, eventually gave Dodgson access to female Oxford undergraduates: when Woodhouse's daughter Ruth, "slightly shy and silent," enrolled at Lady Margaret Hall, Carroll took her to the theater and "promised her to teach her my 'Logic' method—or to give lectures on it to her and others at the Hall, if it were wished" (*The Letters of Lewis Carroll,* ed. Morton N. Cohen, with the assistance of Roger Lancelyn Green [New York: Oxford University Press, 1978], 2:661n.).

13. Samuel Taylor Coleridge, *Biographia Literaria* (London: Dent, 1962), 167.

child, the young fawn. Carroll deliberately avoids specifying its sex. And yet the description of its "soft neck" and "its beautiful brown eyes" seems suggestive (*AW*, 137). Although she had been quite undisturbed by the disappearance of the tearful Gnat, Alice now finds herself "almost ready to cry with vexation at having lost her dear little fellow-traveler so suddenly," thereby indulging the same emotion that Carroll's Looking-Glass surrogates such as the Gnat and White Knight feel on having to part with her. Yet the girl quickly overcomes this momentary bout of nostalgic weakness. She professes to find great "comfort" in the restoration of her identity and name: "Alice—Alice—I won't forget it again. And now, which of these finger-posts ought I follow, I wonder?" (*AW*, 137). Alice has fully recovered her purposiveness, her sense of direction.

Momentarily lost in the amnesiac haze in which she and Fawn could become one, and in which, through a wishful gender-blurring, she could become Lewis Carroll and the velvety fawn turn into a beautiful Alice Liddell, the little pilgrim can once again press forward and try to advance to the next square. Her arrest—which took up almost all of the *Under Ground* and *Wonderland* texts—has been confined to this one brief sojourn in a magical wood. And yet, this time, no tears are shed over a symbiosis lost. The partnership between the man who wanted to be a girl and the girl who wants to be a woman can continue. Indeed, that partnership has been strengthened through the invisible contact between an unnamed player and his agent, the resolute child who has regained her name.

III

Lewis Carroll's temporary delegation of his own narrative powers to the *Looking-Glass* Alice is prefigured in the first chapter just after she has crossed the mirror. Looming over chess pieces who have not yet assumed human sizes, Alice carefully lifts up the tiny White King after he has been accidentally knocked into the ashes by his mate. Despite her solicitude, however, Alice cannot resist treating this Lilliputian monarch with an amused condescension which strongly resembles that shown by the *Wonderland* narrator, in the first chapter of the earlier book, towards the diminished girl who "tired herself out" while trying to climb up the slippery legs of a table (*AW*, 12). When the *Looking-Glass* Alice "gently" picks up the scared little King and dusts him off before she sets him on the table, she cannot help but laugh at his predicament:

She said afterwards that she had never seen in all her life such a face as the King made, when he found himself held in the air by an invisible hand, and being dusted; he was far too astonished to cry out, but his eyes and his mouth went on getting larger and larger, and rounder and rounder, till her hand shook so with laughter that she nearly let him drop upon the floor.

"Oh! *please* don't make such faces, my dear!" she cried out, quite forgetting that the King couldn't hear her. (*LG,* 115)

Carroll uses this interlude to signify several major differences between the *Wonderland* and *Looking-Glass* Alices and between their respective ventures. The phrase, "She said afterwards that . . . ," becomes an important refrain, reiterated throughout the ensuing account of Alice's square-by-square progress on the chessboard. The *Wonderland* Alice half-forgot the dream she retold "as well as she could remember" to an older sister who filtered it further by replaying its salient events (*AW,* 98). Beset by arbitrary changes in size and other unforeseen threats to her integrity, the earlier Alice seemed happy to have evaded the arrested phantasmagoria of mad tea parties, trials, and grinning Cheshire Cats. But the self-assured *Looking-Glass* Alice, who already controls most portions of a dream she has herself induced, proves that her total mastery of remembered details will even extend into the future.

The repetition of the "afterwards" refrain thus guarantees an aftermath that remained in doubt in the *Wonderland* narrative until the waking Alice shattered the timeless present of a dream in which she might have been enisled forever as a flattened underground denizen. The *Looking-Glass* narrative, however, not only depends on Alice's firm point of view *as* she experiences her adventures, but also interjects persistent reminders of her future authority as teller of her own tale. Thus, for instance, in chapter 2, the description of a path which gives "a sudden twist and shook itself" not only purports to be faithful to Alice's sensations as a dreamer but also supposedly is rendered exactly "as she described it afterwards" (*LG,* 120). Retrospection can impose a further order on whatever seemed slightly disorienting in Alice's programmatic advances on the chessboard. Unable to make out how she and the Red Queen managed to accelerate at such a frenzied pace, Alice can slow down the motion by "thinking about it afterwards" (*LG,* 126). The limited perspective of a pawn that Alice has adopted may make it difficult for her to follow the Queen's dizzying movements. But she is hardly as terrified or perplexed by such convulsions as the little King who, when unable to see the giantess who has lifted him and his Queen, is convinced that he has been blown up by a volcano. Like the faster Red Queen, Alice the pawn always moves horizontally; she is not subject to the vertical transpositions that so unsettled her *Wonderland* predecessor and now discomfit the grimacing White King.

When an invisible and unheard Alice raises the King, she assumes an almost god-like stature. But even after she shares the identity of the chess pieces by taking Lily's place, she maintains her superior point of view. Not only will the ineffectual White Queen and King still depend on her upon their reappearance later in the game, but the Gnat, the Tweedles, Humpty Dumpty, the Lion and the Unicorn, the White Knight, and the Old Wasp are also shown to be the subordinates of a child who continues to count on her knowledge and quick intelligence. The amusement with which a Brobdingnagian Alice views the little king will recur in her interactions with several of the other figures. Her laughter becomes a constant. Dancing with the Tweedles in a ring seems so "natural (she remembered afterwards)," that she is unsurprised "to hear music playing": "'But it certainly *was* funny,' (Alice said afterwards, when she was telling her sister the history of all this), 'to find myself singing *"Here we go round the mulberry bush"*'" (*LG,* 139). Unlike the weepy Wonderland Alice, this player thoroughly enjoys most of her adventures. When Tweedledum suggests that she may be unreal, a mere figment of someone else's imagination, she starts to cry, but quickly finds herself "half laughing through her tears" because she reasons that if she weren't real, "I shouldn't be able to cry" (*LG,* 145).

As a fashioner of narratives, Alice competes with all the male storytellers she finds behind the looking-glass. Her superiority to them is immediately established in her encounter with the White King, whose ineffectuality in imposing order on events thus anticipates the difficulties with sequential narratives experienced by all of Alice's later foils. Terribly upset by Alice's efforts to dust him off and smooth "his hair" (after the manner of Dinah's own cleansing operations on her kittens), the White King chooses to play dead. Finding no water around to revive him, Alice considers, significantly enough, pouring out the contents of "a bottle of ink" (*LG,* 115). Instead, finding him revived, she soon chooses to wield another writing tool, the King's very own pencil. For, still reeling from the "horror of that moment," the shocked King has tried to compose himself by placing his experience within some narrative. His first verbal account, already in the past tense, falsifies the trauma: "I assure you, my dear," he tells his hardier wife, "I turned cold to the end of my whiskers" (*LG,* 115). When the Queen points out that he lacks whiskers, he agrees that a better way to bring his emotions under control might be to write them down in his memorandum-book. This distancing tactic, so similar to Lewis Carroll's replaying of memorable events in his diaries as well as in his fictions, seems to be the King's prime defense against speedy changes and abrupt movements—an aversion he will continue to exhibit later in the book:[14]

Alice looked on with great interest as the King took an enormous memorandum-book out of his pocket, and began writing. A sudden thought struck her, and she took hold of the end of the pencil, which came some way over his shoulder, and began writing for him.

The poor King looked puzzled and unhappy, and struggled with the pencil for some time without saying anything; but Alice was too strong for him, and at last he panted out "My dear! I really *must* get a thinner pencil. I ca'n't manage this one a bit: it writes all manner of things that I don't intend—"

"What manner of things?" said the Queen, looking over the book (in which Alice had put '*The White Knight is sliding down the poker. He balances very badly*'). "That's not a memorandum of your feelings." (*LG,* 115)

Alice's appropriation of the King's pencil results in a double mockery of male impotence. Not only is "she too strong" for a monarch who can no more wield his huge pencil than the scepter he vainly brandishes in Tenniel's drawing, but she also underscores the ineffectuality of the King's ally (and Carroll's later impersonation), the White Knight. By forcing a would-be author to write words he did not "intend," Alice is again reversing the hierarchy observed in the *Wonderland* text. There, it was Alice, worried about her identity, who tried to order her feelings by reciting Watts's verses about a busy little bee, only to discover that "the words did not come the same as they used to do" (*AW,* 17). The ventriloquist author who delighted in making Alice's "voice sound hoarse and strange" and who turned a song against idleness and mischief into a mischievous crocodilian parody no longer is an impish presence in *Through the Looking-Glass.* He has now been replaced by Alice herself. It is she who toys with both White King and White Knight, those Carrollian idlers and misfits.

The *Looking-Glass* Alice, then, is quite deliberately presented as a mir-

14. In chapter 7, "The Lion and the Unicorn," Alice comes upon "the White King seated on the ground, busily writing in his memorandum book," apparently recording the movement of the 4,207 horses and men he has vainly sent to put Humpty Dumpty together (*LG,* 170). Informed by Alice that she has seen his Queen running by, pursued by "some enemy," he professes himself unable to help out (given his more constricted movements on the board): "But I'll make a memorandum about her, if you like—She's a dear good creature . . . Do you spell 'creature' with a double 'e'?" (*LG,* 175).

25 John Tenniel, Hands in *Wonderland* and *Looking-Glass*

ror image of the narrator who dominated the heroine of the *Wonderland* text. For the relation between Alice and Carroll's self-personations has now been reversed. The notoriously childish male surrogates of his third attempt to render Alice's adventures are now treated by her in the superior way that she had been treated by Carroll's narrator and by earlier agents, whether hostile, like the Mad Hatter, or friendly, like the Cheshire Cat. The specular inversions observed elsewhere in the text thus also apply to its mode of narration. It is true that the *Wonderland* text had already sporadically anticipated what this sequel carries out much more programmatically. The ineffectual White King is, after all, foreshadowed by the King of Hearts, and, as noted earlier, the Gnat's propensity for tears as well as puns follows the precedent established by the Mock-Turtle. There also are distinct parallels, which Tenniel's illustrations only ratify, between the giantess who toys with the White King and the enlarged Alice who dropped a White Rabbit on a bed of glass (see fig. 25).

Yet Tenniel's pendant drawings also offer a distinct contrast between two kinds of superiority. There is a major difference between the retaliatory aggression of a giantess as childish as any of her underground foils and the solicitude shown by the would-be adult who treats the black kitten and the White King as if they were little children. The claw-like hand that drops a terrified Rabbit is the antithesis of the hand that lifts an equally terrified King. Forced to repeat the fall imposed on Alice by a laughing narrator, the Rabbit becomes a fellow victim who is denied the cushion of Alice's soft landing. Since this timid creature poses no threat to someone who, being "about a thousand times as large," has "no reason to be afraid of it" (*AW*, 29), he is no more of an adversary than those Edenic innocents whom a vengeful and ironic arch-fiend hoped to bring down to the netherworld into which he had himself been plunged. Although the girl who kicks Bill the Lizard and hurts the White Rabbit is certainly not a Satanist, she has been clearly infected by the sadism of Wonderland; her claw-like fingers recall the aggressive Dinah, a hunter of rodents and birds. By way of contrast, the upward moving thumb and forefinger belong to a caretaker who emulates, if not Christ[15] (or even the invisible I Am, Author of all goodness), then at least the maternal *Looking-Glass* Dinah. As authorial deity, this new Alice is neither an angry retaliator nor an ironist content to pare her fingernails.

It seems significant that Alice's eyes should move from the hysterical King—about whose condition she is "still a little anxious" and whom she is still prepared to douse with ink, "in case he fainted again"—to a book lying on the same table. The text of "Jabberwocky" poses a much greater challenge than the blank pages of the little King's memorandum-book. But, like the "beamish boy" of the poem she now tries to decode, Alice passes her first test. The child-hero in the poem is sent on a mission by an adult, much like the mini-knight in Wordsworth's "Nutting," mentioned above, or even the neophyte in Browning's "'Childe Roland To the Dark Tower Came.'" In one of the parenthetical interventions as a commentator so prominent in *Wonderland* but so rare in the *Looking-Glass* text, Carroll questions Alice's notion that she has read a "pretty" poem by informing us that "she couldn't make it out at all" (*LG*, 118). And yet her attempt to summarize its contents seems apt: "*somebody* killed *something:* that's clear at any rate—" (*LG*, 118). If the poem's protagonist manages to behead a

---

15. Still, the similarity between a girl who is willing to adopt the fragile identity of "Lily" the pawn and a deity willing to assume a human shape seems inescapable. Just as portions of *Wonderland* foreshadow the mode of *Looking-Glass*, so are there occasional foreshadowings here (or in "The Hunting of the Snark") of the overtly Christian allegorical mode of the *Sylvie and Bruno* books.

creature with jaws that bite and claws that catch, Alice manages to defuse the threat of total incomprehension. Her extraction of a minimal narrative thread *from* the poem thus seems akin to the beamish boy's own feat *within* the poem itself.

Originally planned as the frontispiece for *Alice Through the Looking-Glass,* Tenniel's full-page illustration for "Jabberwocky" invites the reader to connect Alice and the poem's hero. As Michael Hancher points out, the androgynous child dwarfed by the Jabberwock "closely resembles the Alice" who stares at a perched Humpty Dumpty, the poem's later interpreter, in a drawing for chapter 6.[16] Both child-figures are endowed with flowing locks; both lean back with faces averted from the viewer, looking up at the bizarre creatures who loom over them (see fig. 26). Yet whereas the little knight is about to decapitate the monster, Alice reaches out to shake Humpty Dumpty's proffered hand, "a little anxious" that he might fall off the wall (*LG,* 161). The two drawings thus offer a contrast similar to that noted in my discussion of the dropped White Rabbit and the lifted White King. The motion of the child with the "vorpal sword" anticipates an aggressive action; the motion of the child who extends her hand so carefully in order to avoid pulling Humpty down is solicitous and protective.

The Jabberwock and Humpty Dumpty are far more grotesque than the children they face. Tenniel's caricatures of the levitating dragon and the tottering Egg-Man stress their innate absurdity. If the perilously perched Humpty looks silly in the "beautiful belt" that may actually be a "beautiful cravat" (*LG,* 162), the "whiffling" Jabberwock's scaly chest is covered by a three-button Victorian vest like that worn by the White Rabbit, and his chicken-toes seem to be encased in slipper-like shoes. The creature's carp-like head and human dentures add to his doleful appearance. Is he attacking the little boy or wincing in anticipation of his own pain? He may be less wholesome than the boy whose vorpal sword seems as hard to lift as the pencil with which the White King had been struggling, but he is just as ineffectual.

Carroll may well have decided to follow the advice of mothers who told

---

16. Hancher regards the "child knight" as "the androgynous projection of Alice's own fears" and claims that neither "she nor her chivalric counterpart looks strong enough for self defense" (Michael Hancher, *The Tenniel Illustrations to the 'Alice' Books* [Columbus: Ohio State University Press, 1985], 75). As will become apparent, my own emphasis is rather different.

him that Tenniel's drawing was "likely to alarm nervous and imaginative children"[17] if used as a frontispiece. But such a possibility appears not to have previously occurred to either the author or to an illustrator who had—as Hancher shows—frequently drawn ludicrous dragons wearing Victorian haberdashery. And since Carroll decided to retain the drawing as an integral part of their text, it seems doubtful that it was created solely to exorcise the "terror" and "guilt" caused by the overflow of an eroticized imagination.[18] Instead, as the parallel to the Humpty Dumpty illustration suggests, the vanquishing of a chimerical male creature by a girlish little boy fits into a *Looking-Glass* narrative that mocks a weak adult masculinity as relentlessly as the *Wonderland* narrative had made fun of an adult femininity represented by the hideous Duchess and the irate Queen of Hearts.

The structure of *Through the Looking-Glass* relies on what James Kincaid rightly calls "a series of good-byes," in which the partings from the Gnat and the Fawn "are succeeded by the climactic farewell with the White Knight" and by "yet another farewell, with an old wasp."[19] This list, which omits the less sentimental partings from the Tweedles or from a Humpty Dumpty who fails to reply to Alice's polite "Good-bye!" (*LG*, 168), might also include "Jabberwocky." For the poem Alice reads as a representation of severance is, of course, the first of all the *Looking-Glass* farewells, her own unwitting farewell to an anarchic Wonderland that had still been ruled by Carrollian nostalgia and anger. The boy who looks like a girl in Tenniel's drawing is coaxed by an uncle, who, like the uncle after whom the Baker is named in "The Hunting of the Snark," seems to know all about the deformations of desire. The alliance between these two figures permits Carroll to salvage a debilitated masculinity, the distillation of a manhood that might otherwise become too threatening and repulsive. The man who had vainly hoped to remain a boy-girl had, by 1871, assumed the protective shape of a desexualized and wary Uncle Dodgson. In order to retain access to the Alices and Gertrudes and Ethels and Violets and Irenes so important to his psychological well-being, his past and

17. See Denis Crutch, *The Lewis Carroll Handbook*, rev. ed. (Hamden, Conn.: Archon Books, 1979), 61.

18. Hancher, *Tenniel Illustrations*, 80–81, 83. Carroll told his consultants that "it would be a pity" to omit the drawing altogether (Crutch, *Lewis Carroll Handbook*, 61).

19. James R. Kincaid, *Child-Loving: The Erotic Child and Victorian Culture* (London: Routledge, 1992), 297–98.

26 John Tenniel, Facing the
Jabberwock (opposite), and
Facing Humpty Dumpty

future selves had to combine by either slaying Jabberwocks or being slain by Snarks.

Ironically, however, the *Looking-Glass* Alice is unaware of her relation to the "pretty" poem she wants Humpty Dumpty to decode. Nor will she understand her centrality in the "White Knight's Song," a poem which so ironically opens with the lines, "I'll tell thee everything I can: / There's little to relate" (*LG,* 187). For Kincaid, who much prefers her abused *Wonderland* predecessor, this child is dull and over-complacent, a "Wendy in Wonderland" who offers only "the most unerotic of charms, maternal kindness." Siding with the "hopeless" yearnings that Carroll had already begun to exorcise in *Wonderland,* Kincaid dislikes the *Looking-Glass* sequel, hoping "somehow that we can wish into being" a total union between child and adult, yet finding himself as disappointed as the White Knight by Alice's unsentimental determination.[20]

20. Ibid., 296.

But Carroll reluctantly approves this new Alice's decision to become an adult and his approval goes hand in hand with her solicitude for mutilated males. The vorpal sword used to behead the Jabberwock is connected to Alice's appropriation of the King's pencil to note the dangerous imbalance of the same White Knight who will later fall "heavily on top of his head exactly in the path where Alice was walking" (*LG,* 184). Carved chess pieces such as knights and bishops are notoriously fragile, with heads that often need to be glued back. Alice's note in the memorandum-book thus anticipates a concern with broken or cut-off male heads that will become increasingly pronounced: she ties a pillow around the neck of Tweedledee, "'to keep his head from being cut off,' as he said"; she worries about "what would happen to [Humpty Dumpty's] head" if his mouth were to span the circumference of his entire body: "I'm afraid it would come off"; and she not only frets about the White Knight who brags that his "mind," like the Cheshire Cat's, "goes on working" no matter where his "body happens to be," but also is anxious about the second White Knight: "'I'm afraid you must have hurt him,' she said in a trembling voice, 'being on the top of his head'" (*LG,* 147, 162). And, in the suppressed episode that Carroll decided not to use, Alice helps the Wasp who uses a handkerchief and wig to keep his head from freezing. She encourages him to overcome his anger and fear of death by composing a memorandum, in verse, of a time when he was young and still sported "ringlets" which, like hers or those of the slayer of the Jabberwock, "waved / And curled and crinkled on my head" (*LG,* 213).

At first glance, Alice's obsession with male heads might seem more appropriate for a character such as Charles Dickens's Mr. Dick, the wounded child-man who cannot get the severed head of King Charles out of his broken brain. But the obsession is not really Alice's; it rather comes from the mind of that other Carolus Rex, the royal Charles who purports to doze away in the shape of a Red King. The Wonderland Alice whose head met her toes at one point of her underground adventures was even more disturbed to find it shooting up high above the tree tops. But, despite the White Queen's and King's label, the *Looking-Glass* Alice is no volcano. In a book not prone to eruptions, falls, or convulsions, she moves forward steadily. Bombarded with poems—in addition to "Jabberwocky" and the "White Knight's Song," there is "The Walrus and the Carpenter" recited by Tweedledee, the incomplete piece about the little fishes that Humpty Dumpty claims "was written entirely for your amusement" (*LG,* 166), and the reminiscence which the Wasp casts into rhyme—Alice much prefers the nursery rhymes she already knows. For these familiar verses afford a further means for orientation by allowing her to anticipate, for example, "the monstrous crow" whose arrival cools the Tweedles's eagerness to fight "for a trifle" (*LG,* 148), or, again, the plum-cake and the drums that will put a stop to another boyish fight between the Lion and the Unicorn.

As a reader of nursery rhymes that were traditionally associated, through Mother Goose, with a feminine imagination, Alice has a decided advantage over those *Looking-Glass* males who pre-exist in popular child-verses. For, unlike these characters, she knows the outcome—or last lines—of the poems of which they are a part. If, as mentioned before, the *Wonderland* Alice's confusion was exacerbated when verses she had dutifully memorized did not come out quite "right," the *Looking-Glass* Alice's recollection of familiar rhymes has the opposite effect of giving her the self-assurance and predictive powers of a Sybil. Thus, Alice's worries about Humpty Dumpty's safety stem from her awareness of his ultimate fate. Unlike Humpty, she knows the conclusion of his story: neither the king's horses nor the king's men will be able to put together again the child-Ego who so desperately wants Alice to remain an unhatched fledgling like himself.

Alice soon senses that Humpty's cocky self-assurance merely masks his own anxious intimations of mortality. The creature who finds subtractions so difficult to do also cannot "master" those parts of speech that denote pasts as well as futures. Fortunately for him, he does not have to gloss the later stanzas of "Jabberwocky," thus managing to avoid the account of a whiffling and burbling beast's beheading. Humpty's own poem about little fishes ends quite abruptly, "I tried to turn the handle, but—" (*LG,* 168). Completed narratives are not the *forte* of an imagination, which like that of Dickens's truncated Mr. Dick, finds growth hard to handle. Alice soon senses that she must cater to Humpty's mental insecurity as much as to his physical fragility. For his tenuous belief in his impenetrability crumbles as soon as he nervously learns that, far from being a private secret kept by him and the White King, his story is publicly known to any reader of nursery rhymes:

"Don't you think you'd be safer down on the ground?" Alice went on, not with any idea of making another riddle, but simply in her good-natured anxiety for the queer creature. "That wall is so *very* narrow!"

"What tremendously easy riddles you ask!" Humpty Dumpty growled out. "Of course I don't think so! Why, if ever I *did* fall off—which there's no chance of—but *if* I did—" Here he pursed up his lips, and looked so solemn and grand that Alice could hardly help laughing. "*If* I *did* fall," he went on, "*the King has promised me*—ah, you may turn pale, if you like! You didn't think I was going to say that, did you? *The King has promised me with his very own mouth*—to—to—"

"To send all his horses and all his men," Alice interrupted, rather unwisely.

"Now I declare that's too bad!" Humpty Dumpty cried, breaking into a sudden passion. "You've been listening at doors—and behind trees—and down chimneys—or you couldn't have known it."

"I haven't indeed!" Alice said very gently. "It's in a book."

"Ah, well! They may write such things in a *book*," Humpty Dumpty said in a calmer tone. (*LG*, 160)

The knowledge that his secret compact with the King has been written "in a book" somehow soothes Humpty, perhaps because he knows that the translation of private relations into public texts can become a protection against innuendo and rumor. The verses exhibited at the Knave's trial in the *Wonderland* text proved impervious to public scrutiny. Humpty's firm belief that he can make words mean whatever he chooses is as defensive as his *Wonderland* rudeness. Like the Mad Hatter, he aborts any subject he does not want to pursue: "I mean by 'impenetrability' that we've had enough of the subject" (*LG*, 163). Encased in his stiff but fragile shell, Humpty is paralyzed, rigidified by his fear of change. So immobile that Alice initially mistook him for a "stuffed figure" (*LG*, 159), he abruptly ends their conversation and closes his eyes. Having so "very gently" defused his irrational accusations, Alice at last shows a little irritation at Humpty's failure to reply to her polite "Good-bye!": "of all the unsatisfactory people I *ever* met—" (*LG*, 168). Appropriately enough, the "heavy crash" she hears prevents her from finishing her sentence. There is unfinished business between Alice and the child-man who claimed that his fragmentary poem, now preserved in a book, was, like the "White Knight's Song," especially designed for her. The sentimental White Knight is disappointed by Alice's matter-of-fact reaction to his love-gift. Humpty, however, clings, as long as possible, to his bulbous solipsism. To relate fully is to die.

Linked to the Jabberwock as a residual *Wonderland* creature who cannot survive in Looking-Glass land, Humpty Dumpty also evokes the Cheshire Cat. That other grinning and oval-faced creature had also been shown perched above an Alice whose back was turned to the reader: indeed, Tenniel's drawing for chapter 6 of *Through the Looking-Glass* is clearly meant to match the drawing he had made for chapter 6 of the *Wonderland* text. Each drawing is in the shape of an inverted "L" and thus allows a typographic insert (which renders Alice's exchanges with each creature) to be placed in the lower right-hand quadrant of a rectangle. The short-lived Humpty is the immortal Cat's Looking-Glass foil. Whereas the Cheshire Cat reappears, as he had promised, in the illustration that shows his severed head grinning with aloof impunity over the King and Queen of Hearts, Humpty Dumpty cannot be depicted after the crash in chapter 6. Like the descending vorpal sword that beheads a Jabberwock, his shattering fall signifies Carroll's willed destruction of a madness he no longer finds himself able, or willing, to sustain.

IV

And yet, of course, *Wonderland* irrationality does eventually crack the horizontal world of the chessboard on which Alice has been so steadily advancing. As she approaches her crowning as Queen Alice on the eighth square, the sentimentality and anger that were curbed by Carroll's delegation of his powers to Lily/Alice can no longer be kept down. Whether detained by the doleful White Knight or by the dying Wasp just before jumping across the last brook, Alice must wade through scenes "packed with love and self-pity."[21] And shortly after "something very heavy" presses down "all around her head" (*LG*, 191), Alice discovers that the queenhood she has coveted is hardly a boon. According to the chess diagram Carroll placed after his dedicatory verses, "Alice takes R. Q. & wins" in the eleventh move (*LG*, 104). Still, the victor is not Alice, but an invisible opponent who reasserts the *Wonderland* anarchy he has for so long kept in abeyance.

Whereas Carroll had distanced himself from figures such as the Gnat, the Tweedles, and Humpty Dumpty, he seems far more willing to acknowledge his investment in the White Knight who wants Alice to ad-

---

21. Ibid., 298. Kincaid, however, distinctly prefers the "erotic possibilities" of the first parting scene since it "can be replayed and made to come out differently; or, if all else fails, forced to yield the pleasures of indignation. But Alice as familiar, kindly, mothering Wendy: that is crushing" (298). Maybe so; but if making these encounters "come out differently" is the game, why not build on the Wasp's "expression of admiration" of the girl he mistakes for a honey-bee? Surely there is a considerable "erotic possibility" in the Wasp's hope that Alice might "bite well" and in the "little scream of laughter" with which she responds: "I can bite anything I want" (*LG*, 214). If the love-bite of a human vampire has titillated readers and viewers of Bram Stoker's *Dracula*, why not extend such titillation to girls injecting new life into wasps with desiccated stingers?

mire his crazy inventions and cry over the "very, *very* beautiful song" he intones for her benefit (*LG*, 186). The Gnat and Humpty Dumpty suffered extinction (the impending fate of the old Wasp, the White Knight's deleted successor); the Tweedles fled the monstrous black crow that acted as a possible harbinger of death or at least of the ending of childhood. But the accident-prone Knight, who keeps crashing down from his horse, remains unhurt by his many falls. As invulnerable to head-injuries as the subjects of the Queen of Hearts, he seems a lonely Wonderland survivor. His ability to "go on talking so quietly, head downwards" (*LG*, 185) puzzles an Alice who, in the earlier book, had speculated about antipodians during her own harmless fall.[22]

When Carroll instructed Tenniel that the "White Knight must not have whiskers; he must not be made to look old,"[23] he appears to have wanted his readers to regard Alice's rescuer as a youthful figure like Humpty or the Tweedles, or at least as someone as clean-shaven as the Reverend Dodgson himself. But Tenniel, who had already gone against the text by giving the White King tiny whiskers, drew the Knight as a balding figure whose long mustachios droop as heavily as the tubular bristles that frame the gaping mouth of the ancient Jabberwock in the frontispiece displaced by the later full-page illustration. Whether or not the aged face Tenniel drew was meant to resemble that of his *Punch* colleague, "Ponny" Mayhew, as Hancher believes, or is the artist's self-caricature, as others have proposed,[24] ultimately matters less than his defiance of Carroll's injunction. Like Carroll, Tenniel seems to have had "more than a casual commitment" to the representation of this particular figure.[25]

Carroll's own commitment involves a self-caricature that is quite overt. Editors have drawn parallels between Dodgson's and the White Knight's far-fetched inventions. Moreover, the "self-pity" that Kincaid detects in the Knight's expectation of a weepy response to his song is inseparable from Carroll's impulse to parody the sentimental lyrics that frame his narrative of farewells to a maturing young woman. Just as the Knight vainly

---

22. "I wonder if I shall fall right *through* the earth. How funny it'll seem to come out among people that walk with their heads downwards! The *antipathies*, I think—" (*AW*, 8).

23. Stuart Dodgson Collingwood, *The Life and Letters of Lewis Carroll (Rev. C. L. Dodgson)* (New York: Century, 1899), 130.

24. See Hancher, *Tenniel Illustrations*, 68–74.

25. Ibid., 74.

hopes to bring tears to Alice's eyes through verses that dramatize the non-relation between an "I" and a "you," so are Carroll's frame-poems marked by his fear that a "Thou" separated from an "I" by "half a life" will fail to listen to his "fairy-tale." That fear surely prompted Carroll to consider adding, still before the fateful jump to the eighth square, the sentimental encounter between Alice and the Old Wasp.

But the nostalgia of the *Looking-Glass* verse-frames and of the *Wonderland* closure, with their tentative hopes for perpetuating child-adult bonds and ever-green summer days, directly infiltrates the White Knight episode itself. Carroll thus creates a barrier even before Alice has had a chance to leap over the last row of asterisks. In a paragraph that contains a sentence so long that it exceeds the one which ended the *Wonderland* text,[26] he wrests away from Alice the narrative control he had for so long allowed her to maintain. The refrain of "afterwards" to which Alice had resorted now becomes the sole property of a narrator who assigns emotions to her that are palpably alien to the bored child who is politely "trying to feel interested" in the Knight's loving, but childish, delaying tactics:

> Of all the strange things that Alice saw in her journey Through The Looking-Glass, this was the one she always remembered most clearly. Years afterwards she could bring the whole scene back again, as if it had been only yesterday—the mild blue eyes and kindly smile of the Knight—the setting sun gleaming through his hair, and shining on his armour in a blaze of light that quite dazzled her—the horse quietly moving about, with the reins hanging loose on his neck, cropping the grass at her feet—and the black shadows of the forest behind—all this she took in like a picture, as, with one hand shading her eyes, she leant against a tree, watching the strange pair, and listening, in a half-dream, to the melancholy music of the song. (*LG*, 187)

Seductive and lovely as this passage is, it nonetheless relies on an illusory rhetorical construction. It falsifies our textual experiences and hence is as insubstantial as the gorgeous Bower of Bliss ruthlessly destroyed by a very different sort of knight, Edmund Spenser's Sir Guyon. Alice's earlier recollections of a series of "afterwards"—the jumping road or the warring Tweedles—were always extraordinarily vivid. As a result, the narrator's sudden insistence that we accept his unequivocal assertion that this is the one golden moment she "always" remembered "most clearly" in her later

---

26. There are 99 words in the sentence-paragraph that concludes *Wonderland* and 101 words in the *Looking-Glass* sentence.

life is bound to be met with some skepticism by readers whom he has conditioned to trust Alice's own claims. Forced to weigh the narrator's veracity, such readers may well question his need for making so extravagant a claim. Why must he at all intervene at this point and demand our assent to an authority he has not seen fit to exercise before?

But the sinuous sentence that follows, full of suspended dashes that prolong its duration, seems even more suspect. For the narrator now ascribes to Alice a future nostalgia that a grown-up woman may even be less disposed to feel than the unsentimental girl who just wants to proceed to the eighth square. Would the adult Alice re-experience her encounter so very differently in her later life? Carroll's willingness to sanction the narrator's wishful projection of his desire seems far more self-indulgent than his earlier reliance on Alice's older sister to transmit his own forward-looking thoughts. Indeed, in its greater implausibility, the projection comes closer to the White Knight's own mistaken assumption that Alice must be "sad" simply because he is, and hence in sore need of "a song to comfort" her as much as him (*LG*, 186).

Yet the Knight's distortion of Alice's feelings is immediately exposed by an alert ironist who makes sure to let us know that this subjectivist has misread the quizzical expression on Alice's face: "Alice could only look puzzled: she was thinking of the pudding. 'You are sad,' the Knight said in an anxious tone" (*LG*, 186). By way of contrast, the narrator who now introduces a dazzling "blaze of light" that emanates from a "setting sun" retrieved from the *Wonderland* verses almost seems to be imploring us to forget all the grotesque details of the Knight's earlier characterization. Lost in a "half-dream," as her sister had been at the end of the earlier book, the future Alice must shield her eyes to bear such an excess of effulgence. And so must any half-believing reader willing to be "taken in" by a verbal description that presumably looks "like a picture" yet is so palpably contradicted by Tenniel's drawings of Alice and a bumbler devoid of any aureole or halo. Indeed, the light now "gleaming through [the] hair" of this imaginary Galahad would have quickly bounced off the bald pate of Tenniel's stiff old veteran.

The subjective distortions by which we remake others into imaginary self-reflections preoccupies Carroll throughout the *Looking-Glass* narrative: the living flowers criticize Alice's fading "petals" (*LG*, 121); the Unicorn calls her a "fabulous monster" (*LG*, 176); and Humpty Dumpty and the Old Wasp engage in wishful reconstructions of her face. Carroll renders all these acts of projection as laughable examples of the arbitrariness of assigned meanings. Yet he somehow expects to be exempted from mockery when he asks us to endorse the equally arbitrary reconstruction of a scene to be colored by a future Alice with his own nostalgic tints. The child supposedly exposed to the "melancholy music" of a song that satirizes melancholic excess is wearied by long poems at this late stage of her journey. She is immune to Wordsworthian acts of retrospection or to their parody—a parody that makes the insertion of such heavily nostalgic lyrical prose seem doubly out of place.[27]

Should a future Alice weep tears her present self will not shed? The "White Knight's Song" is unlikely to soften her memories. For the poem's speaker is totally at odds with the narrator who idealizes the Knight with the "kindly smile" and "mild blue eyes" of wonder. Only by dropping a "very heavy weight" upon his toe can this pseudo-sentimentalist bring himself to feel the pain that will make him properly lachrymose in remembering another "mild" interlocutor, met on still another "summer evening long ago" (LG, 189–90):

> I weep, for it reminds me so
> Of that old man I used to know—
> Whose look was mild, whose speech was slow,
> Whose hair was whiter than the snow,
> Whose face was very like a crow,
> With eyes, like cinders, all aglow,
> Who seemed distracted with his woe,
> Who rocked his body to and fro,
> And muttered mumblingly and low,
> As if his mouth were full of dough,
> Who snorted like a buffalo—
> That summer evening long ago,
>   A-sitting on a gate.
>   (LG, 189–90, lines 71–83)

If this last stanza undercuts the sentimentality of Alice's parting from the White Knight, it also anticipates Carroll's deliberate subversion of her coronation in the hurried last third of the book. The systematic progres-

27. For a more sustained reading of Carroll's Wordsworthian underpinnings, see my "Revisiting Wordsworth: Lewis Carroll's 'The White Knight's Song,'" *Victorians Institute Journal* 14 (1986), 1–20.

sion of the first eight chapters is brought to an abrupt halt at the very opening of chapter 9, "Queen Alice" (*LG,* 192). Anarchy now returns, only to accelerate hereafter: the narrator reassumes his *Wonderland* persona and brings in Alice's mad rival queens to spoil all expectations of a "dignified" climax. The would-be adult who addresses herself as "your Majesty" and considers whether "lolling about on the grass" might be demeaning is quickly discredited by a suddenly aroused narrator who can no longer bring himself to endorse Alice's maturation. Sounding exactly like the *Wonderland* predecessor who had told us that the little girl was so "fond of pretending to be two people" that she "sometimes scolded herself so severely as to bring tears to her eyes" and even tried "to box her own ears for having cheated herself in a game" (*AW,* 12), this narrator equates Queen Alice with that more immature child. Imputing his own self-division to her, he insists that she is as schizophrenic as ever, "always rather fond of scolding herself" (*LG,* 192).

But the deflation of Queen Alice is soon given over to the Red and White Queens who refuse to certify her as a fellow monarch until she passes an examination that seems to have been set by Humpty Dumpty or even the Mad Hatter. Far more perturbed than in any of her previous chessboard encounters, Alice is disconcerted by the "dreadful nonsense" of the conversations into which she has been drawn. As in the Mad Tea Party, she finally gives up when confronted with a "riddle with no answer" (*LG,* 194, 195). The discussion, which has centered on a compression of time, challenges the adherence to chronological progress vindicated, until this point, by Alice's own linear advances on the chessboard.

The nursery rhymes that had earlier helped to organize those advances are now subject to comic inversion. Suddenly unable to remember any "soothing lullaby" (*LG,* 196), Alice must delegate that task to a Red Queen who has relinquished the predictive authority she had herself held in the Garden of Live Flowers. Not surprisingly, the queen's nursery song reverses the roles of mother and child: "Hush-a-by lady, in Alice's lap! / Till the feast's ready, we've time for a nap." Soon, both ladies-turned-babies, "fast asleep and snoring loud," drop their heavy round heads in Alice's lap (*LG,* 197). The maternal stance that Alice first assumed when placing the kitten upon her knees served her well in later interactions with boyish combatants such as the Tweedles or even with the Lion and the Unicorn wanting equal shares of the cake she carefully tried to divide. Now, however, she has become the temporary caretaker of the childish matriarchs who will soon ruin the ceremonial banquet over which she would like to preside.

The "shrill voice" that issues, in Alice's name, an invitation to this royal banquet is not her own. Displaced by the queens, Alice must listen to a ventriloquist pronounce words she has not herself uttered: "To the Looking-Glass world it was Alice that said / 'I've a sceptre in hand, I've a crown on my head. / Let the Looking-Glass creatures, whatever they be, / Come and dine with the Red Queen, the White Queen, and me!'" Her prospective guests remain unidentified, but the "hundreds of voices" accepting the invitation allow Carroll to throw more Wonderland discord into the proceedings. The voices enthusiastically vow to "sprinkle the table with buttons and bran; / Put cats in the coffee, and mice in the tea," before dissolving into a "confused chorus of cheering" (*LG*, 199).

And, indeed, when these guests materialize they seem so motley a crew that their composition has either become irrelevant or too amorphous and indistinct for the narrator to handle: "some were animals, some birds, and there were even a few flowers among them" (*LG*, 200). Like the animal jurors at the Knave's *Wonderland* trial, the guests are unaware of regulations or expected roles. Asked to drink to Alice's health by a Red Queen screaming "at the top of her voice," they behave as "queerly" as figures out of a painting by Hieronymus Bosch: "Some of them put their glasses upon their heads like extinguishers, and drank all that trickled down their faces—others upset the decanters, and drank the wine as it ran off the edges of the table—and three of them (who looked like kangaroos) scrambled into the dish of roast mutton, and began eagerly lapping up the gravy, 'just like pigs in a trough!' thought Alice" (*LG*, 202). The infantilism that a growing girl had placed behind her now returns with a vengeance. In the sole "afterwards" reflection she is allowed, Alice will remember that her bodily integrity seemed as threatened by this rabble as by the flying Wonderland cards: "('And they *did* push so!' she said afterwards, when she was telling her sister the history of her feast. 'You would have thought they wanted to squeeze me flat!')" (*LG*, 202).

Alice has no time to think why these aggressors would want to see her as flat as a splattered Humpty Dumpty or as the mice condemned by the Dog Fury. For she is also so strenuously "pushed" by the two queens, "one on each side," that they almost force her to levitate like a Light Princess. When the whole banquet thrusts upward, with candles growing to the ceiling and plates flying like Jubjub birds, Alice erupts with the volcanic rage she has for so long successfully repressed. When even an erect soup ladle impatiently beckons her to get out of its way, Alice has had enough. She turns on the Red Queen, "whom she considered the cause of all mischief" (*LG,* 204), shakes the dwindling figure back into a kitten, and aborts a dream she can no longer control. The book ends with her concession that she may never have possessed that control, having been merely a pawn in someone else's dream.

As noted earlier, James Kincaid, disappointed by Alice's tearless departure from the White Knight, suggests that the farewell scene might be replayed differently, or, at least be "forced to yield the pleasures of indignation."[28] Yet the convulsion at the banquet, which Alice blames on the Red Queen, enacts Carroll's own indignation at his unsentimental dreamchild's drive towards maturity. Indeed, the chapter called "Queen Alice" might well have been named "The White Knight's Revenge." The child who had cut herself away from the Knight is not allowed to slice the Mutton because, as the Red Queen explains, "it isn't etiquette to cut any one you've been introduced to" (*LG,* 200). Lest the link be overlooked, Alice next faces a pudding who talks back to her in an aggressive manner avoided by the hurt Knight who mistook her interest in pudding for sadness. Even the deflection from pudding to recited poetry, which Alice again "politely" agrees to hear (*LG,* 201), follows the sequence observed in the previous chapter. And, most important, the vertical motions that Alice found so laughable as she watched the Knight's repeated falls from his saddle now produce her own unseating. Queen Alice has been dethroned. As far as Carroll is concerned, she should have left off at square seven.

Through the Looking-Glass starts out as a collaboration between adult and child selves, yet ends in an irreconcilable rivalry. Acting like an older sister who could mediate between Tweedledum and Tweedledee, Alice steadily resisted being drawn into skirmishes; she let others do the fighting: even the White and Red Knights must battle it out without her intervention. But when she is at last provoked into fiercely shaking the Red Queen, her presumed chessboard rival, her "capture" of this infantilized figure only ratifies her own return to childish petulance. By deliberately infecting her with his own disappointment and anger, Carroll tries to reclaim Alice as his playmate, the object of a projection he had seemingly been willing to shed. Alice is forced to remember her humiliation when

28. See note 21, above.

she retells "the history of her feast." Christina Rossetti, as we shall see in chapter 10 below, chose to avenge Alice by inviting Carroll to an even more anarchic and sadistic feast in *Speaking Likenesses,* a book in which she reinstated his broken belief that girls ought to become responsible adults in a world of restrictions and rules.

Rossetti's book was written after the appearance of *Through the Looking-Glass,* whereas the next three texts we shall consider, MacDonald's *At the Back of North Wind,* Ingelow's *Mopsa the Fairy,* and Rossetti's own *Sing-Song,* had only the *Wonderland* precedent as their stimulus and foil. Like Carroll's own *Looking-Glass,* these books can therefore be profitably read as responses to *Alice in Wonderland.* Carroll's self-dialogue—between growth and arrest, and between the feminine and masculine components of a divided self—is carried out in important new ways by these writers, as well as by lesser revisionists.[29] MacDonald, whose investment in mythified maternal powers clashes with Carroll's caricatures of adult women, also departs from the emphasis on maturation of his own "The Light Princess." In *At the Back of the North Wind,* the restrictions that Carroll half-accepts in *Through the Looking-Glass* are thrown, quite literally, to the wind. It is MacDonald, therefore, more than Carroll, whom Jean Ingelow will challenge when, in *Mopsa the Fairy,* she will construct a fairy tale which, despite its fantastic flights, eventually grounds a girl who, unlike Alice, is allowed to develop into a caring and nurturant queen.

29. For an overview of such Carrollian offspring, see Sanjay Sircar's two helpful pieces, "Other Alices and Alternative Wonderlands: An Exercise in Literary History" and "A Select List of Previously Unlisted 'Alice' Imitations," *Jabberwocky: The Journal of the Lewis Carroll Society* 13 (1984), 23–48, 59–67; a thoughtful analysis of the relation between the Alice books and one such text, Thomas Hood's *From Nowhere to the North Pole* (1875), can be found in Jan Susina's "Imitations of *Alice*—Lewis Carroll and the Anxiety of Influence," *Proceedings of The Second International Lewis Carroll Conference,* ed. Charlie Lovett (Silver Springs, Md.: Lewis Carroll Society of North America, 1995), 153–66.

S E V E N

Erasing Borders: MacDonald's
At the Back of the North Wind

As still was her look, and as still was her ee
As the stillness that lay on the emerant lea,
Or the mist that sleeps on a waveless sea.
For Kilmeny had been she ken'd not where,
And Kilmeny had seen what she could not declare.
. . . .
But O, the words that fell from her mouth
Were words of wonder and words of truth!
            —JAMES HOGG, *"Kilmeny: A Fairy Legend"*

To me, George MacDonald's most extraordinary, and
precious, gift is his ability, in all his stories, to create
an atmosphere of goodness about which there is nothing
phony or moralistic. Nothing is rarer in literature.
            —W. H. AUDEN, *afterword to "The Golden Key"*

I

In several ways, *At the Back of the North Wind* reverses the sequence I have so far been tracing. Written after *The King of the Golden River, The Rose and the Ring,* "The Light Princess," and *Alice in Wonderland,* George MacDonald's sprawling fantasy-novel ran serially in *Good Words for the Young* from 1868 to 1869 and was reissued in book form in 1871, the same year in which *Through the Looking Glass* was published. The diffuseness and length of a fairy tale that takes up thirty-eight full-blown chapters certainly offers a sharp contrast to the tightly controlled texts of Ruskin, Thackeray, and Carroll, as well as to MacDonald's own well-honed "The Light Princess." Any reader expecting to find a straightforward narrative will be thwarted by the story's abrupt shifts and turns and interpolations.

The book's original publication in separable units, each enhanced by Arthur Hughes's superb woodcuts, partly accounts for its meandering quality. Yet MacDonald's apparent unwillingness to tighten or compress *At the Back of the North Wind* upon reissuing it as a book also suggests that the looser format brought about by the serial mode of publication suited a narrative that challenges our habitual notions of structure even more than "The Light Princess." In that first fairy tale for children, as we saw in chapter 4, MacDonald imitated E. T. A. Hoffmann's *Prinzessin Brambilla* by blurring the demarcations between fantasy and realism, comedy and earnestness, the light and the grave. Yet the decisive closure of "The Light Princess" made it less open-ended than Hoffmann's "capriccio," or, for that matter, than MacDonald's own fantasies for grown-ups, *Phantastes* and "The Portent," had been. For by grounding his Light Princess in a world of generation and social responsibility, MacDonald endorsed the same process of maturation that Thackeray had dramatized and that even Lewis Carroll grudgingly came to accept in *Through the Looking Glass.*

At the Back of the North Wind, however, counters this earlier emphasis on the maturation of a child-protagonist. Since the boy who calls himself "Little Diamond" at the outset does not have to grow into manhood, he seems an ostensible throwback to Ruskin's *The King of the Golden River,* closer to the arrested "little Gluck" than to the maturing princes and princesses of *The Rose and the Ring* and "The Light Princess" or even to an

Alice whose growth Carroll reluctantly comes to accept. Both Gluck and Diamond perform domestic tasks for elders to whom they defer as much as to the personified natural forces with whom they form a special relationship. Nonetheless, Diamond differs substantially from Gluck. Unlike the boy whom Ruskin chooses to reimplant in a this-worldly Eden, MacDonald's dream-child is primarily defined by his obsessive desire for the overpowering female figure who eventually translates him into a numinous order beyond life and death.

The ending of "The Light Princess," in which a parched landscape is refertilized with waters associated with the feminine, was overtly Ruskinian in its emphasis. The opening of *At the Back of the North Wind,* however, furnishes MacDonald with an immediate opportunity to distance himself from the gender stereotypes embedded in *The King of the Golden River.* For MacDonald rejects Ruskin's equation of femininity with an idealized passivity. Apparently recalling the episode in which an avenging gale ravages the bedroom of Schwartz and Hans, MacDonald rewrites the scene from a perspective that establishes the absolute rule of the goddess-figure who will dominate his own narrative.

MacDonald carefully rearranges Ruskin's scene. Gluck's "shivering" brothers found their rooms violated by the intruder who left his calling card, South-West Wind, Esquire. Little Diamond, too, discovers that the blowing wind he has thrice tried to shut out has entered his own sleeping quarters. To avoid the "long whistling spear of cold" that strikes his "little naked chest," Diamond hides his head under the bedclothes. Although the "voice" he hears now seems gentler, even "a little like his mother's," Diamond assumes that he is being addressed by a male invader. Showing Gluck's own deference towards South-West Wind, Esquire, he respectfully addresses "Mr. North Wind," as if his visitor were that earlier figure's brother (*BNW,* chap. 1, 6–7). Yet the intruder quickly corrects the boy's mistake:

A beautiful laugh, large but very soft and musical sounded somewhere beside him, but Diamond kept his head under the clothes.

"I'm not Mr. North Wind," said the voice.

"You told me that you were the North Wind," insisted Diamond.

"I did not say *Mister* North Wind," said the voice.

"Well then, I do; for Mother tells me I ought to be polite."

"Then let me tell you I don't think it at all polite of you to say *Mister* to me." (*BNW,* chap. 1, 7)

Since the child still mistakes the sexual identity of his visitor, the voice asks him, "just a little angrily," to peek out from under the bedclothes. When he refuses, a "tremendous blast" sweeps off Diamond's clothes. The denuded boy must now confront the full-size figure whom MacDonald goes on to describe as combining a maternal authority with something that resembles Diamond's own childlike vulnerability:

He started up in terror. Leaning over him was the large beautiful pale face of a woman. Her dark eyes looked a little angry, for they had just begun to flash; but a quivering in her sweet upper lip made her look as if she were going to cry. What was most strange was that away from her head streamed out her black hair in every direction, so that the darkness in the hay-loft looked as if it were made of her hair; but as Diamond gazed at her in speechless amazement, mingled with confidence— for the boy was entranced with her mighty beauty—her hair began to gather itself out of the darkness, and fell down all about her again, till her face looked out of the midst like a moon out of a cloud. (*BNW,* chap. 1, 8)

Given MacDonald's close personal and literary relations with both Ruskin and Lewis Carroll, it hardly seems unwarranted to read this scene as a friendly corrective of their fearful ambivalence about adult female power. MacDonald had submitted "The Light Princess" to the scrutiny of both men, and had come in conflict with Ruskin over its representation of sexual "passion."[1] He soon twitted Ruskin for his prudery in *Adela Cathcart* and apparently could not resist poking fun at Carroll's self-representation in the opening verses to *Wonderland* as a rower debilitated by female freight.[2] Indeed, as I shall later suggest, it is possible to regard Mr. Raymond, the wealthy bachelor and children's author who becomes Diamond's benefactor, as an amalgam of both Ruskin and Carroll.

By reinstating in a children's book the mighty female presences of his adult fantasies, MacDonald signals the obsession he shares with Ruskin and Carroll. But his two predecessors had resisted the seductive, yet angry, maternal authority to which MacDonald has Diamond submit. Indeed, the boy's initial resistance of North Wind captures Ruskin's and Carroll's own ambivalent response to overpowering women. Ruskin kept female figures out of the all-male cast of *The King of the Golden River;* Carroll confronted Alice with those hideous emblems of maternity, the Duchess

---

1. See chapters 4 and 5, pp. 138–40 and 151, above.
2. See note 5, below.

and the Queen of Hearts. MacDonald, too, acknowledges that an overwhelming maternal figure can be intimidating. The "mighty beauty" who towers over Diamond at first scares the boy as much as a towering Alice intimidated a trembling White Rabbit. But North Wind's "quivering" lip suggests something that Diamond can learn only after his visitor willingly reduces her size; for, like Alice, she too can be naive and vulnerable. North Wind's childlike aspects help to level the differences between herself and the frightened boy. Just as Diamond's regressive imagination furthers the "education" of "a brother-baby" and, later, of a "sister-baby" (*BNW,* chap. 31, 252), so does North Wind often seem more like an older sister. She and Diamond are coworkers, willing agents for an inscrutable power that lies beyond the comprehension of each.

Although Diamond bypasses the process of sexual maturation, MacDonald implies that North Wind's stimulus and tutelage will allow the short-lived boy a privileged existence. In the last third of his narrative, MacDonald repeatedly hints that the unusual child who bears the nickname of "God's baby" may actually have been sent on a special mission during his brief stay among ordinary mortals. Passive during his initial period of apprenticeship, Diamond soon turns into a tiny social activist who succeeds in mending broken lives and inspiring grown-ups by his cheerful rejection of their skepticism and despair. Unlike the dozing Alice or a Gluck immobilized by his older brothers, Diamond is never idle. In the middle portion of the book, he helps redress the destitution caused by his father's joblessness and sickness, the degradation suffered by his friend Nanny (MacDonald's female version of Jo in Dickens's *Bleak House*), the physical abuse inflicted on horses and battered wives, the ennui of the Victorian upper class. Although his abiding cheerfulness often strikes others as odd or even crazy, he inevitably gains their respect—so much so that, in the book's last chapters, a narrator-turned-hagiographer avidly records the boy's last pronouncements.

This unabashed endorsement of Diamond may seem much closer to Charles Lutwidge Dodgson's verse tributes to an adored dream-child than to Lewis Carroll's ironic handling of Alice's misconceptions and blunders. Yet MacDonald's narrator is quite unsentimental about his "goody-goody" hero; he delights in Diamond's many misperceptions and stresses the child's difficulties in articulating, let alone interpreting, the meanings of his dream-encounters. The narrator, however, does not at all feel superior to this slightly addled little boy. Quite to the contrary, he welcomes Diamond's openness to possibilities the adult mind has discarded. The narrator thus repeatedly insists that he respects the elusiveness of meanings that Diamond finds so difficult to express. Such meanings, the narrator acknowledges, cannot really be captured by his own linear narrative. And, by professing to be wholly dependent on Diamond's own accounts, MacDonald as narrator-editor avoids the controlling authorial presence always implied in Carroll's reader-wary narratives.

When Carroll ends *Through the Looking-Glass* by having Alice ask the black kitten "who it was that dreamed it all," he reintroduces the polarities of relations based on power. If the dozing Red King has dreamed Alice as much as Alice has dreamed him, the girl's control over the progression that ended with her crowning is more tenuous than she had reason to believe. As I suggested at the end of the previous chapter, the child who receives no answer from the "provoking kitten" is being displaced by the narrator who now has the last word. Although the *Looking-Glass* Alice may have greater control over her own movements than her *Wonderland* counterpart, this final undermining of her authority puts her on a par with all those tellers of the earlier book—the Mouse, the Dormouse, the Mock-Turtle—who found telling stories to be a most fragile enterprise, fraught with insecurities and dangers.

Unlike Carroll, MacDonald is quite in earnest when he has his narrator defer to the greater authority of a dreamy child-protagonist. The narrator who readily admits his inadequacies as interpreter of North Wind's and Diamond's gnomic utterances almost exults in his lack of control over a story that moves in seeming randomness through stops and starts and diversions. The narrator's deferential relation to Diamond therefore mirrors Diamond's own awed relation to North Wind. Yet North Wind herself, whose visits become fitful and unpredictable after she returns Diamond from the land at her back, professes to serve inscrutable powers far more knowing than herself. Her own authority, she insists with childlike trust, is superseded by these unknown superiors. Like Diamond and the narrator, North Wind thus welcomes a reality impervious to penetration by an adult intellect.

II

When, in chapter 13 of the novel, Diamond's mother looks at the "poverty-stricken shore" near the seaside resort to which she has taken her ill boy, she is reminded of the bleak future awaiting them back in London.

She knows what Diamond has yet to learn, namely, that her husband's dismissal by his bankrupt employer has shattered the family's security:

> "Oh dear!" said Diamond's mother, with a deep sigh, "it's a sad world."
> "Is it?" said Diamond. "I didn't know." (*BNW*, chap. 3, 100)

This simple exchange can be read in two ways. On the one hand, it catches the total innocence of the small boy whom his mother soon calls a "darling stupid" for failing to grasp the extent of the family's destitution and to comprehend the meaning of want or hunger. On the other hand, Diamond's reply also reveals an outlook that counters her own. Having just woken up from a trance his mother regards as a near-fatal illness, Diamond is armed with intuitions confirmed by his contact with a different order of reality. Even before his sojourn in the land at North Wind's back, he was assured by that instructress that events which humans decry as unjust or "sad" may have been simply distorted by their excessive reliance on empirical evidence.

North Wind will not rematerialize until the last chapters of the book, much to Diamond's increasing dismay. But the boy's absolute trust in her is borne out by occasional hints that, though unseen, she is hardly ever absent. Just before Diamond and his mother engage in what amounts to a Blakean dialogue between Innocence and Experience, the narrator informs us, with studied casualness, that a pleasant ocean breeze has been fanning the two speakers: "A sweet little wind blew on their left side, and comforted the mother without letting her know what it was that comforted her" (*BNW*, chap. 13, 100).

The presence of the comforting wind Diamond's mother takes for granted paradoxically validates the boy's ignorance of the-world-as-evil. He has previously accepted North Wind's assurance that even in her most destructive incarnations she somehow serves a benign and purposeful providence. When, earlier, North Wind informed him that, like Shelley's West Wind, she is as much a destroyer as a preserver, Diamond was shaken. How can the mild breeze that so carefully releases a bumblebee imprisoned in a tulip turn into the savage gale that drowns a ship's passengers and crew? North Wind, however, sees no contradiction between the two tasks:

> "I have got to sink a ship tonight."
> "Sink a ship! What! with men in it?"

"Yes, and women too."

"How dreadful! I wish you wouldn't talk so."

"It is rather dreadful. But it is my work. I must do it." (*BNW*, chap. 5, 42)

For a while, Diamond will resist this unquestioning work ethic. But when he protests, more out of wishfulness than actual defiance, "You cannot be cruel," North Wind provides him with all the justification she will ever offer. Assuming both the authority of a knowing parent and the trustfulness of a fellow child, she tells the boy that "I can do nothing cruel, although I often do what looks like cruel to those who do not know what I really am doing. The people they say I drown, I only carry away to—to—to—well, the back of the north wind—that is what they used to call it long ago, only *I* never saw the place" (*BNW*, chap. 5, 44).

Diamond's "You cannot be cruel" echoes Gluck's feeble remonstrance on learning that the King of the Golden River has turned his brothers into stones: "Oh dear me! . . . have you really been so cruel?" (*KGR*, 65) But the little King's cruelty was punitive; his destructiveness, like that of South-West Wind, Gluck's other ally, was designed to avenge the violations perpetrated by the Black Brothers. North Wind, however, causes the death of total strangers. She does not really know—nor cares to know—why she has been chosen to sink a ship that belongs to Mr. Coleman, the employer of Diamond's father, and that carries the young man whom Miss Coleman loves. Nor does she know whose orders she is following:

"East Wind says—only one does not exactly know how much to believe of what she says, for she is very naughty sometimes—she says it is all managed by a baby; but whether she is good or naughty when she says that, I don't know. I just stick to my work. It is all one to me to let a bee out of a tulip, or to sweep the cobwebs from the sky. You would like to go with me to-night?"

"I don't want to see a ship sunk."

"But suppose I had to take you?"

"Why, then, of course I must go."

"There's a good Diamond. I think I had better be growing a bit. Only you must go to bed first. I can't take you till you're in bed. That's the law about the children. So I had better go and do something else first." (*BNW*, chap. 5, 44–45)

North Wind's matter-of-factness makes it difficult to ascertain whether she exists outside the sickly child's imagination. The tasks she sets for herself are as unexpected as her disappearances and reappearances. Before leaving Diamond, she mischievously decides to blow the "mist" out of a poet lost in reverie on a drifting boat beneath the setting sun.[3] As soon as she leaves a tired Diamond rubbing his eyes and wondering "what it was all about," his mother appears, worried about his health (*BNW,* chap. 5, 47). By imploring him to go to bed early, the mother unwittingly helps enact "the law" about sleeping children that North Wind must follow before she can ask Diamond to rejoin her.

Is North Wind a dreaming boy's transformation of the mother who rules his waking life? Or is she that mother's other-worldly anti-type? MacDonald links the two figures from the start. When, on first meeting North Wind, Diamond protests that he cannot follow her outside his room because "Mother never would let me go without shoes," his visitor reassures him by saying: "I know your mother very well. . . . She is a good woman. I have visited her often. I was with her when you were born. I saw her laugh and cry both at once. I love your mother, Diamond" (*BNW,* chap. 1, 10). And, to prove her devotion, North Wind explains that she aided Diamond's parents at his christening by acting as an invisible godmother. She countered the objections about Diamond's name raised by some "man"—a clergyman or a baptismal registrar—who felt that it was impious to name a Christian child after "old Diamond," his father's favorite horse. By blowing the Bible out of the man's hands and allowing Diamond's mother to pick it up conveniently opened on a page that verified the name's scriptural legitimacy, North Wind offered proof of the infant's special election: his name, she now explains to Diamond, is that of the most precious of stones "in the high-priest's breast-plate" (*BNW,* chap. 1, 10).[4]

The mighty figure who occasionally allows Diamond to press against her own "grand bosom" (*BNW,* chap. 6, 51) is assigned a role antithetical to that given to Makemnoit, the malign, anti-maternal figure who had dominated the plot of "The Light Princess." Whereas the excluded Makemnoit spoiled the baptismal ceremony of an infant on whom she conferred the dubious gift of levity, the uninvited North Wind intervenes as

---

3. MacDonald's fondness for twitting literary friends seems to be aimed at Lewis Carroll here: the prefatory poem to *Alice in Wonderland* had linked Carroll's rowboat and the windless afternoon to an inspiration "too weak / To stir the tiniest feather" (lines 7–8). Diamond (still ignorant of writing and spelling) mistakes the "poet" for his "bo-at"; corrected by North Wind and informed that a "poet is a man who is glad of something," he saves face by insisting that the gliding oarsman is "not much of a rower" (*NW,* chap. 5, 46).

4. See Exodus, 28:18.

a supporter of Joseph and Martha, parents of a child whose extraordinariness she understands better than they do.[5] Nonetheless, by retaining some of Makemnoit's destructive aspects, North Wind also undermines the nurturance so steadily offered to an easily excitable, sickly boy by his justifiably worried mother. Whereas Martha tries to rest her child, North Wind brings him to the brink of a heart attack. The "mighty yet musical voice" with which she beckons Diamond is seductive, but it follows a rousing that is more in keeping with the destructive mission she wants him to join. The violent blast that removes the ceiling of Diamond's bedroom in the loft almost chokes him with fear and leaves him with a heart that "was troubled and fluttered painfully" (*BNW,* chap. 5, 48).

If this violation of a protective cover recalls the angry action of Ruskin's South-West Wind, Esquire, it also involves a replay of the aggressive act of perforation MacDonald had assigned to the phallic Makemnoit in "The Light Princess." As I suggested in discussing this scene,[6] the snake that emanates from Makemnoit's loins to drill a hole in the roof of a subterranean cave becomes both a weapon and a suckling child. This duality underscores Makemnoit's own perversely parodic combination of male destructiveness with female nurturance. When the snake withers back into nothingness, its absence exposes the witch's own lack, her hatred of the sexual contraries she wants to prevent from blending.

Although MacDonald seems eager to suggest that North Wind's dual role as preserver and destroyer allows her to blend what Makemnoit wanted to sunder, his attempts to press contraries together reveal a still troubled relation to the feminine. There is something deeply disturbing about the metonymic description of the "gigantic, powerful, but most lovely arm" that Diamond sees extended towards him through the "big hole in the roof" before he finds himself lifted high into the sky. The arm is not only detached from its invisible owner but also separated from "a

5. By naming Joseph's wife Martha, rather than Mary, MacDonald wisely avoided allegorical implications that would have troubled the Evangelical readership of *Good Words for the Young.* His own theology regards Diamond's parents as receptors of God's own "child-like" aspects. Diamond's residence, with "hay at his feet and hay at his head" above a stable that is even called a "manger," suggests that he is a type of the child Jesus (*NW,* chap. 1, 2). Yet, as MacDonald insists in "The Child In the Midst," Jesus behaved like other children: "If he looked like them and was not like them, the whole was a deception, a masquerade at best. I say he was a child, whatever more he might be" (*Unspoken Sermons* [London: Strahan and Co.], 9).

6. See pp. 134–35, above.

hand whose fingers," we are told, "were nothing the less ladylike that they could have strangled a boa-constrictor, or choked a tigress off its prey" (*BNW*, chap. 5, 48).[7] Raised by those all-powerful fingers, the trusting boy becomes dizzied by "the swiftness" with which his "invisible assailant" enforces a levitation more terrifying than that which Makemnoit had inflicted on the Light Princess: "Cowering," he clings to "the huge hand which held his arm, and fear invaded his heart" (*BNW*, chap. 6, 49).

When Diamond tries to protest this rough handling, his words get stuck like soap bubbles in "the mouth of a pipe": "They couldn't get out at all, but were torn away and strangled" (*BNW*, chap. 6, 49). Diamond has become a mute infant, separated from a figure so tall and so distant that she has become unrecognizable, threatening, an assailant rather than a nurturer. But even though Diamond's words have become inaudible, he is heard by the giantess who finally breaks her silence. The narrator's sudden adoption of a soothing tone prepares us for North Wind's own delayed words of compensation to a child deprived of all his familiar bearings:

[J]ust because she was so big and could not help it, and just because her ear and her mouth must seem to him so dreadfully far away, she spoke to him more tenderly and graciously than ever before. Her voice was like the bass of a deep organ, without the groan in it; like the most delicate of violin tones without the wail in it; like the most glorious of trumpet-ejaculations without the defiance in it; like the sound of falling water without the clatter and clash in it: it was like all of them and neither of them—all of them without their faults, each of them without its peculiarity; after all, it was more like his mother's voice than anything else in the world. (*BNW*, chap. 6, 49)

Yet the voice that asks the little boy to "be a man" and assures him that what may be "fearful to you is not the least fearful to me" hardly seems as melodic as the narrator's lyrical description of it. What is more, it emanates from a being whose "face" Diamond still finds hard to discern, since he can at best "persuade himself that he saw great glories of woman's eyes

7. Nina Auerbach cites this passage in order to stress the "totemistic aura" that "parts of a woman's body acquire in disjunction from the woman herself" (*Woman and the Demon: The Life of a Victorian Myth* [Cambridge, Mass.: Harvard University Press, 1982], 48). I would only add that the "eerie potency in dissociation" that Auerbach notes even goes beyond the metonymies and size changes that convey North Wind's dual nature. The dissociation between demon and woman is also evident in the increasing split between North Wind and the biological mother she claims to "love" and aid.

looking down through the rifts in the mountainous clouds over his head" (*BNW*, chap. 6, 51). The rift that exists in his own head cannot be breached as long as he remains puzzled by the contradictory aspects of this benign yet awful goddess. When North Wind boasts that she needs only one arm "to take care of you," while using the other "to sink the ship," his difficulties return. Once more, his objections are met by North Wind's obdurate insistence that the duality Diamond perceives is entirely of his own making.

MacDonald deploys his skills as a casuist in the interminable dialogue that ensues. But it is the circularity of North Wind's argument that finally leads an exhausted little boy to accept her as indivisible: she cannot be cruel, he concludes, because the intensity of his desire for her necessitates that he regard her as kind. North Wind first compels Diamond to acknowledge that contradictions may coexist in a single "me." When he complains that her "taking care of a poor little boy with one arm, and . . . sinking a ship with the other," cannot "be like you," she questions his construction of that "you":

"Ah! but which is me? I can't be two mes, you know."
"No. Nobody can be two mes."
"Well, which me is me?"
"Now I must think. There looks to be two."
"Yes. That's the very point. You can't be knowing the thing you don't know, can you?"
"No."
"Which me do you know?"
"The kindest, goodest, best me in the world," answered Diamond. (*BNW*, chap. 6, 52)

Armed with this profession of belief in the goodness of a known "me," North Wind now proceeds to persuade Diamond that any unknown "me" he fears must be just as good. When the boy asks, justifiably, why she should not be just as "good to other people as well as to me?" her reply almost seems obscurantist:

"That's just what I don't know. Why shouldn't I?"
"I don't know either. Then why shouldn't you?"
"Because I am."
"There it is again," said Diamond. "I don't see that you are. It looks quite like the other thing."
"Well, but listen to me, Diamond. You know the one *me*, you say, and that is good."

"Yes."

"Do you know the other *me* as well?"

"No. I can't. I shouldn't like to." (*BNW,* chap. 6, 53)

North Wind therefore exhorts Diamond to cling to the "me" he is sure of being kind. Once again, he is asked to go, not by appearances, but by a trust based on the intensity of his desire.

But even after Diamond professes himself to be "quite satisfied," North Wind asks him to entertain the possibility that her kindness may only be a mask, "a pretence for the sake of being more cruel afterwards." The thought so unsettles Diamond that he feels compelled to make a passionate avowal of his unquestioning devotion to North Wind's mysterious ways:

> Diamond clung to her tighter than ever, crying:
> "No, no, dear North Wind; I can't believe that. I don't believe it. I won't believe it. That would kill me. I love you, and you must love me, else how did I come to love you? How could you know how to put on such a beautiful face if you did not love me and the rest? No. You may sink as many ships as you like, and I won't say another word. I can't say I shall like to see it, you know." (*BNW,* chap. 6, 54)

As soon as Diamond utters this pathetic confession of total submission, a wild North Wind hurls upward, pressing the boy "close to her heart." The apocalyptic imagery of a "jubilation of thunderous light" and clouds dissolved by gusts, "eddying and wreathing and whirling and shooting and dashing about," may strike MacDonald as theologically appropriate. But this sublime reward for the boy's act of submission also activates a residual demonism: the winds swirling around Diamond are described as resembling "a storm of serpents." Although the child feels secure now that one "arm of North Wind was about him" and laughs in glee when "leaning against her bosom," he cannot see the havoc that her other arm is causing as she streaks towards the sea. The huge threads of her hair mingle with the darkness of the night, making it difficult for Diamond to tell "which was hair and which was black storm and vapour." Even though the narrator also finds description "quite impossible," his blurred vision only contributes to the dissolution (*BNW,* chap. 6, 54–55).

The radiating "threads of the lady's hair" dominate this outdoor scene even more strongly than in Diamond's first encounter with North Wind's "mighty beauty." On that eerie occasion, wonderfully portrayed in Arthur Hughes's representation of a spiraling figure that retains her human dimensions as she hovers over a crouching child (fig. 27), the "darkness in the hay-loft looked as if it were made of her hair" (*BNW,* chap. 1, 8). But the hair of the giantess who now looms above the rooftops extends to the firmament. In Hughes's corresponding illustration (fig. 28), North Wind is coiled, stooping only to pick up the boy who holds on to her foot in the attitude of a supplicant. Her streaming hair can no longer be contained within the rectangular borders of the woodcut. Yet, by anchoring North Wind and freezing her impending movement, even Hughes cannot do full justice to a verbal text that insists on the blurred confusion of a wild kinetic flow that words fail to render. The narrator halts his account by saying, "I must not go on describing what cannot be described, for nothing is more wearisome" (*BNW,* chap. 7, 56).

MacDonald is at his most suggestive whenever he protests the presumed inadequacy of his descriptions. Straining to portray the half-blinded Diamond's sensations, the narrator conjectures that the "mist-muddy" billows appear to have been woven "out of the crossing lines of North Wind's infinite hair, sweeping in endless intertwistings" with Diamond's own locks, "which his mother kept rather long" (*BNW,* chap. 6, 55). The animation such "interwistings" produce may have something to do with the maternal lock MacDonald held dear as a precious lifeline to the mother he lost in early childhood.[8] For despite its theological overlay, Diamond's need to adore an overwhelming maternal figure so repeatedly associated with absence and death has much to do with the stubborn desire of Helen MacDonald's son to recover the irrecoverable.

III

When Diamond's mother plaintively informs him about a "sad world" where indigence and suffering are the norm, she comes in collision with North Wind's previous indoctrination of her son. But her worldview also clashes with an outlook he has gained on his own. Diamond's seven-day sojourn in the strange region at North Wind's back, during an illness in which he hovered between life and death, has radically altered his perspective. Having been sent to the seaport of Sandwich to be cared for by an aunt, Diamond is unaware of his illness or of its gravity. He only recalls his journey to—and from—the limbo in which North Wind deposited him. His contentment there, which the narrator cryptically calls "some-

8. See p. 122, above.

27 Arthur Hughes, North Wind Indoors

thing better than mere happiness" (*BNW,* chap. 10, 87), jarred with his yearning for both North Wind and his mother. While perched on a tree, Diamond suddenly longed to go home again, "for he saw his mother crying"; her desolation also reminds him how much he has missed North Wind, who promptly returns him to his sickbed (*BNW,* chap. 11, 89).

The crying figure whom Diamond thinks he has glimpsed from a tree-top corresponds to the mother who has hurried to Sandwich to attend her comatose child. But when the boy finally awakes, it becomes apparent that he has expected a rather different reunion:

[A] face was bending over him; but it was not North Wind's; it was his mother's. He put out his arms to her, and she clasped him to her bosom and burst out crying. Diamond kissed her again and again to make her stop it.

"What is the matter, Mother?" he said.

"Oh, Diamond, my darling! you have been so ill!" she sobbed.

2 8 Arthur Hughes, North Wind Outdoors

"No, Mother dear. I've only been at the back of the north wind," returned Diamond.

"I thought you were dead," said his mother. (*BNW,* chap. 12, 96)

As in Diamond's later exchanges with his mother and other grown-ups, MacDonald here expects the reader to side with the perspective of a child unbound by the constraints of temporal experience. Just as Diamond will assume functions his parents cannot perform, so does he here reverse roles by soothing a crying adult. The boy is mother of the woman.

Yet Martha's assumption that her son has been dead hardly seems off the mark. The woman named after the sister of Lazarus is confronting one who has indeed come back from a realm of death. Hereafter, Diamond ceases to depend on her common sense, and to his parents the boy seems odd and alien. Martha is repeatedly baffled by Diamond's elliptical pronouncements and strange behavior. Although she rightly attributes his quirks to the aftereffects of his illness, the narrator offers a more mystical explanation to account for the child's new visionary powers. Diamond's trespass into a zone from which few have returned gives him a privileged perspective on what we, like Martha, are too prone to regard as "real."

Diamond has "forgotten" so much about his stay in this hazy twilight zone that the narrator must supplement his account with those furnished by two other travelers. Of these two, the sparse "testimony" of the peasant girl Kilmeny, relayed by "a Scotch shepherd who died not forty years ago," the Romantic poet James Hogg, seems closer to Diamond's story than to the ornate narrative told by "a great Italian of noble family, who died more than five hundred years ago," Dante Alighieri (here called "Durante," *BNW,* chap. 10, 84, 85).[9] MacDonald's narrator hints that, since Durante "was an elderly man" eager to purge his sins, his account of "la divina foresta spessa e viva" cannot be wholly reconciled with the pastoral landscapes encountered by Diamond and "bonny" Kilmeny, young children still "free frae stain."[10] It is Kilmeny's "report," as recounted by Hogg, "telling her story as I tell Diamond's," that therefore offers the narrator a better analogue for his protagonist's faint recollections. Like Kilmeny (and unlike Durante),[11] Diamond remembers a windless region; he also recalls a river whose "tunes" he still can hear—in his head rather than in his ears. There is little else to be passed on to the book's "child readers." For the narrator, who prizes artlessness so much that he feels compelled to point

---

9. MacDonald notes that this name "means Lasting, for his books will last as long as there are enough men in the world worthy of having them" (*NW,* chap. 10, 85). Critics who relate MacDonald and Dante usually dwell on common tropes—the dark forest of error, the purging fire; Rolland Hein also finds some Beatrice figures in both the fantasies and the realistic novels (*The Harmony Within: The Spiritual Vision of George MacDonald* [Grand Rapids, Mich.: Christian University Press, 1982], 128–29). A detailed analysis of the way in which MacDonald integrates *Purgatorio,* canto 28 into the tenth chapter of *At the Back of the North Wind* might be useful. Only C. S. Lewis seems to have fully appreciated the Dantean dimensions of MacDonald's fantasies: in *The Great Divorce,* where MacDonald acts as Virgilian guide for his own travels in hell and heaven, Lewis professes that the youthful purchase of *Phantastes* became for him "what the first sight of Beatrice had been to Dante: *Here begins the New Life*" (ibid., ix).

10. *Purgatorio,* canto 28, line 2; "Kilmeny: A Fairy Legend," line 118.

11. See *Purgatorio,* canto 28, lines 7–8: "*Un'aura dolce, sanza mutamento / avere in se, mi feria per la fronte*" ("A sweet breeze that had no variation in itself was striking on my brow," *The Divine Comedy,* translated by Charles S. Singleton [Princeton: Bollingen Series, 1973], 302–3).

out that two lines in Hogg's poem were actually "the shepherd's own remark, and [hence] a matter of opinion," absolutely refuses to embroider
his informant's meagre narrative (*BNW,* chap. 10, 85–87).

Yet Diamond's dramatic struggle to gain admission into this drab place
is extraordinarily vivid. The boy assumed that North Wind would deposit
him in a vernal region that MacDonald situates, as Coleridge and Mary
Shelley had done, amidst frost and ice.[12] But he finds himself as deserted
as Dante was when his guide, too, departed before he could enter the divine forest in *Purgatorio.* North Wind, her face "worn and vivid," vanishes
before Diamond can reach his destination. As he stares on "in terror," he
sees that "her form and face were growing, not small, but transparent, like
something dissolving, not in water, but in light" (*BNW,* chap. 9, 80).

North Wind's fading form disconcerts Diamond much more than the
waning Cheshire Cat discomfits Alice. Death in Wonderland could be
comically defused. But for the tubercular writer who wrestled with the
illness that killed his mother, siblings, and children, such wanings carry
morbid associations. Diamond does not yet know that after melting away,
North Wind will reappear as an animated corpse:

He could see the side of the blue cave through her very heart. And she melted
away till all that was left was a pale face, like the moon in the morning, with two
great lucid eyes in it.

"I am going, Diamond," she said.

"Does it hurt you?" asked Diamond.

"It's very uncomfortable," she answered; "but I don't mind it, for I shall come
all right again before long. I thought I should be able to go with you all the way,
but I cannot. You must not be frightened, though. Just go straight on, and you will
come all right. You'll find me on the doorstep."

As she spoke, her face too quite faded away, only Diamond thought he could
still see her eyes shining through the blue. When he went closer, however, he found
that what he thought were her eyes were only two hollows in the ice. North Wind
was quite gone; and Diamond would have cried if he had not trusted her so thoroughly. (*BNW,* chap. 9, 80)

True to her promise, North Wind materializes at the margin of a land
that Diamond approaches more guardedly than curious Alice when she

---

12. See the "region of beauty and delight" that Walton expects to find as he sails to
the pole, while "a cold northern breeze plays upon my cheeks" (Mary Shelley, *Frankenstein, or, The Modern Prometheus,* ed. James Rieger [Chicago: University of Chicago Press,
1982], 9–10).

crossed forbidden borders in her adventures. The seated, sphinx-like figure he sees is numb and motionless; dressed in a "greenish robe" that resembles a shroud, with a face as "white as snow," she seems cadaverous.
Growing frightened again, Diamond is convinced that North Wind "must
be dead at last" (*BNW,* chap. 6, 82). Yet like Keats's Moneta, this frozen
"form" offers a feverish dreamer the higher status of a visionary seer.

North Wind asks the child who gazes so "fearfully" at her body to penetrate it if he truly wants to reach the country at her back. The crossing
she asks Diamond to undertake involves a transgression of the barriers
between life and death. At the same time, however, this passage through
a maternal body also offers an eroticized fantasy of return to a place of
origination. If the *Looking-Glass* Alice moved forward by stepping backward, Diamond moves backward—into a realm that antecedes conception
and birth—by boring forward, past the recumbent North Wind's lifted
knees. Like the snake that drilled a hole into the roof of Makemnoit's cave,
like North Wind herself as she ripped open the ceiling of the hay-loft, the
boy with the hard, gem-like name must now aggressively pierce through
the icy body of the same maternal figure who had pressed him against her
warm breast only a short while before. The wondrously opened mountain
cleft that irrigated Gluck's Treasure Valley has been replaced by the aper-
ture demanded by a desire so overwhelming that it needs to thrust itself
against all inhibiting barriers.

MacDonald makes it clear that North Wind considers the entry into
her body as still another test of the immensity of Diamond's unbounded
and unquestioning love—a love she more than ever finds difficult to re-
quite in the manner of a living, biological mother. When the boy mistakes
her paralysis for indifference, he reproaches her much as a small child
might reproach a dying parent for failing to return its hungry passion.
North Wind's reply suggests that his compulsive need for reciprocity may
be satisfied only after he adopts her own condition. He, too, will have to
fade, dissolve, and blend with her before moving on:

> "You don't care for me any more," said Diamond, almost crying now.
> "Yes, I do. Only I can't show it. All my love is down at the bottom of my heart.
> But I feel it bubbling there."
> "What do you want me to do next, dear North Wind?" said Diamond, wishing
> to show his love by being obedient.
> "What do you want to do yourself?"
> "I want to go into the country at your back."
> "Then you must go through me."

"I don't know what you mean."

"I mean just what I say. You must walk on as if I were an open door, and go right through me."

"But that will hurt you."

"Not in the least. It will hurt you, though."

"I don't mind that, if you tell me to do it."

"Do it," said North Wind. (*BNW,* chap. 9, 82–83)

As obedient as ever, Diamond is ready to undertake a journey that will radically alter his future behavior in the everyday world. "Durante" passed a gate that asked all those who entered to abandon hope; Diamond, however, is guided by a yearning that MacDonald equates with trust and hope. The mixture of ice and fire that now overpowers Diamond can be traced back to the trope that Petrarch applied to the lover of both a living and a dead Laura. It thus conveys an ecstasy that is as sensual as it is spiritual. Similarly, the excruciating pain that this little lover now experiences, though associated with the afflictions of martyrs and faithful pilgrims, seems to carry an almost orgasmic intensity:

Diamond walked towards her instantly. When he reached her knees, he put out his hand to lay it on her, but nothing was there save an intense cold. He walked on. Then all grew white about him; and the cold stung him like fire. He walked on still, groping through the whiteness. It thickened about him. At last, it got into his heart, and he lost all sense. I would say that he fainted—only whereas in common faints all grows black about you, he felt swallowed up in whiteness. It was when he reached North Wind's heart that he fainted and fell. But as he fell, he rolled over the threshold, and it was thus that Diamond got to the back of the north wind. (*BNW,* chap. 9, 82–83)

By recrossing this same threshold seven days later, Diamond undergoes a second birth. He now resembles the radiant boy in Wordsworth's "Intimations" ode, who, after entering the world "trailing clouds of glory," can dimly remember an effulgence in moments of "joy."[13] Diamond's own recollections, however, are preeminently aural. What Wordsworth calls the "master-light of all our seeing" remains more elusive for Diamond than the sounds that continue to reverberate in his head. And whereas the Wordsworthian child is destined to "forget the glories he hath known," Diamond will not allow "the light of common day" to extinguish his inti-

13. William Wordsworth, "Ode: Intimations of Immortality from Recollections of Early Childhood," lines 64, 70.

mations of immortality. Unlike the child in the ode, Diamond cannot be diverted by his "mother's kisses" or by the light that shines from a proud father's eyes.[14]

As Roderick McGillis has noted, MacDonald thus actually rejects the view of childhood advanced in the "Intimations" ode he is so very fond of quoting. For Wordsworth, childhood remains a valued phase because it allows grown-ups to recall a short-lived epoch in which there seems to be no death; for MacDonald, however, childhood "is a state of being which everyone must aspire to"[15] because it must be recovered as a gate for passing into a higher order. Although "muted by sin and age," childhood therefore "cannot be annihilated."[16]

In "A Sketch of Individual Development," a remarkable essay first published in 1880, MacDonald tried to revise Romantic psychology from a Christian perspective. Like Wordsworth, MacDonald places special emphasis on a boy's early awareness of "being surrounded, enfolded" by a sustaining atmosphere of maternal love: "the sky over him is his mother's face; the earth that nourishes him is his mother's bosom."[17] But whereas Wordsworth remains nostalgically attached to a "living Nature" that, in a later mental phase, replaces the lost childhood mother, MacDonald regards severance from the mother as a crucial preparation for the "cold, pain-soothing embrace of immortal Death" that awaits all humans.[18]

MacDonald anticipates twentieth-century psychologists in welcoming the child's early resistance to the mother as a needed first step in the road to socialization: "the power of the mother having waned, the power of the neighbour is waxing." Freed from overdependence on a maternal will, recognizing in himself a freedom of action, "of doing or of not doing," the boy who slips from his mother's lap can boldly explore what lies beyond his immediate circle. But MacDonald also gives a spiritual twist to this first manifestation of what he calls "the real Will—not the pseudo-will, which is the mere Desire." The child's willed severance from a mother

14. Ibid., lines 152, 83, 76, 88–89.

15. Roderick McGillis, "Childhood and Growth: George MacDonald and William Wordsworth," in *Romanticism and Children's Literature in Nineteenth-Century England,* ed. James Holt McGavran, Jr. (Athens: University of Georgia Press, 1991), 152.

16. Ibid., 153.

17. George MacDonald, "A Sketch of Individual Development," in *The Imagination and Other Essays* (Boston: D. Lothrop, 1883), 44.

18. Ibid., 59, 65.

whose face was "God" anticipates more difficult acts of assertion in later life. For the adult eventually must cut off all temporal ties to recover something akin to the "undivided bliss" of his first relation. Paradoxically, then, this repetition of willed loss may, in later life, restore unity with a higher being: "There is no type so near the highest idea of relation to God, as that of a child to his mother." For the boy, the "old heaven, the face and will of his mother, recede farther and farther" as he enters a "world of men," which he "foolishly" magnifies. Those who need to become a child again must therefore reverse the process. Whereas the growing boy deified a mother he was compelled to reject, the dying man must bring himself to accept an "Unseen Power" whom his skeptical understanding is reluctant to deify.[19]

IV

Though written long after *At the Back of the North Wind,* the essay on "individual development" helps to explain some of the roles MacDonald assigns to Diamond after the boy's return from "the good place" he has internalized (*BNW,* chap. 10, 88). With North Wind gone during the middle third of the book, her former pupil takes over her identity as teacher of the uninformed. MacDonald delights in Diamond's perverse unreason. He suggests that the child's return from a borderland between life and death has given him the authority—and a newly found "Will"— to challenge experiences his mother regards as axiomatic. When Martha tries to impress upon Diamond the gravity of hunger, he shocks her by parading his incomprehension:

"There *are* people in the world who have nothing to eat, Diamond."

"Then I suppose they don't stop in it any longer. They—they—what you call—die—don't they?"

"Yes, they do. How would you like that?"

"I don't know. I never tried. But I suppose they go where they get something to eat."

"Like enough they don't want it," said his mother petulantly.

"That's all right then," said Diamond, thinking I dare say more than he chose to put in words. (*BNW,* chap. 13, 101)

19. Ibid., 48, 47, 44.

The narrator's last remark seems puzzling. Is the resurrected boy thinking of his contentment, "better than mere happiness," in the land at the back of North Wind? When questioned about "the people there" by the narrator who will become his biographer, Diamond allows that they looked "quite pleased," albeit a "little sad" at finding themselves in a mere way station between their past and a "gladder" future (*BNW,* chap. 10, 88). Even Diamond's unwillingness to verbalize the knowledge he has gained stems from his kinship with figures who can silently communicate when they "only look at each other, and understand everything" (*BNW,* chap. 10, 87).

His anti-verbal stance, however, also allows Diamond to undercut his mother's condescending use of the stale similes she deems appropriate for a child of his limited understanding. Provoked by his quietism, Martha insists that hunger and death are not abstractions, but directly applicable to the family's predicament. She tries to rattle the boy by telling him that "we shall have nothing to eat by and by" (*BNW,* chap. 13, 101), and becomes exasperated when he points to a piece of gingerbread in the basket before them:

> "O you little bird! You have no more sense than a sparrow that picks what it wants, and never thinks of the winter and the frost and the snow."
> "Ah—yes—I see. But the birds get through the winter, don't they?"
> "Some of them fall dead on the ground."
> "They must die some time. They wouldn't like to be birds always. Would you, Mother?"
> "What a child it is!" thought his mother, but she said nothing. (*BNW,* chap. 13, 102)

Martha's underestimation of a child who has just come back from a journey through "frost" and "snow" becomes apparent in the chapters that follow. For Diamond not only acts as the family's chief provider but also takes care of other victims, such as the much-abused Nanny and her crippled friend Jim. When Diamond decides to find Nanny's dwelling place in a foul London slum, a policeman urges him to stay away from the place, lest accompanied by an adult. The unabashed boy ignores the advice. On finding Nanny gravely ill in her filthy lodgings, he is promptly attacked by vicious denizens of the Victorian underworld. The policeman, who has warily followed Diamond, afraid that the child might get "torn" apart, routs the assailants. Gently reproaching Diamond for his excessive trust, he points out that the boy might have suffered great harm "if I hadn't been at hand." Diamond's prompt reply is disarming: "Yes; but you were at hand, you know, so they couldn't." The narrator glosses this truism by saying, "Perhaps the answer was deeper in purport than either Diamond or the policeman knew" (*BNW,* chap. 21, 163).

MacDonald seems to recognize, however, that he must rely on something more than such dialogues between coy Innocence and wary Experience if he is to succeed in vindicating Diamond's unconscious awareness of a "deeper purport." He therefore suggests Diamond's consonance with higher harmonies through more symbolic means. The river sounds that still flow in Diamond's mind have made him attuned to unheard melodies. Whereas earlier, the boy still needed North Wind to explain that a poet was someone "glad of something," he now responds to the incantatory rhythms of a certain kind of free-flowing and free-associational verse. The automatic, self-propelling rhymes he tries to master, even before learning how to read and write, strike Diamond as a better medium for his intuitions than the linguistic precisions demanded by adults. In its preference of sound over sense, this formless type of poetry conveys the feelings of well-being and trust that Diamond finds so difficult to articulate through causal and linear discourse.

Diamond's first experience of such a different mode of utterance occurs, significantly enough, when he is still at the seashore debating with his mother. Pointing to "something fluttering" in the sand, he gets his mother to retrieve what turns out to be "a little book, partly buried in the sand" (*BNW,* chap. 13, 104). When Diamond asks her to read aloud to him what she identifies as nursery rhymes, Martha is frustrated by a poem that strikes her as incomprehensible. She offers to "find a better poem," but a puff of wind thrice blows "the leaves rustling back to the same verses," and Diamond, "of the same mind as the wind," urges her to continue reading. After more than two-hundred lines (and five pages of printed text!) of euphonious, unpunctuated, repetitious yet ever-varying combinations of a limited number of words, Martha has had enough; unlike the pleasantly lulled Diamond, she cannot relax her expectations of direction or meaning:

> "It's such nonsense,!" said his mother. "I believe it would go on for ever."
> "That's just what it did," said Diamond.
> "What did?" she asked.
> "Why, the river. That's almost the very tune it used to sing."
> His mother was frightened, for she thought the fever was coming on again. So she did not contradict him.

"Who made that poem?" asked Diamond.

"I don't know," she answered. "Some silly woman for her children, I suppose—and then thought it good enough to print."

"She must have been at the back of the north wind some time or other, anyhow," said Diamond. "She couldn't have got a hold of it anywhere else. That's just how it went." And he began to chant bits of it here and there; but his mother said nothing for fear of making him worse. (BNW, chap. 13, 112)

The nameless song that so stimulates Diamond is MacDonald's own version of Carroll's "Jabberwocky." Already displaying the adult's interest in definitive meanings, Alice wanted Humpty Dumpty to decode the words of the elusive poem that so intrigued her. Diamond, however, prefers to submit himself to the sounds and rhythms of a catalogue of nouns and verbs that yield no action, no crowning event in which "*somebody* killed *something*" (as Alice so shrewdly noted). We are offered no vorpal sword cutting through gordian knots, no climactic welcoming of a "beamish boy." The never-ending song that the mother of a radiant boy dismisses as errant "nonsense" features no human agent.

Despite occasional conjunctions ("and," "or," "but") and connectives that seem to suggest some causal logic ("for," "so," "and so"), the poem MacDonald has Martha ascribe to a "silly woman" is the kind of antinarrative that Julia Kristeva would call a "genotext": the attempted reconstruction of a process that is "ephemeral" and "unstable" as it "organizes a space" and moves through zones that have only "relative and transitory borders."[20] The only threads that can be said to run through this drawn-out canticle are provided by its opening reference to "a river" and by the recurrent introduction of "the wind" that becomes identified with that river. The flowing river whose waters "run run ever" (line 3) blends with the blowing wind found everywhere: "it's all in the wind / that blows from behind / and all in the river / that flows forever" (lines 199–203). But this fluidity has neither a source nor a destination: "but never you find / whence comes the wind / that blows on the hollows / and over the shallows / where dip the swallows / alive it blows / the life as it goes / awake or asleep / into the river / that sings as it flows / and the life it blows" (lines 129–140). There is no middle or end or beginning to the circularities that Diamond finds so familiar (*BNW,* chap. 13, 106–111). No longer in need of Martha's rendition of the verses, Diamond chants snippets from it be-

20. Julia Kristeva, "Revolution in Poetic Language," in *The Kristeva Reader,* ed. Toril Moi (New York: Columbia University Press, 1988), 121.

fore falling "fast asleep and dreaming of the land at the back of the north wind" (*BNW,* chap. 13, 112). He is in that state described as an entry into a "higher life" in MacDonald's 1880 essay on the growth of a boy's mind: upon recognizing "certain relations, initiated by fancies, desires, preferences that arise within himself" in the "world that is not his mother," the boy opens himself to an "existence and force of Being other and higher than his own."[21]

Yet the narrator of *At the Back of the North Wind* is as slippery as ever when he warns us that the verses he has reproduced are not to be construed as the actual words that fluttered in a seaside breeze: "Now I do not know exactly what the mother read, but this is what Diamond heard, *or thought afterwards that he had heard*" (*BNW,* chap. 13, 104; italics added). Lines that MacDonald has obviously composed himself thus are divested of any authorial imprint. The letter of the text is unimportant. It is Diamond's receptivity that is being stressed when the narrator reminds the reader that Diamond was, after all, "very sleepy" at the time and that, although "he thought he understood the verses" recited to him, "he may have been only dreaming better ones" (*BNW,* chap. 13, 104–105).

Later, when Diamond's father uses "those very rhymes" as a "lesson-book" to teach the boy how to read, Diamond immediately hunts for "the poem he thought he had heard his mother read." He fancies he might identify it merely from "the look of it," yet even after he can make out individual words, the poem continues to elude him. He therefore settles for verses that also appeal to him, although they "were certainly not very like those he was in search of" (*BNW,* chap. 20, 150). Unlike the earlier poem, this enigmatic retelling of "Little Boy Blue" has a slight narrative thread: like Carroll's slayer of the Jabberwock, a little boy triumphs by vanquishing a snake. Diamond readily identifies the snake with the biblical serpent; still, he halts his exegesis by confessing that he cannot extract much more. When Martha calls him "a silly" for taking the poem so seriously and for holding it "true," he responds: "That killing of the snake looks true. It's what I've got to do so often" (*BNW,* chap. 21, 159). The snake, he implies, stands for a negativity he daily combats in others.

Chapter 13 marks a division between the obedient child who had deferred to North Wind as well as to Martha and the newly resolute boy

21. MacDonald, "Sketch of Individual Development," 45–46.

who navigates throughout a bleak Dickensian London, armed only by his faith in an unseen North Wind. MacDonald now validates Diamond's credentials by giving us more instances of his unusual poetic consciousness, and by making us privy to a dream that suggests the boy's subconscious awareness of otherworldy origins. At the same time, however, we follow Diamond's activities as a social worker whose engagements with the everyday world also validate his visionary status. Dream and actuality now intersect. They can no longer be kept apart if a child's innocence is to act as a guide for the higher Innocence that MacDonald, like Blake before him, regards as the vanquisher of empirical Experience.

In his 1880 essay, "A Sketch of Individual Development," MacDonald explained that his ideal "child of man" should reject solipsism: "He is capable not only of being influenced merely, but of influencing."[22] "Influence"—a word derived from the supposed effect of fluids emanating from heaven—becomes the main task of a boy who identifies himself with flowing winds and rivers, and who, in the dream that takes him back to origins, seems himself to have descended from the stars above. After chapter 13, Diamond must do more than frustrate a literal-minded mother. His task is to influence others through the glad tidings he can bring. This hero of a serial published in the Evangelical children's magazine that took its name from the Gospels—*Good Words for the Young*—must now become a gospel worker. He will affect others through good words and good deeds before he can once more blend with his beloved North Wind, the extraterrestrial worker of strange ways.

V

While asleep, Diamond still hears the "far-off sounds of the river" he later converts into songs for his baby sister. But the waking Diamond confers a new sheen on the common world around him. By the time he takes his sick father's place on the hansom cab, he has earned the respect and admiration of rival cab drivers, policemen, passengers, and pedestrians. Even Martha basks in her son's achievements. When he starts to help her around the house, she proclaims him "as good to your mother as if you were a girl," and swears, in a compliment undercut by the narrator's ironic

---

22. Ibid., 48.

stance towards Fairyland,[23] that "a body would think you had been among the fairies" (*BNW,* chap. 16, 120). And when Diamond becomes the family's sole breadwinner, Martha's "pride in her boy" even exceeds "her joy in the shillings" he contributes (*BNW,* chap. 25, 185). She is no longer his foil.

As Diamond's parents become more dependent on him, however, their point of view also recedes in importance. MacDonald therefore introduces two other figures to act as Diamond's prime foils: Nanny the street-sweeper and Mr. Raymond, the "tall gentleman" who first meets both children at the crossing that Nanny has made passable for his "nice boots" (*BNW,* chap. 19, 144). Unaware at first of the boy who stands beside Nanny, Mr. Raymond seems far "more interested in her," attracted by the "sweet smile" that greets his penny-tip. Yet he becomes uneasy—not knowing "what to say next"—when he realizes that this picturesque child suffers from a drunken grandmother's physical abuse. Sensing the gentleman's embarrassed discovery "that such a nice little girl should be in such bad keeping," Diamond tries to mediate. But instead of being allowed to explain Nanny to Mr. Raymond, he finds himself being characterized by her: he is a "good boy," she confides, but "not right in the head" (*BNW,* chap 19, 145).

Diamond's presumed idiocy is easier to handle for Mr. Raymond than Nanny's victimization. He engages the boy in a condescending chat, "for, accepting what the girl had said, he regarded the still sweetness of Diamond's face as a sign of silliness, and wished to be kind to the poor little fellow." After a perfunctory set of questions, Mr. Raymond declares him to be "a useful little man," gives him a penny of his own, and tries to slink away. Hardly expecting to be taken up on a prospect that strikes him as unlikely, he invites Diamond "to come to me" upon having learned how to read and offers a reward of "sixpence and a book with fine pictures in it" (*BNW,* chap. 19, 146). Yet Diamond surprises this guarded child-lover.[24] He demands the gentleman's address and, after pocketing the card,

23. See chap. 2, 13: "I have seen this world—only sometimes, just now and then, you know—look as strange as I ever saw Fairyland. But I confess that I have not yet seen Fairyland at its best. I am always *going* to see it some time."

24. MacDonald's rejection of eternal punishment somehow prompts James R. Kincaid to group him among "Victorian pedophiles." But the ironic handling of Mr. Raymond suggests a contrary story; moreover, MacDonald's investment in the boy Diamond is far less erotic than his identification with Diamond's arousal by the voluptuous body of

allows Nanny to keep his own penny. Mr. Raymond is about to be enlightened. The boy, he begins to think, may not be such a "silly," after all.

Although the narrator insists that Mr. Raymond is "one of the kindest men in London" (*BNW,* chap. 21, 165), MacDonald also makes it clear that the sympathetic capacities of this genteel philanthropist are greatly inferior to Diamond's. When Diamond seeks help for the gravely ill Nanny, he finds access barred by Mr. Raymond's servant. Even after the gentleman finally materializes, Mr. Raymond mistakes his visitor's purpose by assuming that Diamond has come to claim the promised sixpence. Upon being corrected, he must be reminded of Nanny's identity. Mr. Raymond's forgetfulness anticipates his later, more damaging, lapse; his benign neglect of Diamond's father will cause the family renewed hardship.

MacDonald's treatment of the man on whose protection not only Diamond and his parents, but also Nanny and Jim, will rely involves more than a critique of the bourgeois benevolence so often upheld by Victorian ideologues. Mr. Raymond's interest in the poor not only lacks an engagement with real-life penury, but is also curiously aestheticized. When Lewis Carroll had Alice Liddell shed her fashionable cotton and muslin dresses to pose in the suggestively arranged rags of a pathetic "Beggar Child," he produced a photograph memorable for its fetishism. The expression of the little girl, who stares at the camera so seductively, suggests that she is complicitous as a participant in the masquerade: no true beggar would radiate such coquettish self-assurance, let alone be provided with a rug carefully placed beneath the pleasingly plump foot she has been invited to bare. It is the *idea* of such pretty "begging" that appeals to Carroll, just as the idea of an alternate childhood in which he might have been forced "to lie on stone beds and eat black soup" struck Ruskin as an exciting antidote to his coddled bourgeois upbringing.[25]

Mr. Raymond exerts his influence by having Nanny taken to a children's hospital, where, we are told, "he was well known to everybody, for he was not only a large subscriber, but he used to go and tell the children stories of an afternoon" (*BNW,* chap. 21, 165). The faintly ironic sentence once again suggests that this childless gentleman's sporadic involvement with children is at a remove from childhood itself. Such an inference is confirmed as soon as MacDonald contrasts the freshness of Diamond's

---

a super-seductive North Wind. See *Child-Loving: The Erotic Child and Victorian Culture* (London: Routledge, 1992), 245n.

25. See chapter 2, p. 39, above.

imagination to Mr. Raymond's afternoon fancy. Aware that his acquaintance is a storyteller and poet, Diamond hands Mr. Raymond "the torn and crumpled book" of verses he found at the seashore. But when asked to explicate the enigmatic version of "Little Boy Blue" that so appeals to the boy, Mr. Raymond offers no true insights beyond Diamond's own sense that "the snake had something to do with it." Moreover, when Mr. Raymond ceremoniously presents Diamond with a book he has written "chiefly for the children of the hospital," he feels compelled to explain that he did not himself print the book but nonetheless "made it" (*BNW,* chap. 22, 166, 167). To his surprise, Diamond not only understands perfectly well the idea of authorship but also announces that he is a "maker" himself:

> "I know what you mean. I make songs myself. They're awfully silly, but they please Baby, and that's all they're meant for."
> "Couldn't you let me hear one of them now?" said Mr. Raymond.
> "No, sir, I couldn't. I forget them as soon as I've done with them. Besides, I couldn't make a line without Baby on my knee. We make them together, you know. They're just as much Baby's as mine. It's he that pulls them out of me."
> "I suspect the child's a genius," said the poet to himself, "and that's what makes people think him silly." (*BNW,* chap. 22, 167)

The brief exchange dramatizes a reversal of roles: the author who hopes to add Diamond to his audience of child readers now begs the boy to let him hear one of Diamond's own productions. But Diamond's songs require the cooperation of a prelinguistic infant who actually fits the narrator's peculiar gloss of "genius" for his own "child readers": "one who understands things without any other body telling him what they mean" (*BNW,* chap. 22, 168).

Mr. Raymond's work—as we discover from one of his poems, "The True History of the Cat and the Fiddle," as well as from the fairy tale of "Little Daylight" which MacDonald attributes to him—relies on antecedent texts for parodic effects. Diamond, however, by-passes such a self-conscious mode of subversion in verses that stress sound and image over sense. It therefore seems significant that by the time he offers his baby brother a song taken "out of Mr. Raymond's book" rather than composed by himself, he and Baby no longer enjoy the same unreflecting partnership. Although neither has appreciably aged, Diamond, who has just brought home his first earnings, somehow seems correct when he prefaces the borrowed song by saying, with humorous exaggeration, "Baby, baby! I haven't seen you for a whole year" (*BNW,* chap. 24, 182).

Still, Diamond's imagination remains untarnished when contrasted to that of a child as badly bruised by adults as Nanny or to that of an actual adult like Mr. Raymond, whose Carrollian veneration of childhood is marked by nostalgia and irony. Known as "Sal's Nanny," the girl possessed by her sadistic grandmother is also crippled by self-distrust. Her sense of worthlessness helps explain why she prefers to associate herself with "cripple Jim" rather than with the buoyant Diamond. For his part, Mr. Raymond also seems insecure when he tries to test the "genius" he has praised by asking the boy to solve a riddle he has written for his child readers. He sends Diamond home with instructions to "think over" this artificial construct. The narrator intervenes to challenge the action as a debasing form of one-upmanship. Addressing "some little reader" of his own, he explains that a true genius ought to be asked only to ferret out "truths, not tricks" (*BNW*, chap. 22, 169).

MacDonald upholds Diamond's truth-finding capacities by contrasting the boy's "very curious dream" in chapter 25 with both the fairy tale that Mr. Raymond tells the hospital children in chapter 28 and the dream that Nanny, still at the hospital, tries to relay to Diamond in chapter 30. There is a distinct hierarchy suggested by these three interpolated narratives. By placing Diamond's dream first, MacDonald ranks it as the least contaminated, healthier by far than the two therapeutic fantasies told in a hospital ward. Although Mr. Raymond's story of "Little Daylight," which Nanny acknowledges as a source for some of her dream-images, precedes the girl's account, it should be placed lowest on the imaginative scale that Mac-Donald invites us to build.

Mr. Raymond's tale is the most public of these three fantasy-constructs. Like *The King of the Golden River*, it recycles materials from well-known fairy tales—as MacDonald's narrator cannot forbear pointing out; and it is told to other children besides Diamond and Nanny. This varied audience of young and older children allows the author to test his narrative on a trial audience—as Lewis Carroll actually did with the Liddells and the MacDonalds. Publication is deferred by a man of leisure who can implant refinements that future tellings might bring about. Further listeners, Mr. Raymond knows, surely will provide questions and "amusing remarks" he can incorporate (*BNW*, chap. 29, 226).[26]

---

26. There may well be a personal subtext to the narrator's remark that Mr. Raymond had the leisure to "make his stories better" after "every" one of his retellings and rewritings (*BNW*, chap. 28, 206). An impoverished professional writer as rushed as MacDonald

Nanny's confidential account of her dream is told to a single auditor. But the tale also reveals how much she doubts her right to a private vision. She concludes that her banishment from a fantasy-realm dominated by a female presence is fully deserved. Seeing herself as an unworthy trespasser, Nanny questions her qualifications as a dreamer. As a result, her narrative is halting, tentative, constantly interrupted by the supportive comments of Diamond, who wants to help her put a more positive construction on events she regards as bleak. Diamond's mediating efforts are sincere, but they only confirm the narrator's belief that Nanny cannot be trusted as teller or interpreter of her own dream:

My readers must not suppose that poor Nanny was able to say what she meant so well as I put it down here. She had never been to school, and had heard very little else than vulgar speech until she came to the hospital. But I have been to school, and although that could never make me able to dream so well as Nanny, it has made me able to tell her dream better than she could herself. And I am the more desirous of doing this for her [since] I have already done the best I could for Diamond's dream, and it would be a shame to give the boy all the advantage. (*BNW*, chap. 30, 233)

The remark rings untrue. By having his narrator call attention to Nanny's deficient imagination, MacDonald most assuredly gives Diamond "all the advantage."

For the same narrator relays Diamond's dream without any such hint of his own editorial skills; quite to the contrary, he deferentially reproduces a narrative that he presumably heard in the course of his later interactions with the boy. Proud of having been chosen as exclusive confidant, the narrator obscures himself in recounting the boy's "very curious dream." Although he renders it in the third person, he minimizes his role far more than the chatty narrator who relayed Alice's own "curious dream" of Wonderland. Sure that "my readers" will be "as fond of nice dreams as I am, and don't have enough of them of their own," he seems content to act as a mere transmitter (*BNW*, chap. 25, 186). His self-suppression, so unlike Diamond's interruptions of Nanny's dream, is crucial if the dreamer's

---

clearly lacked the time available to wealthy and perfectionist authors such as the fictional Mr. Raymond or the real-life Lewis Carroll. Since the story of "Little Daylight" is of MacDonald's own coinage, however, the joke also seems to be aimed at himself: the version of the fairy tale that appeared in the 1871 text of *At the Back of the North Wind* is identical to that published, in the same year, in the ninth volume of MacDonald's *Works of Fancy and the Imagination* (227–270).

unself-consciousness is to be preserved. For MacDonald wants to keep the narrative free from the contaminations he deliberately injects in the tales told by Nanny and Mr. Raymond.

VI

Diamond's unbroken dream, Nanny's dream fragment, and Mr. Raymond's story of "Little Daylight" are competing versions of the core fantasy that shapes the plot of *At the Back of the North Wind*. For each of these interpolated narratives dramatizes the same yearning for incorporation with a female Other that so powerfully fuels MacDonald's imagination. Each story centers on a wanderer's venture into a magical space. Diamond first dreams about "waiting for North Wind" in the "old garden" in which he met her when he was smaller. Vainly looking for her in a lush and ever-expanding landscape—"a beautiful country, not like any country he had ever been before"—he settles contentedly under a "rose-bush" to be transported into a more exotic realm in a new dream-within-a-dream (*BNW,* chap. 25, 186, 187). Nanny, who claims to have been affected by the role the moon had played in Mr. Raymond's story, dreams of exchanging London's moonless, muddy streets for a beckoning "garden place with green grass, and the moon shining upon it!" (*BNW,* chap. 30, 236). The young prince in Mr. Raymond's tale is even more volitionless. "[C]ompelled to flee for his life, disguised like a peasant" after a massacre of his country's patriarchy, he comes to "the outside of the forest" he merely wants to traverse, when he, too, stumbles upon a "lovely spot" that is moon-bathed and grassy (*BNW,* chap. 28, 213, 215).

Each of these three travelers has been specially chosen to enter a space that offers unexpected sights to their aroused imaginations. Diamond hears "a child's voice" inviting him to "come up" to an unseen location he finds by intuitively choosing to go down (*BNW,* chap. 25, 187, 188). Nanny and the young prince, however, lack Diamond's ability to "look through the look of things," and therefore require the assistance of adults to get to their destinations. When a huge, shiny moon descends next to Nanny, "a curious little old man" steps out to "fetch" the paralyzed girl (*BNW,* chap. 30, 239). This dwarf, Nanny soon discovers, is her superior, though himself a servant to the beautiful lady of the moon. Just as Nanny's servitude is mirrored by the dwarf, so the prince's reliance on a lowly disguise is adopted by the "very nice tidy motherly woman" who feeds him yet refuses to show him how "to get out of this wood" (*BNW,* chap. 28, 214). The matronly figure is actually a fairy who wants to steer this young man towards her ward, Princess Daylight.

The new setting entered by the dreaming Diamond reverses the image of draining that MacDonald had dramatized in "The Light Princess." Lifted by the waters of an upward bubbling stream, Diamond pushes his way out of a subterranean hole into an open place where he is embraced by a host of shouting "naked little boys" with wings (*BNW,* chap. 25, 189). Feeling light and carefree in the company of other children, Diamond seems at the opposite extreme of the sad and uncomfortable prince who had risked death when he "corked" the hole in Lake Lagobel. The prince had demanded a kiss from the child-woman whose gravity—and adult sexuality—he helped restore. Diamond, however, cavorts with levitating angel boys whose kisses make his heart melt "from clear delight." He has regained a prenatal Eden.[27] The place where a wind blows "like the very embodiment of living gladness" seems superior to the windless realm at the back of North Wind (*BNW,* chap. 25, 190). Possibly the "gladder" haven that travelers such as Kilmeny and Durante had yearned for (*BNW,* chap. 11, 88), it seems a place of origination that Diamond has half-forgotten in his waking life. His angelic dream-companions, however, recognize him as one of their own; by "constantly coming back to Diamond," they acknowledge him "as the centre of their enjoyment, rejoicing over him as if he had been a lost playmate" (*BNW,* chap. 25, 190).

MacDonald uses the remainder of this joyful dream to tease us into constructing a mythic genealogy for Diamond that neither the boy nor the narrator ever propound. Diamond may indeed be a wingless angel boy who—like one of the playmates he observes—has zoomed to earth through a hole created by digging "up a small star" of a color to his liking (*BNW,* chap. 25, 191). The shining lumps of precious stones unearthed by these boy miners—rubies or emeralds or amethysts—may, in effect, influence their naming after their incarnation in the world below. That everyday world, however, has given Diamond an awareness that the angel boys lack: "I don't see any little girls," he astutely remarks. His companions are baffled, having never met such complementary beings. They allow that "those others—what do you call them?—" may do repair work to undo the damage the boys cause by their own digging and trampling. But

27. Unlike the Greek word *paradisos* (a walled garden), the Hebrew *edhen* simply means "delight."

if so, they reason, these creatures must make their rounds whenever "we fall asleep." Diamond eagerly awaits the arrival of "girl-angels," since "I, not being an angel, shall not fall asleep." But sleep overcomes him as much as the others. The best he can do is try to remember some of the "nonsense" verses sung by the boy-angels; still, the few lines he recalls are "so near sense" that he doubts their genuineness (*BNW,* chap 25, 192, 193, 194).

The female sexuality that Diamond's dream manages to erase plays a more prominent role in Nanny's dream and altogether dominates the plot of Mr. Raymond's "Little Daylight." Both narratives offer variations of the concern with the passage from girlhood to womanhood that had preoccupied MacDonald's three male predecessors, Ruskin, Thackeray, and Carroll. Nanny's dream dramatizes a pubescent girl's difficulty in negotiating this passage without the support and example of a maternal model. The tale of "Little Daylight," on the other hand, dramatizes a male perspective that MacDonald well understood from his contacts with Ruskin and Carroll: Mr. Raymond's true protagonist is not the story's titular heroine, but rather the prince who must overcome his aversion to menstrual women. Through Nanny's dream and by revising his own story of "The Light Princess," Macdonald subtly repudiates the hankering for ever-pure little girls harbored by his two fellow fantasists.

There were several reasons why MacDonald may have wanted Nanny's dream to follow, rather than precede, Mr. Raymond's story. He implies that the emotional needs of this maltreated street-child cannot really be met by a story that merely reshuffles the habitual trappings of fairy tales familiar to well-read Victorian middle-class children. But more than a gap in class affiliations is involved. For MacDonald also seems to hint that the male point of view that shapes the erotics of "Little Daylight" is of dubious help to any girl on the threshold of puberty. Although Nanny derives her imagery from Mr. Raymond's tale of still another cursed princess released by a lover's kiss, the dream itself has been induced by her hypnotic attachment to a ruby ring that a kind lady visitor has temporarily lent the sick child. This philanthropic gentlewoman, who eventually rescues Mr. Raymond himself from perpetual virginity, is transformed into a yearned-for, yet ultimately inaccessible, figure of female authority in Nanny's dream. The dwarf's "beautiful mistress," the "moon-lady," seems too removed from the lowly servant pressed into service at her lunar abode (*BNW,* chap. 30, 240).

After Nanny tells her dream, Diamond asks her to fall asleep again and try to complete what she has aborted. His response seems justified.

Nanny's account painfully thwarts the reader's desire to witness a fulfillment of the wishes of a child whose psychological health requires something other than the nostrums prescribed by a Victorian middle-class culture that stressed the importance of virtuous parental control and example. After her trials in Wonderland, a waking Alice could return to the comforts offered by her elders. Nanny, however, finds that her dream-trials are no different from those she experiences in her everyday life. Tested in her dream as window cleaner by the dwarf who has become too old for the job, Nanny desperately wants to please the motionless white lady of the moon who averts her "whole face" from her new servant. Although Nanny wants the lady to turn her head "full upon me, or even to look at me" (*BNW,* chap. 30, 245), she accepts the disdain as a mark of her own unworthiness. Her fears of inadequacy come true when she opens, Pandora-like, a box of fiery bees that should have remained shut.

Although the moon-lady professes to pity Nanny, she banishes her from her feminine domain. A girl who cannot "be trusted" to repress her impulse to experience the forbidden, she declares, is "only fit for the mud" (*BNW,* chap 30, 247). Further aggravating Nanny's guilt feelings, the employer in the dream accuses her of having stolen the ring she is wearing and orders the dwarf to twist it off. Unable to protest her innocence, a profoundly "ashamed" Nanny wakes up. Diamond's assurances that she might still have "nice talks with the moon-lady" strike her as impossible. "Sal's Nanny" cannot become the moon-lady's ward. Although she finds herself cared for, hereafter, by Mr. Raymond and his bride, she will prefer the acceptance of "Cripple Jim" to the company of the "little girl-angels" that the cheerful Diamond is sure she might have met (*BNW,* chap. 30, 240).

Mr. Raymond centers his story of "Little Daylight" on the predicament of a princess whose health is tied to the cycle of the moon. But his narrative seems almost as removed from its feminine sources as Nanny was when banished by the moon-lady. Claiming to be unable to come up with the "true story" demanded by a girl auditor, Mr. Raymond complies, instead, with a little boy's request by offering "a sort of a fairy tale" (*BNW,* chap. 27, 205). His fantasy about a young woman whose appearance degenerates every month exaggerates the revulsion over female aging so prevalent in Victorian male fantasies from *Alice in Wonderland* to Rider Haggard's *She.* Princess Daylight is more of a freak than her counterpart in "The Light Princess." Asleep during the day, this night creature, too, finds ways of "enjoying her moonlight alone" (*BNW,* chap. 28, 212). But the child-woman who steals away on nightly swims proves irresistible to the prince who so quickly "falls in" with her. In "Little Daylight," however, it seems "inconceivable" that "any prince" might "find and deliver" a princess whose monthly cycles transform a fresh beauty into a wizened monster:

As she grew older she had grown more and more beautiful, with the sunniest hair and the loveliest eyes of heavenly blue, brilliant and profound as the sky of a June day. But so much more painful and sad was the change as her time came on. The more beautiful she was in the full moon, the more withered and worn did she become as the moon waned. At the time at which my story has now arrived, she looked, when the moon was small or gone, like an old woman exhausted with suffering. This was the more painful that her appearance was unnatural; for her hair and eyes did not change. Her wan face was both drawn and wrinkled, and had an eager hungry look. Her skinny hands moved as if wishing, but unable, to lay hold of something. (*BNW,* chap. 28, 212)

The "something" this hungry, almost vampiric creature desires whenever her "change" comes upon her is a fresh prince who might replenish her waning life-blood. Yet as soon as her vitality is restored by a crescent moon, a male lover becomes inconsequential. Self-sufficient, ecstatic, the princess celebrates the full power of her femininity in a private ritual, "singing like a nightingale, and dancing to her own music, with her eyes ever turned to the moon" (*BNW,* chap. 28, 215–16). The good fairy who draws the disguised prince into the forest glade to watch this performance makes sure that he will see a figure of radiant Innocence, "a girl dressed in white, gleaming in the moon-shine," before he ever faces the loathly hag he eventually must kiss (*BNW,* chap. 28, 215). As voyeuristic and sentimental as his counterpart in "The Light Princess," the young idealist at first resists the notion that this apparition may be as human as himself. He dares not approach her, lest "she should vanish from his sight." After more furtive gazings, he becomes "incapable of thinking of anything" but this beautiful dream-child (*BNW,* chap. 28, 216, 218).

Only an accident emboldens the prince to approach the object of his desire. A lightning bolt—no doubt unleashed by the fairy to whom Mr. Raymond assigns a role akin to that which MacDonald assigns to North Wind—leads the young man to assume that the princess has been stunned or even killed. Their brief exchange ends when she makes "a repellent gesture" which only exacerbates his desire (*BNW,* chap. 28, 221). Like Diamond patiently waiting for North Wind to reappear, he abides his time. But the creature he finally meets on a "night in which there was no moon at all" (*BNW,* chap. 28, 223) is not the seductive figure he has expected:

He sprang to his feet, but his heart throbbed so that he had to lean for a moment against the tree before he could move. When he got round, there lay a human form in a little dark heap on the earth. There was light enough from his fire to show that it was not the Princess. He lifted it in his arms, hardly heavier than a child, and carried it to the flame. The countenance was that of an old woman, but it had a fearfully strange look. A black cloak concealed her hair, and her eyes were closed. He laid her down as comfortably as he could, chafed her hands, put a little cordial from a bottle, also the gift of the fairy, into her mouth; took off his coat and wrapped it about her, and in short did the best he could. In a little while she opened her eyes and looked at him—so pitifully! The tears rose and flowed down her grey wrinkled cheeks, but she said never a word. (*BNW,* chap. 28, 224–25)

Here, as at the end of "The Light Princess," the flow of tears proves to be redemptive. Yet instead of the weeping Light Princess who nurtures an inert prince with the aid of her old nurse, it is the prince himself who uses the "motherly" fairy's bottle to revive the bundled figure, light as a child, whom he cradles in his arms. Convinced that the moaning creature is about die, the young man, "very near crying," implores her to stay alive. His pity is overpowering: "'Mother, mother!' he said. 'Poor mother!' and kissed her on the withered lips." His spontaneous act of love breaks the spell. Abasing himself once again, he falls at a young woman's feet, not daring to "look up until she laid her hand upon his head" (*BNW,* chap. 28, 225).

Even before Mr. Raymond begins this fantasy of recuperation, the narrator steps in to question its appeal: "I do not know how much of Mr. Raymond's story the smaller children understood; indeed, I don't quite know how much there was in it to be understood, for in such a story everyone just has to take what he can get" (*BNW,* chap. 27, 206). Given the tale's adverse effect on Nanny as demonstrated by her subsequent dream, and given, too, Diamond's failure to respond to it, the narrator's remark adds still another note of distrust to MacDonald's habitual reservations about fairy tales for children. The insertion of "The Light Princess" into *Adela Cathcart* supposedly allowed an adult heroine to recover a child-like faith; the insertion of "Little Daylight" into *At the Back of the North Wind,* however, only underscores the freshness of Diamond's nonliterary imagination. The narrator snidely stresses Mr. Raymond's derivativeness: "I cannot help myself thinking that he was somewhat indebted for this to the old story of The Sleeping Beauty" (*BNW,* chap. 27, 206).

Why does MacDonald express hostility towards a tale he readily acknowledged as his own in other collections? And why is his grave narrator so unappreciative of its fine Thackerayan wit? Diamond's earnest biographer seems deaf to the wonderfully comic deflation of standard fairy-tale paraphernalia in the story's early portions; nor does he appear willing to concede that "Mr. Raymond" freshens, not just "Sleeping Beauty" or "The Frog Prince," but also the subtext of the tale which Chaucer assigned to his Wife of Bath. As I have been suggesting, the ironic handling of Mr. Raymond's imagination allows MacDonald to distance himself from falsifying constructions of female purity that he recognized in other male fantasists. The "gentleman-prince" who worships a distant figure in white must be taught what Mr. Raymond himself has to learn—namely, that "femininity" involves more than aestheticized female shapes gazed from afar. The prince's voyeurism resembles that of two gentlemen of MacDonald's acquaintance. Princess Daylight's story has much to do with Lewis Carroll's wishful constructions of perennially young dream-children and with Ruskin's confessions to MacDonald about the shattering discovery that Effie Gray had become a menstrual woman.

Yet MacDonald's attempt to distance himself from Mr. Raymond's fantasy can also be read as an act of self-protection. For the prince who kisses the dying woman he thrice calls "mother" enacts the same incestuous yearning dramatized when Diamond penetrated the cold body of a seemingly dead North Wind. MacDonald's implied critique of Carroll and Ruskin for allowing their stories to be shaped by adult preoccupations can, after all, be applied to his own work. For MacDonald cannot refrain from using Mr. Raymond's fairy tale as a vehicle for the same obsessive longing that eventually leads him to grant Diamond the fulfilling death-embrace the novel has so long delayed.

Read in this fashion, "Little Daylight" satisfies a male's desire to resuscitate a mother associated with death. The transformation of an old woman into a desirable bride demands the parallel transformation of a young prince into a maternal nourisher. Just as Diamond nurses his infant brother and sister as an expression of his unfulfilled desire for North Wind's comforting breast, so does the orphaned prince who stills a sobbing, child-sized woman seek compensation for his own lack. Both figures therefore enact MacDonald's lifelong yearning for the lost young mother who pitied the crying infant she had been forced to wean.[28]

28. See pp. 122–23, above.

It seems significant that MacDonald has little left for Diamond to do after the telling of "Little Daylight." Like the prince who patiently waits for the princess to reappear, Diamond lapses into his earlier passive stance. He has become useless to others. Replaced by a second baby in his parents' home and by lame Jim in Nanny's heart, he is "installed as a page" in the country house of Mr. Raymond and his new bride (*BNW,* chap. 35, 277). His main function in the home called "The Mound" is to delight his employers with his pretty appearance in "a suit of blue" that nicely brings out the pallor of his skin. He also acts as Mr. Raymond's consultant by giving his "opinion" on the children's books that gentleman continues to write. Diamond cannot tell stories that others call "clever" apart from those they call "silly," but he always knows whether he likes a story or not. It remains unclear, however, whether he likes the "story of the Little Lady and the Goblin Prince" that the narrator finds him reading (*BNW,* chap. 35, 277). For he dies before he can pass judgment on what is obviously MacDonald's next work, *The Princess and the Goblin,* serialized in 1871.

The last chapters of *At the Back of the North Wind* restore the dialogic form of Diamond's earlier exchanges with North Wind. The boy now worries that the moon-bathed figure who revisits him after her long absence may be unreal: "How am I to know that it's not a dream?" Her answers no longer seem to satisfy him:

> "I'm either not a dream, or there's something better that's not a dream, Diamond," said North Wind, in a rather sorrowful tone, he thought.
>
> "But it's not something better—it's you I want, North Wind," he persisted, already beginning to cry a little.
>
> She made no answer, but rose with him in her arms. (*BNW,* chap. 36, 292–93)

When, in the novel's final paragraphs, a weeping Mrs. Raymond leads the narrator to Diamond's room at the "top of the tower," he finds the boy frozen into a "lovely figure, as white and almost as clear as alabaster," an image of North Wind herself (*BNW,* chap. 38, 308).

Gerard Manley Hopkins, whose theology was far more orthodox than MacDonald's, ended one of his most famous poems with lines that have a bearing on Diamond's death and transfiguration. Insisting, as MacDonald does, that a higher order—"something better"—is imbedded in the empirical reality our senses behold, Hopkins imposes the "Comfort of the Resurrection" on a Heraclitean world of flux:

Flesh fade, and mortal trash
Fall to the residuary worm; / world's wildfire, leave but ash:
In a flash, at a trumpet crash,
I am all at once what Christ is, / since he was what I am, and
This Jack, joke, poor potsherd, / patch, matchwood, immortal diamond,
Is immortal diamond.[29]

MacDonald, too, wants to convert a mortal "Jack"—an ordinary, humble boy—into a Christlike immortal. The child whom the narrator beatifies cannot be soiled by the residues that weigh down Nanny or his own mother. Having discharged his earthly duties, he can be carried off by North Wind into a mystic abode. Despite its originality and power, there is something complacent about a fantasy that ultimately extricates Diamond from further engagement with error, poverty, and evil. And, despite his apparent efforts to distance himself from a Carrollian worship of an arrested female innocence, MacDonald's own privileging of the virginal boy he refuses to ironize makes him open to rather similar charges of distortion. As we shall see in the next chapter, *At the Back of the North Wind* elicited an indirect response from the first of the three women writers who set out to reclaim fairy tales as a literature of their own. Jean Ingelow was a valued contributor to both *Good Words,* a magazine which also published MacDonald's writings for adults, and *Good Words for the Young,* the journal in which he serialized *At the Back of the North Wind* and which he subsequently edited. In *Mopsa the Fairy,* Ingelow not only extended MacDonald's subversion of a male-constructed "femininity" but also rejected the privileged role he assigned to his boy-hero. The boy who flies into female fantasylands in her own fiction is not a visionary dreamer. For instead of an immortal Diamond, Ingelow deliberately chose as her protagonist a most ordinary and unimaginative little boy called, quite simply, Jack.

29. Gerard Manley Hopkins, "That Nature Is a Heraclitean Fire and of the Comfort of the Resurrection," lines 21–24.

EIGHT

Sundering Women from Boys: Ingelow's *Mopsa the Fairy*

Yet—to gaze on her again
(As my tale has taught thee),
Potent Fairy, I am fain,
Therefore have I sought thee—
Through the forest, through the lea,
Through the tangled wildwood,
For I know she dwells with thee,
*And her name is—*CHILDHOOD!
              —JEAN INGELOW,
          "Mimie's Grass Net," 1850

It is almost strange in these days to find how quietly a
popular writer could live with the world's bustle all
around her, almost like one moored among the
flowering rushes of a peaceful backwater, while the
noisy race went by upon the river. But, indeed, if it had
not been so, I think she could not have written at all;
unless she had been cherished, shielded, sheltered, as she
was, she could hardly have given to us the message
entrusted to her in the form that it comes to us.
—ANONYMOUS, *Some Recollections of Jean Ingelow,* 1901

I

In 1865, in the same year that Lewis Carroll published his first *Alice* book, Jean Ingelow capitalized on her growing reputation as a poet by expanding an earlier collection of didactic stories in a volume she now retitled *Stories Told to a Child*. Among the offerings was a fictitious biographical sketch, "The Life of John Smith." In this deceptively simple narrative, Ingelow uses only six pages to recount the details of the earthly progress of a "great and good man" from his birth "in the parish of Cripplegate Within, at half-past ten on Friday, the 1st of April, 1780," to his burial at "the age of seventy" in the "cemetery at Kensall Green" (*STC*, 185, 190).

Ingelow's narrator seems curiously unselective in giving equal weight to all the details of Mr. Smith's prosaic life. We thus learn that this worthy cut his first tooth at seven months, mastered the whole alphabet "as early as three years old," and "soon learned to distinguish between tin tacks, tenpennies, and brass heads" in his father's hardware store, thereby showing capacities for discrimination that almost appear to excel the narrator's own. Mr. Smith's adult life turns out to be just as drab. We are asked to note his "valuable remarks on the lateness of the season in the North," to which he had traveled after leaving the shop to his eldest son. And, as proof of the retention of "his superior faculties to the last," we are regaled with Mr. Smith's memorable observation that the Niniveh Marbles in the British Museum "did not answer his expectations: as there was so much marble in the country, and also Derbyshire spar, he wondered that the Government had not new articles manufactured, instead of sending abroad for old things which were cracked already" (*STC*, 190).

Yet Ingelow's account of a life exemplary for its uneventfulness does not end with the burial of this "universally respected" patriarch. For the narrator who has so complacently reproduced the contours of Mr. Smith's existence now turns on a reader whom she accuses of having yearned for something more stimulating. We are hauled into a dialogue, relentlessly pounded for our presumption in wishing for a narrative spiced by more extraordinary events:

"And is this all?" cries the indignant reader.

All? I am amazed at your asking such a question. I should have thought you had enough of it! Yes, it *is* all; and to tell you a secret, which, of course, I would not proclaim to the world, I should not be in the least surprised if *your* biography, up to the present date, is not one better worth writing.

What have *you* done, I should like to know? and what are you, and what have you been, that is better worth recording than the sayings and doings recorded here? You think yourself superior? (*STC,* 190–191)

The "you" harangued in this passage is presumably a child reader who would, by 1865, have had good reasons to suppose that a collection entitled *Stories to a Child* might contain more fanciful fare. But Ingelow's narrator is clearly extending her attack to all those tempted to indulge grandiose fantasies. Adults, too, it would seem, might benefit from a homely realism that insists on limits.[1] Curiously enough, the moral pushed by John Smith's artless biographer thus resembles the one which closes that most artful of all Victorian narratives, *Middlemarch.* For the biographer of Dorothea Brooke also relies on a tonal shift when she instructs a "you" to remember that "the growing good of the world" does not necessarily depend on extraordinary deeds. Adopting the familiarity of a kindly aunt addressing a small child, the sophisticated narrator of *Middlemarch* exhorts us to accept the constraint of ordinariness: "[T]hat things are not so ill with you and me as they might have been, is half owing to the number who lived faithfully a hidden life, and rest in unvisited tombs."[2]

The narrator of "The Life of John Smith," however, is confrontational rather than soothing. Whereas George Eliot asks us to recognize the extraordinariness of figures too easily dismissed as inconsequential, Ingelow punctures our very notions of consequence by insisting on her protagonist's inconsequence. Never a character in his own right, Mr. Smith is

1. The anonymous author of *Some Recollections of Jean Ingelow* (London: Wells Gardner, Darton, & Co., 1901) alludes to one such reader in the "following anecdote" about an "aged lady," who was "slowly dying, in a house filled with every luxury": "At a time of great suffering she wanted something very difficult for her perplexed nurses to get, namely, a book which would not be incongruous in her circumstances, and yet would charm away her pain. In the end they procured for her *Stories told to a Child,* which pleased her so much that she never would let it go out of her sight again while life lasted" (131–32).

2. George Eliot, "Finale," in *Middlemarch: A Study of Provincial Life,* ed. Gordon S. Haight (Boston: Houghton Mifflin, 1956), 613.

not nearly as engaging as Sophia and Rosamond, the spry girl-heroines, respectively, of "The Grandmother's Shoe" and "Deborah's Book," two longer psychological studies also included in *Stories Told To a Child*. Away from their homes, Sophia and Rosamond travel to locales in which elders curb and channel their precocious imaginings. These austere figures—a Quaker grandmother and a gentleman who restores Rosamond to her hosts—are nonetheless quite tolerant of childish excesses. In "The Life of John Smith," however, the narrator seems impatient with the expansive cravings of her readers. Whereas Sophia and Rosamond were treated with understanding, here we find ourselves chided for a hunger that Ingelow's antinarrative has deliberately induced.

The unexpectedness of the narrator's harsh assault on a "you" who might reasonably feel superior to poor Mr. Smith causes the reader a much greater discomfort than that experienced by Sophia and Rosamond. Surprised at finding ourselves thrust into the narrative we are reading, we have become more vulnerable than these two transgressive children. Whereas they freely admit their small trespasses, we are harangued for our presumed misreading, embarrassed by a narrator whose cunning turns out to be so superior to Mr. Smith's. We have been tricked, mocked for assuming that the life of a dull boy born on April Fool's Day in 1780 might have yielded something far more exciting. We have underestimated the imagination of an author who has crafted a defiantly anti-imaginative text. Truculent to the very end, Ingelow's narrator prefers to identify herself with the naif who found "cracked" antiques inferior to brand new "articles." Battered and ejected, we have ourselves been "cracked." And, to make sure that no residual hunger for the extraordinary lingers in any reader still reluctant to admit having "had enough," the narrator fires off one parting shot: "I cannot forbear telling you that, whether you are destined to be great or little, the honour of writing your biography is not desired by your obedient servant the biographer of Mr. John Smith" (*STC*, 191).

I shall return to "The Life of Mr. John Smith" after a slight detour. I have started with it because it raises important questions about the nature of Ingelow's ideology and art, and also because it anticipates a dilemma that Christina Rossetti and Juliana Ewing would face as well in their own fictions for children. Ingelow's parable about ordinariness reveals a deep distrust of a subjectivity that can cause us to magnify our own import as well as to project our desires on admired others. Ingelow extended that distrust to her own career as a writer. Despite her literary prominence and her association with major intellectuals and artists of her time—notably John Ruskin, a steady admirer and frequent caller at her Kensington home[3]—she chose to lead as unobtrusive a life as possible. In fact, she was so successful in obscuring herself that the surviving details of her private and public life almost seem scantier than those she allowed to the fictional Mr. Smith.

It is hardly accidental, therefore, that we should lack a full-scale biography to match those devoted to Ingelow's male contemporaries or to Christina Rossetti, the writer to whom she was most often compared by her reviewers. Aware "of a new eminent name having arisen among us," Rossetti herself rather nervously regarded "Jean Ingelow, the wonderful poet" as "a formidable rival to most men, and to any woman."[4] Yet, for all her inventive powers, Ingelow retained much of her Calvinist mother's suspicion of art, artists, and artistic rivalry. Rossetti's letters and manuscripts were readily available to late Victorian editor-biographers such as her brother Michael and Mackenzie Bell. Ingelow's scattered correspondence—though probably just as copious—survives primarily through excerpts included in what is bound to remain the most reliable account of her life, the 1901 *Some Recollections of Jean Ingelow.*[5]

3. Ingelow was a year younger than Ruskin, and died three years before he did. The two writers first became acquainted in 1867–68, when he was forty-eight and she was forty-seven; Ruskin begins to cite lines from her poems soon thereafter in his writings, and, by 1877, he lists her name among those of his eleven "best friends" (*CW,* 36:lxxxvii). The "private house at Kensington" where Ruskin gave an illustrated lecture, in June of 1883, on the art of Kate Greenaway and Francesca Alexander to a group that included Matthew Arnold, James Russell Lowell, Frederick Leighton, Edward Burne-Jones, and Ingelow, may well have been her own (*CW,* 32:535). Although she ceased to write after the death of her favorite brother in 1886 and Ruskin's productivity was affected by bouts of mental illness, they continued to correspond. Her comments on the first chapters of *Praeterita* are as supportive as they are astute (*CW,* 35:lvi). For a fuller discussion of their relationship see my "Male Patronage and Female Authorship: the Case of John Ruskin and Jean Ingelow," *Princeton University Library Chronicle* 57 (Autumn 1995): 13–46.

4. Rossetti to Dora Greenwell, 31 December 1863, and to Alexander Macmillan, 1 December 1863, in *The Rossetti-Macmillan Letters,* ed. Lona Mosk Packer (London: Cambridge University Press, 1963), 22n, 21.

5. Although Maureen Peters was able to draw on some unpublished family papers for her *Jean Ingelow: Victorian Poetess* (Ipswich, England: Boydell Press, 1972), her well-intentioned biography is riddled by factual and typographical errors and marred by an insufficient command of the Victorian literary world in which Ingelow moved. Her

That this modest but insightful study should have been written by a younger friend or relative who concealed her name seems very much in keeping with the tenor of Ingelow's own self-effacing life. Indeed, the anonymous author of *Some Recollections* astutely characterizes that self-effacement by drawing on a floral metaphor devised by Ingelow's friend, John Ruskin, in his grandiosely entitled *Proserpina: Studies of Wayside Flowers, While the Air Was Yet Pure Among the Alps, and in the Scotland and England Which My Father Knew* (1879).[6] Ruskin's moralized anatomy of "all the essential parts of a flower"—its pistil, style, ovary, and stigma—relies on the prime example of the poppy. He has chosen that "impatient and luxury-loving" red flower, he says, because it differs from its more modest peers by boldly displaying its separate parts, having been "at first too severely restrained and then casting all restraint away" (*CW*, 25:260).[7] To characterize her own subject's temperament, Ingelow's 1901 biographer draws on Ruskin's contrast between the showy young poppy and a more decorous rival: though similarly "confined" in its youth, the primrose never chooses to cast off its early "tutorial leaves" in poppy-like abandon.[8]

The anonymous author of *Some Recollections of Jean Ingelow* carefully edits Ruskin's floral symbolism in order to create what she regards as an apt emblem for a woman writer who refused to leave the confines of her family, opting to reside first with her parents and then, upon her mother's death in 1878, with younger brothers. The passage Ingelow's biographer enlists for her analogy deserves to be closely examined. In reproducing it,

---

single-minded thesis could hardly be pushed by someone better acquainted with the nineteenth-century poetics of loss: thus, a young Ingelow's parting from some "faceless and nameless" lover whom Peters finds most "pleasant to think of" as being both "handsome and young" is regarded as the key to her "entire" literary output (29).

6. For the best discussion of this curious book, see Frederick Kirchhoff, "A Science Against Sciences: Ruskin's Floral Mythology," in *Nature and the Victorian Imagination*, ed. U. C. Knoepflmacher and G. B. Tennyson (Berkeley: University of California Press, 1977), 246–58.

7. Ruskin's fascination with the sexuality of the poppy he avoids calling a "she" is obvious. He breaks open a virginal "poppy bud, just when it shows the scarlet line at its side," yet notes that the ripe flower "remains visibly crushed and hurt to the end of its days." In a remark that has a retrospective bearing on the open cleft in Gluck's Treasure Valley, Ruskin downplays the resemblance between human and floral parts: "Instead of 'ovary,' I shall say 'Treasury' (for a seed isn't an egg, but it *is* a treasure)" (*CW*, 25:260, 259).

8. Ibid., 260.

I am also reinstating—in brackets and in italics—some of the infantiliz-ing attributes that Ruskin conferred on his symbolic primrose, attributes that Ingelow's biographer wisely elides:

Ruskin, in his 'Proserpina,' gives a faithful delineation of a primrose both in pen and pencil. The words might stand for a description of Jean Ingelow. They occur in what could be used as an allegory for parents, and begin with a picture of a poppy, whose scarlet cup cannot be developed until it has split up and tossed away the cruel cap that has held it in bondage and left its petals marked for ever. 'Not so flowers of gracious breeding,' says the sage of his primrose, 'first confined as strictly as the poppy, with five pinching green leaves, whose points close over it'; [*the little thing is content to remain a child and finds its nursery large enough*] then 'the little yellow ones peep out . . . [*like ducklings*] they find the light delicious, [*and open wide to it;*] and grow, and grow, and throw themselves [*wider at last*] into their perfect rose' . . . [*But they never leave their old nursery for all that; it and they live on together; and the nursery seems a part of the flower.*][9]

Instead of stressing what might be construed as a regressive attachment to the nursery, as Ruskin had done, Ingelow's biographer prefers to em-phasize the primrose's conservative allegiances. She therefore disrupts Ruskin's sequence and concludes the paragraph with a sentence about the calyx (which Ruskin simply calls the "*hiding* part"; *CW,* 25:261, Ruskin's italics) that does not occur at this point in *Proserpina:*

. . . 'but the primrose remains always in its calyx, its first home; they are never sepa-rated, and the calyx remains part of the flower, which dies in it when its day is over.'

So it was with Jean Ingelow.

Although she gladly hailed every effort made by her friends to enlarge and en-rich their lives by any sort of intellectual or philanthropic work, she certainly be-longed to the old school of thought so far as regards public life for women, and she experienced a veritable shock each time that anyone she cared for stepped across the old barrier, as she deemed, needlessly; still, she differed in silence; it was far from her to discuss these points, and she sometimes let herself be reminded with a smile that she, in her day, had gone to the verge by publishing her poems. To the genera-tion before her such writing was but the graceful and interesting diversion of a gentlewoman, to be kept for the delectation of her own circle. . . .[10]

9. *Some Recollections,* 128–29; the interspliced passages from Ruskin occur in *CW,* 25:260–61.

10. *Some Recollections,* 129.

Significantly enough, Ingelow's biographer censors Ruskin's character-ization of the primrose as a perennially sheltered child who, like Gluck in *The King of the Golden River,* remains in its original green cradle. To re-move the imputation that a mature woman never managed to break free from the nursery, the author of *Some Recollections* stresses the voluntari-ness of her subject's confinement. She suggests that Ingelow's decision to stay within the narrow "calyx" of her immediate family stemmed from her cultural affiliation. The writer who belongs to an older "school of thought" still exhibits the Evangelical values of a generation that had placed a premium on female domesticity. Women of letters such as Maria Edgeworth, who worked closely with her father in fashioning her educa-tional texts, or the Taylor sisters Jane and Ann, whose poems for children complemented their own father's more prosaic instructional works, had also discharged a public role while staying firmly implanted within a pa-rental calyx. Jane Taylor died when Jean Ingelow was only four years old; but the friendship between the Taylors and Ingelows gave Jean access to a domestic atmosphere very different from that existing in her own home. Her visits, as a teenager, to the household of Isaac Taylor introduced her to an intellectual atmosphere far more receptive to creativity than that offered by her own parents, the cultivated but repressive Jean Kilgour and the witty but literal-minded William Ingelow.[11]

Yet if Ingelow was shocked by Victorian women writers who had "stepped across the old barrier" (a possible allusion to George Eliot or even Elizabeth Barrett Browning), her own quietism was hardly without con-flict. The author of *Some Recollections* provides enough information to allow us to construct an "allegory for parents" that strongly suggests that the conformity demanded by Jean and William Ingelow was hard to bear even for one as "docile" as their eldest child. She implies that there was a

11. The story of the prohibitions placed on Jean's "poetic leaning" has been often told: only after her mother found verses scribbled all over the white shutters of the girl's bedroom was paper finally doled out to the fourteen-year-old. The author of *Some Recollections* passes no judgment on these and other instances of parental insensitivity; yet she wonders about the origins of a talent strong enough to flourish under such utterly inhospitable circumstances: "Where Jean got her poetic temperament it would be hard to say. Not from her witty, business-like father, and certainly not from her mother, who, though truly delighted to wake up one day to find her eldest child famous, had no really poetic tendencies herself" (15, 13).

continued tension between the ideology of self-suppression Ingelow accepted and her dogged need to find a creative outlet for her emotions. The poet had, after all, gone to "the verge" by refusing to remain silent. She was a poppy as well as a primrose.

There are contradictions, then, which do not escape the shrewd author of *Some Recollections*. Is Ingelow's art conformist or self-expressive? Did a lingering attachment to her "first home" result in writings that merely reasserted "old barriers" at a time of major social and institutional changes? Or did she use her work to break away from the "cruel cap" of an inhibiting nursery? To counter the notion that Ingelow's art was unaffected by the larger life around her, her biographer points to the popularity that her "comforting, consoling, prophetic" verses gained in the United States immediately after the Civil War: "As American homes were just then building up again, families reuniting after the cruel strain and anguish, the heart of the great people was tuned to take part in the melody."[12]

But even this example may not necessarily rescue Ingelow's work from the charge that it promoted an insulation associated with women and children. Her lyrics might have appealed to adults eager to find an anodyne for the horrors of war. Yet if so, had she not merely found a public forum for private verses that a "gentlewoman" of an earlier generation might have "kept for the delectation of her own circle"? That Ingelow aided a male ideology which valued a segregated female "purity" seems clear from Ruskin's investment in both herself and her writings. He was drawn to her for some of the same reasons that made the little girls at Winnington school so attractive to him. The prepubescent "little birds" Ruskin adored and the spinster whose company he relished struck him as equally virginal, and hence unthreatening. In his *Ethics of the Dust* (1866), Ruskin assigns Ingelow's verses to one of the little girls whom the Old Lecturer teases: having told the children that because they are small, they "should have very little play, and because I'm big, I should have a great deal," Ruskin allows himself to be outwitted by one child who recalls verses from "Miss Ingelow": "The lambs play always—they know no better" (*CW,* 18:211).

With this background in mind, we can at last return to Ingelow's "The Life of John Smith." As I noted, the biographer of this fictional patriarch

---

12. Ibid., 130.

pushes the same restraining ideology with which Ingelow is identified by her own biographer in *Some Recollections.* Yet, as I also hinted, this identification remains problematic. Despite its final put-down of a childish reader, Ingelow's text involves more than a defense of unimaginativeness. For in exhibiting so fully the dullness of its male subject, the narrative comes close to satirizing the patriarchal ideology it supposedly endorses. The narrator's final act of severance is so intemperate that it calls our attention to the dull temperance of a life in which the domestic and the public never seem to clash: "his father died, leaving him the braziery business, and four thousand pounds in the Funds. Mr. Smith was a kind son. His mother lived with him, and her old age was cheered by the sight of his honors, worth, and talents. About this time he took out a patent for a new kind of poker." (*STC,* 188). Is this monotonous conflation of a life's material and emotional aspects really endorsed by the author or is that author slyly detaching herself from her Gulliverian narrator?

Each answer seems as plausible as the other. Acquiescence and resistance are somehow left unresolved. The docility that her biographer attributes to Ingelow, though genuine, is never without a quietly subversive underside. "The Life of John Smith" therefore can be read as a straightforward narrative, as Ruskin seems to have done (although perhaps not without tongue in cheek) when he applauded the "becoming reverence" shown by "Miss Jean Ingelow" toward a "tranquil magnate and potentate, the bulwark of British constitutional principles and initiator of British private enterprise."[13] Or it can be read as a satire of those hagiographic accounts of little boys destined for greater things with which the Victorians liked to regale their young. For the story simultaneously endorses and ridicules a mentality that strongly resembles that of William Ingelow, who had little use for art in his world of business. Professing to have no time to pose for the portrait his worshipful daughter had commissioned with her first earnings as a writer, Mr. Ingelow at last relented and "graciously allowed the artist to take him as he sat working before his desk."[14] Smith's utilitarian perspective on products of art thus may owe much to the "calyx" that restrained Jean Ingelow's early flowering.

How would John Smith or the stolid persona Ingelow adopted to tell that gentleman's life have reacted to *Mopsa the Fairy,* the fairy-tale novel

13. Lecture 5, "The Fireside: John Leech and John Tenniel," in *The Art of England* (*CW,* 33:365).

14. *Some Recollections,* 128.

she published in 1869, only four years after the appearance of *Stories Told to a Child*? The didacticist who had discouraged all youthful flights of fancy in her collection of tales now produced an extravagant venture into a series of fantasylands in sixteen chapters marked by an unresisting "acceptance of wonders."[15] Had Ingelow suddenly repudiated her earlier insistence on limits and barriers? Her shift in mode, though acute, does not necessarily betoken a new outlook. Nor is it necessary to attribute that switch in mode, as critics have done, to her desire to capitalize on the recent success of *Alice in Wonderland*.[16] Instead, if we are willing to allow that "The Life of Mr. John Smith" covertly undermines the constraints it supposedly endorses, we can actually glimpse in that realistic sketch the seeds for Ingelow's fantastic masterpiece for children.

For *Mopsa the Fairy* only brings to the surface the clash already embedded in the account of a Mr. Smith who, we learn, once was a boy called Jack. A fantasy that features as its protagonist not Mopsa, the fairy-girl who becomes a queen, but rather a good and very dull middle-class boy called Jack, thus offers a dramatic extension of the polarities still half-concealed in "The Life of Mr. John Smith." The same preference for the ordinary and everyday promoted in Ingelow's didactic tales for children paradoxically finds its way into a text that seems unrestrained in its indulgence of the extraordinary. A narrative that starts out with Jack as its ostensible hero, the patron of the still nameless fairy child he carries in his pocket, ends with her eminence as a grown-up visionary and with his abasement and exile. Yet it is precisely the boy's unimaginativeness, his lack of prevision, that protects him as he penetrates the dangerous magical realms that Ingelow genders as "feminine." Though welcome as an antidote to Jack's Smith-like stolidity, the superior imagination of Mopsa and her sister-queens is painful, vulnerable, and unstable. The girl who grows beyond Jack in the innermost fairyland into which they have ventured

15. Roger Lancelyn Green, *Tellers of Tales: Children's Books and their Authors from 1800 to 1964* (London: Edmund Ward, 1965), 70.

16. "Undoubtedly the inspiration for *Mopsa the Fairy* was the amazing success of *Alice in Wonderland*" (ibid., 69). Green's remark is repeated by Humphrey Carpenter and Mari Pritchard in *The Oxford Companion to Children's Literature* (Oxford: Oxford University Press, 1984), 357: "It is one of the more successful children's books written under the influence of *Alice's Adventures in Wonderland*." It is reiterated once more in Carpenter's *Secret Gardens: The Golden Age of Children's Literature* (Boston: Houghton Mifflin, 1985), 57: "[C]loser in spirit to *Alice* is one of the first imitations to appear, *Mopsa the Fairy*."

ultimately suffers far more than he. She becomes a wise woman, while he remains a boy. Their union is impossible. An unusual fairy queen must be severed from the ordinary British boy who will soon forget her as well as his imaginative venture. Still, even though she divorces fantasy from realism, Ingelow also tries to reclaim the former mode from boyish worshipers of the "feminine."

II

The decision to have Mopsa outgrow the boy who had enclosed her in his pocket may well be the most salient of Ingelow's many departures from *Alice in Wonderland* and *At the Back of the North Wind,* the two male fantasies *Mopsa the Fairy* so subtly revises. Midway in the novel, Jack is unsettled to discover, as he measures Mopsa's height, that the girl who had barely reached his knee only "the day before" now comes "as high as the second button of his waistcoat." Vaguely anticipating the separation that awaits him, Jack tells Mopsa "I hope you will not go on growing so fast as this," and then wistfully adds, "or you will be as tall as my mamma is in a week or two—much too big for me to play with" (*MF,* chap. 9, 269).

In distancing herself from the precedents of Carroll and MacDonald, Ingelow is seldom as overt or as pugnacious as Christina Rossetti, whose more radical acts of dissociation I shall consider in my next two chapters. Ingelow carefully avoided polemics whenever called upon to pronounce "upon the authors of her own time"; nonetheless, as her 1901 biographer points out, although she was "very reticent in speaking either of current literature or of people, she had her strong partialities as regarded both." The writer whom this biographer calls a "lover of peace" thus engages Carroll in ways that are often so oblique that they can easily be missed.[17]

17. *Some Recollections,* 165. Ironically enough, Ingelow uses a Carrollian pun on the word "peace" to undermine Jack's lyric peace offering before his ejection from Mopsa's world: the maternal "dame" presiding at the banquet for the new Queen refuses to accept Jack's refrain, "give us peace." Insisting that he has made a "mistake," she contends that the dove about whom he sang must have said "Give us peas," since doves and pigeons are notoriously fond of peas. Asserting her own authority over his text, she overrules Jack's protest and orders the court historian to write "it down as the dame said it ought to be" (*MF,* chap. 16, 309–10). The dame's intransigence seems designed to match that of the King whose "angry" puns and destruction of verses at the trial so infuriated Alice that she willed her exit from Wonderland. By placing this comic inter-

Still, Jack's complaint about the rapidity of "his" little Mopsa's growth seems a fairly direct rebuttal of the fantasy devised by a man who did his imaginative best to retard the maturation of little Alice.

After reaching the innermost regions of fairyland, Mopsa develops at a much faster pace than Jack. Yet her growth is steady and deliberate. The compressions and elongations imposed on Alice in Wonderland—or the abrupt changes in size that North Wind repeatedly undergoes in her various encounters with Diamond—are pointedly avoided in the fantastic lands that Jack visits. The boy falsely assumes that Mopsa will not grow beyond the other fairies he has hauled back from England. Once Jovinian and Roxaletta, Mopsa's brother and sister, have attained their full size of one foot and one inch, they can join the tiny inhabitants of the country that turns out to be their—but not Mopsa's—final destination. Unlike Mopsa, who lingers on Jack's knee, her siblings are ready to fly away. Their mobility, however, is hardly a mark of maturation. For these miniscule adults resemble drones and worker bees subordinated to the larger queen grounded in her hive. Important only as foils to Mopsa, they can be dismissed from the story. The lavish adult attire each wears before flitting away only makes these droll miniatures seem all the more parodic of full-grown men and women. Mopsa, however, still dressed in a "white frock" that shows off her "soft, fat arms, and a face just like that of a sweet child" (*MF*, chap. 7, 258), has the human capacity for a higher development.

Yet Mopsa not only outgrows Roxaletta and Jovinian, but also proves to be superior to her older sister, the taller, human-sized fairy queen whom Jack saves from slavery and restores to her subjects. Ingelow offers two contrary explanations for Mopsa's elevation. She hints, on the one hand, that Jack's own decided preference for this "little dear" over the other survivors (a fourth fairy child has been lost through his carelessness) resulted in a kiss that had effects as beneficial as the princely kisses bestowed in "Sleeping Beauty" or in MacDonald's / Mr. Raymond's story of Little Daylight. Nonetheless, Ingelow also claims that Mopsa's election as queen of a fairy race she will redeem and rule was predestined by a higher female authority, the mysterious figure referred to—in the book's later chapters—as "Mother Fate." The two explanations are not, of course, mu-

---

lude just before Jack's pathetic separation from Mopsa, Ingelow may signal her distrust of the emotional sincerity of Carroll's love-gift to the child from whom he must part. There is little "peace" (or appeasement) in a text that challenges both Carroll and MacDonald.

tually exclusive. Indeed, Jack's selection of a child who might otherwise have remained as ordinary as Roxaletta and Jovinian could, after all, itself have been mandated by "Mother Fate."

But it seems futile to look for any such reconciliation in a text that thwarts Jack's own desire to obtain an "explanation" or "reason" for every strange event that befalls him (*MF,* chap. 8, 264; chap. 15, 299). The reader accustomed to realistic narratives will share Jack's frustration in his repeated encounters with creatures uninterested in cause and effect. Enigma and unreason are readily accepted in the fantasylands he visits. Indeed, Mopsa's ready acquiescence to an inexplicable "Mother Fate" gradually alienates her from the human boy who keeps asking "why" to the very end of his adventures:

> "But why?" asked Jack.
>
> Mopsa, however, was like other fairies in this respect—that she knew all about Old Mother Fate, but not about causes and reasons. She believed, as we do in this world, that
>
> > That that is, is,
>
> but the fairies go further than this; they say:
>
> > That that is, is; and when it is, that is the reason that it is.
>
> This sounds like nonsense to us, but it is all right to them.
>
> So Mopsa [thought] she had explained everything . . . (*MF,* chap. 15, 299–300)

Ostensibly, Ingelow here co-opts the "nonsense" that both Carroll and MacDonald had promulgated in their own forays into fantasy. Yet she appropriates that nonsense for distinct purposes of her own. By having Jack venture into fairylands ruled by a female logic he cannot decode, Ingelow questions the uses to which fantasy had been put in both *Alice in Wonderland* and *At the Back of the North Wind.* The two explanations she offers for Mopsa's exaltation—her selection by Jack and her selection by Mother Fate—thus help to illuminate Ingelow's divergence from these male fantasists and to suggest that, like Rossetti and Ewing after her, she felt challenged by the subjectivity of each man's appropriation of female energies.

Although Ingelow does not question the sincerity of Jack's attachment to his little Mopsa, she does suggest that there is something quite arbitrary and proprietary about his preference. The smitten Lewis Carroll chose "Secunda" over a "Prima" who was too old and a "Tertia" who was too young to act as his ideal playmate. Since, originally, Mopsa was of the same age and appearance as the siblings who were hatched in the same nest,

Jack's choice seems even more capricious. Inspected by the fairy queen who will add Roxaletta and Jovinian to her subjects, Mopsa seems to have been retarded in her development. Whereas her siblings greet their future sovereign with the *politesse* of seasoned courtiers, Mopsa coyly hides her face and blushes "with pretty shyness." The fairy queen whom Jack has rescued from slavery is puzzled by this remarkable difference:

> "These are fairies," said Jack's slave; "but what are you?"
>
> "Jack kissed me," said the little thing; "and I want to sit on his knee."
>
> "Yes," said Jack, "I took them out, and laid them in a row to see if they were safe, and this one I kissed, because she looked such a little dear."
>
> "Was she not like the others, then?" asked the slave.
>
> "Yes," said Jack; "but I liked her the best; she was my favourite." (*MF,* chap. 7, 254)

Jack's favoritism, Ingelow seems to suggest here, has somehow slowed down Mopsa's development. Imprinted by a human, the child who was once "like the others" has become far more dependent on him than the two siblings who have reached their maturity as fairies. Like the self-restricted Jean Ingelow, who felt herself bound by her strong allegiances to a parental "calyx," Mopsa finds Jack's possessive love to be inhibiting rather than liberating. When the slave-turned-queen continues to interrogate her, she falls back on the same refrain. To the question, "How comes it that you are not like your companions?," she can only repeat, "in a pretty lisping voice: 'It's because Jack kissed me.'" The queen, who later startles her visitors by informing them that Mopsa is her younger sister and hence a potential rival as ruler of her fairy hive, now soberly acknowledges that "the love of a mortal works changes indeed" (*MF,* chap. 7, 256).

But what kind of "love" did Jack exhibit when he bestowed an impulsive kiss on the fairy child that struck him as "such a little dear"? It seems rather poignant that, immediately after this exchange has taken place, Ingelow should turn away from Jack's relation to the girl Mopsa in order to reinspect his relation to a more mature female figure, the "lovely slave" who has yet to reveal her identity as fairy queen. There is a marked difference between the two relationships. Whereas Jack can continue to patronize the little girl he regards as his possession, he wants to end the ties that bind him to the wrinkled fairy woman who has changed—as unexpectedly as George MacDonald's Little Daylight—into a radiant young beauty. Even before her transformation, Jack was troubled by the master-slave relationship that linked him to this elderly female. Finding that she had spent his money on purchases he considered to be frivolous, Jack adopted a severe parental tone in making his reproof. At the same time, however, he admits the insecurity of his assumed position of authority: "What do you mean by being so silly? I can't scold you properly, because I don't know what name to call you by, and I don't like to say 'Slave,' because that sounds so rude" (*MF*, chap. 7, 253). But after discovering that the slave-woman wisely used her purchases to bring about her magical transformation, Jack feels even less secure. He is no longer in command of the boat that carries his group to the fairyland interiors they are approaching. Eventually, in the innermost of these realms, where the mandates of Mother Fate become most fully manifest, poor Jack will shed the last remnants of his male authority and boyish self-esteem.

"Captain Jack" senses the waning of his former mastery. He is disturbed by the subservience Roxaletta and Jovinian show to someone who still addresses him as her "master" and tells himself that he is "tired of admiring" the slave-woman's beauty. When he also finds himself "wondering at the respect" shown to her by the assiduous little courtiers who adorn her with flowers and fan her with feathers, his jealousy becomes overt. Jack's dominance, always unquestioned in the borderlands and outer fairylands he has so far traversed, has been eroded. The slave-woman seems an intruder in the boat he shared with creatures smaller than himself as happily as Carroll with his own "merry crew" in the prefatory poem to *Alice in Wonderland*. Jack therefore prefers to indulge in some regressive play with the one crew member whom he can still dominate: "he curled himself up in the bottom of the boat with his own little favourite, and taught her how to play at cat's cradle" (*MF*, chap. 7, 256).

As a quick learner and willing playmate, Mopsa only intensifies Jack's desire to single her out. He has no interest in the puppet-like Roxaletta and Jovinian. For her part, Mopsa's older sister displays new powers he finds threatening. Lewis Carroll seized on Secunda as a median neither as childish nor as sexually developed as her younger and older sisters; likewise Jack, having already broken away from his baby sister and from her nurse before embarking on his adventures, dismisses Mopsa's tiny siblings and tries to dissociate himself from the regal lady whose emerging authority and higher status he now finds so troubling.

Jack therefore gladly rids himself of his former slave. Yet his discomforts are hardly over. For Jack will become even more entangled with the magical powers he finds so inexplicable. These powers, which are at their strongest in the matriarchal heartlands he is about to penetrate, will further reduce his significance, sap his self-confidence, and, eventually, demand his banishment from Mopsa's domain:

> When they had been playing some time, and Mopsa was getting quite clever at the game, the lovely slave said: "Master, it is a long time since you spoke to me."
>
> "And yet," said Jack, "there is something I particularly want to ask you about."
>
> "Ask it, then," she replied.
>
> "I don't like to have a slave," answered Jack; "and as you are so clever, don't you think you can find out how to be free again?" (*MF*, chap. 7, 256)

A reversal of roles is set in motion. By asking one he respects for being "so clever" to bring about her own freedom, Jack tacitly admits that he is no longer her master nor even master over his own actions. He seeks his own release from the slave who has become his superior. But the freedom Jack expects cannot be attained through such a separation. The former queen, we later discover, became enslaved only after she fled from the responsibilities that bound her to her subjects. What is more, the severance that Jack now regards as liberating ironically anticipates his strenuously resisted parting from Mopsa. Jack cannot foresee that the little pupil who has become "quite clever" at the game he has taught her will soon surpass him as well as the "clever" sister whose help he solicits.

Despite her greater cleverness, however, the slave-woman is dependent on the unimaginative little boy who is her master. Their interdependence, stressed in the ensuing exchange, suggests Ingelow's own predicament as a writer in a field that had been co-opted by male "masters" of a regressive art:

> "I am very glad you asked me about that," said the fairy woman. "Yes, master, I wish very much to be free; and as you were so kind as to give the most valuable piece of money you possessed in order to buy me, I can be free if you can think of anything you really like better than that half-crown, and if I can give it to you."
>
> "Oh, there are many things," said Jack. "I like going up this river to Fairyland much better."
>
> "But you are going there, master," said the fairy woman; "you were on the way before I met with you."
>
> "I like this little child better," said Jack. "I love this little Mopsa. I should like her to belong to me."
>
> "She is yours," answered the fairy woman; "she belongs to you already. Think of something else."
>
> Jack thought again, and was so long about it that at last the beautiful slave said to him: "Master, do you see those purple mountains?"
>
> Jack turned around in the boat and saw a splendid range of purple mountains.

They were very great and steep, each had a crown of snow, and the sky was very red behind them, for the sun was going down.

"At the other side of those mountains is Fairyland," said the slave; "but if you cannot think of something that you should like better to have than your half-crown I can never enter in." (*MF*, chap. 7, 25–7)

The fairy woman insists on the urgency of her predicament. Thousands of "small people" are waiting to tow their queen through a narrow passage into a mountain enclave that closely resembles Ruskin's Treasure Valley. But they are impotent, as dependent as she is on the little boy's effort to find something more precious than his half-crown. Unless she ceases to be Jack's nominal subordinate, the "strength and skill" of her subjects are of no avail and she will be forced to remain at the margins of her domain, unable to resume her rule.

The fairy woman's dilemma, and Jack's attempt to resolve it, allow Ingelow to allegorize the paradox that confronted Victorian women writers who found themselves simultaneously stimulated and repelled by the "femininities" featured in the fantasies of their male contemporaries. Ingelow, Rossetti, and Ewing are not sure whether they can—or want to— reenter a realm of pure fantasy. The Treasure Valleys, Wonderlands, and regions at the back of North Wind are female domains and hence rightfully theirs. Yet a reclamation of these lands remains problematic. The repossession of such female fairylands required a preliminary cleansing. Any woman writer eager to exercise her own powers of fantasy needed to dissociate herself from men who tenaciously clung to their boyish equation of childhood with femininity. That equation could be crippling. The queen of fairies—whose identity Jack has yet to penetrate—is his dependent as much as his superior. She can shed her enslaved condition only by making the boy acknowledge that he covets something that antecedes his regressive desire to sail "up this river to Fairyland" with the little mate he loves and wants at all cost to retain. That something is, as Ingelow shrewdly knew, a boy's lingering attachment to his first parent, the mother he may continue to invest with magical powers even after he has attained manhood. Whether emulating or repudiating a father's engagement with, and presumed authority over, the material world, Victorian boys, as this older sister well understood, were bound by their unusually strong ties to the mother.

Although Jack will return to his father's garden and bask in the seeming might of that *paterfamilias,* the boy exhibits few patriarchal traits during the early stages of his fantastic journeys. He is uninterested in material possessions. In order to purchase the slave-woman, still wrinkled and feeble, from her abusive master, Jack was more than willing to part with "the half-crown that his grandmamma had given him on his birthday" (*MF,* chap. 6, 250). From the very start of his story, Jack has been affiliated with females. Though breaking away from the triangle in which he was flanked by the nurse and his baby sister, he soon became a nurturer himself. For Jack emulates the nurse by promptly feeding the fairy babies nestled in the hollow trunk of the "old thorn tree" with a piece of the plum cake she gave him for his own consumption (*MF,* chap. 1, 215). He is eager to help deliver the nestlings seemingly deserted by their "old mother." He not only assists in their passage out of the womb-like structure but also uses his waistcoat pocket as an incubator.

Like Diamond, that other boy-nurturer of babies, Jack seems to relish his adoption of maternal surrogacy. And, just as Diamond adopted Nanny as a sister, so does Jack's immediate identification with Mopsa, while still in the tree-hollow, also place him in something like that androgynous relation of brother-sister complements so dear to the imagination of Victorian women writers such as Emily Brontë and George Eliot.[18] The adventurous "Captain Jack" is certainly far less of an androgyne than Gluck or even Diamond. Still, despite his masculine strutting (he offers to fight the slave-woman's master in order to win her release), he is most at ease when playing with the chubby little girl he wants to own forever. It is, in fact, his Carrollian identification with this female dream-child that licenses his forays into the symbolic dreamscapes offered by female fantasylands.

Nonetheless, the manifestations of the female imagination that Jack encounters in these fantasylands also involve power struggles that go beyond the empty threats of Carroll's Queen of Hearts. Not only the fairy queen cruelly enslaved by a rival race of fairies, but also many inhabitants of the other borderlands and fairylands Jack visits are engaged in sustained tribal wars. Jack's humanity and, above all, his male identity make him immune to the abuses of enchantment better understood by those involved in cycles of submission and domination. His naiveté and the palpable possessions found in the trouser pockets of any middle-class Victorian boy—a dog whistle (*MF,* chap. 4, 235), a handkerchief, a pocketknife, as well as coins

---

18. Ingelow's own adult novel, *Off the Skelligs* (1872), narrated by a sister with "a brother two years older than myself," bears interesting resemblances to *The Mill on the Floss,* as well as to *Mopsa the Fairy.*

of various denominations—turn out to be prime assets in his dealings with fairy people.

Jack's desire to free a grown-up slave befits a good British boy brought up on the abolitionist principles of Ingelow's own Evangelical religion. He is sincere in wanting to avoid relations that demand the subjugation of the weaker by the stronger. But the boy who hopes to avoid a power conflict with the woman he suspects to be more than a slave has no compunction in trying to maintain his supremacy over little Mopsa. He sees no contradiction in wanting her to "belong" to him. Like Lewis Carroll, he cannot admit that a loving playfulness may be inseparable from a desire to dominate. When Jack expresses his hope that Mopsa will not become "too big for me to play with," he implies that he wants to control her development. But neither she nor he can stay arrested in wonderlands of the imagination. His hope of perpetual play is not only undermined by the reality of growth, but also compromised by his own desire for power.

When Jack at long last comes up with the wish he has found so difficult to formulate, he demands, significantly enough, a share of the power shown by the fairy woman who is no longer a powerless slave. He asks her for a piece of the silk ribbon that she had magically stretched, first into a child-sized handkerchief, then into a domestic apron, and finally into a "most beautiful robe of purple silk" suited to the resumption of her royal duties. Such stretching powers clearly appeal to Jack as much as to Lewis Carroll or George MacDonald, fellow appropriators of that "esemplastic" imagination that Wordsworth and Coleridge had gendered as feminine yet also equated with male desire:

> "All these sailors to tow my slave!" said Jack. "I wonder, I do wonder, what you are?" But the fairy woman only smiled, and Jack went on: "I have thought of something that I should like much better than my half-crown. I should like to have a little tiny bit of that purple gown of yours with the gold border."
>
> Then the fairy woman said: "I thank you, master. Now I can be free." So she told Jack to lend her his knife, and with it she cut off a very small piece of the skirt of her robe, and gave it to him. "Now mind," she said; "I advise you never to stretch this unless you want to make some particular thing of it, for then it will only stretch to the right size; but if you merely begin to pull it for your own amusement, it will go on stretching and stretching, and I don't know where it will stop." (*MF*, chap. 7, 257)

The fairy woman's warning is meant to instruct Jack about the proper uses of a fantastic imagination. Its stretching powers ought not be wantonly deployed to indulge irrational or subjective wishes that can border on the masturbatory. Such unrestraint, as the former slave knows from her own bitter experience, can be dangerous. The queen's insistence on limits reveals Ingelow's distrust of the stretchings to which Carroll had subjected his Alice and which MacDonald had dramatized through his expanding goddess, North Wind. But Ingelow's distrust is also directed at her personal venture into fantasy. As Alice reached a height of nine feet, she felt that her own feet, which remained on the ground, were so removed from her torso that they seemed to have been amputated. In *Mopsa the Fairy,* the slave-woman has also experienced mutilation. Severed from her subjects because she had become "discontented with my own happy country" (*MF,* chap. 8, 259), she was accidentally captured by wooden-legged townspeople whose original limbs were just as accidentally cut off by fairy rivals after they had tried to make "themselves invisible" (*MF,* chap. 6, 250).

Jack's wish for magical power is hardly inordinate, since he modestly asks for a "tiny bit" of the royal gown. But he misuses the sliver from the robe by creating a protective envelope, a hymen-like "canopy" or "awning," for the boat in which he and Mopsa will try to float away. Worried about enclosures that might "melt away," he wants this shelter to screen and ward off all unsettling changes (*MF,* chap. 9, 265). But the possession of this piece of matriarchal cloth does not allow Jack to stretch out his childish sense of omnipotence; he cannot arrest Mopsa's development nor fend off change. The permanent childhood abode he seeks for himself and Mopsa is as fragile as those harboring youthful shelter-seekers in Victorian novels such as *Wuthering Heights* and *David Copperfield.*[19]

Neither Jack nor Mopsa nor even Mopsa's magical older sister can ever be truly "free" in realms ruled by a female imagination. For they must

---

19. Catherine Earnshaw and Heathcliff, "snug" in the "closet" of the oak-case they use as a bed, are surprised by the servant Joseph who tears down the "pinafores" that act as a "curtain" for their oneness (Emily Brontë, *Wuthering Heights,* ed. William M. Sale, Jr. [New York: W. W. Norton, 1963], chap. 3, 27). Born with an attached placenta, David Copperfield discovers that he cannot transfer his adoration of his mother to the "most beautiful little girl" he first meets at Mr. Peggotty's womb-like boat house: "little Em'ly and I made a cloak of an old wrapper, and sat under it for the rest of the journey. Ah, how I loved her! What happiness (I thought) if we were married, and were going away anywhere to live among the trees and in the fields, never growing older, never growing wiser, children ever, rambling hand in hand" (Charles Dickens, *David Copperfield* [New York: Bantam, 1981], chap. 3, 29; chap. 10, 136).

defer to the inscrutable dictates of Mother Fate. When Mopsa deplores that she is "so big now" and wishes to burrow back into "Jack's waistcoat pocket again," her sister reminds her that their growth as coequal queens was mandated by the "old mother" herself: "She is much more powerful than we are" (*MF,* chap. 11, 278). And that maternal power, for Ingelow, inevitably produces a pain that women are bound to remember but boys are allowed to repress.

III

When Mopsa surpasses Jack in height, she does not just become as "tall as [his] mamma" but also assumes the maternal functions of a queen who is the antitype of Lewis Carroll's irresponsible Queen of Hearts. As I have been implying, Jack's relation to Mopsa permits Ingelow to review Carroll's strenuous resistance to female growth. In dramatizing the boy's grief over his enforced separation from the playmate who has become a queen, Ingelow taps Carroll's pained response to his own loss. Her genuine sympathy with Jack suggests her capacity for appreciating the intensity of that pain. Nonetheless, aware of the transformation of Carroll's nostalgia into anger, she counters her precursor in two distinct ways. She questions his possessive attempts to dominate a girl he resents for growing up and, even more important, she challenges his undisguised hostility towards adult women. It is hardly coincidental that Jack's weeping farewell from Mopsa should come during sunset at "the edge of the reed-bed" that borders the river on which the two had traveled in their little boat, still undivided by sex and age (*MF,* chap. 16, 313). For the landscape which Ingelow treats with a mixture of lyricism and irony pointedly recalls the one traversed by another well-remembered boat. The discordance between the tearful Mr. Dodgson's prefatory poem and Carroll's final loosening of the denizens of a mad underground was not wasted on his shrewd revisionist.

Ingelow's last chapter revises the closure of Carroll's text. Attacked by the encircling cards, Alice aborted her increasingly unpleasant dream. On awaking, she discovered that the aggressive cards merely were fluttering "dead" leaves, emblems of her own march towards maturity and death. Jack, however, cannot bear leaving the wonderland that now has Mopsa at its center. Attacked by the reeds that are "growing up" all around him with their "long spear-like leaves," he nonetheless strains to get a glimpse of her vanishing castle, vainly hoping to penetrate the thicket and find a path that might lead him back to the maiden chamber of an ever-young Sleeping Beauty. But the growing reeds are relentless: "it was of no use, they sprang up and grew yet more tall" (*MF,* chap. 16, 311). And the setting sun which gilds the "rosy sky" until the gold begins "to burn itself away" only acts, as in Carroll's sad recollection of a golden gleam, as a further reminder of the relentlessness of temporal change. Defeated, the boy throws himself on the ground, "burst into tears again, and decided to go home" (*MF,* chap. 16, 313).

Ingelow also scrutinizes Carroll's wishful attempt, in the last paragraph of *Wonderland,* to find compensation in the possibility that Alice may remember—and then transmit to others—the blissful summer days of a briefly shared "child-life." As I have noted in chapter 5, Alice's sister acts as Carroll's agent in her concluding reverie. Through a surrogate who is no longer a child but not yet a grown-up, he can indulge his wish that a grown Alice might remain his double, a child-lover who will disseminate the story he created for her. By gathering "other little children" around her after attaining "riper years," she can perpetuate his Alice-centered narrative and hence reassert their former oneness (*AW,* 99). Ingelow undercuts this fantasy of cooperation through an unsentimental handling of the relation between Mopsa and her older sister, the slave-woman turned queen of fairies. Unlike Alice's older sister, who can half believe herself in Wonderland, Mopsa's sister insists, with a cruel realism grounded in natural science, that their joint maturation has made them rivals: "There cannot be two Queens in one hive" (*MF,* chap. 11, 279). If Carroll tried to find some form of fusion to compensate him for the pains of separation, Ingelow prefers to insist on the irrevocability of loss and change.

Mopsa must be driven out of her sister's domain in order to find a hive of her own; once there, the newly crowned queen cannot afford to be ruled by nostalgia. She must view Jack from a new perspective and admit that this immature human is unfit to be a fairy queen's mate. Her only concession is to imprint Jack's features on the fairy prince she is destined to marry. By keeping Jack's clone at her side, Mopsa can always remember the boy who had imprinted her with his kiss. Jack, however, must forget her if he is to become a grown-up man. They belong to separate worlds.

Ingelow's calculated subversion of *Alice in Wonderland* has been misread, as I have mentioned, as a slavish dependence on Carroll's text. This misreading, so similar to that which has impeded a fuller understanding of Christina Rossetti's *Speaking Likenesses* as a response to *Through the Looking-Glass,* is deplorable yet understandable. For Ingelow's dilemma, as she herself seems to hint, resembles that of the slave-woman: despite a wisdom born from her much wider experience, Mopsa's sister cannot by herself re-enter the fantasy world in which she once ruled supreme. Mopsa's dependence on Jack is even stronger; yet, much like the fairy-mother who left her brood in an English thorn-tree, she eventually needs to push the boy away. Ingelow must likewise acknowledge her ties to the male child-lovers she warily follows. Yet just as Mopsa sadly rejects Jack's incongruous desire to be an adult woman's boy-mate, so does Ingelow gently repudiate Carroll's, MacDonald's, and Ruskin's investment in an arrested childhood.

Ingelow's allusions to Carroll therefore involve more than an attempt to capitalize on the children's book that had become a best-seller in the four years that preceded her own book's publication. The links that Roger Lancelyn Green and others have interpreted as signs of Ingelow's attempt to repeat Carroll's "success" always signal subtle dissociations.[20] Some of these connections are, to be sure, rather strained: the immobile flamingo soldiers who guard the shores of the river traversed by Jack's boat, for instance, simply seem to have been introduced as sturdier versions of the slippery flamingoes whom Alice used as croquet mallets. Most other links, however, suggest the sophistication of Carroll's sly revisionist.

Green was right in observing that Ingelow's textual allusions to *Wonderland* are most noticeable in the opening chapter of *Mopsa*. It is there, of course, as well as in her narrative's climax, that she renegotiates the traffic between fantasy and the everyday that framed Alice's adventures and then were featured in Diamond's night-excursions with North Wind. Ingelow's initial allusions to Carroll's text operate as playful inversions. In each opening, a curious child who breaks away from an older female who is reading a book and squeezes through a hole in order to venture into a space that lacks the behavioral and linguistic signposts of Victorian civilization. Still, whereas Alice's descent into the "antipathies" proves so disorienting that she soon questions her identity, Ingelow's Jack, always secure in his identity as a self-possessed little Victorian male, remains unfazed. Whereas Alice's transgressive sip from a bottle not marked "poison" produces the first of her many bodily discomforts, Jack's matter-of-factness is evident when he calmly notes that the hole he had entered

---

20. See note 16, above; unlike later critics, however, Green allows that *Mopsa* "is not in any sense an imitation, though the first pages suggest that it is going to be" (*Tellers of Tales*, 69).

"must have closed up all on a sudden." Unlike the ravenous Alice who eventually aborts her hunger-dream, this stolid young explorer contentedly settles down to munch the provisions he has brought along: "'Well,' said Jack, 'I may have to stay inside here for a long time, and I have nothing to eat but this cake'" (*MF,* chap. 1, 216).

Ingelow's inversion of gender-stereotypes, however, goes well beyond her decision to replace the little girl who soon bursts into tears with a stoic little boy who will cry only upon his banishment from Mopsa's castle. Lured by a rabbit dressed in male attire, Alice falls down, down, down the hole which that Carrollian surrogate has dug; immured in the hollow tree that also holds the fairy nestlings, Jack is shot, up, up, up, by a female albatross who materializes out of nowhere in order to propel him "through the hole" at the top (*MF,* chap. 1, 218). The difference is palpable. The White Rabbit finds the girl who towers over him as intimidating as the "savage" Duchess and the angry Queen of Hearts. The huge bird who acts as midwife in delivering a small boy and the fairies in his pocket solicitously hovers above Jack during his entire adventure and promptly descends, on his call, to take him back to his father's garden. The rabbit known only by his pallor remains marooned in Wonderland, clothed in the livery of hearts that symbolize both love and hatred. But the albatross so reassuringly called Jenny acts as a ferrier between the everyday world and a world of fantasy. She is even more supportive as guide and guardian than the hovering Cheshire Cat whom Alice regarded as her sole Wonderland friend.

Although Jenny merely appears at the outset and close of Jack's quest, Ingelow implants other female caretakers in almost all the borderlands and fairylands the boy visits. One of the most sympathetic of these, the apple-woman, is, like Jenny, a mediator between human beings and fairies. Herself an ordinary mortal who has resettled in the country ruled by Jack's former "slave," the apple-woman relishes her position of privilege among the tiny fairies, who revere her almost as much as their tall sovereign. Separated from grown-up sons she has left behind in Victorian England, she welcomes Jack and Mopsa and treats them as children of her own. Although she cannot accompany them on their last outing and makes erroneous predictions, this nurturant woman acts as a foil, through her warmth and good humor, to fairies who find it difficult to cry.

The insertion of an actual human in a story that, unlike the narrative of Alice's adventures, never purports to be a dream, serves Ingelow's apparent intention to create a much wider spectrum of female figures than those Alice encountered. Unlike the two Wonderland matriarchs, equally flat, violent, and grotesque, the soft-hearted apple-woman and the unsentimental fairy queen who is Mopsa's older sister are pointedly contrasted, though equally compelling. And even a highly unsavory female character, the "powerful" gypsy woman who turns out to be a "very malicious" enchantress in chapter 5 of *Mopsa,* is given a role that becomes more complicated than that played by her counterpart, the hideous Duchess whom Carroll added to his original *Underground* text.

Indeed, the complexity of this deceptive gypsy woman, a character who poses as a mother, stems, to a large extent, from Ingelow's attempt to evoke Carroll's Duchess. Jack's near-seduction by this pseudo-matriarch provides a commentary on the *Wonderland* text that seems subtler than the links I have so far examined. Alice disliked the Duchess's "tone," even before that matriarch sang to her howling baby; Jack, on the other hand, though warned by a caged parrot about the gypsy's cunning, is mesmerized as soon as she approaches him with a baby in her arms and sings a seductive song:

He felt as if there were some cobwebs before his face, and he put up his hand as if to clear them away. There were no real cobwebs, of course; and yet he again felt as if they floated from the gipsy-woman to him, like gossamer threads, and attracted him towards her. So he gazed at her, and she at him, till Jack began to forget how the parrot had warned him. (*MF,* chap. 5, 238–39)

Jack's hoodwinking by the gypsy singer allows Ingelow to react to Carroll's hostile caricature of the Duchess. But more than his misogyny, the assignation of a brutal "lullaby" to the Duchess probably caught her attention. As a poet who wrote within the domestic tradition of predecessors such as Jane Taylor (whose *Rhymes for the Nursery* Carroll's Mad Hatter so memorably parodies), Ingelow may have felt reasonably offended by the deformations of a kind of poetry that Victorian culture had labeled as "feminine." Yet "Speak Gently," the anonymous 1848 verse upon which Carroll's parodic "Speak Roughly" was based, would have been just as offensive to Ingelow. Though it pretends to adopt the saccharine point of view of a female speaker, the original nine-stanza effusion was actually written by a man, most likely David Bates.[21] The song that Ingelow assigns

21. Roger Lancelyn Green, in his "Appendix: 'Jabberwocky' and Other Parodies," prefers Bates to G. W. Langford (*The Lewis Carroll Handbook,* revised by Denis Crutch [Hamden, Conn.: Shoe String Press, 1979], 310).

to the gypsy-woman thus seems as much directed at Bates's "Speak Gently" as at Carroll's parody. For the gypsy-woman who holds "a baby on her arm" while singing to Jack is neither the deficient mother whom Carroll ridicules nor the soothing nurturer who advises others to address fragile children in "accents soft and mild" in Bates's 1848 version. Seduced by the gypsy's own "accents" and caught in the paralyzing cobwebs of a pseudo-maternal imagination, Jack soon discovers that this impostor is, in fact, no mother at all.

Pitying the screaming baby whom the Duchess so "violently" tosses to the beats of her sadistic lullaby, Alice welcomed the opportunity to assume the role of nurturer offered by the derelict mother who prefers to "get ready to play croquet with the Queen" (*AW,* 49). Jack, the nurturer of fairy babies, also finds himself drawn to the infant, "wrapped in a shawl" and with a "handkerchief over its face," whom the gypsy woman seems to treat so gently. He wonders, solicitously, whether this child of indeterminate sex might be too "heavy for her to carry and wished he could help her." Noticing that the woman "seemed very fond of it," the respectful boy "softly" approaches this tender domestic tableau, "till the gypsy-woman smiled, and suddenly began to sing" (*MF,* chap. 5, 239).

Although the gypsy's song is called a "selling song" by the narrator, Jack, charmed by the melodic voice, pays no attention to the words or intentions of the two verses he hears as a lullaby (*MF,* chap. 5, 238). Alice, too, "could hardly hear the words" of the Duchess's two-stanza lullaby amidst the din of the baby's howling (*AW,* 49). But whereas Alice remained conscious of the squalling child, Jack forgets the quiet little bundle the gypsy woman pretends to be "hushing." Like Diamond's submission to the "baby" rhythms of nonsense verses his mother could not decipher, Jack's obliviousness to sense stems from the primal, hypnotic spell of sound. The chanted two stanzas are rhythmically so seductive that the boy stops paying attention to their possible meaning. His sudden lack of interest in the singer's infant thus is a mark of his own regression. For he has dropped his quasi-maternal investment in small creatures as a result of his own relapse into babyhood. As immobile as the wrapped-up form cradled in the gypsy-woman's arms, Jack has allowed himself to become infantilized by succumbing to a preverbal symbiosis:

When the gipsy had finished her song Jack felt as if he was covered all over with cobwebs; but he could not move away, and he did not mind them now. All his wish was to please her, and get close to her; so when she said, in a soft wheedling voice:

"What will you please to buy my pretty gentleman?" he was just going to answer that he would buy anything she recommended, when, to his astonishment and displeasure, for he thought it very rude, the parrot suddenly burst into a violent fit of coughing, which made all the customers stare. (*MF,* chap. 5, 239)

To Jack's great surprise, the old parrot's "very rude" behavior worsens when that disrespectful bird chooses to turn into a full-fledged parodist: "he began to beat time with his foot, and sing, or rather scream out, an extremely saucy imitation of the gypsy's song, and all his parrot friends in the other cages joined in the chorus" (*MF,* chap. 5, 239). The screeching cacophony of this parrotic chorus seems far more grating than the roughness of the chorus of "*Wow! wow! wow!*"—"(in which the cook and baby joined)"—chanted in the Duchess's kitchen (*AW,* 48). Enraged at finding her prisoner "thus daring to imitate her," the gypsy turns on the offender. But Jack, too, is outraged at the shattering of his regressive absorption in a maternal lullaby. Aware of his effect, the parrot offers another stanza in which he mimics the gypsy's versification but not her intended meaning: "[H]e began to sing another verse in the most impudent tone possible, and with a voice that seemed to ring through Jack's head, and almost pierce it" (*MF,* chap. 5, 240).

As Jack bursts into laughter, the spell is broken. Vainly hurling everlarger objects at the parrot cage, the furious gypsy woman now openly follows a precedent set by Carroll's Duchess, who, after dodging all the saucepans, plates, and dishes thrown at her and at her baby, had so blithely tossed her precious infant at the surprised Alice:

But nothing did the parrot any harm; the more violently his cage swung the louder he sang, till at last the wicked gipsy seized her poor little young baby, who was lying in her arms, rushed frantically at the cage as it flew swiftly through the air towards her and struck at it with the little creature's head. "Oh, you cruel, cruel woman!" cried Jack, and all the small mothers who were standing near with their skinny children on their shoulders screamed out with terror and indignation; but only for one instant, for the handkerchief flew off that had covered its face, and was caught in the wires of the cage, and all the people saw that it was not a real baby at all, but a bundle of clothes, and its head was a turnip.

Yes, a turnip! You could see that as plainly as possible, for though the green leaves had been cut off, their stalks were visible through the lace cap that had been tied on it.

Upon this all the crowd pressed closer, throwing her baskets, and brushes, and laces, and beads at the gipsy, and calling out: "We will have none of your goods, you false woman! Give us back our money, or we will drive you out of the fair.

You've stuck a stick into a turnip, and dressed it up in baby clothes. You're a cheat! a cheat!" (*MF,* chap. 5, 240–41)

Ingelow here offers her own version of the surprised reaction that we share with Alice as she discovers that the baby she tried to protect has abruptly turned into a grunting pig. Carroll's narrative claims that Alice is "quite relieved" by this unexpected change. Indeed, the girl who wonders what to do with the "creature" she has inherited, seems far less interested in being a little mother than Jack, Diamond, or, for that matter, the Looking-Glass caretaker of Dinah's kittens. Unlike Fern in E. B. White's *Charlotte's Web,* who feeds Wilbur with a baby bottle and wheels the piglet in her doll's carriage, Alice has no great maternal investment in the chubby porker she allows to scurry away: "'If it had grown up,' she said to herself, 'it would have made a dreadfully ugly child: but it makes a rather handsome pig, I think'" (*AW,* 50).

Ingelow turns a *Wonderland* deformation into a case of fraud. The bawling baby held by the hideous Duchess in Tenniel's illustration for "Pig and Pepper" *was* human before its porcine incarnation. But the "poor little young baby" a fictitious mother hurls at her imitator's cage never was anything but a turnip stuck on a stick. By cleverly exposing the gypsy woman's trick, the satirical parrot has freed Jack from those smothering cob-webs. Just as Carroll transforms a stanza taken from "Speak Gently" into the two verses of "Speak Roughly," so do the two verses so crudely sung by the parrot undo the effect of the two verses sung by the "false woman" who falsified motherhood.

Like Carroll, Ingelow punctures the mindlessness of Victorian baby-worship. But she goes beyond the comic inversions of the man who greatly worried that boys born to unfeminine women might grow into hoggish beasts. If she, too, indicts the falsified sentimentality of highly popular poems such as "Speak Gently," she does so because such products perpetuate the falsification of male authors who adopt a purported female point of view they find culturally marketable. By adopting the pious female voice of "Speak Gently," David Bates does a disservice to genuine women poets. This man (who can rightly be accused of being a "false woman") offers, as the gypsy does, tainted "goods." And, what is more, he also offers an all-too-easy target for parodists who feel licensed to caricature mindless women as hideous singers and impotent queens. The originator of a bad poem that exploits his culture's sentimental view of the mother-child relation and the clever parodist who exposes that outlook in order to vent his own anger at Victorian matrons are thus equally culpable. And, ironically enough, each can find a wider audience for their products than Elizabeth Barrett Browning's talented trio of poetic successors—Dora Greenwell, Christina Rossetti, and Jean Ingelow.

In authoring *both* the gypsy woman's song and the old male parrot's "saucy imitation," Ingelow wants to reclaim the female authority subverted by both Bates and Carroll. And, whereas Carroll inverted Bates's ideological emphasis by simply altering the wording of the lines he parodied, Ingelow creates elliptical texts to support her belief that tonal skills are more important than the phrasing of versified thoughts. Although the poetic pendants she offers through the gypsy woman and the parrot are snippets taken from ballads and hence hardly resemble the antinarrative verses that MacDonald has Diamond recite to his baby sister, they, too, primarily organize an emotional "space," as Kristeva puts it in her description of genotexts.[22] Lulled by the variations of the call to "buy," Jack may be deaf to the import of the actual words used in the gypsy woman's "selling song."[23] But the reader becomes aware of certain complications: the voice that Jack hears is thrice removed—the gypsy woman reproduces the speech of a "young, young wife" who, in turn, reproduces the call of the gypsies (*MF,* chap. 5, 239). The regressive effect that the song has on Jack thus may have something to do with a transmission that spirals back into layers of the past. Later in the narrative, Mopsa will have to wake the dreaming Jack, once more in danger of becoming entangled as he moves through the diminishing spiral coils of a many-ringed Craken, the primal creature that Tennyson had depicted as an unconscious underwater foetus.

Whereas the two stanzas of the gypsy's song flow into each other, the parrot craftily defers reciting his second verse until he has had a chance to observe the effect of the first. Appropriately, his own song stresses the abruptness of change. In the first half of his ballad-fragment, a male speaker who tries to woo a "dear lady"—who may well be the young wife in the gypsy's song—finds himself repudiated. Yet, in the second verse, set after "another day" has passed, the lady urges the man she has jilted to renew his suit. He fails to do so, however, apparently content with a purely

22. See p. 252n, above.

23. The variation in the final line, "Buy, maids, buy," seems a rather deliberate bow to the hypnotic effect of "Come buy, come buy," the seductive sales pitch of the eerie vendors who lure "maids" in the opening lines of Rossetti's "Goblin Market."

mental possession of the inaccessible woman he now calls "my own, own lady."

The hints of erotic tension and displacements of the gypsy's poem (in which vendors urged young wives to "Buy, buy laces, / Veils to screen your faces") are now more openly confronted. The lady who rejected her lover has become a lonely Madeline or sequestered Mariana as she acknowledges the intensity of her desire through a Keatsian/Tennysonian "moan." This unconsummated affair is as potentially pathetic as Dodgson's love for Alice Liddell or Ruskin's love for "Rosie" La Touche. But the parrot's raucous rendition and the comic chorus provided by the parrot's wife cause Jack to burst out in laughter. Still, seduced into mistaking a "selling song" for a lullaby, the boy cannot grasp the veiled import of a romance he only hears as a burlesque. The plight of male and female selves who cannot reciprocate each other's love because of poor timing anticipates, of course, the final division between Jack and his "own, own" Mopsa. But if the parrot's song seems to predict Jack's separation, it also bears on the wooing of dream-children who can only be wedded in a lonely imagination.

How consciously ironic is Ingelow in her handling of the Carrollian precedents she seems to have implanted in this episode? If, as I have tried to argue, she intends to rehabilitate the female voice comically ventriloquized by Carroll through the medium of the Duchess, why is her own female singer exposed as a "cheat" and the male parrot hailed as a brave liberator from imprisoning female fancies? However impertinent or crude, the parrot not only is ingenious enough to break the spell that had subjected his people to female domination but also frees Jack from submitting to the woman who had masked herself as a mother. Since the clever parrot thus resembles the clever parodist who tried to puncture the matriarchal rule of both the Duchess and the Queen of Hearts, can Ingelow really be said to dissociate herself from her predecessor?

Unlike Christina Rossetti who chose to tap Carroll's own anger in *Speaking Likenesses,* Ingelow does not have to hurl missiles back at the "saucy" creator of the Duchess and Queen of Hearts. Her critique of Carroll, if it can be called that, is based, I think, on her intuitive understanding of the psychic agony that caused his split between adult and child, male and female, satirical and sentimental selves. She understood such conflicts because they stemmed from conditions quite similar to her own. Living the unobtrusive life of a Victorian gentlewoman, a primrose bound by her enduring ties to the nursery, she was, as I have suggested, resentful of the cultural restraints she nonetheless accepted and helped to propagate. What

Ingelow opposes to Carroll's oscillations between nostalgia and anger, then, is a fatalism rooted in her sense of the perpetuity of such strife. Whereas Carroll insists on resolving "antipathies" only to oscillate between emotional extremes, Ingelow finds comfort in the enigmatic fairy dictum that she has Mopsa enunciate for Jack's benefit: "That that is, is; and when it is, that is the reason that it is."

Ingelow's ultimate disagreement with Carroll is artistic, however, and has more to do with his chosen mode of presentation than with the content of *Alice in Wonderland.* His aggressive comedy deflects from his obsession with loss. By having the parrot sing a song about male and female divided selves, Ingelow seems to suggest that Carroll's comic deformations—his use of parody, satire, and burlesque—may only veil his affinities with poets of loss such as Wordsworth, Keats, and Tennyson. To a lyricist and latter-day Romantic like herself, his romanticism is therefore enveloped in constructs that are too cerebral. To invert the work of a poetaster such as David Bates is to misuse creative energies capable of much subtler forms of romantic irony. The pleasures of *Wonderland* are intellectual. Yet beneath this condensed, consummately crafted text lies the unconsummated desire for Alice that Ingelow chooses to handle so differently in her diffuse and episodic drama of divided selves she casts as woman and boy. If Lewis Carroll cannot bring himself to part from the girlish self he wants to retain as an adult, Jean Ingelow must—as Mopsa does—bid farewell to the boyish self who remains imprinted in her female imagination. She relies on her own art of indirection, diffusion, and transposition to intermix the contrary emotional states so central to her and Carroll's creativity. It is not necessary for the gypsy woman to be deformed as a caricature if her song of experience can cause an innocent boy to indulge his yearning for fusion; nor is it necessary to sever parody from nostalgia if a satirical parrot can recite a burlesque that preserves the pathos of its sub-text. Ingelow thus prefers to recombine opposites. In something not unlike a Keatsian "negative capability," she can simultaneously identify herself with both fantasy and anti-fantasy, with the powers of illusion unleashed by the mesmeric gypsy woman and the powers of disenchantment wielded by the clever parrot.

Ingelow's interest in the conflicts of gender and generation certainly is as pronounced as that of any of the male fantasists before her. But, as her opposition of the two singers in chapter 5 shows, she resists their desire to resolve these conflicts. She neither tries to restore an androgynous oneness through fantasies of regression or early death, as Ruskin and MacDonald had done in *The King of the Golden River* and *At the Back of the North Wind,* nor tries to dramatize the sexual consummation of chastened women and men forced to abandon childhood illusion, as Thackeray had done in *The Rose and the Ring* and MacDonald in "The Light Princess." Instead, she simply prefers to transpose the gender stereotypes accepted by her culture. Just as Jack is a boy who has feminine traits despite his pronounced masculinity, so is there something decidedly masculine about the aggressive gypsy who makes a mockery of motherhood, and something maternal about the old parrot who worries about Jack's welfare as much as about the fate of his own kin. The strange chapter ends in a final reversal: the gypsy woman, exposed at last as a power-hungry fairy, now becomes transformed into a bird, "an ugly great condor," while the parrot-people, who belonged to a rival race of fairies, are allowed to resume their former shapes as miniature human beings. There has been no resolution, however, for both tribes continue their never-ending strife. As they knock "each other about," these antagonists become ultimately indistinguishable to Jack; "tired of the noise and confusion," the boy takes refuge in the magical boat that proceeds to move "down the wonderful river" (*MF,* chap, 5, 244–45).

IV

Jack's flight on the giant bird of the imagination who takes him in and out of a fantasyland not only marks a revision of Alice's Wonderland entry and exit but also allows Ingelow to signify her distance from the second major children's book she wants to evoke, *At the Back of the North Wind.* Indeed, her dissociation from MacDonald's fantasy seems more serious and sustained than her rather playful revisions of *Alice in Wonderland.*[24] For Ingelow challenges the text on ideological grounds rooted in her own Evangelical theology. A fable that privileges a boy's dreamy enchantment with North Wind and rejects his mother's mundane reality is contrary to her emphasis on this-worldly ties and her belief in an allegiance to the

---

24. Still, MacDonald's own textual twitting of his friend's introductory *Alice* poem in chapter 5 of *North Wind* may have provided her with a model for her own playful handling of Carroll: by making Jack's self-propelling boat easier on the boy than the craft that had placed demands on a "weak" oarsman, Ingelow extended MacDonald's little joke (see note 3 in the previous chapter).

familiar calyx of our "first home." The escapism that leads MacDonald's narrator to endorse Diamond's night-flights and to encourage his final death wish thus is repeatedly challenged throughout *Mopsa.*

Ingelow's ruddy-cheeked Captain Jack is cast, as I have intimated, as the exact anti-type of that pale and haunted "god's baby," the tubercular Diamond. Both of these naifs are given the role assigned to the "Dummling" figure whose kindness is rewarded with a treasure or a princess in more traditional fairy tales. Viewed superficially, then, both are feminized caretakers, like Ruskin's Gluck. If Diamond ministers to family, neighbors, and strangers enslaved by poverty and despair, Jack looks after Mopsa and her siblings, the little fairies he transports to safety as well as the slave-woman he frees. Yet the missionary activities each boy discharges only underscore the acute differences between them. Having repaired the lives of those who depended on him for their well-being, Diamond is free to leave the world of parents and friends; having become increasingly dependent on the powers of those he initially patronized, Jack resumes a subordinate position in his parental home.

Whereas MacDonald's narrator treats Diamond as a fellow mystic, "as much interested in metaphysics" (*BNW,* chap. 38, 306) as himself, Ingelow asks her readers to regard Jack's ordinariness as an asset. Able to "look through the look of things" (*BNW,* chap. 25, 188), Diamond preferred the company of angel boys to that of unimaginative children such as Nanny and Lame Jim. Jack, however, welcomes the return to normalcy Jenny brings about at the end of his adventures. His strong ties to the everyday world, always manifest throughout his travels, shielded him from the blandishments of the fantastic. Ultimately, not even a fully empowered Mopsa can—or wants to—detain the boy infatuated with her incarnation as a wise and sexually matured woman. She thus helps to redirect Jack's quasi-maternal love for a chubby toddler to its primary object, his own mother. Not surprisingly, his last words in the narrative will be "Mamma!" (*MF,* chap. 16, 316).

Freed of all family ties, "little Diamond" finally gave in to his desire for fusion with the numinous figure who haunted his waking life. Yet Jack is rather easily nudged back into a social order in which he never had been anything other than a coddled little middle-class boy. It is a safer, because more tangible and familiar, order of reality. And it is also the source of all those material talismans Jack so generously shared with the denizens of Fairyland—the plum-cake, his dog whistle, his handkerchief, the half-crown that redeems the slave-woman, and the "silver fourpence" that

Mopsa molds into a magical wand to redeem male fairies entombed in a Carrollian underground. These fragments of a solid actuality define Jack's identity. They become staples in a form of traffic or exchange that always confirms his superior status as a human among fairies and endows him with a certain inviolability. As reminders of the greater stability of Jack's world, of a solid actuality to which he clings so much more persistently than Diamond, these objects leave no doubt about Ingelow's own priorities.

These priorities are also underscored by the mighty albatross who takes Jack from one world to another. Soaring above the clouds, Jenny offers Jack her downy back much in the way that North Wind allowed Diamond to huddle in the "woven nest" of her streaming hair. But Jack regards his guide to new marvels with none of Diamond's terrified awe of the intruder who asked him to tear off the protective plaster his mother had pasted over the hole above his bed. Diamond's morbid infatuation with North Wind led to his reckless disregard of his mother's claim on his life. The cautious Jack, however, is reluctant to follow Jenny through the hole that acts as a passageway into the unknown. He wants to be reassured that she will restore him to his family:

> "I should be more comfortable," replied Jack, "if I knew how I could get home again. I don't wish to go home just yet, for I want to see where we are flying to, but papa and mamma will be frightened if I never do."
>
> "Oh no," replied the albatross (for she was an albatross), "you need not be at all afraid about that. When boys go to Fairyland, their parents never are uneasy about them."
>
> "Really?" exclaimed Jack.
>
> "Quite true," replied the albatross. (*MF,* chap. 1, 218)

Jenny's prediction turns out to be correct. After the bird brings him back, Jack finds that—although it is evening now—neither his father nor mother are at all surprised to see him. Diamond's first trip to the realm at North Wind's back was regarded with great anxiety by his weeping mother; his second departure was mourned by Mrs. Raymond and the narrator. But Jack's absence has gone unnoticed. There has been no disruption of everyday routines.

When Diamond hesitated to follow North Wind, she overcame his resistance by identifying herself with his mother. Yet, as noted in the previous chapter, these two female figures became rivals. Jenny, however, essentially remains a parental surrogate. She almost resembles a diligent

Victorian governess, carefully repeating the instructions she wants Jack to follow. And when the boy meekly asks her to take him home, she is aware of his bruised self-esteem. Diamond's longing to "be nearer" to North Wind could only be sated through his death (*BNW,* chap. 36, 289). Jack's thwarted desire to remain at Mopsa's side, however, is delicately handled by Jenny. Aware that she cannot replace the love-object he has lost, she acts as a mediatrix between Mopsa and Jack's mother. She strongly endorses his wish to go back. And by lulling him to sleep with her rhythmic wing-beats, she starts the boy on a process of forgetting that proves more therapeutic than his many memory lapses among the fairies:

> As Jack's feet were lifted up from Fairyland he felt a little consoled. He began to have a curious feeling, as if all this had happened a good while ago, and then half the sorrow he had felt faded into wonder, and the feeling still grew upon him that these things had passed some great while since, so that he repeated to himself: "It was a long time ago."
>
> Then he fell asleep, and did not dream at all, nor know anything more till the bird woke him.
>
> "Wake up now, Jack," she said; "we are at home."
>
> "So soon!" said Jack, rubbing his eyes. (*MF,* chap. 16, 313)

The repression of painful memories is completed upon Jack's return to the domestic landmarks of his former life. Upon crossing the threshhold of his home, he hears his mother's voice. She is a reader, a disseminator of texts, just like the nurse he left behind in the book's opening.

> He drew a little nearer. His mother sat with her back to the open window, but a candle was burning, and she was reading aloud. Jack listened as she read, and knew that this was not in the least like anything he had seen in Fairyland, nor the reading like anything that he had heard, and he began to forget the boy-king, and the apple-woman, and even his little Mopsa, more and more. (*MF,* chap. 16, 314)

Ingelow devotes her novel's last pages to the sense of well-being Jack experiences as he readjusts himself to familiar coordinates. The *Wonderland* Alice shared her adventures with the older sister who then discharged the task of adjusting a surreal dream to "dull reality." But Jack is delighted to find his parents asking "no questions" about his venture into a realm that Ingelow never treated as a dream-world. The boy basks in a sense of uninterrupted oneness. When he lays his head on his father's waistcoat, he fitfully recalls having carried Mopsa and her siblings in his own waistcoat pocket. But he is more than willing to relinquish his desire to rule as a paternal fairy-king. Looking up admiringly at the father who insists that it is time for this little "man of ours" to go to bed, Jack thinks "what a great thing a man was; he had never seen anything so large in Fairyland, nor so important; so, on the whole, he was glad he had come back, and felt very comfortable" (*MF*, chap. 16, 316, 314). Unlike a Diamond who never reaches manhood or a Carroll who wishes to be Alice's permanent playmate, Jack welcomes the adult male identity that lies ahead.

The patriarchal coordinates Jack gladly embraces also may appeal to child readers comforted by familiar landmarks and resumed routines. But Ingelow does not allow older readers to forget the wonders of the matriarchal fairylands that had tantalized Jack. She keeps our memories of Mopsa and Mother Fate alive by shifting from Jack's placid position on "his father's knee" to the authority of the mother she has cast as a reader of unnamed texts. This figure's adult voice subtly undermines Jack's and the narrator's complacency. The paragraph that began, "At last his father noticed him," thus ends with the acknowledgment of Jack's mother: "Then his mother, turning over the leaf, lifted up her eyes and looked at Jack, but not as if she was in the least surprised, or more glad to see him than usual; but she smoothed the leaf with her hand, and began again to read, and this time it was about the Shepherd Lady" (*MF*, chap. 16, 314).

By allowing her to come last and by assigning her the longest of the many cryptic verses interpolated throughout the narrative, Ingelow makes Jack's mother the most important of all the female singers in *Mopsa the Fairy*. Earlier lyrics—the lullabies sung by the gypsy woman in chapter 5 or by the stone-woman in chapter 13, the hymn welcoming Mopsa's sister in chapter 8, the Mopsa-led ditty in chapter 15—always pointed to ironies and meanings embedded in the prose narrative. Nor were these songs limited to fairyland natives. The old apple-woman, who taught the fairies the words of the welcoming hymn, is given four songs in chapters 9, 10, and 11. Her lyrics often act as counterweights or antidotes to fairy songs, much as the parrot's song had offset the gypsy's pseudo-lullaby.

Like the solid objects in Jack's pockets or like his own effort to come up with a song "that he had often heard his nurse sing in the nursery at home" (*MF*, chap. 16, 309), the apple-woman's verses are imports from an actual world. Through them, this immigrant challenges the ascendancy of the fantastic. The human figures that Diamond saw in his first visit to the limbo at the back of North Wind swayed to the "tunes" sung by the magical river running through that strange country. Mute, unnamed, indistinguishable from each other, these settlers were not eager to return to their world of origin. The apple-woman, too, cannot bring herself to return to the pain and hardship bequeathed to humanity by the apple-eaters of Eden. Yet she remains unseduced by the fairies who cosset and flatter her; she maintains her individuality by wearing her former attire and by clinging to many a "stupid old song" she has committed to memory (*MF,* chap. 11, 280).

Although Jack's mother does not reside in Fairyland, she is as much a mediator as the apple-woman and Jenny. For, like them and like Mopsa, the fairy child altered by human love, she seems keenly aware of the links between competing realities. Indeed, her song about the Shepherd Lady calls attention to the contact between two antithetical orders. The tripartite, nine-stanza poem about the lady entrusted with the flock of a mysterious "piper" is open to conflicting interpretations. If read as a romantic allegory in the mode of Keats's "Eve of St. Agnes" or Tennyson's "The Lady of Shalott," the lady may stand for an aroused poetic imagination. If read as a religious allegory, however, the "shepherd lord" who disappears after leaving his "crook" to his beloved is no demon lover but a rather Divine Bridegroom.[25] In either case, however, the mother's song about the Shepherd Lady calls attention to the burden borne by imaginative women who see and understand more than those entrusted to their care. Such women may be fairy queens compelled to raise their subjects to a higher level, mothers charged with the socialization of their children, or unmarried writers who, like Ingelow or Rossetti, deploy their gifts as poets and storytellers to help young readers ill-served by the subjective constructions of male fantasists. Mother Fate has assigned a similar role to all these caretakers.

Jack, however, fails to see that his mother's song preserves, however subliminally, his fading memories of Mopsa. The mother who kisses him upon finishing the long poem steers the boy to "some strawberries on the sideboard in the dining-room" (*MF,* chap. 16, 316). Denied access to her awareness of anything other than his desire for an evening snack, we are once more tied to Jack's own limited perceptions:

25. In reviewing *Forbidden Journeys,* Gwyneth Jones cogently notes that most Victorian nurseries would have "probably contained a print of the 'Good Shepherd'": "That it should be the lady, rather than St. Peter or a male cleric, who receives and undertakes the pastoral charge of the flock of human souls is a decidedly interesting innovation on the part of Ingelow" (*Victorian Review* 19 [1993]: 66).

So he ran out into the hall, and was delighted to find all the house just as usual, and after he had looked about him he went to his own room, and said his prayers. Then he got into his little white bed, and comfortably fell asleep.

That's all. (*MF*, chap. 16, 316)

The narrator's uninflected tone helps to make this quietistic ending seem anticlimactic. The final matter-of-factness is in marked contrast to the sharper tonal shift at the close of "The Life of Mr. John Smith," that much simpler celebration of uneventfulness. There, a hortatory narrator had suddenly materialized to reprove all readers who dared ask whether they had indeed been told "all." Here, however, by insisting on our acceptance of the commonplace, the narrator tacitly asks wary older readers to re-adopt the repressive faculties of a small child. The demand is hard, and even contradictory, for it invites us to erase all memories of the extraordinary and mysterious otherness that Ingelow has kept alive through the indirection of the final song. The narrator's "That's all" thus must be simultaneously accepted and rejected.

V

The many editions *Mopsa the Fairy* has undergone suggest a continued appeal to different generations of readers. But Ingelow's anti-fantastical fantasy is not without its detractors. Readers drawn to the ironic control exerted by Thackeray's or Carroll's narrators want a stronger authorial presence than that of a self-effacing narrator skilled in the art of under-statement. And readers interested in pinpointing an author's "meaning" are disturbed by Ingelow's fragmentation of her story into a succession of discrete episodes more memorable for their dream-like vividness than for advancing a plot or sustaining a symbolic cohesion. Even the interpolation of poetry into prose has contributed to an impression of arbitrariness and lack of design.[26]

Ironically enough, the presumed disjointedness of Ingelow's narrative and the seeming incoherence of individual episodes may have much to do with Ingelow's ties to the antecedents she tries to revise. Despite its power-ful originality, her narrative is essentially reactive. Not only Carroll and

---

26. I am relying here on the responses of undergraduate and graduate students, as well as of colleagues in my National Endowment for the Humanities summer seminars for college teachers.

MacDonald are repeatedly targeted, as I have tried to show, but even the work of Ingelow's friend John Ruskin comes under occasional scrutiny. The account of the stone people whom Jack and Mopsa encounter in chapters 12 and 13 softens the punishment meted out to the Black Brothers, similarly petrified in *The King of the Golden River*. By dwelling on the story of people who were "powerful once" but must now expiate past cruelties, Ingelow anticipates the similar fall of the nation whom Mopsa redeems (*MF*, chap. 13, 289). But the interlude breaks the narrative flow. Imagistically compelling, it nonetheless seems an unnecessary elaboration of Ingelow's insistence on the agency of a Mother Fate who, though just as punitive as Ruskin's little men, is also far less vindictive.

Yet the text most responsible for the seeming diffuseness of *Mopsa* undoubtedly is the serially published *At the Back of the North Wind*. Episodes not wholly woven into Ingelow's narrative often become more understandable when related to MacDonald's sprawling and episodic text. Thus, for instance, Jack's encounter with "the old white horse" Boney and with the "beautiful brown mare" Lady Betty in a border country in which "things are set right again that people have caused to go wrong" (*MF*, chap. 3, 225, 228, 229) gains poignancy if one remembers the major roles MacDonald had assigned to "old Diamond," the horse with the "white lozenge on his forehead" after whom his hero was named, and the "red chestnut" Ruby, who turns out to be an angel-horse (*BNW*, chap. 29, 232).

Able to understand animal language, Diamond was allowed to overhear a conversation between old Diamond, so badly overworked that he has become as "thin as a clothes-horse," and the "plump and sleek" Ruby (*BNW*, chap. 31, 251). The abuse of the bony carriage horse turns out to have been "necessary": both he and Diamond's father were simply ordained to "grow lean" (*BNW*, ch. 32, 259). Ingelow rebels at a mysticism that can condone such suffering. Unlike Diamond, Jack is surprised to find talking horses and even more surprised that both Bony and Lady Betty have died because of human maltreatment. When he finds out that Boney, like the horse Diamond, "used to live in London," he feels personally implicated (*MF*, chap. 3, 226). The horse's caretaker only sharpens Jack's guilt: "I wonder what will be done to all your people for driving, and working, and beating so many beautiful creatures to death every year that comes." The "alarmed" boy lamely defends himself by contending that "he had never been himself unkind to horses, and was glad that Boney bore no malice" (*MF*, chap. 3 227).

Ingelow's consistency is evident in the thoughtful and deliberate responses to male constructions that I have been tracing. Nonetheless, by reclaiming fantasy only to subvert it in the name of the "real," her revisionist art takes risks that can become liabilities. Her rejectionism frequently leads her into exaggerating the very features she wants to redress. Like Rossetti after her, she therefore often magnifies, and hence aggravates, the fantastical elements she wants to subdue. Attracted by fairylands that welcome human visitors such as Jack and the apple-woman, a small child may well prefer Ingelow's tiny fairies to the inhospitable residents of Wonderland. Still, Jack's adventures can be more terrifying than Alice's. The book's many striking instances of violence and pain seem more intense than the discomforts of a dream-child precisely because they do not occur in a dream that can be safely aborted.

Similarly, the inscrutability of Mother Fate's dictates only helps to obfuscate even further the paradoxes through which MacDonald's awesome North Wind tried to justify her own actions. Feared by the fairies, who are "always crying out for an alphabet without the fatal F" (*MF,* chap. 9, 268), this invisible power seems more of an abstraction than North Wind, even though she stands for a deified motherhood as much as the titaness who claimed to serve the providential design of the Christ-child. Ingelow's apparent wish to counter male paternalism through a female mythology remains guarded and sketchy, perhaps deliberately so, given the potential conflict between her patriarchal Christianity and a matriarchal paganism. Are the black, white, and brown fairies who test Mopsa's future subjects the equivalent of Clotho, Lachesis, and Atropos, the spinners who control the threads of all life? If so, is Mother Fate to be identified with Nyx or Night, the parent of the *parcae*? Just as it is difficult to distinguish among the book's myriad fairy races, so is it impossible to grasp the hierarchical arrangement or chain of command that governs a matriarchal fantasyland ruled by the fatal F.

Is *Mopsa* to be read as a proto-feminist text? Although Ingelow names her novel after the child who becomes a queen, she maintains the outer lineaments of a boy's adventure story. There is as much of Jean Ingelow in Jack as in Mopsa. Her empathetic understanding of boys and men was noted by Ruskin in a 1867 letter he wrote to acknowledge her latest volume of poems. As much addressing himself as Ingelow, Ruskin mused: "I never cease wondering—with a wonder that has always been with me—how women know the way men love. We don't know *your* way of loving—it is a mystery to us, which we accept but cannot imagine. But you can imagine ours. How is this?" (*CW,* 36:530).[27] The answer to this rhetorical question is contained in *Mopsa,* which had not yet appeared at the time. Ingelow's novel suggests that the polarization between male and female selves that Ruskin bemoans is not innate. Women know how men love because they can remember what boys try to forget.

Ideally, Jack and Mopsa ought to fuse. But, like Orpheus and Eurydice in the fine sonnet Ingelow uses as an epigraph for her last chapter or like the lovers in her popular poem "Divided," they cannot blend. Mopsa is either smaller than Jack or he is smaller than she; there is only one brief moment in which these divided selves are balanced and coequal. As a child, Ingelow identified herself with brothers and male cousins who moved freely without the curbs imposed on a future Victorian lady. Like Mopsa, boxed up in her castle, Ingelow accepted the restraints placed on her powerful imagination. Yet the world of male action retained its earlier appeal.

Like the children's books of Ruskin, Thackeray, and Carroll, *Mopsa the Fairy* is dedicated to a girl, "my dear little cousin, Janet Holloway." She was the daughter of a favorite cousin, George Holloway, from whom Jean Ingelow became separated when she was thirteen. Ingelow reappropriated and redirected the constructions of "femininity" undertaken by her male predecessors. But, like Mopsa, she treasures Jack. She does not censure the boy whose return to the father's law allows him to forget Mopsa. Her own nostalgia and her accommodation of the patriarchy thus separate Ingelow from Christina Rossetti, in whose "Goblin Market" there were no human men and whose *Speaking Likenesses* would not feature boy heroes such as Gluck, Diamond, or Jack. Rossetti's texts are more uncompromising than Ingelow's. Her repudiation of Carroll necessarily involved a rejection of the gentler sister-poet who could empathize with a child-lover's nostalgia. Female rivalry, featured in many of Rossetti's poems, thus also makes its way into her relentless deconstructions of the *Alice* books. As both Ingelow and Rossetti knew, there really could not be two Queens in a single hive.

27. For a fuller discussion of Ruskin's letters to Ingelow, see the 1995 article cited in note 3, above.

N I N E

Razing Male Preserves: From "Goblin Market" to *Sing-Song*

If a pig wore a wig
  What could we say?
Treat him as a gentleman,
  And say "Good day."

If his tail chanced to fail,
  What could we do?—
Send him to the tailoress
  To get one new.
      —CHRISTINA ROSSETTI,
          Sing-Song

*Went over to Mr. Rossetti's, and began unpacking the
camera, etc. While I was doing so Miss Christina
Rossetti arrived, and Mr. Rossetti introduced me to
her. She seemed a little shy at first, and I had little time
for conversation with her, but I much liked the little I
saw of her.*
      —LEWIS CARROLL, 6 October 1863

I

After sundry reviewers had extravagantly hailed Jean Ingelow's 1863 *Poems,* Christina Rossetti seemed startled by the emergence of a new competitor for the position vacated through Elizabeth Barrett Browning's death in 1861. "I want to know who she is, what she is like, where she lives. All I have heard is an uncertain rumour that she is aged twenty-one and is one of three sisters resident with their mother. A proud mother, I should think."[1] Although Rossetti soon discovered that Ingelow was no novice but rather a forty-three-year-old published poet and hence her elder by ten years, the tentative identity she had conferred on this potential rival rather fitted her own domestic situation as a youngest daughter "resident" with a mother whose approval was crucial to her well-being. Significantly left out of this situation are men—not just dead fathers (Rossetti's had died in 1854 and Ingelow's in 1855) but also living brothers, such as Jean's younger brothers William (with whom she lived after her mother's death) and Benjamin Ingelow, and, of course, Christina's older brothers Dante Gabriel and William Michael Rossetti.

Rossetti's conversion of Ingelow into a youthful member of a community without men bears a decided resemblance to her devoted life with Frances Lavinia Rossetti, the mother to whom she repeatedly dedicated her works, or to her older sister Maria Francesca's life among an order of Anglican nuns. Yet this construction also poignantly mirrors the final setting Rossetti devised for the poem she had originally named "A Peep at the Goblins" and had "inscribed to my dear only sister."[2] The conclusion of the retitled "Goblin Market" takes place in a maternal enclave of sisters

1. Rossetti's remarks to Dora Greenwell are cited by Frances Thomas in her *Christina Rossetti* (London: The Self-Publishing Association, 1992), 229.

2. In a note written in December 1893, exactly a year before her death, Rossetti claimed that she had chosen the original title to express kinship with a cousin, Mrs. Bray, the author of "'A Peep at the Pixies,' but my brother Dante Gabriel Rossetti substituted the greatly improved title as it now stands." *The Complete Poems of Christina Rossetti: A Variorum Edition,* ed. R. W. Crump (Baton Rouge: Louisiana State University Press, 1979), 1:234.

who are now endowed with "children of their own" (line 545).[3] With "mother-hearts beset with fears, / Their lives bound up in tender lives" (lines 546–47), Laura and Lizzie have become the solicitous caretakers of a female childland. And the space in which Laura reminds a younger generation that "there is no friend like a sister / In calm or stormy weather" not only bars the "wicked, quaint fruit-merchant men" who failed to seduce Lizzie but also seems marked by the absence of father or husbands (lines 562–63, 553).

The narrative poem we now acclaim as a bold and innovative masterpiece, more than equal to Romantic fantasies such as Coleridge's "Christabel" or Keats's "Lamia," might never have appeared had its author accepted the verdict of its first outside reader. When Dante Gabriel Rossetti tried to interest John Ruskin in "the poem about the two Girls and the Goblins,"[4] the older man bristled. Ruskin was convinced that no publisher would take any of the poems he had been asked to read, "so full are they of quaintnesses and offences." He declined to recommend them for publication in Thackeray's *Cornhill Magazine* and insisted that the poet would have to master "Form first" before her "observation and passion" could "become precious."[5]

Upon finding Ruskin to be equally obdurate as a reader of the manuscript of his sexually charged "Light Princess," George MacDonald had emphatically rejected strictures he deemed unacceptable.[6] But Christina Rossetti had no such direct means of appeal. She was forced to rely on both of her brothers as mediators for Ruskin's chilling and condescending advice that she "exercise herself in the severest commonplace of metre

3. Christina Rossetti, "Goblin Market," in *Complete Poems,* 1:25. Unless otherwise noted, all future references to Rossetti's poetry will be to this edition.

4. Dante Gabriel Rossetti to William Michael Rossetti, [18 January 1861], *Letters of Dante Gabriel Rossetti,* ed. Oswald Doughty and John Robert Wahl (Oxford: Clarendon Press, 1965), 2:389.

5. John Ruskin to Dante Gabriel Rossetti, [24 January 1861], *Letters of Dante Gabriel Rossetti,* 2:391. By forwarding Ruskin's note to William, rather than to Christina, Dante Gabriel now pressed his brother into assuming the role of a second intermediary: "It is with very great regret and disgust that I enclose a note from Ruskin about Christina's poems—most senseless, I think. I have told him something of the sort in my answer" (25 January 1861, *Letters of Dante Gabriel Rossetti,* 2:391).

6. For Ruskin's objections to MacDonald's fairy tale, see chapter 4, pp. 138–39, above.

until she can write as the public likes."[7] Unlike the more complacent Jean Ingelow, whom Ruskin always adulated more than he criticized,[8] and unlike Kate Greenaway, who submitted to his patronage, Christina Rossetti resented Ruskin's assumption of an authority that seemed unearned. Yet she also took care to moderate her resentment and keep it private.[9] For his part, Ruskin regarded her with suspicion after she tried to interest others in work that he had declared to be unfit for publication.[10]

Ruskin's confident prediction about Victorian publishers, however, proved to be as faulty as his estimate of Rossetti's craft. As Lona Mosk Packer has shown, Alexander Macmillan, whom Dante Gabriel next approached with his sister's manuscript, turned out to be extremely receptive. Not only did he promptly print Christina's short poem "Up-Hill" in his *Macmillan's Magazine,* but he also decided to "make an exceedingly pretty little volume" out of a selection of her poems to be chosen, not by her, but by Dante Gabriel and himself. The chief "attraction" of such a

7. John Ruskin to Dante Gabriel Rossetti, [24 January 1861], *Letters of Dante Gabriel Rossetti,* 2:391.

8. See my "Male Patronage and Female Authorship: The Case of John Ruskin and Jean Ingelow," *Princeton University Library Chronicle* 57 (1995): 13–46.

9. After Dante Gabriel's death in 1882, Christina was able to justify her animosity toward Ruskin as an act of sororal indignation. Even before she read Ruskin's unkind remarks about her brother's paintings in two 1883 lectures, she claimed to "know enough of their contents to feel not a little wonder and dislike." Later, disturbed by Ruskin's "most irritating sentence" about "Gabriel's having cut himself off from the possibility of studying outdoor nature by living in a 'garret' at Blackfriars," she professed to adopt a posture of "Christian patience" by searching for more "admiring and affectionate" pronouncements. She also claims to make allowances for Ruskin's mental imbalance: "I can well imagine that the lecturer is not his pristine self" (to William Rossetti, 6 and 15 August 1883, *The Family Letters of Christina Georgina Rossetti,* ed. William Michael Rossetti, [London: Brown, Langham and Co., 1908], 132, 136). But her attempts to soften long-standing resentments seem rather unconvincing: "I am not fretting over the Ruskiniana, though at the moment I plead guilty to having felt annoyed. Yet my resumed philosophic calm is not based on contempt for the writer, as I cannot help admiring much of his work. I hope it is based on something more permanent and less discreditable" (to Lucy Rossetti, 15 August 1883, *Family Letters,* 137–38).

10. Whenever, in his copious correspondence with Dante Gabriel, Ruskin asks to be remembered "with deep and sincere respect to your Sister," he is pointedly referring to Maria rather than Christina, because, as William Michael rather disingenuously would have it, "He knew more of the former" (William Michael Rossetti, *Rossetti Papers, 1862 to 1870: A Compilation* [London, Sands & Co., 1903], 13).

volume, he decided, "would be the *Goblin Market,*" to be further enhanced by Dante Gabriel's "designs." Such a "small Christmas book," Macmillan hoped, might catch the "fancy" of a "wise and discerning public." Encouraged by a "tremendous burst of applause" he had received after reading the full text of "Goblin Market" at a "small working-man's society," he expected middle-class readers to respond with equal enthusiasm.[11]

Yet when *Goblin Market and Other Poems* appeared in March of 1862, a year before Jean Ingelow's *Poems,* it was greeted with considerably less fanfare than the older woman's more traditional verses. Christina Rossetti acknowledged feeling "envy and humiliation" after receiving Ingelow's 8th edition as a present in 1864; it would take another year for her own volume to undergo a second printing.[12] Her book's sales not only failed to match those of Ingelow's *Poems,* but also fell short of those which Ruskin's own "small Christmas Book" had attained a decade earlier. *The King of the Golden River* could, after all, be unequivocally marketed as a fairy tale for children; even though many Victorian readers also regarded "Goblin Market" as a fairy tale, its intended audience seemed murkier, for it was followed by shorter poems more overtly directed at adults.

The clearly defined readership of *The King of the Golden River* had undoubtedly contributed to its success. Boundaries between adult and child could be upheld in a bourgeois fable in which the violations of the Black Brothers jarred with little Gluck's retention of a purity identified with an agrarian order that, as in "Goblin Market," was also feminized. Still, even though Rossetti dramatizes transgression and redemption as much as Ruskin, she razes the distinction between child and adult. Sexual innocence and sexual knowledge blend when Rossetti has Laura wake up from the trance into which she had fallen after ingesting the "fiery antidote" dispensed by her older sister (line 559). Laughing and tossing "gleaming" locks that show "not one thread of gray," a sexualized woman has fully recovered her "innocent old way" (lines 540, 538). By conflating girlhood and maturity, Rossetti erases the demarcations that so preoccupied Ruskin and soon would obsess Lewis Carroll in his own creative attempts to preserve his "little Alice" from the presumed taint of womanhood.

11. Alexander Macmillan to Dante Gabriel Rossetti, 28 October 1861; *The Rossetti-Macmillan Letters,* ed. Lona Mosk Packer (London: Cambridge University Press, 1963), 6, 7.

12. Cited by Thomas in *Christina Rossetti,* 230–31. The 1865 edition of *Goblin Market and Other Poems* contained only minor textual revisions.

Lizzie's willingness to be soiled by the fruits her Eve-like sister had so ravenously devoured would be inconceivable in Ruskin's desexualized narrative of purity regained. The "passion" that Ruskin claimed to have found in the manuscript given to him by Dante Gabriel thus would hardly strike him as a "precious" asset. Gluck's passivity is totally unlike Lizzie's inactivity, for her resistance is that of a female Christ or of a defiled, yet victorious martyr. The strength of Lizzie's endurance increases the more she is scratched, kicked and knocked, mauled and mocked by her sadistic tormentors. Her humiliation thus brings about the total defeat of the "evil people" she forces to return into a nether-world: "some writhed into the ground, / Some dived into the brook / With ring and ripple, / Some scud-ded on the gale without a sound, / Some vanished in the distance" (lines 442–46).

"Goblin Market" pits sisters against brothers. If the feminized Gluck is set apart, like an only child, from the abusive older men who seem so improbably cast as his brothers, Lizzie and Laura best a fraternity that is even more unsavory. As an ex officio member of the Pre-Raphaelite Brotherhood, the artistic union that had been inspired and defended by Ruskin and named by Dante Gabriel,[13] Christina Rossetti seems most wary of men's sensual baits. Her goblin men are far more repulsive than the droll little creatures her brother drew on the book's title page. As inter-twined as the sleeping figures depicted in that same "design," Lizzie and Laura are at first difficult to distinguish from each other. Whereas Ruskin immediately asks the reader to separate the fair and blue-eyed Gluck from the boy's repulsive and swarthy older brothers, Lizzie / Laura first appears as a blonde-haired sororal unit. Privileged from the start, Gluck will come to accept the damnation of his kin. Having always been at odds with these brutal farmers-turned-merchants, he must repudiate their masculinity (and hence his own nominal sex) before he can return to a refertilized Treasure Valley. Rossetti's sister-farmers, however, find their shared fe-male sexuality to be an impregnable bulwark. It is this sharing that allows them to triumph over the goblin merchants who leer and signal "each other, / Brother with sly brother" (lines 95–96).

By blurring the differences between the two women, Rossetti can make

---

13. See Holman Hunt's recollection in "The Pre-Raphaelite Brotherhood: A Fight for Art," *The Contemporary Review,* April 1886, 480: "As we bound ourselves together, the word 'Brotherhood' was suggested by [Dante Gabriel] Rossetti as preferable to clique or association."

Laura's "fall" seem reversible and prepare us for the reintegration of her heroines. It is their common femininity, their sexual likeness, rather than the "juices / Squeezed from goblin fruits" which provides Lizzie with the "fiery antidote" that Laura requires (lines 469, 559). Though secreted by her male attackers, the spilled "Goblin pulp and goblin dew" have become female fluids, "my juices," as Lizzie calls them when she joyously offers to Laura's "hungry mouth" the drippings "that syrupped all her face, / And lodged in dimples of her chin" (lines 492, 470, 68, 453–55). By conflating the roles of a seductive lover and a nurturing mother, Lizzie has freed Laura from male blandishments and male treachery.

Although the hungry mouths sated at the close of *The King of the Golden River* are those of the poor to whom Gluck opens his granaries, Ruskin also had invoked female fluids to bring about the redemptive climax of his own fairy tale. The drops of "clear dew" gathered on the "white leaves" of a lily symbolize the Treasure Valley's impending return to a semblance of its lost virginal state. The spring that then gushes out of a rocky "cleft" liquifies the red sand that Ruskin had implicitly likened to dry blood. This arid crust promptly turns into a fecund "moistening soil" (*KGR*, 66–67). And, lest Gluck or the child reader show any inclination to pity the Black Brothers, Ruskin has the King sternly denounce the impurity of water made unholy by male rapaciousness and strife.

In "Goblin Market," however, the restoration of female innocence relies on paradoxes that are more dramatic and powerful than the angry little King's purification of a virginal valley defiled by Schwarz and Hans. Sensual excess facilitates a return to purity when Laura's orgasmic ecstasy forever quenches her thirst for further tastings of goblin fruit. She is now sated by the very same juices that had previously stimulated her appetite. Desire and renunciation blend. By offering herself as a vessel for the products of goblins who have elsewhere fed their "hungry thirsty roots" (line 45), Lizzie can remove her sister's transgression, and, at the same time, make the male sex seem utterly redundant.

Like Ruskin, Christina Rossetti draws on a folkloric "tradition of fable, fairy tale, and nursery rhyme."[14] And, also like her predecessor, she goes to these primitive sources in order to recover a female space she wants to

---

14. Roderick McGillis, "Simple Surfaces: Christina Rossetti's Work for Children," in *The Achievement of Christina Rossetti,* ed. David A. Kent (Ithaca and London: Cornell University Press, 1987), 229.

cleanse of all male contamination. But to purify his Treasure Valley, Ruskin has to rely, as we saw in chapter 2, on tiny, goblin-like agents who are every bit as aggressive as their victims, the huge Black Brothers. By reducing the size of both South-West Wind and the King of the Golden River, Ruskin tried to align them with his frail boy-hero and make their vengeful wrath serve his cause. But Gluck's allies are not children like himself. The punitive West Wind and the irascible little King who lost out to the superior "malice of a stronger king" in a previous struggle belong to a world of competition and domination that is unmistakably adult. Their reduction is therefore a ruse. The ugly intruder with a gigantic phallic hat and the gruff King who changes shape from mug to dwarf to dog are every bit as grotesque, dangerous, and violent as Rossetti's malevolent, tramping "little men" (line 55). Lizzie suffers their sadistic abuse for her sister's sake; Gluck, however, passively watches South-West Wind and the King enact his own unacknowledged anger at his abusive older brothers. Whereas Lizzie bravely exposes herself to snarling and scratching humanoids, Gluck distances himself from male aggression by declaring his benefactors to be unduly "cruel."

Did Ruskin recognize the extent to which Rossetti's fairy tale conflicted with his own fable about purity regained? Even though Dante Gabriel appears to have stressed "Christina's *Goblins,* as having a subject" when he approached his friend with the manuscript,[15] "Goblin Market" is never singled out in Ruskin's dismissive response. Moreover, the older man's animadversions are directed at the form, rather than at the content, of Christina Rossetti's verses. Still, his objections to her use of irregular "measure," which he attributes to a "wilfulness" he blames on Coleridge's precedent, surely stem from an irritation with the rhymes of the longest, most prominent, and most Coleridgean of the poems he had been asked to assess.[16] And, if so, Rossetti's failure to observe proprieties that went beyond versification must have weighed heavily on Ruskin's mind. The unspeci-

---

15. Dante Gabriel Rossetti to William Michael Rossetti, [19 January 1861], *Letters of Dante Gabriel Rossetti,* 2:389.

16. John Ruskin to Dante Gabriel Rossetti, 24 January 1861, *Letters of Dante Gabriel Rossetti,* 2:391. The interlocked bodies of Laura and Lizzie, sleeping "Cheek to cheek and breast to breast" (line 197), would certainly have reminded Ruskin of Coleridge's account of Christabel and Geraldine as another eroticized pair of female sleepers whose "innocent" and "sinful" identities become blurred and interchangeable.

fied "quaintnesses and offences" which, according to him, Victorian publishers would find unacceptable, surely hint at immoderations that go beyond meter.

Indeed, Ruskin could not have failed to be disturbed by Rossetti's subversive handling of the "innocence" that he continued to affix to prepubescent girls. Her reliance on some of the very same fantastic devices he had deployed in *The King of the Golden River* may well have exacerbated his despair of ever finding the unsullied "purity" he identified with the feminine. As noted in chapter 2, Ruskin was embarrassed by the popularity of the fairy tale he had written two decades before Dante Gabriel approached him with Christina's manuscript, for it reminded him (and those privy to his personal life) of his short-lived desire for oneness with a still "innocent" Effie Gray. Although not necessarily intended for child readers, Rossetti's "poem about the two Girls and the Goblins" thus surely affronted Ruskin in his self-appointed role as preserver of the desexualized femininity he associated with childhood. Even more than the sexual innuendoes he found so objectionable in "The Light Princess," the erotics of Rossetti's poem contravened his insistence on female purity. "Goblin Market" thus must have proved to be almost as painful an "antidote" to his own fable about Gluck as that ingested by Laura. Although he acknowledged the "beauty and the power" of the poems Rossetti had assembled,[17] Ruskin could not afford a more generous response to her title-poem.

Even more sympathetic Victorian critics, however, were puzzled by the poem's blending of near-pornographic descriptions with materials highly attractive to child readers. "Is it a fable—or a mere fairy story—or an allegory against the pleasures of sinful love—or what is it?" pondered a reviewer in Alexander Macmillan's own house organ, *Macmillan's Magazine*.[18] Unwilling to decide whether a "mere" fairy tale and a tract against vividly rendered excesses were indeed compatible, the reviewer, Mrs. Charles Eliot Norton, was content to come up with a compromise. She became the first to argue that "Goblin Market" might, in fact, equally appeal to two segregated audiences, the sexually innocent and the sexually

17. Ibid.

18. Mrs. Charles Eliot Norton, review of "The Angel in the House" by Coventry Patmore and "The Goblin Market" by Christina Rossetti, *Macmillan's Magazine* 8 (1863): 401.

mature. The poem could therefore be considered "a ballad which children will con with delight, and which riper minds may ponder over."[19]

By 1904, however, when William Michael Rossetti produced the incomplete and adulterated first "collected" edition of his sister's poetry, the Victorian notion of a dual audience for books "avowedly designed both for children and for grown-up people" had begun to lose its appeal.[20] Still, in his notes for "Goblin Market," William adopted a stance similar to Mrs. Norton's when he stoutly defended the poem's presumed simplicity: "I have more than once heard Christina say that she did not mean anything profound by this fairy tale." Although he refrained from dividing the poem's ideal readers into unreflective children and thinking adults, as Norton had done, he proposed that its "incidents are such as to be at any rate suggestive, and different minds may be likely to read different messages into them."[21] The question of readership still affects our current approaches to the poem. Though not as equivocal as William Michael Rossetti, contemporary critics still ponder whether a text about "the love that exists between the alliteratively linked Laura and Lizzie"[22] is best read as an Anglican tract, a lesbian allegory, a feminist manifesto, or, last but not least, a children's book attractive to such major illustrators as Laurence Housman (1893), Arthur Rackham (1933), and Martin Ware (1980).[23]

Read in the context of some of the "adult" dramatic monologues, lyrics, and narratives Christina Rossetti had gathered in *Goblin Market and Other*

19. Ibid., 402.

20. "On Some Books for Boys and Girls," *Blackwood's* 159 (1896): 391; such books, the anonymous author of this essay remarked, were "apt to please neither" constituency.

21. "Notes By W. M. Rossetti," in *The Poetical Works of Christina Georgina Rossetti* (London: Macmillan and Co., 1904), 459.

22. D. M. R. Bentley, "The Meretricious and the Meritorious in *Goblin Market:* A Conjecture and an Analysis," in Kent, *Achievement of Christina Rossetti,* 72.

23. As Lorraine Janzen Kooistra has noted in her extremely helpful survey of the poem's variegated audiences, "Modern Markets for *Goblin Market,*" the "fairy-tale genre" and "the addition of illustrations" have been far more significant in "the production of *Goblin Market* for a specific community of readers" than the "content of the poem." Kooistra regards Housman as an adult illustrator who feminizes the goblins in order to suggest that they are mere "projections of the female mind"; she considers Rackham as chief illustrator of what she calls "the Children's *Goblin Market,*" but notes that one of his four full-page illustrations "is aimed more directly at the adult viewer" (*Victorian Poetry* 32 [Autumn–Winter 1994]: 249, 254).

Poems, the title-poem does not seem at all idiosyncratic in its privileging of a space denied to male intruders. The female speakers of "No, Thank You, John" and "My Secret" (the superb poem which Rossetti later retitled "Winter: My Secret") are as resolute (and as teasing) in discouraging male suitors as Lizzie was in rebuffing goblin advances. And, if sororal solidarity was upheld in "Goblin Market," its obverse—sororal treachery—is taken up in both "Cousin Kate" and in the ironically titled "Noble Sisters," two poems that were, like "Goblin Market," composed in 1859.

The seduced "outcast thing" in "Cousin Kate" rebukes her "good and pure" rival for having agreed to marry the father of her illegitimate child; had their places been reversed, she avers, "I would have spit into his face / And not have taken his hand" (lines 28, 27, 39–40). Here the "pure" woman is condemned for lacking the solidarity that Lizzie had shown towards a "fallen" sister. Lady Kate, the peasant who commodified her virginity in order to gain a title, remains barren. Thus, despite her wedding ring and her aristocratic position, this proper wife will never possess the "gift" her "unclean" rival can boast of: "my fair-haired son, my shame, my pride" (lines 41, 43, 15, 45). Though simpler, the paradox is not unlike that which underlies the fallen Laura's purification.

In the dialogue of "Noble Sisters," a Laura-like speaker rebukes her "sister dear" for having denied access to the man who had come to "woo me for his wife"; she romantically vows to "seek him thro' the world / In sorrow till I die" (lines 2, 42, 55–56). Significantly enough, however, her older, Lizzie-like counterpart is allowed the last word: "Go seek in sorrow, sister, / And find in sorrow too: / If thus you shame our father's name / My curse go forth with you" (lines 57–60). This sororal exchange dramatizes a self-division that reopens the closure of "Goblin Market." Yet elsewhere in the 1862 volume, Rossetti even resists the earthly fruition she granted to Lizzie and Laura as sisters-turned-mothers. Her yearning for a realm removed from all earthly attachments leads her to impersonate nuns in convents, dead men and women in their graves, androgynous souls detached from their bodies, and a Christ whose agony on the cross has produced a "hiding-place" for all "cleft" individuals beset by conflicting desires.[24]

Still, the kinship between "Goblin Market" and such adult fare hardly invalidates its consideration as a text attractive to children, as Norton

---

24. Christina Rossetti, "The Love of Christ Which Passeth Knowledge," lines 24, 23.

rightly proposed. Laura and Lizzie—whom Dante Gabriel may have called "girls," but then proceeded to draw as voluptuous Pre-Raphaelite beauties—seem adolescents or grown-ups rather than children. At first glance, then, the sisters exhibit none of the similarities to Edgeworth's little Rosamond or Carroll's little Alice that Robert Pattison stresses when he includes the poem in a learned theological discussion of "Children in Children's Literature."[25] Nonetheless, Laura's orality resembles that of a small child as much as that of Milton's Eve. Linked to her fascination with the unknown, her appetite has dangerous consequences, like Eve's; but so do the unfulfilled appetites of curious child-protagonists such as the *Wonderland* Alice and Kipling's Elephant's Child—whom a recent critic defiantly calls a "she" despite the character's male gender.[26] Insatiable hunger, always likened to a "'satiable curtiosity," is, after all, the mark of all Eden-dwellers, whether fully grown or small, theological or childish. Restricted by "innocence," such inmates yearn to taste what those in power label as forbidden.[27]

In this sense, Pattison's notion of Laura as a "fallen child" is, after all, hardly inappropriate.[28] She is far more responsive than Lizzie to elementary pleasures, to the taste of words, to sound. Like a small child, she takes a sensual delight in the hypnotic, sing-song effect of the lush opening lines—so free-flowing in their rhymes that Ruskin surely had them in mind when, assuming the authority of Milton's God, he censured Rossetti for her avowed infractions against proper "Form." Lizzie tries to impress on Laura her own temporal consciousness when she asks her sister to "remember" the story of Jeanie, who "dwindled and grew grey" after accepting goblin gifts (lines 147, 156). Yet Laura, like a child again, still prefers to remain immersed in a pleasurable present of pure sound and pure taste. By the end of the poem, however, she shows her maturation through

25. Robert Pattison, *The Child Figure in English Literature* (Athens: University of Georgia Press, 1978), 141–45.

26. Howard R. Cell, "The Socratic Pilgrimage of the Elephant's Child," *Children's Literature* 20 (1992): 143n.

27. James R. Kincaid's witty remark seems most pertinent here: "If Milton's God created man according to His whim and then damned him for it, we have created children as we wanted and then protected them from it" (*Child-Loving: The Erotic Child and Victorian Culture* [London: Routledge, 1992], 361).

28. Pattison, *Child Figure in English Literature,* 143. As the remainder of this paragraph will make clear, however, I cannot go along with his presentation of Lizzie as a redemptive child figure.

her own mastery, as a teller of tales, of progressions that involve cause and effect. The allure of male songs has been replaced by her dissemination of a monitory female discourse. In a closure that Lewis Carroll would rather reluctantly adopt in order to signify his own heroine's eventual maturity, an older and a younger sister are allowed to overlap, fused as maternal tellers of tales about past encounters with the denizens of a grotesque fantasy world.

At the end of both the *Underground* and the *Wonderland* texts, Alice's older sister (and Lewis Carroll behind her) stabilizes the narrative through the projection of a matron who can recapitulate childland adventures for the benefit of the young entrusted to her care. Roderick McGillis asks why, at the end of Rossetti's poem, "does Laura, not Lizzie, become a storyteller?"[29] His sensible answer deserves further elaboration. Having been previously "silenced" by her "baulked desire" for goblin fruit (line 267), Laura can now invite children to taste the more intangible "fruit" of Lizzie's and her own experiences. "Goblin Market" thus can be read as a progress-poem. Having mastered the meaning of a story she began as an unreflecting participant, Laura can affirm her final maturation: she has become the equal of the sister who had asked her to outgrow her narcissism by relating the cautionary tale of Jeanie. By now converting Lizzie into the heroine of a second cautionary tale, Laura has moved past her earlier dependence on the seductive voice of male rhymesters. When first asked by Lizzie "to make much of me" (line 472), she still reverted to a childlike sucking of the juices she had tasted before. Now, however, having become a mother and an aunt, Laura has truly learned to make much of the sister she renders as a female exemplar, a model for cousins and siblings whose "little hands" she joins in a tighter grasp. The goblin music has been dissipated, banished, and replaced by a more controlled voice. And that voice is at last her very own.

Read in this fashion, "Goblin Market" is as much a narrative about female growth as Jean Ingelow's *Mopsa the Fairy*. And Laura, like Ingelow's Queen Mopsa, stands for the awareness reached and the authority assumed by a writer who must overcome her dependence on male precedents. It is no coincidence that two of the longer poems also included in Rossetti's 1862 volume, "The Convent Threshold" and "From House to Home," should involve a reworking of Tennyson's "The Palace of Art"

---

29. McGillis, "Simple Surfaces," 210.

and *Maud,* respectively.[30] Like Laura, Christina Rossetti wanted to free her voice. Yet in her attempt to sell her own wares, to invite potential readers to "Come buy, come buy," she was still dependent on male commodification: the hawking of her manuscript by Dante Gabriel; the patronage of influential critics and publishers, such as Ruskin and Macmillan; the appropriation of her voice, as Macmillan read "Goblin Market" to assembled working men; the liberties taken with her wording, her titles, her arrangements, whenever Dante Gabriel and Macmillan (and later William Michael Rossetti) violated her textual integrity as much as the goblins had assaulted Lizzie; and, finally, the dependence on reviewers who clearly preferred Ingelow's verses to her own—reviewers, who, with a few notable exceptions such as Mrs. Norton, were mostly literary men and not women.

I raise this issue to explain why, in her subsequent writings for children, the successful *Sing-Song* (1872) and the unsuccessful *Speaking Likenesses* (1874), Christina Rossetti should still have found herself on a collision course with male rivals whose appropriation of "femininity" she increasingly came to resent. "Goblin Market" had indirectly set her in apposition to *The King of the Golden River.* I have tried to pinpoint why and how Rossetti's fable about Laura's maturation conflicted with Ruskin's fable about Gluck's arrested boyhood. And I have assumed that this conflict was probably "unwitting" on her part, that she had not consciously chosen to fashion a fairy tale that trespassed on Ruskin's own. But in the sections that follow I will contend that her later subversions were quite deliberate: still mild and sporadic in the verses she gathered in *Sing-Song,* her rivalry with male authors became harsher in the overtly anti-Carrollian trio of stories she called *Speaking Likenesses.*

Ambitious, eager to find a wider audience, Christina Rossetti was hardly insensible to the possibilities offered by the vastly expanded market for children's books that had been opened by the 1865 publication of *Alice in Wonderland.* Carroll's success, as we have seen, paved the way for MacDonald's *At the Back of the North Wind* and for Ingelow's own incursion into fantasy in *Mopsa the Fairy.* Rossetti knew that reviewers such as Norton had been correct in proposing that "Goblin Market" might easily be

---

30. See Anthony H. Harrison, *Christina Rossetti in Context* (Chapel Hill: University of North Carolina Press, 1988), 130–31, 138. The link between "From House to Home" and Tennyson's "The Palace of Art" was first observed by Dante Gabriel Rossetti, as William Michael Rossetti recalled ("Notes," 461).

read "as a ballad which children [would] con with delight." After the publication of *The Prince's Progress and Other Poems* (1866) and her unsuccessful foray into adult fiction with *Commonplace, And Other Short Stories* (1870),[31] she decided to follow Ingelow's example by directly competing with the "quaint fruit-merchant men" who had offered their honeyed wares to young readers. But her opposition to the rival texts of MacDonald and Carroll soon went beyond Ingelow's more cautious acts of dissociation. The taste of the *Alice* books in particular, as we shall eventually see, "was wormwood to her tongue, / She loathed the feast" (lines 494–95). But she had also to reckon with MacDonald, a writer originally known to her and to Ingelow as a fellow-poet.[32]

II

In preparing her second volume of poems, *The Prince's Progress and Other Poems* for publication by Macmillan, Christina Rossetti found herself even more dependent on her brother Dante Gabriel than she had been for her first collection. Assuming the role of editor and censor, as well as a middleman who embarrassed her by rashly asking Macmillan for an extravagant cash advance, Dante Gabriel took control of the volume by questioning her choices, demanding changes in arrangement, and insisting on rephrasings. He was most domineering in his supervision of the title-poem Christina found difficult to write according to his directions. However well-intentioned, his meddling finally led the poet to insist that "my actual *Prince* seems to me invested with a certain artistic congruity not lightly to

---

31. It is tempting to speculate whether, in naming her novella (at 142 pages, hardly a "short story"), Rossetti remembered Ruskin's advice to discipline herself "in the severest commonplace of metre until she can write as the public likes." Yet the public did not like this venture into unmetrical form. Two of the shorter pieces, "Nick" (reprinted in Nina Auerbach and U. C. Knoepflmacher, eds., *Forbidden Journeys: Fairy Tales and Fantasies by Victorian Women Writers* (Chicago: University of Chicago Press, 1992) and "Hero," actually were fairy tales.

32. Rossetti had contributed "A Royal Princess" to *Poems: An Offering To Lancashire* (1863), a collection designed to raise money for factory workers affected by the closing of mills during the so-called "Cotton Famine" caused by the American Civil War. Mac-Donald, her brother Dante Gabriel, Mary Howitt, and a host of other poets also were among the contributors. See William Michael Rossetti's "Notes," 461.

be despised."[33] She remonstrated further by wondering "whether all the painstaking at my command would result in work better than—in fact half so good—as what I have actually done on the other system." That "system," she implied, was very much her own, and it was "vain comparing my powers (!) with yours."[34]

Always the ironist, Christina Rossetti also recognized that, by causing her to delay the appearance of *The Prince's Progress and Other Poems,* her brother was, in effect, enacting a role quite similar to that played by the idling Prince in her title-poem. Energetic and "strong" (line 13), yet easily diverted, this Prince keeps straying from his avowed "progress" towards a princess who, like Sleeping Beauty or Tennyson's Mariana, can only be released from her torpor by his intervention. The poem's opening emphasis falls on the immobilized bride rather than on her straying rescuer: "The long hours go and come and go, / The bride she sleepeth, waketh, sleepeth, / Waiting for one whose coming is slow:— / Hark! the bride weepeth" (lines 3–6). Whereas the juices Lizzie brings back restore a "dwindling" and graying Laura and help to remove this sister from "death's door" ("Goblin Market," lines 320–21), the elixir of life that the protagonist of Rossetti's new fairy-tale poem brings to his own graying bride can hardly restore life to one who has fallen asleep forever: "Too late for love, too late for joy, / Too late, too late! / You loitered on the road too long. / You trifled at the gate: / ... / The enchanted princess in her tower / Slept, died, behind the grate" ("The Prince's Progress," lines 481–88).

The elixir for which Christina Rossetti herself was waiting in 1865 and 1866 was her brother's promised woodcuts—illustrations which, she felt, would greatly help her new volume's sales. Yet he tarried, just like the easily distracted Prince, having decided to work on a painting instead. She purported to accept the delay quite cheerfully: her Prince, she suggested to Dante Gabriel, "having dawdled so long on his own account" could hardly be expected to "grumble at awaiting your pleasure"; yet she also subtly hinted at her Princess-like dependence by reminding her brother that his "protecting woodcuts help me face my small public."[35] When the first preliminary sketches finally materialized, she professed to notice a

33. Christina Rossetti to Dante Gabriel Rossetti, 10 [February 1865], *Rossetti Papers,* 77.

34. Cited by Lona Mosk Packer in *Christina Rossetti* (Berkeley and Los Angeles: University of California Press, 1963), 193.

35. Ibid.

distinct resemblance between "my phiz" and the physiognomy of "the severe female who arrests the Prince" in the narrative's first episode.[36] She asked Dante Gabriel to conform to her wording by giving the cleanshaven Prince the "curly black beard" he sports in the text (line 64), but her curly-bearded brother ignored her request. At least his demand for the prompt return of his "charming sketches" could be safely subverted, however, for Christina insisted on taking the "liberty of lending them" to their mother for her own "pleasure" and approval.[37]

The postponement of work Christina Rossetti had executed "at such high speed," as well as Dante Gabriel's wranglings with Macmillan, not only left her "exhausted," as Packer notes, but also desirous of a greater creative autonomy.[38] She told her brother that "I hope that after this vol. (if this vol. becomes a vol.) people will respect my nerves, and not hint for a long while at any possibility of vol. 3." To protect herself, however, she portrayed herself as being as slow and torpid as her languid Princess: "I am sure my brain must lie fallow and take its ease, if I am to keep up to my own mark."[39] Yet her desire to work independently with marks set by herself was again thwarted when Dante Gabriel persuaded her to change publishers. Although she wanted F. S. Ellis to give primacy to a volume of "some Nursery Rhymes I have just completed," a volume she first called "SingSong," new delays were occasioned by a search for proper illustrators and by Ellis's promotion of Dante Gabriel's own first volume of poems, which, unlike Christina's previous collections, proved to be an immediate success.[40] When Dante Gabriel suggested that she gather her prose stories while waiting for the publication of *Sing-Song,* she dutifully agreed, only to find him condescending about the end product. After declaring the col-

---

36. Christina Rossetti to Dante Gabriel Rossetti, 6 [March? 1865], *Rossetti Papers,* 83; in a note, William Michael Rossetti assures his readers that the "'severe female' *may* be a little—but only a little—like Christina" (83n).

37. Ibid., 84.

38. Packer, *Christina Rossetti,* 206.

39. Ibid.

40. Christina Rossetti to F. S. Ellis, 23 and 28 February 1870, *Rossetti-Macmillan Letters,* 74, 76. For the full account of Rossetti's involvement with Ellis's firm and her eventual decision to give *Sing-Song* to another publisher, see pp. 72–96. Given the success of her brother's poems, the failure of *Commonplace* was even harder to bear; as she wrote to Ellis, "Still I am glad that so many, even though so few copies have sold. We are not all D.G.R.s" (Summer 1870, *Rossetti-Macmillan Letters,* 90).

lection to be "not dangerously exciting" but "far from being dull," he was, he told her, surer than ever that her "proper business" was to write "poetry, and not *Commonplaces.*"[41]

The opportunity to write poetry without fraternal impediments finally arose when Christina Rossetti found a new publisher and a more congenial illustrator. *Sing-Song* was published in 1872, not by Ellis but by Routledge, and illustrated, not by the artists who had repeatedly failed her, but by Arthur Hughes, whose drawings had enhanced MacDonald's *At the Back of the North Wind* and whose fine grasp of her intentions now undoubtedly contributed to the success of her own "vol. 3." Victorian reviewers who praised the appeal of lyrics wonderfully attuned to "baby ears" were quick to stress the poetry's simultaneous importance for a "more complex" readership. Thus, according to Sidney Colvin, who reviewed Rossetti's volume together with MacDonald's *The Princess and the Goblin* and Carroll's *Through the Looking-Glass,* the momentum created by her carefully crafted poetic sequence allows both children and a "properly constituted grown-up reader" to accept a "self-consciousness" that either group might otherwise regard as a painful adult "affliction."[42]

Colvin's astute insight is valuably developed by Sharon Smulders in her attempt to restore to *Sing-Song* a critical attention the volume has lost because of our academic depreciation of "its status as children's verse."[43] The unified poetic sequence Smulders helpfully reconstructs suggests that Rossetti envisioned *Sing-Song* as a progression that might counter her earlier progress-poems, as well as her ill-fated venture into prose fiction. Whereas she had placed "Goblin Market" and "The Prince's Progress" at the start of her previous two volumes in order to attract Victorian readers conditioned to story-telling, she now fashioned a continuum based on separate yet related lyric moments. The volume of 121 lyrics thus offers, even more than the episodic tales of MacDonald and Ingelow, an anti-narrative narrative. Moving from "cradle to grave, from winter to fall, from sunrise to

41. Dante Gabriel Rossetti to Christina Rossetti, [23 March 1870], *Rossetti-Macmillan Letters,* 81.

42. Sidney Colvin, review of *Sing-Song* by Christina Rossetti, *The Princess and the Goblin* by George MacDonald and *Through the Looking-Glass* by Lewis Carroll, *The Academy* 3 (15 January 1872): 23.

43. Sharon Smulders, "Sound, Sense, and Structure in Christina Rossetti's *Sing-Song,*" *Children's Literature* 22 (1994): 3.

sunset, *Sing-Song* invites readers," as Smulders so persuasively shows, "to understand life as an ordered totality."[44]

Whereas the opening and concluding lyrics are cradle-poems that celebrate an unself-conscious symbiosis between mother and child, the sequence soon accommodates a growing awareness of temporal units, diurnal and seasonal, and dwells on contraries that a maturing "self-consciousness" must acknowledge and master. Any wishful elision of differences is discouraged. Thus, even distinctions of gender are introduced long before the sequence directs the child auditor to consider relationships between grown-up men and women. The thirty-first lyric—at the exact quarter-point of the collection—offers an exchange between a small girl and a loving, but patronizing, boy. A seemingly innocuous celebration of childhood friendship, the dialogue carries resonances rightly picked up by contemporary reviewers as being pertinent to Victorian debates about sexual inequality.[45] The eight-line poem, as coupled with the illustration at its head, also marks the first of several instances in which Rossetti and Hughes teamed up to produce a distinct criticism of some of her immediate predecessors in the field of children's literature.

The eye of the reader falls first on Hughes's illustration of tiny tots perched on a huge heart-shaped throne. Although the girl, and not the boy, wears a crown, her pushy playmate has lifted himself up the throne by stepping on the royal orb and cross placed on the stool before them. The scepter has been dropped. Instead of leaning on her side of the throne, it points to the uncrowned upstart rather than to the diminutive queen. Hughes's drawing thus prepares the reader for the ironies embedded in the poem that follows it (see fig. 29).

As the poem itself makes clear, codes that call for female subservience are ingrained so early in little Victorian girls that they even undercut their fantasies of empowerment. Although the girl speaks first, her words anticipate her male counterpart's innate sense of his superiority. Thus, whereas the boy who would be king smugly confers his own status to the partner he is willing to elevate, she raises him to the throne only to wait on him. "Waiting" is a charged word for a Christina Rossetti who had to wait on—and for—brothers who insisted on their powers and privileges.

44. Ibid.

45. Smulders quotes reviews published in 1872 in *Scribner's Monthly* and *Nation,* both of which note the relevance of this particular poem to "the woman's-rights question" (ibid., 15).

If I were a Queen,
  What would I do?
I'd make you King,
  And I'd wait on you.

If I were a King,
  What would I do?
I'd make you Queen,
  For I'd marry you.
              (*S-S*, 33)

29 Arthur Hughes, "If I Were a Queen"

The eight-line "If I were a Queen" thus offers a miniaturized version of the five hundred forty–line "The Prince's Progress," with its passive and dependent princess. The crowned girl on the throne in Hughes's drawing sits demurely, with legs firmly pressed together; it is unclear whether she is welcoming or resisting the "progress" of the active little boy who has crawled up beside her and still seems in the midst of an advancing motion. Is her arm propped up to help him up or is it leaning on the armrest in order to resist his encroaching effort to occupy more than his half-share of the seat?

On a more indirect level, Rossetti's poem also seems to convey her perennial awareness of the woman she regarded as her chief poetic rival. She had vainly tried to capture Jean Ingelow's public of adult readers with her first two volumes of poetry, and she was now competing with her once again in the lucrative juvenile market. The girl queen who subordinates herself to an active but ordinary little boy had, of course, been prominently featured in *Mopsa the Fairy,* a work Rossetti and Hughes apparently also wanted to evoke in at least two other sing-songs, "Three plum buns" (*S-S,* 60) and "I have a Poll parrot" (*S-S,* 109). Although in her own opposition to male fantasists such as Carroll and MacDonald Ingelow was unquestionably Rossetti's ideological ally, her fascinated attraction to the feminine realm of fantasy and wishfulness over which Queen Mopsa is left to preside must have struck Rossetti as overly sentimental, and, as so many other *Sing-Song* lyrics suggest, even potentially dangerous.

Thus, the boy given a plum bun by an adult female in lyric 53 is not allowed to share it with fairies immured in a hollow tree, as Ingelow's Jack had done after his nurse gave him a portion of a similar treat. Instead, Rossetti's matronly speaker—a young mother or a governess whom Hughes pointedly depicts leaning on a tree stump—instructs her young ward to give their third bun to one who is less privileged, a shepherd "boy who shouts / To scare sheep from the clover" (*S-S,* 60; lines 7–8). The lyric therefore stresses the need for a social conscience in the child reader whose growth the collection subtly charts; in the pendant poem on the opposite page an older girl vows to care for a "motherless" lamb until "he's strong and bold" (*S-S,* 61, lines 1, 8).

If these two evocations of Ingelow seem warranted by the verses themselves, it must be admitted that it is only through Hughes's illustration for "I have a Poll parrot" that one can possibly consider that poem, a mere four lines long, as being similarly intertextual. For it is the artist, to whom Rossetti may well have shown her own initial drawings,[46] who seems interested in conflating two highly memorable scenes in *Mopsa the Fairy.* In the first of these scenes, Jack is horrified when a caged old parrot asks him to twist off his head. Yet the mutilation helps to free a male fairy from his confinement and leads to a spirited rebellion against the Circe-like enchantress who posed as a gypsy. In the second scene from *Mopsa,* however, decapitation has no such happy ending. After another deceptive female, a

---

46. On first approaching Ellis with the manuscript of *Sing-Song,* Christina Rossetti worried that he might have "misconceived" in assuming that she wanted him to reproduce her own illustrations, "as they are mere scratches and I cannot draw" (Christina Rossetti to F. S. Ellis, 23 February 1870, *Rossetti-Macmillan Letters,* 74). I have not had an opportunity to compare Hughes's illustrations to Rossetti's original sketches.

raven, tricks Jack into showing her one of his charges—a boy fairy who is Mopsa's brother—she quickly bites off the fairy's head and gobbles up all but the fluttering and empty garments. Hughes's illustration (fig. 30, with Rossetti's text) seems less gruesome, since the depicted victim is now a doll and not a living creature. Still, the adult woman who has stumbled on this scene is clearly horrified by the savagery of a mayhem she cannot control: sawdust still trickles from the torso from which the doll's head has just been wrested, and a discarded limb lies on the floor in front of the cage.

I have a Poll parrot,
And Poll is my doll,
And my nurse is Polly,
And my sister Poll.
(*S-S,* 109)

30 Arthur Hughes, "I Have a Poll Parrot"

Hughes's drawing features three figures—the uncaged parrot, the mutilated doll, and a beak-nosed woman who appears to have left the parrot cage unlatched. His uncomplimentary rendition of that older woman may well subvert a poem that stresses kinship. The verses involve two more personages: there is not only Poll parrot, Poll doll, and nurse Polly, but also the speaker who owns the doll, as well as "my sister Poll," mentioned at the very end. By omitting these two sisters, Hughes may be "parroting" the violence of two scenes that even today's readers of *Mopsa* find excessive. Yet he could also be contributing to a sororal dialogue already adumbrated in "If I were a Queen" and "Three plum buns." For the controlled singer of *Sing-Song* may have wanted to oppose the poet-novelist of *Mopsa the Fairy,* a work Rossetti would have deplored for yielding to the very imaginative excesses of the male fantasists Ingelow supposedly set out to correct. By insisting on a "commonplace" reality in her own prose fiction, Rossetti had already tried to veer as far as possible from such excesses; and, as we shall see in the next chapter, she would even more strenuously try to dissociate herself from Carroll's fantastic mode in *Speaking Likenesses.* The possibility that Hughes might have been abetting a sororal debate about how best to reclaim female childlands is not as far-fetched as it might seem. After all, Rossetti's next poem, lyric 102 (examined at the end of this chapter), involves the "fall" of a house of cards that has been lovingly constructed by a girl-builder to whom Hughes unmistakably gives the features of the *Wonderland* Alice.

Before I turn to the particulars of Rossetti's and Hughes's joint subversion of the Carroll-Tenniel collaboration, however, it is important to stress that their parodic—or "parrotic"—acts of dissociation in *Sing-Song* are always placed in the service of a larger ideological agenda and hence still transcend the pointedly personal intertextual rivalry that boiled over in *Speaking Likenesses.* The specific targeting of Carroll did not come until Rossetti felt challenged by *Through the Looking-Glass,* which had appeared a few weeks after *Sing-Song* and hence could not have been seen by either Hughes or herself.[47] A contemporary Victorian reader looking at both volumes might have noticed a distinct physical resemblance between the crowned Alice that Tenniel drew for chapters 8 and 9 of *Looking-Glass* and the girl-monarch whom Hughes drew for "If I were a Queen," or, again, between Tenniel's drawing of Alice in the Garden of Live Flowers and Hughes's rendition of a pensive girl gardener who tends flowers that are given human faces (*S-S,* 74). Yet Hughes's depictions of such Alice look-alikes here, as well as in his illustrations for the girl dreamer in lyric 99 and the card-builder in lyric 102, are always based on the *Wonderland* Alice and not on her *Looking-Glass* successor.

47. Whereas Rossetti received her first copy of *Sing-Song* on 18 November 1871, Carroll's first copy of *Through the Looking-Glass* did not arrive until 6 December.

The fact that Hughes had been the illustrator for *At the Back of the North Wind,* a work which *Mopsa the Fairy* had also tried to counter, was an obvious asset for Rossetti's own opposition to wishful and regressive flights of fancy. Hughes's illustration for lyric 113, "If the moon came from heaven" (*S-S,* 122), might easily have been inserted in MacDonald's text to capture Diamond's infatuation with nightscapes bathed by a mystic moon. Here, too, the sex of the gazing child who turns its back on the reader is indeterminate; North Wind might soon appear at the open window casements to reward this androgyne's dreamy longings (see fig. 31). By insisting on temporal and spatial constraints, Rossetti's text discourages the transcendent hankerings Hughes depicts. Night-reveries can at best tell

> If the moon came from heaven,
>   Talking all the way,
> What could she have to tell us,
>   And what could she say?
>
> "I've seen a hundred pretty things,
>   And seen a hundred gay;
> But only think: I peep by night
>   And do not peep by day."
>   (*S-S,* 122)

31 Arthur Hughes, "If the Moon Came from Heaven"

half of the story. Unlike the mighty and discursive North Wind who had ferried Diamond through a succession of radiant nightscapes, "talking all the way," this heavenly visitor offers no intimations of an extrasensory otherness. In the chapter he had called "Diamond's Dream," MacDonald even allowed the moon-child who "had learned to look through the look of things" to converse with angel boys who chatted while trying to dig up shiny stars. Rossetti, however, suggests that if the moon "could speak" at all, she would merely confirm the perceptual limits accepted by anyone willing to "think." Indeed, like all the other sing-songs that begin with a hypothetical "if" that is then subverted in the name of an empirical reality,[48] this poem discourages fantastic constructions. The child in a nightgown should really go back to bed.

By subverting a traditionally feminized lunar icon, Rossetti's lyric 113 also forces the reader, as Sharon Smulders rightly notes,[49] to reconsider the preceding poem about the sun. Invested with male reason—and, sometimes, with divine omniscience—that emblem is even more severely undercut. For that mighty orb, too, can at best "tell us half / That he hears and sees." And, what is more, half of that half also proves to be a rather depressing sight. The child reader who might have rejoiced in the happy *allegretto* beats of birds fluttering in the sunshine must now be brought to admit that the same sun also shines on "cruel boys who take / Birds that cannot fly" (*S-S,* 121; lines 1–2, 7–8). Once again, flights of fancy have been clipped. Forced to consider the helplessness of fledglings who cannot escape their tormentors, the grounded child reader must adopt a daytime pensiveness. Sentimentality has been replaced by a reflectiveness that encourages a greater sense of social responsibilities.

Rossetti's most sustained attack on flighty escapism, however, occurs in the dialogue she dramatizes in lyric 36, "Twist me a crown of windflowers" (*S-S,* 38). The puffy flower whose English name follows the Greek etymology of *anemone* (wind's daughter) was habitually associated with "rising" aspirations. Ruskin, for instance, remarks on the ambi-

---

48. There are seven other such poems in *Sing-Song:* lyrics 25, 31, 40, 60, 64, 110, and 112 (on pp. 25, 33, 42, 68, 72, 119, 121); of these, only sing-song 25, "If all were rain and snow," allows the possibility of transcending the constraints all the others insist upon: the heavenly "bow" that can "span" the contraries of life and death also acts as a bridge to the previous lyric's grim insistence on infant mortality: "bow and die" (*S-S,* line 8; 24).

49. Smulders, "Sound, Sense, and Structure," 17.

tiousness of this wind-tossed flower, an ambitiousness also attributed to avian wind-riders by poets from George Chapman to Gerard Manley Hopkins.[50] Yet Rossetti, as might be expected, sets out to curtail such breezy aspirations. Her Blakean dialogue endorses the Nurse of Experience far more definitively than its precedent.[51]

The reader first hears the voice of a speaker who, like Laura in "Goblin Market," infects us with her wish to catch the strains of alien sounds: "Twist me a crown of wind-flowers; / That I may fly away / To hear the singers at their song, / And players at their play." The next quatrain introduces a second speaker's guarded response: "Put on your crown of wind-flowers: / But whither would you go?" By producing the crown she was asked to make and by limiting herself to a cautious question, this Lizzie figure seems to offer no real resistance to the desire now forcefully reasserted by the first speaker: "Beyond the surging of the sea / And the storms that blow" (S-S, 38; lines 1–4, 5–6, 7–8).

Had the poem ended at this point, it would have endorsed a longing for the same fantastic flights over turbulent oceans taken by child-travelers such as Diamond and Jack. But the second speaker now reveals her impatience with such escapist voyages. Her authority becomes manifest as she treats her interlocutor with the confident resolve that Lizzie had shown in her dismissal of goblin lures: "Ah! your crown of wind-flowers / Can never make you fly: / I twist them in a crown to-day / And tonight they die" (S-S, 38; lines 9–12). By waiting until the next-to-last line before introducing this second and stronger "I," Rossetti produces a brilliant *volta* or "twist." She transforms a questioner who wants to know "whither" her interlocutor would go into a directress as capable of "withering" edicts as the speaker who was given the last word in "Noble Sisters." And, what is more, the text now suggests an identification that has been deliberately delayed: the activity of twisting flowers into wilting crowns serves a poet eager to twist child readers away from the seductive singers and playful players who try to prolong the fading childhood of prepubescent girls and androgynous boys.

---

50. Ruskin also considers the breezy anemone to be "more firm and pure in line" than its cousin, the tulip (*CW*, 25:xxxvi). Chapman casts a rival as an "envious Wind-fucker" (the kestril Hopkins prefers to call "wind-hover") "engrossing all the air with his luxurious ambition" (*The Oxford English Dictionary* [Oxford University Press, 1933], 12: WI-160).

51. See chapter 1, p. 7, above.

Arthur Hughes, significantly enough, renders the two speakers of lyric 36 as older and younger sisters. He places this pair between wind-flowers whose roots are exposed and a wind-borne swallow that is about to veer out of their (and the viewer's) orbit. And he assigns the two young women positions that suggest the dialogue's aftermath: the younger of the two, horizontally grounded, now submissively cradles her head in the lap of her upright sister. Although the artist's interpretation certainly accords with Rossetti's own emphasis in the poem, the second "I" in her dialogue could just as well have been drawn as a nurse or governess or mother rather than a girl who is only slightly older than her sibling. Hughes's decision to give the dialogue a sororal "twist" thus not only allows the reader to associate this poem with "Goblin Market" and "Noble Sisters," as I have done, but also links it to the important modulation on the volume's title undertaken in lyric 65, "Sing me a song." In that poem, three "merry sisters / Dancing in a ring" must come to a halt when their number is abruptly reduced (*S-S*, 73; lines 3–4). A creature whom Hughes depicts as a winged angel of death separates a Tertia from her two older dancing partners. What starts out as a trio's "light" and carefree "song" thus becomes an elegiac "tale" to be processed by two chastened and "mournful sisters" (lines 5, 7, 9).

In his drawing for lyric 65, Hughes gives one of the older sisters the face and hairdo of Tenniel's Alice. The illustration thus reinforces the lyric's subversion of the nostalgic celebration of a "merry crew" of three undertaken in the verses that Lewis Carroll had placed in the front of *Alice in Wonderland*.[52] Similarly, the sororal identity that Hughes confers on the speakers of the wind-flower poem helps to set this dialogue in apposition to Carroll's opening and concluding contrasts between a dreamy Alice and her more reality-oriented sister. Unlike Rossetti, however, Carroll had sided with the dreamer he had also drawn in a recumbent position on the first page of his "Underground" text. Alice's straying interest in underground denizens as bizarre as Rossetti's goblin men must eventually be processed, rather than be rejected, by her older, upright, sister.

---

52. For a discussion of MacDonald's and Ingelow's own subversions of Carroll's nostalgic celebration of the gliding boat, see pp. 236n and 302n, above.

III

With *Sing-Song,* Rossetti and Hughes entered a market in which their competition with Carroll and Tenniel had to be openly confronted. Yet when Carroll first flitted into Rossetti's orbit in 1863, he had come as a photographer rather than as a rival author. Although soon after his contact with the Rossettis he began to draw his Alice as a little pre-Raphaelite beauty, it is doubtful that he would have shown any of them the "Underground" manuscript he shared in 1864 with the MacDonalds and their children. Impressed by the treasure-trove he found in Dante Gabriel's studio, Carroll photographed an entire gallery of female portraits, young and old, "most of them only half finished," and soon turned his camera on the painter himself "and his mother and sister."[53] Charged with the task of ordering prints from "My dear Mr. Dodgson," Christina listed the subjects (headed by "My sister") and the desired number of copies before politely fending off his invitation for a visit to Oxford. In its subtle distancing, her refusal anticipates the letter she would write later, after receiving an inscribed copy of *Alice in Wonderland:*

> Delightful it would be, that possible visit to Oxford. We contemplate it in a spirit of vague approbation. Stirred up by the kind offer of such a Showman, and by a wish to see the sights of Oxford in general and Gabriel's handiwork in particular; weighed down by family immobility;—we tremble in the balance, though I fear the leaden element preponderates. It is characteristic of us to miss opportunities. A year or two ago I had a chance of seeing Cambridge and of course missed it.[54]

As in "Twist me a crown of wind-flowers," this letter professes to entertain a voyage it unequivocally winds up rejecting. And, as in that dialogue,

---

53. *The Diaries of Lewis Carroll,* ed. Roger Lancelyn Green (Westport, Conn.: Greenwood Press, 1971), 30 September 1863, 1:201–2. Carroll writes that, as he was unpacking his photographic equipment, "Miss Christina Rossetti arrived, and Mr. Rossetti introduced me to her. She seemed a little shy at first, and I had very little time for conversation with her, but I much liked the little I saw of her. She sat for two pictures, Mr. Rossetti for one, and also two friends of his, a Mr. Cayley, and a Mr. Legros" (1:203–4). Carroll did not know, nor would Christina Rossetti have volunteered, that her desire to see Cayley probably accounted for her unexpected arrival a day before the picture-taking session had actually been planned. The next day, the arranged sittings resulted in group pictures she much preferred: Mrs. Rossetti with all four children, Mrs. Rossetti with Christina and her two brothers, Mrs. Rossetti with Christina.

54. Written in early 1864, the letter is quoted in Helmut Gernsheim, *Lewis Carroll Photographer* (New York: Dover Publications, 1969), 55.

a seemingly indecisive speaker turns into the decisive "I" who unexpectedly appears in the very last sentence. Absent in the inverted syntax of an
opening sentence devoid of all personal pronouns, hiding behind a collec-
tive "we" and "us" to which it attributes an exaggerated vacillation, this
ironic "I" finally signifies its absolute control. The final sentence, still indirect, leaves no doubt that the writer intends to miss Cambridge's rival
university town. Rather than a result of indecision, her proclaimed inertia
thus conveys a Lizzie-like resolve. She is indebted to the photographer for
the group pictures she has ordered, but refuses him any attendant privileges. She will not be drawn into the darkroom of "such a Showman."
Despite its association with the artwork of her brother, the male bastion
of Oxford will remain unvisited.

Yet Carroll's presentation to Christina Rossetti of an inscribed copy of
Alice in Wonderland, a text that opens and ends with sisters placed in the
countryside near the university town she had refused to visit, demanded
an even more carefully worded response on her part. Did she object to—
or even recognize—Carroll's likely appropriation of the closure of "Goblin Market" for the sororal ending of his own book? Her letter's pointed
omission of any of the female characters in the *Wonderland* text seems curiously suspect. Not only are Alice and her sister, the Duchess and the
Queen, Dinah and the pigeon, never mentioned, but even the book's title
is studiously avoided. Instead, Rossetti dwells exclusively on her reaction
to Carroll's male creatures. Although she professes to like three of these
and only distances herself from the sadistic Hatter and Hare, she appears
to regard all five of them as agents of Carroll's own ambivalence towards
his female dream-child.

Whether consciously or not, Rossetti's letter of November 1865 seems
to adopt the mode Carroll himself had used in shrinking the *Wonderland*
Alice. If the imperious dream-child extolled in his opening verses found
herself reduced soon after tumbling down a rabbit-hole, so does the recipient of this letter undergo a diminution. Starting out as the author of a
"funny pretty book," he winds up as little more than a capable resort photographer:

My dear Mr. Dodgson,

A thousand and one thanks—surely an appropriate number—for the funny
pretty book you have so very kindly sent me. My Mother and Sister as well as myself
made ourselves quite at home yesterday in Wonderland: and (if I am not shamefully
old for such an avowal) I confess it would give me sincere pleasure to fall in with
that conversational rabbit, that endearing puppy, that very sparkling dormouse. Of

the hatter's acquaintance I am not ambitious, and the March hare may fairly remain an open question. The woodcuts are charming. Have you seen the few words of praise already awarded to your volume by the *Reader*?

To descend to very prosy prose. Please do not forget that we are still in your debt for the last vignettes of my Sister: 9 copies, I think. Two or three months ago her carte was taken at Harrogate and turned out an admirable likeness.

My Mother and Sister unite in cordial remembrances. Pray believe me very truly yours.

Christina G. Rossetti[55]

Why does Rossetti, who begins with such fulsome thanks to the creator of Alice's descent underground, feel compelled, as she closes, to "descend to very prosy prose" by reminding her interlocutor of quite another sort of unfinished business between them? She notes that he still lacks payment for nine prints of a photograph he had taken of her sister, and, in what seems a digressive free-association, informs him that a commercial photographer recently managed to turn out "an admirable likeness" of the same subject. The allusion to this photographer introduces a note of rivalry. It not only pits an Oxford don for whom photography is an avocation against a Harrogate professional, but also invites an implicit question. Which of the two men can produce the better representation of an older sister? A casual aside thus introduces questions about a very different kind of rivalry. The creator of Lizzie seems eager to reduce the creator of Alice. Embedded in an ostensible thank-you note are the beginnings of an antagonism that is still kept in check in *Sing-Song* but will eventually burst out in *Speaking Likenesses*.

When read closely, Rossetti's letter to Carroll turns out to proffer very little praise for his imaginative achievement. For a "few words of strong praise," she seems to hint, this new author had better go to the review of his "volume" in the *Reader*. If she and her mother and sister did indeed make themselves "quite at home" in Wonderland, the images retained by such "shamefully old" readers hardly seem to resemble those that impressed the original trinity of Liddell sisters. Why is the hardly "sparkling" Dormouse, a hibernating cousin of Dante Gabriel's own beloved wombat, lifted out from the threesome to which he belongs? The

---

55. Christina Rossetti to Lewis Carroll, [28] November 1865, Berg Collection, MS. 244520-B, Q. 716, through the kind permission of the New York Public Library; a truncated version appears in *The Letters of Lewis Carroll,* ed. Morton N. Cohen, with the assistance of Roger Lancelyn Green (New York: Oxford University Press, 1978), 1:81n.

timid creature is dubiously placed in the company of the White Rabbit, whom the enlarged Alice so cruelly drops on splintered glass, and of the monstrous mastiff, whom the shrunken girl falsifies as a "dear little puppy" (*AW,* 33). Nor do the epithets assigned to these new companions fit their character. Far from being "conversational," the tongue-tied Rabbit fears the "savage" Duchess, flees from Alice's overtures, mistakes her for his servant, and, at the end, abjectly defers to the Queen whose livery he now wears. And the puppy, far from being "endearing," might well tear the dream-child to pieces. What does it mean, then, for Rossetti to claim "sincere pleasure to fall in" with this trio? Is she trying to signify her penetration of a sadistic subtext Carroll has covered with layerings of nostalgia and charm? Or is she pointing to a countertext of her own?

In upholding the Dormouse over his ruder male companions Rossetti seems eager to affirm her belief in the power of a creative inertia. She protests that she is "not ambitious" of making the acquaintance of Hatter and Hare, figures whose mobility, like the Cheshire Cat's, allows them to dominate others. If the madness of the Hatter and Cat sets them apart, the Dormouse is more accommodating. Whereas Hatter and Cat refuse to act as guides, this drowsy creature at least tries to please Alice's desire for narratives, as did the "too weak" storyteller of the opening poem. Despite his ineffectuality, he thus resembles the tutorial figures of the didactic tradition that Rossetti would try to revive in *Sing-Song* and *Speaking Likenesses.*

By the time she received *Alice in Wonderland* Christina Rossetti had added her portrait of the lethargic princess in the still unpublished "The Prince's Progress" to her earlier depiction of Lizzie's passive resistance to goblin men. Her letter to Carroll seems to affirm her distrust of those who privilege an aggressive mobility. When her brother had purchased a hibernating wombat, she drafted a witty Italian poem, "*L'Uumibatto*" (1869), in which she exhorted the creature to stop burrowing down, down, down, lest he "turn up in the Antipodes" that Alice had called "the antipathies."[56] And she added an English distich that converted this sleeper into a personal muse: "When wombats do inspire, / I strike my disused lyre."

The lyre struck in *Sing-Song* allowed Christina Rossetti to carry out an agenda that is barely adumbrated in her letter about *Wonderland.* Poems such as Carroll's "Lobster Quadrille" and "Twinkle, Twinkle, Little Bat"

---

56. "Notes by William Michael Rossetti," 494.

had mocked the verses of earlier women didacticists such as Mary Howitt and Jane Taylor. Rossetti's own verses now reinstated the practical education these and similar didacticists had favored. Thus, for example, her poems about addition and expansion—"1 and 1 are 2" (lyric 42) and "How many seconds in a minute?" (lyric 43)—defy the "lessenings" and faulty arithmetics Carroll had exulted in. Yet in their freshness and playfulness these poems hardly display the sober excesses of the branches of learning the Mock Turtle had called Ambition and Uglification.

The sing-songs that involve puns must also be read as spirited Rossettian correctives to the "very sparkling" word-plays offered by a Victorian punster extraordinaire. Whereas Carroll indulges the novel associations his incongruous yokings create, Rossetti entertains such associations only in order to uncouple them. Thus, for example, lyric 48 ("A pin has a head") offers no less than fourteen negative definitions: "A pin has a head, but has no hair; / A clock has a face, but no mouth there; / Needles have eyes, but they cannot see; / A fly has a trunk without lock or key" (*S-S*, 54; lines 1–4). Carroll, who would ask Tenniel to draw faces and mouths on clocks in *Through the Looking Glass*, might well have been tempted to create a hairy pin or an insect shaped as a suitcase and hence known as a trunk-fly. Rossetti also exploits such possibilities, yet immediately undercuts them with a "but" or "yet" or "without." The last line of lyric 48 returns the reader to the child who must still be taught to desynonimize what irrationalists such as Carroll and MacDonald had playfully pressed together: "And baby crows, without being a cock" (line 14). Appropriately enough, Hughes illustrates lyric 48 by showing such a baby being firmly held by its mother or nurse; it is thus prevented from joining little chicks (not yet male "cocks") who have scurried through bars that restrain a worried mother hen.[57]

If Rossetti and Hughes expose false likenesses through contraries, they also encourage their child readers to find similitude in dissimilitude. Alice was thwarted by the Hatter's demand that she find some likeness between a raven and a writing desk; by way of contrast, lyric 63 volunteers that "Half the answer" of its riddle "hangs on a thread!," thus embedding a third pun in its last line (*S-S*, 71; line 5). Hughes's illustration even furnishes a clue for children still too young to master the verbal text: a mater-

---

57. With its more elaborate syntax and more conceptual associations, lyric 57 seems intended for a slightly older child: "No dandelions tell the time, / Although they turn to clocks" (*S-S*, 65; lines 5–6).

nal figure is depicted as holding in the sewing kit on her lap the answer to the riddle she appears to have told to a pensive little girl. Pricked by the drawing, a tot thus is given the opportunity denied to the older Alice. By recognizing a needle, the little problem-solver can thread her way back to the first line of the poem and pinpoint the other half of the answer.

IV

The disjunctive mode that Rossetti and Hughes perfected in their collaborations for *Sing-Song* relied on affiliations that both verbal text and graphic image then proceed to dismantle. But their dissociations also involved them in an inevitable paradox. For, despite their joint belief that growing children are ill-served by fantasists who flatten all kinds of differences, Rossetti and Hughes cannot insist on differences without first establishing likenesses. They must thus evoke the constructs of Ingelow, MacDonald, and of their two most formidable rivals, Carroll and Tenniel, in order to promote the distinctiveness of their own undertaking.

Given the novelty of a format that relies on the exquisite calibration of 121 lyrics and 121 illustrations, *Sing-Song* could not be misread, as *Speaking Likenesses* would be only two years later, as a mere copy of antecedent texts. Indeed, reviewers like Sidney Colvin stressed the volume's originality. He lavishly praised the poems he considered "as finished and individual, sometimes as beautiful in regard of their theme, as they can be," and valued the supportive role played by a graphic imagination capable of "seconding the suggestions of the verse."[58] Yet this sympathetic emphasis on the freshness of their undertaking also prevented Victorian readers from seeing the extent to which Rossetti and Hughes had engaged in a dialogue with their immediate predecessors. Ironically enough, in the same essay in which Colvin upholds the novelty of *Sing-Song,* he faults *Through the Looking-Glass* for necessarily lacking, as a mere sequel, the "originality" of the first *Alice.*

In their inattention to the dialogic nature of Rossetti's and Hughes's art, the reviewers who would soon dismiss *Speaking Likenesses* as a sequel to a sequel clearly helped to make *Sing-Song* a publishing success. Yet the full achievement of these nursery rhymes can only be grasped if they are also

58. Colvin, review of *Sing-Song, The Princess and the Goblin* and *Through the Looking-Glass,* 24.

read, as I have been trying to show, as playfully indirect replies to earlier expostulations. Ironically enough, the deceptive likenesses we are asked to decode and to question greatly contribute to the unique mix of pleasure with pedagogy that Rossetti and Hughes managed to fashion. Literary critics may have learned from Harold Bloom that the "intertexuality" of novels and poems written for adults can heighten our appreciation of subtleties and intricacies we might otherwise overlook. But, like Colvin, we still seem to demand that children's books offer totally fresh perspectives suited for young minds unsullied by adult preconceptions. The same post-Romantic notions of "originality" that Colvin followed thus cloud our own ability to appreciate the genuine inventiveness of the dialogic interplay so prominent in all major Victorian child-texts, or, for that matter, in the children's books by later writers such as Edith Nesbit and Rudyard Kipling, or, in our own day, Randall Jarrell and Maurice Sendak.

For the seven writers examined in this book, however, textual rivalries always involved a contest that was also extraliterary, since it involved contrary views about the nature and psychology of childhood. A deceptively simple poem such as sing-song 56 carries extra freight for a child reader previously exposed to the metamorphic and anthropomorphic creatures who populate *Alice in Wonderland.* That child reader may have been amused by the conversion of a fish into a liveried footman or by the lizard handyman whom Alice first kicks up "like a sky-rocket" and then teases after he has become a "poor little juror" (*AW,* 31, 87). The fun of imagining a footless fish pressed into the role of footman is further accentuated by Tenniel's drawing at the opening of chapter 6: there, the creature's fish-face jars with his splendid human attire, and his leg-stockings and buckled shoes are made to conform to the outline of a fish tail. Tenniel's drawing of Bill the lizard being propelled out of a smoldering chimney with tightly shut eyes also builds on Carroll's license by exaggerating a comic defiance of the laws of gravity. And Bill's return to terra firma in the jury-box allows Alice (and the child reader) to adopt the superior attitude that an older child might feel towards one who is physically and intellectually slow. Alice first subjects Bill to the same practical joke she will play on the white chess-king in *Through The Looking-Glass:* she wrests away his pencil, confusing him so much that he is forced to write with one of his fingers, a useless action, "as it left no mark on the slate" (*AW,* 87). She then knocks him out of the jury-box, only to realize that she has put him back "head downwards"; yet on rectifying this inversion, Alice smugly concludes that, given Bill's stupidity, the change hardly "signifies much." In-

32 Tenniel vs. Hughes: Lizards

deed, unlike the other jurors, Bill continues to sit in a motionless stupor "with his mouth open, gazing up into the roof of the court" (*AW,* 93).

Sing-song 56 also invites the child reader to feel superior to fishes and lizards who have adopted human attire and hence are potentially given human characteristics. On the surface, the umbrellas and parasols these creatures have appropriated are every bit as ridiculous as the Fish-Footman's stockings or Bill's pencil and slate. Yet whereas the Fish-Footman and the lizard handyman/juryman were passively pressed into service by a humorist who revels in the anarchic incongruities of a topsy-turvy world of his own creation, Rossetti's fishes and lizards are funny because they seem unaware that the props they have chosen are totally unnecessary to their well-being. Carroll encourages the child reader to laugh at a fish who has been dressed up in the finery chosen by his superiors (and by Carroll himself), or to lord it over a lizard who is too stupid to

serve as a juror. Rossetti, however, wants to discourage this same child reader from indulging fantastic transpositions that she, too, purports to entertain. She expects her audience to understand that, however funny, such anthropomorphic exercises go against the fixed slots assigned to different species that coexist within a natural order.

The reader of lyric 56 first confronts a drawing of two lizards placed in a horizontal composition that seems to challenge the vertical composition which Tenniel had used for his own memorable drawing of Bill's flight (cf. fig. 32, right and left). Kicked by a child of the opposite sex, the terrified Bill was depicted with closed eyes. The male lizard in Hughes's drawing, however, ogles the female lizard who has coyly draped her tail around her neck and who has embellished herself further by using her parasol as a seductive prop. His own tail is not pressed between his legs, as Bill's was, but rather is prominently and frontally displayed as a horizontal axis for the entire drawing. This rather frank depiction of a process of sexual selection (Darwin's *Descent of Man* had just appeared in 1871) at first seems rather arbitrary; for by dwelling on lizards with parasols, Hughes has simply left out the fishes with umbrellas of the poem's first two lines:

> When fishes set umbrellas up
> If the rain-drops run,

>   Lizards will want their parasols
>   To shade them from the sun.
>   (*S-S,* 64; lines 1–4)

Even the smallest child reader of this poem will quickly realize that fishes whose natural element is water would hardly need umbrellas to protect them from the rain. Whether or not that child already is sophisticated enough to know that cold-blooded reptiles actually welcome the rays of the sun, it probably can figure out—by a process of analogy which the poem encourages—that parasols, too, would impede something that lizards might actually want. An adult reader, however, may detect even more in these four lines. For Rossetti's poem also opposes the false wishfulness of those who would segregate the child by "shading" it from the sun of adult reason and common sense. It is not the silly aspirations of fishes and lizards that she wants to correct, but rather the effect of fantasies that rely on such creatures.

Hughes's illustration for lyric 56 thus is not as inappropriate as it might have seemed. By relocating Bill the lizard and by giving him a mate of his own size, the artist not only matches Tenniel as a delineator of animal shapes but also creates a corrective for Carroll's own fantasy of a dream-mate. When Carroll has a huge Alice humiliate Bill by exposing this slow and tiny male reptile's inadequacies, he creates a sadomasochistic mismatch that allows him to dramatize some of his own frustrations. The abuse of Bill thus seems prompted by more than a joke shared with child readers. As noted earlier, Rossetti had used her lyric about the sun to excoriate "cruel boys" who torture creatures "that cannot fly" (*S-S,* 121; line 8). Although the indignities suffered by Bill are attributed to a little girl, it is a boyish Carroll who seems to relish tossing about the dull lizard with closed dormouse eyes.

That a potentially destructive little boy should appear in a drawing in which Hughes extends the anti-Carrollian implications of still another Rossetti text, "A house of cards" (lyric 102), thus hardly seems surprising. Here the little girl who carefully balances playing cards she is erecting into a pyramidal structure is again given the unmistakable features of Tenniel's Alice; perched on a table top, she appears to be wholly unaware of a watching boy whose lower extremities are concealed. Her obliviousness to this observer's presence befits a verbal text that stresses the instability of all constructs built on flimsy cards (fig. 33).

Rossetti's poem makes no distinction between the activities of boys and

A house of cards
  Is neat and small:
Shake the table,
  It must fall.

Find the Court cards
  One by one;
Raise it, roof it,—
  Now it's done:—
Shake the table!
  That's the fun.
                (S-S, 110)

33 Arthur Hughes, "A House of Cards"

girls. But its contrast between construction and destruction, between a deliberate upward motion and a sudden downward "fall," and, of course, its emphasis on "Court cards" or face cards, seemed to have encouraged Hughes to suggest an opposition between girl builders and boy shakers. For the little fellow so intently watching an Alice who is absorbed with her cards may merely be biding his time for some mischief. This potential anarchist can abort the girl's game. The cards will not fly up at her as they did in *Wonderland,* but simply come tumbling down. Yet it is possible, of course, that the girl-builder will herself choose to destroy the house of cards she has erected. If so, this little poem is curiously proleptic. For when Rossetti teamed up with Hughes again in *Speaking Likenesses* she was determined to bring down Carroll's house of cards. Yet, as we shall see in the next chapter, the "neat and small" structure she erected in her next book came tumbling down when subversion was misread as mere imitation.

T E N

Avenging Alice: From *Sing-Song* to *Speaking Likenesses*

The Children's books are—what you said. . . . The
worst *I consider Christina Rossetti's* [Speaking
Likenesses]. *I've kept that for the mere wonder of it:
how could she or Arthur Hughes sink so low after their
pretty nursery rhymes?*
— JOHN RUSKIN to F. S. Ellis, 21 January 1875

*Stroke a flint, and there is nothing to admire:
Strike a flint, and forthwith flash out sparks of fire.*
— CHRISTINA ROSSETTI, added to *Sing-Song* in 1893

I

When, a year before her death in 1894, Christina Rossetti prepared a new edition of *Sing-Song,* she inserted five new poems and also enlarged four others. Her expansions often allowed her to clarify meanings not as explicit in some of the 1872 lyrics: thus, for instance, the extra stanza for "I have a Poll parrot" makes the text more congruent with the scene of mutilation that Arthur Hughes had depicted.[1] But the two stanzas added to what had been lyric 93 in the 1872 text provide an unforeseen sequel to Hughes's drawing of a little boy who is walking hand in hand with a stiff-legged doll (fig. 34). The original four lines had rendered this tot's preference for a playmate whose inertia ensures that she will never elude his grasp. The eight lines added in 1893, however, stress the disenchantment and unfulfilled yearning that have replaced childish contentment. What could be read as a song of innocence in its first version now seems to have become a song of experience:

> I caught a little lady bird
> That flies far away:
> I caught a little lady wife
> That is both staid and gay.
>
> Come back, my scarlet ladybird,
> Back from far away;
> I weary of my dolly wife,
> My wife that cannot play.
>
> She's such a senseless wooden thing
> She stares the livelong day;
> Her wig of gold is stiff and cold
> And cannot change to grey.[2]

1. See chapter 9, pp. 332–34. The added lines increase the poem's polytonal playfulness by animating all four Pollies: "'Polly!' cried Polly, / 'Don't tear Polly dolly'— / While softhearted Poll / Trembled for the doll." Christina Rossetti, "I have a Poll parrot," lines 5–8 in *The Complete Poems: A Variorum Edition,* ed. R. W. Crump (Baton Rouge: Louisiana State University Press, 1986), 2:46.

2. Rossetti, "I caught a little lady bird," ibid., 44.

34 Arthur Hughes, "I Caught a Little Lady Bird"

By transferring his attachment from a live "lady" to her "staid" counterpart, the boy in the original one-stanza poem had hoped to avoid the pangs of separation. Yet his act of transference has now lost its appeal. He has presumably grown older in the two stanzas Rossetti added twenty years later. Just as Sara Crewe, in Frances Hodgson Burnett's *A Little Princess,* turns on her doll Emily when its frozen smile no longer fits the girl's emotional needs, so does this boy feel thwarted by a "dolly wife" of his own creation. The "senseless wooden thing" is a stock he can no longer animate. His idol may be unaging, but her fixity is contagious: her inability to initiate play now drains him of his former playfulness. Symbiosis is impossible.

Christina Rossetti's decision to re-issue *Sing-Song* in 1893 probably had nothing to do with Lewis Carroll's 1890 entrance into the same market for nursery books with still another version of Alice's Wonderland adventures. In a preface addressed to "Any Mother," Carroll explained why he had chosen to shrink his 1865 volume into the baby-text of *The Nursery "Alice"*:

And my ambition *now* is (is it a vain one?) to be read by Children aged from Nought to Five. To be read? Nay, not so! Say rather to be thumbed, to be cooed over, to be dogs'-eared, to be rumpled, to be kissed, by the illiterate, ungrammatical, dimpled Darlings, that fill your Nursery with merry uproar, and your inmost heart of hearts with a restful gladness! (*NA,* xxi–xxii)

Carroll's fourth published *Alice* book removes all materials an older child might have found enticing: the wonderful parodies, word-plays, riddles, and ironies that an adult intelligence had injected are gone, and even the character of Alice's older sister is no longer needed in a text dominated by the cloying, over-eager voice of a child-man. The narrator who wants his favorite picture book "to be cooed over" makes sure to control the responses of the dolly listeners and viewers. Tenniel's illustrations are themselves infantilized. Thus, for example, after helpfully identifying all but one of the twelve animals Alice has knocked out of the jury-box, the narrator professes to be momentarily stumped by the drawing he has scanned:

> But that only makes eleven: we must find one more creature.
>
> Oh, do you see a little white head, coming out behind the Mole, and just under the Duck's beak? That makes up the twelve.
>
> Mr. Tenniel says the screaming bird is a *Storkling* (of course you know what *that* is?) and the little white head is a *Mouseling*. Isn't that a little *darling*?
>
> Alice picked them all up again, very carefully, and I hope they weren't *much* hurt! (*NA*, 53)

The attempt to have child auditors recognize the triple repetition of "ling" seems as strained as the narrator's pious hope. Alice's rude treatment of Bill the lizard is now much missed.

Carroll ends *The Nursery Alice* by asking auditors "aged from Nought to Five" to "shut your eyes and pretend to be dear little Alice" (*NA*, 56). In the original text, Alice's older sister well knew that she had to reopen her eyes. But the narrator who no longer requires this agent can now hold on to the fetishized dream-child he first met in 1856 when she was not yet four years old. Unlike the growing boy in the revised sing-song, he is more than happy to replay old games. He thus comes closer to the painter Christina Rossetti had depicted in a sonnet that also went back to 1856, but was posthumously published: "In An Artist's Studio." Whereas the boy in her sing-song eventually rejected the deanimated "thing" that "stares the live-long day," the artist whom Christina endows with Dante Gabriel's own obsessiveness cannot wean himself of his fixation on a female Other. As Christina describes the painter's production, the "face that looks out from all his canvases" is always the same; its "loveliness" can be superimposed on figures who sit or walk or lean, on bodies of girls or adult women: "A queen in opal or in ruby dress, / A nameless girl in freshest summer-greens, / A saint, an angel."[3]

Carroll, too, had presumably found a common denominator among the "lovely pictures" he had photographed in Dante Gabriel's studio back in 1863: sketches of an "Irish girl," of pretty Miss Annie Miller, of a nameless "female head, profile," of Lizzie Siddal in various poses, of a girl and grapes, of Jane Burden, of a "Miss Herbert," and many others.[4] The photographer who had already captured Alice Liddell in sundry poses and the author/illustrator who would soon try to depict her in pre-Raphaelite attitudes and superimpose two versions of her "head" at the end of the *Underground* manuscript was clearly inspired by Dante Gabriel's example. He congratulated himself on the "great treat" he had found in the "house and garden" that had been opened for him: the treasure-trove of female portraits, more "exquisite" than any he had ever seen before, and the birds and beasts inhabiting the garden apparently left an indelible impression.

For Carroll correctly sensed a kinship between himself and the artist who was only four years older than himself (and two years older than Christina). That kinship stemmed from their similar longing for a female epi-psyche, a longing that Christina so well captured in the sestet to her 1856 sonnet. Whereas Dante Gabriel sought such a complement in the full-blown women who acted as his models and mistresses, Carroll sought it in the prepubescent girls and androgynous boys who posed for his camera. Yet both men, as Carroll seems to have realized in 1863, were drawn to the same unfading feminine essence. Christina's summation for "In An Artist's Studio," though directed at Dante Gabriel's art, thus applies just as well to the work of the child-lover who would feast on a dream-child for over forty years:

> He feeds upon her face by day or night,
>   And she with true kind eyes looks back on him,
>   Fair as the moon and joyful as the light:

3. Rossetti, "In An Artist's Studio," lines 5–7, ibid., 3:264. Composed as early as 1856, in the same year that Carroll first met Alice Liddell, the poem went unpublished until 1896, when it appeared in the collection William Michael Rossetti rather deceptively called *New Poems*. Presumably, Christina decided to keep private its implicit critique of Dante Gabriel's art.

4. *The Diaries of Lewis Carroll,* ed. Roger Lancelyn Green (Westport, Conn.: Greenwood Press, 1971), 30 September 1863, 1:201.

Not wan with waiting, nor with sorrow dim;
Not as she is, but was when hope shone bright;
Not as she is, but as she fills his dream.[5]

My previous chapter examined what might be called the first phase of
Christina Rossetti's entanglement with Lewis Carroll. In *Sing-Song,* which
appeared only a few weeks before *Through the Looking-Glass,* her conflict
with Carroll had been ideological and was abetted by Arthur Hughes's
own evocations of Tenniel's *Wonderland* Alice. But the success of *Looking-
Glass,* which Rossetti seems to have regarded as an obsessive repetition of
the same features to which she had objected in *Wonderland,* perhaps convinced her (and, possibly, Hughes) that a stronger repudiation was needed.
Their subtle dissociations in *Sing-Song,* not just from Carroll, but also
from MacDonald or Ingelow, had been completely ignored by reviewers.
As I noted before, Sidney Colvin had praised the originality of *Sing-Song*
in the same review in which he complained that *Looking-Glass,* as a text
that was too close to the first *Alice* book, lacked "the sense of freshness and
the unforeseen" offered by the previous "dreamland." Colvin, however,
also found a further flaw or "weak point" that had nothing to do with the
new book's being a sequel: he detected in it "a certain ugliness at times
which seems to run near the edge of the vulgar."[6]

It seems likely that Christina Rossetti recalled both of Colvin's strictures
when she decided to team up with Hughes once more in order to produce
a pseudo-sequel to the *Alice* books. Her new book would be filled with
ironic cross-references that could not be missed. Moreover, by exaggerating, in the first and last of her three stories, the "ugliness" bordering
on the "vulgar" which Colvin professed to have found in *Through the
Looking-Glass,* she could also obtain a license for her own love of the grotesque. The imagination which had created goblin merchant men could
thus be reactivated in the service of the ideology that already had informed
Sing-Song. She would deploy the fantastic in order to reassert once and for
all the "dull reality" that Alice's older sister (and Carroll behind her) had
so half-heartedly accommodated.

Rossetti's previous volume of prose fiction had been headed by the no-

5. Rossetti, "In An Artist's Studio," lines 9–14.

6. Sidney Colvin, review of *Sing-Song* by Christina Rossetti, *The Princess and the Goblin* by George MacDonald and *Through the Looking-Glass* by Lewis Carroll, *The Academy*
3 (15 January 1872): 24.

vella called *Commonplace*. After first entertaining another numbing title for the three interlinked stories designed to wrest children away from fantastical wonderlands, she rejected the negative "Nowhere" and settled on the more cryptic title of *Speaking Likenesses*. Remembering Dante Gabriel's depreciation of *Commonplace and Other Stories,* she made sure to anticipate him by personally derogating her new venture. It was nothing more, she assured him, than a simple "Christmas trifle, would-be in the *Alice* style with an eye to the market."[7] As usual, however, such self-belittling contains carefully implanted inferences designed to tease the letter's recipient. Since Christina first tells her brother that, this time around, she has taken matters into her own hands by returning to the publisher from whom he had wrested her *Sing-Song* and by personally intervening with Macmillan to enlist Arthur Hughes as the illustrator, her willingness to produce a mere trifle cast in Carroll's "style" seems rather suspect.[8] She soon reports that "I have seen all Mr. Hughes's illustrations to my little story, and hope they are pretty enough to please you in due course," and, upon the book's appearance, keeps insisting, "I hope Mr. Hughes will meet with your approval, even if you skip my text."[9] One can safely assume that the brother whose delayed woodcuts had affected her earlier work and whose fault-finding of *Commonplace* Christina surely remembered, is no more expected to skip this new text than his erstwhile associate, Mr. Dodgson.[10]

As I pointed out in chapter 9, Rossetti went out of her way to repudiate the sadistic Hatter and Hare in the 1865 letter in which she so cautiously thanked Carroll for her copy of *Alice*. By casting her mother, sister, and

7. Christina Rossetti to Dante Gabriel Rossetti, 4 May 1874, in *The Family Letters of Christina Georgina Rossetti,* ed. William Michael Rossetti (London: Brown, Langham, & Co., 1908), 44.

8. Writing to Macmillan on 20 April 1874, Rossetti informs the publisher that nothing "would please me more than Mr. Arthur Hughes" doing the artwork, and adds that his illustrations for "my Sing-Song were reckoned charming by Gabriel, not to speak of other verdicts." *The Rossetti-Macmillan Letters,* ed. Lona Mosk Packer (Berkeley and Los Angeles: University of California Press, 1963), 100.

9. Christina Rossetti to Dante Gabriel Rossetti, 1 October and 5 November 1874, *The Family Letters of Christina Georgina Rossetti,* ed. William Michael Rossetti, (London: Brown, Langham and Co., 1908), 47.

10. The reaction of Lewis Carroll, who owned a copy of *Speaking Likenesses,* apparently uninscribed, will, alas, forever remain unknown, since Christina Rossetti destroyed his letters to her.

herself as sole respondents to the book, she could exclude her brother's far more enthusiastic reaction to his friend's text. Unlike Christina, Dante Gabriel had especially relished Carroll's aggressive deformations of the moralistic primers that Mrs. Rossetti had used in rearing her four children.[11] Christina, on the other hand, had come to side with the female didacticists. She therefore upheld the Dormouse as a tepid alternative, not just to the Hatter and Hare who tried to detain Alice in their mad, atemporal world, but also to Carroll's hostile portraits of matriarchs such as the Duchess and the Queen of Hearts. The creature who tells Alice a sequential tale about three sisters who draw all manner of things that begin with the letter M at least acknowledges origins Christina herself tried to honor when she dedicated *Speaking Likenesses,* like most of her other volumes, to "My dearest Mother, in grateful remembrance of the Stories with which she used to entertain her children."[12] By casting a stern mentoria as the narrator of *Speaking Likenesses* and by giving primacy to adult female figures in all three of the tales, she could now, more strongly than ever, counter Carroll's unflattering portraits of grown-up women as well as his desire to arrest the growth of his little heroine.

Speaking Likenesses is an antagonistic work. The roots of its antagonism surely go beyond Christina Rossetti's desire to settle a score with the writer who had reintroduced Hatter and Hare in *Looking-Glass* and created still another irascible matriarch in the figure of the Red Queen. The unity of Christina's family life had been recently splintered. When her brother William Michael chose to take a young wife, who would soon regale Christina with a succession of nephews and nieces, her sister Maria had opted to remove herself to an Anglican sisterhood. Dante Gabriel, claiming that "solitude" had become "the habit of my life," did not join the wedding party, and soon Christina and her mother "had to face the prospect of becoming guests in their own home, subservient to a new female

---

11. Dante Gabriel Rossetti wrote to Carroll on 2 February 1866: "I saw *Alice in Wonderland* at my sister's, and was glad to find myself still childish enough to enjoy looking through it very much. The wonderful ballad of Father William and Alice's perverted snatches of school poetry are among the funniest things I have seen in a long time" (*The Letters of Lewis Carroll,* ed. Morton N. Cohen, with the assistance of Roger Lancelyn Green [New York: Oxford University Press, 1978], 1:81n). A year later, Dante Gabriel wrote again to congratulate Carroll on the book's "decided and continuous success," adding that nothing "could be better deserved."

12. Christina Rossetti, *Speaking Likenesses* (London: Macmillan, 1874), v.

head" who, to their chagrin, turned out to be less religious than William.[13] Nor was Christina's temperament helped by the continuing aftereffects of the severe case of Graves' disease that she had contracted in 1871.

The irascible narrator of *Speaking Likenesses* thus is more than a parody of Carroll's Red Queen, but she is that as well. This impatient aunt-figure counters the avuncular voice of the *Alice* books by adopting the tone of the character who had snapped at Alice at the beginning of *Through the Looking-Glass:* "Where do you come from? . . . And where are you going? Look up, speak nicely, and don't twiddle your fingers all the time" (*LG,* 124). The *Looking-Glass* Alice's anger at the rival who marred her coronation party mimicked the *Wonderland* Alice's final outburst at the Queen of Hearts; by shaking the Red Queen back into a kitten she hoped to reassert her dominance. The children in *Speaking Likenesses,* however, can no more challenge their domineering aunt than the girl heroines in the aunt's three stories can usurp the power wielded by the adult women who are their indisputable superiors. Surrounded by her five little nieces, Rossetti's narrator is even more hortatory than Carroll's Red Queen:

Come sit round me, my dear little girls, and I will tell you a story. Each of you bring her sewing, and let Ella take pencils and colour-box, and try to finish some one drawing of the many she has begun. What Maude! pouting over that nice clean white stocking because it wants a darn? Put away your pout and pull out your needle, my dear; for pouts make a sad beginning to my story. And yet not an inappropriate beginning, as some of you may notice as I go on. Silence! Attention! All eyes on occupations, not on me lest I should feel shy! Now I start my knitting and my story together. (*SL,* 325)

The *Looking-Glass* Alice had adopted a similar tone of admonition when she addressed the Black Kitten in the story's opening: "Now, if you'll only attend, Kitty, and not talk so much, I'll tell you all my ideas" (*LG,* 110). But, as Carroll had made clear, Alice's assumption of authority was just another manifestation of "let's pretend," a form of play. Alice refuses to punish the naughty kitten and even gives it a "little kiss to make it understand that it was in disgrace" (*LG,* 107). No such concessions are allowable under the absolute rule of Rossetti's Aunt. Alice may have grown beyond the kitten who chases its own tail in never-ending circles; the girl who soon starts her linear voyage on the chessboard dutifully tries

---

13. Frances Thomas, *Christina Rossetti* (London: The Self-Publishing Association, 1992), 295.

to wind up the ball of worsted, "all knots and tangles," that her naughty playmate has undone (*LG,* 107). But the kitten who will become the Red Queen still remains Alice's self-projection. By way of contrast, the Aunt who will enlist a dereliction as a fit "beginning" for her narrative is a moralist who always wants to accentuate the wide gulf that separates her from her naive little wards.

Ostensibly, the utilitarian opening of *Speaking Likenesses* harks back to *Sing-Song,* where the title page had featured Hughes's fine drawing of a little girl industriously hemming a pocket-handkerchief with needle and thread. Yet *utile e dolce* were inseparable in Rossetti's sing-songs. Despite her steady adult point of view, the lyricist always produced, in Colvin's words, "a music suited to baby ears." The narrator of *Speaking Likenesses,* however, is anti-lyrical. Her matter-of-factness often veers into irritation. When the children interrupt her story-telling with questions, as they frequently do, she impatiently turns on Ella, Maude, Jane, Clara, and Laura. She repeats their questions only to dismiss them: "How many children were there at supper?—Well, I have not the least idea, Laura, but they made quite a large party: suppose we say a hundred thousand" (*SL,* 339). The knitting of stories seems less important than needlework to this practical figure. Yet if she seems a highly prosaic version of the *fatas* and fairies entrusted with the threads of human lives, the Aunt's cleverness must not be underestimated. For it is hardly a coincidence that her opening story should begin on the "birthday morning, at half-past seven," of a little sleeper who happens to be "Eight years old to a minute" (*SL,* 325).

Still seven in Wonderland, Alice had only aged half a year when Humpty Dumpty, finding "Seven years and six months" to be an "uncomfortable age," had told her that with "proper assistance, you might have left off at seven" (*LG,* 162). Blonde, blue-eyed, asleep, the eight-year old Flora, whose physical resemblance to Alice is again brought out in Hughes's drawings, is the first of the three girl heroines the Aunt dangles before listeners who later reveal their familiarity with Carroll's work. These listeners form a unit such as the three little girls whom Carroll and the Dormouse tried to memorialize. But whereas Carroll clung to a single heroine, Rossetti's three protagonists—Flora, Edith, and Maggie (whose initials spell out the word "FEM")—are carefully differentiated. And the first of these, who resembles Alice much more than the other two, will be forced to dream about a party in which she suffers indignities far more uncomfortable—or even "vulgar," to use Colvin's term—than those which Alice suffered at either the Mad Tea-Party or the coronation banquet. The Aunt who derogates her capacities as a storyteller thus must be distrusted as much as the author who derogated her production of a mere trifle in Carroll's style.

II

The narrator who wants her little listeners to keep their "eyes on occupations, not on me," claims to be too "shy" to bear direct eye-contact. Yet there is nothing shy about the autocrat who steadily thwarts her audience's desire for something more "wonderful" and Carrollian than she is prepared to deliver. Indeed, her lack of shyness is akin to the determination of an author who now addresses her publishers with none of her earlier deference. Even while convalescing at a "grand Hospital" where she was staying with her mother, Rossetti tells Macmillan that he simply "must" defer to her wishes about the text. His demand for a different title is unacceptable, because, as she rather undiplomatically points out to him, it is based on far too superficial an understanding of her text:

And then I really must adopt "Speaking Likenesses" as my title, this having met with some approval in my circle. Very likely you did not so deeply ponder upon my text as to remark that my small heroines perpetually encounter "speaking (literally *speaking*) likenesses" or embodiments or caricatures of themselves or their faults. This premised, I think the title boasts of some point & neatness."[14]

Such self-assertiveness certainly is in marked contrast to the enforced submission, earlier in Rossetti's career, to misreaders like Ruskin or merchant-appropriators of her organic wares. Yet the explanation she offers to Macmillan remains problematic because incomplete.

Rossetti's contention that the "likenesses" faced by her heroines offer magnifications of their faults best applies to her first and most violent tale, which, not coincidentally, also happens to be the most overtly anti-Carrollian of the three. Told by her mother that she will be allowed to preside as "queen of the feast, because it is your birthday," Flora soon misuses her privileges (*SL,* 326). Instead of acting like a responsible eight-year old, she allows herself to be infected by the anarchic childishness that ruins her party, despite the valiant efforts of her older siblings, Susan and Alfred.

---

14. Christina Rossetti to Alexander Macmillan, 27 July [1874], *Rossetti-Macmillan Letters,* 101.

Jealousy and rivalry (emotions not unknown to the youngest of the four Rosssetti siblings) become so intense that the disgruntled Flora wanders off, falls asleep, and finds herself the victim of a nightmare. Abused and soiled by horrid child-monsters whose sadism even exceeds that of Lizzie's tormentors in "Goblin Market," Flora is denied the triumph Laura's older sister had savored. Instead, the girl who sees her face mirrored "fifty million-fold" in the "looking-glasses" that line the tea party into which she has stumbled, must also see a self-reflection in the arrogant and angry "birthday Queen," herself "reflected over and over again in five hundred mirrors" (*SL*, 332, 334).

At her own party, Flora had insisted on her primacy: "'It's my birthday,' cried Flora; 'it's my birthday'" (*SL*, 328). In the dream-party in which she is an uninvited guest, however, a scowling, red-faced girl "enthroned in an extra high chair" denies Flora the food she wants to eat by acting as her speaking likeness: "'You shan't, they're mine,' she repeated in a cross grumbling voice: 'it's my birthday and everything is mine'" (*SL*, 333). Just as multiple mirrors in the room create "not merely simple reflections, but reflections of reflections, and so on and on and on, over and over again," so is this birthday queen curiously prone to repetition and duplication (*SL*, 334). In the melee that ensues, in which a girl called Sticky counters a girl called Slime by hurling back the same insult and saying, "You're another," the birthday queen herself, suddenly challenged by the boy Hooks, cannot come up with a smart retort of her own:

> "You're another!" shrieked the Queen (the girls all alike seemed well-nigh desti-tute of invention).
> Her words were weak, but as she spoke she stooped: and clutched—shook—hurled—the first stone.
> "Oh don't, don't, don't," sobbed Flora, clinging in a paroxysm of terror and with all her weight, to the royal arm. (*SL*, 341)

The raging Queen who acts as Flora's speaking likeness is Rossetti's most conspicuous example of the "embodiment" or "caricature" she de-scribes in her letter to Macmillan. This discontented creature and the party she cannot control unmistakably present Flora with a distorted image of her unsuccessful rule as queen over her own birthday party. Yet Flora's dream involves another sort of caricature, as well, for Rossetti almost seems more eager to exaggerate the "faults" of a rival creator than the shortcomings of an eight-year-old. The room "lined throughout with looking-glasses" and the "playground" in which chaos spoils a child's desire for order may seem vaguely familiar settings to the Aunt's little listeners. And an irascible red Queen, the increasing "hunger and thirst" felt by a dreaming child for whom lamps "twinkling" like "stars" and looking "like illuminated peaches, apples, apricots, plums" are no substitute for the food others devour (*SL*, 340), the sadistic behavior of highly bizarre male companions, and, lastly, a strong urge to break off this increasingly frustrating dream, evoke further "speaking likenesses." Rossetti engages in a back-talk that involves the hurling of reflections of reflections, and so on and on, and over again. "Half mad with fear," Flora flings herself through the exit created by a "ponderous stone" that crashes through the glass (*SL*, 342, 341). She cannot bear to hear still another "You're another!"

The eight-year-old who is half mad with fear thus is herself a speaking likeness of the seven-year old who "gave a little scream, half of fright and half of anger" when attacked by the Queen of Hearts (*WL*, 97). And since Rossetti quite obviously regards both Alices as duplicates of each other, Flora also acts as the double of the seven-and-a-half-year-old who turned so "fiercely upon the Red Queen." Neither of Carroll's heroines can stand "any longer" the indignities inflicted on her by the demented matriarchs whose authority each one finally challenges (*LG*, 204). But if the queens who thwart the *Wonderland* and *Looking-Glass* Alices are fellow spoilers whom Rossetti seems to regard as repetitious likenesses of each other, it is not Flora's red-faced double, "the birthday Queen of her troubled dream" (*SL*, 342), but an older woman who is determined to ruin the dream of this third Alice. And that older woman, who upholds the matriarchal tradition Carroll had challenged, is, of course, none other than the storyteller herself.

Rossetti's firm insistence, to Macmillan, on the absolute necessity of her elliptical title thus stems from considerations that go beyond the plots of small heroines who meet talking self-embodiments. The Aunt's caustic asides to her squirming listeners suggest a hyperawareness of the antecedents she wants to shatter. When Ella protests that the "horrid game" of Hunt the Pincushion proposed by the birthday Queen, and described with great relish by the Aunt, "surely" can have no precedent in real life, the narrator responds by saying: "Certainly not, Ella; yet I have seen before now very rough and cruel play, if it can be termed play" (*SL*, 336). Ella again registers her discomfort when the Aunt proceeds to explain the rules of the next game, called Self Help: although "no adventitious aids were tolerated," she tells the children, every "natural advantage, as quill or fishhook, might be utilized," as it indeed is by Hooks and his accomplices,

Angles and Quills, who soon drag, "goffer," prick, and scratch their girl-victims in true goblin style. Although Ella's puzzled expression may simply reflect her response to the word "adventitious," the Aunt sees her opportunity to lambaste earlier occasions of sadistic play: "Don't look shocked, dear Ella, at my choice of words; but remember that my birthday party is being held in the Land of Nowhere. Yet who knows whether something not altogether unlike it has not ere now taken place in the Land of Somewhere? Look at home, children" (*SL,* 338).

The Aunt's admonition is double-edged. She is asking her listeners to remember that the unpleasant discord she is dramatizing ought to be well known to them, since they too have surely experienced—or even participated in—some version of excessively cruel games. But the Land of Nowhere that licenses such sadistic play can also be found at "home" among their beloved nursery books. Something *not altogether unlike,* and hence something remarkably like, these games has taken place in other imaginary lands they ought to be able to identify. The children the Aunt dominates thus are more than naive foils to an ironic adult. They are, quite specifically, Victorian girl-readers who have too passively accepted, as far as Rossetti is concerned, their transportation into wonderlands or other realms of "marvel." The Aunt's attempt to re-educate her five wards thus serves Rossetti's purpose. Carroll had tacitly acknowledged that Alice's wishfulness stemmed from a desire to dominate as insatiable as his own. The *Looking-Glass* heroine, we are told, once "had really frightened her old nurse by shouting suddenly in her ear, 'Nurse! do let's pretend that I'm a hungry hyaena, and you're a bone!'" (*LG,* 110). The older women whom the Aunt holds up as exemplars in *Speaking Likenesses* can never be frightened by tiny fantasists. If Carroll resented Alice Liddell for having grown far beyond the age of the fictional Alice, Rossetti is impatient with children who take too long before maturing into grown-up women. It is her narratress who poses as a hyaena and the little girls who are, if not exactly bones to be crushed, then at least silly cubs in need of discipline and correction.

It is no coincidence, therefore, that the Aunt's first story should end with an awakening that leaves both her heroine and her listeners rather shaken, though happy to have escaped the unflattering mirrors of "a hall of misery" (*SL,* 342). The rumpled Flora is grateful for the subordinate place she is allowed to reoccupy, at a real-life tea-table, next to her parents, Alfred, Susan, and her five guests. She contritely apologizes for her earlier crossness, yet it is the Aunt who insists on having the last word: "And I think if she lives to be nine years old and give another birthday party, she is likely on that occasion to be even less like the birthday Queen" (*SL,* 342). Growing up is a goal that little girls should covet.

When the Aunt's listeners politely request a second story, they signify a willingness to entertain more sober fare. Susan, Flora's older sister, had vainly tried to restore order by trying her hand at some animal fable in the manner of Aesop or LaFontaine. Yet the Aunt, more interested in Flora's negations, had relayed a mere snippet *in medias res:* "'—So the frog did not know how to boil the kettle; but he only replied: I can't bear hot water,' went on Susan telling her story. But Flora had no heart to listen, or to care about the frog. She lagged and dropped behind" (*SL,* 330). By now asking the Aunt to complete a tale unheard by the immature Flora, the girls seem to align themselves with Susan's greater maturity. Still, despite their implicit repudiation of the choosy brat who found that the ordinary food prepared for her birthday party did not suit her refined tastes, the five girls still evince a Laura-like hunger for exotic fruit.

Always the ironist, the Aunt seizes this opportunity to discourage an appetite for fantastic sequels. Even a simpler animal fable, she pleads, might tax her powers of invention. Here, as elsewhere, the Aunt assumes the pose of a strict literalist:

"Aunt, do tell us the story of the frog who couldn't boil the kettle."

"But I wasn't there to hear Susan tell the story."

"Oh, but you know it, Aunt."

"No, indeed I do not. I can imagine reasons why a frog would not and should not boil a kettle, but I never heard any such stated."

"Oh, but try. You know, Aunt, you are always telling *us* to try."

"Fairly put, Jane, and I will try, on condition that you all help me with my sewing."

"But we got through our work yesterday."

"Very well, Maude, as you like: only no help no story. I have too many poor friends ever to get through *my* work. However, as I see thimbles coming out, I conclude that you choose story and labour. Look, these breadths must be run together, three and three." (*SL,* 342–43)

If the Aunt's first story had magnified the sadism of a Duchess or Mad Hatter, the second tale revels in the sort of feigned impotence that Carroll himself had delighted in when pleading "a breath too weak / To stir the tiniest feather" (*AW,* 3). The Aunt contends that she is utterly unoriginal, totally ruled by precedent. She can only repeat narratives told by others, and having neither heard Susan tell the frog-tale nor run across any authoritative explanation that might account for a froggish aversion to boiling water, she claims to be inadequate to the task. After allowing the girls to coax her into telling a tale about a tail-less amphibian, she promptly produces a story that turns out to be story-less, an embodiment or caricature of the imaginative impotence she had pleaded. Her new heroine is not an older child like Susan, but a girl who is actually younger than Flora. Indeed, little Edith is so immature that she cannot perform the simple task of lighting a match.

Read superficially, this antinarrative merely illustrates the homely moral that little girls should not play with matches. Yet, as I have had occasion to argue before, and will again a little later in this chapter, the brilliant tour de force is crucial to the subversive strategies of a tripartite construct, in which stories that "must be run together, three and three" form a third alternative to the two Alice books of 1865 and 1871. Having first thwarted her audience's hunger for novelty by regaling them with the unpleasant excesses of Flora's story, the Aunt disappoints them once again by employing an exactly contrary tactic in the story of tiny Edith's insufficiencies. Her nieces justifiably feel unfulfilled. They have been denied a sequel such as Carroll had provided. A pendant to the Flora story is still missing, given the incompleteness of Edith's adventures in animal-land. And so, remembering that Lewis Carroll had balanced an outdoor summer story with an indoor tale in which the "window-panes" of Alice's room were caressed by "nice and soft" snow (*SL,* 109), two of the girls muster enough courage to demand a complementary winter's tale:

> "Well then, Jane and Maude, what is it?"
>
> "We were only saying that both your stories are summer stories, and we want you to tell us a winter story some day. That's all, Aunty dear."
>
> "Very well, Maudy dear; but don't say 'only,' as if I were finding fault with you. If Jane and you wish for a winter story, my next shall freeze hard. What! now? You really do allow me very little time for invention!"
>
> "And please, Aunt, be wonderful."
>
> "Well, Laura, I will try to be wonderful; but I cannot promise first-rate wonders on such extremely short notice. Ella, you sitting down too? Here is my work for you all, the same as yesterday, and here comes my story." (*SL,* 350)

Although the Aunt claims to be unable to produce "first-rate wonders" on such short notice, she nonetheless serves notice that these five girls with "dreaming eyes of wonder" had better not expect "the love-gift of a fairy-tale" (*LG,* 103). She first mocks Maud's attempt to endear herself to an adult. She refuses to accept the sincerity of Maud's self-belittlement and converts the girl's "Aunty dear" into a parodic "Maudie dear." And her unexpectedly quick acquiescence to a "winter story" becomes suspect as soon as she promises to come up with a narrative that shall "freeze hard." As in "Winter: My Secret," where the speaker so effectively chills the expectations of her male interlocutor, Rossetti knows all too well how to deploy the slaying power of winter frosts. The Aunt will tell a Christmas story in which the protagonist's concussion, rather than a dream, becomes the starting point for "marvellous adventures" (*SL,* 352). The story begins with poor Maggie seeing "sparks, flames and flashes of lightning" after having slipped on a "loose lump of ice," gone "down" in a "fall," and injured her head so badly that her brain might well have been "damaged by the blow"—suggesting that this third story is potentially more serious than its counterparts (*SL,* 352). Flora, too, had fallen in the first tale. But her fall, like Alice's and unlike Maggie's, had occurred within the safety of a dream, allowing the Aunt to minimize the effect of such imaginary accidents.[15]

The Looking-Glass Alice never is thrust into the cold outer world she describes to the Black Kitten. The snow, she sentimentally assumes, must love the trees and fields it so solicitously covers with a "white quilt" and to whom it "perhaps" says, "'Go to sleep, darlings, till the summer comes again'" (*LG,* 109). Rossetti, however, forces her heroine to traverse a landscape "coated with thick sheet ice"; the shivering and hungry birds that sit on "leafless bows" offer a very different sort of analogue for the resolute little girl who has offered to deliver goods left behind in her grandmother's store. Injured by her fall, cold, hungry, and tired, she might well succumb to death by being lulled into sleep. As the Aunt unsparingly notes, "I only know that many a thrush and sparrow died of cold that winter" (*SL,* 352).

Thus, the temptation to enter an evergreen world in which "speaking likenesses" might loosely frolic seems all the more alluring to the working-class orphan who has volunteered to act as her grandmother's delivery agent. Right after her fall on the ice, Maggie, with head still reeling, thinks that the wind-driven clouds and wind-tossed boughs must be "at play." Like the first speaker in "Twist me a crown of wind-flowers," the sing-

---

15. "Do you fancy the fall jarred her? Not at all: for the carpet grew to such a depth of velvet pile below her, that she fell quite lightly" (*SL,* 336). Rossetti the realist is clearly impatient with the light-falling Alice who "was not a bit hurt" after she lands upon a heap of sticks and dry leaves (*AW,* 9).

song discussed in my previous chapter, Maggie envisions a wind-borne escape from her dire surroundings. The speaker of the poem was prevented from joining exotic "players at their play."[16] But as soon as Maggie vows that she "should dearly like a game of play," fantasy-players materialize: the bleak ice-scape dissolves and, abruptly, "an opening in the forest disclosed to her a green glade, in which a party of children were sporting together in the very freest and easiest manner possible" (*SL,* 352).

Surprisingly enough, the Aunt seems disinclined to disparage Maggie's eagerness to join levitating acrobats as immune to the laws of gravity as MacDonald's Light Princess. Indeed, quite to the contrary, she even encourages Ella, Maude, Clara, Jane, and Laura to consider the plausibility of such a wish: "we must bear in mind," she volunteers, "that Maggie had no playfellows at home, and that cold winter was just then at its very coldest." It therefore seems logical, the Aunt suggests, that a lonely girl might want to participate in activities that promise to be "so sociable, or so warming on a cold day" (*SL,* 354). Maggie, after all, is not a sulking bourgeois child such as Flora, dissatisfied with the fine food and jolly games made available to her in the opulent mansion of her wealthy parents. The "orphan granddaughter" of Dame Margaret, the kindly and charitable old shopkeeper, seems far worthier of empathy. Poor Maggie's eagerness to join games offering a temporary release from heavy duties ought hardly be held against her by little girls who have themselves been pressed into the service of a philanthropist who helps "too many poor friends" with her needlework (*SL,* 351, 343).

As usual, however, the crafty Aunt has laid a trap for her listeners. For just as Maggie complacently asks the revelers who have clustered around her "what shall we play at?" we discover that these potential playmates belong to the same nasty bunch who ruined Flora's dream. Having already been forced to share Flora's unpleasant experiences with this group, the Aunt's listeners must now reconsider their identification with Maggie's wish. Unwilling to revisit the same cruel games, they know more than a Maggie who, unschooled in ironic narratives, is still in the state of innocence the five girls have lost. Not being privy to Flora's dream, or, for that matter, to Alice's two dreams, the naive Maggie remains blissfully unaware of what might be in store for her if she were to agree to the game of "Hunt the pincushion" eagerly proposed by "a glutinous-looking girl"

16. See pp. 336–37, above.

or the game of "Self-Help" stoutly insisted upon by "a boy clothed in something like porcupine skin" (*SL,* 354).

The Aunt's listeners feel tricked. When alert and outspoken Ella protests, "Oh, Aunt, are these the monstrous children over again?" the Aunt sarcastically replies, "Yes, Ella, you really can't expect me not to utilize such a brilliant idea twice" (*SL,* 354). The sarcasm, however, is not only directed at the girls who foolishly demanded a winter-pendant for a summer tale whose nasty "wonders" the Aunt now compels them to recall. It is also a further shaft aimed at the author whose duplication of wonders Rossetti set out to undermine. If Carroll could replicate his brilliant ideas in texts in which he professed to deny the very powers of invention he simultaneously asserted, why should not the Aunt, a female "speaking likeness" of his own avuncular narrator, try to hoist him on his own petard?

Still, to the relief of Ella and her fellow listeners, there is no need for an actual repetition of the "brilliant idea" they find so intimidating. No more sadistic games are needed, because Maggie, the sole ideal character among Rossetti's three girl heroines, will on her own accord repudiate Slime and Sticky and Quills and Hooks and all the other players the Aunt has threatened to re-release. As a child who has not been exposed to the fantasylands created by Victorian authors, Maggie can come up with resistances of her own. She instinctively rejects the allurements which the Aunt's little slaves, busily stitching and hemming, know only from hindsight to be false. On the verge of joining the players, the excited Maggie, "twirling and leaping in emulation," suddenly aborts all play because she remembers the "promise to make haste" that she had given to her worried grandmother. As her matriarch's agent, this child does not need to be reindoctrinated by the mentorias of the Victorian upper-middle-class. Steadying her swinging basket, she "resolutely though sadly" discourages the players' further attempts to draw her into play and walks away, as dignified as Lizzie in "Goblin Market," immune to peals of "mocking laughter" (*SL,* 354). Although she will encounter two more temptations in her forward passage through the dark woods, Maggie has ceased to be childish.

Unlike the stories of Flora and Edith, Maggie's involves progress and a fruition of sorts. Having rejected an infantile desire for perpetual play, she must next overcome temptations to which even adults might succumb. Though hungry, she denies herself a bite from the chocolate her granny's clients had so carelessly left behind in the shop; though drowsy, she refuses to give in to a sleep which, as the Aunt does not fail to point out to her wards, might well have proven to be fatal. On both occasions, Maggie meets new embodiments of the desires she must stifle. And both of these embodiments involve further evocations of *Through the Looking-Glass.* The first is the grotesque Mouth Boy whom Hughes draws as a horrid blend of Tweedledum and Lewis Carroll; the second is the group of male sleepers, each of whom Hughes endows with the same sleeping cap worn by the snoring Red King, that other Carrollian self-projection.

Although Maggie would never consider eating the delicacies in her basket, the plight of hungry wood-pigeons vainly pecking in the frozen path makes her "hungry from sympathy." Like Ruskin's Gluck, who gave the thirsty dog his last drops of holy water, Maggie is about to be tested. She is *"almost* ready to break off the *least little* corner" of the sweets that might have failed to nurture the birds, when she is stopped by a frightful apparition (*SL,* 355, italics added). The repulsive creature who "hastily" causes her to shut her basket is far more disgusting than the goblin men who vainly tried to pry open Lizzie's firmly shut mouth in "Goblin Market"; indeed, he seems an embodiment of those "blind mouths" Milton had excoriated in "Lycidas":[17]

A boy: and close at his heels marched a fat tabby cat, carrying in her mouth a tabby kitten. Or was it a real boy? He had indeed arms, legs, a head, like ordinary people: but his face exhibited only one feature, and that was wide mouth. He had no eyes; so how came he to know that Maggie and a basket were standing in his way I cannot say: but he did seem somehow aware of the fact; for the mouth, which doubtless could eat as well as speak, grinned, whined, and accosted her: "Give a morsel to a poor starving beggar." (*SL,* 355–56)

Like the episode in which Hooks, Quills and Angles had abused Flora, the scene carries unpleasant sexual overtones. Yet whereas Flora's boy-tormentors could be diverted by other victims, this potential attacker is "all alone" with Maggie. She is understandably frightened when he starts to "grind" the "teeth and tusks" of that wide mouth. Yet when the determined Maggie holds firm, the creature "hung his head, shut his mouth, and turned to go away faster and faster" (*SL,* 356). Like the goblins scattered by Lizzie's steadfastness, this emblem of excess has been vanquished.

The Mouth Boy represents a male imagination that is as unsated as that of the painter who fed on female features in Rossetti's sonnet. Portrayed

17. The startling metaphor (in line 119 of the poem) had been brilliantly analyzed by Ruskin in his lecture "On King's Treasuries" in *Sesame and Lilies* (*CW,* 18; 71–72).

as a highly aggressive beggar in Hughes's illustration, he extends his arm towards a recoiling Maggie, who is placed next to the innocent wood-doves perching on a branch behind her (fig. 35, top). As a mirror image of the drawing in which Tenniel had drawn Alice extending her own arm towards a hideous and adult-looking Tweedle twin (fig. 35, bottom), Hughes's drawing offers a gender reversal. He has produced what amounts to a looking-glass image. It is a pushy boy, rather than an empathetic girl, who is juxtaposed to one whose posture suggests an unwillingness or incapacity to relate.

But Hughes also extends the feline associations Rossetti has embedded by evoking still another Tenniel illustration. The boy's toothy mouth and the huge striped cat that sticks out from between his legs evoke the Cheshire Cat whose long claws and "great many teeth" had at first made Alice uneasy. In Tenniel's drawing of the grinning Cat, its huge tail was propped between two branches of the tree on which it was perched. In Hughes's drawing of the Mouth Boy, the protruding arm that matches the portruding cat is also wedged between the forked branches of a gnarled tree. Here, however, there is a distinct suggestion of sexual threat. The Cat whom Alice addressed as "Cheshire Puss" and whom Carroll calls an "it" rather than a "he," helpfully erased its tail before its head. But Hughes's cat is far less innocuous. Thrust out of the crotch of a hideous male, with a bushy tail that follows the contours of human trousers, this creature is no maternal Dinah.

Rossetti describes this animal as a "fat tabby cat, carrying in *her* mouth a tabby kitten" (*SL,* 355, italics added). Yet the creature depicted by Hughes as a part of a fat boy's anatomy seems male rather than female. Given the boy's association with hunger, we almost expect the cat to devour the kitten it carries in its mouth, or, at the very least, to drop it before pouncing on the doves perched behind Maggie. Indeed, the feral cat will drop the kitten, whom Maggie later finds, "all alone" and pitifully mewing, on her return trip (*SL,* 359). Discovered in the same spot where she had met the Mouth Boy, the abandoned, "helpless creature," who "seemed to beg for aid," is a worthier recipient of Maggie's charity. An orphan like Maggie herself, this kitten is not a tool to be shaken and harangued by an Alice who projects on her pet the same unsatisfied hunger for power that motivates her thwarted male creator.

Alice shakes the Red Queen back into a kitten she can dominate. Maggie, however, pours the kitten—and a frozen dove and a cold puppy—out of her grandmother's basket to be "thawed" at the old woman's matri-

35 Hughes vs. Tenniel: Maggie/Alice Facing Mouth Boy/Tweedle Twin

archal hearth (*SL,* 360). Alice's domination of her kitten is undercut by a narrator who resurfaces at the end of *Through the Looking-Glass* to remind us that, though dozing like the Red King, it was he who has dreamed her. By closing her own book with Dame Margaret and Maggie going to bed, Rossetti abjures the power-game she had imitated through her "speaking likenesses." Significantly enough, there is no return to the frame story. The domineering Aunt and her nieces are no longer necessary. The two Margarets, grandmother and granddaughter, suffice as embodiments of the matriarchal tradition Rossetti has tried to reinstate. Just as in her third and last temptation, Maggie resisted the allurements of a Carrollian doze by walking past the adult male dreamers whom Hughes endows with the Red King's sleeping cap, so does Rossetti no longer need to remind her readers that she has crafted a response to the man who dreamed Alice's dream. She can now drop her competitive game of "You're another."

The allegorical mode of this last tale allows Rossetti to sidestep her dialogic engagement with the components of Carroll's own fantasies. Indeed, her ultimate denial of the Carrollian antecedents to which she and Hughes had been so closely bound fits the thematic importance accorded to denial in *Speaking Likenesses.* Unlike Flora and Edith, and unlike the five little seamstresses who are schooled in the art of self-abnegation, Maggie is the heroine of a denial that requires the death of desire and a confrontation with death itself. Even after this brave little pilgrim reaches her destination and delivers the contents of her basket, her progress remains incomplete. Maggie's expectations are severely undercut: she had hoped to receive some recognition for her delivery of goods which she regarded as precious, but which the wealthy occupants of the house could dismiss as trivial. Unrecompensed, she is not "asked indoors, warmed by a fire, regaled with something nice, and indulged with a glimpse of the Christmas tree bending under its crop of wonderful fruit." As always in *Speaking Likenesses,* sanguine projections are undercut, even for a child who well deserves some such reward: "Alas, no! The door opened, the parcel was taken in with a brief 'Thank you,' and Maggie remained shut out on the sanded doorstep" (*SL,* 358). And, in a narrative that calls attention to its allegorical and religious texture, Maggie must walk through the dark forest all over again, as deprived and hungry and tired as ever before. It is only on her return to her grandmother's house that the three negative "speaking likenesses" she encountered on her voyage out can be replaced by positive emblems of the charity that she has practiced.

III

Despite its final avoidance of competition and strife, *Speaking Likenesses* derives its prime energy from the author's relentless assault on what she regarded as an unhealthy obsession with girlhood. But the most mischievous and destructive component of the book also happens to be the least dynamic. Neither the first story featuring Flora's violent abuses nor the last story with its account of Maggie's stout resistance, but rather the innocuous middle story about Edith's incompetence, most fully realizes Rossetti's subversive aims. In an irony that she surely savored, the most incendiary of her three stories dwells on a little girl's futile efforts to light a fire with lucifer matches.

Although younger than proud Flora, Edith also regards herself to be "by no means such a very little girl, and at any rate as wise as her elder brother, sister, and nurse." Eager to be considered an important member of the household, she volunteers—as Maggie does in the last story—to help the adults. Discovering that her "loving mother" has planned an outdoor party for the family and friends, Edith tells the cook that she will take a tea kettle into a little grove which to her looks "no less than a forest" (*SL,* 343):

> "I will carry the kettle out ready."
> "The fire will have to be lighted first," answered cook, as she hurried her tarts into the oven, and ran out to fetch curled parsley from the kitchen garden.
> "I can light the fire," called out Edith after her, though not very anxious to make herself heard: and thus it happened that the cook heard nothing beyond the child's voice saying something or other of no consequence. (*SL,* 344)

If less busy, the cook, who even earlier was "not attending" to the child's prattle, might have instructed her in the proper use of matches. But her inattention perfectly captures that of adult readers easily lulled by a tale seemingly tied to Edith's puerile point of view. Such unwary readers may well dismiss the account of Edith's shortcomings as nothing but a trite narrative without any "consequence" whatsoever.[18]

18. See Ralph A. Bellas, *Christina Rossetti* (Boston: G. K. Hall, 1977), 103–7, and Thomas Burnett Swann, *Wonder and Whimsy: The Fantastic World of Christina Rossetti* (Francestown, N.H.: Marshall Jones, 1960), 60–64. Both critics complain about the dullness of the middle story, which, they note with some puzzlement, even seems to lack the overt moral of the first.

Indeed, in what must surely be the most consummate hoax in English children's literature, Rossetti makes sure that the story about a tiny girl who could not light a match will never catch a fire of its own. The reader's expectations are steadily subverted. Edith immediately drops most of the lucifers from the matchbox as she sallies out of the house with her pets—a cockatoo, a Persian cat, and the Newfoundland dog who helpfully carries the kettle. When she gets to the grove, she wastes four of the remaining matches. Joined by a group of forest animals, she and the reader anxiously hope that some friendly assistance might set in motion a limping plot.

When a "leisurely" hopping frog appears among the forest animals, the Aunt's listeners excitedly cry out, "*The* frog, Aunt?" (*SL,* 346). Told that this is indeed the same frog whose prominence in Susan's story had stimulated their interest, the girls now eagerly settle back to discover his connection to the boiling kettle. But, as always, the Aunt thwarts their hope. For the frog is immediately displaced by a series of talking animals who try to respond to Edith's call for assistance. In his prefatory poem to *Alice in Wonderland,* Lewis Carroll had claimed that his heroine was engaged in "friendly chat with bird or beast." Yet Edith's interlocutors are far more friendly than the pigeon who had called Alice a "serpent" or the March Hare who accused her of being uncivil for sitting down without being invited. Still, despite the solicitude they show, their attempts to help her light the fire turn out to be just as unproductive as her own. Two pigeons advise Edith to fly away; a squirrel promises to fan nonexistent flames with his tail; a mole volunteers to rearrange the sticks; two hedgehogs remain silent. When the frog at last shows a "sudden appearance of interest" in the proceedings, his remark is dismissed because it appears to be unrelated to the task at hand. A cousin of his, a toad singled out for being "cleverer" than the other creatures, helpfully suggests that the match be applied "inside," rather than outside, "the heap" of kindling (*SL,* 348).[19]

When the sixth and final match results in a "first spark of success" yet is followed by "a dim, smoky, fitful smouldering," the frog at last seems ready to assume his long-awaited role. "Now to boil the kettle," he exults, "hopping up and down in his excitement and curiosity" (*SL,* 349). Of all

19. When the girls ask the Aunt why the toad should be "so much cleverer," she explains that he and his ancestors have lived "inside stones" (*SL,* 348). Though masculine, he thus resembles the walled-in female figures in several of Rossetti's poems, notably "An 'Immurata' Sister."

the congregated animals, he alone had remembered the actual goal of this enterprise when he inquired whether the kettle might not "want filling," although he became convinced that it was "full already" when nobody "noticed what he had said" (SL, 348). As a "speaking likeness" of the girl whose words to the cook had also gone unheard, the frog remains her superior. For, unlike the frog, the unthinking Edith had forgotten to fill the kettle with water. It is therefore fortunate that the fire she has lit should quickly die out. Still, its extinction also quells the frog's not-so-promising role:

> "Now," cried the frog once more, "now for the kettle."
> "Boil it yourself," retorted Edith.
> *So the frog did not know how to boil the kettle; but he only replied, "I can't bear hot water."* This you may remark was a startling change of tone in the frog: but I suppose he was anxious to save his credit. Now if he had only taken time to look at what was under his very eyes, he might have saved his credit without belying his principles: for
> The fire had gone out! (SL, 349–50; italics added)

Having promised Jane that she would "try" to build on the one-sentence fragment of the frog-story introduced in the tale about Flora, the Aunt halts her non-narrative as soon as she has found an opportunity to insert that earlier (italicized) sentence. She has kept the terms of her bargain. Presumably as eager as the frog to save her "credit," she has done so without compromising her principles. But the Aunt's own abrupt "change of tone" is even more "startling" than the frog's. Like her little auditors, Rossetti's reader is being teased by the steady squelching of the story's multiple narrative possibilities. Any lingering expectations of further openings are undercut when Edith's old nurse comes with a new box of matches and some newspapers as kindling, and sends the crestfallen child home. As did the endings of Flora's and Maggie's stories, this closure insists on the authority—and greater competence—of the adult.

Rossetti allows us a glimpse at her objectives in *Speaking Likenesses* when a seemingly minor detail catches the attention of one of the Aunt's listeners: the kettle happens to be hung on a tripod. When Maude wants to know, "Why a tripod, Aunt?" (SL, 345), the narrator's answer turns out to be suggestive. The Aunt explains that three sticks are "the fewest that can stand up firmly by themselves; two would tumble down, and four are not wanted" (SL, 345–46). Having already constructed a children's book out of a hundred twenty-one carefully calibrated lyrics, Rossetti had now

produced a narrative tripod that stood on the bare minimum of three stories. A fourth tale would have been excrescent. But since the two stronger
legs of her structure, the first and third stories, depend on the two Carrollian antecedents that Rossetti is contesting, her own structure needs the
support of an independent middle prop. Thus, Edith's story, whose awake
heroine moves in a highly "commonplace" world, actually best serves Rossetti's attempt to collapse the constructs on which Carroll had tried to hang
his own bubbling kettle. By strengthening her own tripod, this seemingly
shaky and weakest unit allows her to challenge the expectations of child
readers recently exposed to the fantasylands of Carroll, as well as MacDonald and Ingelow. By its steady avoidance of a fiery imagination, this drab
little story paradoxically proves to be essential to the production of a satirical "Christmas trifle, would-be in the *Alice* style."

The story of Edith's inability to light a fire of her own, however, also
betrays Rossetti's insecurities and self-doubts about her ability to recapture
the adult readership who had welcomed her first two volumes of poetry.
Had she not, by becoming a writer for children, lost that earlier public?
Was she not therefore destined, like little Edith, to be ignored by adults?
It seems significant that, in the very same letter she wrote to accompany
the manuscript of *Speaking Likenesses,* Rossetti should have resorted to the
metaphor of a dead fire in responding to Macmillan's call for "additional
matter" in a new collection of her poetry: "I fear there will be little indeed
to offer you. The fire has died out, it seems; & I know of no bellows potent
to revive dead coals."[20] Although ahead still were major poems such as
"Monna Innominata" and others collected in *A Pageant, and Other Poems*
(1881), it is true that her later work would lack some of the earlier intensity. The two-line sing-song inserted as an epigraph for this chapter thus
also seems to enfold some self-criticism: "Stroke a flint, and there is nothing to admire: / Strike a flint, and forthwith flash out sparks of fire."

But even in *Speaking Likenesses,* Christina Rossetti courted a fate that
resembled little Edith's unsuccess. By inviting her readers to regard her
highly original book as nothing but an inferior version of the *Alice* stories,
she became excessively reliant on the success of the imagination from
which she had so badly wanted to distance herself. Misread as lesser copies
rather than as burlesques, her two Carrollian analogues obscured the novelty of her clever enterprise and caused her book to be remembered only

20. Christina Rossetti to Alexander Macmillan, 4 February, 1874, *Rossetti-Macmillan
Letters,* 99n.

in conjunction with *Alice in Wonderland* and *Through the Looking-Glass,* the two components of the tripod she had tried to topple. By having the Aunt so repeatedly insist on her literalism and unoriginality, Rossetti had, in effect, only managed to reinforce the originality of her avuncular rival. The invention of the monster-children who torture Flora hardly led to a banishment of Hatter and Hare. Rossetti's repression of Flora and Maggie and the restraint she placed on her own powerful imaginative fire in the story of Edith thus merely augmented Carroll's reputation. Despite her brilliant efforts, she failed to undermine the "very sparkling" wit that she had, in her 1865 letter to Carroll, so sarcastically attributed to his sleepy Dormouse.[21]

21. Christina Rossetti's interactions with Lewis Carroll did not end with the publication of *Speaking Likenesses.* Readers interested in the aftermath of the relation between the two writers may wish to look at pp. 324–27 of my "Avenging Alice," *Nineteenth-Century Literature* 41 (1986): 298–327, an essay that bears a title similar to that of this chapter but is otherwise completely superseded by it.

E L E V E N

Repairing Female Authority: Ewing's "Amelia and the Dwarfs"

I

Victorian fantasies for children seldom move at a leisurely pace. Oscillating between the contraries of generation and gender, protagonists and readers are subjected to rapid horizontal and vertical movements. They are hurled into rabbit holes, shot out of hollow trees, forced to fend off grotesque attackers, to jump over hurdles or walk through barriers as hard as North Wind's frozen form. Still, readers who have ventured into my own narrative re-creation of such bizarre motions have also been treated to a much more tempered tour through a portrait gallery of nineteenth-century authors. For, like William Hazlitt, who produced his own guided tour of pre-Victorian worthies in *The Spirit of the Age, Or, Contemporary Portraits* (1825), I have insisted on a rather old-fashioned relation between texts and authorial selves. As I have tried to show in several of my previous chapters, texts written by adults for the young are quite likely to reactivate and to reprocess personal emotions that go back to the circumstances of the writer's own childhood and adolescence.

The analogy between Hazlitt's undertaking and mine, however, also operates on another level. For, like Hazlitt, I now conclude my gallery-tour by asking my readers to consider a writer not as well known as those discussed earlier. Hazlitt surprised his 1825 audience by claiming that he could not end his book without introducing "the name of the author of *Virginius,*" a certain John Sheridan Knowles, who, although "the most unconscious, the most artless, the most unpretending of mortals," was somehow to be esteemed as "the first tragic writer of the age."[1] My own claims for Juliana Horatia Ewing (1842–1885), however, require no such special pleading. As the wife of an impecunious officer in Queen Victoria's army, she may have lived in circumstances as modest as Mr. Knowles's; but, as a highly gifted writer of children's stories which had sold 200,000 copies by the early twentieth century and had "won the approval of Ruskin, Char-

---

1. William Hazlitt, *The Spirit of the Age, Or, Contemporary Portraits* (London: Oxford University Press, 1970), 301–2.

lotte Yonge, Henry James, Kipling, and Arnold Bennett,"[2] she certainly was far from "artless." Indeed, it is no exaggeration to say that Juliana Ewing became as self-assured and polished an artist as Maria Edgeworth and Jane Austen had been in Hazlitt's own time (although neither forerunner was featured in his all-male gallery). The "author of *Virginius*" is as slighted today as he was by contemporaries undoubtedly surprised to find him placed in the company of Byron and Scott or Wordsworth and Coleridge. Yet "Mrs. Ewing," as she was known by her own contemporaries, deserves to recapture the readership her work enjoyed at the high point of her career in the mid-1870s and early 1880s and continued to enjoy for at least one more generation thereafter.[3]

To the Victorians, Ewing's name was inextricably linked with that of her mother, Margaret Scott Gatty (1809–1873), the author of five successive volumes of the highly popular *Parables of Nature* (1855–1871) and the indefatigable editor of an elite journal for children called *Aunt Judy's Magazine* (begun in 1866). When Ewing died only twelve years after her mother, eulogists insisted on relating the two writers by considering their "lasting influence on our juvenile literature."[4] According to Mary Louisa Molesworth, the loss of the daughter who ought to have enjoyed, like her mother, at least twenty more years of productivity, had created a vacuum lamented "inconsolably" by a Victorian "child-world": "For it was on Juli-

2. Margaret Howard Blom and Thomas E. Blom, *Canada Home: Juliana Horatia Ewing's Fredericton Letters, 1867–1869* (Vancouver: University of British Columbia Press, 1983), x.

3. Although interest in Ewing persists, her stories and poems are, ironically enough, less accessible than the letters and drawings collected by Margaret Howard Blom and Thomas E. Blom in *Canada Home*. One may still find used copies of several of her seventeen titles re-issued in 1896 in both England and the United States by the Society for the Promotion of Christian Knowledge (SPCK), but most works by Ewing have gradually gone out of print. Everyman's Library last reprinted its two volumes of assorted early and late tales from the 1860s and 1880s in 1954; and Schocken re-issued *A Great Emergency* (1874) and *A Very Ill-Tempered Family* (1874–75) in a 1969 volume in its ill-fated "Victorian Revival" series. "Christmas Crackers" (1869–70) and "Amelia and the Dwarfs" (1870) are currently in print in Nina Auerbach and U. C. Knoepflmacher, eds., *Forbidden Journeys: Fairy Tales and Fantasies By Victorian Women Writers* (Chicago: University of Chicago Press, 1992). Yet the other 1870 fantasies discussed in this chapter, "Benjy in Beastland" and eight "Old Fashioned Fairy Tales," are unavailable.

4. Mary Louisa Molesworth, "Juliana Horatia Ewing," *The Contemporary Review* 49 (May 1886): 675–86, reprinted in Lance Salway, ed., *A Peculiar Gift: Nineteenth Century Writings on Books for Children,* (Harmondsworth: Kestrel Books, 1976), 503.

ana Ewing, of all the Gatty family, that the mantle of her mother's rare and sweet gifts most fully descended."[5] And even today, more than a century later, as Christabel Maxwell has so rightly maintained in her exquisite dual biography, "no study of Mrs Ewing is complete without the mother."[6]

Margaret Gatty first created the fictional figure of a young storyteller she called "Aunt Judy" in her 1859 *Aunt Judy's Tales.* This "elder girl in a large family, amusing what are called *the little ones,*"[7] discharges the role actually played in Gatty's own teeming nursery by her precocious daughter Juliana (or Julie), nicknamed both "Punch" and "Judy." When Gatty herself became widely known as "Aunt Judy," the creative identities of mother and daughter were intertwined even further: the adult moralist who had rather awkwardly tried to blend didacticism and fantasy in earlier efforts such as *The Fairy Godmothers and Other Tales* (1851), had, in effect, become dependent on the inventiveness of her still unpublished daughter. Soon, however, there were wider dividends to be reaped from this collaboration between a literary mother and the daughter whose creative talents Margaret Gatty had shrewdly recognized and fostered. For Julie Gatty (not yet "Mrs. Ewing") began to publish children's stories in Charlotte Yonge's *Monthly Packet,* the same journal to which her mother had contributed. And, after these stories had been collected in book form and after her marriage to Major Alexander Ewing, she could help her mother by gradually becoming the main contributor to *Aunt Judy's Magazine.*

As that nineteenth-century rarity, a woman writer with a living literary foremother as an immediate model and inspiration, Juliana Ewing was perfectly prepared to go beyond the role of nursery entertainer. By following her husband to sundry localities in England, Canada, and Malta, she could widen her scope in ways closed to her formidable, yet harried, mother. For Margaret Gatty's life was more restricted than her daughter's. Despite her close friendship with figures like Tennyson and notwithstanding the high respect she garnered from fellow naturalists who valued her researches on seaweeds and zoophytes, this multitalented woman was hampered by her parochial position as wife of a poor country rector and mother of the eight surviving children she bore from 1840 to 1851. Juliana Ewing's career, however, was less constrained. Distance from the pres-

---

5. Ibid., 504.

6. Christabel Maxwell, *Mrs Gatty and Mrs Ewing* (London: Constable, 1949), 15.

7. Margaret Gatty, *Aunt Judy's Tales* (London: Bell and Daldy, 1859), 1.

sures exerted by parents and siblings, an exposure to different communities, a relative life of leisure, and the intellectual stimulation provided by her widely traveled and well-educated husband allowed her to broaden her education, and gave her time to perfect her craft before placing it in the service of her mother's efforts to revitalize a pre-Romantic tradition of children's literature.

Although Christina Rossetti and Jean Ingelow had also tried to recover the legacy of those earlier women writers whose moral realism had been displaced by male fantasy, Juliana Ewing was better suited to play the role of transmitter. The supportive environment she had enjoyed, first as her mother's student-helper and then as the traveling wife of a gifted fellow intellectual, yielded opportunities unavailable to the other two women. It was she, therefore, more than Ingelow and Rossetti, who could best fuse moral realism and fantasy. And she could do so, moreover, by remaining aloof from the rivalries and acts of subversion that had characterized the work of Victorian fantasists and anti-fantastists alike. Although her writings for children display an awareness of gender roles and sexual difference that is as acute as that of any of the six writers we have so far considered, she does not privilege one sex over the other. And her insights into the psychology of boys are as shrewd and as sensitive as her sympathetic understanding of the emotional lives of girls.

Lewis Carroll delegated to Alice's older sister the forward-looking projection his *Wonderland* narrator finds so difficult to make. As a clergyman's daughter, and, moreover, as an older sister like Frances and Elizabeth Dodgson or Lorina Liddell, Julie Gatty can be seen as the female counterpart to Charles Dodgson, himself a nursery entertainer and fashioner of funny family magazines.[8] Yet unlike the pseudonymous Lewis Carroll and very much like Rossetti's fictional Aunt in *Speaking Likenesses,* the young woman whom her mother had cast as "Aunt Judy" also resembled that matriarch by wanting her young wards to grow up. The passage from childhood into maturity became Ewing's steady leitmotif, whether treated realistically or fantastically or, as in the important 1870

---

8. A close comparison of the nursery magazines edited by Julie Gatty and Charles Dodgson should definitely be undertaken. I suspect that Carroll's *Rectory Magazine* and *The Umbrella* are less inclusive of other Dodgson family members than the forum for Gatty children created by Julie's management of *Anon* (begun in 1856, when she was fourteen), *Le Caché* (1859–61), and *The Gunpowder Plot* (1862–71, continued by her siblings after she left home). See Maxwell, *Mrs Gatty and Mrs Ewing,* 113–14.

fictions I shall consider in later sections of this chapter, through a clever mixture of both of these modes.

II

Given this concern with transition, Ewing's narratives are often set at thresholds or crucial turning points. In "Friedrich's Ballad," a story she added to an 1862 volume containing her contributions for *The Monthly Packet,* and hence composed well before Lewis Carroll's or George Mac-Donald's ventures into childland, the twenty-year-old Julie Gatty (not yet Juliana Ewing) dramatizes the uneasy passage from boyhood to manhood undertaken by a young genius. There is a break between the self-absorbed and ambitious Friedrich and his mostly younger seven siblings, ordinary and placid children. And there is an equally sharp internal fissure that still plagues him as a successful adult poet: the adulation of a public oblivious to his early circumstances fails to compensate him for a lost cohesion he painfully remembers. Urged to confide in a well-meaning aristocratic patron, Friedrich Schiller (whose last name the sly narrator pointedly omits) recites a ballad he wrote just before his life took a decisive new turn. He will never publish the verses he asked his older sister Marie to read aloud to the other family members. The poem launched his career; yet it acts as a private reminder of his incompletion, of limits he had yet to recognize while a boy. The sickly poet, who will soon die at the prime of life, is left wandering between two worlds:

"Your story has entertained and touched me beyond measure," said the Duke. "But something is wanting. It does not (as they say) 'end well.' I fear you are not happy."

"I am content," said Friedrich. "Yes, I am happy. I never could be a child again, even if it pleased God to restore me the circumstances of my childhood. It is best as it is, but I have learned the truth of what Marie told me. It is the good, and not the great things in my life that bring me peace; or, rather, neither one nor the other, but the undeserved mercies of my God!" (FB, 258)

In emphasizing a contentment based on the acceptance of restrictions, "Friedrich's Ballad" rather remarkably foreshadows the sentimental but powerful *Laetus Sorte Mea* ("Happy in My Lot"), retitled *The Story of a Short Life* (1882), written two decades later when an ailing Ewing was, like

Schiller, herself near the end of her literary career.[9] Yet by dramatizing the plight of a budding genius, the story is even more compelling as the production of a young writer whose career had barely been launched. Friedrich must wrest himself away from the parents and younger siblings who have been his first audience, and yet cannot wean himself from the influence exerted by his older half-sister who has recognized the boy's uniqueness. At the outset of a promising career, Julie Gatty thus tries to integrate these two figures: she is both Friedrich and Marie, an aspiring, gifted, but necessarily hesitant writer-to-be, and a self-effacing, yet strongly intuitive and pious, nurturer of younger brothers and sisters. Friedrich's world lies all before him; Marie's future holds only marriage to a "man in no way worthy of her" (FB, 258).

Friedrich's relation to Marie thus provides the story with its axis. When a kind pedagogue imparts "to her a slight knowledge of Latin, and of the great Linnaeus's system of botany" (FB, 226), Friedrich is jealous, full of "envious admiration" of a dual training in foreign languages and science quite similar to that which Julie Gatty received from her own mother. But as the child of a first wife who died in childbirth, Marie lacks the biological mother on whose loving solicitude the boy can always count. The girl's adoption of a quasi-maternal role thus stems from want as much as from a sense of obligation. Marie is eager to repay the woman who nursed her as an infant by emulating her as a surrogate mother to Friedrich and to his younger siblings. Friedrich at first depreciates "Our Marie" for not being as clever as he is, but he soon regards her as an indispensable moral alter ego. He asks her to read aloud an original ballad he wrote to replace the more traditional rhymed fairy tales his growing siblings have rejected. Insecure about its merits, he needs her approval. When, "with a strange emotion on her face," Marie certifies to the adults who have overheard the poem, that he is indeed its author, Friedrich becomes validated for the first time in his life. The "huddled miserable figure" who winced during Marie's reading is now recognized as "the Genius of the family" (FB, 249).

"Friedrich's Ballad" can be read as a text which resembles Ingelow's "The Life of Mr. John Smith" in its ideological emphasis on the worthiness of obscure and commonplace lives. Yet unlike Ingelow's tongue-in-cheek

9. For a fine discussion of this tale, see Judith A. Plotz, "A Victorian Comfort Book: Juliana Ewing's *The Story of a Short Life*," in *Romanticism and Children's Literature in Nineteenth-Century England,* ed. James Holt McGavran, Jr. (Athens: University of Georgia Press, 1991), 168–89.

paean to ordinariness,[10] Julie Gatty tries to make the homely precepts of Marie an integral component of a major Romantic poet's productions. By having both Friedrich and Marie adopt a role invented by the five younger children in the nursery, the fledgling writer tries to present brother- and sister-selves as co-equal transmitters or bridge-builders. The five children have instituted a ritual built around "an old book of ballads and poems, which they were accustomed to read in turn with special solemnities, on one particular night in the year; the reader for the time being having a peculiar costume, and the title of *Märchen-Frau,* or Mother Bunch, a name which had in time been familiarly adopted for the ballad-book itself" (FB, 223). Their annual celebration, however, breaks down after they discover that "whenever the book was brought out, there was the same feeling that the magic of it was gone" (FB, 234). Before, each reader, wrapped in "huge hood and cloak," could joyfully assume the identity of "the 'Märchen-Frau' or Story Woman," with the others excitedly providing a chorus of antiphonal responses. Now, however, the book's familiar contents have worn thin. Even the "pet ballad of Bluebeard, at the exciting point that sister Anne is looking out from the castle window" (FB, 233), has lost its former appeal.

The collaboration of Friedrich and his quasi-maternal sister thus revitalizes a tradition that might otherwise have withered away. Marie can be credited as much as Friedrich for reanimating "the imaginary personage who is known in England by the name of Mother Bunch, or Mother Goose" (FB, 223). Continuities—between childhood and maturity, old folktales and artistic innovation—are preserved under the Märchen-Frau's ample cloak, a vesture concealing sexual differences. And Romanticism, with its masculine emphasis on a fantastic imagination, must accommodate the moral realism and pragmatism of feminine mentorias. "Friedrich's Ballad" thus offers a blueprint for a self-aware author at the outset of her career: the future "Mrs. Ewing" would seek forms of transmission that might go beyond the rivalries of gender and genre.

As we have seen, the question of transmission had become a major concern for writers of children's books after the publication of *Alice in Wonderland.* Lewis Carroll's hope that a matured Alice might want to disseminate his own Wonderland fantasy offended both Ingelow and Rossetti in its implied notion that female imaginations were subservient to his own.

10. See chapter 8, pp. 271–73, 279–80, above.

Yet their efforts to reinstate a female literary tradition were fraught with considerable difficulties—difficulties that bear rehearsing before we turn to Ewing's "Amelia and the Dwarfs" and her other 1870 productions. The acquisition of authority by the female protagonists of *Mopsa the Fairy* and *Speaking Likenesses* is beset by conflicts and frictions that have much to do with each author's uneasy relation to fantasy and hence with her own textual authority. For, in trying to reclaim children's fairy tales as a literature of their own, these women writers warily confronted a genre that had served the constructions of "femininity" by their male predecessors.

Ingelow plants Jack into a female fantasy world from which he must be banished. Yet by also asking him to forget the realm in which Mopsa attains queenhood, she segregates that female fantasyland from an ordinary world she genders as masculine. Unremembered and isolated, fairy queens thus exercise, in a world of their own, the imaginative powers that Victorian mothers must keep half-concealed from literal-minded husbands and sons. For Rossetti, fantasy becomes even more suspect. Her very attraction to its anarchic energies needs to be expunged if little girls are to grow into reality-minded matriarchs. Rossetti therefore engages in a divisive operation that is more radical than Ingelow's. By attributing fantasy's potential for violence to masculinity, she can turn the tables and deploy sadism on behalf of a threatened femininity. When she creates male antagonists for girls and women to overcome, Lizzie's and Laura's goblin torturers turn into grotesquely deformed boys: Angles and Hooks try to violate Flora's integrity and the horridly Carrollian Mouth-Boy threatens to devour Maggie as well as the contents of her basket. Transmission is possible only through coercion: the Aunt must intimidate her wards with terrifying nightmares.

Ewing is as concerned as Rossetti and Ingelow with problems of transmission and just as eager as they are to effect the full recovery of a female authority. To realign fantasy with the reality of everyday, to connect it to the domesticity that Victorian middle-class culture had assigned as a proper sphere for its queen-like matrons, is therefore a task that she, too, sets out to accomplish. And, if the discomforts experienced by girl heroines like Mopsa and Flora enacted Ingelow's and Rossetti's own ambivalent relation to the fantastic, Ewing chooses little Amelia as her own replacement for Carroll's *Wonderland* Alice. Indeed, Amelia, as we shall see, plunges into a sadistic underground world that tests her mettle and allows her to resurface as a substantially altered member of Victorian society. Yet, even though Ewing is as much of a moral realist as the other two women writers, she neither banishes fantasy, as Ingelow so reluctantly does, nor feels compelled to exorcise it, as Rossetti insists on doing. Instead, she allows a traffic between fantasy and realism that befits her assumed role of bridge-builder. To reinstate an unimpeded female literary tradition is as important to her as to mediate between the masculine and the feminine.

In her 1873 eulogy, "In Memoriam, Margaret Gatty," Ewing surveys her mother's many talents—calligrapher, etcher, natural historian, expert on sun-dials, propagandist for animal rights. Yet, in a characteristic move, she makes no extravagant claims for Gatty's authorship of "popular" children's books. Instead, Ewing prefers to stress her mother's role as an educator whose investment in her "numerous child-correspondents" allowed her to become a maternal guide for "what one might call her magazine children"(IM, 479). Having modeled herself, "in a very early fit of hero-worship," after Elizabeth Smith (whose example led her to study German literature), Margaret Gatty was prepared to act as a model, later in life, for a host of young correspondents. These eager learners, girls and boys, were "of all ages and acquirements, from nursery aspirants still barely out of pothooks" to a published author "who still calls her his 'literary god-mother'" (IM, 479). Ewing thus grants Margaret Gatty an authority that stems from her assumption of a role quite similar to that which Marie had discharged in "Friedrich's Ballad":

> Whatever interest this little record of some of my mother's tastes and acquirements may have had for her young readers, its value must be in her example. Whatever genius she may have had, her industry was far more remarkable. The pen of a ready writer is not grasped by all fingers, and gifts are gifts, not earnings. But to cultivate the faculties GOD has given us to His glory, to lose petty cares, ignoble pleasures, and small grievances, in the joy of studying His great works, to be good to His creatures, to be truthful beyond fear or flattery . . . —these things are within the power as well as the ambition of us all.
>
> I must point out to some of the young aspirants after her literary fame, that though the date in Elizabeth Smith's *Remains* shows my mother to have only been eleven years old when she got it, and though she worked and studied indefatigably all her girlhood, her first original work was not published till she was forty-two years old. (IM, 482–83)

Coming from one who began to publish fiction at the age of nineteen and whose powers of imagination her mother rightly placed far above her own, Ewing's sobering tribute seems rather chastening. She might easily have been forgiven for exaggerating the artistry or importance of Margaret Gatty's children's books. But Ewing is a truth-teller. The opening paragraph of her essay clearly establishes her priorities: "My mother became editor of *Aunt Judy's Magazine* in May 1866. It was named after one of her most popular books—*Aunt Judy's Tales;* and Aunt Judy became a name for herself with her numerous child-correspondents" (IM, 479). It is the "ordinary work of editorship," increased by Gatty's "kindness to tyro authors, and to children in want of everything, from advice on a life-vocation to old foreign postage stamps," that Ewing chooses to stress. For the woman who inspired one such "tyro" in her very own nursery was able to extend her sympathy and knowledge to "child-correspondents" all over the British Empire (IM, 479).

Ewing therefore wants Gatty to be remembered by past, present, and future readers of *Aunt Judy's Magazine* as an inspirational force rather than as the author of stories that popularized the daughterly "name" of Aunt Judy. Not even her bodily paralysis during "ten years of affliction and pain" could slow down a "brain as vigorous as ever" or reduce Gatty's many "interests" to a "fretful circle of invalid fancies and fears" (IM, 483, 482). Ewing wants this matriarch to be valued as an empowering public figure. The gifted daughter who will try to carry out her mother's ideological agenda thus sees herself as being no more exceptional than any of Gatty's more commonplace "magazine-children." She is merely better acquainted with personal details she is willing to share with all those others who are in Gatty's debt. For the editor of *Aunt Judy's Magazine* is not the private maternal censor to whom Ingelow deferred or to whom Rossetti so abjectly presented all her productions. Her mantle, like that of the Story Woman, spreads far beyond a single nursery.

Exactly four years earlier, the December issue of the eighth volume of *Aunt Judy's Magazine* (November 1869 to October 1870) also tried to signify Gatty's influential authority by featuring a medallion engraving of "The Editor" as its frontispiece. Seen in profile, looking benign yet autocratic, Margaret Gatty's face resembles the representations of Queen Victoria on postage stamps of the time (fig. 36). "The Editor's" content expression may reflect her satisfaction with the success of a magazine that no longer requires translations of Hans Christian Andersen or a story by the celebrated Lewis Carroll ("Bruno's Revenge") to attract a wider audience of middle-class juveniles. For this volume can count on the inventiveness of a more accessible author. No longer an apprentice, Ewing is ready to become the journal's major contributor (fig. 37).

In the span of eleven months, Ewing supplied her editor-mother with no less than fourteen separate contributions: eight short stories in a series

36 G. W. Brookes, Margaret Gatty

37 Randolph Caldecott, Juliana
Horatia Ewing

called "Old Fashioned Fairy Tales" and three novellas, each in two monthly installments, "Christmas Crackers" (December 1869 and January 1870), "Amelia and the Dwarfs" (February and March 1870), and "Benjy in Beastland" (May and June 1870). The importance this author now holds for the journal can be deduced from the quality of the artists assigned to illustrate her work: A. W. Bayes for the eight fairy tales, and the aged, but still brilliant, George Cruikshank for the three novellas.[11] The author's name also becomes increasingly prominent: at first omitted at the beginning or end of a text, then noted only through the initials "J. H. E.," the

11. With the exception of his full-page illustration for the seventh of the "Old Fashioned Fairy Tales," Bayes's illustrations take up three quarters of a page. Cruikshank's drawing for the second installment of each of the three novellas is given a full page, and the one for "Amelia and the Dwarfs" (reproduced in Auerbach and Knoepflmacher, *Forbidden Journeys*) acts as the frontispiece of the March issue. About that one drawing, Horatia K. F. Gatty, Juliana's first biographer, noted: "The dwarfs inspired Mr. Cruikshank to one of his best water-colour sketches: who is the happy possessor thereof I do not know, but the woodcut illustration very inadequately represents the beauty and delicacy of the picture" (*Juliana Horatia Gatty and Her Books* [London: SPCK, 1885], 22).

writer's identity soon is designated as "By the Author of Mrs. Overthe-way's Remembrances," and finally set down as "By J. H. Ewing" and "Juliana H. Ewing."

Impressed by the texture of "Amelia and the Dwarfs," Margaret Gatty urged her daughter to continue to blend the real and the fantastic: "you seem to have such a tendency to it that I say it is a vocation, and I should at any rate have my fling at it in the new volume."[12] But that collection, *The Brownies and Other Tales* (1870), in which "Christmas Crackers" and "Amelia and the Dwarfs" were joined by the fine title-story Julie Gatty had published in *The Monthly Packet* as far back as 1865, contained little that was truly new. A collection published three years later, *Lob-Lie-By-the-Fire, and Other Tales,* brought together the title story and "Timothy's Shoes" (1870–71), both of which Gatty's sister considered "of the same type as 'Amelia'"[13] with the previously published "Benjy in Beast-land." With the release of that volume, Ewing's foray into fantasy was essentially over. Even though she continued to produce occasional "Old Fashioned Fairy Tales" until 1876 (collected, with a preface, in an 1882 volume), she moved away from a mode she had initially mastered in the Gatty nursery. After her mother's death, she first assisted her sister in editing the journal and then helped its circulation by contributing a flow of poems and the more realistic tales prized by her contemporaries. The superb "Amelia and the Dwarfs," its more somber pendant, "Benjy in Beast-land," and "Timothy's Shoes," and "The Brownies" thus stand out as Ewing's major ventures into fantasylands. Still, even if anomalous, the quality and importance of all four tales, especially of "Amelia," makes them the perfect culmination for the sequence I have been tracing in the course of this book.

III

When Ewing collected her "Old Fashioned Fairy Tales" near the end of her career, she wrote a brief preface to set down her ideas about the genre. To distinguish her enterprise from that of other Victorian authors, such as Dinah Mulock Craik or Maria Louisa Molesworth, she explains that she never attempted to offer her readers "old fairy tales told afresh." In-

---

12. Quoted in Maxwell, *Mrs Gatty and Mrs Ewing,* 185.
13. Gatty, *Juliana Horatia Ewing and Her Books,* 25.

stead, much like Ruskin in *The King of the Golden River,* she tried to produce original *Kunstmärchen,* "written in conformity to certain theories respecting stories of this kind."[14] These "theories," however, turn out to be far more concrete than those advanced in Ruskin's 1868 essay on "Fairy Stories." For Ewing addresses, not the presumed "purity" of the genre Ruskin idealizes, but rather what she calls the "common 'properties' of Fairy Drama." Like a folklorist or ethnologist, she therefore singles out common leitmotifs extracted from diverse cultures and reimplanted in stories of her own. And, ever the stylist concerned with the craft of fiction, Ewing also notes that such stories should not surrender to a Victorian fondness for the ornate but must retain a mode of telling that respects the sparseness of an oral tradition.

To explain why she considers original stories to be "old-fashioned," Ewing lays out essentials she wants her readers to understand:

> First, that there are ideas and types in the myths of all countries, which are common properties, to use which does not lay the teller of the fairy tales open to the charge of plagiarism. Such as the idea of the weak outwitting the strong; the failure of man to choose wisely when he may have his wish; or the desire of sprites to exchange their careless and unfettered existence for the pains and penalties of humanity, if they may thereby share in the hopes of the human soul.

> Secondly, that in these household stories (the models for which were originally oral tradition), the thing to be most avoided is a discursive or descriptive style of writing. Brevity and epigram must ever be the soul of their wit, and they should be written as tales that are told.[15]

Ewing's 1870 fairy tales adhere to this program, and so do "Amelia," "Benjy," and "The Brownies," despite their more "discursive or descriptive" mode. By dramatizing the dynamic clash between humans and "sprites," Ewing can simultaneously invigorate seemingly contrary traditions. More comfortable with what her mother called "supernatural machinery" than were any of the earlier women moralists, she can deploy her genuine fascination with the particularities of dwarfs, Brownies, Boggarts, wizards, sorceresses, giants, nixies, and an assortment of water sprites by placing such creatures in the service of a this-worldly and pragmatic ethic. The external changes in fortune that the shorter fairy tales dramatize with their rewards and punishments become internalized as psychological

14. Ibid., 36.
15. Ibid.

changes in some of the longer tales or in novellas about growing children such as Amelia, Benjy, and Tiny.

Although most of the human protagonists in the old-fashioned fairy tales are adults rather than children, when the young do appear, their contact with alien creatures reinforces their own marginality. Eager to annoy "the whole stupid race" of humans, a water sprite in "The Nix in Mischief" plays his tricks on the washerwoman's daughter who has scooped him up in her pail and causes the child to be wrongly accused of incompetence.[16] Contact between humans and nonhumans here proves detrimental to both races. Even though Bess's good name is reinstated and the nix gets his comeuppance, the girl shares his outcast status. Ewing's sympathies clearly lie with an older water sprite's complaint about human affronts against his race: "[D]o them what good you may, in the long run you will reap nothing but ingratitude. From how many waters have they not already banished us?"[17]

Whereas Rossetti endorsed Lizzie's repudiation of repulsive goblin men, Ewing identifies herself with the plight of affronted little people who, unlike small children, have the power to retaliate for injuries suffered at the hands of adults as well as a capacity to reward their benefactors. "The Hillman and the Housewife" thus immediately reverses the emphasis of "The Nix in Mischief," published in the previous month. Now it is the alien creature, a rightly vindictive goblin, who punishes the mean-spirited peasant woman who tried to cheat him. And, in the more complicated plot of "Under the Sun," another such "dwarf or hill-man" gets the better of a miserly farmer who covets his industrious neighbor's land. This unsavory bargain-maker shows a canny awareness of traditional fairy tales when he assures his wife that he has no intention to repeat the mistakes made by sundry predecessors: "[W]e will not be like the foolish couple who wasted three wishes on black-puddings. Neither will I desire useless grandeur and unreasonable elevation, like the fisherman's wife. I will have a solid and substantial benefit."[18] Nonetheless, despite such generic sophistication, this clever man gets tripped up by a simple

16. Juliana Horatia Ewing, "The Nix in Mischief," *Aunt Judy's Magazine* 8, no. 48 (April 1870): 365.

17. Ibid., 363.

18. Juliana Horatia Ewing, "Under the Sun," *Aunt Judy's Magazine* 8, no. 48 (April 1870): 572.

linguistic trick child readers would cherish as much as the humiliation devised for him by the witty dwarf.

Ewing does not shy away from brutality. In "The Magic Jar," the last of the 1870 series, a young peasant defends a Jewish peddler from the abuse of country louts who threaten to beat up the old man and to smash his fragile wares. When the grateful merchant asks his protector to choose one jar as his reward, the youngster selects the most natural and least adorned. His choice, immediately commended by the donor, matches Ewing's belief in the value of restoring an unadorned tradition of oral tales told by *vieilles* or *Märchenfrauen*. For, appropriately enough, the old Jew explains that he serves a wise woman by dispensing magic to help those elect who differ from a mean-spirited multitude. Buyers coveting this same beautiful jar, he explains, have reviled him, incensed to hear that it costs as much as vases covered with gold and silver ornamentation. The jar benefits its new possessor, yet also kills a treacherous king who tries to steal it after the peasant has once again generously volunteered his help. The courtiers, sensing the young man's unusual qualities, immediately offer him the dead monarch's crown. Years later, after this kindly peasant-king's own death, the Jewish peddler reappears among the mourners. Undetected, he retrieves the precious jar, to be bestowed, presumably, on someone as worthy as this singular man.[19]

"The Magic Jar" is a fable that conveys Ewing's complete awareness of her own task. For the story's plot dramatizes her desire to place the contents of a once-potent tradition in the service of a quotidian reality. The young protagonist who rules so unselfishly resembles both Ewing and her putative readers. As the recipient of the deceptively simple jar, he obtains a container for a lost wisdom identified with forgotten foremothers. Yet he does not use the gifts he has earned for any self-indulgent motives or as an instrument of revenge. Uninterested in greater riches or further aggrandizement, he is content, like the old Jew, to act as a humble link between past and future. Like so many of Ewing's protagonists and narrators, he modestly assumes the role of mediator or transmitter.

The recovery of a female tradition by a male protagonist is even more overtly dramatized in "The First Wife's Wedding-Ring," which appeared a month before "The Magic Jar." Like *The King of the Golden River,* this

19. Juliana Horatia Ewing, "The Magic Jar," *Aunt Judy's Magazine* 8, no. 53 (September 1870): 697–701.

tale features a male Cinderella who might well have stepped out of the pages of the Brothers Grimm, or perhaps Ludwig Bechstein, Ewing's preferred author of German fairy tales.[20] But unlike Ruskin's feminized Gluck, this disinherited hero is quite masculine, an only "son, who soon after his mother's death, resolved to become a soldier, and go to foreign lands."[21] Yet shortly before returning to his remarried father, the discharged soldier discovers that his mother's wedding ring, which he always carried with him, has mysteriously disappeared. The loss of the ring jeopardizes his birthright and, indeed, strips him of his identity as his father's son. Although the feeble patriarch trusts the bronzed stranger who claims to be his firstborn, the old man's "artful and malicious" second wife, eager to push the interests of her own offspring, so strenuously discredits his narrative that he leaves the parental home, dispossessed and utterly marginalized.

Yet like Amelia and Benjy, the child-protagonists of the novellas examined in the next sections, the young soldier actually benefits from his exile into a different order of reality. Strong and resilient, but also hopelessly naive, he is confident that he can meet the terms set by a giant who proposes that he cut a pathway through a dense forest. If he reaches the other side of the woods after a year and a day, the soldier can keep royal jewels he will find there; but if he fails to reach the clearing, he must remain the giant's perpetual slave. As trustful as a small child, the muscular veteran starts wielding his axe. But the giant—who also happens to have been the thief who stole the maternal ring—is as treacherous as the king in "The Magic Jar." Without the opportune help of a "small weazened old woman," the energetic young man would surely have been cheated for a second time. For, as she promptly explains, the giant has deliberately placed him in the wrong spot. Having relocated the young man and asked him to start anew, the old woman, herself enslaved, must still teach him how to become more artful. She thus performs essentially the same task Ewing assigns to the slave woman who, in "Amelia and the Dwarfs," shows crafty Amelia how to outwit her captors. Yet, by acting as the boyish soldier's second mother, the woman also discharges the role Marie had played in "Friedrich's Ballad" and that Julie Gatty herself had presumably fulfilled when looking after the interests of her younger brothers.

20. See Gatty, *Juliana Horatia Ewing and Her Books,* 6–7.
21. Juliana Horatia Ewing, "The First Wife's Wedding-Ring," Aunt Judy's Magazine 8, no. 52 (August 1870), 579.

Despite her brief appearance, this wily mentoria is every bit as important to the plot of "The First Wife's Wedding-Ring" as the unseen wise
woman was in "The Magic Jar." For the young soldier who seems so irre-
trievably lost without his mother's ring is in sore need of some maternal
tutoring. To outwit the giant, the old woman suggests, he must learn the
art of fiction. The deceptions used by adults (or giants) must be mastered
and redirected. To lull the giant into believing that the woodcutter is still
on the wrong path, a decoy is needed. The old woman therefore advises
her ward to do a little "cutting at the old place from time to time, as a
blind."[22] The soldier is a quick learner: after each day's foray into the forest, he pretends to have made little progress by looking every bit "as
gloomy as before."[23] Able to reach the clearing on the appointed day, he
not only finds the jewels stolen from a king but also the purloined wedding ring. As honest as the protagonist of "The Magic Jar," he returns the
treasure to its owner, who promptly allows the young man to wed the
princess and become the royal heir. The defeated giant simply slinks away,
and so does the father's second wife, who, unlike the joyous old man, is
barred from the palace wedding.

"The First Wife's Wedding-Ring" follows the archetypal patterns of
Perrault's "Cendrillon" and the Grimms's "Aschenputtel": the death of a
mother leaves her offspring unprotected, at the mercy of a stepmother
whose influence causes the father to ignore his first child's legitimate
claims. But by changing the sex of the protagonist and by adding the giant
as a second villain, Ewing complicates the gender-politics of a plot of great
interest to other Victorian women writers.[24] The "good man" who marries
for a second time is hardly as uncaring as Cinderella's father. Worried that
he might not recognize the son who will grow up away from home, he
entrusts the youth with his first wife's ring as a token of the legitimacy of
claims he intends to honor as fully as the blind Isaac respected the birthright of Esau, his own firstborn, warrior son. Nor is the "artful and mali-

---

22. Ibid., 582.

23. Ibid.

24. Anne Thackeray Ritchie, Dinah Mulock Craik, Maria Louisa Molesworth, Florence Bell, and others prefer Perrault's version to that of the Grimms, since he features
the godmother's aid rather than a magical tree's agency, and makes the stepmother and
stepsisters less repulsive than their counterparts in the German version. Charlotte
Brontë, however, denies Jane Eyre the support of a female protector such as Cinderella's godmother.

cious" stepmother ever as cruel and unreasonable as her fairy tale prototypes: the child whose interests cause her to discredit the soldier is, after
all, the old man's own second son, a Jacob to his Isaac. The giant's inordinate greed, on the other hand, is less pardonable; not only does he hoard
stolen treasures, but wants to enslave men and women alike. Devious and
power-hungry, this robber disrupts basic human relations preserved in the
continuities of family, vocation, and labor. Although the Grimms would
surely have had the soldier decapitate him at the end of the story, his ostra-
cism seems a fitter punishment. He must now suffer the isolation he had
inflicted on others.

The young man's repossession of his mother's ring involves the recovery of a matrilineal heritage already aided by the old woman who, in godmotherly fashion, taught him something of the "artful" ways his stepmother had used against him: he can now place the ring on the finger of
his princess-bride and mend a broken circle. At the same time, however,
a debilitated patriarchal tradition, represented by the two fathers—the
soldier's and the princess's—has also been invigorated. Ironically enough,
the resolution of Ewing's terse and economical five-page tale thus happens
to be far more inclusive than the lush symbolic closure that Ruskin devised
for his five-chapter account of another male Cinderella's recovery of a maternal valley. Whereas Ruskin places Gluck in a world devoid of women,
Ewing's nameless soldier needs mothers, stepmothers, and godmothers to
succeed in a social order in which neither benevolent fathers nor treacherous employers can guarantee an industrious young man the rewards he
amply deserves.[25]

An enfeebled tradition also preoccupies Ewing in "Amelia and the
Dwarfs." Here, however, as in "Benjy and Beastland" and "The Brownies," the archetypal patterns so sparsely enlisted in the "Old Fashioned
Fairy Tales" are brought to bear on a vividly rendered and richly detailed
Victorian present. The parenting of permissive middle-class adults is so
deficient that their children need to be abducted and taken directly into a
more ruthless primal world in order to be re-educated. Thus, in "Amelia,"
it is not merely the symbolic loss of a dead mother's ring but rather a living
mother's lack of authority that fuels the plot. Wordsworth idealized the
child as father of the man. Ewing, however, charts the course by which an
extraordinarily clever little girl can eventually become mother to her well-

---

25. See note 32, below, for biographical links between Ruskin and Ewing.

meaning, but totally incompetent, "mamma." The superior child who so easily circumvents this ineffectual matriarch's rule must acquire self-control in a climate that is less "soft" than the cushioned drawing rooms through which she has been ushered. Before recovering his patrimony, the soldier in "The First Wife's Wedding-Ring" had to be toughened by his military life in "foreign lands" and then by his onerous servitude to the giant who lived at the forest's edge. Before she can be reunited with her mother, Amelia, too, must be tested in a hardy and alienating netherworld as servant to sadistic dwarfs. Although by the time she resurfaces in the parental home she is far wiser than the frazzled matron who thinks that Amelia is dying, the girl—a young woman now—can at last bring herself to love "the poor lady" unrestrictedly as "my dear, dear mother!" (AD, 125).

IV

The opening of "Amelia and the Dwarfs" immediately establishes a textual authority for the ensuing narrative. Whereas Ewing insisted that her "Old Fashioned Fairy Tales" were not old tales told anew, her novella retailors and greatly enriches materials that had once been orally transmitted in a venerable folkloric tradition. Ewing's narrator places herself at the end of a succession. The testimonials of five previous generations of female storytellers presumably authenticate the narrative she will relay:

My godmother's grandmother knew a good deal about the fairies. *Her* grandmother had seen a fairy rade on a Roodmas Eve, and she herself could remember a copper vessel of a queer shape which had been left by the elves on some occasion at an old farm-house among the hills. The following story came from her, and where she got it I do not know. She used to say that it was a pleasant tale, with a good moral in the inside of it. My godmother often observed that a tale without a moral was like a nut without a kernel, not worth the cracking. (AD, 105)

By invoking foremothers to verify her story, Ewing's narrator updates a folk wisdom once energized through periodic human contacts with fairy folk. She can thus, paradoxically, become closer to the story's protagonist than Amelia's own mother ever will. Hampered by her adherence to superficial routines, that genteel lady cannot bring herself to believe in Amelia's account of her rough underground apprenticeship among dwarfs.

The kinship between clever Amelia and the clever narrator, also manifest in several other ways, thus makes this story much more than an adult homily about the redemption of an insufferably bratty bourgeois child. For the godmother's point of view is quickly invoked again to validate Amelia's superiority over her parents. Their origins in Southern England, this northerner implies, may have prevented them from having their wits honed through encounters with the little folk still found in the more primitive regions of the British isles:[26]

They were an easy-going, good-humored couple; "rather soft," my godmother said, but she was apt to think anybody "soft" who came from the southern shires, as these people did. Amelia, who had been born farther north, was by no means so. She had a strong, resolute will, and a clever head of her own, though she was but a child. She had a way of her own too, and had it very completely. Perhaps because she was an only child, or perhaps because they were so easy-going, her parents spoiled her. She was, beyond question, the most tiresome little girl in that or any other neighborhood. From her baby days her father and mother had taken every opportunity of showing her to their friends, and there was not a friend who did not dread the infliction. (AD, 105–6)

In contrasting these "soft" parents to their strong and clever daughter, Ewing closely follows the precedent of "Wee Meg Barnileg and the Fairies," an Irish folktale she probably heard as a child—as did a modern transcriber of folktales, Ruth Sawyer, from a traditional storyteller. Just as the narrator of "Amelia" respects the point of view of the godmother who acts as her informant, so does Sawyer celebrate the "living art" of her Irish childhood nurse, Johanna. Johanna's telling of this particular story of child-power lost and regained profoundly impressed Sawyer: "I can hear the soft Irish burr on her tongue which made the words join and dance, making a fairy ring that completely encircled me. I can hear her begin the tale of 'Wee Meg Barnileg,' knowing it already well myself, and feeling the stinging mortification of Meg's behavior, which might well have been mine. But Johanna pointed no moral and drew no application. There was the tale—I could take it or leave it; and I always took it."[27]

If Sawyer's reconstruction of "Wee Meg" attempts to retain the cadences and the vocabulary of her nurse's voice, Ewing's freer adaptation still seems to preserve expressions that some other Johanna derived from

---

26. Whereas Margaret Scott was born in Essex and Alfred Gatty in London, all their children were born in Yorkshire; like Amelia, then, Juliana Gatty was "born farther north" than her parents (AD, 105).

27. Ruth Sawyer, *The Way of the Storyteller* (London: Penguin, 1986), 16, 17.

her own Irish precursors. Although both the narrator and the "gentlefolk" in "Amelia and the Dwarfs" speak in a language that is more cultivated than the dialect used by the farm folk in "Wee Meg Barnileg," it seems noteworthy that both versions should retain identical words, such as "soft," or identical phrases, such as "she had a way of her own," in order to accentuate the opposition between over-indulgent parents and their wayward child:

> There lived once by Lough Erne a rich farmer. He and the wife were a soft good-natured pair; come-easy-go-easy was the way they took the world and the world took them. They had one child, a girl by the name of Meg—Wee Meg Barnileg, they called her. Now there be's childher and childher, as ye well know; and ye might have traveled the world over to find one the match of Meg. She had a way of her own, and she had it entirely.
>
> It was: "Come hither and go yonder. Fetch that and take this," all with a stamp of the foot and a toss of the head and a spoiled look in the eye.
>
> When the pair went anywhere they fetched Meg with them, to fairs and feises, weddings and wakes; and when the neighbors put their eye to the window and saw the three of them coming they'd raise a wail ye could hear to Malin Head . . . (WMB, 205)

When Ewing changes colloquialisms such as "come-easy-go-easy" to "easy-going" and parcels out a phrase like "soft good-natured pair" by turning it into "good-humored couple; 'rather soft,'" she highlights words that can accrue further meaning in the course of her leisurely unfolding narrative. An original adjective like "soft" will soon come to connote parental soft-headedness and not just a permissiveness that stems from a kindly disposition.

Even more charged is the word "observing," used ironically both in Johanna's and Ewing's versions. Carroll's *Wonderland* narrator mocked Alice for being a "curious child." But when the farmwife calls Meg "a terribly observing child" and Ewing's "soft" gentlewoman calls Amelia "a very observing child," the irony is directed at the mother rather than at the offspring on whom she bestows that label. For the label only calls attention to each parent's own decidedly deficient powers of observation. Proud of their child's quick discernment, each chooses to overlook the misuses of that quickness. In both stories, neighbors fear the sharp eyes of a little girl who can immediately identify all breakable goods and yet utterly fail in observing proper behavior. Terrified farmers hide their "new butter crock" and best dishes, as well as newly laid eggs, as soon as Meg turns the corner (WMB, 206); and Ewing's gentlefolk, just as intimidated, "snatch up any delicate knick-knacks, or brittle ornaments lying about" in anticipation of Amelia's visit (AD, 106).

Despite this emphasis on an unchecked destructiveness, however, each narrative also validates the uniqueness of a child shrewd enough to see through adult veneers and highly skilled at piercing adult defenses. Meg specializes in publicly embarrassing grown-ups by disclosing what they assiduously try to conceal: "she was one of them pleasant kind that told everything she saw and more that she didn't" (WMB, 206). And Amelia crowns her own public acts of exposure with climactic flourishes calculated to produce the widest possible effect. As deft as Meg in denouncing the inadequacy of "chintz" coverings passed off as more costly materials, she takes even more drastic actions against other forms of imposture. Glued ceramics that belie their broken condition are especially offensive to this scourge of bourgeois pretentiousness. Balancing a mended china bowl "on her finger ends," Amelia carefully waits until her mother gets appropriately flustered:

... and when Amelia flurried her, she always rolled her r's, and emphasized her words, so that it sounded thus:

"My dear-r-r-r Ramelia! You MUST NOT."

At which Amelia would not so much as look round, till perhaps the bowl slipped from her fingers, and was smashed into unmendable fragments. Then her mamma would exclaim, "Oh, dear-r-r, oh dear-r Ramelia!" and the lady of the house would look as if it did not matter, and when Amelia and her mother departed, would pick up the bits, and pour out her complaints to her lady friends, most of whom had suffered many such damages at the hands of this "very oberving child." (AD, 106–7)

As the narrator's carefully placed "perhaps" suggests, Amelia masks design as accidents, thus blunting all adult efforts to hold her responsible for her depredations. Befitting her higher social status, this drawing-room tactitian has refined subversive strategies that go beyond Meg's deliberate brashness. At a wake, Meg loudly asks her father, in everyone's hearing, whether it was not true that he had frequently referred to the deceased, one Barney Gallagher, as "the tightest man in Donegal?" (WMB, 206). But Amelia reserves her craftiest assaults for more intimate social occasions. Although she can wreak havoc in other people's houses, she is at her terrifying best whenever her parents receive "their friends at home" (AD, 107). It is on her home turf, after all, that guests are forced to remain extra polite and hence are least likely to protest her calculated acts of aggression. Amelia chooses her victims carefully. She positions herself near "the person most deeply engaged in conversation" or breaks "by force" one of the delicate "divisions" of a bracelet that some luckless lady allowed her to try on. The visitor may well deduce that such an unusually clever child can hardly have been stumped by the simple "working of a clasp." But she can no more denounce such guerrilla tactics than can the young ladies whom Amelia startles just as they had hoped to settle down in some "quiet corner for a chat" (AD, 107):

> The observing child was sure to spy them, and run on to them, crushing their flowers and ribbons, and crying—"you two want to tell secrets, I know. I can hear what you say. I am going to listen, I am. And I shall tell, too." When perhaps a knock at the door announced the nurse to take Miss Amelia to bed, and spread a general rapture of relief. (AD, 107)

Ewing's narrator might denounce Amelia as "the most tiresome" little girl in the vicinity. But the relish with which she reproduces Amelia's clever assaults on neighbors she herself satirizes for their blandness also suggests that there is a tacit alliance between these two ironists. That alliance does not operate in "Wee Meg Barnileg," where Johanna is less distanced from outspoken neighbors who openly complain about Meg's transgressions.

In "Amelia and the Dwarfs," however, the genteel adults persistently pestered by this crafty child observe codes of restraint that Amelia deliciously exploits and the narrator slyly exposes as being unnatural and even hypocritical. Since "Amelia's mamma's acquaintances were too polite to complain before her face," the narrator informs us, "they made up for it by what they said behind her back" (AD, 109). Their covert sarcasms are pointedly contrasted to the directness with which Amelia's next set of victims respond to her taunts. Though "really fond of dogs," Amelia cannot forbear treating animals much in the way she handles her mother's guests. She treads on tails as readily as she tramples on the "gathers" of ladies' dresses and withdraws expected morsels of food as quickly as she upsets the glasses she spills on gentlemen's shirt-fronts. But the animals she annoys are not inhibited by any false show of drawing-room politeness. Provided with a fine set of front teeth, the bulldog, who will assume a prominent role in Ewing's narrative,[28] does not have to resort to the verbal

---

28. By way of contrast, the animal whom Meg teases—a chained watchdog belonging to neighbors—merely precipitates her flight to the "wee men." He is invoked at the end, but only to suggest the extent of her reformation: "'Dear me,' said Meg, natural-like, 'I hope you didn't shoot the dog. He'd never have nipped me if I hadn't the life plagued out of him'" (WMB, 216).

backbiting through which more inhibited humans express their own frustrations and anger:

Now Amelia's mother's acquaintances were so very well-bred and amiable, that they never spoke their minds to either the mother or the daughter about what they endured from the latter's rudeness, willfulness, and powers of destruction. But this was not the case with the dogs, and they expressed their sentiments by many a growl and a snap. At last one day Amelia was tormenting a snow-white bull-dog (who was certainly as well-bred and as amiable as any creature in the kingdom), and she did not see that even his patience was becoming worn out. His pink nose became crimson with increased irritation, his upper lip twitched over his teeth, behind which he was rolling as many warning Rs as Amelia's mother herself. She finally held out a bun towards him. And just as he was about to take it, she snatched it away and kicked him instead. This fairly exasperated the bull-dog, and as Amelia would not let him bite the bun, he bit Amelia's leg. (AD, 108)

In both "Wee Meg Barnileg" and "Amelia and the Dwarfs," the dog's bite acts as a catalyst by allowing adults to express their own pent-up aggression. But Ewing significantly shifts the emphasis of the original Irish folktale, where the dog's "nip" brings out in public the anger harbored by Meg's long-suffering neighbors:

Ye should have heard the hurly-burly the pair raised the length and breadth of Ireland, Meg crying and the dog howling. The neighbors came running. Some were for killing the dog and burning the leg. They rushed this way and that for a gun and a pair of red-hot tongs, crying and wringing their hands. And so mixed up and muddle-minded did they get that they couldn't tell at the last was it the dog or Meg they'd shoot.

"If it was me ye're asking, I'd say shoot them both and make good work of it," said one of the sour-dispositioned neighbors who had stood more from Meg than most.

"'Tis a good dog—leave him be. But the child is bad entirely. If ye must shoot one, shoot her," was another's bit of advice.

It was Wee Meg herself who settled it; she took one good look at the hard set faces about her, and then she took to her heels and put distance aplenty atween her and the neighbors. (WMB, 209)

Such unvarnished expressions of the hatred Meg has fostered go far beyond a howling dog's harmless nip. Frightened by the threats she overhears, the girl flees from the intense animosity she must at last acknowledge, only to be captured by the equally affronted (and equally sadistic) wee men, who undertake the task of completing her conversion.

In "Amelia and the Dwarfs," however, the same interlude allows Ewing to suggest that a dog may be superior to human adults as an educator of intractable little girls. No threatening neighbors appear in her version of the scene, only a physician who confirms that Amelia's wound is slight and who astutely perceives, on examining the bulldog, that "he looked a great deal more sensible than anybody in the house" (AD, 109). Although Amelia, like Meg, is found "crying bitterly," neither her injury nor fear of a painful treatment causes her tears. Instead, she is worried about the bull-dog's fate: "She was telling him that they wanted to shoot him, but that they should not, for it was all her fault and not his" (AD, 108). The doctor who overhears this conversation finds the dog to be more nurturant than Amelia's mother, who has left her alone, running out in "hysterics," distraught and bonnet-less: "the bull-dog kissed [Amelia] with his red tongue, and rubbed his pink nose against her, and beat his own tail much harder on the floor than Amelia had ever hit it" (AD, 108, 109).

Ewing uses this episode to show Amelia's tractability: the child's responsiveness to the dog's punitive measures as well as to his loving solicitude augurs well for her eventual transformation into a young lady capable of tolerating parental ineptitude. At the same time, however, Ewing also enlists this canine educator as a comic foil for those inept parents. The open anger shown by Meg's "sour-dispositioned" neighbors is now attributed, with a shrewd, pre-Freudian grasp of the mechanics of psychological displacement, to none other than Amelia's well-intentioned, but hopelessly addled, mother. Unlike Ewing's own mother, a firm believer in the virtues of chloroform, this frantic lady is convinced that her child will die if drugged while having her wound cauterized, "for as one in several thousands dies annually under chloroform, it was evident that her chance of life was very small indeed" (AD, 108). Rattled about what course to take, she catches herself in a revealing slip of the tongue: "Whether we shoot Amelia and burn the bull-dog—at least I mean shoot the bull-dog and burn Amelia with a red-hot poker—or leave it alone; and whether Amelia or the bull-dog has chloroform or bears it without—it seems to be death or madness everyway!" (AD, 108).

Amelia's education requires another "sensible" mentor whom Ewing also places in the parental household. The bulldog's "good lesson on manners" causes the girl to behave with "utmost propriety to animals" thereafter (AD, 109); but she remains as unchecked as ever in her social affronts to her fellow humans. When her overworked nurse tries to offer much-needed correctives, she is totally unsuccessful, since her status as a servant prevents her from exercising the authority Amelia's mother has abdicated.

Unable to implant or enforce rules, the nurse can at best appeal to her ward's good sense, only to be insulted in ways that the otherwise amused narrator finds decidedly unfunny. When the nurse protests that some other "poor child" might welcome "what you waste every meal time, Miss Amelia," she is promptly undercut by the mother's permissive habits: "But Amelia's mamma allowed her to send away on her plates what would have fed another child, day after day" (AD, 110–11). And when she remonstrates about the stained frocks and irreparably shredded dresses she must try to wash and mend, the nurse is haughtily rebuffed by this child of privilege:

> "You seem to think things clean and mend themselves, Miss Amelia," said poor nurse one day.
>
> "No, I don't," said Amelia, rudely. "I think you do them; what are you here for?"
>
> But though she spoke in this insolent and unladylike fashion, Amelia really did not realize what the tasks were which her carelessness imposed on other people. When every hour of nurse's day had been spent in struggling to keep her willful young lady regularly fed, decently dressed, and moderately well-behaved (except, indeed, those hours in which her mother was fighting the same battle downstairs); and when at last, after the hardest struggle of all, she had been got to bed no more than two hours later than her appointed time, even then there was no rest for nurse. Amelia's mamma could at least lean back in her chair and have a quiet chat with her husband, which was not broken up every two minutes, and Amelia herself was asleep; but nurse must sit up for hours wearing out her eyes by the light of a tallow candle, in fine-darning great, jagged and most unnecessary holes in Amelia's dresses. (AD, 110)

For the narrator, Amelia's disregard of her social inferiors is a far greater dereliction than any discomforts she might inflict on her parents and their friends. Although Ewing hardly exculpates the girl she now calls rude, insolent, and unladylike, she also suggests that Amelia's total unawareness of the excessive demands she places on those paid to serve her is attributable to her mother. For that lady seems as oblivious as her child to the duties and social responsibilities inherent in the class system to which she belongs. Amelia cannot be expected to become a future "lady" without the kind of palpable example that Margaret Gatty set for her children in real life. As the contrast between the mamma who relaxes in the living room and the servant who must wear out her eyes in a poorly lighted attic suggests, this matriarch has given little thought to the workload her willful daughter imposes on those entrusted with her daily care.

This social critique—the "domestic part" that Gatty found "so *real*"—

sets the stage for the story's second half, with its "supernatural machinery." Unlike Meg, whose sojourn among the "wee men" merely makes her a more tractable farmer's daughter, Amelia needs to be radically lowered in class in order to become a more thoughtful "lady."[29] It is significant that Amelia's nurse—a figure not found in the story told by Johanna, herself a nurse—should also act as a stimulus for Amelia's venture into a fantasyland. For she alludes to the fairies in a fruitless attempt to prevent Amelia from returning to a moon-bathed hayfield in which the child had earlier romped and been "shaken" by a fall:[30] "Now, my dear Miss Amelia, do go quietly to bed, like a dear love. The field is all wet with dew. Besides, it's a moonlight night, and who knows what's abroad! You might see the fairies—bless us and sain us!" (AD, 111). Yet the warning only incites Amelia to undertake the night journey that leads to her capture by the little green men.

The sadism of Carroll's underground denizens, like Alice's bodily changes, seemed at odds with his infatuation with that "curious child." And the tortures inflicted on Flora, the first of Rossetti's three Alice substitutes, greatly exceeded that eight-year-old's faults. But when Ewing's "observing child" is herded underground by dwarfs who pinch her funny bone with "lean fingers" and tread on her heels with "long-pointed" shoes (AD, 113), the sadism seems fully merited. For even though these creatures are contemptuous of the inhabitants of Amelia's world, they also act as retributive avengers. They fool the parents and the nurse by replacing Amelia with a double whose moans attract the humans who promptly carry it indoors with "exclamations of pity and surprise" (AD, 114). Yet the servitude they now impose on Amelia involves tasks of restitution and acts of amendment for each of her infractions in the world above. Forced to wash and darn her own clothes, to eat cold scraps of all the foods she

29. This beneficial "lowering," in which bourgeois characters are reschooled in values that come from ungenteel work, is as much a feature of "adult" Victorian fiction as of children's classics such as Frances Hodgson Burnett's *A Little Princess* (a work actually indebted to Ewing in other ways). Dickens's works are full of such hard apprenticeships, as the young David Copperfield or the older John Harmon enter conditions of servitude before reassuming a place in genteel society. And even in *Middlemarch,* the novel that Virginia Woolf considered more "grown-up" than the "childish" productions of Dickens, Fred Vincy gives up the gentlemanly pretensions and his university education in order to live a productive life with Mary Garth.

30. Like Maggie's in *Speaking Likenesses,* that fall may have caused a slight concussion, thus providing a realistic explanation for Amelia's coma in the "real" world.

rejected, to mend the gimcracks she has broken, Amelia is exempted only from trying to disentangle "the broken threads of all the conversations" she has interrupted, since, as an old dwarf explains to younger goblins, "There are very few drawing-room conversations worth putting together a second time" (AD, 122).

To match the roles she assigned to the bulldog and the nurse in the domestic realm above ground, Ewing creates a third authority figure to guide Amelia throughout her servitude in the dwarfs' murky netherworld and to help her return to her parents. In the original folktale, Meg is taken to washtubs by an "old fairy woman" who cruelly tells the child that her absence surely pleases parents and neighbors now unmolested "for the first time" (WMB, 214). But Ewing converts the elderly woman Amelia meets into a mentoria such as the apple woman in Ingelow's *Mopsa the Fairy* or the crone in her own story of "The First Wife's Wedding Ring." And, what is more, she insists on making her a fellow-captive who "seemed to be a real woman, not a fairy—which was the case, as Amelia afterwards found. She had lived underground for many years and was the dwarfs' servant" (AD, 115).

It is no coincidence that this fellow-laborer should appear just after Amelia learns from the dwarfs that washing her dirty frocks is no longer her nurse's "business," as she persisted in believing: "What nurse can do she has done, and now it's time for you to begin" (AD, 115). Stripped of her superior social position, Amelia now gratefully accepts the identification she had denied to her nurse in the hierarchical world above. This kind female worker thus acts as the nurse's underground double, as well as the new Amelia's kin, and hence functions as what Rossetti would have called a "speaking likeness." Given her ability to help Amelia outwit the dwarfs, she also is Ewing's equivalent for the maternal Lizzie in "Goblin Market." In a fairy tale and in a poem where there seem to be no female fairies, "real" women are called upon to protect girls from the predations of goblin men. But instead of being cast as an inviolate older sister, this maternal instructress and rescuer of a female transgressor is depicted as a figure bent by experience. Given the unmistakable sexual interest that Amelia soon arouses in the dwarfs, the woman who has sojourned among them for so "many years" may well have been abducted when she was herself still young, lively, and desirable.

The old woman warms up to the increasingly docile Amelia, especially after the girl cooks for her and entertains her with "stories and pieces of poetry" (AD, 118). But she cautions Amelia that, paradoxically enough, her attractiveness may have become a liability: "You see, when you first came you were—excuse me!—such an unlicked cub; such a peevish, selfish, wilful, useless, and ill-mannered little miss, that the fairies nor anybody else were likely to keep you any longer than necessary. But now you are such a willing, handy, and civil little thing, and so pretty and graceful withal, that I think it is very likely that they will want to keep you altogether" (AD, 118). Ewing clearly relishes the irony involved. An ideology that values the submissiveness of "pure" little girls also privileges those who are the prettiest and most graceful. Despite her recent domestication, Amelia thus must fall back on the artful subversions she perfected in the world above. To trick the dwarfs, the old woman insists, she should feign to be happy. And, since "dwarfs love dancing," she advises Amelia to dance as provocatively as possible to relax their guard (AD, 119).

Deviousness can now be placed in the service of the social order to which Amelia is ready to return. Confident of her credentials as a "clever" dancer, and, as soon becomes evident, of her sex appeal, Amelia requires no further coaching by the old woman. An especially "grotesque and grimy old dwarf" is so smitten with her performance as she seductively holds "out her little skirt" and begins gyrating in "one of her prettiest dances" that she soon gets him to do her own work (AD, 119–20). Showing a new solicitude for those less fortunate than herself, Amelia offers to help the old servant woman to regain her own freedom. But like Ingelow's apple woman, this exile does not "care to return" to the world she left behind so long ago (AD, 119). Drained of the vitality Amelia so amply enjoys, she accepts her burdens with the same equanimity that Ewing attributed to the ailing and paralyzed Margaret Gatty in the 1873 eulogy of her mother.

In *The Rose and the Ring,* written more than two decades before "Amelia and the Dwarfs," Thackeray had boldly introduced adult sexuality into a fairy tale written for children when he had a succession of lustful autocrats pursue the hapless Rosalba. By dwelling on the "smutty and very old" dwarf who proves to be Amelia's ticket to freedom, Ewing also injects sexual comedy into the folktale she so greatly complicates. Amelia's mazurkas with this "queer partner," who tries to hold on to her waist as tightly as possible while his protruding shoes are "very much in the way" (AD, 121), may not be quite as erotically charged as the intertwining bodies of Laura and Lizzie in "Goblin Market." But the unmistakable erotic overtones serve a double purpose by confirming Amelia's physical matura-tion and by allowing Ewing to satirize, with Thackerayan gusto, the one-sidedness of a dirty old child-lover's infatuation.

Amelia and Ewing have become allies again. They jointly expose the self-delusions of older males who firmly believe that their desire for little girls must automatically be reciprocated by the object of their affections: "'Look how content she is,' said the old dwarf, 'and, oh! how she dances, my feet tickle at the bare thought.' . . . 'We are partners in the dance, and I think we will be partners for life. But I have not fully considered the matter, so this is not to be regarded as a formal proposal'" (AD, 123). Unlike Rossetti, Ewing would hardly have wanted to offend the famous "Author of 'Alice's Adventures in Wonderland,'" who remained an occa-sional contributor to *Aunt Judy's Magazine*.[31] Yet it is difficult not to con-nect her comical underground child-lover to Lewis Carroll's own self-reductions as the permanent partner of an ever-small Alice.

Back in her mother's world, Amelia draws strength from her under-ground schooling in paradox. She is now as socialized as Meg, who, by the end of Johanna's story, is so reformed that she becomes proverbially known as the progenitor of "well-bred" children and great-great-grandchildren (WMB, 216). But the girl who outwitted the dwarfs by craftily engineering an escape that, for Meg, was merely accidental, must continue to rely on her powers of dissimulation. Amelia accepts her dis-tracted and confused mother, but, at the same time, recognizes that her venture into fantasyland will forever place her apart from her more ordi-nary fellow-mortals. She cannot transmit the story of her adventures, for not "even the nurse would believe in them." Only the bulldog can become a secret sharer, who signifies through "sympathetic whines the sentiment 'Of course I would have helped you if I could; but they tied me up'" (WMB, 126, 127). Amelia, too, finds herself "tied up," isolated by virtue of her very uniqueness.

Like Meg, she is now upheld as an example by the adults she had for-

---

31. In December 1870 and January 1871, Carroll contributed the rather negligible "Puzzles from Wonderland" to the magazine. Puzzle Four asks: "What is most like a bee in May? / 'Well let me think: perhaps—' you say. / Bravo! You're guessing well to-day!" (*Aunt Judy's Magazine* 9, no. 56 [December 1870]: 102; and, a month later, the explanation appears: "'Twixt 'Perhaps' and 'May be' / Little difference we see: / Let the question go round, / The answer is found" (*Aunt Judy's Magazine* 9, no. 57 [January 1871]: 187).

merly tortured: "she became so popular with her mother's acquaintances that they said—'We will no longer call her Amelia, for it was a name we learnt to dislike, but we will call her Amy, that is to say, "Beloved"'" (AD, 127). But Ewing ironizes the public approval bestowed by the very same "amiable" folk she had earlier satirized for their secret disapproval. By pointing out that the girl who grows up to be "good and gentle, unselfish and considerate for others," also remains "unusually clever, as those who have been with the 'Little People' are said always to be," she suggests that the old Amelia still survives beneath the new "Amy." The people who rename Amelia to signify her presumed acceptance of their conventionality may have been as hoodwinked as her captors in the world below. Amelia's contrition is genuine, but her acquiescence is self-imposed, a measure of her strength and resolute will. Her observance of manners in no way makes her less observing than before. Her maturation only strengthens her resemblance to a narrator who is hardly an unquestioning member of her society. Amelia has also joined the foremothers invoked at the opening of the tale. For the narrator reminds us in the story's last sentence that "my godmother's grandmother" was as skilled as Amelia in the art of concealment, by resolutely refusing to say whether the girl "had really been with the fairies" or merely had given in to "fever ravings" (AD, 127).

V

In "Benjy and Beastland" (May and June 1870) and "Timothy's Shoes" (November and December 1870; January 1871), Ewing rendered the unusual education of two little boys as vividly and imaginatively as she had depicted Amelia's schooling among the dwarfs. "Benjy," the first installment of which appeared in *Aunt Judy's Magazine* only two months after the concluding portion of "Amelia," was clearly designed as a pendant to the earlier story. In outline, the plots seem near-identical: a child in sore need of a training unavailable at either home or school must be immersed into a harsh fantasy world if it is to grow up into a responsible adult. Yet whereas "Amelia" converts an old folktale into a comedy of manners, "Benjy in Beastland" is a much darker fable, closer to George MacDonald's most somber symbolic fairy tales of destruction and resurrection than to the burlesque mode of Thackeray. The story's highly playful opening thus misleads readers to expect a more genial narrative:

Benjy was a bad boy. His name was Benjamin, but he was always called Benjy. He looked like something ending in jy or gy, or rather dgy, such as *podgy*. Indeed he was podgy, and moreover smudgy, having that cloudy, slovenly look (like a slate *smudged* instead of washed) which is characteristic of people whose morning toilet is not so thorough as it should be.

Now I am very fond of boys. I do not think, with some people, that they are nuisances to be endured as best may till they develop into men. I think that an intelligent and modest boy is one of the most charming of companions. As to an obliging boy (that somewhat rare but not extinct animal), there is hardly a limit to his powers of usefulness; or anything—from emigrating to a desert island to cleaning the kitchen clock—that one would not feel justified in undertaking with his assistance, and free access to his pocket stores. (BB, 411)

The "smudgy" boy described in the opening paragraph clearly falls short of the generic specimens of boyhood the narrator professes to like. Such boys might be entrusted as travel companions of girl fairies such as Mopsa, or, in the actual world, even be counted upon to share this rather scientifically minded narrator's interest in specimens of nonhuman life: "Then what admirable naturalists boys can make. They are none the worse for nocturnal moth hunts, or wading up a stream for a Batrachtosperma, or standing in a pond pressing recruits for the fresh water-aquarium. A 'collection' more or less is as nothing in the vast chaos of their possessions, though some scrupulous sister might be worried to find 'a place for it'" (BB, 410).

Yet the narrator's tone changes as soon as she returns to Benjy himself. She may be fond of boys in general, but this particular boy merits none of the empathy bestowed on the lively and uniquely clever Amelia. With the exception of the bulldog, soon her best friend, Amelia's victims were adults, whose superior powers she challenged and circumvented. But the morose and asocial Benjy, whose sole associate is "a coarse, cruel, and uneducated lad, whose ideas of 'fun' Benjy unfortunately made his own," is a coward who persecutes weaker creatures incapable of retaliating. His cruelty to animals is not just a "fault" but "*the* vice of his character." As a bully, he has developed a "taste for torture, that pleasure in other creatures' pain, which does seem to be born with some boys." The cruelty of the dwarfs who harassed Amelia served a purpose. Benjy's sadism sets him apart; it "certainly seems more near to a fiendish characteristic," according to the narrator, "than to rank as a human infirmity" (BB, 411).

Amelia's rehabilitation could be undertaken by a series of parental surrogates. Ewing suggests that Benjy, too, is "without due control and companionship": his father is "an invalid" and there are "no brothers," only "two little sisters," who are younger and whom he holds in "supreme contempt" (BB, 411–12). Adult women, so prominent in "Amelia," are hardly visible in this story of a boy who belongs to a class known for sneering "at feminine society" (BB, 411). A mother, briefly mentioned in the course of the narrative, seems to have had little effect on her repulsive offspring. Since Benjy's vicious delight in seeing animals tortured and killed cannot be solely attributed to parental permissiveness or the lack of proper role models, his redemption demands more than the reaffirmation of a traditional female authority.

In "Amelia and the Dwarfs," that authority was exercised by a narrator who places her protagonist within the strong matriarchal lineage with which she affiliates herself. In "Benjy in Beastland," however, the narrator refuses to fall back on the folkloric wisdom of foremothers. Instead of relying on a narrative passed down by generations of rustic female storytellers, Ewing concocts a fable that significantly deepens her mother's mixture of theology and science in her own *Parables of Nature*. The narrator who knows all about water creatures such as batrachosperma is very different from the persona Ewing had employed in "Amelia." For this scientific moralist, who engages child readers in a more direct I-you dialogue, sets out to validate the sacredness of a natural order that Benjy daily affronts. There is no need of figures such as the nurse or the old woman captive. Instead, the male bulldog whose role Ewing expanded in "Amelia" is now replaced by two canine protagonists, "Mister Rough," an old terrier whom Benjy has taught how to kill cats, and "Nox," the "big, curly dog, partly retriever and partly of Newfoundland breed" (BB, 412), who, by eventually saving Benjy's life, also brings about the boy's redemption.

Ewing contrasts Benjy the destroyer to Nox the preserver through a series of sharp appositions:

Benjy, to look at, was smudgy and slovenly, and not at all handsome, for he hated tubs, and brushes, and soap, and cold water, and he liked to lie late in a morning, and then was apt to shuffle off his clothes and come down after very imperfect ablutions, having forgotten to brush his teeth, and with his hair still in dusty 'cockatoos' from tossing about in bed.

Nox rose early, delighted in cold water, and had teeth like ivory, and hair as glossy as a raven's wing, his face beamed with intelligence and trustfulness, and his clear brown eyes looked straight into yours when you spoke to him, as if he would say, "Let my eyes speak for me, if you please; I have not the pleasure of understanding your language."

Benjy's waistcoat and shirt-front were often spotted with dirt, and generally untidy.

The covering of Nox's broad chest was always glossy and in good order.

Benjy would come into the drawing-room with muddy boots and dirty hands.

Nox, if he had been out in the mud, would lie down on his return and lick his broad soft brown paws like a cat till they were clean.

It has been said that Benjy did not appreciate the society of girls; but when Nox was petted by his lady-sisters, he put his big head on their shoulders, and licked their faces with his big red tongue (which was his way of kissing). . . .

Benjy destroyed lives with much wanton cruelty.

Nox had saved lives at the risk of his own. (BB, 412–413)

Ewing is careful not to anthropomorphize the dog into someone more human than Benjy. Instead, her juxtapositions have the effect of making Benjy seem all the more unnatural, sub-animalistic as well as sub-human. For Nox merely carries out "his retriever instincts" when he fetches anything that "does not properly or naturally belong to the water": he feels bound to salvage dead animals in various states of decomposition as much as drowning children, always ending the operation by carefully depositing on the shore all the "bodies he rescued from the river" (BB, 414, 413). Moreover, as the narrator quickly notes, these bodies may never have belonged to an animated Nature: "I use the word bodies in the most scientific sense, for it was not alone the bodies of men and animals that Nox felt himself bound to reclaim. He would strive desperately for the rescue of an old riding-boot, the rung of a chair, a worn-out hearthbrush, or anything obviously out of place in the deep waters" (BB, 413).

Having cruelly caused Nox far more pain than the irritations Amelia or Meg had inflicted on dogs, Benjy expects the animal to avenge itself when he is thrust into a situation that makes him as helpless as any of his former victims. But unlike Amelia's justifiably irritated bulldog, Nox is incapable of resentment. By simply remaining true to his natural instincts, the huge retriever discharges a function reserved for humans or fairies in Ewing's other fairy tales. If Ewing transformed a folktale into a social comedy in "Amelia," in "Benjy in Beastland" she blends theology and natural science in a parable of nature that boldly makes an ordinary dog into a savior capable of effecting a conversion. By hauling Benjy out of the water, Nox cleanses the sinner whom the narrator had likened to an unwashed slate. The death of Mister Rough completes Benjy's conversion, washing any remnant of smudginess "away from him body and soul." The boy who seemed utterly beyond redemption will, as a man, become "a first-rate naturalist, and a good friend to beasts" (BB, 461).

Yet Ewing also departs from the mode of Gatty's *Parables of Nature* by once again introducing fantastic elements that powerfully reenforce rather than clash with her tale's moral naturalism. Like Amelia, Benjy undertakes a nocturnal expedition in a moon-bathed landscape before he is rescued by the dog named Night. Having killed a smaller dog, whose corpse he threw into the river, the boy returns to the scene of his crime, hoping to retrieve the body with a pitchfork "and hide or bury it" (BB, 417). It is at this point that he is lured into a hallucinatory Beastland, a realm based on "a book that had been his mother's and now belonged to his sisters, in which it was amusingly pretended that dogs went to the moon after their existence on earth was over" (BB, 417). Trying to climb up towards the large moon, the boy finds himself falling, only to move up, after all, much like MacDonald's Diamond did in his own dream of a lunar voyage.

Benjy's venture into that "beautiful place" begins auspiciously enough: the excited creatures who reside there are "all free" and are as herbivorous as the animals were before the Fall in Milton's Eden (BB, 451). The emphasis is on creativity and construction. Beavers, with faces "as glossy as that of Nox," show off their prowess as builders, as does a small "caddis worm" whose "own house bore witness to similar patience and skill" (BB, 452–53). But when Benjy is exposed as a destroyer of animal life and hauled before a jury composed of victims of human cruelty, the testimony of his old dog, Mister Rough, confirms his guilt. Expelled and humiliated rather than condemned to death, he is chased, with a kettle tied to his back, "till he got to the end of the moon and jumped off, Mister Rough jumping after him" (BB, 456). Alice's fall now has become transformed into a nightmare that accentuates Benjy's fear of death: "Down, down they went past the Great Bear (where were all the ghosts of the big wild beasts); past the Little Bear (where were the ghosts of all the small wild beasts); close by the Dog Star, where good dogs go when they die" (BB, 456). At last landing in the water, Benjy, no more able to swim than the kittens and pups he drowned, chokes and gasps and struggles, "as his victims had so often choked, and gasped, and struggled under his eyes." And, for the first time, as "the remembrance of all his cruelties" floods his mind, Benjy finds that he truly "loathed himself" (BB, 457). He has at last gained a moral sense. As he sinks and rises to the surface for the third and last time, he is rescued by Nox, as efficient and matter-of-fact as ever:

... close to Benjy's pallid face was a soft black nose, and large brown eyes met his with an expression neither revengeful nor affectionate. It was business-like, earnest, and somewhat eager and proud. And then the soft, sensitive mouth he had wounded seized Benjy with a hold as firm and as gentle as if he had been a rare water-fowl, and Nox paddled himself round with his broad, brown paws, and made gallantly for shore. Podgy Benjy was much heavier than a dead cat, and the big brave beast had hard work of it. (BB, 459)

When, later in 1870, Ewing complemented this grim tale with another story about a boy's maturation, she returned to the comic mode she had perfected in "Amelia and the Dwarfs." Despite its deliciously funny mode, however, "Timothy's Shoes" departs from her earlier fairy tales by dispensing with the account of ventures into bizarre fantasylands and importing, instead, a homely but powerful "magic" object into the everyday world. A utilitarian godmother, reminiscent of Thackeray's equally practical Fairy Blackstick, arrives at the christening of her goddaughter's first child with "a small brown-paper parcel in her hand" (TS, 4). The gift is neither a Fortunatus's purse nor the golden mug expected by the university-educated schoolmaster, who has undoubtedly read Ruskin's *King of the Golden River*. The godmother explains "that the experience of many centuries has almost convinced us poor fairies that extraordinary gifts are not necessarily blessings"; she has therefore brought a "mere trifle," a "very common gift" that she nonetheless expects "will prove useful": "*a small pair of strong leather shoes, copper tipped and heeled.*" Since she correctly anticipates that the new mother will eventually be blessed with a large family, the shoes, which will never wear out, can be passed from one child to the next "just at the age when little feet are most destructive" (TS, 5).

When the "sensible, sweet-tempered" goddaughter abandons whatever "ambitious day-dreams" she had harbored and earnestly thanks the old lady, the fairy starts to explain that her gift also possesses magical properties that may hold special value for little boys disposed to stray:

"If your children inherit your good sense and good temper, my love, they will need nothing an old woman like me can give them," said she; "but, all the same, my gift is not *quite* so shabby as it looks. These shoes have another quality besides that of not wearing out. The little feet that are in them cannot very easily go wrong. If, when your boy is old enough, you send him to school in these shoes, should he be disposed to play truant, they will pinch and discomfit him so that it is probable he will let his shoes take him the right way; they will in like manner bring him home at the proper time. And—"

"Mrs. Godmother's broomstick at the door!" shouted the farming man who was acting as footman on this occasion.

"Well, my dear," said the old lady, "you will find out their virtues all in good time, and they will do for the whole family in turn; for I really can come to no more christenings. I am getting old—besides our day is over. Farewell, my love." And mounting her broomstick, the fairy finally departed. (TS, 5–6)

The godmother's parting insistence that the days of fairies are over seems to betoken Ewing's own farewell to the genre she had helped to revitalize. Longer than either "Amelia and the Dwarfs" or "Benjy in Beastland," the comical account of Timothy's repeated attempts to rid himself of shoes he had inherited from his eight older brothers can almost be read as an allegory about the transmission of authority and, hence, of fairy tales as a vehicle for that very process of transmission. Just as the godmother departs on her broomstick at the opening of the tale, so do the magic shoes that Timothy ultimately outgrows disappear to an unknown destination at the story's closure. When the dozing mother hears the clatter of shoes coming down the stairs, the "habit of years" makes her think that a tenth child might soon tumble down the stairs. But the shoes are now empty: "Down the stairs they went, and they ran with that music of a childish patter that no foot in the house could make now." Knowing the house to be locked, the mother hopes that the shoes "can't go right away yet." But she hears the house door turn slowly on its hinges and watches the "little shoes" patter through the garden, through the gate that opens for them until they disappear, "leaving little footprints in the dew" (TS, 160).

The shoes have served their purpose, and so have those other containers Ewing has used for educational purposes, the fairy tales that have also left little print marks on pages as well as on young minds. The mother nostalgically reflects on the value that those training devices held for her growing boys over the last twenty years. Poking fun at the didactic tradition she has so wonderfully revalidated, Ewing deliberately renders the mother's ruminations in the outdated Johnsonian diction of eighteenth-century mentorias: "That early discipline which makes the prompt performance of duty a habit in childhood, is indeed the quickest relief to parental anxieties, and the firmest foundation for the fortunes of one's children." But her narrator endorses these somewhat stilted effusions with an aphoristic wit that is all her own:

Such, and many more, were the excellent reflections of this conscientious woman; but excellent as they were, they shall not be recorded here. One's own experience preaches with irresistible eloquence; but the second-hand sermons of other people's lives are apt to seem tedious and impertinent. (TS, 159)

Fairy tales, no matter how innovative, are likewise bound to be a "second-hand" affair. In "Timothy's Shoes," the agency of those magical shoes allows Ewing to slip in many a slyly parodic allusion to that other wearer of magical footwear, Cinderella. But she freshens up old-fashioned motifs by giving equal status to her own kind of hero: once again, the intervention of a huge dog, this time a giant St. Bernard called "Bernardus," is needed to complement the fairy gift. By returning to school to warn that Timothy, his best friend, and a kindly usher have been lost in a swirling snowstorm, the shoes help the schoolmaster organize a rescue party. But it is Bernardus who saves the trio. As a human member of the rescue party remarks, "It's a rare good thing there's some dumb animals cleverer than we are ourselves" (TS, 157), a tribute that seems to be fully endorsed by the clever author who says farewell to fairy tales in one of her cleverest ventures into the genre.

The shoes that disappear into the distance may make their way back into some fantasyland. But the flat landscape beyond the gate also symbolizes the horizontality of a narrative that places each episode into a separate setting and yet contains no abrupt descents into subterranean fairylands or falls from a lunar Beastland. Cruikshank's illustration for "Timothy's Shoes" (the frontispiece for the November 1870 issue of *Aunt Judy's Magazine*) quite appropriately calls attention to the story's horizontal grounding by its organization into three parallel panels (fig. 38). Only the godmother, whose broom barely hovers above the ground so prominently featured in the upper and lower panels, hovers in the air. The shoes and the human figures adhere to the laws of gravity. The drawing thus markedly differs from Cruikshank's illustration for "Benjy in Beastland" (the frontispiece for the June 1870 issue of the magazine), where three-quarters of the page is devoted to the plummeting figures of Benjy and Mister Rough. The indignant animals who have pushed their tormentor off the moon's nimbus are clustered above; and the dark river whose depth Benjy has yet to fathom lies beneath (fig. 39).

The contrast between these two drawings captures Ewing's own chosen movement after "Timothy's Shoes." Having mastered the rises and falls so central to the fantasies of Ruskin, Carroll, MacDonald, and Ingelow, she was ready by 1871 to return to the planar (and plainer) movements of a temporal world. The little fairy who waves a cheerful good-bye has left a renewable legacy. Looking surprisingly young, this smiling Märchenfrau can, like Marie in "Friedrich's Ballad," be read as the equivalent of a diminutive Aunt Judy. If so, she is entitled to feel content, having not only completed her own fantastic ventures but also refined those published, from 1851 to 1871, by her major fellow authors.[32]

VI

But even though the little fairy looks back in satisfaction, her movement is forward. Ahead in Ewing's career were the realistic fictions that cemented her fame among the late Victorians, longer books such as *Six to Sixteen* (serialized in *Aunt Judy's Magazine* in ten installments from January to October of 1872) and shorter novellas, all much reprinted. And these works, more than her fairy tales perhaps, influenced the two major writers of children's books of the next generation, Edith Nesbit and Rudyard Kipling. Still, Ewing's ability to ground fantasy in a natural order was a legacy she bequeathed to these and other successors. Nesbit, who imitated Ewing in early productions such as *A Book of Dogs* (1898), soon mastered the same delicious interplay between fantasy and reality of a story like "Timothy's Shoes" in her wonderfully inventive *Nine Unlikely Tales,* in which absentee fairy godmothers post letters carried by sundry animals or are turned into ordinary school-mistresses. And, despite Kipling's acknowledged debt to a realistic girl's book in his lavish tribute to *Six to Sixteen* (a book from which Frances Hodgson Burnett also seems to have freely borrowed), his animal tales, both in the *Jungle Books* and in the *Just So Stories,* are even more profoundly indebted to both Aunt Judys: Gatty as well as Ewing.

32. As Maxwell shows, both Ingelow and Ruskin—Ewing's elders by twenty years—were solicitous about her career, and concerned that she was receiving "neither the publicity" nor "the money that she deserved." Whereas Ingelow was indirectly responsible for Ewing's eventual partnership with Randolph Caldecott, the illustrator of all her later works, Ruskin went so far as to volunteer helping her bring out a volume of her tales to be published at his expense, "independent of any publisher," as long as he had control over the illustrations (Maxwell, *Mrs Gatty and Mrs Ewing,* 208). Ewing, who had met Ruskin in 1879 and "got on affably" after discovering that they were equally "soldier mad," turned down his offer, although her younger sister accepted his generous subvention to keep *Aunt Judy's Magazine* in print (ibid., 221).

TIMOTHY'S SHOES.

38 George Cruikshank, Timothy's Shoes

39 George Cruikshank, Benjy in Beastland

There were further legacies, however. Kipling's Mowgli stories, as is well known, were a direct inspiration for Lord Baden-Powell's formation of the Boy Scout Movement.[33] What is less known is that the Brownies, the British Girl Guide Movement, owes its name to the fine experimental fairy tale that Ewing wrote in 1865, before the founding of *Aunt Judy's*

33. Invited to hear more than fifteen thousand Wolf Cubs offering the "biggest howl in history," Kipling managed to miss that occasion. For the most comprehensive discussion of his reluctant affiliation with scouting, see Hugh Brogan, *Mowgli's Sons: Kipling and Baden-Powell's Scouts* (London: Jonathan Cape, 1987).

Magazine and before she returned to the mode in her 1870 fantasies. When "The Brownies" (which Ewing used to introduce the 1870 volume that included "Amelia and the Dwarfs") was reissued in 1946 under Ewing's name, the central figure of a little boy was changed into a girl in order to stress the tale's connection to the girl scout movement, by then thirty years in operation. The link was validated by Lady Baden-Powell, who admitted that, in 1915, she and her husband had not only taken the name but also derived their "ideas for the activities" of the organization from "that story written by Mrs Ewing, and founded their ritual and ceremonies on the tale of the Owl, the quest by the children in the wood, and so on."[34] Whereas Kipling had been consulted about boy scout rites taken from the *Jungle Books,* the appropriation of "the Brownie idea," though more fundamental, went unacknowledged: "But I am afraid that my husband never asked anybody's permission for the right to use the Brownie story, and just brought it into being."[35]

As Lady Baden-Powell's endorsement of this 1946 Scribner's edition that included "The Brownies" suggests, the decision to change the sex of Ewing's boy hero was probably prompted by the publisher's eagerness to heighten the story's appeal for Girl Guides. Whatever motives were behind the text's revision, however, the change in gender merely reinstated a feminization akin to that undertaken by Ruskin in *The King of the Golden River,* the first of the "ventures" I have discussed in the course of this book. And, ironically enough, this twentieth-century reinstatement of segregated male and female stereotypes had the effect of negating Ewing's accomplishment in "The Brownies." For if that story anticipates "Amelia and the Dwarfs" or "Timothy's Shoes" in abolishing the differences between fantasy and everyday, it also succeeds in mediating between adult and child by erasing the difference between too rigidly defined masculine and feminine modalities.

"The Brownies" relies on a complicated web of concentric narratives. As the story progresses, and the interplay between its narrative layers becomes increasingly apparent, the gendered and generational identities of tellers and listeners begin to dissolve and become interchangeable. In the outer circle is the story's prime narrator, a middle-aged doctor who lives alone with his German poodle; his fondness for the six children he regales with stories, and his special investment in two of these, the girl Tiny and

34. Quoted in Maxwell, *Mrs Gatty and Mrs Ewing,* 145.
35. Ibid., 146, 145.

her brother Deordie, seem to stem from the loss of his wife, twenty years ago. In the middle circle, the doctor's role is taken over by another lonely, yet child-loving figure, the aged, superstitious mother of an impoverished tailor, himself a widower in charge of three children, two carefree boys and a baby girl. And, in the innermost circle, the doctor who addresses the six children and the "old lady" who tells folktales to her two grandsons are turned into a third narrator, the Old Owl. Now speaking to an audience of one, the older of the two boys, this oracular creature schools him in the helpful ways of the Brownies or Small Folk, also known as the Good People, domesticated elves whose antitypes are the Boggarts, a rival race of urchins.

Ewing wants her readers to recognize that all these figures are imaginary constructions: if the Doctor acts as surrogate for a female narrator whose voice occasionally supplies added information, the grandmother and the Old Owl, both of whom are referred to as "old lady," are the Doctor's own projections. It is the Grimm story of the Shoemaker and the little Elves, which Deordie and Tiny have read, that leads him to invent his own counter-version of a poor tailor aided, not by elves or Brownies, but rather by his own, very human, children's secret impersonation of these helpful supernatural beings. The self-conscious doctor, who harbors a secret of his own when he holds conversations with his dead wife, finds it difficult to believe in elves; in a joke his child-listeners take seriously, he gives the tailor's son, Tommy Trout, a name he has simply lifted from a nursery rhyme. But old grandmother Trout, who, unlike her skeptical son, fully believes in the existence of Brownies, and who attributes a cryptic wisdom to an elusive figure she calls Old Owl, is capable of constructions as potent as those of the doctor who has invented her. And, to complete these multiple projections, the Old Owl whom Tommy meets—in what is clearly a dream that reprocesses the boy's earlier conversations with his grandmother—is shown to be the boy's own unconscious construction of that other "old lady." As such, however, the wise owl also acts as the doctor's personation of a female folklore that this educated and skeptical modern man cannot bring himself wholly to dismiss.

Near the end of her story, Ewing calls attention to the fluidity she has created through the use of these multiple masks. The Doctor turns to his prime auditor, the girl Tiny, and repeats "in sepulchral tones" the same invitation that the Old Owl had extended to Tommy: "Kiss my fluffy face" (B, 63). Tiny immediately understands the transference in identities. The bearded Doctor is Owl, a female; she is Tommy, a boy. Playfully, she protests that the "owl is too high up" and, upon being lifted by the Doctor, complains that his face is not as soft as that of the bird who was Tommy's re-creation of his grandmother: "'You're not fluffy at all,' said she in a tone of the utmost contempt; 'you're tickly and bristly. Puss is more fluffy, and Father is scrubby and scratchy, because he shaves'" (B, 64). But the Doctor—and a Ewing who drops this bearded male mask—presses Tiny further: "And which of the three styles do you prefer?," he asks. Having been ventriloqually addressed in three very different "styles," Tiny now laughs, "Not tickly and bristly," and runs home (B, 64). The child who signifies her understanding of the voluntary nature of becoming a "Brownie" is as much at ease with this lonely stranger as with her clean-shaven father, who soon protests, "affecting a great appearance of severity, 'you're my Brownie, not his'" (B, 66).

The proprietory attitude of two adult males who vie for possession of a female child might well have been treated more negatively by an author like Christina Rossetti.[36] Ewing, however, uses the father's jocular remark to suggest that the Doctor's story can be appreciated by adults as much as by children. For the father who pities his rival understands that the tale about the Brownies stems from the emotional needs of this childless and mateless storyteller. For her part, Tiny, even more than her brother Deordie, benefits from the story placed at the core of this multi-layered narrative. She is the prime recipient of information which the Owl relayed to a boy, who in turn passed it on to his younger brother and to the baby sister who "grew up into a Brownie, and made (as girls are apt to make) the best house-sprite of all" (B, 59). What is more, both Tiny and Deordie have come to understand that the fluidities of the story they have heard go beyond gender. When the children dislike the Doctor's first closure about the desirability of girl Brownies, he satisfies their desire to hear more about the Owl. And when the bird, now silent, flies away after being accosted by Tommy and his father, they remain unsatisfied:

"Is that the very very end?" asked Tiny.

"The very very end," said the Doctor.

"I suppose there might be more and more ends," speculated Deordie—"about whether the Brownies had any children when they grew into farmers, and whether the children were Brownies and whether *they* had other Brownies, and so on and

36. In *Forbidden Journeys,* 335n, Auerbach and Knoepflmacher suggest that Rossetti may have poked fun at her rival's male-derived middle name.

on." And Deordie rocked himself among the geraniums, in the luxurious imagining of an endless fairy tale.

"You insatiable rascal!" said the Doctor. "Not another word. Jump up, for I'm going to see you home. I have to be off early tomorrow."

"Where?" said Deordie.

"Never mind. I shall be away all day, and I want to be at home in good time in the evening, for I mean to attack the crop of groundsel between the sweet-pea hedges. You know, no Brownies come to my homestead!"

And the Doctor's mouth twitched a little till he fixed it in a stiff smile. (B, 62)

Recognizing the lack that prompts the Doctor's love of Tiny, who will weed this lonely man's garden without necessarily becoming his little bride or dream-child, Ewing shows herself to be more tolerant of adult male child-lovers than Christina Rossetti. As much concerned with female transmission in this story as in "Amelia and the Dwarfs," she allows this incomplete man a place in the line of female progenitors he activates when he has the Owl recite "the whole history of the Brownies, as it has been handed down in our family from my grandmother's great-grandmother, who lived in the Druid's Oak, and was intimate with the fairies" (B, 36–37). Male storytellers like Lewis Carroll or George MacDonald need not be debarred because of their infatuation with the feminine.

Ewing would have been pleased to know that in 1969, a century after its composition, her story would spawn another male narrative about a boy's encounter with a giant owl, Randall Jarrell's *Fly By Night*. And she would undoubtedly have been delighted by the masterful, Blakean illustration that Maurice Sendak fashioned for that text when it appeared in 1976. The two-page drawing in which a levitating dreamer, the boy David, is suspended between the fluffy face of the mother Owl he has met in his dream and the maternal figures, animal and human, placed on earth below, captures a mythology that Ewing would have perfectly understood. Woken up by his mother after his moon-bathed flight to the owl's nest, Jarrell's David accepts the same ordinary world that reclaims Amelia, Benjy, and Tommy Trout—and, before them, Ingelow's Jack, Carroll's Alice, MacDonald's Light Princess, and a host of other Victorian child-dreamers and voyagers. For night ventures into fantasylands, however energizing, demand a return to the slower motions of a world of generation and growth.

Epilogue

Of the three abstractions joined in this book's subtitle—"Victorians," "Fairy Tales," and "Femininity"—only the first seems relatively unproblematic. Thirty years separate the births of the oldest from the youngest of the seven writers I have considered here (Thackeray was born in 1811, and Ewing in 1841). And only one of these seven, MacDonald (who died in 1905), actually outlived Queen Victoria. Moreover, as I have tried to show through my multiple cross-referencings and interchapter connections, the children's books these writers published in a twenty-year period form a remarkably cohesive unit shaped by literary affinities and cultural convergences that not only link them strongly to each other but also align them with the canonized productions of their Victorian contemporaries and Romantic predecessors.

"Fairy Tales," by way of contrast, seems a considerably looser term, barely adequate as an umbrella for the great variety of subgenres I have examined. Even Ruskin's attempt to emulate a Grimm fairy tale substantially differs, as noted in the last chapter, from Ewing's expansion of an actual Irish folktale or from her additions to existing folklore in her "Old Fashioned Fairy Tales." Yet the term becomes far more porous when it must accommodate the disparate modes I have discussed: burlesques, dream-visions, nursery rhymes, verse parodies, narrative poems such as "Goblin Market," adult fantasies such as MacDonald's *Phantastes,* and the *Alice* stories that Carroll expressly did *not* want to be read as ventures into fairylands. The designation "Fairy Tales" thus can at best capture the eclecticism that marks a literature for children that is every bit as experimental as Victorian writings for adults.

"Femininity," however, is by far the most problematic of my three terms. Since the constructions of the feminine greatly vary in each of the children's texts I have discussed, a plural noun would certainly have been more desirable. But even within any single text, the "feminine" is inevitably fractured, split by the markedly different or often inimical characterizations separating children from adults. "Feminine" girls and feminized boys are not only screened from an adult masculinity but also are frequently segregated from grown-up women. That segregation may be seen as desirable by those writers who privilege a desexualized "innocence" they nonetheless invest with considerable erotic affect. Or, conversely, it may be regarded as undermining the maturation process encouraged by a cultural ideology that insists on placing children and adolescents within the strict demarcations set by a heterosexual social order.

Some of the male-authored texts I have examined betray a considerable ambivalence about extending the "femininity" they privilege to grown-up female figures. Ruskin's "little" Gluck recovers a maternal enclave but is screened from contact with any flesh-and-blood women; Carroll's "little" *Wonderland* Alice repudiates grotesque maternal figures such as the Duchess and Queen of Hearts before allowing her older sister to process dreams she may or may not share with children as a prospective matriarch; MacDonald's "little" Diamond much prefers a mystical death-bringer to the biological mother who tenderly tries to nurse him back to life. These child-figures—insulated, slowed down, or lifted out of a world of generation—are at odds with those protagonists who do grow up because tutored by wise godmothers, heroic older sisters, and assorted mentorias: Thackeray's Giglio and Rosalba, Ingelow's Mopsa and Jack, Rossetti's Laura and Maggie, Ewing's Amelia and Timothy.

Still, as my alignment of Thackeray with three women writers already suggests, the male-authored constructions of "femininity" which Ingelow, Rossetti, and Ewing rewrite, unwrite, and replace are hardly uniform. Thackeray challenges Ruskin's earnest construction of a passive "feminine" receptacle for the equally passive Gluck by creating a humorous counter-world in which even the minimal interventions of Fairy Blackstick are sufficient to make a shambles of the amorous and combative posturings of a host of strutting males. Similarly, MacDonald teases both Carroll and Ruskin for aesthetizing girlhood and for avoiding adult women they either elide or deform into grotesque matriarchs. Although MacDonald himself is quite capable of creating the monstrous Princess Makemnoit, his portrait of Mr. Raymond slyly satirizes the guarded child-loving of his two Oxonian bachelor friends.

If such acts of revisionism allow male writers to destabilize rival gender-constructions, they also call attention to the instability of their own formulations. Self-revision is even more prominent than the engagement with competing male texts. Thackeray's first book for children forces him to reinspect and readjust the "juvenile" ideal of femininity he had created in *Rebecca and Rowena,* itself a revision of Scott's *Ivanhoe.* Carroll's obsessive reworking of his shifting relation to a growing dream-child leads him to modify that relation in three successive *Alice* books—and even a fourth, if one also counts *The Nursery Alice.* MacDonald's self-revisings are just as numerous. After reconfiguring adult fantasies such as *Phantastes* and "The Portent" in "The Light Princess," he reverses himself once more by changing the heterosexual consummation of the first tale into an eroticized retrogression into the womb. That hideous enemy of procreation, Makemnoit, can now become a seductive and highly desirable bringer of death; North Wind's embrace thus denies Diamond the resurrection-through-coition granted to the young Prince in the Light Princess's bed.

The very instability, variety, and tentativeness of these male-authored constructs, however, also must be regarded as the prime common denominator that separates them from the counter-texts created by Ingelow, Rossetti, and Ewing. When Ingelow sets out to amend *At the Back of the North Wind* in her own fantasy of a traveling boy, and when Christina Rossetti responds to the *Alice* books in both *Sing-Song* and *Speaking Likenesses,* they operate from the relative security of a mainstream cultural position that endorses their distrust of a gender-bending they consider regressive. Despite their literary marginalization as women and despite their undeniable attraction to the playfulness and subversiveness of experimentations with gender, these women writers oppose male constructions they target as irresponsible. To counter that presumed irresponsibility, they press into service a maternal authority they impart to mature older sisters, maiden aunts, and other female tutors. Although they devise forms that are as inventive and radical as those used by their male counterparts, their ideological position is uniform and their convictions are unchanging.

And yet the cultural authority Ingelow and Rossetti try to assert is compromised by their imaginative closeness to the male texts they set out to revise. Something like the sentimentality of MacDonald's nostalgia or the unsentimentality of Carroll's irony thus permeates their counter-texts. Ingelow's Queen Mopsa so yearns for the little boy she has outgrown that she must clone him into a fairy consort; the intensity of her longing therefore almost replicates, in a looking-glass reversal, that which seized another little boy, Diamond, in his own desire to become reunited with North Wind. Rossetti's acid Aunt in *Speaking Likenesses* may act as a foil for Carroll's ineffectual queens, but the harshness that masks her fine wit may well have the same dire effect on prospective child readers that the Duchess's mishandling of her peppered baby or the Queen's irascibility had on a retreating Alice. In trying to repossess the "feminine," both Ingelow and Rossetti created the misperceptions that led so many intelligent critics to dismiss *Mopsa* and *Speaking Likenesses* as nothing but pale imitations of the universally acclaimed (and canonized) *Alice* books.

It is Ewing, therefore, by sidestepping the intertextual squabbles among the other six writers, who manages to reinstate a female authority in children's texts. Unlike Ruskin's purported transmission of a Styrian folktale or the spurious transmission of Diamond's experiences by MacDonald's worshipful narrator, Ewing's "old-fashioned" fairy tales are authenticated by the time-tested gender-constructs of a long tradition of female storytellers, the anonymous *Märchenfrauen* silenced by male collectors like the Grimms. Yet Ewing also succeeds in revalidating a second female tradition that had influenced the shape of children's literature in England and America for an entire century—the didactic tradition established by the rational women writers whom Romanticism had displaced and whose sense Carroll and MacDonald had converted into anti-sense.

By relaxing the opposition to fantasy maintained by these earlier pedagogues, Ewing could reimplant their definitions of gender as a social construction determined by pragmatism, habit, and observation rather than by the subjectivism of male desire. Ewing's Amelia matures by reconciling herself to norms of behavior culturally marked as "feminine." That "femininity," she recognizes, is merely a conventional veneer, but it is a useful and necessary construction that not only allows an extraordinary child to become a contributing member of her social order, but also permits that child-turned-woman to maintain her distance from a culture she can subtly resist from within. Ventures into an irrational counter-world strike Ewing as useful for future women and men. Not only slave women or goblin men but also male bulldogs, St. Bernards, and other canine retrievers can teach children of both sexes to retrieve basic strengths needed for their acculturation. An Amelia-turned-"Amy" does not have to flee the irrational as the *Wonderland* Alice was forced to do; instead, she masters it during her underground venture and makes it serve her own ends upon returning to the domestic world she had tried to fight. Cleverer than her mother, she should provide her own daughters (and sons) a better model for them to interiorize.

My chapter on Ewing makes much of her own relation to a clever literary mother, Margaret Gatty. Indeed, since the relation to the maternal is featured so prominently in all of the texts I have examined, some biographical speculations may be in order. Are these male and female constructions of "femininity" different only because of a Victorian boy's and a Victorian girl's different relationship to the mother? Or are there other important variables in that relationship that must be taken into account? Helen Mackay MacDonald died in her thirties when her son was eight;

Frances Jane Lutwidge Dodgson (about whom we know almost as little) died at age 46 one day before Charles's nineteenth birthday. Their removal at crucial phases of each son's development may well have led to the creation of compensatory fictions that turn, in excessive anger as much as in excessive love, to maternal surrogates for a sustenance that can never be resupplied.

By way of contrast, Anne Becher Carmichael-Smyth (the remarried mother who outlived Thackeray by a year) and Margaret Cock Ruskin (who died at the age of ninety, when John was 52) were around as arbiter-censors of the writings their only sons produced for both children and adults. Surely the absence of mothers from Treasure Valley and the respect shown for a cane-wielding Blackstick noted for her own absenteeism have something to do with the ambivalent attitudes these long-lived and domineering matriarchs instilled in authors they continued to treat as boys. Thackeray, as I noted, became a male mother when he wrested his daughters away from their grandmother's influence. The unmarried Ruskin, on the other hand, self-anointed and brilliant prophet in the public domain, could not shed his private self-image as Margaret Ruskin's chatty and errant boy.

Unmarried as well, Ingelow and Rossetti also spent their adult lives in the daily company of their strong and durable mothers, Jean Kilgour Ingelow (1799–1876) and Frances Lavinia Polidori Rossetti (1801–1886). Whereas Ruskin could periodically flee to Italy or the Lake Country, these Victorian daughters traveled very little, and when they did were always joined by the mothers to whom they steadily deferred. Ewing's choice of a married life with a male traveler thus stands in marked opposition to the lives led by daughters as immobilized as the immured Mopsa who meekly submits to the mandates of Mother Fate. Although Ewing's ties to the maternal calyx were every bit as strong as those of Rossetti and Ingelow, she signified her allegiance by writing for her mother's children's magazine rather than by remaining implanted as a domestic surrogate in the Gatty nursery. Her greater freedom, however, also involved an Amelia-like submission. For had she been willing to seek other outlets for her prose, as Ruskin suggested, or even to write for adult audiences, as admirers like Henry James and Kipling clearly wanted her to do, the effect of her genius might have been more diffusive. Instead, her impact has been as forgotten as that of the anonymous women, resting "in unvisited tombs," memorialized at the end of *Middlemarch*.

I began this book on a personal note. And I might as well end in the same vein by admitting that my own constructions may suffer from the subjectivism I have sometimes deplored in the course of my narrative. Notwithstanding my credentials as the child of parents born at the tail-end of the Victorian era and as someone who has thought long and hard about a great variety of Victorian texts, I am hardly immune to the charge of engaging in acts of projection. Schooled by thinkers such as Barthes, Benjamin (Jessica, more than Walter), Chodorow, Klein, Kristeva, Winnicott, and others, I am surely imposing twentieth-century notions of "masculinity" and "femininity" on the representation of traits seen rather differently in a pre-Freudian era. Overlaps and nuances now lost to us were taken for granted in a culture in which unmarried women in their twenties could still be seen as dependent "girls." We can never recover the Victorians as they saw themselves. Filtered by hindsight, our reconstructions are necessarily distorted. My own ventures into childlands are therefore surely as over-determined in form and ideology as those of Carroll or MacDonald, or of Ingelow and Rossetti. Still, however literally distanced and culturally conditioned my readings may be, I have tried to enlist them in a refiguring of literary history. And the sequence I have traced in this book should help restore the complexities of a debate that still shapes our changing assumptions about gender and generation.

Index

Adam, 138; boys represented as, 21, 166, 204

Addison, James, 5n

adolescence
  as exile, 26
  as prolongation of childhood, 166

adults, and children
  as collaborators, 91, 109–10, 172, 195, 198, 226, 258
  in conflict, 86, 114, 121, 175, 179, 194–95, 222, 234, 241, 243, 306, 363, 367–68, 400
  as dual readership, xiii, 7, 79, 85, 87, 89, 110–12, 148–49, 188, 320–21, 348
  as components of a single "self," xiv, 300

Agnew, Joan, 37, 38n

Alcott, Louisa May, xiv

Alexander, Francesca, 274n

American Civil War, 278, 326n

Andersen, Hans Christian, 128, 388

androgyny, 131n
  and representations of boys, xii, 48, 163, 163n, 187, 212, 254, 288
  and women writers, xii, 288, 301, 322

angels, 28, 261–62, 303

"Anon" (Gatty nursery magazine), 382n

The Arabian Nights, 80, 117; tale of "The Golden Water," 69–70

Arnold, Matthew, 274n

Auden, W. H., on George MacDonald, 228

Auerbach, Nina, 23, 32, 238n

"Aunt Judy," as shared pseudonym, 381, 382, 417

Aunt Judy's Magazine, 378, 380, 381, 387 et passim; Carroll contributes to, 408n

Austen, Jane, 23, 113, 380

author, as presence in children's texts, xiv, xv, 152, 152–53n, 379

Baden-Powell, Lady Olave, 420

Baden-Powell, Lord Robert, 419

Bagehot, Walter, 78n

Bambi (Disney film), 2

Barbauld, Anna Laetitia, 19, 21, 22, 113

Barks, Carl, 5n

Barnes, Irene, 157, 158

Barnes, Violet, 157, 158

Barrett Browning, Elizabeth, 124, 277, 299, 313

Barrie, James, *Peter Pan,* xvii, 187, 219n

Barthes, Roland, 106, 430

Bates, David, 295–96, 298, 299, 301

Battiscombe, Georgina, 31n

Baxter, Lucy, 83, 84

Baxter, Sally, 83, 93

Bayes, A. W., 389

Bechstein, Ludwig, 394

Bell, Lady Florence, 395n

Bell, Mackenzie, 274

Bellas, Ralph A., 373n

Benjamin, Jessica, 16, 26, 430

Benjamin, Walter, x, 430

Bennett, Arnold, 380

Bentley, D. M. R., 321n

Bettelheim, Bruno, *The Uses of Enchantment,* 51, 54, 55

Bible, 160, 205, 236
  Exodus, 236n
  Genesis, 395
  Song of Solomon, 184

Blackwood's Edinburgh Magazine, 321n

Blake, William, 6, 7n, 11, 22, 234, 251, 254, 423
  "Infant Joy," 7–8
  "The Lamb," 7–8
  "Nurse's Song," 7

Blom, Margaret Howard, 379–80

Blom, Thomas E., 379–80

Bloom, Harold, 345

rivalries, intertextual (*continued*)
MacDonald's *BNW:* as foil for *MF,* xii,
227, 268, 281, 302–6, 309–10, 427; as
foil for *S-S,* 343–48, 427
Ruskin's *KGR:* as foil for *BNW,* 230–
31, 235; as foil for "Goblin Market,"
316–20 passim, 325, 328; as foil for
RR, 18, 70, 72, 80, 89, 105
Robertson, C., 130n
Roosevelt, Franklin Delano, 3
Rossetti, Christina Georgina, xi, xii, 24,
166, 187, 273, 283, 307, 311, **313–77,**
385, 386, 422, 422n
her audiences, 316, 320–21, 321n, 332
and her brothers, 319ff, 326, 327, 353,
354n, 356
and Carroll, 31, 32, 153n, 196–97, 227,
300, 316, 340, 343–48, 356n
Carroll on, 312
her letters to Carroll, 339–42, 356, 377
and Ewing, 382, 422, 422n, 423
on Hughes, 356, 356n
and Ingelow, 274, 281, 292, 299n, 311,
313, 316, 326, 331–33
on Ingelow, 313
and Macmillan, 315–16 et passim
Ruskin on, 6, 314–15, 317, 319–20, 323,
350
clashes with Ruskin, 315n, 319–20,
325
—Works (*see also* rivalries, intertextual)
Commonplace, and Other Short Stories,
326, 326n, 328n, 356
Goblin Market, and Other Poems, 321;
"The Convent Threshold," 324;
"Cousin Kate," 322; "Goblin Market," 31, 299n, 313–14, 322–25, 340,
355, 361, 368, 369, 386, 392, 407:
"From House to Home," 324; "The
Love of Christ Which Passeth
Knowledge," 322; "My Secret," 322,
366; "No, Thank You, John," 322;
"Noble Sisters," 322, 337; "Up-Hill,"
315

A Pageant and Other Poems: "An 'Immurata' Sister," 374n; "Sonnets are
Full of Love," 29
The Prince's Progress and Other Poems,
326–27; "The Prince's Progress,"
327–28, 329, 331, 342
Sing-Song: A Nursery Rhyme Book
(S-S), 227, 325, 329–39, 342–49, 350,
351–52, 355, 375; "A house of cards"
(lyric 102), 334, 348–49; "A pin has
a head" (lyric 48), 343; "I caught a
little ladybird" (lyric 103), 351–52;
"If a pig wore a wig" (lyric 40), 312;
"If I were a queen," (lyric 31), 330–
32, 334; "If the moon came from
heaven" (lyric 122), 335–36; "If the
sun could tell us" (lyric 123), 336; "I
have a Poll parrot" (lyric 101), 332–
34, 350, 351–52n; "Motherless baby"
(lyric 116), xxiv; "The peacock has
a score of eyes" (lyric 57), 343n;
"Shake a flint," 376; "Sing me a
song" (lyric 65), 338; "Three plum
buns" (lyric 53), 332; "Twist me a
crown of wind-flowers" (lyric 38),
336–37, 339, 366–67; "When fishes
set umbrellas up" (lyric 56), 345–48
Speaking Likenesses (SL), 227, 311, 325,
341, **356–77,** 405, 405n; misread as
imitation of Carroll's work, 292,
376–77, 382, 386, 427
Unpublished Poems: "In An Artist's
Studio," 353–55; "L'Uumibatto," 342
Rossetti, Dante Gabriel, 169n, 312–314,
319, 325n, 326
and Carroll, 354, 356, 357, 357n
and sister's work, 325, 326–28, 356
Rossetti, Frances Lavinia Polidori, 28–29,
313, 360, 429
Rossetti, Maria Francesca, 313, 315n,
357
Rossetti, William Michael, 274, 313, 321,
325, 325n, 328n, 354n, 357, 358
Ruskin, John, xi, xv, 3–4, 5, 6, 8–11